THE OXFORD

MW00776896

THE VALLEY OF
THE KINGS

THE OXFORD HANDBOOK OF

THE VALLEY OF THE KINGS

Edited by

RICHARD H. WILKINSON

and

KENT R. WEEKS

OXFORD

UNIVERSITY PRESS

OXFORD
UNIVERSITY PRESS

Oxford University Press is a department of the University of Oxford. It furthers
the University's objective of excellence in research, scholarship, and education
by publishing worldwide. Oxford is a registered trade mark of Oxford University
Press in the UK and certain other countries.

Published in the United States of America by Oxford University Press
198 Madison Avenue, New York, NY 10016, United States of America.

© Oxford University Press 2016

First issued as an Oxford University Press paperback, 2019

Cataloging-in-Publication data is on file at the Library of Congress
ISBN 978-0-19-993163-7 (hardcover); 978-0-19-005207-2 (paperback)

CONTENTS

PART IV TOMB CONSTRUCTION AND DEVELOPMENT

PART V ROYAL TOMB DECORATION

PART VI INDIVIDUAL KV TOMBS

PART VII CONTENTS OF ROYAL KV TOMBS

PART VIII GETTING TO THE AFTERLIFE

PART IX DESTRUCTION, DESECRATION, AND REUSE

PART X HUMAN REMAINS FROM THE KV AND THEIR STUDY

PREFACE

SCHOLARLY and public interest in ancient Egypt, and its royal tombs in particular, has generated many books on the Valley of the Kings (KV). However, recent discoveries, as well as the improved archaeological techniques and initiatives of the past decade, have repeatedly underscored the need for an up-to-date and more comprehensive reference work on the necropolis of the New Kingdom pharaohs. The present volume has been carefully planned to meet that need. With nearly forty chapters and an additional appendix, this work covers many different facets of the history, exploration, analysis, conservation and management of the royal valley, looking both at past and current developments in KV research as well as the future challenges the site will undoubtedly face.

Individually, the volume's chapters are discrete studies by Egyptologists, archaeologists and other scholars who have worked first-hand in the royal necropolis or with its materials, and these studies are arranged in thematic groups.

First, introductory chapters locate the Valley in its natural setting through discussions of the geology, topography and hydrology of the area. Succeeding chapters then move to focused examinations of the development of the royal necropolis and its tombs, their construction, contents, decoration and significance and administration as well as later history. Additional topics such as the ancient desecration and reuse of the tombs, as well as the study of their human remains are also covered. Recent studies of DNA, filiation, cranio-facial reconstruction, and other aspects of the royal mummies have produced important and sometimes controversial results, all of which are considered. Finally, the book discusses the ongoing exploration of the KV along with current issues of great importance for the area's preservation - such as conservation, tourism and site management, and the role of the Valley of the Kings in the lives of modern Egyptians.

No other work on the Valley of the Kings has previously attempted coverage of this scope, and no other work has gathered so many experts to discuss the many aspects of this great archaeological site. Many of the included topics have not been dealt with in detail in earlier works, and other topics have been greatly updated through the discussion of recent studies and archaeological work. It is hoped that the resulting volume will provide a valuable addition to the literature of KV studies, and the Editors thank the contributors for the expertise and experience which they have generously brought to bear on their respective chapters. Our thanks also go to Dr. Stefan Vranka as series editor for proposing this Handbook, to Sarah Pirovitz for her help throughout the preparation of the volume, and to all the OUP staff involved in its production.

The Editors

LIST OF ABBREVIATIONS

AL	*Amarna Letters*
A&L	*Ägypten und Levant*
ASAE	*Annales du Service des Antiquités de l'Égypte*
BARCE	*Bulletin of the American Research Center in Egypt*
BASP	*The Bulletin of the American Society of Papyrologists*
BdÉ	*Bibliothèque d'Étude*
BIÉ	*Bulletin de l'Institute d'Égypt*
BIFAO	*Bulletin de l'Institut Français d'Archéologie Orientale*
BiOr	*Bibliotheca Orientalis*
BSEG	*Bulletin de la Société d'Égyptologie Genève*
BSFÉ	*Bulletin de la Société française d'Égyptologie*
CAJ	*Cambridge Archaeological Journal*
CCE	*Cahiers de la Céramique égyptienne*
CdE	*Chronique d'Égypte*
CRAIBL	*Comptes rendus de l'Académie des Inscriptions et Belles-lettres*
EA	*Egyptian Archaeology*
GM	*Göttinger Miszellen*
JAEI	*Journal of Ancient Egyptian Interconnections*
JARCE	*Journal of the American Research Center in Egypt*
JAS	*Journal of Archaeological Science*
JEA	*The Journal of Egyptian Archaeology*
JESHO	*Journal of the Economic and Social History of the Orient*
JJP	*Journal of Juristic Papyrology*
JNES	*Journal of Near Eastern Studies*
JSSEA	*Journal of the Society for the Study of Egyptian Antiquities*
KMT	*Kmt: A Modern Journal of Ancient Egypt*
LÄ	*Lexikon der Ägyptologie*, 7 vols., ed. W. Helck, E. Otto, and W. Westendorf, 1972/5, Wiesbaden.

MDAIK   *Mitteilungen des Deutschen Archaeologischen Instituts Kairo*

MDOG   *Mitteilungen der Deutschen Orient-Gesellschaft*

MIFAO   *Mémoires publiés par les membres de l'Institut Français d'Archéology Orientale du Cairo*

OBO   *Orbis Biblicus et Orientalis*

PAMR   *Polish Archaeology in the Mediterranean. Reports.*

RdE   *Revue d'Égyptologie*

SAK   *Studien zur Altägyptischen Kultur*

SDAIK   *Sonderschrift des Deutschen Archäologischen Instituts, Abteilung Kairo*

ZÄS   *Zeitschrift für ägyptische Sprache und Altertumskunde*

LIST OF CONTRIBUTORS

Hartwig Altenmüller is Professor Emeritus at the Archaeological Institute of the University of Hamburg.

Susanne Bickel is Professor of Egyptology at the University of Basel.

Judith M. Bunbury is a geologist in the Department of Earth Sciences at Cambridge University.

Filip Coppens is a scholar and lecturer at the Czech Institute of Egyptology, Faculty of Arts, Charles University in Prague.

Stephen W. Cross is an independent Egyptologist who writes and lectures on the Valley of the Kings.

Rosalie David, OBE is Emerita Professor of Biomedical Egyptology, The University of Manchester.

Robert J. Demarée is an Affiliated Fellow at the Faculty of Humanities, Leiden University.

Aidan Dodson is a Senior Research Fellow at the University of Bristol.

Andreas Dorn is Curator of the Egyptian Museum Bonn.

Ogden Goelet is Clinical Professor of Middle Eastern and Islamic Studies at New York University.

Michael Jones is Associate Director, Conservation Projects, at the American Research Center in Egypt, Cairo.

Heather L. McCarthy is Deputy Director of the New York University epigraphic expedition to the Ramesses II temple at Abydos.

Adam Lowe is the director of Factum Arte and founding member of the Factum Foundation for Digital Technology in Conservation.

Ryan Metcalfe is Lecturer in Biomedical Egyptology, KNH Center for Biomedical Egyptology, University of Manchester.

Gregory D. Mumford is Associate Professor, University of Alabama at Birmingham.

Sarah H. Parcak is Associate Professor, University of Alabama at Birmingham.

Lyla Pinch-Brock is Research Associate, Royal Ontario Museum.

Campbell Price is Curator of Egypt and Sudan, Manchester Museum, University of Manchester.

Stephen Rickerby is a private conservator who has worked in the Valley of the Kings.

Joshua A. Roberson Assistant Professor of Art History (Egyptology) at the University of Memphis, Institute of Egyptian Art and Archaeology.

Catharine H. Roehrig is Curator of Egyptian Art at the Metropolitan Museum of Art.

John H. Taylor is Assistant Keeper, Department of Ancient Egypt and Sudan at the British Museum.

Joyce Tyldesley is Senior Lecturer in Egyptology at the University of Manchester.

Martina Ullmann is Privatdozent for Egyptology in the Institute of Egyptology, Ludwig-Maximilian University, Munich.

Kees van der Spek is an independent ethnographer affiliated with the Australian National University in Canberra, Australia.

Carola Vogel is an independent researcher at the Johannes Gutenberg University, Mainz.

Alexandra von Lieven is Privatdozent and currently Heisenberg Fellow at the Egyptological Seminar, the Free University of Berlin.

Kent R. Weeks is Professor Emeritus, the American University in Cairo and Founding Director of the Theban Mapping Project.

Richard H. Wilkinson is Regents' Professor Emeritus, the University of Arizona and Founding Director of the University of Arizona Egyptian Expedition.

Lori Wong is a Project Specialist at the Getty Conservation Institute.

PART I

INTRODUCTION

INTRODUCTION

RICHARD H. WILKINSON AND KENT R. WEEKS

ARGUABLY one of the most important archaeological areas in the world, a World Heritage Site, and unquestionably the single most important site for understanding the funerary beliefs and practices of the pharaohs of ancient Egypt's New Kingdom era, the Valley of the Kings (KV) served as the burial place for most of the kings and several non-royal members of the elite in Egypt's Eighteenth, Nineteenth, and Twentieth Dynasties, a period of some 500 years, approximately 1550 to 1000 B.C.E.

WADI BIBAN EL-MOLUK: THE VALLEY OF THE KINGS

Known since early modern times as the "Valley of the Kings" (Arabic: وادى الملوك Wadi el-Moluk) or more fully as the "Valley of the Gates of the Kings" (Arabic: وادى بيبان الملوك Wadi Biban el-Moluk), the royal necropolis is situated on the west bank of the Nile, opposite modern Luxor (ancient Thebes), in the high cliffs of the "Theban massif" some 500 kilometers (313 miles) south of Cairo (lat 25°44′N, long 32°36′E). Within its rugged setting, the "valley" actually consists of two connected large valleys and clusters of smaller side-*wadis*, together containing some sixty-four known tombs, pits, and caches, and many commencements (initial tomb cuttings), as well as the remains of ancient walls, paths, water diversions, shrines, workmen's huts, guard posts, and other features. The tombs themselves range from small, undecorated, yet carefully cut shafts and single chambers to complex hypogea such as the richly decorated tomb of Seti I (KV 17) and the massively complex tomb of the sons of Ramesses II (KV 5).

Together with the artifacts and inscriptions discovered in the royal valley, these monuments provide a unique window into the riches and afterlife beliefs of the pharaohs interred there, as well as many glimpses into the lives of the workmen who planned, dug, administered, and guarded the royal necropolis.

Explored since classical times and the source of many amazing finds over the centuries (including, but certainly not limited to, the treasures of the boy-king Tutankhamun), new discoveries are still being made in the royal valley (including the only recently uncovered KV 64), each one generating great interest among scholars and the general public alike. As a result, many of the royal tombs have been prepared for tourism, and the royal valley has become one of the largest open-air museums in the world—one that draws as many as two million visitors each year. This influx of people is not without its problems—some of them severe—but for better or worse, the Valley of the Kings today represents one of the great centerpieces of modern Egypt's show-casing of its past. For a number of archaeologists drawn to the area and the specialists who work with them, the royal valley has also become the focus of a virtual subfield of Egyptology.

Studying the Tombs of Pharaohs

The Valley of the Kings has attracted the interest of archaeologists and other schol-ars since Napoleonic times, but no thorough and systematic study of its tombs—their design, content, function, and evolution—was undertaken until the landmark 1966 work by Elizabeth Thomas (1907–1986). *The Royal Necropoleis of Thebes*, privately pub-lished in an edition of only ninety copies, transformed scholars' approaches to KV and laid the foundation for much of the work that has followed, changing it from what had often been little more than random and frantic treasure hunts to systematic surveys con-cerned with meticulous studies of architecture, epigraphy, chronology, funerary prac-tices, and conservation. Today, work in KV is likely to involve not just archaeologists and Egyptologists, but geologists, engineers, art historians, medical and social scien-tists, conservators, and a host of other specialists, as the contributions to this volume demonstrate.

In the decades since the publication of Thomas's seminal work, we have seen sev-eral significant developments in our understanding of KV. Some are the result of fieldwork. Giovanni Belzoni's proclamation, made 200 years ago, that "there are no more" tombs to be found there has regularly been proved wrong, most recently with the discoveries of KV 63 and 64 (see chs 15, 32–34). The re-examination of long-known tombs, such as KV 7, has revealed new chambers, texts, and objects (see chs 16–24). KV 5, whose entrance has been known since 1825, but which was thought to be small, undecorated, and of no importance, was in the 1980s found to be one of the largest tombs ever dug in the New Kingdom, a family mausoleum meant for multiple burials of royal sons. Epigraphic and photographic surveys of decorated tombs are making possible new analyses of the funerary customs and reli-gious beliefs that governed the way in which KV tombs were cut, decorated, and furnished (see ch 35). Biomedical studies are helping to identify human remains and more accurately attribute some tombs (see chs 25–27). Recent excavations of ancient workmen's huts built on the valley floor are changing what we know of how the labor force responsible for cutting and decorating KV tombs operated (see chs 6 and 7).

Equally important are recent syntheses of KV data. Building on Thomas's work, scholars have begun to trace the history of KV tombs with greater accuracy and in more detail and are much closer to understanding the social and religious reasons for the almost constant redesign of royal tomb plans (see chs 8–14). Funerary equipment is being analyzed (see chs 16–18). The funerary texts that so brilliantly decorate KV tomb walls are now being published in detail, their meaning finally becoming clearer to scholars (see chs 10–11, 19–21). Ancient site protection and tomb robbery is now better understood (see chs 29–31). Most important, great care is finally being taken to ensure that these treasures from our ancient past are being recorded, protected, and conserved for future generations (see chs 1–2, 36–38).

KV Studies and the Present Volume

Because the wide range of scholarship employed in this volume embraces the work of numerous archaeologists as well as other specialists, it is natural that there are differences in interpretation regarding some details. These represent neither contradictions of facts nor a failure to harmonize the content of the various chapters of the volume. They are instead a clear indication of the dynamic, ongoing, wide-ranging scholarship, which involves multiple, sometimes conflicting, hypotheses. These differences of interpretation, however, involve only small details; the general knowledge we possess regarding KV is on solid footing.

Although many things are still unknown about the use of some tombs and the identities of their occupants, ongoing research continues to uncover previously unknown pits and tombs, and even rooms within previously known tombs (such as the discovery of the great extent of KV5, as well as the examination being conducted at the present time for hidden rooms in KV62, the tomb of Tutankhamun). These ongoing discoveries and investigations continue to add to our understanding of the history of the Valley, and it is certainly likely that yet more tombs remain to be found in KV and its surroundings.

The rapidly growing content of KV studies is particularly well served by this handbook. Not only are its chapters as up-to-date as possible, but the establishment of dedicated pages related to the volume on the website of the Theban Mapping Project (http://thebanmappingproject.com/resources/handbook.html) means that updates can and will be posted there as new information becomes available. In addition to the illustrations provided within the printed volume, further images will also be found on this website, providing fuller documentation for many of the chapters than is possible in the printed volume.

THE KV TOMBS

Numbering of the Tombs

The twenty-one tombs in the Valley of the Kings known to early nineteenth-century travelers were given numbers by John Gardner Wilkinson in 1827, establishing a system used by Egyptologists to this day. The numbers ran in geographical order through the valley, north to south, east to west. Since 1827 tombs have been assigned numbers in order of their (re)discovery, from KV 22 to 64; see the following table. (KV also contains what are known as "commencements," unfinished shafts that have been given letter designations. See Thomas 1966, 65; Reeves and Wilkinson 1996, 61f., and ch 9 in this volume.)

Tombs in the Valley of the Kings (Excluding Unattributed "Commencements")

KV Number	Dynasty	Owner
1	20	Ramesses VII
2	20	Ramesses IV
3	20	Son of Ramesses III
4	20	Ramesses XI
5	19	Sons of Ramesses II
6	20	Ramesses IX
7	19	Ramesses II
8	19	Merenptah
9	19	Ramesses V/VI
10	19	Amenmesse
11	20	Ramesses III
12	18	Unknown
13	19	Bay
14	19/20	Tausret/Sethnakhte
15	19	Seti II
16	18	Ramesses I
17	19	Seti I
18	20	Ramesses X
19	20	Mentuherkhepeshef
20	18	Hatshepsut
21	18	Two queens
22	18	Amenhotep III (and family members?)
23	18	Ay
24	18	Unknown
25	18	Amarna period (perhaps royal)
26	18	Unknown
27	18	Unknown

(continued)

KV Number	Dynasty	Owner
28	18	Unknown
29	18	Unknown
30	18	Unknown
31	18	Unknown
32	18	A queen?
33	18	temp Thutmose III (a queen?)
34	18	Thutmose III
35	18	Amenhotep II (and family members?)
36	18	Maiherpre
37	18	temp Thutmose III (a queen?)
38	18	temp Thutmose I (perhaps royal)
39	18	Unknown (a queen?)
40	18	Unknown (a princess?)
41	18	Unknown
42	18	Unknown
43	18	Thutmose IV
44	18	Unknown
45	18	Userhet
46	18	Yuya and Thuya
47	19	Siptah
48	18	Amenemopet
49	18	Unknown (a queen?)
50	18	Animal burial
51	18	Animal burial
52	18	Animal burial
53	18	Unknown
54	18	Unknown
55	18	Amarna period (royal or a queen?)
56	18	Unknown
57	18	Horemheb
58	18	Unknown
59	18	Unknown
60	18	Two female commoners
61	18	Unknown
62	18	Tutankhamun
63	18	Unknown
64	18	Unknown (princess?)

THE NEW KINGDOM RULERS OF EGYPT

The following table gives the names and dates of the kings of Egypt's Eighteenth, Nineteenth, and Twentieth Dynasties, who ruled during the period in which the Valley of the Kings was utilized as a royal necropolis, ca. 1550–1100 B.C.E. Dates are based on those given in the online UCLA *Encyclopedia of Egyptology*. Note that some dates are rounded, and some are set according to supposition, given the historical information that is extant. In most cases the dates are not substantially different from those found in other standard lists, such as the one included in *The Oxford History of Ancient Egypt*, edited by Ian Shaw (Shaw 2009).

Birth Name	Throne Name	Regnal Dates B.C.E.
Eighteenth Dynasty		
Ahmose	(Nebpehtyra)	1548–1523
Amenhotep I	(Djeserkara)	1523–1502
Thutmose I	(Aakheperkara)	1502–1492
Thutmose II	(Aakheperenra)	1492–1479
Thutmose III	(Menkheperra)	1479–1425
Hatshepsut	(Maatkara)	1473–1458
Amenhotep II	(Aakheperura)	1425–1399
Thutmose IV	(Menkheperura)	1399–1389
Amenhotep III	(Nebmaatra)	1389–1349
Amenhotep IV/Akhenaten	(Neferkheperura Waenra)	1349–1332
Semenkhkare	(Ankhkheperura)	1332–1328
Tutankhamun	(Nebkheperura)	1328–1319
Aye	(Kheperkheperura)	1319–1316
Horemheb	(Djeserkheperura)	1316–1302
Nineteenth Dynasty		
Ramesses I	(Menpehtyra)	1302–1301
Seti I	(Menmaatra)	1301–1290
Ramesses II	(Usermaatra Setepenra)	1290–1224
Merenptah	(Baenra Hotephermaat)	1224–1214
Seti II	(Userkheperura Setepenra)	1214–1208
Amenmesse	(Menmira)	1208–1206
Siptah	(Akhenra Setepenra)	1206–1198
Tausret	(Sitra Merytamen)	1206–1198
Twentieth Dynasty		
Sethnakhte	(Userkhaura Meryamen)	1198–1195
Ramesses III	(Usermaatra Meryamen)	1195–1164
Ramesses IV	(Hekamaatra Setepenamen)	1164–1156
Ramesses V	(Usermaatra Sekheperenra)	1156–1152
Ramesses VI	(Nebmaatra Meryamen)	1152–1144
Ramesses VII	(Usermaatra Setepenra Merytamen)	1144–1137
Ramesses VIII	(Usermaatra Akhenamen)	1137
Ramesses IX	(Neferkara Setepenra)	1137–1118
Ramesses X	(Khepermaatra Setepenra)	1118–1115
Ramesses XI	(Menmaatra Setepenptah)	1115–1086

Maps of the Valley of the Kings and Surrounding Areas

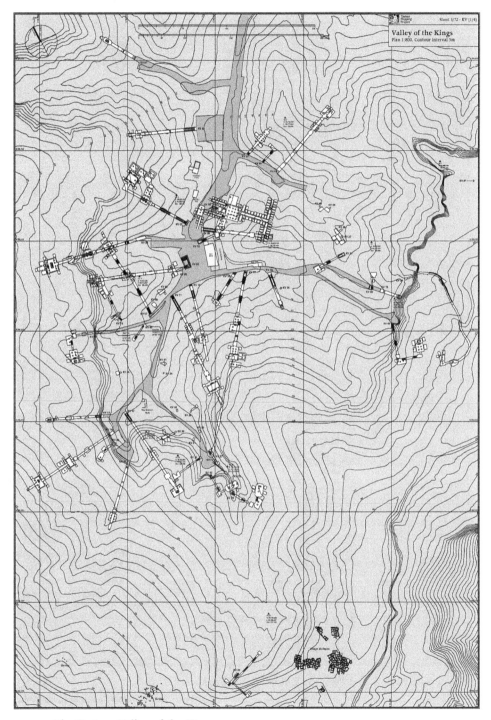

MAP 1 The Eastern Valley of the Kings.

[Map courtesy of the Theban Mapping Project.]

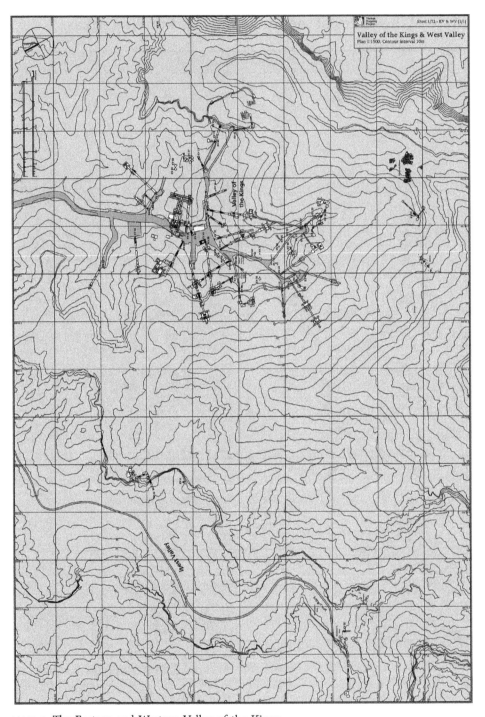

MAP 2 The Eastern and Western Valley of the Kings.

[Map courtesy of the Theban Mapping Project.]

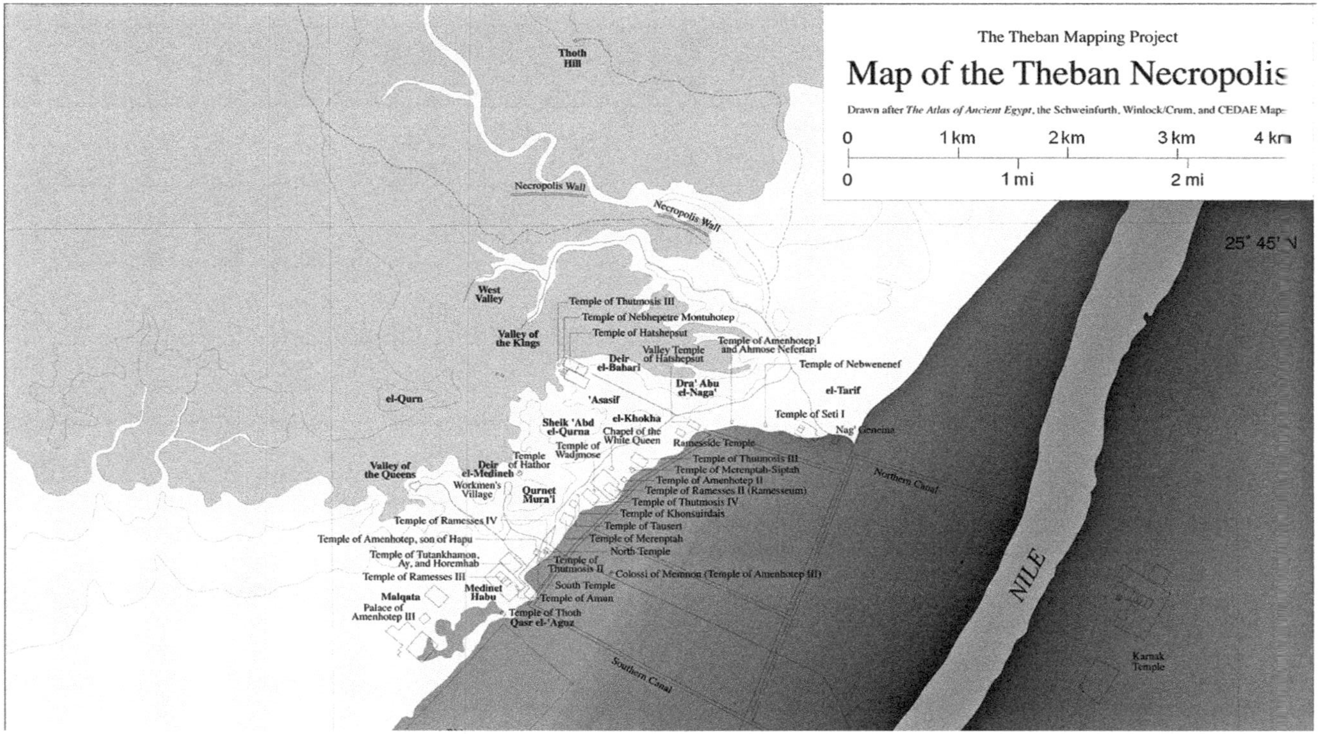

The Theban Mapping Project

Map of the Theban Necropolis

Drawn after *The Atlas of Ancient Egypt*, the Schweinfurth, Winlock/Crum, and CEDAE Maps

NILE

Karnak
Temple

25° 45' N

Thoth
Hill

Necropolis Wall

Valley of
the Kings

West
Valley

el-Qurn

Valley of
the Queens

Temple of Thutmosis III

Temple of Nebhepetre Montuhotep

Temple of Hatshepsut

Deir
el-Bahari

Valley Temple
of Hatshepsut

Dra' Abu
el-Naga'

el-Tarif

Temple of Amenhotep I
and Ahmose Nefertari

Temple of Nebwenenef

Temple of Seti I

Nag'

'Assif

el-Khokha

Sheikh 'Abd
el-Qurna

Chapel of the
White Queen

Temple of
Wahmose

Ramesside Temple

Temple of Thutmosis III

Temple of Merenptah-Siptah

Temple of Amenhotep II

Temple of Rameses II (Ramesseum)

Temple of Thutmosis IV

Temple of Djehutimes

Temple of Merenptah

Temple of Tausert

North Temple

Colossi of Memnon (Temple of Amenhotep III)

Temple of
Thutmosis II

Temple of
Thutmosis I

South Temple

Temple of Amun

Temple of Thoth

Qasr el-'Aguz

Deir
el-Medineh

Workmen's
Village

Temple of
Hathor

Qurnet
Mura'i

Medinet
Habu

Malqata
Palace of
Amenhotep III

Temple of Rameses IV

Temple of Amenhotep, son of Hapu

Temple of Tutankhamon,
Ay, and Horemhab

Temple of Rameses III

Northern Canal

Southern Canal

| 0 | 1 km | 2 km | 3 km | 4 km |
| 0 | 1 mi | 2 mi | | |

MAP 3 Map of the Theban necropolis: The area around the Valley of the Kings.

[Map courtesy of the Theban Mapping Project.]

BIBLIOGRAPHY

Reeves, C. N. and R. H. Wilkinson. 1996. *The Complete Valley of the Kings: Tombs and Treasures of Egypt's Greatest Pharaohs*, London & New York.

Shaw, I. 2009. *The Oxford History of Ancient Egypt*. Oxford.

Thomas, E. 1966. *The Royal Necropoleis of Thebes*. Princeton.

PART II

THE NATURAL
SETTING

CHAPTER 1

··

GEOLOGY OF THE VALLEY OF THE KINGS

··

JUDITH M. BUNBURY

THE Valley of the Kings is the canvas upon which the royal mortuary complex was developed. The geology is fundamental to the topography of the area: the formation of the rocks and their uplift and erosion to form the deep valleys of the Theban massif in which the necropolis was hidden. The geology is also the source of some of the practical difficulties experienced by tomb builders as well as those encountered by archaeologists and conservators of today.

The tombs of the kings at Luxor are excavated into a series of broad, flat-lying limestone beds (see Figure 1.1) that were deposited at a time when the area was buried under a warm, shallow sea (Said 1962; Sampsell 2003). The chalky limestones contain fossils, including sea urchins, from the Eocene period (Nakkady 1950), and these creamy-white stones, which can be relatively easily excavated, also make an excellent base for carving, writing, and painting. The stones were an excellent medium for the production of the many decorated tomb-chapels of the Valley of the Kings. Fragments of the white limestones were also an ideal and freely available substrate for memos and sketches, many of which were found in rubbish deposited in the failed well of Deir el-Medina, the ancient village that was home to the artisans who worked at the Valley of the Kings. From these fragments and jottings on old pottery, a detailed picture of village life for New Kingdom tomb builders emerged.

Although the limestones of the Valley of the Kings were a good medium, into which were built the decorated tomb-chapels, they were not perfect. Beneath the limestone is the clay-rich Esna shale, which expands and contracts with water, providing a treacherous and unstable foundation. In addition, the limestone beds, although generally fine-grained, chalky, and homogeneous, are interrupted by beds of yellow friable marl and shale as well as bands of silicious concretions (nodules) that have grown within the limestone. Minor faults also frequently disrupt the layers of rock of the plateau into which the Valley of the Kings is incised. These various features presented challenges to the tomb builders and required adaptations to the design of the tombs as the excavations proceeded.

FIGURE 1.1 The broad, flat-lying limestones of the Valley of the Kings seen at Deir el-Bahri, with the grey Esna shales visible just above the temple and the Theban limestones above it.
[Photograph courtesy University of Arizona Egyptian Expedition.]

GEOLOGICAL HISTORY

The rocks of North Africa and Egypt are founded on old continental crust that sank under the sea during the Jurassic period (Said 1981; Rutherford and Ryan 1995). The sea was warm and shallow, drowned all of Egypt, and extended southward into northern Sudan. As the sea advanced thick beds of sandstone, the Nubian sandstone, accumulated and eventually became periodically marine, as the waters became more extensive and deeper. With time, terrestrial influences waned from sandy to muddy and eventually almost completely ceased, so that the area became a warm, shallow sea, a rich habitat for sea life somewhat like the Florida of modern times. As the sea animals died they fell to the sea floor, and diagenetic processes formed silicate-rich flint nodules around the rotting bodies. Eventually, during the Cretaceous period (145 to 66 million years ago) conditions became ideal for the deposition of chalk. Chalk forms when the microscopic skeletons of coccoliths (tiny planktonic animals) accumulate on the seabed to form a very fine-grained limestone deposit (Figure 1.2).

Toward the end of the Cretaceous the sediments became muddier again, and a layer of mud several hundred meters thick was deposited. This layer, somewhat compressed and lightly metamorphosed, is now known as the Esna shale, and it straddles

(a)

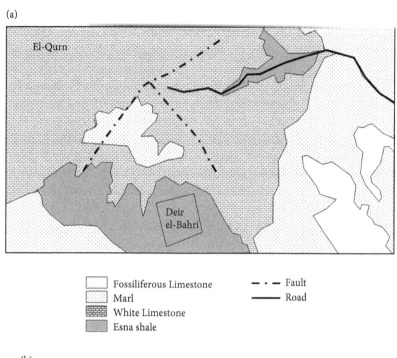

El-Qurn

Deir
el-Bahri

☐ Fossiliferous Limestone   – · – Fault
▢ Marl   —— Road
▦ White Limestone
▨ Esna shale

(b)

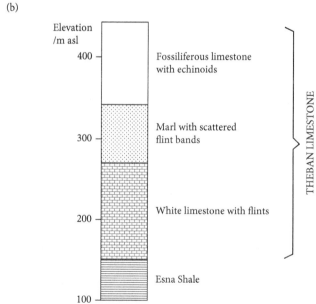

Elevation
/m asl

400 — Fossiliferous limestone
with echinoids

300 — Marl with scattered
flint bands

200 — White limestone with flints

Esna Shale

100 —

THEBAN LIMESTONE

FIGURE 1.2 A and B. Map and section of geology of the Valley of the Kings, showing fault-
ing and extent of outcrop of the Esna shale and Theban limestones in the Luxor area.

[Compiled by J. Bunbury after Said (1962) and Rutherford and Ryan (1995).]

the boundary between the late Cretaceous and the Eocene periods (56 to 34 million years ago). After the muddy interval, limestone-producing conditions returned during the early Eocene to produce the layer in which the Valley of the Kings formed. The chalky, white, Eocene limestone beds are ideal for excavation and decoration, as they are fine grained, can be cut in any direction, and form an excellent white background for paint. Occasionally there were episodes of muddy input from the land, which resulted in thin shale beds, but generally terrestrial input was limited, allowing chalk beds around 10 meters thick to form. As other animals, including sea urchins, died and fell to the seafloor, they were also incorporated into the sediment and occasionally, as they decomposed, silicious (flinty) nodules formed around their remains. Eventually the sea retreated to the north, and now all that remains of it is the Mediterranean Sea.

During all this deposition the ancient crust, already criss-crossed by a network of faults that are generally parallel to either the Gulf of Suez or the Gulf of Aqaba (Youssef 1968), continued to creak with ancient fault lines. These would break through the newer rocks again, leaving discontinuities and fissures in the limestones and, in the Theban area, forming an upstanding block that is skirted by the Nile. The latter forms the backdrop to Luxor and the massif into which the Valley of the Kings is incised. The massif is known locally as al-Qurn, and the remains of temples on Thoth Hill at the highest point seem to date from the Early Dynastic (Strudwick and Strudwick 1999). The earthquakes that result from movements of the faults continue to the present day and have caused damage, particularly in the Valley of the Queens.

FORMATION OF THE VALLEY

While the early history of the geology of the Valley of the Kings is one of deposition and uplift, its recent history is dominated by erosion. Although the modern Nile seems to flow serenely across the broad floodplain of the Luxor area, the river has evolved through a number of phases as glacial and interglacial cycles lowered and raised the sea level affecting the river. Flexing of the African tectonic plates also contributed to the vertical land movements that formed the valley. During the Pliocene (the period 5 to 2.5 million years ago) a profound glaciation lowered the sea level dramatically, drying up most of the Mediterranean Sea. As the sea level fell, the Nile eroded its way down to form a deep canyon that stretched from the Aswan to the Mediterranean basin, matching the Grand Canyon in scale.

Increased rainfall in the Saharan region activated the local tributaries of the Nile, which cut down into the layers of rock to form deep valleys. As the sea level rose again, it invaded the Nile canyon, which became a marine gulf and started to fill with sediment. With time, locally derived rock fragments and abundant sandy sediment from the White Nile catchment helped to refill the Nile valley, and as it did, the tributary radar valleys clogged up with sediment to form the dry wadi system of modern Egypt, of which the valleys of the Theban area form parts. The full extent of these buried valleys can be seen on satellite radar traces, and hence they have become known as "radar valleys" (McCauley et al. 1982).

In the Nile valley, the dark-brown sediments that are so fertile and form most of the agricultural wealth of Egypt are a thin (10- to 20-meter) veneer on the top of the yellower sediments of the marine canyon. The dark-brown, clay-rich sediments were derived from the Ethiopian highlands when the Ethiopian monsoon was switched on at the end of the last glaciation, eroding the Ethiopian basalts and bringing the mineral-rich products to "the black land," as the ancient Egyptians knew it. The dark sediments lap around the remains of the uplifted bedrock massif and into the mouths of the clogged radar valleys.

In addition to affecting sea level and causing the incision of the valley, climate change has also caused rainfall in Egypt to vary over time. After the end of the glaciation around 12,500 years ago, direct rainfall initially increased in the Egyptian region until it peaked at around 6,000 years ago, when it began gradually falling to current levels. During the pre-dynastic period and into the Old Kingdom, there was sufficient water to sustain vegetation, which stabilized the surface of the mountains and valleys, reducing erosion and producing a layer known locally as "tafla." However, by the New Kingdom rainfall was sparse, and no vegetation remained in the valleys. Just as there is occasional rainfall now in the Luxor area, there was also during the New Kingdom period. In the absence of vegetation to absorb the rain, water ran off quickly into the valleys, mobilizing the sediment as it went, and caused flash floods such as those in autumn 1994, described by McLane and colleagues (2003).

Flash floods of this type continued to shape the valley during the construction of the Valley of the Kings, as well as after the necropolis was no longer in use. Construction of the tombs generated large quantities of rubble, which the workers dispersed within the floor of the valley, altering its profile. During flash floods the rubble was further redistributed, so that natural surface rubble as well as that dumped by the tomb builders was transported from the upper part of the valley to the lower, raising the floor of the lower valley above the level of the existing tomb entrances. Although tombs were originally sealed when construction and burial was completed, the majority were reopened and robbed in antiquity, leaving them vulnerable to the elements. Subsequent flash floods entered many of the tombs, damaging and burying the contents. In the case of the tomb of Tutankhamun (Cross 1993), flooding occurred so soon after the completion and initial robbery of the tomb that the remains were completely concealed until their discovery by Howard Carter in 1922. However, it is not clear whether the deep shafts that interrupt the entrance passages of many of the tombs were intended to divert such floodwaters, to trap robbers, or both.

In addition to the management of flash floods, the rocks of the Valley of the Kings provide an additional hazard that was encountered in antiquity and continues to affect the survival of the tombs: the shales below and within the limestones. Thin layers of

FIGURE 1.3 A and B. Star from temple of Seti I and five-pointed star on sea urchin fossil from Theban Plateau.

[Photographs by J. Bunbury.]

shale within the limestone accumulations are of unpredictable position and extent. Piers Litherland's work has shown that when tomb excavators intersected an unexpected shale band, they seem to have adapted their plans and diverted the shafts to avoid the hazard (Litherland 2013). The irregularities of the thin shale beds, taken with the occurrence of flint nodules and abundant cracking of the chalks, meant that the walls of the tomb often had to be made good with a thin layer of plaster before relief and painting could be executed.

In addition to the practical difficulty of creating reliefs in the shale, there was a hazard perhaps unanticipated by the tomb builders. Once the clay in the shale layers is exposed to the air, the flexible structure of the clay minerals absorbs water from humidity in the atmosphere and expands, acting as a hydraulic pad and forcing apart the limestone beds around the clay layer, causing damage to the tombs in which they are found. Large numbers of visitors naturally increase the humidity within the tombs and can exacerbate this effect.

The more extensive metamorphosed muds of the Esna shale that underlie the chalky Eocene limestones can be particularly problematic. In particular, the combination of floodwater and exposure of the underlying Esna shale can cause comprehensive damage, for example that described by Stephen Cross (unpublished Supreme Council of Antiquities, Egypt conservation report). The conservation work of Stephen W. Cross has been directed toward finding ways to minimize the damage to tombs from expansion of the Esna shale, which breaks down the walls and pillars of the tombs and damages the ceilings.

Many of the tombs are cut into the lower chalky limestones, but a number of fossils are found in the surface rocks of the Valley of the Kings, and striking among these are the fossils of echinoids (sea urchins). The sea urchins are characterized by a five-pointed star of small holes in the upper part of the shell, and these have been proposed by Ken McNamara (2010) as the source of the images of stars that have five points, such as those at the temple of Seti I nearby (see Figure 1.3A and B). Perhaps the ancient people of the Valley of the Kings thought that these were stars that had fallen to earth!

BIBLIOGRAPHY

Aston, B. G., J. A. Harrell, and I. Shaw. 2000. "Stone." In *Ancient Egyptian Materials and Technology*, edited by P. T. Nicholson and I. Shaw, 5–77. Cambridge.

Baines, J., and J. Malek. 2002. *Atlas of Ancient Egypt*. Cairo.

Cross, S. W. 1993. "The Hydrology of the Valley of the Kings." *Journal of Egyptian Archaeology* 94: 305–310.

Gupta, A., ed. 2007. *Large Rivers: Geomorphology and Management*. New York.

Hume, W. F. 1925. *Geology of Egypt*. Vol. 1, *The Surface Features of Egypt: Their Determining Causes and Relation to Geological Structure*. Cairo.

Litherland, P. 2013. "Landscape and Human Activity in the Valley of the Kings: Construction Techniques, Geology and Their Implications in the XVIIIth Dynasty." PhD diss., Cambridge University.

McCauley, J. F., G. G. Schaber, C. S. Breed, M. J. Grolier, C. V. Haynes, B. Issawi, C. Elachi, and R. Blom. 1982. "Subsurface Valleys and Geoarcheology of the Eastern Sahara Revealed by Shuttle Radar." *Science* 218: 1004–1020.

McHugh, W. P., J. F. McCauley, C. V. Haynes, C. S. Breed, and G. P. Schaber. 1988. "Paleorivers and Geoarchaeology in the Southern Egyptian Sahara." *Geoarchaeology* 3: 1–40.

McLane, J., R. A. J. Wüst, B. Porter, and J. Rutherford. 2003. "Flash-Flood Impacts and Protection Measures in the Valley of the Kings." *Luxor, Egypt Association for Preservation Technology International Bulletin* 34: 37–45.

McNamara, K. J. 2010. *The Star-Crossed Stone: The Secret Life, Myths, and History of a Fascinating Fossil.* London.

Nakkady, S. E. 1950. "A New Foraminiferal Fauna from the Esna Shales and Upper Cretaceous Chalk of Egypt." *Journal of Palaeontology* 24: 675–692.

Nicholson, P. T., and I. Shaw, eds. 2000. *Ancient Egyptian Materials and Technology.* Cambridge.

Rutherford, J., and D. P. Ryan. 1995. "Tentative Tomb Protection Priorities, Valley of the Kings, Egypt." In *Valley of the Sun Kings: New Explorations in the Tombs of the Pharaohs*, edited by R. H. Wilkinson, 134–156. Tucson, AZ.

Said, R. 1962. *The Geology of Egypt.* Amsterdam.

Said, R. 1981. *The Geological Evolution of the River Nile.* New York.

Said, R. 1993. *The River Nile: Geology, Hydrology and Utilization.* Oxford.

Sampsell, B. M. 2003. *A Traveller's Guide to the Geology of Egypt.* Cairo.

Strudwick, N., and H. Strudwick. 1999. *Thebes in Egypt.* Ithaca, NY.

Wilkinson, R. H., ed. 1995. *Valley of the Sun Kings: New Explorations in the Tombs of the Pharaohs.* Tucson, AZ.

Woodward, J. C., M. G. Macklin, M. D. Krom, and A. J. Williams. 2007. "The Nile: Evolution, Quarternary River Environments and Material Fluxes." In *Large Rivers: Geomorphology and Management*, edited by A. Gupta, 261–292. New York

Youssef, M. I. 1968. "Structural Pattern of Egypt and Its Interpretation." *American Association of Petroleum Geologists Bulletin* 52 (4): 601–614.

CHAPTER 2

TOPONYMS OF THE VALLEY OF THE KINGS AND ITS APPROACHES

KENT R. WEEKS

THE course of the Nile at Luxor has shifted over time, and the river's current west bank lies farther east than it did in the nineteenth century. Maps from that time place it near what is today the Cairo–Aswan highway and the adjacent el-Fadliyya Canal, a kilometer west of its present channel (Bonomi 1906; Winlock 1924, 225, ftn. 3; van der Spek 2011). In the nineteenth century, a great tree, a *Ficus sycomorus*, stood on the river's west bank, directly across from the temples at Karnak. The tree was called the *gemayz Abu Daoud* (*gemayz* is the Arabic word for the sycomore fig tree), and it and an adjacent *saqia* marked the landing spot for boats bringing tourists who began their tour of West Bank monuments here (see, e.g., the 1817 description in Manley 2001, 185). The tree is gone today, but the *saqia* can still be seen, in the courtyard of the Abul Kassem Hotel.

Three thousand years ago, this area was called *ḫft-ḥr nb.s*, "In Front of [i.e., Facing] Her Lord," loosely translated as the "Forecourt of Karnak" (Winlock 1924, 225; Otto 1952,49; Leitz 2002, V, 725), identifying it as part of the domain of the temple of Amun across the Nile. On the shoreline, a stone quay marked the landing where the *gemayz* later grew (Winlock 1924, 224–225), and where religious processions from Karnak docked during festivals and royal funeral ceremonies before passing through an area known two hundred years ago as *Er-Rebek* (Bonomi 1906, 79; more correctly, *Qasr el Rubayq*), and today as *el-Genīna* (van der Spek 2011). From the nearby memorial temple of Seti I, ancient processions and nineteenth- century tourists traveled across low-lying desert that offered a footpath, accessible even during the inundation, southward to royal memorial temples and westward to the Valley of the Kings (KV; Winlock 1924, 224). That path is still today the principal route used by visitors to KV.

In antiquity the West Bank was called *imntt n w3st*, "The West of Thebes," "The Great West," or "The Beautiful West" (Otto 1952, 45). Other names included *st m3ʿt*, "The Domain of Maat," or "The Land of the Two Truths," "The Land of the Truthful Ones" (perhaps a reference to non-royal necropoleis; Ventura 1986, 38–63), and *t3 rj.t (m niwt)*, "This Side (of the City)" (Otto 1952, 46; Černý 1973, 87). Later, *t3mt* or *d3mt*, Djeme, originally a name for the area around Medinet Habu, came to be used for all the West Bank (Vandorpe 1995, 222), as did the Greek term *Memnonia* (Winlock 1926, 4 and pl. 1; Gardiner 1961, 91–94; Thomas 1966, 51;), and even *hft-hr nb.s* (Winlock 1924, 224–225).

From *hft-hr nb.s*, modern tourists and ancient priests proceeded to the Valley of the Kings through a long and winding *wadi* that starts behind the memorial temple of Seti I, between a part of Dira' Abu el-Naga called *Khawi 'Alamat,* and the home of Howard Carter. The area at the beginning of this *wadi* was perhaps *sht 3t,* "The Great Field" (Černý 1973, 90; Wente 1973, 227). From here, it weaves its way 6 kilometers north and west to a modern parking lot and Visitors Center, where the two Valleys of the Kings, the East and the West, begin (Černý 1936, 113). Today, this path is the preferred route of most tourists to KV because it is paved and climbs gradually into the desert, making it suitable for buses and bicycles. Five decades ago, before it was paved, its starting point was called *Dira' Abu el-Nabi.* In antiquity, the path was a sandy track used by funeral processions for New Kingdom pharaohs, and was called *w3t htp r' im-s,* "The Path on Which the Sun Sets" (Spiegelberg 1898, 9; Otto 1952, 56), and there was an official charged to watch over it. One such was Amennakht, son of Ipuy, called "The Royal Scribe of the *w3t*-on-which-the-sun-sets" (Spiegelberg 1898, 9; Thomas 1966, 50). Other references to it include "die Schöne Treppe des Westens," and perhaps "der Weg, mit welchen sich die sonne vereinigt" (Otto 1952, 56). Edward Lane (2000, 370) described the path in the 1820s: "The natural road to the Tombs of the Kings is a narrow, long, and winding valley; the entrance of which is about half a mile from the ruined village of El-Choor'neh [Qurna]. The sides are steep and rugged; and of whitish and sandy hue. Not a blade of grass, nor even a noxious weed, is seen throughout the tedious route; which is well calculated to prepare the mind of the traveler for the contemplation of the solemn and mysterious tombs; and seldom is his attention diverted by any living creature inhabiting the valley. . ." Apparently, Henry Salt cut a road through the *wadi* to transport the sarcophagus of Rameses III to the Nile, but it was destroyed by flash floods soon after completion in 1819 (Thomas 1966, 56), and only a track remained until 1960, when a paved road was laid down.

The track forks at the modern Visitors Center. One path continues forward into the East Valley; the other, on the right, leads to the West Valley of the Kings, "Vallée de l'Ouest," also called *wadyein,* "The Two Wadis," because near its entrance, just beyond the expedition house built a century ago by Theodore Davis, the single *wadi* splits. That on the right is called by the French the "Vallée du gardien Khaouy" (Černý et al. 1969–1970). The main part of the West Valley continues to the left and is called *Bibân el Gurud,* "Les Portes des Singes," or "The Valley of the Monkeys," a reference to a scene in KV 23, the tomb of Ay. Farther along, on the left, lies the "Cirque du graffito de 'Eau du Ciel'," in which KV 22, the tomb of Amenhotep III, was dug. Beside it, we find the "Terrasse de repos des Ouvriers" (Černý et al. 1969–1970). At the end of the West Valley, the path splits again. The branch on the right leads into the "Vallée de la tombe de Ay," that on the left to the "Vallée de la 'Chambre de Hay', " and to a steep path leading over the hill to the East Valley.

Returning to the modern Visitors Center, one walks south along the gently rising *wadi* floor toward the entrance of the East Valley of the Kings. On the left lie two side-*wadi*s, "the Vallée du scribe Houy," and the "Vallée du Puits," with KV 41 (Černý et al. 1969–1970). A few meters beyond, the road climbs more steeply and makes a sharp curve to the right. It was here that a low bedrock cliff once blocked the entrance to KV. Pococke described its appearance (1743–1745, 97): the road "ascended by a narrow steep passage, about ten feet high which seems to have been broken down thro' the rocks." A part of the cliff was cut away in the nineteenth century to provide easier access to KV. Villagers called the cut *el-Manata*, "the jumping-place." A footpath was built around this barrier, on the hill near the cliff's western end; it can still be seen today. (The area is shown in a nineteenth-century sketch by Lane [2000, pl. 48, figure 112 in Thompson's edition]). The entire passage was cut through in the 1960s to complete the paved road leading from *ḥft-ḥr nb.s* into KV itself. Today, the tourist tram from the Visitors Center stops a few meters from here, and the modern entrance to KV is marked by a ticket office and a gate beyond which only official vehicles may pass.

There are two other principal routes to KV. The least frequently used is a steep path that climbs over the ridge separating the temple at Deir el-Bahri from KV. In the nineteenth century, the path was called *Shuq Ismail* (Bonomi 1906, 80; Lane 2000, 370–371). In the New Kingdom, the ridge and the range of hills on the West Bank of which it is a part were referred to generally as *p3 ḏw* or *ḏww imntt* (Černý 1973, 97). The highest point in the hills is the *Qurn*, "Horn," or *el-Tantoura*, "The High Place," in antiquity called *t3 dhnt3t* "The Great Peak" (Otto 1952, 47), which hovers over the southern end of KV. Its pyramidal shape when viewed from KV may have been one reason that KV was chosen as the site for royal burials.

By far the most frequently traveled route to KV in the New Kingdom was the steep path that climbed the southern end of the ridge, from the village at Deir el-Medina along the lower slope of the Qurn. It was the path taken by workmen from their homes in that village to KV, where they were employed cutting and decorating the royal tombs. The path is still used today, and is popular with young, independent tourists. The path, or some part of it, was called *k3y r bwt* (Bruyère 1939, 353; Thomas 1966, 58), and at its highest point, where one begins the descent into KV, a small collection of 64 stone huts known as the "Village du Repos" was built so workmen (the *rmt-ist n p3 ḥr*, "People of the Necropolis") could spend time enjoying the sweet breath of the north wind without having to return home to Deir el-Medina (Peet 1930, I, 10). The village may have been called *ṯhn nfr* (originally the name of a nearby chapel, Bruyère 1939, 353), the col in which it lay perhaps *sḥt*, "the Field," and thus, *t3y.f ˁt nty m sḥt*, "his room that is in the field" (Thomas 1966, 58). Farther west, on the slope of the Qurn, stood a series of nearly two hundred small shrines (Davies 1935–1938, and soon to be published by the Theban Mapping Project).

Along *k3y r bwt* and the path in the northern *wadi*, it is likely that there stood small guard posts manned by the *mḏ3y*, police whose job was to prevent unauthorized entry to KV (Černý 1965; Thomas 1966, 51; Ventura 1986, 171; Eyre 1992, 279). The huts were called *inbt*, "walled enclosures," perhaps similar to the ancient structures still to be seen above KV 9 and other places in the Necropolis (Carter 1917, pl. xix; Thomas 1966, 51). Edgerton (1951, 139, ftn. 10), referring to a mention of them in the Strike Papyrus, described them: "I conceive the five *inbt* of the Necropolis (or of the Tomb?) as five small forts or guardhouses or fortified gateways which had to be passed successively by anyone following the valley route to or from the Tombs of the Kings." *p3 ḥtm n p3 ḥr*, "the Fortress of the Necropolis" (Thomas 1966, 50–51), may refer to similar structures, or to a stone wall that surrounded the royal necropoleis. Traces of that wall, some of it of later, Christian, date, can still be seen today (and parts are shown on Schweinfurth's 1909 map; Winlock 1926).

Wadi Biban el-Moluk, the Valley of the Kings, together with other parts of the royal necropolis, were called *p3 ḥr ʿ3 špsy n ḥḥw n rnpwt n pr-ʾ3 ʿws ḥr imntt w3st*, "The Great, Noble Necropolis of Millions of Years of Pharaoh, May He Live, be Prosperous and Healthy, on the West of Thebes," a term that originally may have referred to a "king's tomb in progress" (Thomas 1966, 50). The general terms for *wadi, int* and *t3 int* (Černý 1973, 92), could also refer to a specific *wadi*, depending on context. It has been suggested, for example, that in some texts, *t3 int* referred to the valley in which Deir el-Medina, called *p3 dmit*, lies (Ventura 1986, 154), while in others it might refer to Deir el-Bahri (Černý 1973, 94). Generally, *t3 int* is to be translated simply as "the valley," unless context requires a more specific term, as in English "the city" might refer to New York or London or another specific urban center, or simply to large urban settings in general, only the context revealing which meaning was intended. Spiegelberg (1921, 588, 897) thought *t3 int* was a term used of every royal *wadi*. Černý (1927, 186; 1973, 92) believed that, while *int* meant simply "valley," *t3 int* might refer specifically to KV, but most Egyptologists (e.g., Peet 1930, 10; Thomas 1966, 50 and 1963, 57) argue that both are general terms (*t3 int ʿ3t*, on the other hand, may refer specifically to the Valley of the Queens [Ventura 1986, 162].) A similar confusion surrounds the modern term *Wadi Biban el-Moluk*, which some Egyptologists use to refer only to the East Valley of the Kings, others to both the East Valley and the West.

ḥr was "a word for 'tomb' generally," and some argue that *p3 ḥr* "means the tomb of the reigning pharaoh, usually in course of construction during his lifetime" (Winlock 1924, 226; Capart, Gardiner, and van de Walle 1936, 186 ftn. 10; Černý 1973, 1–28). Ventura (1986, 1–37), however, believes *ḥr* to be a reference to "the necropolis administration of the workmen," specifically to the administrative district enclosing the royal necropoleis. Other frequently used words for "tomb" included *ḥrt* and *st* or *st ʿ3t* (Peet 1930, I, 9; Gardiner 1947, I, 142*; Thomas 1966; cf. Bruyere and Kuentz 1926, 54; Wente 1973, 225). *p3 b3kw* and *p3 r3-ʾ b3kw*, "that which is in a state of work," may also refer to tombs in prog- ress (Černý 1973, 81 and 1929, 248; Thomas 1966, 61).

t3 st ʿ3 (nty ḥtp pr-ʾ3 im-s), "The Great Place (in Which Pharaoh Rests)," may refer to *Wadi Biban el-Moluk*, as well as to specific KV tombs, as perhaps did *p3 ḥr ḥni* and *p3 ḥr n ḥnw ḥni*, "the Guarded *p3 ḥfr* within (the Gebel)" (Thomas 1966, 50, 1963, 57–73, and

1966, 50, ftn. 13, citing T. G. Allen), and similarly *st nty imnt*, "The Place That Is Hidden" (Černý 1929, 245, 247), but again see Ventura (1986, 1–37).

Not everyone, however, believes that KV had its own, unique name. Peet (1930: 10) thought it did not: "It is singular that these papyri do not furnish us with the name of the Valley of the Kings. Indeed, we know of no ancient name for it save the vague term *t3 int*, 'the Valley.'" Ventura (1986: 185) argued that protecting royal burials in KV required any reference to it be shrouded in secrecy and concealed in circumlocutory phrases: "I believe that a search after the official name of the Valley of the Kings in the documents of the Necropolis that we possess is doomed to failure a priori. I doubt whether such a name ever existed. . ."

We know nothing about ancient terms for geographical features within KV. It seems likely that locations were indicated, as they are today, by reference to visible tomb entrances: "*x* lies near the tomb of Rameses VI," "*y* lies in the side-wadi with two pit tombs," and so on. The French surveys identified small *wadis* in KV in this manner. Their system divides part of the West Bank archaeological zone into four regions: D, the West Valley of the Kings; C, southern Theban *wadis*; B, the Valley of the Queens; and A, the East Valley of the Kings. Region A was subdivided into 10 units: A1, the Valley of the Scribe Houy; A2, the Valley of the Well; A3, the Valley of KV 4; A4, the Valley of KV 1; A5, the Valley of KV 8; A6, the Valley of KV 35; A7, the Valley of KV 15 (and others); A8, the gebel that separates KV 15 from KV 34; A9, the Valley of KV 34; and A10, the eastern slope of the Qurn above KV (Černý et al. 1969–1970, 16–40).

BIBLIOGRAPHY

Baikie, J. 1932. *Egyptian Antiquities in the Nile Valley*. London.

Baillet, A. 1926. Inscriptions grecques et latines des tombeaux des rois ou syringes. *Mémoires de l'Institut Français d'Archéologie Orientale du Caire* 42 (2): 222ff.

Bonomi, J. (edited by P. E. Newberry). 1906. "Topographical Notes on Western Thebes Collected in 1830." *Annales du Service des Antiquités de l'Égypte* 7: 78–86.

Bruyere, B. 1939. *Rapport sur les fouilles de Deir el-Medineh (1934–1935): Le village, les décharges publiques, la station de repos du col de la Vallée des Rois.* (= FIFAO, 16,3). Cairo.

Bruyere, B. and C. Kuentz. 1926. "La tombe de Nakht-Min et la tombe d'Ari-Nefer." *Mémoires de l'Institut Français d'Archéologie Orientale du Caire* 54: 51–54.

Capart, J., A. H. Gardiner, and B. van de Walle. 1936. "New Light on the Ramesside Tomb-Robberies." *Journal of Egyptian Archaeology* 22: 169–193.

Carter, H. 1917. "A Tomb Prepared for Queen Hatshepsuit and Other Recent Discoveries at Thebes." *Journal of Egyptian Archaeology* 4: 107–118.

Černý, J. 1927. "Le culte d'Amenophis Ier chez les ouvriers de la nécropole thébaine." *Bulletin de l'Institut Français d'Archéologie Orientale* 27: 159–203.

Carter, J. 1929. "A Note on the "Repeating of Births." *Journal of Egyptian Archaeology* 15: 194–198.

Carter, J. 1936. "Datum des Todes Ramses' III. und der Thronbesteigung Ramses' IV." *Zeitschrift für Ägyptische Sprache und Altertumskunde* 72: 109–118.

Černý, J. 1965. "Egypt from the Death of Ramesses III to the End of the Twenty-first Dynasty." In Edwards, Gadd, Hammond and Sollberger: Vol. 2:2, 606–657.

Černý, J. 1973. A Community of Workmen at Thebes in the Ramesside Period (= BdE 50). 2nd ed., 2001.

Černý, J., Ch. Desroches Noblecourt, and M. Kurz. (1969–1970). Graffiti de la Montagne thébaine, I: Cartographie et etudes topographique illustrée. Cairo.

Christophe, L. A. 1953. "Les enseignements de l'ostracon 148 de Déir el-Médineh." Bulletin de l'Institut Français d'Archéologie Orientale 52: 113–44.

Davies, N. de G. (1935–1938). "A High Place at Thebes." Mélanges Maspero, I: Orient ancien. (= Mémoires de l'Institut Français d'Archéologie Orientale du Caire 66 (2), 241–250).

Edgerton, W. F. 1951. "The Strike in Ramses III's Twenty-ninth Year." Journal of Near Eastern Studies 10: 137–145.

Edwards, I. E. S., C. J. Gadd, N. G. L. Hammond, and E. Sollberger, eds. 1965. Cambridge Ancient History, 2nd ed. Cambridge.

Eyre, C. 1992. "[Review of Ventura 1986.]" Chronique d'Égypte 67 (134): 277–281.

Gardiner, A. H. 1947. Ancient Egyptian Onomastica. Oxford. 3 vols.

Gardiner, A. H. 1961. "The Egyptian Memnon." Journal of Egyptian Archaeology 47: 91–99.

Lane, E. W. 2000. Description of Egypt. edited by J. Thompson. Cairo.

Leitz, C. 2002. Lexikon der ägyptischen götter und götterbezeichnungen. Leuven.

Manley, D. 2001. "Lord Belmore Proceeds up the Nile in 1817–1818." In Starkey and Starkey, 239–260.

Otto, E. 1952. Topographie des Thebanischen Gaues. (= UGAA 16). Berlin.

Peet, T. E. 1930. The Great Tomb-Robberies of the Twentieth Dynasty: Being a Critical Study with Translations and Commentaries of the Papyri in which These are Recorded. Oxford. 2 vols.

Pococke, R. 1743–1745. A Description of the East, and Some Other Countries. London. 2 vols.

Schweinfurth, G. 1909. Karte der westlichen Umgebung von Luksor und Karnak (Theben) mit Benutzung von Wilkinson's Topographic Survey of Thebes, 1830, in 1:4500 und des Katasteraufnahme von 1904, in 1:2500. Berlin.

Spiegelberg, W. 1898. Zwei Beiträge zur Geschichte und Topographie der Thebanischen Necropolis im Neuen Reich. Strassburg.

Spiegelberg, W. 1921. Ägyptische und andere Graffiti (Inschriften und Zeichnung) aus der thebanische Nekropolis. Heidelberg.

Starkey, P. and J. Starkey, eds. 2001. Unfolding the Orient: Travellers in Egypt and the Near East. Reading.

Thomas, E. 1963. "P3 ḫr ḫni hnw / n hnw ḫni, a Designation of the Valley of the Kings." Journal of Egyptian Archaeology 49: 57–63.

Thomas, E. 1966. The Royal Necropoleis of Thebes. Princeton.

van der Spek, K. 2011. The Modern Neighbours of Tutankhamun: History, Life and Work in the Villages of the Theban West Bank. Cairo.

Vandorpe, K. 1995. "City of Many a Gate, Harbor for Many a Rebel." In Vleeming, 203–239.

Ventura, R. 1986. Living in a City of the Dead: A Selection of Topographical and Administrative Terms in the Documents of the Theban Necropolis (= OBO 69). Freiburg.

Vleeming, S. P., ed. 2011. Hundred-Gated Thebes: Acts of a Colloqium on Thebes and the Theban Area in the Graeco-Roman Period (= Papyrologica Lugduno-Batava 27). Leiden.

Wente, E. F. 1973. "A Princess's Tomb in the Valley of the Kings." Journal of Near Eastern Studies 32: 223–234.

Wilkinson, J. G. 1835. *Topography of Thebes and General View of Egypt*. London.

Wilkinson, J. G. 1843. *Modern Egypt and Thebes: Being a Description of Egypt*. London. 2 vols.

Winlock, H. E. 1924. "The Tombs of the Kings of the Seventeenth Dynasty at Thebes." *Journal of Egyptian Archaeology* 10: 217–277.

Winlock, H. E. 1926. *The Monastery of Epiphanius at Thebes, I: The Archaeological Material (= MMA Egyptian Expedition* 3). New York.

CHAPTER 3

THE HYDROLOGY OF THE VALLEY OF THE KINGS

Weather, Rainfall, Drainage Patterns, and Flood Protection in Antiquity

ANDREAS DORN

WEATHER AND RAINFALL

IN the arid climate of Egypt rainfall occurred rarely, but was not unknown. Since systematic records of rainfall from ancient Egypt are not attested to date, the proof of single rainfall events is only possible in a few cases. The necropolis journal—the document in which official records about events and in which administrative tasks related to the construction of the royal tombs were noted—could well have been the place to record rainfall, but it is unfortunately silent on such matters.

Some rainfall is attested in the desert valleys of the royal necropolis of the New Kingdom on the west bank of ancient Thebes (Valley of the Kings and Valley of the Queens) (Dorn/Müller 2006). Four graffiti mention it explicitly, in a form (*ḥꜣyt jrj.n pꜣ mw n*) that can be differentiated linguistically from Nile flood graffiti (*ḥꜣyt jrj.n pꜣ mw r*) (Janssen 1987, 130–131). The oldest of these graffiti (graffito 3013), which can be assigned to the reign of Ramesses II by the high year date, was inscribed at the far end of the Valley of the Queens at the foot of a waterfall in a canyon-like cut in the rock forming an *abris* (French: "natural rock shelter"):

Graffito 3013:

rnp.t-sp 62 ꜣbd 4 šmw sw 23 hrw pn ḥꜣyt jrj.n pꜣ mw n p.t

Regnal year 62, 4th month of the schemu-season day 23, on this day, rainfall (lit.: the coming down made by water of heaven).

The next oldest graffito was scratched just nine years later in the reign of Merenptah, next to the graffito from the reign of Ramesses II:
Graffito 3012:

rnp.t-sp 4 njswt-bjtj B3-n-R^c 3bd 1 šmw sw 27 hrw pn h3yt jrj.n p3 mw n p.t

Regnal year 4 of the king of upper und lower Egypt Merenptah, 1st month of the schemu-season, day 27 on this day, rainfall.

In another *abris* at the other end of the royal necropolis, close to the modern parking lot in the Valley of the Kings, another mention of rainfall can be found, which could be assigned to year 2 of one of the rulers following Ramesses III, based on the mention of the workman Amenpahapi:
Graffito 2868:

rnp.t-sp 2 3bd 4 šmw sw 2 h3yt jrj.n p3 mw {m} m p3 mw ḥrj m t3 p.t, sḏm- [^{c}š] m s.t m3^c.t Jmn-p3-ḥ^{c}pj sn=f sh3 ///

Regnal year 2, 4th month of the schemu-season, day 2, rainfall (lit.: coming down, made by the water as the upper water from the sky). The workman in the place of truth Amenpahapi, his brother the scribe ///.

An extraordinary graffito was recorded in the second year of Ramesses IV, V, or VI by the necropolis scribe Amennakht, son of Ipui, in the West Valley, not far from the tomb of Amenhotep III (WV 22). It is located in proximity to a depression located at the foot of a cliff, so that when heavy rains occurred, the water rushing down the rock face gathered in this depression and formed a lake. The inscription states that the scribe Amennakht went with three of his sons explicitly to show them this peculiarity:
Graffito 1736:

rnp.t-sp 2 3bd 4 šmw sw 24 r p3 mw n p.t sh3 Jmn-nḫt s3 Jpwy s3=f P3-nfr-m-ḏd s3=f H^c-m-ḥḏt s3=f P3y-nḏm

Regnal year 2, 4th month of the schemu-season, day 24, at the water of heaven, the scribe Amunnakht, son of Ipui, his son Paneferemdjed, his son Khaemhedjet, his son Pinedjem.

When connecting the Egyptian dates with the Gregorian calendar, a date in March is obtained for graffito 3012; a date in May/June for the other graffiti (Sadek 1990, 118–119). Precisely these last dates are clearly after the winter months during which rainfall usually takes place. In modern times, most rainfall has occurred in the months of October and November (Cross 2008, 305 n. 7). The reasons for the recording of these rainfalls are therefore likely to lie mainly in the fact that they were exceptional—it remains open whether they were also severe or long-lasting. Since such rainfalls are not regular, but rather exceptional cases from a historical climate point of view, no conclusions can be drawn from these data about the frequency of precipitation during the period in question.

In addition to these written attestations of rainfall, there is proof of rainfall in a strati-graphic profile east of the tomb of Ramesses X (KV 18). A layer of flash-flood deposition is attested between two layers of *taffl* (Arabic "schist"), characteristic of the construction debris from the lower parts of the tomb of Seti I. The pottery found in both *taffl* layers confirms the dating to the reign of Seti I and suggests that the flash flooding occurred during the construction of his tomb (Dorn 2011, 29–30).

Thanks to this group of graffiti in the royal necropolis and this datable rainwater layer, the first loose series of exceptional rainfalls can be established for the New Kingdom. Beginning with an instance in the reign of Seti I; another is attested more than sixty years later in the sixty-second year of the reign of Ramesses II; one nine years later in the fourth regnal year of Merenptah; and two more about sixty years later, spaced over two of the three reigns of Ramesses IV, V, or VI, at intervals of five to a maximum of thirteen years.

A late Eighteenth Dynasty date has been proposed for the heavy rain and flash flood-ing that purportedly covered over tombs KV 55, KV 62, and KV 63 (Cross 2008). This date cannot be regarded as certain, since the conclusion assumes that no flash-flood debris had been deposited on that spot for the tens of thousands of years before the use of the Valley of the Kings for tombs. The conglomerate layer in the area of these three tombs cannot be dated based on the old excavation photographs and sometimes even contradictory descriptions, and requires the consultation of stratigraphic profiles, lay-ers, or other datable material. It is more likely that the conglomerate layer had built up over thousands of years and was dug through during construction of the tombs, as is the case with similar stratigraphy observed in the area of shaft openings elsewhere in the Theban necropolis, cases in which it is clear from the filling of the shafts and superim-posed brick structures that the conglomerate layer already existed before the shaft was hewn (Polz 1992, 115–117).

The above-mentioned rainfall in the reign of Seti I could have covered the tombs KV 55, KV 62, and KV 63 at the latest, which at least contributed to the locations of KV 62 and KV 63 becoming lost.

Another stratigraphic profile consisting entirely of layers formed after rainfall is located in the last corridor (corridor C) of the unfinished tomb of Ramesses X (KV 18), which was never used for a burial (Dorn 2000, 30–33). The profile consists of thirty layers, which cannot be dated more precisely than to say that they occurred after the tomb's construction, that is to say, after 1115 B.C.E. Similar fill was observed for instance in KV 5 (sons of Ramesses II; Weeks 2000a, 12–13, 16), in KV 7 (Ramesses II; Guillaume and Emery-Barbier 1995), and in KV 8 (Merenptah; Barbotin and Guichard 2004). However, these only happened after the original burial was removed, a chro-nology suggested by the fact that in these tombs, which were at times filled to the top with rainwater debris, only a few objects from the original grave assemblages were found. The tombs seem to have been protected from intruding rainwater until the end of the New Kingdom, as indicated by the tomb robbery papyri, for instance for the tomb of Ramesses II; rainwater entered only after the New Kingdom (Guillaume and Emery-Barbier 1995, 149–150). This observation shows on the one hand that when the tombs of Ramesses VI (KV 9) and Ramesses IX (KV 6) were built, the debris had been dumped in such a way that the entrance of the tomb of Ramesses II could not be reached by rainwater, and on the other hand that water protection still existed after the tomb robberies at the end of the New Kingdom, or was re-established after the inspections.

DRAINAGE PATTERNS AND FLOOD PROTECTION

The geomorphological drainage system of the Valley of the Kings in the time of the pharaohs did not differ significantly from today's, as the map in Figure 3.1 shows (Cross 2008, fig. 1; Rutherford and Ryan 1995, fig. 3). Water drainage patterns were known to the officials responsible for the planning and construction of the tombs in the Valley of the Kings, and they were respected to ensure the protection of the tombs against the ingress of rainwater. They had to take account of both the danger to the tombs of large amounts of flash-flood water as well as the position of the individual tombs in relation to their exposure.

The systematic protection of tombs from water penetration before and after construction can be concluded from two observations: on the one hand, no water damage can be detected in unrobbed tombs, in tombs resealed after robbery, or even in tombs that were at times left open (e.g., KV 36, KV 46, KV 60, KV 62, KV 63); on the other hand, some tombs display constructional features that served explicitly for water drainage.

Rainfall runoff could flow over the valley cliffs in the form of waterfalls. This phenomenon is also linguistically attested by the expression ph n $p3$ mw n $p.t$ "the end (bottom) of the Water of the Sky" in O. JdE 72460 (Thomas 1976, 212; Lakomy 2008, 30–33; Dorn and Polis 2015). The protection against rainwater in the form of waterfalls and streams that threatened to flood shafts and tomb openings was ensured in different ways depending on the tomb type (Romer 1993, 145; Rutherford and Ryan 1995). Large fissures in the rock presented another hazard, both those along which tombs were hewn as well as those occurring perpendicular to the axis of a tomb. The damage caused by water penetrating through these cracks, such as in KV 55 (Romer 1993, 145–150), was usually less severe than the flooding of tombs through the entrance (Parizek 2009).

The oldest type of royal tomb belonging to the New Kingdom, attested from the time of Hatshepsut until the time of Thutmose IV, is the so-called bab or cliff-tomb with hidden entrances. The Nineteenth-Dynasty tombs of Seti II (KV 15), Tausret (KV 14), and Bay (KV 13) and the Twentieth-Dynasty tomb of Mentuherkhepeshef (KV 19) are also built in the same tradition, although in contrast to those of the Eighteenth Dynasty, each has a visible entrance at the foot of the cliff. The hidden entrances of the

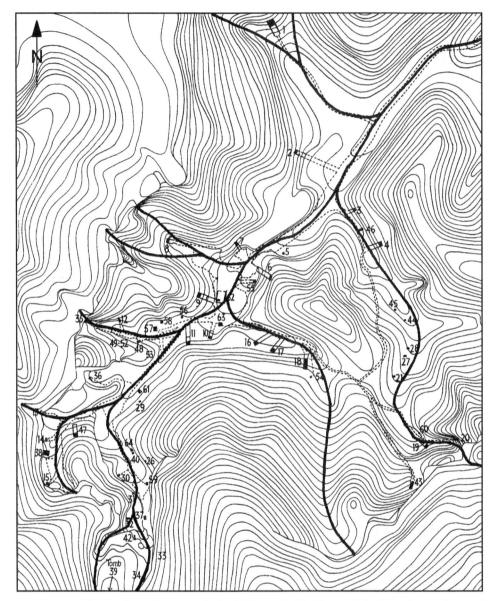

FIGURE 3.1 Stream-flow diagram of the Valley of the Kings, including the position of the tombs.

[Based on Porter and Moss (1964), i2, pl. II. Griffith Institute, University of Oxford, with additions by the author.]

Eighteenth-Dynasty tombs are set in or at the foot of rock fissures that penetrate vertical cliffs, over which waterfalls can pour during heavy rain. The entrances of these tombs were closed with stones and covered with rubble after the burial. Probably the first corridor and possibly even the first three corridors were also filled with stones (Abitz 1974, 114), by which means a seal—a watertight closure—was achieved. Doors are not attested for closing tomb entrances for the oldest royal tomb type (Roehrig 1995). For the entrance to the tomb of Thutmose III (KV 34), located in a crack through which run-off water from a large area (several thousand square meters) could flow, a sequence of walls (see Figure 3.2) was constructed for retaining and draining water via a gorge to the west of the tomb (Romer 1975, 319–321).

The entrance to the slightly older tomb of Hatshepsut (KV 20) is also located at the foot of a crack through which water from above could flow. Today, this crack has been filled up with large boulders in order to protect the underlying entrance from water (Černý et al. 1969, GMT I pl. 33a, b; Reeves and Wilkinson 1996, 92, upper right-hand fig.). It is not clear whether or not this intervention is ancient. If it is modern, the entrance would probably have been closed using the method described above, without further protection.

It seems quite reasonable that following the burial the ground level was lowered around the entrances of tombs such as that of Hatshepsut (KV 20) or Thutmose I (KV 38), as well as of the more recent tombs of the Nineteenth Dynasty with exposed entrances located at the bottoms of cliffs (KV 13, KV 14 and KV 15); this may have ensured that water coming down from the cliffs flowed away from the entrance. Evidence of such interventions, however, has not yet been observed archaeologically.

At approximately the same time as the first *bab* or cliff-tombs are attested, simple shaft tombs or tombs accessible via a steeply descending staircase were constructed for members of the royal family, as well as for some high officials. These tombs can be classified into two different types according to their location and the appropriate type of protection against the ingress of water. Tombs of the first type were constructed at the bottom of *wadis* (e.g., KV 42, Thutmose II [?]; KV 37; KV 36, Maiherpri; KV 39), where it had to be expected that the entrances would be flooded during rainfall. The protection against water of these tombs was achieved by filling the shaft or the descending stairs.

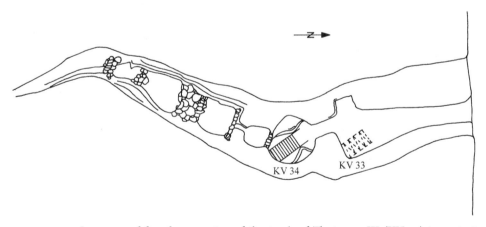

FIGURE 3.2 Sequence of five dams on top of the tomb of Thutmose III (KV 34) to protect the tomb entrance from flooding.

[Drawing by the author based on Romer (1975, 319 fig. 1).]

The specific placement of entrances beneath waterfalls or in water flows at the bottom of *wadis* was in fact an effective strategy for hiding the entrances, since the first rain event after the burial would have left a covering of natural sediment that served as ideal camouflage.

In order to protect the tombs of the second type (e.g., KV 29, KV 30, KV 31, KV 32, KV 40, KV 64) against penetrating rainwater, the entrances were hewn on the slopes a few meters above the bottom of the *wadis* so that they were not reached by water. In addition, the shafts or the descending stairs were filled.

The last royal tomb to have a hidden entrance, the tomb of Seti I (KV 17), also exhibits precautions against penetrating rainwater. To prevent water flowing into the tomb from the front, the construction debris was not dumped immediately before the tomb in the *wadi*, but deposited above the tomb. This elaborate dumping of rubble with a long, uphill trek for the workers shows that the comprehensive protection of a tomb against intrusive water was planned from the beginning. This dumped debris, up to 2 meters high and about 15–20 meters long, also served to drain the runoff water to the west, away from the tomb entrance. Once the small depression above the tomb was completely filled, the debris was carried much farther away, to another *wadi* to the east of the tomb Seti I (to the east of the future location of the tomb of Ramesses X), where the above-mentioned flash-flood layer from the time of Seti I could be observed in a stratigraphic profile.

The large concentration of debris—sharp, bright limestone flakes—produced during the construction of a large tomb made its location obvious, so the successful concealment of a tomb after construction was most likely possible only for smaller ones that were hewn at the bottom of *wadis* and covered by rainwater sediment.

For the royal tombs with visible monumental entrances and double-leafed doors—the third tomb type, characteristic for all subsequent royal tombs from the reign of Ramesses II onward—water protection was achieved via two measures: on the one hand these tombs were usually constructed on rock spurs, so that the water flowed on both sides of the entrance (corridor A)—in pharaonic times most probably with masonry no higher than the surrounding surface; on the other hand they were positioned above the bottom of the *wadi* so that the entrances could not be reached by flash floods. In addition, on the north side of the *wadi* leading up to the tomb of Merenptah a canal—designated as man-made drainage installation—can be observed (Hawass 2007/2008). It probably protected tombs lying in the outflow of the *wadi* such as KV 5, KV 7, KV 55, and eventually also KV 62.

The entrances of the tombs of the third type nowadays strongly affected by rainwater and containing rainwater debris (e.g., KV 7, Ramesses II; KV 8, Merenptah; KV 10, Amenmesse; KV 11, Ramesses III, etc.) were high enough in antiquity. The relocation of nearby debris in ancient times (excavations in the Twenty-first Dynasty) and the deposition of sediment after flash floods led to the elevation of the ground level in front of the tomb entrances and created the possibility for water to flow into the tombs. The height of the pathways in the Valley of the Kings today is in many places 2 meters or more higher than in pharaonic times and gives a very different impression of the position of the tomb entrances. The so-called tomb robber's shafts (shaft room E) have also been considered a measure to protect the royal tombs from the ingress of rainwater (Abitz 1974, 11–13, 115–116; Thomas 1978). Various arguments speak against this function of shaft room E:

- When the king died before his tomb was completed, the shaft was not hewn anymore in the seventy-day period between the death of the king and the funeral (in these cases water protection of the burial by the shaft seems not to have been important).
- In the tomb of Ramesses II (KV 7), the shaft was decorated with the twelfth hour of the netherworld book Amduat (this indicates the primarily religious function/ meaning of the shaft).
- The access to the shaft room had been walled up, plastered, and painted, so that intrusive water would have been dammed up, destroying the decorated walls in the preceding corridor D, before even reaching the shaft (at least from a modern point of view it seems not likely that this was intended).

Bibliography

Abitz, F. 1974. *Die religiöse Bedeutung der sogenannten Grabräuberschächte in den ägyptischen Königsgräbern der 18. bis 20. Dynastie*, Ägyptologische Abhandlungen 26. Wiesbaden.

Barbotin, C., and S. Guichard. 2004. "La tombe de Merenptah: projets et travaux récents." *Memnonia* 15: 153–164 with pl. 28.

Černý, J., et al. 1969–1983. *Graffiti de la Montagne Thébaine (GMT)*. Cairo.

Collombert, P., Lefèvre, D., Polis, S. and J. Winand, eds. 2015. *Aere Perennius*. Orientalia Lovaniensia Analecta. Leuven.

Cross, S. 2008. "The Hydrology of the Valley of the Kings." *Journal of Egyptian Archaeology* 94: 303–310.

Dorn, A. 2000. "Architektur." In *Das Grab Ramses' X. (KV 18)*, Aegyptiaca Helvetica 16, edited by H. Jenni, 30–33. Basel.

Dorn, A. 2011. *Arbeiterhütten im Tal der Könige: Ein Beitrag zur altägyptischen Sozialgeschichte aufgrund von neuem Quellenmaterial aus der Mitte der 20. Dynastie (ca. 1150 v. Chr.)*, Aegyptiaca Helvetica 23. Basel.

Dorn, A., and M. Müller. 2006. "Regenfälle in Theben-West." *Zeitschrift für Ägyptische Sprache und Altertumskunde* 133: 90–93.

Dorn, A. and S. Polis 2015. "A Re-examination of O. Cairo JdE 72460 (= O. Cairo SR 1475). Ending the Quest for a 19th Dynasty Queen's Tomb in the Valley of the Kings." In Collombert, P., Lefèvre, D., Polis, S. and J. Winand, eds. 2015. *Aere Perennius*. Orientalia Lovaniensia Analecta. Leuven.

Guillaume, A., and A. Emery-Barbier. 1995. "Le remplissage sédimentaire de la tombe de Ramsès II." *Memnonia* 6: 147–173.

Janssen, J. J. 1987. "The Day the Inundation Began." *Journal of Near Eastern Studies* 46: 129–136.

Jenni, H., ed. 2000. *Das Grab Ramses' X. (KV 18)*, Aegyptiaca Helvetica 16. Basel.

Johnson, J. H., and E. F. Wente, eds. 1976. *Studies in Honor of George R. Hughes*, Studies in Ancient Oriental Civilisation 39. Chicago.

Lakomy, K. C. 2008. *Cairo Ostracon J. 72460: Eine Untersuchung zur königlichen Bestattungstradition im Tal der Könige zu Beginn der Ramessidenzeit*, Göttinger Miszellen Beihefte Nr. 4. Göttingen.

Owen, J. 2013. "Mummy Mystery: Multiple Tombs Hidden in Egypt's Valley of Kings." December 4. http://www.livescience.com/41675-tombs-hidden-in-valley-of-kings.html (accessed February 17, 2015).

Parizek, K. 2009. "Fracture Zones Endanger Tombs in Valley of the Kings." October 21. http://www.sciencedaily.com/releases/2009/10/091019123105.htm (accessed February 25, 2013).

Polz, D. 1992. "Bericht über die erste Grabungskampagne in der Nekropole von Dra' Abu el-Naga/Theben-West." In *Mitteilungen des Deutschen Archäologischen Instituts Kairo* 48: 115–130.

Porter, B. and Moss, R. 1964. *Topographical Bibliography of Ancient Egyptian Hieroglyphic Texts, Reliefs and Paintings I. The Theban Necropolis. Part 2. Royal Tombs and Smaller Cemeteries.* OxfordReeves, C. N., and R. H. Wilkinson. 1996. *The Complete Valley of the Kings: Tombs and Treasures of Egypt's Greatest Pharaohs.* London.

Roehrig, C. H. 1995. "Gates to the Underworld: The Appearance of Wooden Doors in the Royal Tombs in the Valley of the Kings." In *Valley of the Sun Kings: New Explorations in the Tombs of the Pharaohs*, edited by R. H. Wilkinson, 82–107. Tucson, AZ.

Romer, J. 1975. "The Tomb of Tuthmosis III." *Mitteilungen des Deutschen Archäologischen Instituts Kairo* 31 (2): 315–351.

Romer, J., and E. Romer. 1993. *The Rape of Tutankhamun.* London.

Rutherford, J., and D. P. Ryan. 1995. "Tentative Tomb Protection Priorities, Valley of the Kings, Egypt." In *Valley of the Sun Kings: New Explorations in the Tombs of the Pharaohs*, edited by R. H. Wilkinson, 134–156. Tucson, AZ.

Sadek, A. A. 1990. "Varia Graffitica." *Varia Aegyptiaca* 6: 109–120.

Thomas, E. 1976. "Cairo Ostracon J. 72460." In *Studies in Honor of George R. Hughes*, edited by J. H. Johnson and E. F. Wente, 209–216. Chicago.

Thomas, E. 1978. "The 'Well' in Kings' Tombs of Bibân el-Molûk." *Journal of Egyptian Archaeology* 64: 80–83.

Weeks, K. R. 2000a. "Archaeological and Architectural Description." In *KV 5: A Preliminary Report on the Excavation of the Tomb of the Sons of Ramesses II in the Valley of the Kings*, edited by K. R. Weeks, 7–53. Cairo.

Weeks, K. R., ed. 2000b. *KV 5: A Preliminary Report on the Excavation of the Tomb of the Sons of Ramesses II in the Valley of the Kings*, Publication of the Theban Mapping Project 2. Cairo.

Wilkinson, R. H., ed. 1995. *Valley of the Sun Kings: New Explorations in the Tombs of the Pharaohs.* Tucson, AZ.

PART III

THE DEVELOPMENT OF THE ROYAL NECROPOLIS

CHAPTER 4

···

THE EGYPTIAN CONCEPT
OF A ROYAL NECROPOLIS

···

JOHN H. TAYLOR

INTRODUCTION

THE survival of so many tombs from pharaonic Egypt reflects the ancient inhabitants' perception of human existence, in the context of the eternal cycles of the cosmos. The earthly lifespan of a man or woman was merely a brief phase, to be followed by another, and much more important, life that would last forever. In this afterlife the reborn dead would gain access to the parts of the cosmos where the gods existed, but they would also dwell on earth in their tombs, remaining a part of the wider community and having the ability to move freely between the world of the living and that of the dead. The tomb was the point of contact between these spheres, and hence all Egyptian tombs fulfilled two essential functions. First, they provided a secure resting place for the body, and second, they served as the primary location for the cult activities that were considered necessary to maintain the spirit aspects of the individual: rituals of nourishing, rebirth, commemoration, and protection.

For these reasons tombs were located close to settlements and were clustered into cemeteries. The physical grouping of graves and tombs is a feature of Egyptian culture throughout the pharaonic period, and the Greek term now generally applied to such a cluster—necropolis—is apt, since they often housed the deceased members of entire communities and in their internal arrangement mirrored the social hierarchy of the living (Seidlmayer 2001, 511–512). Egyptian cemeteries were located in liminal regions, chiefly on the desert's edge, just beyond the precious cultivation. These areas were understood to be the entrances to the supernatural realm, ruled over by the gods. Their status is well conveyed by the ancient Egyptian term for cemetery, *kheret-netjer*, literally "that which belongs to the god." The word "god" in this context probably originally denoted the king, by whom the privilege of formal burial was granted to persons of high status, but later it was apparently interpreted as a reference to deities such as

Osiris, Anubis, or Sokar, who were perceived as holding authority over the land of the dead (Seidlmayer 2001, 511). Underlining this interpretation are other common terms for necropolises or parts of them, such as *t3-dsr* ("the sacred land") and *Rˁ-stˁw* ("the beginning of corridors" [under the earth]), associated particularly with Anubis and Sokar, respectively. The cemeteries were predominantly located on the west bank of the Nile, the region of the setting sun; "The West" and "The Beautiful West" were regular circumlocutions for the place of burial, as was "the horizon of eternity." The horizon became from an early date a powerful symbol of transition and rebirth, and the notion that the afterlife was eternal gave strong motivation to construct the tombs using durable materials (preferably stone)—hence the relatively high rate of survival of tombs, by comparison with the impermanent dwellings made for the living.

The burials of rulers were of exceptional importance. The king possessed both mortal and divine qualities, as the son of the sun god Ra and also the earthly incarnation of Horus, and he occupied a pivotal position as mediator between his people and the gods. His role did not end with death, for although the dead ruler was believed to have merged with the being of the creator, he nonetheless retained his individual identity, while also becoming a member of the host of past kings. The dead king was thus the latest link in a continuous chain stretching back to the time of the gods on earth (Quirke 2001, 117). This theoretically unbroken sequence of monarchs offered an assurance of the continuing stability of the Egyptian state on earth, and also of the eternalizing of Maat, the principle of cosmic order. These ideological factors are reflected in recurrent features of the burial places of Egyptian kings.

Kings' tombs were located at centers of political or religious importance: at the sites of the origin of dynastic lines, close to royal residences or administrative centers, and in meaningful spatial relationships with major cult temples. Generally, the tombs were not isolated, but grouped (Thomas 1966, 1), and the use of a particular royal necropolis remained consistent over long periods, suggesting that ideology took priority over personal preference: thus all of the First Dynasty kings were buried in the Umm el-Qaab cemetery at Abydos, and most of those of the New Kingdom in the Valley of the Kings. Where exceptions occur the reason is rarely identifiable, although in the case of Akhenaten the decision that the royal family should be buried at el-Amarna was clearly influenced by religious motives personal to that king.

At least until the New Kingdom, the royal cemeteries were not totally self-contained, but formed part of larger symbolic environments. One function of these "ritual landscapes" was to reflect the hierarchy of the state—the social context of the king on earth, which was to be transferred to the eternal sphere. Hence a "royal necropolis" was often located within a larger cemetery, where the king's subjects were also buried. One enduring manifestation of the stratified society that emerged in Egypt in the later fourth millennium B.C.E. was a differentiation in the elaboration of burial arrangements. The tomb of the king is early distinguished from those of others by its size, by its architectural form, and by its conspicuous consumption of material resources, craftsmanship, and even (in the First Dynasty) the lives of servants and animals. In view of this, another key function was for the kings' tombs to act as focal points within a religious landscape, which might involve orientation toward the cardinal points or stars of the night sky and spatial relationships with significant topographical features (such as the peak of el-Qurn at Thebes) and other religious structures. Kings' tombs were significant features in the development of "ritual landscapes" at three major centers—Abydos, Memphis, and Thebes—from the Early Dynastic period to the New Kingdom inclusive.

These conceptual aspects evolved over time. The following chronological survey highlights the changing principles that underlay the evolution of the royal necropolis, explaining the origin of some of the factors that distinguish the Valley of the Kings.

EARLY DYNASTIC PERIOD—ABYDOS

The earliest distinct "royal necropolis" is at Abydos. Here, at Umm el-Qaab, an elite cemetery was established in the late fourth millennium B.C.E., containing the tombs of the predynastic rulers of Upper Egypt and those of the kings who reigned around the time that the country was unified into a single state. The kings of the First Dynasty, as well as the last two rulers of the Second Dynasty, were buried in this same spot. In the Early Dynastic period, the strong associations of Abydos with the cult of Osiris as supreme god of the dead had not yet emerged (though the siting of the royal tombs at the mouth of a *wadi* may have been in part motivated by an idea of its being the entrance to the netherworld). Hence the choice of this place for the royal burials was probably determined at least in part by its status as the ancestral cemetery of the rulers who had established the centralized state (Kemp 1966, 19–21; O'Connor 2009, 147–148, 177). These tombs at once introduce some of the key features of the Egyptian royal necropolis. Each king was buried separately, his place of interment comprising a subterranean burial chamber with associated storage rooms for grave goods, the burial chambers being topped by a rectangular mound of sand and gravel that was hidden below ground level. The superstructures, built of organic materials, are no longer extant but were probably brick mastaba-like edifices, perhaps with a chapel containing a cult statue of the dead king (O'Connor 2009, 153–155). The tombs were grouped in close physical proximity, but no two are identical in design; evolution is clearly manifested in periodic (though not reign-by-reign) increases in size and in the addition of architectural features such as an access stairway and stone floor (O'Connor 2009, 150).

The "burial" function was only one element of the royal mortuary complex. No less important was the ritual transference of the king to the afterlife and the maintenance of cult, which doubtless took place at the large, rectangular brick enclosures that were situated at the edge of the cultivation at a distance from the tomb proper (O'Connor 2009, 159ff). Several examples for First Dynasty rulers have been excavated, but the two best-preserved enclosures belonged to Peribsen and Khasekhemwy of the Second Dynasty. The space within the high brick walls was occupied by a relatively small chapel, in which libations were poured and incense burned, probably before either a statue or a stela (O'Connor 2009, 159–181). The building of a structure of the same type for

Khasekhemwy at Hierakonpolis indicates that the activities performed in these monuments were not necessarily restricted to one place, a feature of royal cult that recurs in later periods. In addition to acting as a stage for the performance of rituals, it has been suggested that these enclosures also magically eternalized the setting of the royal palace, providing not only a dwelling for the king's spirit, but also the place in which he would participate in the public roles of kingship, such as ceremonies and display of various kinds, as he had done in life.

The dead king was to be supplied with all the necessities of existence, and hence the tomb incorporated storerooms for food, drink, and other commodities, while placing the ruler at the apex of the social hierarchy by providing him with a retinue. The subsidiary graves that surrounded each king's tomb in the First Dynasty contained the burials of servants and members of the court—possibly even relatives of the king—and since these graves were apparently sealed at the same time as the burial of the ruler, it is likely that that their occupants were put to death to accompany him, although this practice declined during the First Dynasty and is not attested afterward (O'Connor 2009, 148, 172–173). The separate mortuary enclosures were also surrounded by subsidiary graves, predominantly of artisans and administrative officials (O'Connor 2009, 181), and here also boats were buried. Excavation beside one of the First Dynasty enclosures has revealed a "fleet" of fourteen large wooden vessels, and while these may have been intended to serve as transport and supply craft for the dead king, a religious function can also be supposed, since they are evidently the precursors of the boat burials in rock-cut pits known from later kings' pyramid complexes, such as that of Khufu. It appears that most of these enclosures at Abydos were intentionally razed to the ground after the funeral, perhaps constituting a ritual "burial" of the cult place to enable it to accompany the king into the afterlife for his eternal use.

OLD KINGDOM—THE MEMPHITE NECROPOLIS

Clay seal impressions found at the tomb and mortuary enclosure of Khasekhemwy at Abydos show that his burial was conducted by his successor, Netjerikhet (Djoser). The new king, however, later counted as the founder of the Third Dynasty, constructed his own tomb at Saqqara, a cemetery associated with Memphis. This city, the administrative focus of the united Egypt, was traditionally supposed to have been established by the kings of the First Dynasty. Saqqara had already become an important cemetery in the First Dynasty, and at least three early to mid-Second Dynasty kings had been buried there, but Djoser's funerary complex was radically innovative in several ways. It unified the burial place and the cult place by locating the tomb within the enclosure. The tomb itself comprised a six-stepped pyramid of stone blocks, perhaps a development of the surface mound of earlier tombs (O'Connor 2009, 195–198). Not only the enclosure and the pyramid were of stone, but also the subsidiary buildings, copying the forms of the brick, wood, and matting of which the now lost structures within the Abydos enclosures were made. The stone enclosure wall replicates the pan-eled brick walls of these First to Second Dynasty cult enclosures, and the form of the dummy shrines and chapels inside indicates that they were settings for the *sed* festival, the ritual by which the powers of the king were magically renewed. There is no explicit contemporary statement of the religious significance of the Step Pyramid itself, but the rise to prominence of Ra at this period may indicate that it symbolized the equating of the king with the sun god.

At the height of the Old Kingdom, in the Fourth to Sixth Dynasties, the kings' tombs were distributed over a wide area, which incorporated the sites of Saqqara, Maidum, Giza, Abu Rawash, Abusir, and Dahshur. The step pyramid was replaced by the "true" pyramid, which steadily increased in size until the reigns of Khufu and Khafra and then diminished under later kings. A strongly standardized set of ele-ments now comprised the royal mortuary complex, with the "valley temple" located at the water's edge, and a causeway connecting this to the pyramid temple. Cult activ-ities would have taken place in both of these structures, focusing on the presentation of offerings to statues of the king, which acted as accessible physical habitations for his spirit.

Although the primary function of the pyramids was to protect the body of the king, their form and architecture make allusion to stellar and solar symbol-ism. They are aligned with great precision on the cardinal points, and the shafts that pass through the core of the Great Pyramid would have been sighted on stars. The northward-pointing entrance passage was aimed at the circumpolar stars, the "immortals," which were equated with the dead kings of the past. The ancient names of some Old Kingdom pyramids (or parts of their complexes) also allude to stellar significance, but solar vocabulary ("to rise," "horizon") is also used in these con-texts, and the shape of the true pyramid is clearly linked with that of the benben, the pointed stone that was sacred to Ra. It has therefore been suggested that the pyra-mid perhaps also acted as the focus of cult activity, and this may explain why not all pyramids contained burials. King Sneferu completed three large pyramids, only one of which would have housed his body, the others perhaps serving his cult, as might also the smaller pyramids that were erected at other sites in Egypt during his reign (Quirke 2001, 122). According to this hypothesis the royal mortuary monuments of this period would have functioned within a ritual landscape that was not restricted to the immediate vicinity of the dead king's resting place.

The three great pyramids of Khufu, Khafra, and Menkaura, with their associated temples and the surrounding tombs of royal relatives and courtiers, dominated the Giza plateau and maintained the symbolic replication of the hierarchy of state in the after-life. For unknown reasons the later rulers of the Old Kingdom abandoned this locality and built their tombs at Saqqara and Abusir. While most of these complexes comprised the elements that were now standard, some of the kings of the Fifth Dynasty also built a solar temple, containing a large obelisk (that of Niuserra at Abu Ghurab being the best preserved). The functioning of the administration and the offering supply in these temples was closely interrelated with that of the pyramid complexes, an indication that despite changes of emphasis, the components of the royal necropolis continued to reflect the great importance of linking the dead king to the cult of major deities such as Ra. The Giza pyramids would have been visible from the solar cult center of Iunu (Heliopolis), and the burial of cedarwood boats in pits beside the Great Pyramid would have served for the king's celestial journeys. The location of the Fifth Dynasty sun temples at Abu Ghurab perhaps gave them a sight line to Iunu, which the pyramids themselves no longer possessed after the move away from Giza (Quirke 2001, 128).

A major innovation in kings' tombs from the late Fifth to the Eighth Dynasties was the inscribing of the words of mortuary liturgy and offering rituals (the "Pyramid Texts") on the walls of the chambers. There can be little doubt that ritual and the use of liturgy played an important (though currently undocumented) part in earlier royal burials, but now the texts were placed in eternal form inside the tomb, a situation that would be repeated in the New Kingdom.

FIRST INTERMEDIATE PERIOD—SAQQARA AND THEBES

The poorly documented kings of the Ninth to Tenth Dynasties had their base at Heracleopolis at the mouth of the Fayum, but inscriptional evidence reveals that at least one of these rulers, Merykara, built a pyramid at Saqqara. It cannot be located today, but its situation indicates that these kings regarded themselves as the heirs of the Memphite traditions of the Old Kingdom. Contemporary with the Heracleopolitan kings were the rulers of the early Eleventh Dynasty, based at Thebes. Previously a provincial center without royal associations, Thebes rose when its governors successfully challenged the Heracleopolitans for control of Egypt, three of them, Intef I–III, adopting royal titularies. These men maintained the traditional burial place of their precursors, and with their tombs at el-Tarif on the west bank, Thebes became for the first time the site of a royal necropolis, a development in which ancestral tradition was evidently an influential factor. The Intefs also retained a provincial style of funerary establishment typical of their home—the so-called *saff* tombs, with an open court surrounded by a columned or pillared portico, but distinguished from others of the same model by their great size and monumental architecture.

Under the porticos were chapels, from which shafts led down to the burial chambers of the king and members of his family. The *saff* tombs lacked pyramids but did possess "valley" temples of brick, and each tomb housed multiple burials, the side porticos giving access to the tombs of courtiers as well as royal relatives, and thus continuing the principle of replicating the hierarchy of the court.

Middle Kingdom—Thebes, Memphis, and the Fayum

Mentuhotep II, the successor of Intef III, restored centralized government, and with him the Middle Kingdom begins. Thebes remained, at least at first, the site of the principal royal necropolis, now focused in the natural amphitheater of Deir el-Bahri. In this setting Mentuhotep adapted the *saff* type of tomb to create a mortuary monument based on a terraced structure, with a central stone element that may have been a pyramid, a rectangular flat-topped mastaba, or a representation of the primeval mound. Burial place and cult place were again combined in one spot, and the monument's wall-reliefs and statuary recall Djoser's complex in making prominent allusion to the *sed* festival. The monument was certainly built and began to function during the king's lifetime (when it underwent development and expansion), and its decoration manifests for the first time a close association between the king and the god Amun-Ra (Ullmann 2007, 12). It is now that the royal necropolis and the Amun temple at Karnak on the opposite side of the Nile emerge as key elements in a local Theban ritual landscape. Mentuhotep II's monument was the first to receive the visit by Amun from Karnak in the annual Festival of the Valley, which would become an important part of the religious calendar in the New Kingdom (Ullmann 2007, 7, 8). As before, the king's tomb acted as the focus of other royal and court burials, with Queen Tem being interred at the rear of the monument, and six females (some of whom were wives of the king) each having a mortuary chapel and burial chamber at the edge of the main terrace. In the immediate vicinity of the monument was the tomb-chapel of Queen Neferu II, while the tombs of officials were cut along the avenue to the cultivation (Dodson 2005, 25–26) and into the cliffs north of the king's monument.

Under the kings of the Twelfth Dynasty there was a clear return to some of the traditions of the Old Kingdom, together with innovations. The siting of the royal necropolises in this period shows considerable variation. Under Amenemhat I and Senusret I the king's tomb was built at el-Lisht, north of the Fayum, probably in order to locate it in proximity to the newly established residence city of Itytawy, founded by the earlier king. The tombs of the later rulers were widely distributed along the west bank, from Dahshur at the southern end of the Memphite necropolis, to Lahun and Hawara in the Fayum, and at least one ruler, Senusret III, also built an elaborate tomb at Abydos, which may have served as his actual burial place. The pyramid form of the late Old Kingdom was revived, but older models were also copied and adapted, the enclosure wall of Senusret I's pyramid recalling that of the Step Pyramid of Djoser. Among the innovations one particularly striking feature is the arrangement of the subterranean parts of the pyramids, first seen in that of Senusret II, which seem to reflect new concepts of the afterlife—specifically an island-like central chamber with surrounding corridors, which were features of the tomb of Osiris, whose importance as supreme mortuary deity became more manifest in this period. Hence now the king's burial united elements relating to both Ra and Osiris, but although the solar and Osirian elements were both important, they could be physically separate (Quirke 2001, 130–132). Amenemhat III returned to the model of a single centralized complex, although (following Senusret III at Dahshur) his pyramid temple at Hawara (the "Labyrinth") was greatly expanded—this being the largest of the period. One feature of late Old Kingdom kings' tombs that was not revived was the inscribing of mortuary texts on the walls of the pyramid; perhaps they were provided through some other medium, such as on papyrus or on the coffins of the king.

Only a few tombs have been identified for the ephemeral rulers of the Thirteenth Dynasty. Some constructed small pyramids in the Memphite necropolis, while others were interred at south Abydos in tombs with a sloping underground passage leading to a stone or stone-lined burial chamber.

SECOND INTERMEDIATE PERIOD

The Asiatics who occupied the Delta after the Middle Kingdom did not in general follow Egyptian mortuary practices, although how their rulers, the Hyksos, were buried is still unknown. The contemporary Egyptian royal line of the Seventeenth Dynasty, based at Thebes, chose to be buried at Dra Abu el-Naga, north of Deir el-Bahri, in small tombs of traditional pyramid form, which united burial place and cult place. While some of these pyramids seem to have possessed only a single burial chamber, the Ramesside Tomb Robbery papyri state that in at least one instance the king and queen were buried together. Traditional elements of the royal necropolis remained strong, the tombs being situated within sight of Karnak and having below them the sepulchres of the ruler's retinue.

NEW KINGDOM—NEW CONCEPTIONS OF THE ROYAL NECROPOLIS

The original tombs of the first four rulers of the Eighteenth Dynasty have not yet been securely identified, although there is strong evidence that Amenhotep I and his mother Ahmose Nefertari were buried in a double tomb at Dra Abu el-Naga (K.93.11–12) (Polz 2007, 172–197), but in the joint reign of Hatshepsut and Thutmose III significant changes in the concept of the royal burial arrangements are recognizable. Beginning with tomb KV 20, the sepulchre of Hatshepsut as female king, the separation of burial place and cult place became the norm, the "Temples of Millions of Years," located on the plain facing the Nile, serving as the setting for the cult of the rulers who were buried in the Valley of the Kings.

The valley functioned as the prime royal necropolis for the next four centuries. Some practical advantages doubtless motivated the choice of this spot, but the symbolic associations of its topography were perhaps the most important—not least the shape of the great limestone massif where the valley lay, which resembled the hieroglyphic sign for "horizon" (*3ḥt*) and received the setting sun each evening. Furthermore, the valley was overlooked by the peak of el-Qurn, which may have been interpreted as a kind of collective natural pyramid, marking the solar symbolism that had already for many centuries played a key part in the religious role of the royal necropolises. In the New Kingdom the adjacent Deir el-Bahri valley and el-Qurn were also sacred to Hathor and to the goddess Meretseger, both of whom were regarded as protectors of the dead.

In their architectural form and in their iconography the tombs of the kings replicate the path of the sun during its nocturnal journey beneath the earth, a course on which the king himself was closely identified with the sun god and through which both deity and dead ruler experienced rebirth. The architectural details and the images and texts that adorn the walls of corridors and chambers show a steady (almost reign-by-reign) evolution, which seems to reflect a continuing elaboration of religious thought about the posthumous destiny of the king.

The names given to the tombs in the valley in the New Kingdom—*t3 št-ʿ3t* ("The Great Place") and *t3 št-M3ʿt* ("The Place of Truth")—reflect their special status (Černý 1973, 29–85), and hint that in conceptual terms the tomb was a place beyond the confines of the material world. The separation of the burial place from the cult establishment also emphasized the desire for secrecy and hiddenness. The king's tomb was no longer conspicuous; it was, as stated in the title to the Book of Amduat, the "hidden chamber," the place where the mysteries of rebirth took place, and was not accessible to profane eyes. The responsibility for the construction of the royal tombs was given to a self-contained community of skilled craftsmen who, with their families, were housed in the walled village of Deir el-Medina, and although they were not "quarantined," their comparative isolation would have contributed to the security of the necropolis. The abundant records that the village has yielded also reveal that access to the Valley of the Kings was strictly controlled.

The powerful ideological significance of the valley drew almost all the New Kingdom pharaohs to this spot for burial, although some (such as Aye, Horemheb, and Ramesses I) are known to have originated in other parts of Egypt. The only break in continuity came with Akhenaten, who developed an extreme and idiosyncratic religious outlook focused on the uniqueness of the solar disc as a divine force, and in which traditional concepts of the afterlife were eschewed. He created a new residence city on a virgin site at el-Amarna, constructing tombs for himself and his immediate family in a *wadi* on the east bank—an "alternative" ritual landscape in which the royal necropolis was situated at the eastern horizon, from which life emerged at dawn. This experiment was short-lived, and with the "return to orthodoxy" under Tutankhamun the Valley of the Kings was reopened for use, and the royal dead who had been interred at el-Amarna were even brought there for reburial.

The principle of one tomb for each king was still generally followed in this period, but the burial arrangements for members of the king's immediate family show chang-ing patterns (Dodson 2005–2006). At the beginning of the Eighteenth Dynasty queens were buried in separate shaft-tombs or cliff-tombs, which were widely distributed on the Theban west bank, some in the southern part of the necropolis (the Valley of the Queens and other *wadis* to the south of this) and others at Deir el-Bahri (DB 358) and Qurna (Dodson 2005–2006, 34). In the middle of the Eighteenth Dynasty there was a change, with some close family members (wives and young children) being given burial within the king's own tomb (as seen with Amenhotep II, Thutmose IV, and probably Amenhotep III), and others perhaps being interred in communal sepulchres such as KV 39 (Dodson 2005, 34–37) and KV 40. Also during the Eighteenth Dynasty the Valley of the Kings accommodated some burials of relatives by marriage (such as Yuya and Tuya) and even of persons apparently unrelated to the king, who perhaps were granted burial there as a special favor (Maiherpri). In the Nineteenth and Twentieth Dynasties, tombs for members of the royal family became more elaborate, having for the first time their own wall decoration. Some of these were situated within the Valley of the Kings itself, such as the massive KV 5 for children of Ramesses II and KV 19, begun by Prince Sethirkhopshef C and ultimately taken over by Prince Mentuherkhepeshef C. The Valley of the Queens, however, now became more clearly defined as a counterpart to the Valley of the Kings, with numerous tombs being prepared for wives and sons of the rulers, as its ancient name *t3-st-nfrw* ("Place of the Royal Children") indicates. There is clear evi-dence of long-term planning for the necropolis, since some of the tombs were prepared in advance, with blank spaces left for the names of the eventual occupants to be filled in (Leblanc 1988, 93–95; Dodson 2005–2006, 38–39). It should be noted, however, that by no means all children of the king were buried in these cemeteries. Prince Khaemwaset, the son of Ramesses II, was interred at Saqqara and another Ramesside prince at Gurob.

Post–New Kingdom

The concept of the royal necropolis underwent radical change after the New Kingdom. The known tombs of kings of the Twenty-first to Twenty-third Dynasties were con-structed within the enclosure walls of cult temples and hence are sometimes termed "temenos tombs." The royal necropolis at Tanis consisted of a cluster of small tombs with stone-built substructures, over which probably stood superstructures of stone or brick, now destroyed. These tombs, as well as those of the Twenty-fifth to Twenty-sixth Dynasty God's Wives of Amun and that of "King" Harsiese at Medinet Habu, were all located within the outer courts of cult temples of Amun, demonstrating the intensifi-cation of the link between the royal burial place and the cult of the major local deity, already attested in earlier periods. It has been suggested that the location and architec-ture of these temenos tombs reflected a delta tradition, perhaps based on the archaic sepulchres of the Lower Egyptian kings of Sais and Buto (Stadelmann 1971, 118–123; Lull

2002, 11, 253). The royal tombs were now physically isolated from those of the extended royal family and persons of lower status, and the identities of their occupants also reflect changing emphases. In the tomb of Psusennes I at Tanis the king and queen originally had paired chambers, and court members such as the general Wendjebauendjed were now granted burial within the king's own sepulchre.

The Twenty-fifth-Dynasty rulers, originating in Kush, were buried in their homeland. The principal royal cemeteries of el-Kurru and Nuri had been used by the ancestors of this Kushite line and were located close to an important local center of the cult of Amun at Gebel Barkal. They broke with the tradition of the temenos tombs, constructing instead monuments of pyramid form, each with a small cult chapel. This pattern of mortuary installation continued in Kush for many centuries after the Twenty-fifth Dynasty's control of Egypt had ceased.

The royal necropolises of the rulers of Egypt from the Twenty-sixth to Thirtieth Dynasties are very poorly documented. Herodotus (II, 169) describes the now-destroyed tombs of the Twenty-sixth-Dynasty kings at Sais as having stood within the temple enclosure of Athene (i.e., the local goddess Neith). This statement, together with the observation that the tomb of Amasis possessed a courtyard with palm-columns and double doors leading to the burial place, indicates that these rulers had probably returned to the tradition of the temenos tomb, which had been current before the Kushite conquest. The discovery of the sarcophagus of Nepherites I of the Twenty-ninth Dynasty in the temple of Banebdjed at Mendes, the residence of that royal line, suggests a continuing tradition of locating the royal burials within the cult temple of the local deity. Little is known of the mortuary arrangements of other members of the royal families in these dynasties, but some of them were certainly buried away from the kings, as exemplified by the tomb of Queen Takhuit, wife of Psammetichus II, at Athribis, and the burial of Nakhtbasteru, wife of Amasis, at Giza. Of the tombs of the rulers of the Thirtieth Dynasty and the Ptolemaic period no traces have yet been identified.

POSTBURIAL ACTIVITY AND LATER ATTITUDES TO ROYAL NECROPOLISES

During the period of use of a royal necropolis, changes to the arrangement of some burials took place. Ideological reasons may have motivated the reinterment of Thutmose I in a new sarcophagus by Hatshepsut and his subsequent transfer to another burial place by Thutmose III. The removal of the bodies of Akhenaten and his immediate family after the abandonment of el-Amarna, and the reburial of some or all of them in the Valley of the Kings, perhaps reflect both a habitual concern for the security of royal tombs and a gesture toward rehabilitation of these persons into a more traditional burial environment by Tutankhamun. However, the tombs of some rulers who were evidently regarded by posterity as illegitimate—such as Amenmesse—might be appropriated for other royal burials once their owner's influence was past (Schaden and Ertman 1998, 151). The only contemporary evidence for official modification of an entire royal necropolis comes from the end of the New Kingdom, when the tombs in the Valley of the Kings were stripped of valuables and the mummies gathered into caches (see Introduction chapter).

After the original phase of their use, some royal necropolises underwent modification and reinterpretation by later generations. The Early Dynastic royal cemetery at Abydos acquired new significance from the Middle Kingdom onward as part of a larger sacred landscape, when the tomb of Djer was identified as the burial place of Osiris. The cemetery became the focal point of local cult activity as the destination of the procession and the ritual re-enactment of the Osiris myth at the god's annual festival. The importance of this occasion at a national level drew pilgrims from all over Egypt, and the tombs became covered with ceramic offering vessels deposited by devotees, which have given rise to the modern Arabic name of the site, Umm el-Qaab ("Mother of Pots").

The Old Kingdom pyramids in the Memphite necropolis also attracted pilgrims in the New Kingdom, as documented by visitors' graffiti. Some of these monuments even underwent a formal restoration in the Nineteenth Dynasty on the orders of Prince Khaemwaset, who inscribed them with gigantic "museum labels" to preserve the names of the kings who had built them. Respect for these monuments may have helped to protect them from reuse and plundering for building material. The excavators of the Step Pyramid enclosure noted the rarity of later material there, at least until the Late Period, when intrusive burials and quarrying are attested (Malek and Magee 1984–1985, 169–170). A late restoration of the burial of Menkaura within the third pyramid at Giza may also point to a continuing desire to connect with the great ages of Egypt's past.

Bibliography

Černy, J. 1973. *A Community of Workmen at Thebes in the Ramesside Period*. Bibliotheque d'Etude 50. Cairo.

Dodson, A. 2005. "An Eternal Harem: The Tombs of the Royal Families of Ancient Egypt; II, The Middle Kingdom." *Kmt* 16 (1): 24–32.

Dodson, A. 2005–2006. "An Eternal Harem: The Tombs of the Royal Families of Ancient Egypt; III, The New Kingdom." *Kmt* 16 (4):32–42.

Dorman, P. F., and B. M. Bryan, eds. 2007. *Sacred Space and Sacred Function in Ancient Thebes*. Studies in Ancient Oriental Civilization 61. Chicago.

Kemp, B. J. 1966. "Abydos and the Royal Tombs of the First Dynasty." *Journal of Egyptian Archaeology* 52:13–22, pls. VII–VIII.

Leblanc, C. 1988. "*T3 St Nfrw*—Une Necropole et son Histoire." In *Akten des Vierten Internationalen Ägyptologen Kongresses München 1985*, Band 2, edited by S. Schoske (*Studien zur Altägyptischen Kultur Beihefte* 2), 89–99, Taf. 8–9.

Lull, J. 2002. *Las tumbas reales egipcias del Tercer Periodo Intermedio (dinastias XXI-XXV): Tradicion y cambios*. BAR International Series 1045. Oxford.

Malek, J., and D. N. E. Magee. 1984–1985. "A Group of Coffins Found at Northern Saqqara." *Societe d'Égyptologie Geneve, Bulletin* 9–10:165–189.

O'Connor, D. 2009. *Abydos: Egypt's First Pharaohs and the Cult of Osiris*. London.

Polz, D. 2007. *Der Beginn des Neuen Reiches: Zur Vorgeschichte einer Zeitenwende*. Sonderschrift des Deutschen Archäologischen Instituts Abteilung Kairo 31. Berlin and New York.

Quirke, S. 2001. *The Cult of Ra: Sun-worship in Ancient Egypt*. London.

Redford, D. B., ed. 2001. *The Oxford Encyclopedia of Ancient Egypt*. Oxford.

Schaden, O., and E. Ertman. 1998. "The Tomb of Amenmesse (KV.10): The First Season." *Annales du Service des Antiquites de l'Egypte* 73: 116–155, pls. I–IX.

Seidlmayer, S. J. 2001. "Necropolis." In *The Oxford Encyclopedia of Ancient Egypt*, edited by D. B. Redford, II, 506–512. Oxford.

Stadelmann, R. 1971. "Das Grab im Tempelhof: Der Typus des Königsgrabes in der Spätzeit." *Mitteilungen des Deutschen Archäologischen Instituts Abteilung Kairo* 27: 111–123, pl. XVI.

Thomas, E. 1966. *The Royal Necropoleis of Thebes*. Princeton, NJ.

Ullmann, M. 2007. "Thebes: Origins of a Ritual Landscape." In *Sacred Space and Sacred Function in Ancient Thebes*, edited by P. F. Dorman and B. M. Bryan, 3–25. Chicago.

CHAPTER 5

EARLIER ROYAL TOMBS, THE ROYAL CEMETERIES OF THEBES, AND THE BEGINNINGS OF THE VALLEY OF THE KINGS

AIDAN DODSON

PERHAPS the first "royal" tombs in Egypt were those constructed in cemetery HK6 at Hierakonpolis, where wood-framed structures were erected above brick-lined burial places whose size and location suggests their ownership by the top elite of the latter part of the Predynastic period (Friedman 2011). At the same site is also found the first known decorated tomb-chamber, in the form of tomb 100 (Case and Crowfoot Payne 1962; Crowfoot Payne 1973). Another Predynastic royal cemetery was established at Cemetery U at Abydos-Umm el-Qaab (Kaiser and Dreyer 1982; Dreyer 1998), to the west of which the kings of the First Dynasty erected there tombs (for these and references to all further individual tombs, see Table 5.1, below). The tombs at Umm el-Qaab comprised brick-lined cuttings in the desert gravel, perhaps topped by mounds of gravel (minimal traces of any superstructure survive; Dreyer 1991). These tombs were surrounded by the brick-lined graves of the royal household, many of which have usually been regarded as having been occupied at the same time as the royal tomb was sealed. On the east side of each royal tomb, a pair of stelae marked an offering place, while a further "public" element of the tomb took the form of a large mud-brick enclosure with a north-south axis, built some two kilometers from Umm el-Qaab, nearer to the edge of the desert (Kaiser and Dreyer 1982, 253–260; O'Connor 1989; Bestock 2009). These enclosures were dismantled after the burial and were thus presumably intended solely for rites surrounding the interment or immediately afterward.

The royal cemetery shifted to Saqqara in the north of Egypt (see Figure 5.1) at the beginning of the Second Dynasty. Rock-cut tombs (known examples being those of

Table 5.1 Pre-Valley of the Kings Royal Tombs

Owner	Location & Tomb Number/ Name	Type	Bibliography
Narmer	Abydos/Umm el-Qaab Bs17/18	B	Porter and Moss 1937, 88; Kaiser and Dreyer 1982
Aha	Abydos/Umm el-Qaab B10/15/19	Bs	Porter and Moss 1937, 88; Kaiser and Dreyer 1982
Djer	Abydos/Umm el-Qaab O	Bs	Porter and Moss 1937, 78–81; Dreyer 2009, 165–166; 2010, 143–144
Djet	Abydos/Umm el-Qaab Z	Bs	Porter and Moss 1937, 82–83; Dreyer 1993, 57
Meryetneith	Abydos/Umm el-Qaab Y	Bs	Porter and Moss 1937, 82
Den	Abydos/Umm el-Qaab T	Bs	Porter and Moss 1937, 83–85; Dreyer 1993, 57–61; Dreyer, Hartung, et al. 1998, 141–164; Dreyer, von den Driesch, et al., 2000, 97–118; Dreyer, Hartmann, et al., 2003, 88–107
Anedjib	Abydos/Umm el-Qaab X	Bs	Porter and Moss 1937, 82.
Semerkhet	Abydos/Umm el-Qaab U	Bs	Porter and Moss 1937, 85–86; Dreyer, von den Driesch, et al., 2000, 119–121; Dreyer, Effland, et al., 2006, 93–98
Qaa	Abydos/Umm el-Qaab Q	Bs	Porter and Moss 1937, 86–87
Hetepsekhemwy	Saqqara A	Rs	Porter and Moss 1974–1981, 613
Ninetjer	Saqqara B	Rs	Porter and Moss 1974–1981, 613; Lacher-Raschdorff 2014
Peribsen	Abydos/Umm el-Qaab P	Bs	Porter and Moss 1937, 81; Dreyer, Effland, et al., 2006, 98–110
Khasekhemwy	Abydos/Umm el-Qaab V	Bs	Porter and Moss 1937, 87; Dreyer et al. 1998, 164–166; Dreyer, von den Driesch, et al., 2000, 122–128;Dreyer, Hartmann, et al., 2003, 108–124, 2006, 110–127
Djoser	Saqqara "Step Pyramid"	SPS	Porter and Moss 1974–1981, 399–415
Sanakht	Abu Rowash "El-Deir"?	SPB?	Swelim 1987, 91–95
Sekhemkhet	Saqqara	SPSu	Porter and Moss 1974–1981, 415–417
Khaba	Zawiyet el-Aryan "Layer Pyramid"	SPS	Porter and Moss 1974–1981, 313; Lehner 1996; Dodson 2000
Huni	Abu Rowash "Brick Pyramid"	SPB	Swelim 1987
Seneferu	Meidum L.LXV	S/TPS	Porter and Moss 1934, 89–90; Maragioglio and Rinaldi 1964–1977, III; Stadelmann 1980
Seneferu	Dahshur "Bent Pyramid"	TPS	Porter and Moss 1974–1981, 877–878

(continued)

Table 5.1 *Continued*

Owner	Location & Tomb Number/ Name	Type	Bibliography
Seneferu	Dahshur "Red Pyramid"	TPS	Porter and Moss 1974–1981, 876; Stadelmann and Sourouzian 1982; Stadelmann 1983
Khufu	Giza "Great Pyramid"	TPS	Porter and Moss 1974–1981, 11–16
Djedefra	Abu Rowash L.II	TPS	Porter and Moss 1974–1981, 1–3; Valloggia 2011
Seth?ka	Zawiyet el-Aryan "Unfinished Pyramid"	TPSu	Porter and Moss 1974–1981, 312–313; Edwards 1994
Khafra	Giza "Second Pyramid"	TPS	Porter and Moss 1974–1981, 19–26
Menkaura	Giza "Third Pyramid"	TPS	Porter and Moss 1974–1981, 26–34
Shepseskaf	Saqqara-South "Mastabat Faraun"	M	Porter and Moss 1974–1981, 433–434
Userkaf	Saqqara L.XXXI	TPS	Porter and Moss 1974–1981, 397–398; Labrousse and Lauer 2000
Sahura	Abusir L.XVIII	TPS	Porter and Moss 1974–1981, 326–335
Neferirkara	Abusir L.XXI	TPS	Porter and Moss 1974–1981, 339–340
Neferefra	Abusir L.XXVI	M (TPSu)	Porter and Moss 1974–1981, 340; Verner 2006
Niuserra	Abusir L.XX	TPS	Porter and Moss 1974–1981, 335–339; Maragioglio and Rinaldi 1964–1977, VIII:8–53
Menkauhor	Saqqara L.XXIX	TPS	Maragioglio and Rinaldi 1964–1977, VIII:59–63; Hawass 2010
Isesi	Saqqara-South L.XXXVII	TPS	Porter and Moss 1974–1981, 424; Maragioglio and Rinaldi 1964–1977, VIII:64–97
Unas	Saqqara L.XXXV	TPS	Porter and Moss 1974–1981, 417–422; Labrousse 1996–2000, I:15–41
Teti	Saqqara L.XXX	TPS	Porter and Moss 1974–1981, 393–396; Labrousse 1996–2000, I:43–72
Pepy I	Saqqara-South L.XXXVI	TPS	Porter and Moss 1974–1981, 422–424; Labrousse 1996–2000, II:1–45
Nemtyemsaf I	Saqqara-South L.XXXIX	TPS	Porter and Moss 1974–1981, 425; Labrousse 1996–2000, II:47–76
Pepy II	Saqqara-South L.XLI	TPS	Porter and Moss 1974–1981, 425–431; Labrousse 1996–2000, II:77–99
Ibi	Saqqara-South L.XLI	TPS	Porter and Moss 1974–1981, 425
Khui?	Dara	M?	Porter and Moss 1934, 258

(continued)

Table 5.1 *Continued*

Owner	Location & Tomb Number/ Name	Type	Bibliography
Intef I	El-Tarif "Saff el-Dawaba"	R	Porter and Moss 1960–1964, 594; Arnold 1976, 19–22
Intef II	El-Tarif "Saff el-Qisasiya"	R	Porter and Moss 1960–1964, 595; Arnold 1976, 25–32
Intef III	El-Tarif "Saff el-Baqar"	R	Porter and Moss 1960–1964, 595; Arnold 1976, 33–38
Mentuhotep II	Deir el-Bahri DBXI.14	Rt	Porter and Moss 1972, 381–400; Arnold 1974–1981, 1979
Mentuhotep III	Thebes-West Thoth Hill	R	Porter and Moss 1972, 340; Weeks 1983: 53–54; Vörös 1998, 2003, 2007, 82–95
Mentuhotep IV	Thebes-West, TT281?	Rtu	Porter and Moss 1972, 400; Arnold 1991
Amenemhat I	Lisht L.LX	TPS	Porter and Moss 1934, 77–78; Arnold 1988, 70–71
Senwosret I	Lisht L.LXI	TPS	Porter and Moss 1934, 81–83; Arnold 1988, 1992
Amenemhat II	Dahshur "White Pyramid"	TPS	Porter and Moss 1974–1981, 885–886
Senwosret II	Lahun L.LXVI	TPB	Porter and Moss 1934, 107–109
Senwosret III	Dahshur L.XLVII	TPB	Porter and Moss 1974–1981, 882–885; Arnold 2002
Senwosret III	Abydos	Rt	Porter and Moss 1937, 92; Wegner 2007, 2009.
Amenemhat III	Dahshur "Black Pyramid"	TPB	Porter and Moss 1974–1981, 887–888; Arnold 1987
Amenemhat III	Hawara L.LXVII	TPB	Porter and Moss 1934, 100–101; Uphill 2000
Amenemhat IV, V or VI?	Dahshur L.LIV	TPB?	Porter and Moss 1974–1981, 887; Swelim 1994, 343, n.16
Ameny-Qemau	Dahshur-South	TPB	Porter and Moss 1974–1981, 890; Swelim and Dodson 1998
?	Mazghuna "North Pyramid"	TPS	Porter and Moss 1934, 76
Hor	Dahshur L.LVIII/1	R	Porter and Moss 1974–1981, 888–889
?	Mazghuna "South Pyramid"	TPS	Porter and Moss 1934, 76
Khendjer	Southern Saqqara-South L.XLIV	TPB	Porter and Moss 1974–1981, 434–435
?	Southern Saqqara-South L.XLVI	TPBu	Porter and Moss 1974–1981, 435
?	Abydos S9	M?	McCormack 2010, 75–77; Wegner 2014

(*continued*)

Table 5.1 *Continued*

Owner	Location & Tomb Number/ Name	Type	Bibliography
Sobekhotep (III, IV or V?)	Abydos S10	M?	McCormack 2010, 75, 76; Wegner 2014
Senebkay	Abydos	Bs	Wegner 2014
Intef VI	Dra Abu'l-Naga	TPB+R	Porter and Moss 1960–1964, 603; Polz 2007, 31–33, 133–138

Key:

Bs Brick tomb-chambers sunk in a shallow pit, with superstructure of uncertain form
M Mastaba
R Rock-cut tomb
Rs Rock-cut tomb, with superstructure of uncertain form
Rt Rock-cut tomb within temple
SPB Step pyramid (brick)
SPS Step pyramid (stone)
TPB True pyramid (brick)
TPS True pyramid (stone)
The suffix "u" indicates unused for burial, either through being incomplete, or some other reason.

Hetepsekhemwy and Ninetjer), with their superstructures now almost totally destroyed, were supplemented as at Abydos by temporary rectangular enclosures, of which two have also been identified. The earlier (the "L-shaped Enclosure") was delineated by piled desert gravel, but the later (the Gisr el-Mudir) was constructed of limestone blocks. However, two later kings of the dynasty were buried back at Abydos, in tombs and enclosures that followed the norms of the First Dynasty in their construction techniques.

The advent of the Third Dynasty marked a fundamental change in royal tomb design, whose location now shifted back to the north for the duration of the Old Kingdom. There, at Saqqara, was built the Step Pyramid of Djoser, which not only combined the formerly separate tomb and monumental rectangular enclosure into a single unit, but also in its final form placed a stepped pyramid above the royal burial place itself. As a further innovation, the whole complex was constructed from stone.

A stepped pyramid—possibly to be regarded as a "stairway to heaven"—apparently also formed the centerpiece of the remaining royal tombs of the Third Dynasty, although two of them reverted to brick for their structures. However, at the beginning of the Fourth Dynasty the stepped pyramid form was replaced by the straight-sided, "true" form—perhaps to be regarded as the petrified rays of the sun. At around the same time, the rectangular enclosure was replaced by a new form of east-west aligned complex, with a mortuary temple against the east face of the pyramid and a valley building on the edge of the cultivation, the two elements joined by a causeway.

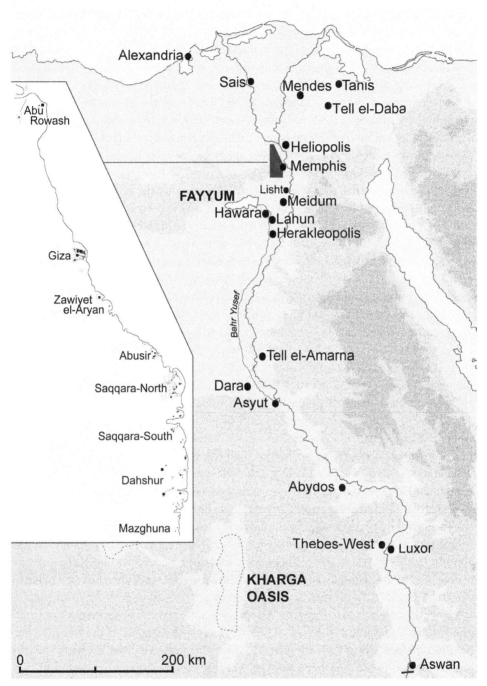

FIGURE 5.1 Locations of the principal sites discussed in this chapter.

A series of innovative monuments of the Fourth Dynasty was ultimately followed by an increasingly standardized set of pyramid complexes during the Fifth Dynasty and then a run of pyramids of all but identical size and design during the Sixth. Only two royal tombs have been identified from the earlier part of the subsequent First Intermediate period, presumably reflecting the lack of resources by the ephemeral rulers of that time.

However, a new sequence of royal sepulchers began with the establishment of a Theban-centered southern kingdom in the person of the Horus Sehertawy Intef (I) around the middle of the twenty-second century B.C.E. in opposition to the Ninth/Tenth Dynasty ruling from Herakleopolis (Ihnasiya) at the mouth of the Fayyum. The earliest known tombs in the Theban necropolis had been constructed at its northern extremity, El-Tarif, during the Fourth Dynasty (Arnold 1976, 11–18). Later in the Old Kingdom, five decorated, rock-cut tomb-chapels were constructed by local governors of the area, in an area 2.5 kilometers south of El-Tarif, now known as Khokha (Saleh 1977).

It was, however, back at El-Tarif that Intef I established his new royal necropolis, probably owing to its location opposite the area that was now coming into existence as the sanctuary of Karnak, whose axis seems to have been important in the layout of the cemeteries on the west bank well into the New Kingdom. The typical of tomb of this period had its offering place fronted by a wide but shallow fore-hall, the front of which consisted of a series of pillars, giving such sepulchers their Arabic name, *saff*, implying a "line" or "many doorways." This was the design followed by Intef I and his two successors on a monumental scale, with huge courtyards sunk into the desert surface, with the royal chapel at the rear and the tombs of officials along the sides of the court. At least one of the royal *saff*s, that of the Horus Wahankh Intef II, had a chapel at the eastern end of the 70-by-250-meter courtyard, perhaps intended as a kind of valley temple (see Figure 5.2).

A description of this sepulcher in a Ramesside tomb-inspection itinerary, Papyrus Abbott (British Museum EA 10221, 2:1–3:14; Kitchen 1983, 469–472), mentions a pyramid as forming part of the tomb; however, no traces have been found. The program of decoration of the royal *saff*s is unclear, although several stelae are known, including one from Intef II's "valley temple" that shows the king attended by his pet hounds.

The Horus Nakhtnebtepnefer Intef III was the last ruler of the line to control the south only, his successor Nebhepetra Mentuhotep II uniting the country and founding the Middle Kingdom midway through his reign of half a century. He also abandoned El-Tarif in favor of a new location, not far from the Old Kingdom governors' tombs at the head of a valley now known as Deir el-Bahri, but still oriented toward Karnak. Although in a very different environment from the flat plain of El-Tarif, the concept of the approach to the royal tomb being flanked by the sepulchers of his court was continued. The rock-cut tomb-chapels of the nobility were cut high in the walls of the valley, overlooking the causeway that led from the edge of the cultivation (and perhaps a valley building) to the site of the royal tomb.

The king's funerary monument took a completely novel form, a temple-tomb on two levels, both fronted by colonnades, which went through four phases of evolution before reaching its ultimate form (see Figure 5.3).

The upper terrace's central focus was a large, square massif, variously reconstructed as a tumulus, a mastaba, or a pyramid (cf. Polz 2007, 200–211), although the latter option is

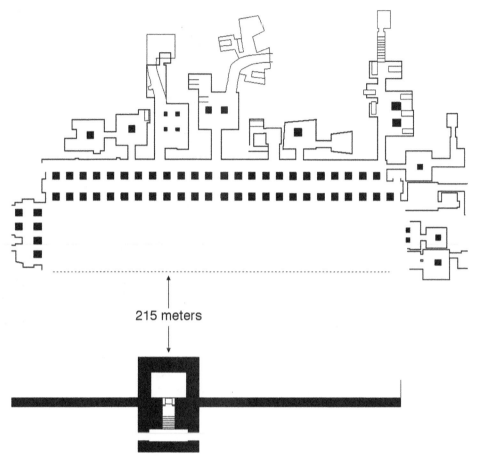

215 meters

FIGURE 5.2 Plan of the Saff el-Qisasiya, the tomb of Intef II at El-Tarif, showing the complex of chapels at the rear and the structure at the eastern end of the structure, which contained a stela showing the king with his dogs.

[Aidan Dodson.]

suggested by the designation of the monument as a pyramid in Papyrus Abbott. This was surrounded by a pillared hall, behind which was a colonnaded court and then a hypostyle hall, at the back of which lies the main offering place, together with the entrance to the king's rock-cut tomb. Mentuhotep's temple was adorned with a wide range of motifs, including military activities, hunting in the desert, agricultural narratives, the king in the presence of the gods, and episodes from the *heb-sed* festival. The temple itself also included the small tomb-chapels of six female members of the royal household, together with the tomb of one of the king's wives, named Tem. Further subsidiary tombs lay outside the temple proper, including the tomb-chapel of another wife of the king, Neferu (Arnold 2008).

The burial place of the king himself lay at the end of a 150-meter-long passageway, partly lined with sandstone, which descended from the rear part of the temple. This gave access to a chamber with a pointed roof, within which was constructed an alabaster shrine that served in lieu of a conventional sarcophagus. This contained a wooden coffin and

FIGURE 5.3 Overhead view of the temple-tomb of Mentuhotep II at Deir el-Bahri. Visible at the top left are the entrance to its cenotaph (the Bab el-Hosan), the tree-pits that flanked the final approach, the square massif that may have been the base of a pyramid, the sloping passage to the king's burial chamber, and the inner hypostyle hall.

[Martin Davies.]

wooden-lidded canopic jars, together with scepters, walking sticks, and bows and arrows, while models of the typical Middle Kingdom type were found not only in the burial chamber, but also in niches in the walls of the descending corridor. The temple complex also incorporated a *heb-sed* jubilee-cenotaph in the form of a passageway—known as the Bab el-Hosan—that descended from the temple forecourt to a chamber under the pyramid and may have been intended to be the actual royal burial chamber during the earliest phase of the temple's evolution. This room contained offerings, an empty wooden coffin, and a sandstone statue of the king in jubilee dress, wrapped in linen, with some wooden model boats in a chamber at the bottom of a shaft below the burial chamber.

Later graffiti refer to priests of the mortuary cult of the next king, Seankhkara Mentuhotep III (Winlock 1947, pls. 42–43), but the identification of the structure within which they officiated has been a matter for debate. It has often been equated with an unfinished structure behind the Sheikh Abd el-Qurna hill, which comprises grading in preparation for the construction of a temple and causeway of the kind built for Mentuhotep II, together with a corridor-tomb and a number of subsidiary shaft-tombs. However, this had never been a functional temple of the kind implied by the aforementioned graffiti, and it has also been suggested that Mentuhotep III's funerary monument should be identified with his temple at Thoth Hill in the northwest of the Theban necropolis, built on the site of a much more ancient sanctuary. This included a *heb-sed* jubilee-cenotaph and a chamber in the cliff below (later forming part of a Coptic hermitage), containing a sarcophagus cut from the living rock, which may represent the king's burial place.

The identification of the tomb of Nebtawyra Menthuhotep IV is also problematic. A text in the Wadi Hammamat records an expedition to obtain the lid for the king's sarcophagus (Porter and Moss 1952, 331), but nothing related to his actual burial place has been identified. It is possible that his may have been the unfinished temple site mentioned above as the potential monument of Mentuhotep III. This has also, however, been identified as possibly an initial tomb begun for Amenemhat I, founder of the Twelfth Dynasty, prior to a decision to return the royal cemeteries to the northern part of Egypt (Arnold 1991).

For the next three-and-a-half centuries royal cemeteries remained primarily in the north of Egypt, although a number of royal tombs were also constructed at Abydos. In contrast to the innovative monuments of the Theban kings, the tombs in northern Egypt took the form of free-standing, large pyramids with adjacent offering places, broadly modeled on Old Kingdom prototypes, although as time went by developments occurred primarily aimed at enhancing security.

The earliest of these monuments, that of Amenemhat I at Lisht, is in poor condition, and little is known about the layout of its temples, although the mortuary temple may have been on two levels and thus reminiscent of the temple of Mentuhotep II. Its substructure followed late Old Kingdom practice in descending from ground level in the center of the north face, although instead of terminating in the burial chamber, it gave access to a vertical shaft under the center of the pyramid. Unfortunately, what lay at the bottom is concealed by infiltrated groundwater that also afflicts the substructure of the nearby pyramid of Senwosret I. On the other hand, enough of Senwosret's mortuary temple is preserved to indicate that its design was heavily influenced by that of late Old Kingdom examples, albeit with a number of innovations.

The next king, Amenemhat II, abandoned Lisht and moved north to Dahshur to find a site for his pyramid. The pyramid itself is so destroyed that even the dimensions of its base cannot be determined, but the substructure also has a number of interesting features, including the concealment of the sarcophagus under the floor of the burial chamber. This theme of enhanced security is seen in the next pyramid, that of Senwosret II, which was built away from any earlier royal necropolis, at Lahun at the mouth of the Fayyum. Here, the entrance to the substructure was shifted from its historic location close to the center of the north side to one at the eastern end of the south side; no subsequent pyramid would have its entrance in the ancient location. The pyramid also switched from stone to brick for its principal construction material, something also found in almost all subsequent royal pyramids in Egypt.

Senwosret III built two funerary monuments. One was at Abydos, comprising an elaborate rock-cut tomb, plus two temples, one above the tomb and one on the edge of the cultivation; it is possible that this sepulcher was his actual burial place. The other was a pyramid complex at Dahshur, a monument in its final phase of construction apparently inspired by the Third Dynasty Step Pyramid of Djoser, with a north-south orientation and approached from the southeast. The pyramid itself is also interesting in that its substructure had an underground link to that of the adjacent pyramid of the king's mother. This was taken a step further by Amenemhat III, in whose Dahshur pyramid the tombs of his wives were placed under the king's pyramid itself—with a separate entrance, but once again with a linking corridor between the two sections.

Apparently abandoning his Dahshur monument owing to structural failure, Amenemhat III built another pyramid complex at Hawara in the Fayyum. This took some of the earlier security innovations further, with dummy blind passages; massive sliding "trapdoors" of quartzite; and a burial chamber that was carved from a single block of the same stone and accessed not via a conventional doorway, but through a movable roofing-block, lowered into place after the burial by a kind of "hydraulic" system using sand.

These and other stratagems—culminating seemingly in the provision of a dummy "decoy" burial chamber in one pyramid—were also employed in pyramids of the succeeding Thirteenth Dynasty, although some—if not all—were left unfinished. The number of identifiable monuments is significantly fewer than the number of potential owners; indeed, only two pyramids of the dynasty are firmly attributed, to Khendjer and Qemau, while the relative chronological order of all remains moot to some degree (cf. McCormack 2010). That many Thirteenth Dynasty kings may have been buried in much simpler forms of sepulcher is indicated by the tomb of King Hor, which lay at the foot of a shaft in the earlier pyramid enclosure of Amenemhat III at Dahshur. In this case, an old shaft had been appropriated and a burial complex reminiscent of contemporary pyramids inserted. Other kings were buried away from the Memphite necropolis, two tombs at Abydos (S9 and S10, adjacent to the tomb of Senwosret III) preserving substructures of Thirteenth Dynasty royal type, one belonging to a king Sobekhotep, almost certainly the third, fourth or fifth king of the name.

The end of pyramid building in the Memphite necropolis—and possibly the appearance of potential royal tombs much farther south at Abydos—was certainly the result of the progressive takeover of the north of Egypt by the Palestinian Hyksos Fifteenth Dynasty. The principal resulting rump Egyptian regime was centered on Thebes (for discussions of its nature and chronology, see, inter alia, Dodson 1991; Ryholt 1997, 151–183; Polz 2007, 20–56), although another(?) line existed at Abydos, with a cemetery close to the tomb of Senwosret III and tombs S9 and S10, including that of a king Senebkay.

The royal cemetery of the Theban regime lay at Dra Abu'l-Naga. Only one of the tombs of this group is currently positively located, but others were seen or plundered in the nineteenth century, and yet more were listed in Papyrus Abbott. Having recorded the inspection of the tombs of Amenhotep I (see pp. 67–68, below) and Intef II (see p. 60, above), the papyrus then notes in turn the condition of the sepulchers of Nubkheperra Intef (VI), Sekhemra-Wapmaat Intef (V), Sekhemra-Shedtawi Sebekemsaf (I), Seqenenra Taa, Seqenenra Taa-aa, Kamose and (prince) Ahmose-Sapairi, before concluding with the tomb of Mentuhotep II at Deir el-Bahri (see pp. 60–62, above).

The remains of the pyramid of Intef VI have been excavated roughly a quarter of the way along the Dra Abu'l-Naga hill, and given that the Papyrus Abbott sequence terminates at Deir el-Bahri, one would assume that it represented the northernmost of a series of Seventeenth Dynasty royal tombs running southward from that point. The papyrus notes that plunderers had attempted to tunnel under the pyramid from the adjacent tomb of Shuroy (TT13), a Ramesside tomb-chapel that lies directly to the right of the pyramid.

The pyramid itself, with a steep slope of approximately 67 degrees (contrasting with the approximately 52 degrees of most earlier monumental pyramids), was built on top of an earlier shaft tomb (K02.2), on the slope of the hill, with the height of the apex (equipped with an inscribed capstone) 9.9 meters above the ground surface at that point. It comprised an outer skin of bricks, now reduced to a few courses, with a rubble fill, surrounded on three sides by an enclosure wall (see Figure 5.4).

The eastern side may have been terraced, and was in any case was adorned by a pair of small obelisks bearing the king's names and titles. Auguste Mariette, who found the obelisks in 1860, reports having uncovered some kind of rock-cut offering place ("hemi-spéos") near them, but this has not been subsequently identified. A number of tombs of the king's contemporaries were built adjacent to the pyramid, including that of the chancellor Teti.

No substructure has been located in the immediate vicinity of the pyramid, which would thus seem to have been some distance from the monument itself. The only information available is that "during researches made by the Arabs in the year 1827, they discovered in the mountain [of Dra Abu'l-Naga] a small and separate tomb, containing only one chamber, in the centre of which was placed a sarcophagus, hewn out of the same rock, and formed evidently at the same time as the chamber itself; its base not having been detached" (Athanasi 1836, xi). This was found intact and contained the (now

FIGURE 5.4 The middle part of the hill of Dra Abu'l-Naga, showing the location of the pyramids of Intef V and VI. The remains of the latter, with a preexisting shaft (with modern tripod over it) in its center, comprise no more than the lowest courses of the brick skin of the rubble-filled monument. The modern shelter directly to its right protects the entrance to the tomb-chapel of Shuroy (TT13), from which Twentieth Dynasty plunderers attempted to tunnel under the pyramid.

[Aidan Dodson.]

destroyed) mummy of the king, within a gilded *rishi* coffin (British Museum EA 6652; Porter and Moss 1960–1964, 602–603; Polz 2007, 22–25).

A similar separate substructure seems to have held the burial of Intef V (to which the coffin of Sekhemra-heruhirmaat Intef VII was later added), Gardner Wilkinson stating in 1855 that their coffins were found (around 1848) "all the way up the [Dra Abu'l-Naga] hill," in a chamber at the end of a corridor accessed by a brick-lined shaft "4 men" deep. In this he corrects his 1849 statement they had been found in a pit-cache (Oxford, Bodleian Library, Wilkinson MS e.67, p. 79). Intef V's gilded *rishi* coffin had been made for him by his brother Intef VI (Louvre E.3019; Porter and Moss 1960–1964, 603; Polz 2007, 29–34), while that of Intef VII was a "stock" piece (Louvre E.3020; Porter and Moss 1960–1964, 603; Polz 2007, 25–28). The burial chamber presumably also held Intef V's canopic chest (Louvre N.491 = E.2538; Porter and Moss 1960–1964, 603; Dodson 1994, 37–47, 117–118[25], 150–151[25]). As for the actual pyramid of Intef V, mentioned in Papyrus Abbott as a "in the course of being tunneled into by the thieves at the place where the stela of its pyramid was set up," fragments of its capstone have been found just southeast of the pyramid of Intef VI. This suggests that the pyramid itself lay close by, reflecting the aforementioned expectations on the basis of the Papyrus Abbott itinerary.

In contrast to these actual remains, the tomb of Sobekemsaf I has yet to be positively identified (Polz 2007, 160–162), nor has anything deriving from it been positively identified, although the latter is not surprising, given that Papyrus Abbott describes it as having been robbed-out shortly before the inspection in Year 16 of Ramesses IX (the canopic chest of a 'King Sobekemsaf' might potentially be from the tomb, although it may actually belong to Sekhemra-wadjkhau Sobekemsaf [Leiden AH.216; Porter and Moss 1960–1964, 604; Dodson 1994, 37–47, 118[26], 152–153[26]]). Interestingly, the account in the papyrus (supplemented by the transcript of the trial of those responsible in Papyrus Leopold II-Amherst; Kitchen 1983, 481–489) does indicate that the tomb included provision for the king's wife (cf. Winlock 1924, 237–243).

No candidates for the tombs of Taa and Taa-aa have yet been localized, and indeed it seems that while the former is a well-attested individual (Ryholt 1997, 397–398), Taa-aa is a complete phantom. For many years it was argued that "Seqenenre Taa-aa" was actually an error for "Senakhtenre Taa-aa" (Winlock 1924, 243–245), but now that Senakhtenre's nomen has been identified as "Ahmose" (Biston-Moulin 2012), this is no longer an option. It thus seems that "Seqenenre Taa-aa" is most likely a scribal phantom, the creation of some confusion by the official who wrote up the notes of the commission of inspection.

The last two tombs of the Papyrus Abbott Seventeenth Dynasty sequence, of Kamose and Ahmose-Sipariri, would presumably have lain toward the southern end of Dra Abu'l-Naga; on this basis, a monument in the Birabi (the southern end of Dra Abu'l-Naga/ western edge of the Asasif) as been posited as one or other of their tombs. Certainly datable to the end of the Seventeenth Dynasty, this comprises a pyramid within a large enclosure, with a built chapel, but with its innermost part set into the pyramid—much like the contemporary pyramid of Tetisherit at Abydos—together with a rock-cut substructure.

On the other hand, it is possible that rather than being strung out along the flank of the hill, the Seventeenth Dynasty royal necropolis was concentrated in the immediate area of the known sites of the pyramids of Intef V and VI. In this case, a large, rock-cut tomb-chapel of late Seventeenth/early Eighteenth Dynasty date (K94.1) that lies high above the Intef tombs on the Dra Abu'l-Naga hill could be a possibility for the sepulcher of Kamose (Polz 2007, 162–172). In any case, his coffin (Cairo TR 14/12/27/12; Porter and Moss 1960–1964, 600) was found secondarily buried at the foot of the hill, perhaps near TT155, at the mouth of the Khawi el-Amwat, some 200 meters north of the Intef VI pyramid (see Winlock 1924, 252). It had presumably been moved at some point after Year 16 of Ramesses IX, when Kamose's tomb was found to be intact.

The matter of the burial place of the founder of the New Kingdom, Ahmose I, has long been a subject of debate. Given the interment of his immediate predecessors and successors at Thebes and the discovery of his mummy in the TT320 cache, the general assumption has been that his own original interment had been in the Theban necropolis, perhaps in the ancestral cemetery of Dra Abu'l-Naga. However, no unequivocal original tomb of his has been identified at Thebes (cf. Dodson 2010, 26), while at Abydos the king constructed an extensive funerary complex, comprising a pyramid, a pyramid-cenotaph for his grandmother, three temples, and a pyramid—plus a subterranean tomb—spread out along a 1.25-kilometer axis across the desert. The (not-quite-finished) pyramid was fronted by a pair of temples, one belonging to queen Ahmes-Nefertiry, the other to the king, and adorned with reliefs apparently depicting the defeat of the Hyksos, with a further terraced structure against the cliffs at the western end of the axis. Some distance in front of the latter was a large, sinuously planned, rock-cut tomb including an eighteen-pillared hall, although like the pyramid, it was not wholly finished.

This whole complex has generally been dismissed as a cenotaph, but in view of its completeness and the lack of any corresponding structures at Thebes, it has been suggested (Dodson 2010) that Ahmose may have originally been interred at Abydos, but reburied at Thebes a few years later. The location of this reburial may have been a tomb behind Dra Abu'l-Naga (AN B), first identified as that of Amenhotep I, but later as that of Ahmes-Nefertiry. The latter identification has now been undermined by the redating of TT320 (later the royal cache) as most probably the original tomb of that queen (Aston 2013), leaving the possibility that AN B might actually have been constructed or extended by Amenhotep I and Ahmes-Nefertiry for a Theban reburial of Ahmose. This would be consistent with the mix of royal names found in the tomb (but see also p. 68, below).

The burial place of Amenhotep I also presents problems, in spite of being mentioned in Papyrus Abbott. It appears at the head of the list, but it is unclear what—if anything—this implies about its position. It is unlikely to have lain north of the tomb of Intef II, while the relative prominence of the king vis à vis the other tomb owners involved (Mentuhotep II excepted) may have led to Amenhotep's tomb being given special attention and being visited out of strict topographical order.

Papyrus Abbott states that the tomb lay 120 cubits below some elevated element (whose exact translation remains moot) and north of the "House of Amenhotep of the Garden." Unfortunately there is no clarity on the location of the latter, and it has variously been identified with a number of structures (cf. Polz 1995 for a summary with references), including the Eighteenth Dynasty temple at Medinet Habu (with which Amenhotep I seems wholly unconnected); the mortuary temple of Amenhotep-son-of-Hapu; the brick temple of Amenhotep I at Deir el-Bahri (buried under Hatshepsut's temple for

350 years by the time of Papyrus Abbott); a potential replacement chapel of Amenhotep I in the "garden" in front of the temple of Mentuhotep II at Deir el-Bahri; and the joint temple of Amenhotep I and Ahmes-Nefertiry in front of Dra Abu'l-Naga. Candidate tombs to the north of one or more of these loci have included KV 39, above the southern end of the Valley of the Kings (which now seems to be a royal family tomb of the middle of the Eighteenth Dynasty; Dodson 2003b, 188–189; Aston 2013, 16–17); a putative yet undiscovered tomb in the cliff above the temples at Deir el-Bahri (Niwiński 2009); Dra Abu'l-Naga AN B; and a rock-cut tomb-chapel high up at Dra Abu'l-Naga (K93.11; Polz 2007, 172–197). Both the latter candidates lie close to the north-south axis of the temple of Amenhotep I and Ahmes-Nefertiry, with the complementary possibility that the unexcavated tomb that shares a courtyard with K93.11 (K93.12) might be that of the queen.

The identification of the owners of K93.11 and K93.12 is complicated by the fact that they were extensively modified by the high priests of Amun Ramesesnakht and Amenhotep G and the God's Wife of Amun Iset E during the late Twentieth Dynasty (Polz 1998; Rummel 2009, 2011, 2014). This would appear to argue against identifying K93.11 with the tomb of Amenhotep I, since his sepulcher is reported by Papyrus Abbott as being intact in Year 16 of Ramesses IX—just the time at which the tomb was being rebuilt as an apparently private monument. On the other hand, it is not impossible that the rebuilding was not intended as a private usurpation, but rather as a new memorialization of Amenhotep I—although extant fragments do not directly support such a conclusion. Thus, in light of the evidence associating Ahmes-Nefertiry with TT320, it now seems not unlikely that AN B is that of Amenhotep I after all—perhaps later shared with Ahmose I on his mummy's aforementioned possible "repatriation" from Abydos (Dodson 2013).

Amenhotep I is the last king definitively known to have been buried outside the Valley of the Kings until the Amarna period. Although it is generally agreed that the first king interred there was Thutmose I, debate continues about the identity of that tomb (Polz 2007, 211–229). The main candidates have been KV 38 (Porter and Moss 1960–1964, 557–559), in which a sarcophagus manufactured for him was found, and KV 20 (Porter and Moss 1960–1964, 546–547), in whose burial chamber a sarcophagus modified for him by Hatshepsut was discovered. Issues also remain over the burial place of Thutmose II, in particular whether KV 42 (Porter and Moss 1960–1964, 559) was intended to be his, whether or not it was ever used for his interment (cf. Eaton-Krauss 2012), or whether his tomb was another monument – perhaps the first phase of KV 20, the tomb later extended for Hatshepsut (Roehrig 2007, 122). Thus the earliest unequivocally identifiable royal tomb in the Valley of the Kings is KV 34, the sepulcher of Thutmose III.

Bibliography

Arnold, Dieter. 1974–1981. *Der Tempel des Königs Mentuhotep von Deir el-Bahari*. 3 vols. Mainz.

Arnold, Dieter. 1976. *Gräber des Alten und Mittleren Reiches in El-Tarif*. Mainz.

Arnold, Dieter. 1979. *The Temple of Mentuhotep at Deir el-Bahari*. New York.

Arnold, Dieter. 1987. *Der Pyramidbezirk des Königs Amenemhet III in Dahschur, I: Die Pyramide*. Mainz.

Arnold, Dieter. 1988. *The Pyramid of Senwosret I*. New York.

Arnold, Dieter. 1992. *The Pyramid Complex of Senwosret I.* New York.

Arnold, Dieter. 2002. *The Pyramid Complex of Senwosret III at Dahshur: Archictectural Studies.* New York.

Arnold, Dieter. 2008. "The Tombs of the Queens of Mentuhotep II." In *Queens of Egypt: From Hetepheres to Cleopatra*, edited by C. Ziegler, 94–101. Monaco and Paris.

Arnold, Dorothea. 1991. "Amenemhat I and the Early Twelfth Dynasty at Thebes." *Metropolitan Museum Journal* 26: 5–48.

Aston, D. A. 2013. "TT 320 and the ḳȝy of Queen Inhapi: A Reconsideration Based on Ceramic Evidence." *Göttinger Miszellen* 236: 7–20.

Athanasi, G. d'. 1836. *A Brief Account of the Researches and Discoveries in Upper Egypt Made under the Direction of Henry Salt.* London.

Bestock, L. 2009. *The Development of Royal Funerary Cult at Abydos: Two Funerary Enclosures from the Reign of Aha.* Wiesbaden.

Bietak, M. 2010. "From Where Came the Hyksos and Where Did They Go?" In *The Second Intermediate Period (Thirteenth-Seventeenth Dynasties): Current Research, Future Prospects*, edited by M. Marée, 139–181. Leuven.

Biston-Moulin, S. 2012. "Le roi Sénakht-en-Rê Ahmès de la XVIIe dynastie." *Égypte nilotique et méditerranéenne* 5: 61–71.

Case, H., and J. Crowfoot-Payne. 1962. "Tomb 100: The Decorated Tomb at Hierakonpolis." *Journal of Egyptian Archaeology* 48: 5–18.

Crowfoot-Payne, J. 1973. "Tomb 100: The Decorated Tomb at Hierakonpolis Confirmed." *Journal of Egyptian Archaeology* 59: 31–35.

Dodson, A. 1991. "On the Internal Chronology of the Seventeenth Dynasty." *Göttinger Miszellen* 120: 33–38.

Dodson, A. 1994. *The Canopic Equipment of the Kings of Egypt.* With contributions by O. J. Schaden, E. C. Brock, and M. Collier. London

Dodson, A. 1996. "The Mysterious 2nd Dynasty." *Kmt* 7 (2): 19–31.

Dodson, A. 2000. "The Layer Pyramid at Zawiyet el-Aryan: Its Layout and Context." *Journal of the American Research Center in Egypt* 38: 81–90.

Dodson, A. 2003a. *The Pyramids of Ancient Egypt.* London.

Dodson, A. 2003b. "The Burial of Members of the Royal Family during the Eighteenth Dynasty." In *Egyptology at the Dawn of the Twenty-first Century: Proceedings of the Eighth International Congress of Egyptologists, Cairo, 2000*, edited by Z. Hawass and L. Pinch-Brock, II:187–193. Cairo.

Dodson, A. 2010. "The Burials of Ahmose I." In *Thebes and Beyond: Studies in Honour of Kent R. Weeks*, edited by Z. Hawass and S. Ikram, 25–33. Cairo.

Dodson, A. 2013. "On the Burials and Reburials of Ahmose I and Amenhotep I." *Göttinger Miszellen* 236: 7–20.

Dreyer, G. 1991. "Zur Rekonstruktion der Oberbauten der Königsgräber der 1. Dynastie in Abydos." *Mitteilungen des Deutschen Archäologischen Instituts, Kairo* 47: 93–104.

Dreyer, G. 1993. "Umm el-Qaab: Nachuntersuchungen im frühzeitlichen Königsfriedhof. 5./6. Vorbericht." *Mitteilungen des Deutschen Archäologischen Instituts, Kairo* 49: 23–62.

Dreyer, G. 1998. *Umm el-Qaab. Band 1, Das prädynastische Königsgrab U-j und seine frühen Schriftzeugnisse.* Mainz.

Dreyer, G. 2009. "Report on the 21st Campaign of Reexamining the Royal Tombs of Umm el-Qaab at Abydos 2006/2007." *Annales du Service des Antiquités de l'Égypte* 83: 165–175.

Dreyer, G. 2010. "Report on the 22nd Campaign of Reexamining the Royal Tombs of Umm el-Qaab at Abydos 2007/2008." *Annales du Service des Antiquités de l'Égypte* 84: 143–156.

Dreyer, G., A. Effland, U. Effland, E.-M. Engel, R. Hartmann, U. Hartung, C. Lacher, V. Müller, and A. Pokorny. 2006. "Umm el-Qaab: Nachuntersuchungen im frühzeitlichen Königsfriedhof 16./17./18. Vorbericht." *Mitteilungen des Deutschen Archäologischen Instituts, Kairo* 62: 67–129.

Dreyer, G., R. Hartmann, U. Hartung, T. Hikade, H. Köpp, C. Lacher, V. Müller, A. Nerlich, and A. Zink. 2003. "Umm el-Qaab: Nachuntersuchungen im frühzeitlichen Königsfriedhof, 13./14./15. Vorbericht." *Mitteilungen des Deutschen Archäologischen Instituts, Kairo* 59: 67–138.

Dreyer, G., U. Hartung, T. Hikade, E. C. Köhler, V. Müller, and F. Pumpenmeier. 1998. "Umm el-Qaab: Nachuntersuchungen im frühzeitlichen Königsfriedhof, 9./10. Vorbericht." *Mitteilungen des Deutschen Archäologischen Instituts, Kairo* 54: 77–167.

Dreyer, G., A. von den Driesch, E.-M. Engel, R. Hartmann, U. Hartung, T. Hikade, V. Müller, and J. Peters. 2000. "Umm el-Qaab: Nachuntersuchungen im frühzeitlichen Königsfriedhof, 11./12. Vorbericht." *Mitteilungen des Deutschen Archäologischen Instituts, Kairo* 56: 43–129.

Eaton-Krauss, M. 2012. "Who Commissioned KV 42 and for Whom?" *Göttinger Miszellen* 234: 53–60.

Edwards, I. E. S. 1994. "Chephren's Place among the Kings of the Fourth Dynasty." In *The Unbroken Reed: Studies in the Culture and Heritage of Ancient Egypt in Honour of A. F. Shore*, edited by C. Eyre, A. Leahy, and L. M. Leahy, 97–105. London.

Friedman, R. F. 2011. "The Early Royal Cemetery at Hierakonpolis: An Overview." In *Recent Discoveries and Latest Researches in Egyptology: Proceedings of the First Neapolitan Congress of Egyptology, Naples, June 18–20, 2008*, edited by F. Raffaele, M. Nuzzolo, and I. Incordino, 67–86. Wiesbaden.

Harvey, S. P. 2001. "Tribute to a Conquering King: Battle Scenes at Abydos Honor a Pharaoh's Triumph over Hyksos Occupiers and his Reunification of Egypt." *Archaeology* 54 (4): 52–55.

Harvey, S. P. 2004. "New Evidence at Abydos for Ahmose's Funerary Cult." *Egyptian Archaeology* 24: 3–6.

Harvey, S. P. 2008. "Report on Abydos, Ahmose and Tetisheri Project, 2006–2007 Season." *Annales du Service des Antiquités de l'Égypte* 82: 143–155.

Hawass, Z. 2010. "The Excavation of the Headless Pyramid, Lepsius XXIX." In *Perspectives on Ancient Egypt: Studies in Honor of Edward Brovarski*, edited by Z. Hawass, P. Der Manuelian, and R. B. Hussein, 153–170. Cairo.

Kaiser, W., and G. Dreyer. 1982. "Umm el-Qaab: Nachuntersuchungen im frühzeitlichen Königsfriedhof: 2. Vorbericht." *Mitteilungen des Deutschen Archäologischen Instituts, Kairo* 38: 211–269.

Kitchen, K. A. 1983. *Ramesside Inscriptions: Historical and Biographical*, I. Oxford.

Labrousse, A. 1996–2000. *L'architecture des pyramides à textes*. 2 vols. Cairo.

Labrousse, A., and J.-Ph. Lauer. 2000. *Les complexes funéraires d'Ouserkaf et de Néferhétepès*. Cairo.

Lacher-Raschdorff, C.M. 2014. *Das Grab des Königs Ninetjer in Saqqara. Architektonische Entwicklung frühzeitlicher Grabanlagen in Ägypten*. Wiesbaden: Harrassowitz.

Lehner, Mark. 1996. "Z500 and the Layer Pyramid of Zawiyet el-Aryan." In *Studies in Honor of William Kelly Simpson*, edited by P. Der Manuelian, 507–522. Boston.

Maragioglio, V., and C. A. Rinaldi. 1964–1977. *L'architettura delle Piramidi Menfite*. Vols. III–VIII. Rapallo.

McCormack, D. 2010. "The Significance of Royal Funerary Architecture for the Study of Thirteenth Dynasty Kingship." In *The Second Intermediate Period (Thirteenth-Seventeenth Dynasties): Current Research, Future Prospects*, edited by M. Marée, 69–84. Leuven.

Niwiński, A. 2009. "The Tomb Protection in the Theban 21st Dynasty: Unknown Archaeological Facts Gathered during the Excavation of the Polish-Egyptian 'Cliff Mission' at Deir el-Bahari in the Seasons 1999–2006." In *The Libyan Period in Egypt: Historical and Cultural Studies into the 21st–24th Dynasties; Proceedings of a Conference at Leiden University, 25–27 October 2007*, edited by G. P. F. Broekman, R. J. Demarée, and O. E. Kaper, 277–289. Leiden.

O'Connor, D. 1989. "New Funerary Enclosures (*Talbezirke*) of the Early Dynastic Period at Abydos." *Journal of the American Research Center in Egypt* 26: 51–86.

Polz, D. 1995. "The Location of the Tomb of Amenhotep I: A Reconsideration." In *Valley of the Sun Kings: New Explorations in the Tombs of the Pharaohs*, edited by R. H. Wilkinson, 8–21. Tucson, AZ.

Polz, D. 1998. "The Ramsesnakht Dynasty and the Fall of the New Kingdom: A New Monument in Thebes." *Studien zur altägyptschen Kultur* 25: 257–293.

Polz, D. 2007. *Der Beginn des Neuen Reiches: Zur Vorgeschichte einer Zeitenwende*. Berlin.

Polz, D., and A. Seiler. 2003. *Die Pyramidenanlage des Königs Nub-Cheper-Re Intef in Dra' Abu el-Naga*. Mainz.

Porter, B., and R. L. B. Moss. 1934. *Topographical Bibliography of Ancient Egyptian Hieroglyphic Texts, Reliefs and Paintings*, IV: *Lower and Middle Egypt*. Oxford.

Porter, B., and R. L. B. Moss. 1937. *Topographical Bibliography of Ancient Egyptian Hieroglyphic Texts, Reliefs and Paintings*, V: *Upper Egypt: Sites*. Oxford.

Porter, B., and R. L. B. Moss. 1952. *Topographical Bibliography of Ancient Egyptian Hieroglyphic Texts, Reliefs and Paintings*, VII: *Nubia, the Deserts and Outside Egypt*. Oxford.

Porter, B., and R. L. B. Moss. 1960–1964. *Topographical Bibliography of Ancient Egyptian Hieroglyphic Texts, Reliefs and Paintings*, I: *The Theban Necropolis*. 2nd ed. Oxford.

Porter, B., and R. L. B. Moss. 1972. *Topographical Bibliography of Ancient Egyptian Hieroglyphic Texts, Reliefs and Paintings*, II: *Theban Temples*. 2nd ed. Oxford.

Porter, B., and R. L. B. Moss. 1974–1981. *Topographical Bibliography of Ancient Egyptian Hieroglyphic Texts, Reliefs and Paintings*, III: *Memphis*. 2nd ed. by J. Málek. Oxford.

Roehrig, C. 2007. "Chamber Ja in Royal Tombs in the Valley Of The Kings." In *Sacred space and sacred function in ancient Thebes. Occasional proceedings of the Theban Workshop*, edited by P.F. Dorman and B.M. Bryan, 117–138. Chicago.

Rummel, U. 2009. "Grab oder Tempel? Die funeräre Anlage des Hohenpriesters des Amun Amenophis in Dra' Abu el-Naga (Theben-West)." In *Texte—Theben—Tonfragmente: Festschrift für Günter Burkard*, edited by D. Kessler, 348–360. Wiesbaden.

Rummel, U. 2011. "Two Re-Used Blocks of the God's Wife Isis at Deir el-Bakhit/Dra' Abu el-Naga (Western Thebes)." In *Ramesside Studies in Honour of K.A. Kitchen*, edited by M. Collier and S. Snape, 423–431. Bolton.

Rummel, U. 2014. "War, death and burial of the High Priest Amenhotep: the archaeological record at Dra' Abu el-Naga." *Studien zur altägyptschen Kultur* 43: 375–397.

Ryholt, K. S. B. 1997. *The Political Situation in Egypt during the Second Intermediate Period, c. 1800–1550 B.C.* Copenhagen.

Saleh, M. 1977. *Three Old-Kingdom Tombs at Thebes. 1, The Tomb of Unas-Ankh no. 413. 2, The Tomb of Khenty no. 405. 3, The Tomb of Ihy no. 186*. Mainz.

Stadelmann, R. 1980. "Snofru und die Pyramiden von Meidum und Dahschur." *Mitteilungen des Deutschen Archäologischen Instituts, Kairo* 36: 437–449.

Stadelmann, R. 1983. "Die Pyramiden des Snofru in Dahschur: Zweiter Bericht über die Ausgrabungen an den nördlichen Steinpyramide." *Mitteilungen des Deutschen Archäologischen Instituts, Kairo* 39: 225–241.

Stadelmann, R., and H. Sourouzian. 1982. "Die Pyramiden des Snofru in Dahschur: Erster Bericht über die Ausgrabungen an der nördlichen Steinpyramide." *Mitteilungen des Deutschen Archäologischen Instituts, Kairo* 38: 379–393.

Swelim, N. 1987. *The Brick Pyramid at Abu Rowash, Number '1' by Lepsius: A Preliminary Study.* Alexandria.

Swelim, N. 1994. "Pyramid Research from the Archaic to the Second Intermediate Period: Lists, Catalogues and Objectives." In *Hommages à Jean Leclant*, edited by C. Berger, G. Clerc, and N. Grimal, I:337–349. Cairo.

Swelim, N., and A. Dodson. 1998. "On the Pyramid of Ameny-Qemau and its Canopic Equipment." *Mitteilungen des Deutschen Archäologischen Instituts, Kairo* 54: 319–334.

Uphill, E. P. 2000. *Pharaoh's Gateway to Eternity: The Hawara Labyrinth of King Amenemhat III.* London and New York.

Valloggia, M. 2011. *Abou Rawash 1: Le complexe funéraire royal de Rêdjedef.* 2 vols. Cairo.

Verner, M., ed. 2006. *Abusir IX: The Pyramid Complex of Raneferef; The Archaeology.* Prague.

Vörös, G. 1998. *The Temple on the Pyramid of Thebes: Hungarian Excavations on Thoth Hill at the Temple of Pharaoh Montuhotep Sankhkara 1995–1998.* Budapest.

Vörös, G. 2003. "The Ancient Nest of Horus above Thebes: Hungarian Excavations on Thoth Hill at the Temple of King Sankhare Montuhotep III (1995–1998)." In *Egyptology at the Dawn of the Twenty-first Century: Proceedings of the Eighth International Congress of Egyptologists, Cairo, 2000*, edited by Z. Hawass and L. Pinch-Brock, I:547–556. Cairo.

Vörös, G. 2007. *Egyptian Temple Architecture: 100 Years of Hungarian Excavations in Egypt, 1907–2007.* Budapest.

Weeks, K.R. 1983. "The Berkeley Map of the Theban Necropolis: report of the fifth season, 1982." *Newsletter of the American Research Center in Egypt* 121: 41–58.

Wegner, J. 2007. *The Mortuary Temple of Senwosret III at Abydos.* New Haven, CT.

Wegner, J. 2009. "The Tomb of Senwosret III at Abydos: Considerations on the Origins and Development of the Royal Amduat-tomb." In *Archaism and Innovation: Studies in the Culture of Middle Kingdom Egypt*, edited by D. P. Silverman, W. K. Simpson, and J. Wegner, 103–168. New Haven, CT, and Philadelphia.

Wegner, J. 2014. "Kings of Abydos, solving an Ancient Egyptian Mystery". *Current World Archaeology* 64: 21–27.

Winlock, H. E. 1924. "The Tombs of the Kings of the Seventeenth Dynasty at Thebes." *Journal of Egyptian Archaeology* 10: 217–277.

Winlock, H. E. 1947. *The Rise and Fall of the Middle Kingdom in Thebes.* New York.

PART IV

TOMB CONSTRUCTION AND DEVELOPMENT

....

CHAPTER 6

THE WORKMEN WHO
CREATED THE ROYAL TOMBS

....

ROBERT J. DEMARÉE

ACCORDING to a much later Ramesside tradition, King Amenhotep I and his mother Ahmose-Nefertari of the early Eighteenth Dynasty were worshipped as the patrons of a settlement in a small valley on the west bank of Thebes. Archaeological evidence, however, seems to point rather to Thutmose I as the founder of this little village, which was meant to house a group of specialized craftsmen/artisans responsible for the construction and decoration of the impressive final resting places of the kings and other royals of the Egyptian New Kingdom in the Valley of Kings and the Valley of Queens. The modern name of their village, Deir el-Medina (named after a former Coptic cloister on the site), has become the token designation for all research into and study of the life and times of these necropolis workmen and their monumental achievements.

Already in the early decades of the nineteenth century antiquities hunters like Henry Salt and Bernardino Drovetti explored the site of Deir el-Medina and added many objects from there to their collections, which later became the nuclei of several European museums. The first scientific excavations were undertaken by E. Schiaparelli for the Turin Museum in 1906–1909 and G. Möller for the Berlin Museum in 1911–1913, but the village was almost completely excavated between 1917 (1921) and 1951 by B. Bruyère for the French Institute of Cairo (Bruyère 1924–1953; Andreu 2002, 19–41) (Figure 6.1).

Very little documentation has survived from the earliest history of the community of Deir el-Medina. All too often general conclusions are drawn regarding institutional and other topics of both administration and labor during the whole time span of the New Kingdom. The archaeological and textual record does not provide us with a complete picture. Whereas the tombs of most rulers of the New Kingdom are known, our information concerning those who were responsible for their construction only covers some disconnected periods within this whole era. Little is known of how the royal workmen were organized during the Eighteenth Dynasty. Certainly the first building phase of their village dates from that period, as also do some of their private tombs in the western cemetery, but all these archaeological remains provide us with very few data concerning

FIGURE 6.1 The village of Deir el-Medina.

[Photograph by R. J. Demarée.]

their one-time owners. In fact, even the title indicating their profession—*sḏm ꜥš* or *sḏm ꜥš m S.t.-Mꜣꜥt* , "servant" or "servant in the Place of Truth"—and the designation of the workforce as *is.t*, "crew," are only first attested in the final decades before the Amarna period.

Textual records are scarce, and any firm evidence concerning the workforce or the institution responsible for the construction of the royal tombs during the Eighteenth Dynasty is lacking. Only a few examples testify to the fact that different officials controlled the works in the Valley of Kings, like the Theban mayor Inene, the high priest of Amun Hapusonb, or the overseer of the treasury Maya. Most scholars (e.g., Megally 1974) up till now have just postulated the existence of such a workforce as a kind of predecessor to its well-known counterpart of the later Ramesside period. In support they have usually referred to similar units known to have been active in building the temples of Queen Hatshepsut and King Thutmose III at Deir el-Bahri. The points of similarity are, however, restricted to some very general aspects, like the existence of gangs of workmen divided into two halves, each led by a chief or foreman and a scribe, working on orders of high authorities. Noteworthy is the fact that these gangs of builders were composed of groups of men brought in from various places around Thebes—this in contrast to the standing workforce of later, Ramesside Deir el-Medina.

In view of the small size of the Eighteenth Dynasty royal tombs and their comparatively modest decoration, the question may be raised as to whether at any time during that period there existed a permanent institution for the one main task: creating tombs for royals. It seems quite possible that these projects were executed by temporary established and varying groups of necropolis workers, quarrymen, and members of artists'/draughtsmen's ateliers, such as those known from Amarna and Memphis (Zivie 2013, 97–110).

Contrary to this poor record for the Eighteenth Dynasty, information about "Deir el-Medina" as an organization during the Ramesside era, starting with the re-establishment of the institution after the Amarna interlude in year 7 of King Horemhab, is definitely much better documented. Knowledge of both the internal and the external administration is still far from complete, but gradually the overall image of the necropolis workers' community is evolving from a vague pencil sketch into a colorful picture.

Thanks to the vast amount of archaeological data and administrative and other texts on both papyri and ostraca related to the construction of the royal tombs in the Theban necropolis, the organization of this "department of works" is no doubt the best-documented structure of its kind within the history of ancient Egypt.

Since the appearance of the fundamental monographs (Černý 1973 and 1973/2001; Valbelle 1985) on the workmen responsible for these monuments, a great number of detailed studies have been published on various aspects of the organization and the history of their community. The mass of data concerning most of the employees of the institution and their family members has even made it possible to draw up a "who's who" (Davies 1999). Publications of ostraca and papyri in museum collections, as well as some discovered by more recent excavations, have added a substantial number of "new" textual sources to the already rich corpus available for the study of this institution and its organization.[1]

Yet also for the Ramesside period we are faced with some serious limitations. The problems are to a large extent caused by the unevenness and partiality of the evidence. As for the archaeological record, data about domestic architecture, private tombs, stelae, and chapels or little shrines concern almost exclusively the early half of the Nineteenth Dynasty, and only a few belong to the middle of the Twentieth Dynasty. Consequently, any attempt to study these elements of village life and its organization in general for the whole of the Ramesside period has to take into account this only partial and unbalanced data record.

With regard to the written documentation—papyri, ostraca, graffiti, etc.—the situation is slightly different, but nonetheless comparable. With just a few exceptions, records on papyri are only known dating from the Twentieth Dynasty, while those on ostraca mainly date to the later decades of the Nineteenth Dynasty and the middle of the Twentieth Dynasty (Figure 6.2).

After the Amarna period a new workforce was established at Deir el-Medina, with craftsmen and artisans brought in from different places. The workmen were employees of a department of state, the already mentioned *S.t-M3ʿt*, and in inscriptions in their tombs and on stelae they bore the title *sḏm ʿš m S.t-M3ʿt*, "servant in the Place of Truth." A more daily name of this institution was "the Great and Noble Tomb of Pharaoh on the West of Thebes," clearly so named after its first and foremost task, the construction and decoration of the royal tomb. In most cases, however, the name of the institution was abbreviated to *p3 Ḥr*, "the Tomb." In this short form it appears in some titles, but it is also found in expressions like *n3 rmṯ n p3 Ḥr*, "the men of the Tomb," referring to the complete crew, or *n3y.w n p3 Ḥr*, "those of the Tomb."

FIGURE 6.2 A delivery of firewood and pottery noted on an ostracon (private collection), dated to year 3 of Seti I.

[Photograph by R. J. Demarée.]

In administrative and private documents the Deir el-Medina workforce was designated as *t3 is.t,* "the crew" (after the word for a ship's crew), and its members were all *rmṯ-is.t,* "man of the crew." The whole group was divided into two parts, the "Right Side" (*wnmy*), and the "Left Side" (*smḥy*), each led by a "foreman" (*ꜥn is.t,* or in an earlier stage *ḥr.y-is.t*), who was assisted by a "deputy" (*idnw*). Responsible for reporting to the higher authorities was originally one local administrator, the "scribe of the Tomb" (*sš n p3 Ḥr*). Together, the two foremen and the scribe were usually designated the "captains" (*ḥwty.w*).

As expert craftsmen/artisans, the men of the crew boasted titles like "draughtsman" (*sš-qd*) or "chiseler, sculptor" (*ṯ3y-mḏ3.t*). Within the community some workmen acted as local doctors (*sinw*) or as scorpion charmers (*ḫrp-Srqt,* i.e., magicians or specialists in controlling venomous animals). Closely connected with the affairs of the work-force were two doorkeepers, one or two guardians (controlling the tools and other work-ing materials), and a number of servant women (making bread and wicks for torches). Furthermore, the gang of workmen enjoyed the services of a large group of servants or assistance personnel (the *smd.t*), consisting of woodcutters, water carriers, fishermen, gardeners, washermen, gypsum-makers, potters, confectioners, and probably copper-smiths (e.g., Janssen 1997; Janssen et al. 2003), catering for the specific needs of the work-men and their families in the village. All these people were on the same payroll as the workmen. Remarkably, in order to fulfill their tasks, the woodcutters and water carriers were often obliged to hire donkeys from the workmen (Janssen 2005). This practice regu-larly led to disputes, usually caused by nonpayment of the hire price. The servants and the members of a small police force (*mḏꜣy.w*), who had to keep order and prevent unauthor-ized entry into the necropolis, were settled outside the confinement of the village. Some of these functionaries or laborers may well have been more loosely connected to the orga-nization or worked on a temporary base. Although in recent years several detailed studies on some have appeared, we are still lacking a clear picture of their work, responsibilities, and status within the whole framework of the organization.

The village proper was enlarged in the early decades of the Ramesside era to pro-vide accommodation for forty to fifty families and later, at its greatest extent around the middle of the Twentieth Dynasty, for more than sixty families, some dwellings even being constructed probably outside the original circuit. The place was called *pꜣ dmi* by its inhabitants, who built their own private tombs in a cemetery nearby on the slope of the western desert hills.

In older general descriptions of the village, reference is often made to the existence of a wall or walls. In fact, however, no real wall in the sense of a separate structure encir-cling the settlement has ever been located. There is just a continuous line of the back walls of the houses, which all had their sole entrance opening from the central main street. Most scholars are by now convinced that the so-called *inbw.t* were not "walls" but guard posts (Dorn 2009).

When they became a member of the workforce, the workmen were entitled to a house in the village, the *pr*, a hut, the *ꜥ.t*, and a tomb, the *mꜥḥꜥ.t*. Beside their houses in the vil-lage, where they lived with their wives (Toivari-Viitala 2001) and children, the workmen thus also had at their disposal the so-called huts, in a settlement on the col between the village and the Valley of the Kings, in the Valley of the Kings, and in the Valley of the Queens. These clusters of small buildings, probably denoted by the term *tꜣ wḥꜣ.t*, have long been vaguely described as places where the workmen could rest or take a nap. Recent studies and excavations have shown, however, that these settlements served not just as simple dormitories, but rather as places where the crew members stayed dur-ing the building process of the royal tomb under construction (Dorn 2011). The word *ꜥ.t* as it occurs so often in Deir el-Medina texts, but also in other administrative docu-ments, may therefore better be translated as "workplace," which more aptly describes the purpose and use of such a building than the rather vague term "hut."

An important architectural and institutional feature near the village was the *ḫtm* or *ḫtm n pꜣ Ḫr*. The precise localization is still a hotly debated issue (Eyre 2009), but this "gatehouse of the Tomb" may be identified as the administrative and storage center of the organization, the office that served as the place of contact between the locals and all outsiders, whether authorities, messengers, or those carrying deliveries and equipment to the crew. The gatehouse had its own storehouse or magazine, and the whole complex must have been large enough to house meetings of a number of people and store sub-stantial amounts of products and equipment. Possibly near or around this gatehouse were also located simple sheds or stables for the number of donkeys that we know sev-eral workmen possessed and that could never have found a home within the confine-ment of the village itself. All these constructions were not necessarily built completely in stone, probably rather in mud brick and wattle, which would explain why only small traces of architectural remains may have been left, difficult to interpret. Almost cer-tainly, however, this complex was not located directly near the northern main entrance to the village, where there is hardly enough space, but rather somewhere between this spot and the southwestern corner of the Ramesseum.

The workmen as well as local lesser officials were employees of the reigning king, and as such appointed by him, at least in name. In practice, from the beginning of the Ramesside period this power was delegated by the monarch to his vizier. The appoint-ment is several times explicitly referred to—for example, in the words of the famous chief of police Montumose: "Pharaoh has placed me to guard his house."

As state employees the workmen were administered and paid by the pharaoh, the embodiment of the state. The full workforce numbered some 40 men dur-ing the Nineteenth Dynasty and the beginning of the Twentieth Dynasty. It was then increased to some 60 men, and temporarily in the middle of the Twentieth Dynasty even to 120 men. At all times the group was divided into two parts, each led by a foreman and his deputy. Administrative records were kept by the scribe of the tomb (sometimes assisted by junior scribes or apprentices). Some of these scribes not only diligently fulfilled their main tasks of administration, but also were real men of letters, such as an owner of a small library or an author of literary works. Several have become famous characters in the literature on Deir el-Medina, such as Qenherkhepeshef, Amennakhte and his son Horsheri, and Dhutmose and his son Butehamun. The senior scribe and the two foremen constituted the leaders of the village, the captains. They were the liaison between the community and the higher authorities, notably the vizier ("our superior"). Their duties included, among oth-ers, overseeing all aspects of the construction of the royal tombs, running the daily affairs of the community, distributing the rations/wages among the workmen, and recommending candidates for vacancies in the workforce. As chief magistrates at least one or two of them sat on the local court (the *qnb.t*), accompanied by some ordi-nary workmen, who may have been chosen due to their seniority or esteem in the vil-lage. This court—or rather council of elders—had the power to settle all civil action and disputes (McDowell 1990). They could even decide minor criminal matters, but capital offences had to be referred to a higher court in Thebes. When the ruling of the local court was disputed, one could consult the deified patron king Amenhotep I by oracle. Such consultations, which usually took place during the free weekends, were mainly concerned with claims to property. Questions were either read before the image of the god or deposited before him in the form of two written petitions, one positive and one negative. The god then could answer a specific question or indicate which petition he favored.

Changes were made in the local administration and leadership during the Twentieth Dynasty. We still do not know exactly when or why, but most probably in the last decade of the reign of Ramesses III, the scribe of the tomb became assisted by a junior scribe, and as of the middle of the Twentieth Dynasty, the three captains were joined by the chief draughtsman, to form a leadership of four men. Possibly the main task of the junior scribe was to administer the large contingent of service personnel, the *smd.t* (Figure 6.3).

Various sources provide indications that the administrators of the crew—that is, the scribes—for several purposes made use of lists of the workmen in sequence order. A complete list would comprise all members of both the Left Side and Right Side, in that order, starting with the names of the chief workman, the scribe, and the deputy, followed by those of the ordinary workmen according to seniority. Newly appointed members of the gang were added at the bottom of the list. This sequence order was definitely used, for example, for the lineup of the watch roster during the later years of Ramesses III and the first years of Ramesses IV—the so-called turnus of first nineteen and later thirty men of probably each side responsible for the reception and distribution of the daily rations.[2] Recent studies have shown evidence for the existence of this turnus-system already in the late Nineteenth Dynasty (Collier 2004). Moreover, similar name lists according to

FIGURE 6.3 Journals with daily notes concerning work and related subjects at Deir el-Medina were written on papyri such as this fragment from P. Milan RAN E 0.9.40126 verso.

[Photograph by R. J. Demarée.]

seniority, length of service, clearly formed the basis for the regularly updated registers of the "Stato Civile" census documents as far as we know these from the second half of the Twentieth Dynasty (Demarée and Valbelle 2011).

An important aspect of labor organization in general is of course the matter of remuneration—the payment of wages or salaries. As civil servants the royal necropolis workmen were paid by their employer, the state, or in other words the pharaoh (Janssen 1975, 455–493; 1997, 13–35). The total of their remunerations was termed *ḥtri*, the so-called dues in another context, provided by temple institutions. These wages consisted of the most important monthly rations (the *diw*) of emmer and barley for making bread and beer, supplemented by regular deliveries of water, fuel (firewood and dung), fish, oil, other foodstuffs like vegetables and dates, pottery, occasionally meat, and also clothes. Sometimes the men were given extra deliveries, in most cases some special products.

A great number of texts on papyri and ostraca provide detailed information about the payments of the grain rations, the "standard salaries" (also known as "full deliveries"). According to our documentation, these rations remained more or less the same in the period between Seti I and Ramesses X, but after that they were a little lower. Probably no fixed payday existed, but distribution of the grain rations was expected at the beginning of each month, although in the course of time the responsible authorities had increasing difficulty supplying the demand. With regard to fish, fuel, and pottery, members of the assistance personnel were required—at least in certain periods—to deliver specific amounts per week or month, but it is nowhere said how these totals were distributed among the families of workmen. For the other products, it is not clear whether the workmen were entitled to fixed amounts.

Distribution lists of the grain rations show that the two foremen each received monthly 5½ *khar* emmer-wheat and 2 *khar* barley. The first mentioned amounts are usually written in red and the last mentioned in black ink (1 *khar* = ca. 75 liters).

The senior scribe received similar rations, but his "salary" is divided in the distribution lists, half with the "right side of the crew" and half with the "left side of the crew."

All ordinary workmen received monthly 4 *khar* emmer and 1½ *khar* barley. A still puzzling phenomenon in the ration lists is the distribution of the very small quantities to several separately mentioned men.

Besides the real workmen, other people attached to the workforce were also entitled to "salaries." The "youngsters" or apprentices (*mnḥ.w*) got 1½ *khar* emmer and ½ *khar* barley monthly. Some "old men" (*i3w*—seniors or "pensioned workmen") received small quantities, just like a group of female servants (*ḥmw.t*) (in some cases a "widow" received a small amount). The doctor and the scorpion charmer were ordinary workmen who received something extra above their regular salaries. The doorkeepers (sometimes two, sometimes three) usually received 1 *khar* emmer and ½ *khar* barley.

The guardians (sometimes one, sometimes two) probably received the same salary as the regular workmen. And finally, the assistance personnel, always mentioned as a group, received small quantities.

Whereas the general mechanism of this distribution system is well known by now, many details still have to be elucidated. The number of published written sources on the subject has been greatly augmented in recent years, several others await publication, and altogether they should provide us with a much clearer insight. One point still to be explored is the payment of the grain rations in installments, the *dni diw*. The question is whether this was a regular phenomenon or just a matter of inadequate administration and/or supply. Another problem is posed by long lists, actually journals or daybooks, in which the deliveries of very small quantities of bread and beer were enumerated daily. These texts are known from ostraca, but also from at least one long, unpublished papyrus scroll (now in many fragments) in the Turin collection, dating to the years 29–31 of Ramesses III. In such lists each day's entry is followed by the notice: "2 loaves, 4 jars of beer" (or similar small amounts). Such deliveries to the workmen have been called "extra provisions" coming from the temples. The problem then is whether these small amounts are really meant to be divided among all workmen. And this of course is immediately followed by the question of how they would be divided. Or were these loaves and jars of beer in fact only intended for the two workmen who were "on duty" each day? And if so, why keep such detailed records? Was this just red tape, bureaucracy, or a standard response to the demand for accountability?

Also not yet fully understood are the so-called attendance registers or absentee lists. These registers were very differently kept and noted in different periods, but they all contain records of the days when specific workmen were absent, or at least not working, either because they were ill or for some other reasons, which are sometimes but not always specified. Such reasons for absences and the special technical terms for absenteeism/not working in these lists have been studied, and other research has contributed a great deal on the private scribal traditions of some of the scribes who kept these records (Donker van Heel and Haring 2003). But a fundamental question not yet answered is: To what purpose were such lists written down? Were the local authorities just simply interested in knowing who was ill or absent? That is not likely. Were these records intended to enable an easy counting of the number of available workers, in connection with calculations on how much work had been and still had to be done? Or was illness or absenteeism a reason for a cutback in rations/salaries? The answer is still lacking, but such reasons may explain why in several of the distribution lists of rations, some workmen are specifically mentioned as receiving less than the full amounts.

Another important aspect of labor relations is found in the administrative system used by the employer to keep control over his employees and their work and activities (Häggman 2002). Although everything Deir el-Medina stands for was in fact aimed at the eternal benefit of the pharaoh, the king for all we know never (or hardly ever) inspected his royal final resting place in person. As far as our documentation permits us to tell, during the Nineteenth Dynasty it was always the vizier who kept control over the ongoing construction process, either by visiting and inspecting personally or by sending his subordinates or messages (the often mentioned letters from the vizier) (Janssen 1997, 147–173). Such inspection visits were briefly indicated by the term *šsp b3kw*, "to receive the work." Detailed records of the construction or building operations were kept and regularly sent to the office of the vizier, mentioning how much progress had been made and even indicating the precise amount of stone hacked out and how much still had to be quarried away, which rooms were finished, and so forth (Demichelis 2004). Special reasons for visits or messages seem to have been instigated by important events such as the death, or imminent death, of a king and the nomination of a new ruler. Soon after the installation of a new king, orders were sent to the crew of workmen to start building a new royal tomb. These orders were often accompanied by a special reward (the *mkw*) for the whole gang. Basically the idea behind this system of keeping control over what was called *p3rꜥ-b3kw*, "the work in progress" (the royal tomb under construction), did not change in the Twentieth Dynasty. However, some important alterations were made, probably after the famous strikes of the year 29 of Ramesses III. It was no longer only the vizier with his assistants who made inspection or control visits. From then on he was accompanied by a team of higher authorities, consisting mostly of royal butlers. Another remarkable change in the direction of the institution is that from the middle years of the Twentieth Dynasty onward, records appear of (inspection) visits by the high priest of Amun.

Life in Deir el-Medina during the almost two centuries of the Ramesside era will have had its up and downs, following the general economic development of Egypt. From some of their richly decorated tombs, grave goods, stelae, and personal belongings, we may conclude that the members of the first generations of craftsmen/artisans in this period were well to do. In the course of time this situation definitely changed, but as long as the authorities ensured their income by regularly supplying rations and other provisions, the workmen had not much to complain about. Several crew members, notably the expert craftsmen or artisans, cleverly used their skills to execute all kinds of jobs for both fellow workmen and outsiders—for example, manufacturing wooden objects and leatherwork and decorating tombs and tomb furniture. This work within what has been called "an informal workshop" (Cooney 2007) guaranteed extra income, which was most welcome in times when the state, due to economic and political factors, was no longer able to care for the needs of its employees. Although the workmen sometimes may have exaggerated the effects, at the end of the reign of Ramesses III (but possibly already earlier), the delivery of rations and other supplies failed to arrive on time. In combination with complaints about irregularities in the necropolis administration, these delays in payment led to the famous strikes or sit-down demonstrations in the twenty-ninth regnal year of this king. Emergency measures by local officials resulted in the arrival of at least part of the requested provisions, but the fat was in the fire, and strikes erupted again later in the same year and several times during subsequent reigns (Figure 6.4).

The final stage of the history of the workmen of Deir el-Medina is still shrouded in mystery. Part of the community may have left their houses in the village at the end of the Twentieth Dynasty to go live somewhere near the temple of Ramesses III at Medinet Habu. Whether this move had anything to do with incursions of Libyans, as has often been asserted, still lacks unequivocal proof. It is true, however, that in this period the living conditions deteriorated. Members of at least two families of workmen were involved in activities described in the judicial documents concerning the so-called tomb robberies at the end of the reign of Ramesses IX and in the following period. A comparison between a list of workmen drawn up in the last years of the reign of Ramesses IX and

FIGURE 6.4 The family of the foreman Anhorkhew, depicted in his tomb, TT 359, at Deir el-Medina, second half of the Twentieth Dynasty.

[Photograph by R. J. Demarée.]

a similar list filed in the early years of Ramesses X shows that these men were removed from the workforce.

An as yet unpublished dossier of ostraca and a number of graffiti seems to prove that—based at a kind of workshop at Deir el-Bahri—the last generations of workmen (Butehamun and colleagues and their sons and grandsons) took part in what can best be described as the recycling of the contents of royal tombs. On orders of the new rulers of the Twenty-First Dynasty, they systematically "robbed" these places of their valuable objects. It is ironic that this "work" had to be done by the heirs of those who had contributed so much to the creation of these royal sepulchers.

Notes

1. For publications of texts and all other Deir el-Medina matters, see the regularly updated bibliography on The Deir el-Medina Database at http://www.leidenuniv.nl/nino/dmd/dmd.html.
2. For this duty roster, see The Deir el-Medina Database at http://www.leidenuniv.nl/nino/dmd/dmd.html.

Bibliography

Andreu, G., ed. 2002. *Les artistes de Pharaon*. Paris.
Andreu, G., ed. 2003. *Deir el-Médineh et la Vallée des Rois*. Paris.

Bierbrier, M. 1982. *The Tomb-Builders of the Pharaohs*. London.

Bruyère, B. 1924–1953. *Rapport sur les fouilles de Deir el-Médineh*. 14 vols. Fouilles de l'institut francais d'archéologie orientale du Caire Cairo.

Černý, J. 1973. *The Valley of the Kings*. Cairo.

Černý, J. 1973/2001. *A Community of Workmen at Thebes during the Ramesside Period*. Cairo.

Collier, M. 2004. *Dating Late XIXth Dynasty Ostraca*. Egyptologische Uitgaven 18. Leiden.

Cooney, K. M. 2007. *The Cost of Death: The Social and Economic Value of Ancient Egyptian Funerary Art in the Ramesside Period*. Egyptologische Uitgaven 22. Leiden.

Davies, B. 1999. *Who's Who at Deir el-Medina*. Egyptologische Uitgaven 13. Leiden.

Demarée, R. J., and A. Egberts, eds. 2000. *Deir el-Medina in the Third Millennium AD: A Tribute to Jac. J. Janssen*. Egyptologische Uitgaven 14. Leiden.

Demarée, R. J., and D. Valbelle. 2011. *Les Registres de recensement du Village de Deir el-Medineh (Le "Stato Civile")*. Leuven, Paris, and Walpole, MA.

Demichelis, S. 2004. "Le projet initial de la tombe de Ramsès IV?" *Zeitschrift für Aegyptische Sprache und Alterthumskunde* 131: 114–133.

Donker van Heel, K., and B. J. J. Haring. 2003. *Writing in a Workmen's Village: Scribal Practice in Ramesside Deir el-Medina*. Egyptologische Uitgaven 16. Leiden.

Dorn, A. 2009. "Die Lokalisation der '5 Mauern'/Wachtposten (*t3 5 jnb.t/n3 jnb.wt/t3 jnb*)." *Journal of Egyptian Archaeology* 95: 263–268.

Dorn, A. 2011. *Arbeiterhütten im Tal der Könige*. Aegyptiaca Helvetica 23. Basel.

Eyre, C. 1980. *Employment and Labour Relations in the Theban Necropolis in the Ramesside Period*. Liverpool.

Eyre, C. 2009. "Again the #tm of the Tomb." In *Texte—Theben—Tonfragmente: Festschrift für Günter Burkard*, edited by M. Goecke-Bauer et al., 107–117. Wiesbaden.

Goecke-Bauer, M., et al., eds. 2009. *Texte—Theben—Tonfragmente: Festschrift für Günter Burkard*. Ägypten und Altes Testament 76. Wiesbaden.

Häggman, S. 2002. *Directing Deir el-Medina: The External Administration of the Necropolis*. Uppsala Studies in Egyptology 4. Uppsala.

Janssen, J. J. 1975. *Commodity Prices from the Ramessid Period*. Leiden.

Janssen, J. J. 1997. *Village Varia: Ten Studies on the History and Administration of Deir el-Medina*. Egyptologische Uitgaven 11. Leiden.

Janssen, J. J. 2005. *Donkeys at Deir el-Medina*. Egyptologische Uitgaven 19. Leiden.

Janssen, J. J., E. Frood, and M. Goecke-Bauer. 2003. *Woodcutters, Potters and Doorkeepers*. Egyptologische Uitgaven 17. Leiden.

Kákosy, L., and E. Gaál, eds. 1974. *Studia Iuvenum in Honorem V. Wessetzky*. Studia Aegyptiaca I. Budapest.

Lesko, L. H. ed. 1994. *Pharaoh's Workers*. Ithaca, NY and London.

McDowell, A. G. 1990. *Jurisdiction in the Workmen's Community of Deir el-Medîna*. Egyptologische Uitgaven 5. Leiden.

McDowell, A. G. 1999. *Village Life in Ancient Egypt: Laundry Lists and Love Songs*. Oxford.

Megally, M. 1974. "À propos de l'organisation administrative des ouvriers à la XVIIIme dynastie." In *Studia Iuvenum in Honorem V. Wessetzky*, edited by l. Kákosy and E. Gaál, 297–311. Budapest.

Toivari-Viitala, J. 2001. *Women at Deir el-Medina*. Egyptologische Uitgaven 15. Leiden.

Valbelle, D. 1985. *Les ouvriers de la Tombe: Deir el-Médineh à l'époque ramesside*. Cairo.

Zivie, A. 2013. *La Tombe de Thoutmes, Directeur des Peintres dans la Place de Maât*. Toulouse.

CHAPTER 7

CHOOSING THE LOCATION FOR A ROYAL TOMB, THE WORKMEN'S TECHNIQUES AND TOOLS, UNITS OF MEASUREMENT, KV HUTS, AND WORKPLACES

ANDREAS DORN

CHOOSING THE LOCATION FOR A ROYAL TOMB

THE site where a royal tomb was to be built was identified by the vizier. This is attested by an ostracon, O. DeM 45, rto. 15–17, which tells us about the vizier Neferrenpet, who in the Twentieth Dynasty came to the Valley of the Kings, accompanied by two royal butlers, in order to find (choose) a suitable site for the construction of the tomb of Ramesses IV. Foundation deposits discovered in front of tomb entrances suggest that foundation rites similar to those known from temple contexts were performed as part of the process for choosing the appropriate construction site for a royal tomb. Various tombs had foundation deposits in front of the entrances, in the center and/or on the sides; they include KV 20 (Hatshepsut), KV 34 (Thutmose III), KV 38 (Thutmose I), KV 42 (Meritre-Hatshepsut), KV 43 (Thutmose IV), WV 22 (Amenophis III), KV 2 (Ramesses IV), KV 18 (Ramesses X), and KV 4 (Ramesses XI). The deposits contained various miniature tools (chisels, axes, knives), vessels, picks, symbols of protection, and faience objects, some of which bore the name of the king (Reeves and Wilkinson 1996: the figure on p. 28 shows a selection of objects from the foundation deposits for Amenophis III).

However, no concrete evidence has come down to us regarding the foundation rite and how it was performed as part of the process of choosing a site for the construction of a tomb.

The identification of a site would probably have been preceded by an inspection of the Valley of the Kings by a local building committee, since one cannot assume that nonlocal officials from the residence in the delta (from the Nineteenth Dynasty onward; before that they would have lived in Thebes) were familiar with the features of the local rock and the topographical conditions suitable for the construction of a tomb.

During the period when the Valley of the Kings was used as a royal burial ground, from the Eighteenth to the Twentieth Dynasties, the demands on the construction sites changed. During the Eighteenth Dynasty the royal tombs were built either halfway up the sheer rock faces (KV 34, Thutmose III) or at their bases (KV 20, Hatshepsut; KV 38, Thutmose I; KV 42, KV 35, Amenhotep II; KV 43, Thutmose IV). While in the Nineteenth Dynasty they were located either on rock ridges (KV 7, Ramesses II; KV 8, Merenptah; KV 10, Amenmesse; KV 47, Siptah) or at the base of a rock face (KV 14, Tausret/Sethnakht; KV 15, Seti II), the entrances were no longer buried under layers of rubble, as had been the case in the Eighteenth Dynasty, but were now monumental and highly visible constructions. The tradition of building royal tombs with monumental entrance portals on rock ridges continued in the Twentieth Dynasty (Ramesses III–Ramesses XI).

In several cases the rock had a crack running along the axis of the tomb (KV 8, Merenptah; KV 1, Ramesses VII; KV 18, Ramesses X). Since it was easier to excavate the bedrock along these cracks, their presence probably had a bearing on the choice of site.

THE WORKMEN'S TECHNIQUES AND TOOLS

Excavating the rock and building corridors and chambers entailed quarrying out the natural limestone. The tools used were wooden hammers and hardened copper chisels. Such tools have mainly been found in or in the vicinity of private tombs in Thebes, and a small number have come to light in the Valley of the Kings (for examples of hammers see Reeves 1990, 99 n.21, from above the tomb of Seti I; for chisels see Reeves 1990, 327, from the area to the east of the entrance to the tomb of Merenptah, KV 8). On the one hand, there were large, pointed (stonemasons's chisel: $kr\underline{d}n$) or flat chisels ($m\underline{d}з.t$), which were used to excavate the rock, depending on the hardness and other features such as cracks; the flat chisels were mainly used to shape the walls and ceilings to a regular finish (smoothing of the walls). On the other hand, there was a variety of smaller chisels ($ʿn.t$) that were used to decorate the rendered walls with sunken reliefs. Such stucco chisels had large wooden handles, allowing the workman to apply pressure with the heel of his hand and to cut into the plaster without using a hammer.

The tools, and more important the precious copper, were owned by the royal tomb administration. Some of the texts that have survived list the issuance of copper chisels, while others mention the collection of worn chisels to be melted down.

Numerous stone weights bearing the inscription "six," "seven," or "four *deben*" (1 *deben* = 91 grams) have been found in the Valley of the Kings, which actually corresponded to their weights. They were probably used to check the weights of newly issued chisels, either by the workers themselves or by the foremen responsible; chisels were regularly monitored in order to prevent copper from being stolen. In accordance with the six *deben* stone weights, intact chisels often weigh approximately 550 g (6 *deben*) (Valbelle 1977, 14), which supports the theory that such checks were indeed made. Stone weights weighing significantly less and bearing different inscriptions, consisting of a date, a chisel weight, and a person's name, have also been found. They would have been used to check or determine the actual weight of a chisel on a particular day after a period of use, during which its weight would have decreased due to copper chipping off. The fact that the weight of these precious chisels was worth monitoring is illustrated by records of court cases dealing with thwarted chisel thefts.

Besides tools such as hammers and chisels, measuring instruments and other aids were also used. Right-angled corners of rooms were determined and checked using square tools, some of which had a plumb line attached. The lengths, widths, and heights of chambers and corridors were defined and checked using wooden cubit rods and measuring cords. Boning rods were used to check whether the walls were consistently level (Arnold 1991, 45, 256f.; Stocks 2003, 187–191). Their use was attested to by black and red dots discovered underneath the original plaster when it crumbled off the walls of KV 47 (Siptah).

These tools were made of two wooden rods of approximately 15 cm in length, the top ends of which were linked by a cord. The rods were held against the wall with the cord tautened. A third rod of the same length was then used to check whether the wall was smooth; if this rod lifted the cord, more rock had to be removed. The axes and widths of corridors and chambers were checked by using pieces of cord covered in wet paint, which were then stretched the lengths of the corridors. By slightly lifting the cord and then letting it go, a perfectly straight line of red paint was left on the ground, from which further measurements could then be taken. Other straight lines, for instance tracings of doors and pillars and the grids used to lay out the paintings of figures, were also created using such cords. Lines left by them have been identified on the ceilings in the corridors of KV 43 (Thutmose IV) and on the vaulted ceiling in the sarcophagus hall of KV 47 (Siptah).

Various paintbrushes were used. The paint was mixed on plates or in the bases of broken ceramic storage vessels.

UNITS OF MEASUREMENT

The basic unit of measurement used in the construction of the royal tombs was the royal cubit (*mḥ*), which roughly measured 52.5 cm and could vary between 52.3 and 52.9 cm. The lengths, widths, and heights of corridors were usually measured by multiples of this unit. It was further divided into ½ cubits, palm widths (*šsp* = 7.5 cm; 7 palm widths = 1 cubit), and digit widths (*ḏbꜥ* = 1.875 cm; 4 digit widths = 1 palm width).

The information about the units of measurement used in the construction of royal tombs stems on the one hand from tomb plans with measurements (Demarée 1992; Dorn and Polis 2015) and on the other from deducing the units from the dimensions of preserved chambers (see the plans with measurements in meters and royal cubits at www.kv5.com).

Two ostraca dating from the end of the Nineteenth Dynasty have been shown to contain a progress report on the ongoing work at a tomb (Helck 1992, 267 n.1; 2002, 167–171). They provide information about the progress of the work during the first two years of King Siptah's reign (KV 47). They tell us that corridors A–C were completed in less than a year. Numerous red lines, some of them vertical, were found underneath the crumbling plaster in Siptah's tomb; they were identified as measuring aids and construction lines, which probably helped calculate the excavated amount of rock on the one hand (see Figure 7.1) and measure the length of the corridors on the other.

There was a tendency from one king to the next or from one tomb to the next to exceed the size of the tomb of one's predecessor. This was achieved on the one hand by building longer corridors and on the other by constructing wider and higher corridors and chambers (Hornung 1978). The number of pillars in the first pillared chamber (F) and in the sarcophagus chamber (J) gradually increased from one or two pillars in the Eighteenth Dynasty to four (in chamber F) and eventually up to eight (in chamber J) in the Twentieth Dynasty. The pillars usually measured 2 cubits in width, although those in the tomb of Ramesses XI (KV 4) were wider.

HUTS IN THE VALLEY OF THE KINGS

Workmen's huts have been found at various sites throughout the Valley of the Kings—in both the Eastern and Western Valleys and also beside the pathway between the Valley of the Kings and Deir el-Medina. Based on the finds and features uncovered, it has been possible in some cases to ascertain the functions of the huts in more detail; other huts, however, provided no distinguishing features, which has made it difficult to determine their function and date.

The earliest evidence attesting to the presence of workmen in the Valley of the Kings in the vicinity of the tomb under construction was an occupation surface (possibly the floor of a hut?) found in a *wadi* east of the tomb of Ramesses X, which contained pottery dating from the reign of Thutmose IV (Dorn and Paulin-Grothe, 2015). A little more recent in date are three groups of huts found in the Western Valley near the tombs WV 24 and WV 25 and also along the eastern slope of a *wadi* to the south of these huts (Aubriot and Kurz 1971, plans 88–90, 100). The latter group, visible since antiquity and recorded on the maps of the CEDAE, were newly surveyed and excavated by a team from the Supreme Council of Antiquities (SCA) between 2009 and 2011. The associated

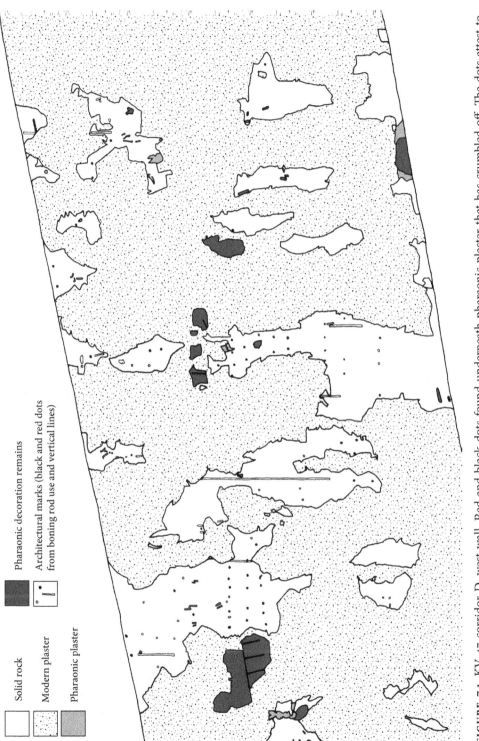

Solid rock

Modern plaster

Pharaonic plaster

Pharaonic decoration remains

Architectural marks (black and red dots from boning rod use and vertical lines)

FIGURE 7.1 KV 47 corridor D, west wall. Red and black dots found underneath pharaonic plaster that has crumbled off. The dots attest to the use of a boning rod.

finds have not yet been published, which means that its preliminary dating to the late Eighteenth Dynasty (Amarna and post-Amarna periods) rests almost solely on the location of the huts in the immediate proximity of tombs WV 23–25, of which only WV 23 is definitely associated with a particular ruler (Aye); another clue is the pottery found by O. Schaden, which besides Eighteenth Dynasty vessels also included much later material ("late Roman redware cooking pot") (Schaden 1979, 1991, 55).

A hut discovered immediately northeast of the entrance to the tomb of Seti I (Nineteenth Dynasty), has been associated with the construction of the tomb, based on its location and given the lack of datable finds (Dorn and Paulin-Grothe, 2015). Other huts found farther east, which yielded no identifiable features, may also date from the reign of Seti I. Numerous other huts from the Nineteenth Dynasty were uncovered by Howard Carter above the tomb of Tutankhamun and farther south near the entrances to the tombs of Ramesses VI (KV 9), Amenmesse (KV 10), and Ramesses III (KV 11). Excavations carried out by the Amarna Royal Tomb Project (ARTP; see Reeves 2002) by Otto Schaden, and by the SCA under the leadership of Zahi Hawass, brought to light yet more huts, which, based on current knowledge, can also be dated to the Nineteenth Dynasty. A cluster of huts is still visible to the east of the entrance to the tomb of Siptah (KV 47), and more huts probably stood to the north of this entrance, as is suggested by small remnants of floors found at the foot of the vertical rock faces and by more than 200 ostraca-bearing, mainly administrative texts. Some of them were recovered during excavations mounted around 1900 and are today stored in the Egyptian Museum in Cairo, while others came from the spoil heap of those excavations, which was investigated by the University of Basel between 2001 and 2005. Based on an analysis of the ostraca, these huts can be dated to the late Nineteenth Dynasty and associated with the construction of the nearby tombs of Seti II (KV 15), Siptah (KV 47), Tausret / Sethnakhte (KV 14), and Bay (KV 13).

No significant numbers of ostraca dating from the reign of Ramesses III have been found to date in the Valley of the Kings that would allow us to identify workmen's huts from that period. During the reign of his successor, Ramesses IV, however, more than sixty workmen's huts were constructed east of where the tomb of Ramesses X (KV 18) would later be constructed. The huts continued to be used until the reign of Ramesses VII. More huts from the reign of Ramesses IV probably stood in the area between tombs KV 6 and KV 9 (Ramesses IX and Ramesses VI), as suggested by significant amounts of ostraca dating from that period. Both clusters of huts—those near the two tombs just mentioned and those to the east of the tomb of Ramesses X—were situated at some distance from the building site instead of being erected, as in earlier periods, in close proximity to whichever royal tomb was under construction at the time (huts in the Western Valley and north of the entrance to the tomb of Siptah [KV 47]). Numerous huts east of the tomb of Ramesses X (KV 18) yielded intact features, which has allowed us to ascertain how workmen's huts were used in the mid-Twentieth Dynasty (Dorn 2011). Most of them measured approximately 2–2.5 m by 3 m at the most, and they contained several plates, a number of jugs, and sometimes a storage vessel buried up to its neck in the ground. Besides these basic hut furnishings, molds made of limestone for small amulets and different ostraca were also found. Some of these showed workers worshipping the gods (ostraca acting as stelae), which made it possible to identify the inhabitants of the individual huts. At that time huts were usually occupied by a father and one of his sons. This was probably due to the fact that under Ramesses IV the crew was increased from 60 to 120 workers, which was probably achieved by taking on the sons of the existing workmen. Besides administrative texts, all of which together provide only limited information about the work, a large number of ostraca contain images, which were drawn by inexperienced draftsmen. This suggests that on the periphery of the workplace children/students were instructed in drawing by their fathers/teachers. Moreover, some copies of literary texts attest to students learning the art of writing. One text that mentions the issuing of grain to the individual workers, cooking vessels, and other features shows that in the mid-Twentieth Dynasty the workers lived in these huts during the working week.

The most recent huts found in the Valley of the Kings again would have been situated in the areas of tombs KV 6 and KV 9 (Ramesses IX and Ramesses VI). Perhaps the huts that had stood there during the reign of Ramesses IV continued to be used, as shown by the most recent ostraca, which can be dated to the reigns of Ramesses IX–XI.

Besides the huts in the Valley of the Kings and in the Western Valley, which were directly associated with the royal tomb under construction, another settlement of huts was situated approximately halfway between the Valley of the Kings and Deir el-Medina, where the workers and their families lived, on a mountain ridge between the Valley of the Kings and the fertile lands (Bruyère 1939; Toivari-Viitala 2012). Based on the finds recovered, this cluster of 115 huts, known as "station de repos" or "village du col," was used from the reign of Ramesses II to the Twentieth Dynasty. Perhaps the absence of huts in the Valley of the Kings during the reign of Ramesses III can be explained by the fact that the huts on the mountain ridge were in use. In contrast to those in the Valley of the Kings, they were sturdier, and some even had rendered walls. Some of them contained a masonry-built bed and solid seats made of limestone, as well as head rests also made of limestone. The finds included gaming pieces, stelae, administrative texts, and picture ostraca, all of which suggests that the huts were used as dwellings. Twisted rags used as lamp wicks indicate that they served also as ateliers or workplaces. It is entirely possible that they were used particularly in the summer months, since their location on a mountain ridge made them more exposed to the cooling winds than the huts down in the Valley of the Kings. Based on their strategic location on one of the access routes into the Valley of the Kings and on the fact that a path ran straight through the cluster of huts, they have also been interpreted as a site where incoming goods and people were inspected. While this possibility cannot be excluded, it cannot be further confirmed by actual finds or written sources. Given the topographical situation and the fact that access controls are known to have been carried out in Deir el-Medina, this function of the site remains at best doubtful.

Recent research, which has included not just the royal tombs but also the traces left behind by the workers who constructed and decorated the tombs, has yielded a different view of the Valley of the Kings. On the one hand, it was the final resting place of the pharaohs, some members of the royal family, and certain officials, and on the other it was an almost constant building site—except on days when funerals or feasts took place—beside which the workers lived in simple huts. This was where they cooked their food, slept, wrote, drew, prayed, and so forth. However, the workers not only stayed in their huts, but also frequented other places, for instance the shaded areas at the foot of the rock faces near KV 34 (Thutmose III), where they drew graffiti on the rock, which usually consisted of their names and filiation information. Some of the graffiti record actual events, for instance the visit of a vizier, a particularly heavy rainfall, or a funeral. Some of the carved images show gods, in rare cases accompanied by a worshipper. The workers also established small religious sites, which allowed them to worship the gods not only using ostraca in their huts but also elsewhere. One such site was found above the entrance into KV 37, an Eighteenth Dynasty tomb, which would have been covered by several meters of rubble at the time the niche was constructed (Reeves and Wilkinson 1996, 183, fig. on bottom right). Another site probably also dating from the Twentieth Dynasty was found southwest of the tomb of Ramesses III (KV 11) (Reeves 2002, figs. 46, 58, 59). There Meretseger was worshipped, as is attested to by an ostracon found *in situ* and by numerous other ostraca found in the huts from the period of Ramesses IV situated to the east of the tomb of Ramesses X (KV 18) (see above). Ritual acts involving sacrifices, which were probably performed at one of the niches, can be deduced from a delivery of grain, which explicitly included grain for a serpent-deity (Dorn 2011, 392 with pl. 493–495; O. BTdK 617). This deity, not actually named in the context of the delivery, was most likely Meretseger. That the worshipping of Meretseger was so prominent is explained by the fact that the goddess was the patron of the local workers, sharing this function with Ptah, the god of craftsmen.

WORKPLACES

The tomb under construction (*p3 r3-ꜥ-b3kw*) was the workplace. During the rough cutting stage, two and sometimes three or four chiselers, depending on the width of the corridor, were working at the front. The rock was quarried from the ceiling to the bottom, and the workers were split into two groups, each responsible for one side of the tomb. The limestone lumps were carried out of the tomb using baskets (see Figure 7.2). At the same time that the rough cutting was advanced, the roughly cut walls were smoothed, rendered, and decorated.

The fact that these different stages of the work took place at the same time can be seen in tombs that were never finished—in the Valley of the Kings this includes KV 18 (Ramesses X), KV 19 (Mentuherkhepeshef), and KV 4 (Ramesses XI). Before the limestone walls were decorated, for example with raised relief, sometimes covered with stucco, and then painted, they were smoothed using sandstones, numerous fragments of which were found, abraded on all sides, during the excavations carried out by the University of Basel (1998–2005) at various sites, for instance the area to the east of the tomb of Seti I. Howard Carter also found similar stones, identifying them as "stone

FIGURE 7.2 O. BTdK 53 showing workmen constructing a tomb. Two men sitting on scaffolding are working with chisels, while other workers carry baskets of rubble on their shoulders out of the tomb.

rubbers." They were recovered east of the entrance to KV 8 (the tomb of Merenptah), together with two plumb bobs and a paintbrush (Reeves 1990, 327). Lime or lime finish was delivered to the site by specialized workers in quantities specified in advance. It cannot be ascertained whether the lime finish was already processed or whether this was done on-site, which is more likely (mixing with water). No archaeological evidence has yet come to light in the Valley of the Kings that would point to a mixing site.

As the tomb grew in length, a point was soon reached at which artificial light was required so that the workers inside could see what they were doing. Lamps (*ḥȝbs*), consisting of simple bowls filled with fuel, *sgnn*-oil, and wicks, were used. The wicks were made from old textiles, probably clothes, and had to undergo similar inspections as the chisels by members of the tomb administration, because textiles were also of considerable value. Textile deliveries were weighed by the foreman of the crew, as is attested to by stone textile weights bearing names.

The study of texts recording the distribution of wicks for the lamps revealed that the wicks were handed out twice a day (Černý 1973, 43–54). Černý concluded that the workmen probably worked two four-hour shifts each day. Thanks to the spectacular discovery of a sundial by a team from the University of Basel (Bickel and Gautschi 2013; Bickel and Gautschi 2014) in the winter of 2012–2013 in the Valley of the Kings, we now know how they divided the days into the two shifts. Another interesting feature of the sundial is that besides the hours, the sundial also showed the passage of half hours. This fine tuning would have allowed the foremen to arrange for the chiselers, who had the most physically demanding task, to be regularly relieved and to ensure that the shifts were always of the same duration.

In order to ensure that the work on the royal tomb progressed as desired, the workmen had to be supplied with whatever they needed. This, of course, would have included all manner of tools and other aids, such as baskets and scaffolds, but also food and water. We may thus assume that donkeys were brought to the Valley of the Kings several times a day, carrying the huge number of water bags needed to supply the 60 and sometimes even 120 workmen.

BIBLIOGRAPHY

Arnold, D. 1991. *Building in Egypt: Pharaonic Stone Masonry*. Oxford.

Aubriot, L., and M. Kurz. 1971. *Graffiti de la montagne thébaine II.2: Plans de position*, Centre de Documentation et d'Étude sur l'Ancienne Égypte 25. Cairo.

Bickel, S., and R. Gautschi. 2013. "A Sundial found in the Egyptian Valley of the Kings." *British Sundial Society Bulletin* 25 (4): 2–7.

Bickel, S., and R. Gautschi. 2014. "Eine Ramessidische Sonnenuhr im Tal der Könige." *Zeitschrift für Ägyptische Sprache und Altertumskunde* 141: 3–14.

Bruyère, B. 1939. *Rapport sur les Fouilles de Deir el-Médineh (1934–1935)*. Fouilles de l'Institut Français d'Archéologie Orientale 16. Cairo.

Černý, J. 1973. *The Valley of the Kings*. Bibliothèque d'Étude 61. Cairo.

Cilli, D. 2011. "Delivery Ostraca Discovered Adjacent to KV 47." In *Ramesside Studies in Honour of K. A. Kitchen*, edited by M. Collier and S.Snape, 95–110. Bolton.

Collier, M., and S. Snape, eds. 2011. *Ramesside Studies in Honour of K. A. Kitchen*. Bolton.

Collombert, P., Lefèvre, D., Polis, S. and J. Winand, eds. 2015. *Aere Perennius*. Orientalia Lovaniensia Analecta. Leuven.

Demarée, R. J. 1992. "Royal Riddles." In *Village Voices: Proceedings of the Symposium "Texts from Deir el-Medîna and their Interpretation," Leiden, May 31–June 1 1991*, edited by R. J. Demarée and A. Egberts, 9–18. Center of Non-Western Studies Publications 13. Leiden.

Demarée, R. J., and A. Egberts, eds. 1992. *Village Voices. Proceedings of the Symposium "Texts from Deir el-Medîna and Their Interpretation," Leiden May 31–June 1 1991*. Center of Non-Western Studies Publications 13. Leiden.

Dorn, A. 2011. *Arbeiterhütten im Tal der Könige: Ein Beitrag zur altägyptischen Sozialgeschichte aufgrund von neuem Quellenmaterial aus der Mitte der 20. Dynastie (ca. 1150 v. Chr.)*. Aegyptiaca Helvetica 23. Basel.

Dorn, A., and E. Paulin-Grothe. 2015. "Ausgrabungen im Tal der Könige 1998–2008: Grabungsareale und Spuren früherer Ausgräber." In *Zur modernen Geschichte des Tals der Könige*, Aegyptiaca Helvetica 25, edited by H. Jenni, 55–74. Basel.

Dorn, A. and S. Polis 2015. "A Re-examination of O. Cairo JdE 72460 (= O. Cairo SR 1475). Ending the Quest for a 19th Dynasty Queen's Tomb in the Valley of the Kings." In P.

Collombert, D. Lefèvre, S. Polis and J. Winand, eds. 2015. *Aere Perennius*. Orientalia Lovaniensia Analecta. Leuven.

Helck, W. 1992. "Begräbnis Pharaos." In *The Intellectual Heritage of Egypt*, Studia Aegyptiaca 14, edited by U. Luft, 267–276. Budapest.

Helck, W. 2002. *Die datierten und datierbaren Ostraka, Papyri und Graffiti von Deir el-Medineh*. Ägyptologische Abhandlungen 63. Wiesbaden.

Hornung, E. 1978. "Struktur und Entwicklung der Gräber im Tal der Könige." In *Zeitschrift für Ägyptische Sprache und Altertumskunde* 105: 59–66.

Jenni, H., ed. 2015. *Zur modernen Geschichte des Tals der Könige*. Aegyptiaca Helvetica 25. Basel.

Luft, U., ed. 1992. *The Intellectual Heritage of Egypt*. Studia Aegyptiaca 14. Budapest.

Reeves, C. N. 1990. *Valley of the Kings: The Decline of a Royal Necropolis*. London.

Reeves, C. N. 2002. Newsletter of the Valley of the Kings Foundation. http://www.nicholas-reeves.com/item.aspx?category=Writing&id=102.

Reeves, C. N., and R. H. Wilkinson. 1996. *The Complete Valley of the Kings*. London.

Schaden, O. J. 1979. "Preliminary Report on the Re-clearance of Tomb 25 in the Western Valley of the Kings (WV-25)." *Annales du Service des Antiquités de l'Égypte* 63: 161–168.

Schaden, O. J. 1991. "Preliminary Report on Clearance of WV24 in an Effort to Determine Its Relationship to Royal Tombs 23 and 25." *Kmt* 3 (2): 53–61.

Stocks, D. A. 2003. *Experiments in Egyptian Archaeology: Stoneworking Technology in Ancient Egypt*. London.

Toivari-Viitala, J. 2012."Finnish Team at the Workmen's Huts." http://xy2.org/lenka/Finnishteam.html.

Valbelle, D. 1977. *Catalogue des Poids à Inscription Hiératiques de Deir el-Médineh: Nos 5001–5423*. Documents de Fouilles de l'Institut Français d'Archéologie Orientale 16. Cairo.

CHAPTER 8

THE COMPONENT PARTS OF KV ROYAL TOMBS

KENT R. WEEKS

INTRODUCTION

THIS chapter deals with 23 of the 24 royal tombs in the Valley of the Kings (KV). KV 62, the tomb of Tutankhamun, is excluded for reasons of space and, in a few instances, relevance. Much of the data on which discussions here are based are to be found in an Appendix at the end of this *Handbook*, and its 16 tables are referred to throughout the text. Much of the discussion is presented in highly abbreviated form, and readers are referred to the Theban Mapping Project (TMP) website, cited below as Weeks 2002, for further details.

Many labeling systems have been proposed for KV tomb chambers (for examples see Porter and Moss 1964). The chamber designations used here (Figure 8.1) follow the generally accepted system of Elizabeth Thomas (1966), with a few minor modifications by the Theban Mapping Project (TMP). The letters Thomas assigned, A through L, indicate both a chamber's position within a tomb and its possible funerary function: for example, A is always the tomb's entrance, F its "First" or "Chariot Hall," J its burial chamber. Some tombs, such as KV 14 and 11, have all the chambers on Thomas's list. Others have only a few: KV 18, for example, has only three chambers—A, B, and C. Every KV royal tomb includes chambers A and B; most frequently absent are H, I, K, and L (Appendix table 2). Side chambers are given letter designations (e.g., Ja, Jb, Jc), moving clockwise from the left front of the chamber off of which they are cut. Multiple, subsidiary side chambers are lettered Ja, Jaa, Jaaa, etc. Side chambers are usually, but not always, smaller than chambers (see also Arnold 1991, 2003; Schacht and Hansen 2010).

The modern architectural terms used here are those adopted by the TMP (Schacht and TMP staff 2003). They are meant to regularize past inconsistent usage in which a "chamber" might also be called a "passage," a "cell," a "room," a "corridor," or a "hall."

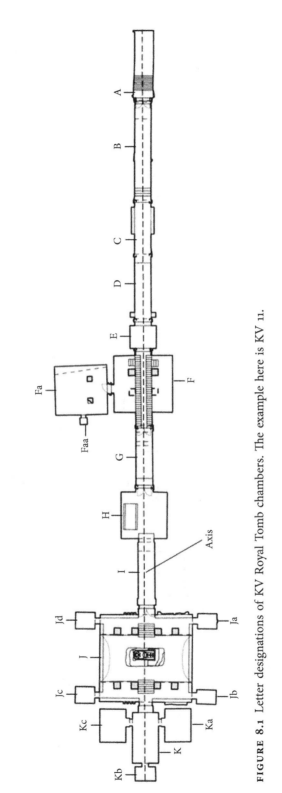

FIGURE 8.1 Letter designations of KV Royal Tomb chambers. The example here is KV 11.

"Chamber" is the TMP's most general designation. "Corridor" refers to a chamber, longer than it is wide, on a tomb's principal axis. "Hall" is a chamber, also on the main axis, nearly square in plan and often pillared. We use "hall" only for Chambers E, F, and I. The TMP's system for labeling parts of chambers is illustrated in Figures 8.2, 8.3, and 8.4.

Gates are chamber entrances with single or compound jambs. Gates and entrances are identified by the chamber into which they lead: for example, Gate C leads into Chamber C from Chamber B (see later, Gates). "Doors" refer to the single or double leaf wooden doors installed in many gates.

Egyptian architectural terms are given in the text that follows. The term most commonly used for a KV royal tomb chamber was *st3-ntr*, "God's Passage." Carter and Gardiner (1917, 135) said it "always referred to a sloping construction, whether passage or ramp," and was "the sloping axial passage of a royal tomb," but many examples (see later and Thomas 1966, 278) clearly show that the term also referred to level corridors, and the TMP translates it simply as "corridor." The second most common term was *wsḫt*, "hall." (In other contexts, *wsḫt* referred to rooms on the main axis of a temple in which

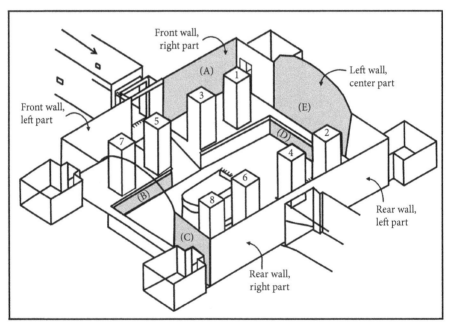

FIGURE 8.2 TMP's terms and phrases used to identify walls and pillars in KV royal tomb chambers. As you enter a chamber, the tomb entrance is at your back, the chamber's front wall is behind you, and its rear wall ahead of you. When referring to the parts of a wall, assume you are facing that wall. This figure is a simplified drawing of KV 8 J. (A) Upper level, front wall, right part. (B) Lower level, front wall, left part. (C) Upper level, right wall, left part. (D) Lower level, left wall. (E) Upper level, left wall, center part. Pillars are numbered from left to right, front to back (see figure 8.3).

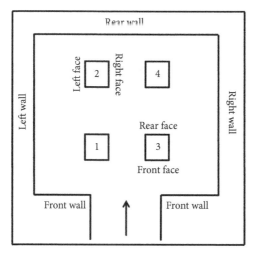

FIGURE 8.3 TMP's system for numbering pillars and labeling their faces.

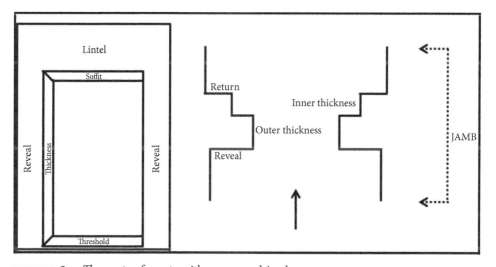

FIGURE 8.4 The parts of a gate with compound jambs.

offerings or important ceremonies took place, or to important rooms in royal palaces [Spencer 1984, 71–85].)

Several classifications of KV royal tombs have been proposed. Abitz (1989b), for example, grouped them according to changes in their principal axis (distinguishing axes that curve, turn 90°, make two 90° turns, make a parallel shift, run straight, etc.). Other classifications include Kemp and Rose (1991) and Badawy (1968); see also Preys (2011, 322–329). The most useful is that of Hornung (1978), who divided the tombs into four groups based on the gradually increasing width and height of their chambers and the increasing width of their gates (see also Thomas 1966, 64; Romer 1981, 279). Here, we refer to his groups as Stages 1, 2, 3, and 4. (The divisions between the stages are less precise than Hornung suggests, especially between Stages 2 and 3, but the system is sound.) His stages are as follows (measurements are approximate):

Stage 1   Early Eighteenth Dynasty, including KV 20, 38, 34, 35, and 43. Corridor width varies from ca. 1.5 to 2.0 m; corridor height from 1.7 to 2.3 m; gate width from 1.0 to 1.8 m.

Stage 2   Late Eighteenth and early Nineteenth Dynasty, including KV 22, 23, 57, 16, 17, and 7. Corridor width varies from ca. 2.5 to 2.6 m; corridor height from 2.5 to 2.8 m; gate width from 2.0 to 2.1 m.

Stage 3   Late Nineteenth and early Twentieth Dynasty, including KV 8, 10, 15, 14, 47, and 11. Corridor width varies from ca. 2.6 to 2.8 m; corridor height from 3.1 to 3.3 m; gate width from 2.0 to 2.2 m.

Stage 4   Late Twentieth Dynasty, including KV 2, 9, 1, 6, 18, and 4. Corridor width varies from ca. 3.1 to 3.3 m; corridor height from 3.6 to 4.1 m; gate width from 2.5 to 2.8 m.

SOURCES

Studies of the component parts of KV royal tombs rely on three sources: ancient texts, ancient tomb decoration, and modern surveys. Broadly speaking, texts give us the names of tomb components, decoration offers clues to their function, and surveys provide their measurements. (Tomb decoration is discussed in chs 11–14 and 19–21.)

Ancient Textual Sources. Nineteen papyri and ostraca describe the architecture of various Theban royal tombs. Three others refer to a prince's tomb (source 7). Some provide considerable detail; others are frustratingly vague. It has been possible to identify the specific tomb in many ancient sources by dating those sources palaeographically and comparing their measurements and descriptions with actual KV tombs (e.g., Weeks 1979). Most sources are of Ramesside date and refer to tombs KV 7, 2, 9, and 8. Many were found in ancient debris in the central section of KV, where the tombs they describe are located. The following list is in roughly chronological order. Our chamber descriptions rely heavily for nonmetric data on Rossi (2004), Demarée (1992), Eigner (1984), Černý (1973b), Carter and Gardiner (1917), and the works cited in the text that follows.

1.   Ostracon Michaelides 53. Measurements of a Nineteenth Dynasty royal tomb (Goedicke and Wente 1962).
2.   Ostracon British Museum 8505. Measurements of KV 16 or QV 51. Thomas (1966) suggests it refers to KV 22 or KV 23, or perhaps to KV 57 or KV 17.
3.   Ostracon Cairo 51936. Sketch of a four-pillared hall, perhaps Chamber F in KV 15 or Chamber J in KV 17 (Reeves 1986).

4. Papyrus Cairo JdE 86637, verso. Measurements of chambers A–E of KV 7 (Bakir 1966).
5. Ostracon Michaelides 92. Measurements of rooms behind the burial chamber of a late Nineteenth Dynasty tomb, probably KV 8 (Goedicke and Wente 1962).
6. Ostracon Cairo CG 25581, recto. Written by Kenhirkhopeshef; refers to work in chambers A and B of KV 8.
7. Ostracon Turin 57036 and 57037. Notes on rooms in the Valley of the Queens (QV) tomb of a son of Rameses III, from regnal year 24 (Lopez 1978). See also Ostracon Strasbourg H.112, perhaps QV 44 (Kitchen 1989).
8. Papyrus Turin 1885, recto. A plan of KV 2; drawn after the tomb was cut.
9. Ostracon Cairo unnumbered. A plan of a flight of stairs and a doorway, perhaps the entrance to KV 2 (Reeves 1986, 1990).
10. Papyrus Turin 1885 verso. Measurements of KV 9, made after the tomb was completed (the sarcophagus is shown in place; Hornung 1988, 1990b).
11. Papyrus Turin 1923, verso. Report on quarrying in KV 9 during Years 2–3 of that king (Ventura 1988).
12. Ostracon Berlin B and ostracon Nash 10 (= ostracon British Museum 65944). Measurements of most of KV 9, KV 15, or KV 10.
13. Ostracon Cairo CG 25538, 4–6. Notes progress of work in KV 15; dated Year 6, II *šmw* 25 (Černý 1935).
14. Ostracon Cairo CG 25536, recto and 25537. Describes work in Chamber A and Gate B of KV 47, in Year 1 during II and IV *3ḥt*.
15. Ostracon Cairo JdE 72452. Note on starting work in KV 14 in Year 2, II *pr.t* 8 of Seti II (Kitchen 1982; Altenmüller 1983, 1984; Helck 1990).
16. Ostracon Michaelides 71, verso 2–3. Late Nineteenth Dynasty reference to *wtn* (breaking through) *p33 sb3 n t3 s.t n ẖ'w n*, "the Door of the 'Place of Weapons' [or Equipment].”
17. Ostracon Deir el-Medina. A list of measured tomb doorways in a Nineteenth or Twentieth Dynasty tomb, probably KV 8 (the more likely choice) or KV 15.
18. Ostracon Cairo 25184. Plan, with dimensions, of KV 6 (Rossi 2001b).

Modern Sources. The earliest modern plans of KV royal tombs were made by eighteenth- and nineteenth-century travelers. The list of visitors begins with Pococke in 1737 and is followed by many others (see Porter and Moss 1964; Thomas 1966; Romer 1976; Reeves and Wilkinson 1996; Weeks 2001; Roehrig 2002). The plans they drew were simple sketches, often crudely measured and not to scale. A few, however, were more accurately planned by early twentieth century excavators; an early example is KV 2 (Carter and Gardiner 1917), which includes Carter's taped measurements of the tomb itself. Among several others are Carter and Newberry (1904) and Guilmant (1907). More recent tomb plans include those by Hornung (1975, 1978, 1988, 1990b), but these, too, were taped, not surveyed. (Taped surveys usually wrongly assume that corners and angles are 90°.) In 2000, the publication of the TMP's *Atlas of the Valley of the Kings* (Weeks 2000) made available for the first time detailed, surveyed plans of KV tombs (see also Weeks 2001; Schacht and TMP Staff 2003). Complete TMP data and plans may be consulted at the TMP's website, www.thebanmappingproject.com.

CHAMBERS, CORRIDORS, AND HALLS

Entrance A The entrance to a KV royal tomb was called *p3 sṯ3-nṯr n w3t šw*, "The God's Passage of the Way of Shu" (sources 4, 6, and 12); *p3 sṯ3-nṯr tpy ḥr w3.t šw* "The First God's Passage which is upon the Sun's Path" (sources 8 and 18); "The Open-Air Corridor"; or "The [First] Corridor" (sources 8 and 14). A is generally open to the air, especially in Stages 3 and 4, when it also has a gently sloping floor or a ramp-stair combination with widely spaced sides of hewn bedrock and little additional construction. In Stage 1, A includes a steep stairway; in Stage 2, slope and stairs appear in combination (KV 22, 16, 17, and 7). A was undecorated until KV 7, when the lintel of Gate B was decorated with a solar disc and figures of Isis and Nephthys, and the thicknesses with a figure of Maat. KV 11 and 6 have pilasters cut on the left and right walls. Tombs in the first half of the Eighteenth Dynasty generally were dug near the base of sheer cliffs, often below clefts—sometimes called waterfalls—over which rainwater might pour during heavy storms and bury their entrance under tons of flood debris. That debris, and the deliberate filling of the tomb's first chambers with stone, was meant to protect the inner chambers from flooding and theft. In the last half of the Eighteenth Dynasty and all of the Nineteenth Dynasty, however, A was located on gently sloping hillsides and there was little internal protection. This resulted in serious flood damage to many tombs. Tombs of the Twentieth Dynasty lay at the base of hills away from the most common flood path and were not much affected.

Corridor B B is found in every royal KV tomb and is the tomb's first fully enclosed chamber. It has a simple, rectangular plan (Appendix table 3), and is consistently the largest corridor, in cubic meters, in KV royal tombs (except for D in KV 23 and 14). It is the third-largest tomb chamber generally, after F and J.

B was called "The Second God's Passage [of Re]" (source 18); *p3 sṯ3-nṯr nty r-mḥ 2*, "The Second God's Passage Which Is Behind It," "It" being Entrance A (sources 6, 12, and 14); or *p3 sṯ3-nṯr n r'*; "The God's Passage of Re," (source 18); and variations (including sources 2, 8, and 11). The absence of decoration in the first corridors of early KV tombs (corridors B, C, and D) may confirm that they were filled with debris after the burial was installed. The earliest decoration of Chamber B is found in KV 17.

The reference to Re in the chamber's name may reflect the change in plan that B underwent in the Nineteenth Dynasty. In the steeply descending tombs of the Eighteenth Dynasty, B lay in perpetual darkness. But in the nearly level, more open tombs of the Nineteenth and Twentieth Dynasties, when the name "Second God's Passage of Re" first appeared and its walls were first decorated, the chamber might be bathed in sunlight when Gate B was open. Appropriately, the sunlit chamber walls featured scenes of solar deities.

In only three KV royal tombs does B have side chambers. The earliest is KV 10, with one side chamber. The others are KV 11, with two, and KV 6, with four.

Corridor C C is found in all KV royal tombs except KV 1. (Appendix table 4; Thomas (1966) identifies two C corridors in KV 20; see also Preys [2011].) C was called *pA sṯз-nṯr n ///* "The God's Passage of..." (sources 12 and 18); *ky sṯз- nṯr nty r-mḥ 3*, "The Third God's Passage" (source 4); or "The Hall Wherein They Rest" (Černý and Gardiner 1957). "They" refers to statuettes of deities placed inside recesses cut in the side walls of C, or to their figures painted on the recesses' walls. Thirty-seven such figures were painted in KV 17. In KV 2, the figures in two niches continue rows of deities on adjacent walls that are a part of the Litany of Re.

The recesses in Corridor C were called *nзḥ ḥm.y nty ḥtp-w nз nṯr.w iзb.t/iwn.t im-w* "The Recesses [some translate 'Sanctuaries'] in which the Gods of the East/West Reside" (source 18; Černý 1973b, 28). (The position of the "east" and "west" niches mean that a visitor was considered to be walking northward when entering the tomb, regardless of his actual orientation.) Recesses are found in all C corridors in KV royal tombs except KV 20, 38, 15, 14, and 47. C niches (in KV 20) vary from 2.5 to 2.7 m wide. C recesses vary from 3.25 to 5.75 m. All are 1.0 to 2.0 m high and generally 0.50 to 0.55 m deep.

In Stages 1 and 2, C nearly always had a staircase. In Stage 1, these had about 15 treads, but by the end of Stage 2, the number grew to 29. Early examples descend at an angle of about 40° (51° in KV 34); that is reduced to 20–30° in KV 17 and 7. Only in KV 7 is there a ramp–stair combination instead of steps (cf. KV 20 C1, D1).

KV 11, uniquely, has eight C side chambers, Ca–h. They were later additions to the tomb, their gates cut through already decorated walls. The side chambers were decorated with scenes of offerings and vignettes from the Book of the Dead, and measure about 1.77 m high, 2.0 m wide, 1.75 m deep, about 6.2 m³ each. These side chambers, and perhaps Ba–d in KV 6, were given names that apparently described their contents: "House of Food," "Fields of *Iaru*," "Treasury," etc., written in hieratic above their gates. The texts were badly damaged when Champollion saw them, and have since disappeared (Černý 1973b 32–33).

Corridor D D is absent from KV 38, 16, 1, and 18. It occurs twice in KV 20 and KV 11 because of unanticipated changes in the tomb's axis (Appendix table 5). It was called *ky sṯз-nṯr nty r-mḥ 4*, "The Fourth God's Passage" (sources 4 and 12). A ramp in the chamber floor of KV 2 was called *p3 r3-sṯз*, "the passage's mouth" (*Wb.* reads "Gang") which Carter and Gardiner (1917, 137) read as "the sarcophagus-slide" (source 8; Černý 1973, 28). It descends at an angle of 9.3°.

Niches are found first in Chambers D1 and D2 of KV 20, and not again until KV 8 (if that is not the cutting for a gate). Niches in D are common thereafter. KV 10, 15, 47, 11, 2, 9, and 6 each have two niches at the end of their side walls. Each measures about 68–75 cm wide, 60–75 cm deep, and 94–110 cm high, with its floor about 30–50 cm above the chamber floor. (Their size is discussed in Ventura 1988, 141.) The ancient name was *'.t iry-'з 2*, "the two doorkeepers' rooms" (sources 11 and 12; Černý 1973b, 28–29 and, more generally, 1973a, 161–174), suggesting that two guardians were symbolically posted here to block access further into the tomb. Architecturally, these "rooms" are niches, and the TMP assigns them no chamber designations. It has been suggested that D marked the beginning of the most sacred part of the royal tomb, and was officially sealed with stone and plaster after the burial had been installed (Thomas 1966).

Hall E From the reign of Thutmosis III, Hall E was a part of most royal KV tombs (Appendix table 6). Called "The First Hall" by early Egyptologists, E is usually rectangular in plan, from 1.00 to 1.54 times wider than long. The ceiling is horizontal and varies in height from 1.7 m to 4.09 m, gradually and regularly increasing through the New Kingdom. E is the smallest of the axial chambers in KV royal tombs.

In 19 tombs, E has a shaft (also called a well or pit) cut through its floor. The top of the shaft is as broad and wide as the chamber itself, but below it varies in size and plan; in some cases, it was unfinished. Its depth ranges from 6.27 m to 9.10 m below the chamber's ceiling. If tomb AN–B was a royal tomb (perhaps for Amenhotep I [Polz 1995]), its shaft was the first to be cut at Thebes. If not, then the earliest is KV 34. The last was KV 11. Between KV 34 and KV 11, the shaft was a regular part of the royal tomb: of 14 tombs, 13 had E chambers, and of those, 10 had shafts.

In Papyrus Turin (sources 8 and 18; varr. 4, 10, 11, and 12), E was called *t3 wsḫt isḳ*, "The Hall of Waiting," "The Hall of Hindering," or simply, *p3 isḳ*, "The Waiting." Ventura (1988), followed by Rossi (2004: 140), suggest "The Hall of Denial of Access." We are not sure what function these names imply, but four suggestions have been made.

1. E was a waiting room. Earlier Egyptologists, taking literally the translation "Hall of Waiting," suggested that E was just that. Černý (1973b, 29) claimed that "the dead had to wait here before being admitted to the burial chamber." Carter and Carnarvon (1917, 138) believed it "was intended to designate the place where relatives, courtiers and subjects might wait before being admitted to the august presence of the Pharaoh." But it is unlikely that a chamber that often had a deep pit instead of a level floor was a place where people stood about or a mummy awaited burial.

2. E was a flood control device. Since Belzoni first described the shaft in KV 17, many writers have called it a well, a catch basin for the water and debris that poured down KV hillsides during occasional torrential rainstorms, preventing them from washing farther into the tomb and damaging the burial chamber. It is true that the shaft could stop floods (at least until it filled with debris), but surely it would have made more sense to locate the pit nearer the tomb's entrance, and to dig no pit at all if the tomb was in a location unlikely to flood. Further, several well shafts have side chambers at their bottom: the earliest is KV 35; others are KV 43 and 22, and perhaps 57, 17, and 7. Some side chambers are plastered and decorated (e.g., Romer 1975), odd features if the shaft's only purpose was to trap floodwater (see also Dorn, ch 3).

3. E was meant to discourage thieves. It has been called a "tomb-robbers' pit" ("Grabräuberschächte"). The gate immediately after E was walled up after the body of pharaoh was interred, thereby blocking access to the interior of the tomb. Traces of such blocking can still be seen in several tombs (Abitz 1974, 1978). The

pit has been described as a barrier: thieves could neither cross it nor, seeing only a solid wall beyond, would want to. Yet, the wall blocking Gate F was covered with painted decoration, not carved relief like the other walls in E, and would have made a hollow sound if hit, surely a hint to thieves that something was amiss.

If E was meant to prevent theft, it did not work. Thieves could easily knock a hole in the blocked Gate F, lay a plank across the pit, and continue into the tomb (Wilkinson 1835, 102). In both KV 7 and 34, excavators found lengths of ancient rope hanging down the shaft, tied to pillars in neighboring chambers. Thieves may have rappeled down one side of the shaft and climbed up the other (Reeves 1990).

4. E had a religious purpose. Egyptologists have also argued that the shaft and its side chambers were the symbolic burial place of Osiris, Sokar, or Osiris-Sokar. Abitz (1974, 1978), Hornung (1988), and Rossi (2004) argue that, in the Eighteenth Dynasty, the shaft symbolically connected the tomb to the subterranean "aquatic region" of the Imyduat. Hornung (1990a) describes it as "a passage from this world to the Beyond, serving the resurrection of the deceased." Scenes and texts on its walls support this religious association. But if the shaft regularly had such a purpose, its presence in the royal tomb at Amarna (Martin 1989) is difficult to explain.

Thomas (1966) believed none of these four theories adequately explained every shaft. A theory apparently valid for one tomb is not valid for others. She suggested that several explanations together played a role, and most Egyptologists today would agree. The shaft disappeared from KV tombs after the reign of Rameses III, presumably because of changing religious views.

Hall F F first appeared in KV 34 and is present in most tombs thereafter (Appendix table 7). F is rectangular in plan in KV 34, 35, 43, and 22, but from KV 57 onward it was nearly square. It is the second largest chamber in KV royal tombs after Chamber J, and its pillars doubtless played a structural as well as a symbolic role (Arnold 1984). Following Romer (1976), the TMP considers F in KV 20 to more correctly be labeled J1, a burial chamber.

Prior to KV 17, two pillars stood in the center of F at right angles to the axis of previous chambers; thereafter, F had four pillars, 2 by 2. (KV 8 originally had four pillars, but two at the rear were removed in antiquity.) One source (12; Černý 1973b), perhaps referring to KV 9, mentions them: "What is in it [Chamber F]: four pillars."

Six F chambers, all late Nineteenth Dynasty or Twentieth Dynasty, have side chambers. One side chamber, Fa, may be seen in six tombs, KV 17, 7, 8, 11, and the unfinished KV 10 and 15. The first three of these had pillars: two in KV 17 and 8, four in KV 7. In KV 10, F was begun, perhaps with two pillars, but not completed. All side chambers lie on the right side of F, except KV 17, where Fa was cut through the rear wall, and KV 15, which has an unfinished gate, Fa, on the left.

KV royal tombs from the reign of Thutmosis III can be said to have two parts, religiously based and physically defined by their architecture and decoration (Abitz 1989b; Hornung 1995; Wilkinson 1995; Robinson 2010). The tomb's upper part, chambers A through F, emphasized the god Re and female deities and was associated with the east;

the lower part, chambers G through J, emphasized Osiris and male deities and was associated with the west. From the late Eighteenth Dynasty, a shrine to Osiris and the Book of Gates appeared in Chamber F, and the Litany of Re, which had appeared in the lower part of KV 34, was moved to the upper part. (Decorated pillars do not appear until KV 17.) Chamber F marked the divide between the upper and lower parts, and Gate G was "the the beginning of the truly sepulchral part of the tomb" (Thomas 1966, 275). Although the plans of the two parts of the tomb parallel one another, there are also architectural features that distinguish them. In Stage 1 tombs, there was a 90° shift in the tomb's axis at F. In Stage 2 (KV 57 and 17), the tomb's axis jogged left in F. In both, a staircase leads from F down to G (or, in KV 34, to J). These staircases descended at about 40–44° and had 16–20 treads. In Stage 3, F had a central ramp/stairway combination with about 15–20 treads descending at 22–33°. In Stage 4, KV 9, 6, and 4 have sloping floors without steps (Abitz 1989a).

F may have been the burial chamber in earlier royal tombs (Romer 1976), but by the Eighteenth Dynasty it served another function. It was called *t3 wsḫt mrḥt* "The Chariot Hall" (source 11), and pieces of actual chariots have been found in KV 43 and 22. It was also called *kt wsḫt dr sbi(.w)* "Another Hall of Repelling the Rebel(s) [or Enemies]" (source 12; Thomas 1966; Demarée 1992), suggesting that it served as "a back-up deterrent," in effect another "Hall of Hindering" (Chamber E). In KV 9, beheaded figures are shown on one wall, and its name may refer to this scene. On the Cairo plan (source 3), the chamber is called *t3 wsḫt //// pr-ḥd*, "The Hall /// the Treasury" (Thomas 1966).

Chamber G G is called *ky st3-nṯr qr tpy n wp.t*, "Another God's Passage," or "First (God's Passage) of the *wp.t* ['zenith of the sun's journey through the night' or, perhaps, 'judgment']" (Černý 1973b; Demarée 1992). Note that the second name inaugurates a new chamber count: G is the "First" passage after F. G first appears in KV 20 and 35, and in 65 percent of all later tombs (except KV 23, 16, 15, 2, 1, 6, and 18). It has a simple, rectangular plan (a W:L ratio of 1:3) with no unusual features except a vaulted ceiling in KV 10 and a small side chamber in the left wall in KV 14 (Appendix table 8).

Chamber H Called *ky st3-nṯr*, the term also used for G, H was more precisely *p3 ky st3-nṯr r-mḥ 2*, "The Other, Second, God's Passage." It first appears in KV 43 (Appendix table 9). Recesses in H occur only in KV 17 (see also later, Chamber J in KV 47).

Hall I Sometimes called the Antechamber, I was *t3 wsḫ.t m3'.t*, the "Hall of Truth." Whenever they occur, G, H, and I appear together from KV 43 onward, except in unfinished KV 10 and 4 (Appendix table 10; see also the section on Gates).

Burial Chamber J Called *wsḫ.t nty ḥtp-tw m-im*, "The Hall in Which One Rests" (source 2), or *pr n nbw*, "The House of Gold [in Which One Rests]" (source 8), J was the most important chamber in the royal tomb and usually the largest (Appendix table 11). It was here that the pharaoh's mummy was interred, surrounded by funerary texts and goods. J is found in every tomb except the unfinished KV 10 and 18. In some tombs, J was a chamber originally intended for another purpose and converted when the tomb was hastily completed. P. Turin describes J in KV 2: "The House of Gold [a reference to shrines placed here], wherein One rests, of 16 cubits; breadth, of 16 cubits; height, of 10 cubits; being drawn with outlines, graven with the chisel, filled with colours, and completed; and being provided with the equipment of His Majesty. . . on every side of it, together with the Divine Ennead which is in the Netherworld" (Carter and Gardiner 1917, 139).

There are variations in the plan of J, and some show chronologically meaningful distribution. Two J chambers in Stage 1 (KV 38 and 34) have an oval plan (perhaps copying the supposed shape of the underworld [Hornung 1990a]). J1 and J2 in KV 14, and less precisely J in KV 16, 8, 11, and 2, are nearly square. Most are rectangular: in KV 23, 47, and 9 J is wider than long; the others are longer than wide.

Burial chambers with flat ceilings are most common in Stages 1 and 2. Vaulted or partly vaulted ceilings are common in Stages late 2, 3, and 4; only in KV 10, 2, 1, and 6 does the vault parallel the tomb's axis and not lie at a right angle to it. Other vaulted ceilings are KV 17, 7, 8, 14, 47, 11, 9, and 4. The floor of that part of J housing the sarcophagus (sometimes called the "crypt") was usually cut at a lower level in the rear third of J in late Stages 1 and 2, but moved to the middle of J in Stages 3 and 4. Steps lead from one level to the other as follows: stairs on center axis, front of chamber: KV 35, 43, 22; stairs on center axis, front and rear: KV 8, 11; stairs on center axis and left side, both front and rear: KV 57, 7. Instead of steps, there is a ramp on center axis, front in KV 9, and ramps on center axis, front and rear in KV 14. Benches, sometimes called shelves, are narrow horizontal areas above floor level along the walls of J, or the depression in its floor, or in a side chamber. They are found along all four walls of J in KV 6 and 8, along three walls in KV 7 (Jc, Jd, Jddd; 17 Jb; 47 J), two walls (KV 7 J), or one wall (KV 14 J1).

The number of pillars in J varies: there are three in KV 20; four in KV 47, 9 (also with 4 pilasters), and 4; six in KV 35, 43, 22, 57, and 17; and eight in KV 7, 8, 14 (in both J1 and J2), and 11. Six tombs, all among the smallest in KV and with hastily abbreviated plans, have no pillars in J: KV 38 (but see later, the section on Pillars), 23, 16, 2, 1, and 18. The pilasters in the rear wall of J in KV 9 are in fact unfinished cuttings for pillars, probably altered to speed completion of the tomb. (On J2 in KV 20, see Romer 1976.)

J side chambers are found in nearly all tombs of Stages 1, 2, and 3 (except KV 15 and 47), but not in Stage 4. KV 7 has 10 J side chambers, more than any other tomb (Hornung 1978, 65). Usually, four gates or more lead into side chambers, but KV 38 and 23 have only one. Chamber J with four gates: KV 34, 35, 43; five: KV 22, 57, 17, 8, 14 (both J1 and J2), 11; six: KV 7. (In KV 47, J1 was converted to H2 when workmen unexpectedly encountered KV 32, and J2 was then added to the plan. J1a is therefore not an unfinished side chamber, but the abandoned start of work to enlarge the original J1. It should be labeled H2 and not J1.)

Multiple side chambers (e.g., Jc plus Jcc and Jccc) are found only in Stage 2. There are doubles in KV 57, triples in KV 57 and 7. In Stage 2, every J chamber has one single or one multiple side chamber behind its rear wall: KV 22 has Jc and Jcc; KV 23 has Ja; KV 57, Jc, Jcc, and Jccc; KV 16, Jb; and both KV 17 and KV 7 have Jc. Side chambers lie behind the left and/or right walls of Chamber J in Stages 1 and 3.

The most important side chamber seems to be Ja, and Roehrig (2007) and Thomas (1966, 279) note that the foot end of all *in situ* sarcophagi in Stage 1 and 2 tombs are oriented toward its gate. Rather than being simply a storeroom for offerings of food and

drink, Ja's contents were "intended to facilitate the king's journey through the underworld and his successful transformation into Osiris" (Thomas 1966, 279). Figures of
Osiris are painted on the chamber's walls in KV 57, 16, and 17. In KV 7, there is a carved
figure of Osiris in the back wall of Je, and in KV 8 Ja, as there is in the rear wall of
Corridor 7 in the non-royal KV 5.

J varies greatly in size. The largest date to Stages 2 and 3 and include KV 8 (1112 m³),
KV 11 (882 m³), and KV 7 (870 m ³). The smallest are scattered through all stages and
include KV 16 (104 m ³), KV 1 (188 m³), and KV 23 (225 m ³); all of the smallest are tombs
in which work was cut short and the original plan abbreviated.

A special type of niche is found in Chamber J in Stages 1 and 2 (KV 35, 43, 22, 23, 57, 16,
17, and 7). Called "magical brick niches," Roth and Roehrig (2002, 121) have suggested
that they held bricks associated with "women during childbirth," their presence "meta-
phorical, replicating the equipment of an earthly birth in order to ensure the deceased's
rebirth in the other world." Two were cut in each of the chamber walls facing the ends
of the sarcophagus (KV 43, 57, 16, 17, 7, with only 2 total cut in 11), or singly in each of J's
four walls (KV 43?, 22, 23). Usually, they were cut in walls immediately surrounding the
sarcophagus, that is, in the walls of the J "crypt." Each was associated with amuletic figures mentioned in chapter 151 of the Book of the Dead: a mummiform figure, the Anubis
jackal, a reed or flame, and a *djed*-pillar. Their arrangement in J varied (see also Thomas
1964, Weeks 2002, Report for 2011). Those in Stage 1 and early Stage 2 tombs were apparently sealed; later examples were left open (Roth and Roehrig 2002, 125; their suggestions
in footnote 22 about chambers having more than four brick niches are not convincing).

Chamber K The room immediately behind Burial Chamber J was called *p3 st3-ntr nty
ms.t š3bty.w*, "The God's Passage Which Is in the Shabti-place," or *p3 st3-ntr nty m t3 w3.t
hnw n pr-nbw*, "the God's Passage Which Is on the Inner Side of the House of Gold." K
is found in six KV tombs, all dating to Stages 3 and 4 (Appendix table 12). KV 11 and 14
have two chambers, K1 and K2. (The long corridor beyond J in KV 17, although sometimes labeled K, is not; see Corridor M). Tombs having chamber K have all other chambers, A through J, as well, except tomb KV 2, which lacks F, G, H, and I, and KV 1, which
lacks all chambers but A, B, J, and K.

"The Shabti-place" is a misnomer: there is no evidence that K housed such figures.
More likely, they were placed in two side chambers (Ka and Kc in KV 2), referred to as
pr-hd smhy/wnmy, "Left/Right Treasury" (sources 2 and 8). In three instances, K has
side chambers: KV 8 and KV 2 have three, in their left, right, and rear walls; KV 14 has
two, in K1, and perhaps also in K2 (if indeed these are unfinished entrances and not
niches). KV 1 has one niche in the chamber's rear wall; KV 2 has two recesses. The location of *s.t t3 rsy hr wnmy*, "The Place of *t3 rsy* on the Right," shown following J on the
Turin plan (source 8; Demarée 1992), is uncertain.

Chamber L In KV 14, L lies between K1 and J2. It was perhaps called *p3 st3-ntr r-mh
2 nty hr ph n pr-nbw*, "The Second God's Passage Which Is at the Back of the House of
Gold," or *pr-hd n p3 nfrw*, "Treasury of the End [or Innermost] Room" (source 8). It is a
simple, rectangular corridor with a flat ceiling and two niches in its side walls. In KV 11,
L has five large, decorated recesses and a vaulted ceiling.

Corridor M The long tunnel extending beyond Chamber J in KV 17 has been labeled Corridor K in several studies, including the TMP's *Atlas*, but there is little to justify that designation. (Its ancient name, if any, is unknown.) Instead of being a "Shabti-place" or a "Treasury," this long passage may have been an attempt to connect J to ground-water, loosely copying the Osireion at Abydos (Weeks 1979; Lipinski 1994), but that theory remains unproved. A recent clearing (in 2007–2010) of the passage indicates that M was well-carved, with stairways and stair–ramp combinations along its path. It extended 174.5 m beyond J before work on it was abandoned in antiquity. The question of its function remains unresolved. We have assigned to it the letter M to indicate that it differs significantly in plan and almost certainly in function from corridors A through L. It may someday be necessary to divide M into several components when its plan is better known.

GATES

Every tomb chamber has an entrance. It may have been left open, blocked with mud and stone, or closed with a door. Most entrances had gates, by which we mean they had simple or compound jambs (Figure 8.4; Appendix table 13). Only seven chamber entrances lack gates (KV 43 B; 22 H; 17 K; 14 K1a, K1b; 9 K; and 4 J). Where gates were lacking, the change from one chamber to the next was marked only by a change in ceiling level or the slope of the floor, or by the beginning or end of a stairway. The reveals in gates along the main axis of KV 8 were cut away and then rebuilt in ancient times (Thomas 1966, 109).

The first tomb to have wooden doors installed in a gate was KV 34 (Appendix table 13), and we can still see wooden strips, to which single-leaf doors were attached, fitted into the soffits and threshold of its Gates Ja–d. The first single-leaf door to be installed along a tomb's main axis was in Gate J in KV 35. Uniquely, that door was hung to open outward (Roehrig 1995, 85–86). Double-leaf wooden doors first appeared in KV 7, and from then on we find no single-leaf doors except as follows: KV 9 F, KV 8 Fa; KV 11 Ba–b, Ca–h, D1, and Fa; all J side chamber doors, and doors into I. Gates B, C, D, E, and K are always double-leaf (except KV 11 D1). KV 7 boasts the largest number of wooden doors (15), followed by KV 2 with 6, and KV 9, 6, and 4 with 5 each. Single-leaf doors are generally found in Gate J and J's side chambers, double-leaf doors only in gates on a tomb's main axis (see also Clarke and Engelbach 1930).

The modern architectural terms used by the TMP for the parts of gates are shown in Figure 8.4. Ancient terms are as follows (see Sethe 1920; Černý 1973b; Spencer 1984, 155–161): *ḥꜣy.t* refers to the entire gate. The reveals are called *wmt* (Spencer 1984), although Černý (1973b) suggests the word refers only to the thickness of the gate. Spencer says *sbꜣ* referred to the "door frame" or the entire doorway, but by the Nineteenth Dynasty came to refer to a "door leaf." Other terms include *bnš*, door jamb (see also Carter and Gardiner 1917, 146); *wmt n bnš*, thickness of the door jamb; *wsḫt* the "breadth" of the opening; *ḥy-bnš* the height of the door jamb or opening; *'ryt* a stone lintel; *ḥr.f* the frame of a wooden door (see also Carter and Gardiner 1917: 146–148; Thomas 1966: 278).

PILLARS AND PILASTERS

Pillars were never constructed but cut from solid bedrock. We find them in many tombs in chambers F, Fa, J, Jb, Jc, Jd, and Jddd (see also appropriate chamber discussions in the preceding text; Appendix table 15). There are only minor differences in the sizes of pillars: most range from 0.97 to 1.10 m wide. The largest are in KV 17, 20, 34, and 4; the smallest are in side chambers of various tombs. Only in KV 7, 9, and 4 do the pillars in Chamber J differ significantly in size from those in Chamber F (see also Chamber J); J pillars are always the larger (Hornung 1978, 62; Arnold 1984). The remains of an oddly positioned pillar seen by Loret in KV 38 J may have been cut by ancient workmen as a safety measure while working in that chamber, then removed by them when their work was finished (Weeks 2002, notes on KV 38 J).

Pilasters are found only in Entrance A of KV 11 (two on each wall near Gate B) and A of KV 6 (three on each wall near Gate B), none of them finished. See also comments on pilasters in KV 9, Chamber J.

STAIRCASES, STEPS, AND RAMPS

Staircases are common in chambers A and C in Hornung's Stage 1 and 2 tombs, extending the full width of the chamber (except in KV 20), and descending steeply, sloping 30–40°. They are also found in H (in KV 43, 22, 57, and 17), sloping 27° to 44°. In Chamber F (KV 34, 35, 43, 22, 57, and 17, but not 7), stairs descend off-axis through the floor to Gate G (or to J in KV 34). From KV 7 onward, fewer tombs have staircases, and these are often stair–ramp combinations (KV 7, 10, 47, 11, 2, 6, and 18), usually with sloping rather than horizontal treads (Arnold [2003, 228] refers to them as "sloping treads"), sloping at 4° to 15°. Risers of stairs with sloping treads are not always vertical but cut at right angles to the tread (Clarke and Engelbach 1930, 178). Small sets of steps (usually with only two to four risers) may be seen in Gate J of KV 35, in Gate F (KV 57), Gate Fa (KV 17), Gate Ja (KV 7), Gate H (KV 8), and in Gate B (KV 9 and 18). Steps (either one set or two) descend from the upper to the lower level of J in KV 35, 43, 22, 57, 8, and 11; there are four sets in KV 7. The steps in KV 20 and in Chamber M of KV 17 are unique in number and design.

Ramps are common in chambers B and D in Stages 1 and 2, much less common later. They usually slope at less than 15°. Ramps in chamber F in Stages 3 and 4 are steeper. (See Chamber D; Carter and Gardiner 1917; Rossi 2001a).

NICHES AND RECESSES

In TMP usage, niches are smaller than recesses, higher than they are wide, located low or at mid-level in a wall. Recesses are larger than niches, generally wider than high, and located at the top of side walls in chambers lying on a tomb's principal axis. They are also found on the faces of benches in KV 17 Jb. (For magical brick niches see Chamber J.) The occurrence of niches and recesses is shown in Appendix table 16 (see also Chambers C and D). Note that recesses are found almost exclusively in Chamber C (the exceptions are KV 17 H, 2 E and K, 8 J, and 11 L). Niches are usually found only in Chamber J in Stages 1 and 2, and in Chamber D in Stages 3 and 4 and usually were cut in the walls of the "crypt" in J in which the sarcophagus was placed (Roth and Roehrig 2002, 125). The Egyptian terms for niches and/or recesses included *ḥm.y* and *'t iry(w)-'3* (Černý 1973b, 28; Ventura 1988).

Put-logs, also called beam holes (Arnold 1991, 2003), have two parts: a roughly square hole in one wall near the top of a ramp or ramp–stair combination and, in the wall opposite, a wedge-shaped cutting. Together, the two temporarily held a beam around which a rope was wrapped to control the descent of a sarcophagus into the burial chamber. They are found in KV 20 B, C, C2, D1, D2; 16 B; 7 A, B; 8 A, B, Gate C; 14 C, D, H; 47 C; 11 C; 9 G. The put-log in KV 1 K is uniquely placed.

ACKNOWLEDGMENTS

I am delighted to again acknowledge the skills of the Theban Mapping Project field staff, 1970–2012, whose hard work produced the architectural and archaeological data on which this chapter is based. Their names are listed on the TMP website, but I must again give special credit to David Goodman, Catharine Roehrig, and Walton Chan. In addition, Lori Lawson was responsible for painstakingly organizing the complex tables here. Ilka Schacht prepared the figures. Magdy Abu Hamad Ali ensured the smooth running of our Cairo office, and Ahmed Mahmoud Has'san oversaw our many Luxor activities with customary skill and patience.

BIBLIOGRAPHY

Abitz, F. 1974. *Die religiose Bedeutung der sogenannten Grabräuberschächte in den ägyptischen Königsgräbern der 18. bis 20. Dynastie (=ÄgAbh 26). Wiesbaden.*
Abitz, F. 1978. "The 'Well' in the King's Tombs of Bibân el-Moluk." *Journal of Egyptian Archaeology* 64: 80–83.
Abitz, F. 1989a. *Baugeschichte und Dekoration des Grabes Ramses' VI* (= OBO 89). Freiburg.
Abitz, F. 1989b. "Die Entwicklung der Grabachsen in der Königsgräbern im Tal des Könige." *Mitteilungen des Deutschen Archäologischen Instituts, Abteilung Kairo* 45: 1–25.

Altenmüller, H. 1983. "Bemerkungen zu den Königsgräbern des Neuen Reiches." *Studien zur Altägyptischen Kultur* 10: 25–61.

Altenmüller, H. 1984. "Der Begräbnistag Sethos. II." *Studien zur Altägyptischen Kultur* 11: 37–47.

Arnold, D. 1984. "Pfeiler." In Helck and Otto: IV, 1008–1009.

Arnold, D. 1991. *Building in Egypt*. Oxford.

Arnold, D. 2003. *Encyclopaedia of Ancient Egyptian Architecture*. London.

Badawy, A. 1968. *A History of Egyptian Architecture: The Empire (the New Kingdom) from the Eighteenth Dynasty to the End of the Twentieth Dynasty, 1580–1085 B.C.* Berkeley.

Baines, J. et al., eds. 1988. *Pyramid Studies and Other Essays Presented to I.E.S. Edwards* (= *EES, Occasional Papers* 7). London.

Bakir, A. M. 1966. *The Cairo Calendar, No 86637.* Cairo.

Carter, H. and A. H. Gardiner. 1917. "The Tomb of Ramesses IV and the Turin Plan of a Royal Tomb." *Journal of Egyptian Archaeology* 4: 130–58.

Carter, H. and P. E. Newberry. 1904. *The Tomb of Thoutmôsis IV* (= *Davies Excavations, 1*). Westminster.

Černý, J. 1935. *Ostraca hiératiques* (= *CGC* 95). Cairo.

Černý, J. 1973a. *A Community of Workmen at Thebes in the Ramesside Period* (= *BdE* 50). Cairo.

Černý, J. 1973b. *The Valley of the Kings: Fragments d'un manuscrit inachevé* (= *BdE* 61). Cairo.

Černý, J. and A. H. Gardiner. 1957. *Hieratic Ostraca*, I. Oxford.

Clarke, S. and R. Engelbach. 1930. *Ancient Egyptian Masonry: The Building Craft*. Oxford.

Demarée, R. J. 1992. "Royal Riddles." In Demarée and Egberts, 9–13.

Demarée, R. J. and A. Egberts, eds. 1992. *Village Voices: Proceedings of the Symposium* "Texts from Deir el-Medineh and their Interpretation." *Leiden, May 31–June 1, 1991* (= *CNWS* 13). Leiden.

Dodson, A. 1988. "The Tombs of the Kings of the Early 18th Dynasty at Thebes." *Zeitschrift für Ägyptische Sprache und Altertumskunde* 115: 110–123.

Dorman, P. and B. Bryan, eds. 2007. *Sacred Space and Sacred Function in Ancient Egypt* (= *SAOC* 61). Chicago.

Eaton-Krauss, M. 2012. "Who Commissioned KV 42 and for Whom?" *Göttinger Miszellen* 234: 53–60.

Eigner, D. 1984. *Die monumentalen Grabbauten der Spätzeit in der thebanischen Nekropole* (= *DÖAW*, 6). Vienna.

Engelbach, R. 1927. "An Architectural Project from Thebes." *Annales du Service des Antiquités de l'Égypte* 27: 72–75.

Eyre, C., A. Leahy and L. Montagno, eds. 1994. *The Unbroken Reed: Studies in the Culture and Heritage of Ancient Egypt in Honour of A.F. Shore* (= *EES Occasional Papers* 11). London.

Goedicke, H. and E. F. Wente. 1962. *Ostraka Michaelides*. Wiesbaden.

Graindorge-Héreil, C. 1994. *Le Dieu Sokar à Thèbes au nouvel empire* (= *GOF IV, 28, 1–2*). 2 vols. Wiesbaden.

Guilmant, F. 1907. *Le tombeau de Ramsès IX* (= *MIFAO* 15). Cairo.

Helck, W. 1990. "Drei ramessidische Daten." *Studien zur Altägyptischen Kultur* 17: 205–214.

Helck, W. and E. Otto, eds. 1984. *Lexikon der Ägyptologie*. Wiesbaden.

Hornung, E. 1975. "Das Grab Thutmosis II." *Revue d'Égyptologie* 27: 125–131.

Hornung, E. 1978. "Struktur und Entwicklung der Gräber im Tal der Könige." *Zeitschrift für Ägyptische Sprache und Altertumskunde* 105: 59–66.

Hornung, E. 1988. "Zum Turiner Grabplan." In Baines, 138–142.

Hornung, E. 1990a. *The Valley of the Kings: Horizon of Eternity*. New York.

Hornung, E. 1990b. *Zwei Ramessidische Königsgräber: Ramses IV. Und Ramses VII.* (= *Thebes* 11). Mainz.

Hornung, E. 1991. *The Tomb of Pharaoh Seti I (Das Grab Sethos' I.)* Zürich.

Hornung, E. 1995. "Studies on the Decoration of the Tomb of Seti I." In Wilkinson, 70–73.

Kemp, B. J. and P. Rose. 1991. "Proportionality in Mind and Space in Ancient Egypt." *Cambridge Archaeological Journal* 1: 103–129.

Kitchen, K. A. 1982. *Ramesside Inscriptions: Historical and Biographical,* IV, 13–15; V, 6–11; VI, 12–6. Oxford.

Kitchen, K. A. 1989. *Ramesside Inscriptions: Historical and Biographical,* VII, 1–5. Oxford.

Leblanc, C., ed. 2010. *The Temples of Millions of Years and the Royal Power at Thebes in the New Kingdom: Science and New Technologies Applied to Archaeology (= Memnonia, Cahier Supplèment* 2). Cairo.

Lipinski, J. 1994. "The Mysterious Tunnel." In Eyre, Leahy and Montagno, 193–194.

Lopez, J. 1978. *Ostraca ieratici N.* 57001–57092 (= *Catalogo del Museu egizio di Torino* ser. 2, 3, 1). Milan.

Martin, G. T. 1989. *The Royal Tomb at el-'Amarna: The Rock Tombs of El-'Amarna, VII, II: The Reliefs, Inscriptions, and Architecture (= ASE, 39),* 5–17, 19 by Mark Lehner. London.

Polz, D. 1995. "The Location of the Tomb of Amenhotep I: A Reconsideration." In Wilkinson, 8–21.

Porter, B. and R. L. B. Moss. 1964. *Topographical Bibliography of Ancient Egyptian Hieroglyphic Texts, Rekliefs and Paintings,* I, 2: *The Theban Necropolis: Royal Tombs and Smaller Cemeteries.* 2nd ed. Oxford.

Preys, R. 2011. "Les tombes non-royales de la Vallée des Rois." *Studien zur Altägyptischen Kultur* 40: 315–338.

Reeves, C. N. 1986. "Two Architectural Drawings from the Valley of the Kings." *Chronique d'Égypte* 61, 121: 43–49.

Reeves, C. N. 1990. *Valley of the Kings: The Decline of a Royal Necropolis.* London.

Reeves, C. N. and R. H. Wilkinson. 1996. *The Complete Valley of the Kings.* London.

Robinson, P. 2010. "Some Observations on the Route to the Afterlife from Late 18th Dynasty Royal Tombs." *Journal of the Society of the Study of Egyptian Antiquities* 37: 59–77.

Roehrig, C. H. 1995. "Gates to the Underworld: The Appearance of Wooden Doors in the Royal Tombs in the Valley of the Kings." In Wilkinson, 82–107.

Roehrig, C. H. 2002. *Explorers and Artists in the Valley of the Kings.* Cairo.

Roehrig, C. H. 2007. "Chamber Ja in Royal Tombs in the Valley of the Kings." In Dorman and Bryan, 117–138.

Romer, J. 1975. "The Tomb of Tuthmosis III." *Mitteilungen des Deutschen Archäologischen Instituts, Abteilung Kairo* 31: 315–351.

Romer, J. 1976. "Royal Tombs of the Early Eighteenth Dynasty." *Mitteilungen des Deutschen Archäologischen Instituts, Abteilung Kairo* 32: 191–206.

Romer, J. 1981. *Valley of the Kings.* New York.

Rossi, C. (2001a). "Dimensions and Slope in the 19th and 20th Dynasty Royal Tombs." *Journal of Egyptian Archaeology* 87: 173–180.

Rossi, C. 2001b. "The Plan of a Royal Tomb on O. Cairo 25184." *Göttinger Miszellen* 184: 45–53.

Rossi, C. 2004. *Architecture and Mathematics in Ancient Egypt.* Cambridge.

Roth, A. M. and C. H. Roehrig. 2002. "Magical Bricks and the Bricks of Birth." *Journal of Egyptian Archaeology* 88: 121–139.

Schacht, I. and TMP Staff. 2003. *Image Database (IDB): Documentation and User Manual (= Publications of the Theban Mapping Project).* 2nd ed. Cairo.

Schacht, I. and N. Hansen. 2010. "The Theban Mapping Project: Archaeological and Image Databases." In Leblanc, 305–313.

Sethe, K. 1920. "Die Türteile bnš und ʿrj.t zu Totb. Nav. 125 Schlußrede 28–34." *Zeitschrift für Ägyptische Sprache und Altertumskunde* 67: 115–117.

Spencer, P. J. 1984. *The Egyptian Temple: A Lexicographical Study*. London.

Thomas, E. 1964. "The Four Niches and Amuletic Figures in the Royal Tombs." *Journal of the American Research Center in Egypt* 3: 71–78.

Thomas, E. 1966. *The Royal Necropoleis of Thebes*. Princeton.

Vandersleyen, C. 1975. «Le Sens symbolique des puits funéraires dans l'égypte ancienne.» *CdE* 50: 151–157.

Ventura, R. 1988. "The Largest Project for a Royal Tomb in the Valley of the Kings." *Chronique d'Égypte* 74: 137–156.

Weeks, K. R., ed. (1979). *The Berkeley Map of the Theban Necropolis: Report of the Second Season, 1979*. Berkeley.

Weeks, K. R. 1998. *The Lost Tomb*. New York, London and Cairo.

Weeks, K. R., ed. 2000. *Atlas of the Valley of the Kings* (= Publications of the Theban Mapping Project 3). Rev. study ed. Cairo.

Weeks, K. R., ed. 2001. *The Treasures of the Valley of the Kings: Tombs and Temples of the Theban West Bank in Luxor*. Vercelli and Cairo.

Weeks, K. R. 2001. "Introduction to the Valley of the Kings." In Weeks (2001): 112–123.

Weeks, K. R. 2002. Retrieved from: www.thebanmappingproject.com.

Weeks, K. R. 2005. *The Illustrated Guide to Luxor: Tombs, Temples, and Museums*. Vercelli and Cairo.

Wilkinson, J. G. 1835. *Topography of Thebes and General View of Egypt*. London.

Wilkinson, R. H. 1995. "Symbolic Orientation and Alignment in New Kingdom Royal Tombs." In Wilkinson, 74–81.

Wilkinson, R. H., ed. 1995. *Valley of the Sun Kings: New Explorations in the Tombs of the Pharaohs*. Tucson.

CHAPTER 9

COLLISIONS, ABANDONMENTS, ALTERATIONS, TOMB COMMENCEMENTS/PITS, AND OTHER FEATURES IN THE VALLEY OF THE KINGS

LYLA PINCH-BROCK

THIS chapter[1] discusses three subjects pertinent to the construction of tombs and the general setting of the Eastern Valley of the Kings: collisions, tomb abandonments, architectural alterations, man-made pits and tomb commencements, and new discoveries in the latter category. Other features of the valley, such as ancient walls, shrines, and graffitti are also considered.

COLLISIONS

Instances where masons cutting one tomb inadvertently broke into another.

Examples: KV 10 (Amenmesse); KV 11 (Ramesses III); KV 47 (Siptah); KV 32 (Tia'a); KV 14 (Setnakht); KV 9 (Ramesses V and Ramesses VI); KV 12 (unknown); KV 55 (Amarna Cache/ Akhenaten); KV 6 (Ramesses IX).

The fact that collisions occurred in ancient times during tomb construction suggests which tombs were known in antiquity. It also indicates that a plan of the necropolis was not known. It seems masons did not do "soundings," but rather simply tunneled into areas of good rock. But looking at how KV 9 (Ramesses V and Ramesses VI) and KV 8 (Merenptah) passed over KV 57 (Horemheb), one wonders if the later architects knew there was something below. Masons also tried to avoid the veins of calcite that were found in a number of tombs, including KV 8 and KV 9 (see Theban Mapping Project[2] website for calcite locations). The subject of collisions is well addressed on the TMP website under "tombs in collision" (see Weeks 2003).

KV 10/KV 11

Sometimes collisions can help modern investigators, as Otto Schaden found in the tomb of Amenmesse (KV 10). Schaden entered through the breakthrough into KV 11 (Ramesses III): "With rubble reaching to near the ceiling in C and D chambers, the only immediate access to the pillared hall was through a hole or breech connecting Ramesses III's tomb (KV 11) with the unfinished side chamber (Fa) in KV 10. KV 11 was originally hewn for Ramesses II's father, Setnakht. The tomb was abandoned after hitting the KV 10 side chamber. Ramesses III later adapted KV 11 for his own use. The hole is now covered by a grate" (Schaden 1992).

Corridor D1a of KV 11 was meant to extend into the burial chamber, but the architects changed direction when they found the route collided with KV 10. Strangely, chamber Fa of KV 10, just below, was also abbreviated, suggesting that there was poor rock at this point. Schaden cleared Fa in 1995–1996, but he does not elaborate on the condition of the rock.

KV 47/KV 32

KV 47, the tomb of Siptah, was cleared of flood debris by the Supreme Council of Antiquities in 1992. From 2001 to 2002, the University of Basel reinvestigated the interior of the tomb and cleared the area in front of it, uncovering workmen's huts of the Nineteenth Dynasty. Their investigations included the breakthrough into what was believed to be the tomb of Tia'a (KV 32). "This planning error was the unexpected space J1, replacing the original plan of broad sarcophagus hall" (Jenni 2000). The plan was changed, and the sarcophagus hall was begun behind it, but never completed, apparently interrupted by the death of the king. During excavations in this area, some hidden decoration was found. The team now concludes: "This undecorated tomb, which until now could not be attributed to any possessor, can now, with good reason, be attributed to a queen of the Eighteenth Dynasty: Amenhotep II's wife Tiaa."

KV 9/KV 12

KV 9 was started under the reign of Ramesses V and continued to be constructed under that of Ramesses VI, but when the latter began to lengthen the tomb, the masons ran into KV 12 (owner unknown) at the end of corridor H. The resulting break was carefully plastered over, and the architect changed the plan, lowering the burial chamber in order to bypass the tomb above. The vein of calcite shown on the TMP website plan 7 meters farther on may have played a part in this, preventing further construction in KV 12.

KV 55/KV 6

A brief mention should be made of an anomaly between the east wall of KV 55 (Akhenaten/Amarna Cache) and the niche Bd in KV 6 (Ramesses IX). On the TMP plan (Weeks 2003) it looks like a collision, but in fact it is probably either bad rock or a vein of calcite going through both tombs, not visible in KV 55 because of the plaster covering this area. In KV 6 it has resulted in the abbreviation of the niche Bd, and in KV 55 it caused plans for what would have been the first pillared hall to be abandoned (see "Alterations," below).

ABANDONMENTS

Instances where there is no solid evidence a tomb was ever used for its intended occupant.

Examples: KV 4, KV 3, KV 11, KV 12, KV 18, KV 19, KV 24, KV 25, KV 33, KV 42, KV 49, KV 53, KV 58, KV 61, KV 56, KV 39

Tombs that were cut but apparently never used for their intended occupant can be identified, some with more certainty than others. These include KV 4 (Ramesses XI); KV 3 (a probable son of Ramesses III); KV 12 (originally cut in the Eighteenth Dynasty but enlarged in either the Nineteenth or Twentieth Dynasty, but with no evidence of use, and only sketched decoration); KV 18 (intended for Ramesses X but left unfinished); and KV 19, originally for Twentieth Dynasty prince Sethherkhepeshef, but unfinished and unused by him. The latter was subsequently decorated for prince Montuherkhepeshef, son of Ramesses IX, but apparently not used by him either (Thomas 1969, 151). Also included in this list are KV 24 and KV 25 (two unfinished Eighteenth Dynasty tombs in the Western Valley) and KV 33, which can be attributed to the reign of Thutmose III. KV 42 (Eighteenth Dynasty), which was perhaps cut for the wife of Thutmose III—Meryet-Ra Hatshepsut—contains unfinished sarcophagi and substantial ceramic remains, but nothing that conclusively points to an actual burial. KV 49 (Eighteenth Dynasty, reign of Tutankhamun/Horemheb?) may have been used as an embalming cache, as suggested by remains of whitened store jars and linen. KV 53 and KV 58, although apparently used as caches for material from a late Eighteenth Dynasty royal burial, left no evidence of use for an actual burial. KV 61, according to Elizabeth Thomas (1969, 161), may have been an embalming cache that was extended to become a tomb, although again with no signs of ever having been used. KV 11, undecorated and with no remains of a burial found inside, can also be added to this list.

KV 56

KV 56 was originally excavated by Harold Jones (Davis 1908, 3). It is a small, single-chambered tomb and while it contained no evidence for an actual burial, a minor horde of jewelry inscribed with the names of Tausret, Ramesses II, and Seti II was found packed in the mud that filled its bottom. This also contained bits of a small coffin, leading Cyril Aldred (1963, 176) to conclude that the tomb might have been cut for the burial of a child of Seti II and Tausret. But the mud could have been flood debris, washed in from a nearby tomb, covering a thief's cache. More material was retrieved from KV 56 during a clearance by the Amarna Royal Tombs Project in 2000 (Reeves 1998, season 2001). This consisted of Nineteenth Dynasty gold jewellery—three necklace pendants, a mandrake fruit, and a Hathor-mask amulet. Reeves believes, on the basis of the tomb's architecture and "a number of significant Amarna fragments found close by in 2000," that the jewelry was associated with a secondary phase within the chamber, and that the tomb had actually been cut for the burial of a late-Eighteenth Dynasty queen, purportedly from the Amarna royal family. But other than KV 63, the plan does not fit the other small Amarna period tombs in the area, notably KV 55, 62, and 46.

KV 39

KV 39 could also be an abandoned tomb. The tomb is undecorated. Its position at the foot of three watercourses may have caused it to be abandoned shortly after its construction, perhaps in the Eighteenth Dynasty. Although it has been suggested that it was built for Amenhotep I, it is difficult to confirm from the published reports (Willockx 2010, 60) if the king's burial was actually made there. The tomb was investigated in 1989, and from 1991 to 1994 by Rose (2000), then beginning in 2001, after the Theban flood of 1994, by Buckley and colleagues (2005). Their publication includes a new tomb plan and a valuable assessment of the masons' marks in this undecorated tomb. It also includes an analysis of the materials from Rose's excavation kept in the west bank storehouse—ceramics, human, and botanical remains. The team believes that some of this comes from a high-status burial. But could it be an embalming cache and not an actual burial? They note: "The tomb has three separate sections, which is probably the result of modifications of the original basic design .... the rough construction of the south passage suggests either a design for a cache or an unfinished tomb." They conclude: "The sequence of re-use in the tomb and the identification of material found there with specific burials are still unresolved but this season's work has reinforced the fact that the assemblage of ceramics and other artifacts derive from at least two different periods."

ALTERATIONS

Changes to a tomb as a result of a collision, and/or information derived from masons' marks, tomb plans, or other evidence.

Examples: KV 1, KV 5, KV 6, KV 8, KV 9, KV 10, KV 14, KV 15, and KV 55

Such a high percentage of tombs underwent alterations that it is easier to note exceptions. Certainly most were occupied before completion, as masons' marks often show. (See also alterations mentioned above in "Collisions" and "Abandonments"). Most alterations were probably made to circumvent water entry, bad rock, or veins of calcite. In the tomb of Merenptah (KV 8), the sarcophagus must have presented difficulties, as it was necessary to remove the jambs of gates B to H. to make the descent. Parts of these jambs were found by Howard Carter in debris near the tomb (Carter 1920, 18).

In KV 1 (Ramesses II), the second corridor was converted into a burial chamber. This may also have been done because the rock in the tomb is badly cracked, especially on the ceiling. The general length of the tomb seems to have been abbreviated. According to the TMP website (Weeks 2003): "The original plan of the tomb was altered after the death of the king, and the chamber which would have been pillared chamber F was used for burial chamber J. Two plans of the tomb are known: a plan of the whole tomb drawn on a papyrus now in the Turin Museum (Cat. 1885), and a sketch of the doorway of the tomb on an ostracon found in the rubble at the entrance." KV 5, according to the website, "may originally have been a Dynasty 18 tomb (consisting of chambers 1, 2, and part of 3) usurped by Ramesses II as the burial place for several of his principal sons." In KV 6, "a corridor following descent F was enlarged to be used as the burial chamber." In KV 9, "the jambs of gate B through gate F were originally inscribed for Ramesses V but were re-carved by Ramesses VI. KV 10 was originally decorated for Amenmesse, but subsequently re-decorated for Takhat and Baketwerel. In KV 14 as in Merenptah, and possibly for the same reason . . . the thickness of gates before the first burial chamber J1 were cut back. Names and images were altered from Tausret to Setnakht and from Siptah to Seti II." In KV 15, "a rectangular recess, cut at some later date into the beginning of the first corridor's left wall, damaged the raised relief figure of the king."

KV 55

KV 55, the tomb of Akhenaten, but also known as, "the Amarna cache," contains many masons' marks indicating planned alterations to this small tomb (see Figure 9.1). Part of the tomb's plan, painted on a small ostracon, was found during a clearance in 1993 (Pinch-Brock 1997). The ostracon may represent the corridor and the cracked north jamb of the burial chamber entrance (originally done in red, corrected in black)—showing divisions and subdivisions. The small ticks may represent cubits. There were red sight marks in the corridor about 2.7 meters apart; there were red lines on the north stairwell wall—probably directions for recutting the entrance. In the burial chamber, numerous

FIGURE 9.1 Photo of the masons' marks on the east wall of the burial chamber in KV 55, taken in 1992 during re-excavation of the tomb.

[Photograph by L. P. Brock.]

black strokes, about a meter in length and a cubit apart, were painted on the south part of the east and west walls. These may be indications either for removal of rock or for the cutting of columns, as in the tomb of Ramesses VI (KV 9). Two red *nefers*—masons' marks indicating "end" or "level"—one halfway under the plaster, were painted on the north end of the east wall, about halfway up; below there appears to be the hieroglyph for "height," a man with raised arms.

KV 55 was one of three similar tombs possibly planned to be much larger; KV55, KV 46, and KV 62 are all variations on a theme. Figure 9.2 shows that the floor of KV 55 might have been lowered to allow the entry of shrine parts found by Theodore Davis in 1907 (Davis 1910, 1). If the KV 62 plan is swung around counterclockwise (Reeves 1997, 70), Ja becomes the canopic niche in KV 55, and the annex would have been precisely where a preliminary cutting in the wall in KV 55 is visible.

COMMENCEMENTS/PITS

A pit or cutting in the rock, suggesting by location, size, or filling, that it is man-made.

Examples: KV 54 and KV 59; KV B, C, E, F, G, H, L, M, N, O, P, Q, R, S, and T; and cache near KV 8

This section is confined to the "'Tomb-commencements' and Pits" published by Nicholas Reeves and Richard Wilkinson (1996, 207) and only those in the Valley

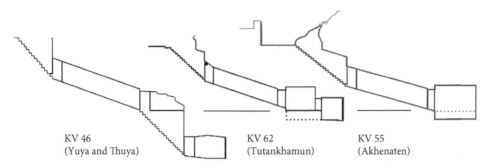

FIGURE 9.2 Comparison of plans of three Amarna period tombs in the Valley of the Kings.
[Computerized illustration by Lyla Pinch-Brock, based on plans from the Theban Mapping Project.]

of the Kings. There seems to be only one map of these pits readily available (Reeves 1990, 173).

The published entries bear closer investigation—if they can be found. Unfortunately, some digging in the Valley of the Kings in recent years may have obscured or destroyed some of these pits, which were often vaguely defined at best. In 1969 Thomas mentioned nineteen pit tombs and at least four others (KV H–K; I, J, and K being located in the Western Valley). She wrote that small pits were probably a regular part of the Theban necropolis, used as caches for embalming materials, or possibly infant burials. Once they were robbed, or the materials were displaced, the pits may later have been "converted into true pit tombs." As examples she cites KV 29, 61, 50, and 52 (Thomas 1969, 156, 164).

I conclude that most pits can be divided into two categories: workmen's pits (workmen's materials) and pits containing, or meant to contain, embalming materials.

Workmen's Pits

The following are probably workmen's pits, as their contents seem to be related to tomb construction, that is, cutting tools and provisions for the workmen. It has been suggested that these pits were carefully covered up to hide evidence of the location of the tomb (Reeves and Wilkinson 1996, 187) or even to deter animals. Most were found very near tombs.

KV P, KV Q, and KV R were discovered by Harold Jones (Jones and Burton 1879). The contents were burnt wood, potsherds, flint flakes, straw, and bone. Similar material was found in KV S (outside KV 47), KV T (near KV 36), and apparently outside KV 55. The latter is cited as KV C, but this is the cache of jars; perhaps there was also a pit of workmen's materials. The burnt pits were mentioned by Jones *reis* (Reeves 1990, 175).

KV D and E were discovered by Davis and Ayrton during excavations in the watercourses before the discovery of KV 47 (Siptah) (Davis 1908, 3, n.1). They contained the same burnt materials listed above.

Embalming Pits/Caches

The presence of embalming pits/embalming deposits in or near tombs in the Valley of the Kings has recently been discussed by Dylan Bickerstaff (2007), Marianne Eaton-Krauss (2008), and Susan Allen (2000).

Embalming materials may be identified as bags of natron, dishes (usually broken), and strips of linen stuffed into large jars and sealed. The jars are usually of the tall, waisted, white-painted variety, but note that the KV C jars were reused Canaanite wine jars (Pinch-Brock 2013), and the thirteen found by Carter near KV 8 in the watercourse south of the tomb were made of alabaster and carried the names of Ramesses II and Merenptah (Carter 1920, 18).

Thomas suggests that KV C–E and pits H–J/K (J/K are in the Western Valley) qualify as embalming pits (1969, 163). Reeves mentions three caches of embalming material (KV 54, KV C, and KV P, none in a tomb) (1990, 174, 172). It seems at least three pits of embalming materials may be firmly identified in the VOK: KV54 (Tutankhamun), the cache of jars associated with the KV 55 (Reeves's KV C), and the KV 8 cache of alabaster jars. To these might now be added KV 63, which is possibly the commencement for a larger tomb and while it contained no human remains, material associated with a burial was found, including a substantial amount of embalming materials (Schaden 2007).

As the aforementioned authors point out, while it is more usual from a magico-religious point of view for embalming materials to be buried with the deceased, their removal to a nearby pit may have occurred for one of two reasons. (A) It may have been done intentionally, to fill the entrance to the tomb with rubble as a deterrent against tomb-robbing (e.g., Allen's [2000] theory about KV 62), which seems to have been done in both KV 55 and KV 62. In KV 55 the height of the debris is still visible on the walls of the corridor. (B) In the case of the Ramesses XI, Ramesses II, and Merenptah embalming cache materials, perhaps these were displaced when the royal burials were dismantled during the late Twenty-first Dynasty.

KV B

KV B was found by Davis and Ayrton, 325 meters south of the tomb of Thutmosis IV (KV 43) near the cliffs. "We removed our work to the extreme east of the valley, slightly to the south of the tomb of Thothmes IV. . . . Here Ayrton dug up the slope to the face of the cliffs, finding nothing except the unfinished entrance to a tomb which had barely been begun" (Davis 1908, 6). Apparently it is no longer visible. Thomas dates the tomb to the reign of Thutmosis IV (1969, 149).

KV C

This pit, which cannot be precisely located, other than that it was found south of the tomb of Ramesses IX and on the western face of the mound, contained "several jars of the 20th Dynasty type," according to Ayrton (1910, 7). Only two of the jars now remain, given to the Metropolitan Museum of Art by Davis and subsequently deaccessioned to the Oriental Institute of the University of Chicago. The jars do indeed seem to be associated with nearby KV 6 (Ramesses IX), because the "*nefer*" decoration on one pot dates to that period (Pinch-Brock 2013). Reeves believes the contents of these jars were not recorded: The jars might have been broken open and their contents discarded for entertainment during the visit of Sir Elwyn Gorst (Pinch-Brock 1999, 223). When I saw the jars at the University of Chicago, their necks were, in fact, broken. Lindon-Smith, the artist working for Davis during the excavation of KV 55, wrote that, among the material that Davis sent off to the MMA from his storehouse in the Western Valley were; "broken jars and an unbroken one containing the entrails of the body not preserved in a canopic jar" (1956, 128). There are no viscera in the canopic jars from KV 55, only indentations in the unguent. The origin of the viscera mentioned by Lindon-Smith remains puzzling.

When the old resthouse in the Valley of the Kings was torn down, a feature came to light just south of KV 55, which might be KV C: Ayrton described it as "a cut face with squared corners on either side, showing that a tomb had at least been begun on this spot" (1910, 7). It appears to be the commencement for a tomb measuring approximately 2.3 m by 3.78 m by 2.4 m deep (Pinch-Brock 1999). Now it is almost completely obscured by the new rest house.

KV D, KV E

Two of three tomb commencements were found by Ayrton in 1907 while excavating his way down the valley before he found KV C (the third) and then KV 55 (Thomas 1969, 149). There is no description other than that the cuttings were in the watercourse, and the masons probably concluded that they were vulnerable to flooding and abandoned their work. According to Thomas, "Their location, form and extent would in fact indicate whether they were embalming caches" (1969, 149). There is no mention of these pits during the Hawass excavations in the area beginning in November 2007, although he did re-examine KV C (Hawass 2007), believing it was an actual tomb.

KV F

Found by Carter in 1921 at the base of a sheer cliff (see detail on map I/J 22-55 from Carter MSS I.G.51, on the Griffith Institute website, (http://www.griffith.ox.ac.uk.). KV F is well documented on the TMP website as quoted below. Its measurements are 1.34 m by 1.34 m by 2.16 m deep. Its owner is unknown.

> KV F is located in the south branch off the southwest *wadi*. Carter noted this rectangular tomb commencement in the rear of the cleft forming the bottom of the

waterfall channel in which KV 34 is cut. No details are given as to whether it was a shaft or stairwell. To the west, Carter found four foundation deposit pits outlining a square. One of the deposits was intact and contained objects with the name of Thutmes III. Their proximity to KV F, led Carter to believe that they were associated with that abandoned commencement. Due to the presence of nearby foundation deposits bearing the name of Thutmes III as well as its position beneath the tomb made for that king, Carter believed it was an abandoned commencement for that same king's tomb. However, others such as Thomas feel that the foundation deposits are to be associated with KV 34 and not with KV F. This site was used during the following period(s): New Kingdom, Dynasty 18, *temp* Thutmes III (dated according to proximity to KV 34). The tomb is inaccessible and filled with debris.

(Weeks 2003)

At the time Thomas was writing, "F" was still detectible as a "slight depression." See also her extensive comments on this pit (Thomas 1969, 140). No further information from the University of Basel's clearance of this area is available (Bickel 2009, season 2013).

KV G

As noted by Thomas: "Just off the path to the south, right, 10–15 m east of KV 18 and in the first low rise on the way to 19, 20 and 43, a potential door about 180 cm wide is well cut at the top and sides for its visible height of perhaps 150 cm; its depth is 100 cm at most. It is called G, but the purpose may have been other than a tomb, possibly a niche to serve as shrine like that above the entrance of KV 37, for [workmen's] huts lie a few meters further east"(1969, 149). KV G is shown on Reeves's map of pit tombs.

KV H

According to Thomas, "KV H represents explorations a few meters east of KV 39, where one pit or possibly two may have been discovered and almost entirely refilled" (1969, 156). There is no mention of the discoverer, but it could have been Loret or Micarios and Andraos around 1900 (Thomas 1969, 98; Willockx 2010, 61). Thomas believes one pit might have been an embalming cache like KV 54—a large quantity of embalming materials was found in the tomb proper.

There was no specific mention of these pits during excavations by Rose, although the area outside was covered by 2 meters of debris. A number of items were found in these strata, which could be part of an embalming cache: ceramics, bones, and a limestone bowl (Rose 2000). The pit may be seen in the Willockx photo above the opening of KV 39 (Willockx 2010, 73).

KV L–KV M

According to Reeves, pits KV L–T were not known to Thomas at the time of her survey. Jones noted KV L–M as discovered in 1898 by Loret (Reeves and Wilkinson 1996, 207) on the north side of the *wadi* leading to the tomb of Amenhotep II (KV 35). They contained materials from that tomb (Reeves 1990, 174).

KV N

KV N, on the west side of the tourist path south of KV 53, was a meter-square pit, five feet deep, discovered by Jones on December 21, 1908 (Reeves 1990, 174).

KV O

This pit was found by Jones in 1909 and described as an "unfinished pit with stone wall built around." It was possibly a workman's hut; a funerary cone with the name of Montuemhet (TT 34) was found close by (Reeves 1990, 174).

KV P, Q, R

These three pits were noted by Jones; P and Q were found on December 12 and 13, 1909, respectively. Both were undisturbed. They contained ashes, broken ceramics, flints, twigs, straw, and burnt bones. Were they workmen's pits? (See comments above.) No specific discovery date was noted for KV R, simply "December, 1909." The pits had the same contents: "burnt Rubbish" (Reeves 1990, 175).

KV S

This pit was found before the discovery of KV 47 (Siptah) by Ayrton, working for Davis in 1908. (Ayrton mentions finding two or three pits of this type.) It was filled with workmen's debris. Was this Thomas's KV D/E? (Reeves and Wilkinson 1996, 207; Reeves 1990, 175). The area where KV S was found is within the concession of the University of Basel Mission, but there is no mention of any rediscovery of this pit.

KV T

Is this another pit discovered by Loret? It was marked on Jones and Burton's sketch-map, entries for December 15–27, 1909 (Reeves 1990, 176). It is located opposite the tomb of

Siptah (KV 47), an area recently cleared by the University of Basel, where they found workmen's huts (Jenni 2000).

KV 54

This pit has attracted attention ever since its discovery in December 1907 by Ayrton, working for Davis (Davis 1912). The cache consists of a single, shallow, square-cut pit, 1.17 m by 1.17 m by 1.69 m deep (Weeks 2003). It was associated with Tutankhamun, whose burial Davis thought it was. When found, about 110 meters southeast of what was later known as KV 62 (Tutankhamun), the pit was covered with chippings from the ancient excavation of the tomb of Ramesses VI. It contained embalming materials, clothing, faunal and botanical material, and ceramics, mostly packed into twelve to fifteen large, white-painted jars. Since only the whole vessels were removed and sent to the Metropolitan Museum of Art, presumably this meant broken material was left behind (but see photo [Bickerstaff 2007, 47] showing an empty pit). Davis thought KV 54 was an actual tomb, but much later Winlock (1944) proved it was the remains of a funerary feast for Tutankhamun. The pit was apparently still visible in 1969 (Thomas 1969, 163). In 1999 the University of Basel re-excavated it (Jenni 2000); they "found south of KV 54—not in the pit—in modern disturbed debris, fragments of two natron bags (if they belonged to the original fill is hard to say but it cannot be excluded). KV 54 was filled with modern rubble containing different objects not belonging to the original filling" (Adreas Dorn, personal communication 2012).

Two scholars have recently added some information to the history of KV 54. Reeves (1983) suggested that a small cartonnage mummy mask, considered to be part of this cache, actually came from another Davis excavation—KV 51. It was mixed up with the small gilded mask from the *foeti* in the tomb of Tutankhamun, found in one of the KV 54 jars (now in the Cairo Museum). Allen (2000) has done an analysis of the material found in the corridor of KV 62 and has concluded that the KV 54 embalming materials and jars were originally placed in the entrance to that tomb. They were subsequently moved to KV 54 after the first tomb robbery, and the corridor was filled with debris by necropolis officials as a deterrent.

KV 59

The history of this small pit tomb, owner unknown, is well chronicled by Campbell (2012, 159, 160). The TMP website gives the size of this tomb as roughly 2 m by 2 m by 3 m deep, located at the foot of the cliffs, in the south branch of the southwest *wadi* near the tomb of Thutmose III (Weeks 2003). It was known to Burton, Lefebure, and Carter, and thus open to view until at least 1921, when Carter apparently examined and numbered it (Thomas 1969, 141), although exactly when is not clear. Preys, on the basis of the tomb's dimensions and location, believed it could be an important tomb (2011). It was dated to *temp.* Thutmes III on the basis of its proximity to tombs of the same era (Weeks

2003), and apparently now there is confirmation of this: the tomb was re-excavated by the University of Basel in 2011 (Bickel 2009). It turned out to be a shaft with a small room at the bottom, completely empty except for a few fragments of New Kingdom ceramics.

Recently Discovered and Unnumbered Pits and Commencements

An unfinished tomb cutting has been noted by Brock (personal communication 2012) located at the end of the *wadi* running SW from KV 1. The upper corners of the cutting are visible. The feature has not been investigated or excavated (see Figure 9.3).

An embalming cache was found by Carter near KV 8 (Carter 1920, 18, with photo): "A cache comprising thirteen alabaster vases of Ramesses II and Merenptah—these were placed side by side in one group, covered with stones, as if carefully buried. They afterwards were much crushed by weight of rubbish accumulated above." There is no mention of the contents. This cache is a little difficult to pinpoint, since Carter's map

FIGURE 9.3 Tomb cutting at the end of the *wadi* running southwest from KV 1 in the Valley of the Kings, discovered recently by E. C. Brock.

[Photograph by E. C. Brock]

is not precise. "West end of lateral valley, near the entrance to the tomb of Merenptah" seems the closest description.

Carter also mentions another pit, left unnumbered, at the "extreme end of Thothmes III valley, below rift containing king's tomb" (1921). There he found the foundation deposit for the tomb of Thutmose III, a hole, and "near this a commencement for a tomb." On his map the latter seems to be of a considerable size. It has yet to be investigated by the University of Basel which has the concession for the area. However, while investigating the terrain to the north of it, the team found a new feature near KV 40, which they have dubbed "KV 40b." (See map 2011 excavations, Bickel 2009.)

OTHER FEATURES

Features in the Valley of the Kings not corresponding to any of the aforementioned.

Examples: shrines, graffiti, walls

Walls

The "Five Walls"

The "Five Walls," mentioned in the Turin Strike Papyrus, were purportedly located somewhere near the workmen's village of Deir el-Medina. It is not known whether these "walls" were real walls or guard posts, or even where they were located. There is considerable debate about these points in the articles cited in this chapter (Dorn 2009; Frandsen 1989, Ventura 1986). The subject is timely because Reeves's Amarna Royal Tombs Project claims to have located one of the "walls" near KV 57:

> Here, running across the Valley, ARTP encountered a solid limestone bluff, swinging round at the north to give restricted access to the Valley beyond. It was a natural checkpoint, protected by guards whose water jars and hearth we uncovered . . . situated between the tombs of Horemheb (KV57) and Ramesses III (KV11). We believe it is very likely one of the mysterious "five walls" of the Valley. If the identification is correct, then we may assume that further "walls" of the same type, dividing the interior of the Valley into easily patrolled sectors, remain to be uncovered at key points beneath the tourist pathways. The principal of these "walls" has in fact long been known: the so-called "gate" at the entrance to the Valley, which was demolished many years ago to facilitate public access to the site.
>
> (Reeves 1998)

Ancient Flood-Protection Walls

A few ancient flood-protection walls have been noted: On February 17, 1920, Carter "investigated canyon above Thutmose III where there were many boulders artificially placed there"[Carter 1920, 16, and see photos, Griffith Institute website]. These boulders and debris, from an excavation of a tomb of early date, are very puzzling. Possibly they may comprise the debris from tomb No. 39 at the head of the upper valley—hidden like that of the tomb of Amenhetep I. (The ground above around the edges of the canyon still requires exploration.) It is now believed by local archaeologists that these boulders may constitute the remains of an ancient flood-protection barrier.

Channels with walls were found by Hawass during his excavations behind the tomb of Merenptah in 2007: "In the cliffs behind the tomb we discovered channels that the ancient Egyptians dug to redirect the "tears of the gods," the flood, in order to preserve the tombs" (Hawass, 2007, with good photo).

John Rutherford and his team, investigating ancient flood-protection installations in the valley, found some channels as well, but unfortunately the locations are not mentioned in their article on the subject (McLane et al. 2003).

Graffiti

Graffiti may also be considered a "feature" of the Valley of the Kings, as it dots the tombs, their walls, and the hills and *wadis* all around. The largest survey done so far, *Graffiti de la Montagne Thebaine*, was begun by Černý in 1969 (Černý 1969). Since then, other researchers, notably Lukaszewicz (who worked mainly in KV 9), Cruz-Uribe, and Vincent (unpublished) have also carried out surveys, mainly looking in the tombs and on their exterior walls, focusing on Demotic graffiti. Lukaszewicz continued his survey of Greek and Latin graffiti in the valley from 2010 and 2013 (Lukaszewicz 1995, 1999, 2010a, 2010b).

Sanctuaries/Shrines

There are at least two recently reported features in the Valley of the Kings that might qualify as sanctuaries or places for votive offerings. The first is a cutting in the rock face above the entrance of KV 37 on the left (east) side of the path up to the modern stairs leading up to the entrance to the tomb of Thutmosis III (KV 34) and KV 33 (owner unknown), an area currently being investigated by the University of Basel. The UB website has two photos and a brief report (season 2010, figs. 10, 11; Bickel 2009). It appears to be about 40 cm by 20 cm by 50 cm in size. According to Bickel, this feature was already mentioned in the reports of early excavators, and as a result of being quite visible, it has suffered from casual vandalism. There are traces of painted plaster left on the back and on one of the sides in the niche, apparently indicating a seated figure wearing the Hathor crown. The niche may have been some sort of shrine, perhaps for Hathor, and date to either the Nineteenth or Twentieth Dynasty (Weeks 2003, sheet 52/70, n.1). There is also a group of square cuttings on either side of the modern steps leading up to KV 34 and in the passageway at the top. According to E. C. Brock, who is studying post-Amarna royal sarcophagi, these may have been beam emplacements used to raise the sarcophagus up to the tomb from the valley path below (Brock, personal communication 2012).

The second, possibly votive, feature was found in 2002 by the Amarna Royal Tombs Project between the tomb of Ramesses III (KV11) and the tomb of Horemheb (KV57) beneath the modern tourist path, ". . . a small, rock-cut shrine cut into this natural 'wall': Amun and Horus in the upper register, Atum, Isis, Meretseger and Seth in the lower. And within the shrine—undisturbed for thirty centuries—a votive stela still remained *in situ*, painted in relief decoration with a scene showing a Ramesside official in adoration before Meretseger, the serpent goddess of the Theban mountain" (Reeves 1998, season 2002).

NOTES

1. I would like to acknowledge the help of the following for providing me with information for this chapter: Ted Brock, David Aston, Robert Demarée, Susanne Bickel, Andreas Dorn, Steve Cross, Richard Wilkinson, Roger Sharp, and Catharine Roehrig.
2. Hereinafter referred to as TMP.

BIBLIOGRAPHY

Aldred, C. P. 1963. "Valley Tomb No 56 at Thebes." *Journal of Egyptian Archaeology* 49: 176–178.

Allen, S. 2000. "Tutankhamun's Embalming Cache Re-considered." In *Egyptology at the Dawn of the Twenty-first Century: Proceedings of the Eighth International Congress of Egyptologists*, edited by Z. Hawass and L. P. Brock, 23–29. Cairo.

Ayrton, E. R. 1910. "The Excavation of the Tomb of Queen Tiyi." In *The Tomb of Queen Tiyi*, edited by T. M. Davis et al., 7–10. London.

Bickel, S. 2009. Reports of the University of Basel Valley of the Kings Expedition, 2009–2013. http://aegyptologie.unibas.ch/forschung/projekte/university-of-basel-kings-valley-project/report-2010/.

Bickerstaff, D. 2007. "Embalming Caches in the Valley of the Kings." *Kmt* 18: 46–53.

Brock, E. C. 1996. "Clearance around the Tombs of Sety I and Ramesses I for Contractors C. C. Johnson and Malhorta." Unpublished manuscript.

Buckley, I. M, P. Buckley, and A. Cooke. 2005. "Fieldwork in Theban Tomb KV 39: the 2002 Season." *Journal of Egyptian Archaeology* 91: 71–82.

Campbell, A. R. 2012. "Forgotten Sepulchers: The Uninscribed Tombs in the Valley of the Kings in Luxor, Egypt." MA thesis, University of Montana.

Carter, H. 1920. "Carter Excavations, 3rd Season: Notebook E." Griffith Institute. http://www.griffith.ox.ac.uk.

Carter, H. 1921. "Carter Excavations, 4th Excavation Season: Notebook E." Griffith Institute. http://www.griffith.ox.ac.uk.

Černý, J., Ch. Desroches-Noblecourt, M. Kurz, et al. 1969. *Graffiti of the Theban Hills*. Vols. I–IV. Cairo.

Cross, S. W. 2008. "The Hydrology of the Valley of the Kings." *Journal of Egyptian Archaeology* 94: 303–310.

Danforth, R., ed. 2010. *Preserving Egypt's Cultural Heritage: The Conservation Work of the American Research Center in Egypt, 1995–2005.* San Antonio.

Davis, T. M., G. Maspero, G. Daressy, and L. Crane. 1912. *The Tombs of Haremhabi and Touatânkhamanou.* London.

Davis, T. M., G. Maspero, G. E. Smith, E. R. Ayrton, G. Daressy, and E. H. Jones. 1908. *The Tomb of Siphtah, the Gold Tomb and the Monkey Tomb.* London.

Davis, T. M., G. Maspero, G. E. Smith, E. R. Ayrton, G. Daressy, and E. H. Jones. 1910. *The Tomb of Queen Tiyi.* London.

Dorn, A. 2009. "Die Lokalisation der 5 Mauern/Wachposten (tẏ 5 jnb.t/nẏ jnb.wt/tẏ jnb." *Journal of Egyptian Archaeology* 95: 263–268.

Eaton-Krauss, M. 2008. "Embalming Caches." *Journal of Egyptian Archaeology* 94: 288–292.

Ertman, E. L., R. Wilson, and O. Schaden. 2006. "Unraveling the Mysteries of KV 63." *KMT* 17 (3): 18–27.

Frandsen, P. J. 1989. "A Word for 'Causeway' and the Location of 'the Five Walls." *Journal of Egyptian Archaeology* 75: 113–123.

Hawass, Z. 2007. Excavations in the Valley of the Kings. http://voices.nationalgeographic. com/2009/04/06/valley_of_the_kings_egypt/.

Hawass, Z., and L. P. Brock, eds. 2000. *Egyptology at the Dawn of the Twenty-first Century: Proceedings of the Eighth International Congress of Egyptologists.* Cairo.

Hoffmeier, J., ed. 2013. *Excavations in North Sinai: Tell el-Borg I.* Winona Lake.

Jenni, H. 2000. Excavations of the University of Basel Mission, Tombs of Siptah, Ramesses X, and Environs. https://aegyptologie.unibas.ch/forschung/projekte/university-of-basel-kings-valley-project/.

Jones, E. H., and H. Burton. 1879. *Tombs of the Kings Excavation Journal.* New York.

Jones, M. 2010. "Protective Walls in the Valley of the Kings." In *Preserving Egypt's Cultural Heritage: The Conservation Work of the American Research Center in Egypt, 1995–2005,* edited by R. Danforth, 59–62. San Antonio.

Lembke, K., M. Minas-Nerpel, and S. Pfeiffer, eds. 2010. *Tradition and Transformation: Egypt under Roman Rule.* Leiden and Boston.

Lindon-Smith, J. 1956. *Tombs, Temples and Ancient Art.* Norman, OK.

Lukaszewicz, A. 1995. "Memnon, King of Egypt." *Journal of Juristic Papyrology* 25: 131–146.

Lukaszewicz, A. 1999. "Valley of the Kings: Epigraphical Survey in the Tomb of VI (KV 9)." *Polish Archaeology in the Mediterranean XI, Reports 2000:* 191–194.

Lukaszewicz, A. 2010a. "Autour du tombeau de Memnon." In *L'organisation matérielle des cultes dans l'antiquité,* edited by B. Anagnostou-Canas, 87–92. Paris.

Lukaszewicz, A. 2010b. "Memnon, His Ancient Visitors and Some Related Problems." In *Tradition and Transformation: Egypt under Roman Rule,* edited by K. Lembke et al., 255–263. Leiden and Boston.

McLane, J. R., A. J. Wust, B. Porter, and J. Rutherford. 2003. "Flash-Flood Impacts and Protection Measures in the Valley of the Kings." *Arizona Technical Bulletin* 1 (34): 37–45.

Philips, J., ed. 1997. *Studies in Honour of Martha Rhodes Bell 1.* San Antonio, TX.

Pinch Brock, L. 1995. "Theodore Davis and the Rediscovery of KV 55." In *Valley of the Sun Kings: New Explorations in the Tombs of the Pharaohs,* edited by R. H. Wilkinson, 34–42. Tucson, AZ.

Pinch Brock, L. 1997. "The Final Clearance of KV 55." In *Studies in Honour of Martha Rhodes Bell 1,* edited by J. Philips, 121–136. San Antonio, TX.

Pinch Brock, L. 1999. "The Real Location of KV 'C'?" *Journal of Egyptian Archaeology* 85: 223–226.

Pinch Brock, L. 2014. "Red-painted Nefer Jars and the Example from Tell el-Borg." In *Excavations in North Sinai: Tell el-Borg I*, edited by J. Hoffmeier, 506–509, Winona Lake.

Preys, R. 2011. "Les tombes non-royales de la Vallée des Rois." *Studien zur Altagyptischen Kultur* 40: 315–338.

Reeves, N. 1983. "On the Miniature Mask from the Tut`ankhamun Embalming Cache." *Bulletin, Societe d`Egyptologie Geneve* 8: 81–83.

Reeves, N. 1990. *Valley of the Kings: The Decline of a Royal Necropolis.* London.

Reeves, N. 1997. *The Complete Tutankhamun.* London.

Reeves, N. 1998. Amarna Royal Tombs Project, 1998–2002. http://www.nicholasreeves.com/item.aspx?category=Archaeology&id=152.

Reeves, N., and R. H. Wilkinson. 1996. *The Complete Valley of the Kings: Tombs and Treasures of Egypt's Greatest Pharaohs.* London.

Romer, J. 1981. *Valley of the Kings.* New York.

Rose, J. 2000. *Tomb KV 39 in the Valley of the Kings: A Double Archaeological Enigma.* Bristol.

Schaden, O. 1992. Amenmesse Project. http://www.kv-10.com/.

Schaden, O. 2007. "KV 63: An Update. The Final Stages of Clearances." *Kmt* 18 (1): 16–25.

Thomas, E. 1969. *The Royal Necropoleis of Thebes.* Princeton, NJ.

Ventura, R. 1986. *Living in a City of the Dead: A Selection of Topographical and Administrative Terms in the Documents of the Theban Necropolis.* Schweiz and Gottingen.

Weeks, K. 2000. *Atlas of the Valley of the Kings.* Cairo.

Weeks, K. 2003. Theban Mapping Project. http://www.thebanmappingproject.com/.

Wilkinson, R. H., ed. 1995. *Valley of the Sun Kings: New Explorations in the Tombs of the Pharaohs.* Tucson, AZ.

Willockx, S. 2010. "Three Tombs Attributed to Amenhotep I; K93.11, AN B and KV39." http://www.egyptology.nl/3TA1.pdf.

Winlock, H. E. 1944. *Materials Used at the Embalming of King Tut-Ankh-Amun.* New York.

PART V

ROYAL TOMB
DECORATION

CHAPTER 10

THE TECHNOLOGY OF ROYAL TOMB DECORATION

STEPHEN RICKERBY AND LORI WONG

THE decoration of the tombs in the Valley of the Kings fulfilled a significant religious role during the New Kingdom, by ensuring rebirth and eternal life for their royal occupants. The tomb was a meeting place of both physical and metaphysical worlds, in which painting and relief carving not only functioned as religious imagery, but were also considered to possess magical animating powers (Dodson and Ikram 2008, 13–22). An intimate relationship between the physical decoration and its empowering force in the world beyond imbued tomb technology. Understanding how tombs were decorated to render them effective houses of eternity is therefore of fundamental importance.

More than twenty royal tombs survive with decoration. Many of these are large, and decoration is extensive and well preserved. Insights of how decoration of tomb interiors were planned and executed are richly embedded in the physical record, and knowledge of workshop practice and the division of artisanal tasks within tombs has been retrieved from original sources (Ĉerný 1973; Bogoslovsky 1980, 89–111). However, although there is considerable scientific analysis of Egyptian paintings generally, very little exists for tombs in the Valley of the Kings. In the literature, an emphasis has been placed instead on textual and iconographic interpretations of decoration. Descriptions of original materials and their methods of application are often inaccurate, and changes in technology over time—associated with developments in tomb plans and their iconography—have been overlooked.

INFLUENCES ON ROYAL TOMB DECORATION

A number of circumstances specifically influenced technological developments in the kings' tombs, where defining differences relate to issues of resources, both natural and human.

The most important natural resource is the geology of the valley. The generally excellent quality of the limestone rock enabled a majority of tombs to be cut with extraordinary precision, and, from the late Eighteenth Dynasty, contributed to virtuosic relief carving; on this substrate too, plastering was usually applied and carved with relative ease. Available human resources associated with ambitious tomb plans were the other driving influence, promoting tomb construction and decoration on an unprecedented scale over a period of almost 500 years, from the Eighteenth to the Twentieth Dynasties.

Tombs such as those of Seti I and Merenptah demonstrate lavish expenditure, labor availability and organization, materials procurement, and technology. But the employment of large teams of craftsmen, whose multiple tasks were divided among different parts of a tomb, led to divergent practice. Extensive decorative programs, and those that spanned long reigns, were interrupted by stoppages caused by labor and funding problems. A short reign or sudden death of a tomb's owner imposed different problems, resulting in hasty completion. Periods of political crisis or economic decline also curtailed the extent and standard of decoration in several tombs (Bierbrier 1982, 27, 41, 43, 50).

Tomb decoration is therefore characterized by a number of trends: continuity and conservatism, development and innovation, and technical shortcuts in response to constrained circumstances. To appreciate this fully requires a consideration of all the materials and technological procedures that contribute to a tomb interior, beginning with the rock support. In addition, technical outcomes must also be related to the diverse circumstances and events associated with royal dictate and the collective work of the original craftsmen.

ROCK SUPPORT: INFLUENCE ON INTERIOR DECORATION

Methods of utilizing the rock in tomb decoration in the Valley of the Kings evolved gradually. Awareness and use of its potential coincided with developing trends in tomb architecture and with increasingly elaborate programs of funerary iconography.

Thutmose I's tomb, probably the earliest in the valley, seems not to have received much direct decoration. In its burial chamber, funerary texts were instead inscribed on limestone blocks, which were probably meant to line its rock walls (Reeves and Wilkinson 1996, 92–93). Thutmose III's tomb is the first surviving royal tomb to preserve substantial applied decoration, most famously in the antechamber and burial chamber, with their scroll-like depictions of the Amduat and the Litany of Re (Roehrig 2006). But other parts of its interior intentionally appear to have been left roughly cut and undecorated, as in Thutmose I's tomb.

A significant change occurs in the tombs of Thutmose III's successors. Their more complex interiors were cut with greater regularity, although areas of decoration remained localized to only certain chambers, since tomb iconography was still at an early stage of development (Reeves and Wilkinson 1996, 35–37). But an absence of painted decoration in parts of these tombs does not necessarily denote their unfinished state. In the carefully cut entrance corridor of Amenhotep III's tomb, for example, black dots were painted in grid-like intervals directly on the rock, to guide cutting back a further few millimeters to provide a smoother finish. In its decorated chambers, however, the rock walls were left in a rougher state, in order to receive plaster and painting. In some parts of this tomb, therefore, finely cut but undecorated walls were originally regarded as a finished treatment as much as those with painting.

This type of rock working was probably reserved for conspicuous parts of tombs, in particular entrance corridors. Being a time-consuming task, it was frequently left incomplete. This was the case in the tombs of Tutankhamun and Aye, whose corridors were exquisitely cut, although neither was quite finished. Both these tombs appear to have been completed hastily, due to the relatively short reign of both occupants (Dodson and Ikram 2008, 245–246; Wong et al. 2012, S322–S330). Nevertheless, the efforts made in cutting their corridors indicate a significant allocation of resources for "finishing" areas in which painting was probably never planned.

A distinction between painted and unpainted areas was most likely also intended in Horemheb's tomb, although outcomes here were very different. This was the first royal tomb to combine painting with relief, which, however, was completed only in two of its chambers, and was left incomplete in the burial chamber (Hornung 1971). Since tomb iconography was still quite limited at this date, it is unlikely that decoration was planned for the tomb's stairways and entrance corridors, where the rock walls were left roughly hewn. But these were almost certainly meant to be finely cut, as in Tutankhamun's and Aye's tombs; the introduction of relief carving as a new technical endeavor seems to have taken precedence over their completion.

Such differences over how to utilize the rock substrate for decoration and finishing persist in the royal tombs. Advantages offered by the rock were reflected in greater regularity of tomb interiors, and, for a time, in a preference for leaving some corridors or rooms with exposed rock walls. This fashion declined with the onset of more extensive iconographical programs. But regard for the potential of the rock was next transferred to superb relief carving. As a means of conveying the revivifying power of decoration, relief—either raised above or sunk below the plane of the wall—came to signify an ideal form of representation. Its pursuit led to a number of outcomes, which are considered later.

PLASTERS: USES, TYPES, AND APPLICATION PROCEDURES

Plasters in Egyptian tombs were used to repair rock fractures, level uneven rock-cut surfaces, and provide a suitable substrate for painting. In the kings' tombs, their nature and appearance allowed unrivaled aesthetic qualities in relief carving and painting.

New Kingdom plasters are usually described as being either earth or gypsum based (Lucas and Harris 1989, 76; Arnold 1991, 292–293; Dodson and Ikram 2008, 48). Although both types were used, this misrepresents what is a more complicated and nuanced situation. Earth plasters, in which clay minerals provide the main binder, were likely sourced from alluvial deposits left by the inundation of the Nile. In the kings' tombs, such plasters were reserved for leveling layers or for repairing defects in the rock. Plasters with gypsum as the dominant binder were probably not widely employed, but were likely utilized when circumstances required a faster set; in Tutankhamun's burial chamber, gypsum plaster was used for expedient patching and repairing (Wong et al. 2012, S325–S326).

The main plasters present are almost certainly those known as *hib*, sourced from the clay-containing calcitic deposits of the Theban area, which also contain varying amounts of anhydrite and gypsum. They therefore had a number of potential binding properties, including from clays, calcium sulfate, and calcite-clay combinations. These minerals also provided natural aggregates. *Hib* plasters vary considerably in their physical characteristics, reflecting different sources and mixing of component materials to achieve desired strength properties or rates of set. The ancient craftsmen were empirically aware of these properties, skillfully manipulating them for various purposes.

Thick plaster layers, packed with limestone fragments, were used to conceal rock defects, such as may be seen in parts of Thutmose I's tomb. This approach was also adopted for shaping vaulted roofs, as in Merenptah's burial chamber. Elsewhere, procedures varied, both within and between tomb interiors. In Amenhotep III's tomb, for example, the use of two and sometimes three plaster layers is recorded (Uda 2004, 79). Different considerations, as discussed later, influenced the plaster stratigraphies of relief decoration. There has been no study of the sections into which walls were divided for plastering, although major divisions seem to have been guided by horizontal scaffolding lifts, as evidenced in Ramesses I's burial chamber. But methods of large-scale plastering were probably subject to numerous logistical variations.

The limited iconographical programs of Eighteenth Dynasty tombs had a positive impact on plastering quality. For example, the plastered walls of Thutmose III's tomb are relatively few, but are very skillfully applied, with a smooth finish. Similarly, plastered walls that also imitate unrolled papyrus scrolls feature in the tombs of Amenhotep II and Amenhotep III. In these tombs, limited areas of high-quality plastering and painting alternate with rooms and corridors exhibiting refined rock leveling to produce superbly designed interiors.

In contrast, the rough plasters found in the burial chambers of the tombs of Tutankhamun and Aye are anomalous. In Tutankhamun's tomb, plaster types and mixes—and numbers and sequences of layers—vary from wall to wall (Wong et al. 2012, S325–S327). Trowel and hand marks indicate that plasters were applied quickly and roughly, and they were also brushed on as slurry in some areas. In such a small decorative program, these variations and discrepancies appear slapdash. Aye's burial chamber betrays similar characteristics. Its walls seem also to have been coated with plaster slurry, while corrective patches were smeared on by hand. This is far removed from the accomplished plastering of preceding tombs, providing further evidence that Tutankhamun's and Aye's burials were probably hastily completed.

Expanded iconographical programs were a motivation for constructing larger tombs during the Nineteenth Dynasty (Reeves and Wilkinson 1996, 137). Almost comprehensive interior plastering became the norm, and sunk relief the predominant form of decoration. Immense demands were placed on the scale of plaster production and on the nature and function of plastered surfaces. The technical challenges of providing a plaster that could be reliably carved over huge surface areas were considerable.

Plastering standards inevitably varied, for a range of reasons. In Seti II's tomb, a decorative program that was begun to a high standard was interrupted by political upheaval and the king's early death (Dodson 1999). With little time for completion, the burial chamber was hastily fashioned from an abbreviated corridor, and its interior was roughly plastered and painted, particularly on the ceiling. Ramesses IX's burial chamber was similarly rapidly adapted, presumably following the king's demise, which also resulted in expedient plastering (Reeves and Wilkinson 1996, 168–170). In the tomb of Ramesses V and Ramesses VI, a decline in plastering quality occurs shortly after the first pillared hall, which probably reflects a change in workmanship between the reigns of these kings (Ventura 1988).

RELIEF DECORATION: IDEALS
AND REALITIES

The technology of raised and sunk relief overlaps considerations of both rock treatment and plastering, as the previous sections demonstrate. But perceptions of the hierarchical significance offered by these different approaches to carving deserve closer examination.

Although the long-lasting appeal of relief decoration throughout the Nineteenth and Twentieth Dynasties was rooted in the preferred technology of rock carving, this approach quickly became unsustainable. In Horemheb's burial chamber, carving of the multiple small scenes and texts from the Book of Gates was abandoned, despite their design having been painstakingly worked out in red and black outline; the demands of completing this three-dimensional endeavor in the rock were hugely underestimated (Figure 10.1).

Indeed, this ideal was only realized in Seti I's tomb. Its immense interior is decorated almost throughout with painted raised relief of the highest quality (Brand 2000, 289–293) (Figure 10.2). Remarkably, Seti's reign was not very long—only around a decade—suggesting that time was not, in this case, the most important resource governing decorative ambition. But funding and expertise were provided in abundance, allowing the near completion of this magnificent program.

Such resources were never to be repeated. In Seti II's tomb, an attempt to carve a decorative program in the rock met with failure. Here, the walls of the entrance and first

FIGURE 10.1 Scene from the Book of Gates in Horemheb's burial chamber, showing preliminary sketching in red, with corrections in black, and raised relief carving only partially completed.

[Francis Dzikowski 1999. © Theban Mapping Project. Image Ref. # 13771.]

FIGURE 10.2 Painted raised relief carving of the highest quality was completed almost throughout the Tomb of Seti I. Here the goddess Hathor is shown welcoming Seti I.

[© RMN-Grand Palais/Art Resource, NY.]

corridor were coated with a thin skim-plaster, to repair geological defects. The skim was then mostly carved away in the process of executing sunk relief into the rock. The deepest relief, which allowed the rock to be modeled to maximum effect, was prioritized for the king's image panel at the entrance. The walls of the second and third corridors were also coated with skim-plaster, with the intention that they too would be carved. But the plan to continue high-quality relief seems to have been too ambitious, and work in the corridors did not progress beyond the drawing phase.

In other tombs, rock carving was limited to a few areas, and sunk relief in plaster became the principal medium. For large interiors, this was a practical and economical choice. Plaster could not be carved as finely as good quality rock, but results were more easily attained. Technical differences were also manipulated for hierarchical effect. Beginning with Merenptah, tomb entrances were made wider than their internal corridors (Reeves and Wilkinson 1996, 147). Important figure carvings, showing full-sized or larger than life, high-quality reliefs of the king before Ra-Horakhty and other gods, were displayed here. Differentiated architecture and relief technology were thus coordinated to emphasize the pharaoh's godlike power. Superb raised reliefs of Merenptah and the gods were carved into smoothed rock at the entrance of his tomb, alternated with sunk relief texts in the first corridor (Figure 10.3). In the second corridor, sunk relief was partly carved in rock, and partly in skim-plaster. But in the third corridor, a changeover occurred to sunk relief in thicker plaster—although in many places carving was still incised through to the rock beneath.

This trend was continued in other tombs, with variations. Although much damaged by flooding, sunk relief in plaster appears to have been executed throughout Siptah's large tomb. Once again, the finest work—which exploited the underlying rock for subtle modeling—was reserved for the king standing before Ra-Horakhty at the entrance, although here this was done in sunk rather than raised relief. Elsewhere, texts and images seem mainly to have been carved into a single plaster layer. This general approach was also adopted in Tauseret's tomb, in the combined tomb of Tauseret and Sethnakhte, and in Ramesses III's tomb.

If conditions allowed, use of a single plaster layer seems to have been preferred, presumably because this offered easy carving into the rock beneath when deeper modeling was required. Inevitably, there were variations. In Seti II's tomb, two or more plaster layers were applied in the pillared hall. In the tomb of Tauseret and Sethnakhte, a transition to the use of two plaster layers occurs after the first burial chamber, coinciding with that part of the interior constructed for Sethnakhte alone. In Ramesses IV's tomb, the plastered walls are extremely smoothly applied, with one layer apparently used at the front of the tomb, and two or more layers present elsewhere. Carving and painting of the sunk reliefs, though, were cursorily done: the purpose of the careful plastering here seems instead to have been to enhance the architectural regularity of the interior.

Painted relief, whatever its quality, continued to be valued over painting alone. This is clear in tombs that ran into completion difficulties. In Sethnakhte's large burial chamber, relief was started, but most of the chamber was left undecorated: painting does not seem to have been considered as an alternative option. Relief decoration was also curtailed

FIGURE 10.3 Magnificent painted raised relief of the pharaoh standing before Ra-Horakhty, carved into the rock at the entrance to the tomb of Merenptah.

in Ramesses IX's tomb, but this was managed by a gradual substitution of painting: full relief decoration stopped after the second corridor, relief and painting were combined in the third corridor, and remaining chambers were only partly adorned with painting. Inferior painting was carried out as an abrupt substitute for halted relief decoration in such tombs as Seti II, Ramesses IV, Ramesses V and Ramesses VI, and Ramesses VII.

Setting-out and Drawing Procedures

The many examples of unfinished decoration in the royal tombs provide remarkable insights into setting-out and drawing techniques prior to and during painting and relief carving. Since these procedures were not just confined to early stages of the decorative process, much evidence also remains visible on finished painting.

Compositional zones and borders, guidelines for text, and proportioning of figures and other features were set out using horizontal and vertical lines, either snapped against the wall or ceiling with a cord dipped in paint or drawn, usually between registration marks, freehand or with the aid of a straight edge. Red paint was used most frequently, but yellow, black, and white lines were also applied. Approaches to drawing were similarly varied. A common procedure involved draftsmen making preliminary sketches in red paint, which were then redone and corrected in black by the master draftsman. But less formal methods were also employed. As in setting-out techniques, yellow, black, and white paint was also used.

Plaster incisions were also sometimes employed. Incised setting-out lines and drawing survive on two unfinished figures in Seti II's tomb. In Tutankhamun's burial chamber, incisions were used for partial drawing of the figures on the north wall only, and for their rudimentary proportioning to the twenty-square Amarna grid. This is a significant departure in setting out and drawing from other walls of the chamber and points to two different teams of craftsmen working side by side (Wong et al. 2012, S327, S329). Incisions were also used as drawing aids in the tombs of Amenhotep II, Aye, and Ramesses I, and probably others. The evidence suggests that incisions were not relied upon for extensive setting out and drawing, but were mainly employed in a supplementary capacity.

For the cursive painting that is a hallmark of Thutmose III's tomb—and which occurs also in the tombs of Amenhotep II and Amenhotep III—efforts to disguise setting-out techniques were a stylistic priority. In Thutmose III's tomb, inconspicuous red lines were ruled to align details of the Amduat against the neutral walls of the burial chamber; similarly thin, white lines were ruled against yellow backgrounds. In Amenhotep II's tomb, barely perceptible white paint was used for registration marks and setting-out lines on the neutral walls of the burial chamber. Little or no preliminary drawing was employed for this style of painting, reflecting its scribal nature.

The emergence of major figure painting in Eighteenth Dynasty tombs coincided with the use of squared grids for proportioning. These are visible in the tombs of Thutmose IV and Amenhotep III. This method of setting out allowed figures to be drawn simply in red outline, without recourse to further correction. But reliance on the grid system seems to have been short-lived (Robins 2001). Certainly by the time of Horemheb's death, figures in his tomb were set out with snapped horizontal lines that defined only their feet, shoulders, and tops of their heads.

Horemheb's tomb is marked too by altogether more rigorous drawing procedures, with the first known use of preliminary designs in red meticulously corrected in black. This was a corollary of the introduction of relief decoration; quality control in drawing was critical when subsequent carving represented an irreversible step in the decorative process. This exacting approach was followed in most subsequent tombs with relief decoration; unfinished areas, such as in the burial chambers of Tauseret and Sethnakhte, allow glimpses of this practice. An exception is Ramesses IV's tomb, where preliminary drawing appears to have been confined to red outline alone. This may have influenced the quality of its relief carving, which is poorer than in many other tombs and may have been completed in haste.

As in other areas of technology, resource issues were influential. Rudimentary setting-out and drawing characterize the decoration of Tutankhamun's tomb, probably reflecting hasty completion circumstances (Wong et al. 2012, S327, S329). This is also evident in the decoration of Ramesses I's tomb, much curtailed by the king's extremely brief reign of less than two years (Reeves and Wilkinson 1996, 134–135). Although it was probably painted by the same artists who worked in Horemheb's tomb, time constraints apparently prevented the artists achieving the same standard of painstakingly corrected drawing, or indeed relief decoration: cursory red and yellow setting-out lines and sketches, of varying quality, are the only basis for subsequent painting. Ramesses VII's reign, beset by economic crises, appears to have resulted in a very limited tomb program, typified by rapid drawing techniques (Shaw 2000, 308).

With the widespread implementation of relief decoration in the Nineteenth Dynasty, approaches to setting out and drawing diverged between walls and ceilings. Ceilings never received relief decoration and were only painted with figurative subject matter following the innovation of Seti I's astronomical ceiling. Thereafter, tomb ceilings expanded in iconographical complexity (Reeves and Wilkinson 1996, 137). In response, setting-out and drawing procedures sometimes became expedient or were incorporated into final painting with little effort to disguise their presence, as occurred on the extensive astronomical ceilings in the tomb of Ramesses V and Ramesses VI. Vaulted ceilings also inhibited setting-out techniques such as snapped and ruled lines, leading to basic drawing measures, as may be seen in the unfinished burial chambers of Tauseret and Sethnakhte.

PAINT APPLICATION AND COLOR SYMBOLISM

In the Egyptians' conception of the universe, discernment of cosmic qualities associated with colors was immensely important, a disposition that is reflected in the lexicographic evidence (Tiradritti 2008, 24–61; Pinch 2001, 183–184; Quirke 2001). In the royal tombs, this worldview was distilled through only six colors—white, black, red, yellow, blue, and green—but this basic palette was subtly enhanced, through specific pigment choices and paint application procedures, to convey both naturalistic and symbolic meaning.

Scientific analysis has established a range of pigments used in New Kingdom painting. Three whites are recognized: calcium carbonate, calcium sulfate, and magnesium calcium carbonate, known as huntite (Heywood 2001). Blacks are mainly of fine-grained carbon, derived from lampblack or soot (Lee and Quirke 2000, 105, 108), but crushed charcoal was also used, as for example, in Tutankhamun's tomb (Wong et al. 2012, S327). The black manganese ore pyrolusite is occasionally reported (Lee and Quirke 2000, 105, 108, 198). Hematite was widely utilized to achieve a variety of red to brown shades. Much rarer is the intense orange-red pigment, realgar, which was selectively used in Amenhotep III's tomb to define details in royal figures, an indication of its precious nature (Capriotti 2008, 74). Yellows include, most commonly, the basic ochres, goethite and limonite, but also jarosite and natrojarosite, and, occasionally, orpiment (Colinart 2001). The only blue pigment is the synthetic calcium copper tetrasilicate, Egyptian blue (Tite et al. 1987); closely related to this is Egyptian green, the most widely used green pigment in the New Kingdom, although malachite is also sometimes reported (Scott 2010).

Before their decoration, walls and ceilings were brushed over with preparatory washes. These probably acted as a sealant and provided a uniform surface for painting. Clay and gypsum washes were used in Tutankhamun's burial chamber, and similar applications are visible in other tombs (Wong et al. 2012, S325–S327). These sometimes also functioned as ground layers, modifying the final appearance of the painting. The painting of Ramesses I's burial chamber, for example, is notable for its distinctive blue-grey background, achieved by carrying a thin layer of Egyptian blue over a greyish ground.

More usually, ground layers were white, applied either selectively or universally (Lucas and Harris 1989, 354–355). In Tutankhamun's burial chamber, a white ground was used on three of its four walls, consisting primarily of huntite, extended with calcium sulfate and calcite (Wong et al. 2012, S326–S327). In Horemheb's tomb, the white ground is composed of calcite (Shoeib 1998, 137, 139–141). Varying combinations of these white pigments were probably used, depending on their availability and cost and on the extent of surfaces to be covered. The choice of white was important for enhancing the brilliance of upper paint layers, achieving not just an aesthetic effect, but also the symbolic concept of brightness, which had auspicious connotations associated with sunlight.

Brightness as an innate quality informed a number of paint techniques. Huntite, favored for its bright white appearance, was sometimes further enhanced by the addition of particles of Egyptian blue. This was done for the white clothing of figures in the paintings in Tutankhamun's tomb, conferring on them associations of purity and spirituality (Ragai 1986, 75). Gold was associated with divinity and eternity, and in wall paintings the color yellow signified its presence. As a stand-in for gold, orpiment was regarded as a superior pigment, due to its rarity and brilliance. Its presence is attested in a number of Eighteenth Dynasty tombs, but usage was evidently restricted. On the walls of Thutmose III's tomb, orpiment was glazed over yellow ochre, in imitation of gold (Shaaban et al. 2009, S6–S7). This correlation was given added significance in Amenhotep III's tomb, where orpiment was glazed over pink to signify the skin of female deities and imply their incorruptibility (Capriotti 2008, 83).

Selective glossiness was another important paint quality. Discrete coatings are widely reported in Egyptian painting, and identified materials include beeswax, egg white, animal glue, and mastic resin (Newman and Halpine 2001). Mastic is known to have been burnt as an incense and was referred to as "that which makes divine" (Serpico and White 2001, 36). Its application as a varnish was therefore also emblematic of conveying divinity. Although this area of technology is unexplored in the royal tombs, flesh painting on figures is often distinguished by its glossy appearance; the likely presence of differentiated coatings requires further study.

Matte and glossy effects also need to be considered in relation to pigment-binder combinations. The most widely recognized type of Egyptian paint binder is acacia gum, though additional binders—including other plant gums, plant nectars and honey, animal glue, and resins—are identified on a wide range of Egyptian objects (Newman and Serpico 2000, 488–489; Newman and Halpine 2001, 25). Little analysis has been carried out in the kings' tombs, but acacia gum is the principal paint binder in Tutankhamun's burial chamber (Wong et al. 2012, S325, S327), and probably also in Horemheb's tomb (Shoeib 1998, 140–142). However, various binders were probably also employed in the royal tombs, expertly mixed with different pigments to create a range of visual effects.

Texture, like brightness, was also used to lend color added stimulus. Different grindings of Egyptian blue and green were utilized to create *impasto* effects, which were contrasted with areas of smoothly applied paint, mixed from finely ground pigments. Huntite was chosen not only for its brightness, but also because its small particle size produced a compact and intense paint layer. The connection between color intensity and purity was important and prompted other paint techniques: single colors were built up in successive layers of pure pigment to increase their intensity and depth. This process was sometimes left unfinished, as occurred in Thutmose IV's tomb.

Variations of hue and tone were created by a number of techniques. Different grindings of Egyptian blue and green altered their optical properties, ranging from dark, intense tones to gradually more translucent ones (Scott 2010, 32–34). Variations in the manufacturing process of these pigments, and their layering over black or white, also resulted in a wide range of hues (Tite et al. 1987, 42). In parts of Thutmose III's tomb, in addition to being applied over black, Egyptian blue was overlaid with hematite, then another layer of blue (Shaaban et al. 2009, S7). In Amenhotep III's tomb, Egyptian blue was combined with a manganese black pigment to intensify its appearance and is suspected to have been mixed with yellow ochre to create an alternative green (Yoshimura and Kondo 2004, 45, 143; Uda 2004, 81, 82). In Tutankhamun's tomb, Egyptian blue was added to yellows and reds to increase the range of flesh colors.

These and other methods of pigment preparation, layering, and blending demonstrate how the search for "symbolic" colors promoted technological development. But New Kingdom painting is also celebrated for its innovative naturalism (Ragai 1986, 78–79). Semitransparent glazes and skillfully juxtaposed colors were used to simulate features such as diaphanous garments and subtle gradations of skin tone. In the kings' tombs, these techniques achieved their apogee in combination with relief carving and the discriminating use of glossy and matte painting.

Final Considerations: Sequencing and Finishing

A consideration of the diverse materials and procedures involved in the decoration of the royal tombs demonstrates their complexity and sophistication. But this still says little about sequencing decisions in the decorative process and the manner in which tomb interiors were regarded as finished.

Although tomb decoration was marked by distinct stages, sequencing often seems random. Very different states of completion exist side by side, not only between chambers, but also within a single chamber, and on the same wall or ceiling. The fact that decoration of the highest quality could be completed alongside very poorly executed or unfinished work can now seem odd. But this is to impose modern notions of completion on the original function of royal tomb decoration and to misjudge the processes of workshop organization that produced it.

Many of these inconsistencies can be explained. Well chambers were often decorated as a priority, because of their important role in simulating the eternal chamber of the tomb to prevent plundering (Dodson and Ikram 2008, 46). Some unfinished chambers show that decorative features were completed at different times from figurative painting, indicating hierarchical divisions of labor. The workshop practice of dividing tomb decoration between two principal "gangs" led to different levels of completion in adjacent areas (Černý 1973, 36–38; Keller 1991, 51); on the walls of Horemheb's tomb, work areas completed to different stages also reflect the separation of teams by scaffolding height (Dodson and Ikram 2008, 49).

In summary, reasons for the discontinuous nature of royal tomb decoration include the many logistical matters related to workshop practice and a wide range of economic and political factors. But tombs were also left in varying states of completion because they were regarded as ritualistically "finished" on the interment of the deceased pharaoh. This has left vivid evidence of technical procedures with respect to rock cutting, setting out, drawing, preparatory layers and plastering, and painting and relief carving, allowing us also to appreciate the royal tombs as a high point of artistic and technical expression in ancient Egypt.

BIBLIOGRAPHY

Arnold, D. 1991. *Building in Egypt*. New York: Oxford University Press.

Bierbrier, M. L. 1982. *The Tomb Builders of the Pharaohs*. London: British Museum Press.

Bimson, M., and I. C. Freestone, eds. 1987. *Early Vitreous Materials*. London: British Museum Press.

Bogoslovsky, E. S. 1980. "Hundred Egyptian Draughtsmen." *Zeitschrift fur Ägyptische Sprache und Altertumskunde* 107: 89–111.

Brand, P. 2000. "The Monuments of Seti I and Their Historical Significance: Epigraphic, Art Historical and Historical Analysis." PhD thesis, University of Toronto.

Capriotti, G. 2008. "The Technique of Egyptian Wall Painting." In *Egyptian Wall Painting*, edited by F. Tiradritti, 62–84. New York: Abbeville Press.

Černý, J. 1973. *The Valley of the Kings: Fragment d'un Manuscrit Inachevé*. Institut Français d'Archéologie Orientale du Cairo, Bibliothque d'Étude T 61. Cairo: Institut français d'archéologie orientale du Caire.

Cline, E. H., and D. O'Connor, eds. 2006. *Thutmose III: A New Biography*. Ann Arbor, MI: University of Michigan Press.

Colinart, S. 2001. "Analysis of Inorganic Yellow Color in Ancient Egyptian Painting." In *Color and Painting in Ancient Egypt*, edited by W. V. Davies, 1–4. London: British Museum Press.

Davies, W. V., ed. 2001. *Color and Painting in Ancient Egypt*. London: British Museum Press.

Dawson, J., C. Rozeik, and M. M. Wright, eds. 2010. *Decorated Surfaces on Ancient Egyptian Objects: Technology, Deterioration and Conservation*. London: Archetype Publications.

Dodson, A. 1999. "The Decorative Phases of the Tomb of Sethos II and Their Historical Implications." *Journal of Egyptian Archaeology*, 85: 136–138.

Dodson, A., and S. Ikram. 2008. *The Tomb in Ancient Egypt: Royal and Private Ssepulchers from the Early Dynastic Period to the Romans*. London: Thames & Hudson.

Heywood, A. 2001. "The Use of Huntite as a White Pigment in Ancient Egypt." In *Color and Painting in Ancient Egypt*, edited by W. V. Davies, 5–9. London: British Museum Press.

Hornung, E. 1971. *Das Grab des Haremhab im Tal der Könige*. Bern: Francke Verlag.

Keller, C. 1991. "Royal painters: Deir el-Medina in Dynasty XIX." In *Fragments of a Shattered Visage: The Proceedings of the International Symposium of Ramesses the Great*, edited by E. B. and R. Freed, 50–86. Monographs of the Institute of Egyptian Art and Archaeology 1. Memphis, Tenn.: Memphis State University.

Lee, L., and S. Quirke. 2000. "Painting Materials." In *Ancient Egyptian Materials and Technology*, edited by P. T. Nicholson and I. Shaw, 104–120. Cambridge: Cambridge University Press.

Lucas, A., and J. R. Harris. 1989. *Ancient Egyptian Materials and Industries*. London: Histories & Mysteries of Man.

Newman, R., and S. M. Halpine. 2001. "The Binding Media of Ancient Egyptian Painting." In *Color and Painting in Ancient Egypt*, edited by W. V. Davies, 22–27. London: British Museum Press.

Newman, R., and M. Serpico. 2000. "Adhesives and Binders." In *Ancient Egyptian Materials and Technology*, edited by P. T. Nicholson and I. Shaw, 475–494. Cambridge: Cambridge University Press.

Nicholson, P. T., and I. Shaw, eds. 2000. *Ancient Egyptian Materials and Technology*. Cambridge: Cambridge University Press.

Pinch, G. 2001. "Red Things: The Symbolism of Color in Magic." In *Color and Painting in Ancient Egypt*, edited by W. V. Davies, 182–185. London: British Museum Press.

Quirke, S. 2001. "Color Vocabularies in Ancient Egyptian." In *Color and Painting in Ancient Egypt*, edited by W. V. Davies, 186–192. London; British Museum Press.

Ragai, J. 1986. "Color: Its Significance and Production in Ancient Egypt." *Endeavor* 10: 74–79.

Reeves, N., and R. H. Wilkinson. 1996. *The Complete Valley of the Kings: Tombs and Treasures of Egypt's Greatest Pharaohs*. London and New York: Thames & Hudson.

Robins, G. 2001. "The Use of the Squared Grid as a Technical Aid for Artists in Eighteenth Dynasty Painted Theban Tombs." In *Color and Painting in Ancient Egypt*, edited by W. V. Davies, 60–62. London: British Museum Press.

Roehrig, C. H. 2006. "The Building Activities of Thutmose III in the Valley of the Kings." In *Thutmose III: A New Biography*, edited by E. H. Cline and D. O'Connor, 238–259. Ann Arbor, MI: University of Michigan Press.

Scott, D. A. 2010. "Greener Shades of Pale: A Review of Advances in the Characterisation of Ancient Egyptian Green Pigments." In *Decorated Surfaces on Ancient Egyptian Objects: Technology, Deterioration and Conservation*, edited by J. Dawson et al., 32–45. London: Archetype Publications.

Serpico, M., and R. White. 2001. "The Use and Identification of Varnish on New Kingdom Funerary Equipment." In *Color and Painting in Ancient Egypt*, edited by W. V. Davies, 33–42. London: British Museum Press.

Shaaban, A., A. Korman, A. Stonert, F. Munnik, and A. Turos. 2009. "Ion Beam Analysis of Ancient Egyptian Wall Paintings." *Vacuum* 83: S4–S8.

Shaw, I., ed. 2000. *The Oxford History of Ancient Egypt*. Oxford: Oxford University Press.

Sherratt, S. ed. 2000. *The Wall Paintings of Thera: Proceedings of the First International Symposium*. Vol. 1. Athens: Thera Foundation.

Shoeib, A. 1998. "Examination of Pigments and Organic Binding Media Applied on Ancient Egyptian Wall Paintings Dating from the New Kingdom (1348–1320 B.C.)." *Zabytkoznawstwo i Konserwatorstwo* 30 (327): 132–142.

Tiradritti, F., ed. 2008. *Egyptian Wall Painting*. New York: Abbeville Press.

Tite, M., M. Bimson, and M. R. Cowell. 1987. "The Technology of Egyptian Blue." In *Early Vitreous Materials*, edited by M. Bimson and I. C. Freestone, 39–46. London: British Museum Press.

Uda, M. 2004. "In Situ Characterization of Ancient Plasters and Pigments on Tomb Walls in Egypt Using Energy Dispersive X-Ray Diffraction and Fluorescence." *Nuclear Instruments and Methods in Physics Research B* 226: 75–82.

Ventura, R. 1988. "The Largest Project for a Royal Tomb in the Valley of the Kings." *Journal of Egyptian Archaeology*, 74: 137–156.

Wong, L., S. Rickerby, A. Phenix, A. Rava, and R. Kamal. 2012. "Examination of the Wall Paintings in Tutankhamen's Tomb: Inconsistencies in Original Technology." In *The Decorative: Conservation and the Applied Arts*, 2012 IIC Congress, Vienna, S322–S330. London: Maney Publishing.

Yoshimura, S., and J. Kondo. 2004. *Conservation of the Wall Paintings in the Royal Tomb of Amenophis III: First and Second Phases Report*. Tokyo: Waseda University.

....

CHAPTER 11

ICONOGRAPHY, PALAEOGRAPHY, DECORATIVE ELEMENTS, DISTRIBUTION, AND DEVELOPMENT OF SCENES

....

HEATHER L. MCCARTHY

EACH royal tomb in the Valley of the Kings cosmographically embodies an imagined afterlife landscape. Together, the architecture and decoration create a three-dimensional representation of the netherworld experienced by the king. The tomb plan delimited the physical boundaries of the king's personal netherworld, and the decorative program reinforced the tomb's cosmographic values, evoking the events comprising the sun god's—and by extension the king's—afterlife journey, including his rebirth and regeneration.

This representation of a "kingly" netherworld was not static, as the notion of what a king's tomb should be evolved during the New Kingdom, and no two pharaohs' tombs were identical. However, one common thread linked all pharaohs' tombs in the Valley of the Kings: the use of a genre of royal funerary art and literature that was employed solely in kings' tombs.

EIGHTEENTH DYNASTY KINGS' TOMBS

....

The decorative programs of Eighteenth Dynasty kings' tombs (see Table 11.1) emphasize the nocturnal journey of the sun through the earth (Wilkinson 1994, 82–83; 1995, 75–76; ch 20, this volume). These tombs were each envisioned as having an ideal, symbolic north-south orientation, its entrance in the south and its burial chamber in the north,

Table 11.1 Chart Showing Distribution of Scenes in Eighteenth Dynasty Theban Kings' Tombs*

Tomb	Well-Room	Pillared Hall	Antechamber	Sarcophagus Chamber	Annex(es)
KV 38: Thutmose I	X	X	X	Amduat scene fragments	X
KV 20: Hatshepsut (reburial of Thutmose I, burial of Thutmose II)	X	X	X	Amduat scene fragments in second sarcophagus chamber (J2)	ND
KV 34: Thutmose III	*Kheker* frieze on walls; stars on ceiling	Catalog of 741 Amduat deities	X	Amduat hours 1–12 on walls; Litany of Re gods, Isis as tree-goddess, and royal women on pillars	ND
KV 35: Amenhotep II	ND	ND	X	Amduat hours 1–12 on walls; divine scenes on pillars	ND
KV 43: Thutmose IV	Divine scenes: king before deities	ND	Divine scenes: king before deities	ND	ND
WV 22: Amenhotep III	Divine scenes: king and his *Ka* before deities, including the deified Thutmose IV	ND	Divine scenes: king and his *Ka* before deities	Amduat hours 1–12 on walls; divine scenes on pillars	ND
KV 62: Tutankhamun	X	X	ND	Amduat 1st hour, funeral scene, Opening of the Mouth scene (with Aye), divine scenes with king and his *Ka*	ND

(continued)

Table 11.1 *Continued*

Tomb	Well-Room	Pillared Hall	Antechamber	Sarcophagus Chamber	Annex(es)
WV 23: Aye	X	X	ND	Amduat 1st hour, marsh hunting scene (with queen), divine scenes with king and his *Ka*, texts from BD 130 and 144	ND
KV 57: Horemheb	Divine scenes: king offering to and receiving favors from deities	ND	Divine scenes: king offering to and receiving favors from deities	Book of Gates hours 1–6 on walls	Depiction of enshrined Osiris-Khentyamentiu (Jb)

* This chart includes only architectural features that were decorated. ND indicates that the chamber was not decorated; X indicates that the tomb does not have this feature.

where the nocturnal sun was believed to be at its zenith. The side walls of these tombs were thus the east and west. The curved or bent axes of these tombs were meant to evoke the circular path of the sun (Barta 1974; Wilkinson 1993, 46).

In the earliest known Eighteenth Dynasty tombs, those of Thutmose I, KV 38, and Hatshepsut, KV 20, only the sarcophagus chambers were decorated, and the surviving relief fragments from both tombs consist of Amduat scenes (Hornung 1990, 208–209; Richter 2008, 73–74), which formed the sole decorative scheme used on the walls of kings' burial chambers until the Amarna period.

Beginning with Thutmose III's tomb, KV 34, kings' tombs had more extensive programs, with decoration often employed in the well-room, pillared hall (KV 34 only), antechamber, and/or sarcophagus chamber (Hornung 1990, 27, 209). KV 34's well-room has a *kheker*-frieze on the walls and a star-patterned ceiling, while the pillared hall contains a unique pictorial catalog of 741 Amduat deities. In the sarcophagus chamber, all twelve hours of the Amduat adorn the walls, and the two pillars are decorated with images of the sun god's forms from the Litany of Re; representations of royal women; and a scene depicting Thutmose III suckling at the breast of the goddess Isis, who appears as a semi-anthropomorphic tree (Hornung 1990, 62–63, 209; 2001b, 139).

In KV 35, the tomb of Amenhotep II, Thutmose III's son and successor, only the sarcophagus chamber is decorated. As with KV 34, its walls are covered by the entire Amduat. The six sarcophagus chamber pillars were decorated with divine scenes showing the king before one of the three deities that evoke and summarize the processes of regeneration in the afterlife: Hathor, Osiris, and Anubis (Hornung 1990, 55). Afterward, similar divine scenes, with a greater variety of deities, became the usual pillar decoration in New Kingdom royal tombs.

Beginning with Thutmose IV's tomb, KV 43, the well-room and antechamber have divine scenes depicting the king standing before various deities (Hornung 1990, 209), though KV 43's sarcophagus chamber was undecorated. Amenhotep III, who cut his tomb, WV 22, in the Western Valley, combined schemes used by his predecessors and added innovations of his own. Like his father, Thutmose IV, he decorated the well-room and antechamber with divine scenes (Thomas 1966, 84), but for the first time, the king's royal *Ka* accompanies him (Reeves and Wilkinson 1996, 112–113), and his well-room program includes the deified *Ka* of Thutmose IV among the gods. Like his grandfather, Amenhotep II, Amenhotep III adorned his sarcophagus chamber walls with the complete Amduat and divine scenes, each showing the king before Osiris, Hathor, or Anubis, on its six pillars.

THE AMARNA AND POST-AMARNA PERIOD, FROM AKHENATEN TO AYE

The rules governing the decoration of kings' tombs changed during the reign of Akhenaten, who cut the Amarna royal tomb, TA 26 (Martin 1974, 1989), in the eastern cliffs of his new capital. The program of TA 26 contains subject matter specific to the Amarna period; three chambers have scenes reflecting the central roles played by the royal family in the Aten cult. In the sarcophagus chamber, Akhenaten and his great royal wife, Nefertiti, offer to the Aten (Martin 1989, 23–26, pls. 22–30 and 31–32). Funerary scenes showing the royal family mourning the death of Princess Meketaten (and possibly that of a second royal woman) appear in two of the three connected chambers comprising the tomb's "Meketaten suite" (Martin 1989, 42–46, pls. 63–71).

After the death of Akhenaten's successor, Semenkhkare, Tutankhamun restored the practice of traditional Egyptian religion and re-established the royal necropolis in western Thebes. His early death led to a hasty burial in KV 62, a small, specially adapted, nonroyal tomb in the Valley of the Kings, perhaps originally meant for Aye (Thomas 1966, 89). Only KV 62's sarcophagus chamber was decorated, and its abbreviated program demonstrates an attempt to conform to "kingly" conventions, despite the tomb's small size, while also employing funerary scenes previously reserved for private tombs. As with pre-Amarna kings' tombs, Tutankhamun's sarcophagus chamber program includes the Amduat, though it is limited to a condensed representation of the first hour on the left wall. The rear wall includes divine scenes showing the king, followed by his royal *Ka* being welcomed by Nut and by Osiris, while Anubis, Hathor of the West, and Isis greet the king on the left half of the entry wall. Tutankhamun's funeral cortege is shown on the right wall, and the adjacent scene on the right corner of the rear wall represents his successor, Aye, performing the Opening of the Mouth ritual on the king's mummy. The employment of these two previously nonroyal scene types may have been influenced by the use of similar funerary tableaux in the Amarna royal tomb (Thomas 1966, 90).

Aye was buried in WV 23, a Western Valley royal tomb probably originally intended for Tutankhamun (Thomas 1966, 89). As with KV 62, only the sarcophagus chamber is decorated, and its program comprises a similar blend of condensed "kingly" scenes and erstwhile private tomb motifs (Piankoff 1958, 247–251, pls. 21–25). An abbreviated version of the Amduat's first hour, similar to that in KV 62, adorns the right lateral wall. The upper half of the left wall depicts the goddess Nephthys standing between two solar barks, while text from Book of the Dead 130 and 144 is arranged in contiguous vertical columns below. The rear wall has scenes showing Aye, twice followed by his royal *Ka*, being received by Hathor of Thebes, Hathor of the West, Nut, and Osiris. Another scene, above the rear annex doorway, depicts the four sons of Horus as enthroned, mummiform gods wearing the crowns of Upper and Lower Egypt. The entry wall scene is a marsh hunting tableau, previously employed only in private tombs, featuring Aye accompanied by his chief queen, Tiy.

TRANSITION TO THE NINETEENTH DYNASTY: HOREMHEB AND RAMESSES I

At the end of the Eighteenth Dynasty, Horemheb instituted several innovative changes to the decoration of his own tomb, KV 57 (Hornung 1971, 26–31, 44–49, 55, pls. 1–10, 13–61, 66). He used painted relief, which became the standard royal tomb decoration for the rest of the New Kingdom. Thereafter, painting alone was only employed on ceilings and when haste was required to complete a tomb. Like Thutmose IV and Amenhotep III, Horemheb decorated his tomb's well-room and antechamber with divine scenes. However, these scenes evince a change in the relationship between the deceased and the deities depicted. Horemheb, for the first time, is shown actively offering to the gods as well as receiving favors from them, suggesting a heightened emphasis on the *do ut des* relationship between king and gods in the mortuary realm.

In J, Horemheb eschewed the Amduat and Litany of Re in favor of the first six hours from the new Book of Gates, including, for the first time in a king's tomb, a representation of the judgment of Osiris (Book of Gates, sixth hour), on the sarcophagus chamber's rear wall. KV 57 is also the only Eighteenth Dynasty king's tomb with a decorated annex. This annex, Jb, on the left side of the sarcophagus chamber, has a rear wall scene depicting Osiris-Khentyamentiu inside a shrine, supported by a *djed*-pillar, a precursor of the decorated "Osiris niche" or "Osiris annex" employed in the sarcophagus chambers of Ramesses I, Seti I, Merenptah, and Ramesses III.

Ramesses I, the first king of the Nineteenth Dynasty, was Horemheb's chosen successor. Because he was an elderly man when crowned, the architectural and programmatic scope of his tomb, KV 16, was necessarily abbreviated (see Table 11.3). Its

Table 11.2 Chart Showing Distribution of Scenes in the Front Sections of Nineteenth and Twentieth Dynasty Kings' Tombs*

Tomb	Doorway A	Corridor B	Corridor C	Corridor D	Well Room E	Pillared Hall F	Pillared Hall Annex Fa and/or Niche Faa
KV 16: Ramesses I	ND	ND	X	X	X	X	X
KV 17: Seti I	ND	Litany of Re frontispiece and texts	Litany of Re figures; Amduat 3rd hour text, BD 151 motifs	Amduat hours 4, 5	King with deities	Book of Gates hours 5, 6, and Osiris shrine scene; gods and king on pillars	Amduat hours 9–11; divine scenes on pillars
KV 7: Ramesses II	Isis and Nephthys adoring sun disk on lintel; Maat on thicknesses	Litany of Re frontispiece and texts	Litany of Re deities, BD 151 motifs	Amduat hours 4, 5	King with deities on chamber walls; Amduat hours 6, 12 on shaft walls	Book of Gates hours 5, 6; Osiris shrine scene; gods and king on pillars	Decoration damaged
KV 8: Merenptah	Isis and Nephthys adoring sun disk on lintel; Maat on thicknesses	Litany of Re frontispiece and texts	Litany of Re deities, BD 151 motifs	Amduat hours 4, 5	King and Osiris, deities	Book of Gates hours 5, 6 and Osiris shrine scene; divine scenes on pillars	ND in Fa; Osiris–Ramesses II and deities (Faa)
KV 15: Seti II	Isis and Nephthys adoring sun disk on lintel; Maat on thicknesses	Litany of Re frontispiece with Nefertum behind Re-Horakhty, Ra-Horakhty, and Sokar, Litany of Re texts	Litany of Re deities, Amduat 2nd and 3rd hour text, BD 151 motifs	Amduat hours 4, 5	Paintings of divine and funerary statues	Book of Gates hours 5, 6 and Osiris shrine scene; divine scenes on pillars	X

Table 11.2 *Continued*

Tomb	Doorway A	Corridor B	Corridor C	Corridor D	Well Room E	Pillared Hall F	Pillared Hall Annex Fa and/or Niche Fa
KV 10: Amenmesse (reused for Queens Takhat and Baketwerel)	Isis and Nephthys adoring sun disk on lintel; Maat on thicknesses	Litany of Re frontispiece and texts	Litany of Re deities	Amduat hours 4, 5	Takhat before deities	Baketwerel before deities	ND
KV 47: Siptah	Isis and Nephthys adoring sun disk on lintel; Maat on thicknesses	Litany of Re frontispiece and texts	Litany of Re deities, BD 151 motifs	Amduat hours 4, 5	Decoration damaged	Traces of Osiris shrine scene	X
KV 14: Tausret (later usurped for Sethnakhte)	Isis and Nephthys adoring sun disk on lintel; thicknesses cut away	Modified Litany of Re frontispiece scene, divine scenes with Tausert (twice with king)	BD 145, divine scenes	BD 145	Deities	BD 145, modified Osiris shrine scene	X
KV 11: Ramesses III	Isis and Nephthys adoring sun disk on lintel; Maat on thicknesses	Litany of Re frontispiece and texts; two lateral annexes with damaged decoration	Litany of Re deities, BD 151; eight decorated lateral annexes	Divine scenes (D1); Amduat hours 4, 5 (D2)	Deities	Book of Gates hours 5, 6 and Osiris shrine scene; divine scenes on pillars	Book of Gates 7th hour, king with Osiris, Horus, and Thoth on entry wall
KV 2: Ramesses IV	Isis and Nephthys adoring sun disk on lintel; king's names on thicknesses	Litany of Re frontispiece and texts	Litany of Re	Book of Caverns divisions 1, 2	X	X	X

(*continued*)

Table 11.2 Continued

Tomb	Doorway A	Corridor B	Corridor C	Corridor D	Well Room E	Pillared Hall F	Pillared Hall Annex Fa and/or Niche Faa
KV 9: Ramesses V/VI	Isis and Nephthys adoring sun disk on lintel; king's names on thicknesses (R VI carved over R V)	Pendant scenes of king before Re-Horakhty and Osiris, Book of Gates hours 1–3, Book of Caverns 1st division	Book of Gates hours 4–6, Book of Caverns division 2 and beginning of 3	Book of Gates hours 7–8, Book of Caverns divisions 3, 4, and beginning of 5	Book of Gates hours 9–10, Book of Caverns 5th division	Book of Gates hours 11–12, Book of Caverns 6th division on right wall and three faces of rear, right pier; divine scenes on all other pillar faces	X
KV 1: Ramesses VII	Isis, Nephthys, and king adoring sun disk on lintel, king's names on thicknesses	King offers to deities, Book of Gates 1st scene, Book of Caverns 1st division, Iunmutef purifying Osiris king (both walls)	X	X	X	X	X
KV 6: Ramesses IX	Isis, Nephthys, and king adoring sun disk on lintel (with Nut's head and arms above disk); king's names on thicknesses	King and Re-Horakhty, king and Osiris, Litany of Re; Iunmutef purifying Osiris king, king, Amen-Re-Horakhty, and Meretseger, Book of Caverns 1st division	Litany of Re deities, BD 125 and 126, king and Hathor, king and Khonsu–Shu–Neferhotep, ram-headed god, Book of Caverns divisions 2–4; astronomical ceiling	Amduat hours 2, 3, king offers to Ptah, enigmatic scenes	Pendant Iunmutef figures on rear wall	ND	X

Table 11.2 *Continued*

Tomb	Doorway A	Corridor B	Corridor C	Corridor D	Well Room E	Pillared Hall F	Pillared Hall Annex Fa and/or Niche Faa
KV 18: Ramesses X	Isis, Nephthys, and king adoring sun disk on lintel; king's names on thicknesses	King and Re-Horakhty, king, Amen-Re-Horakhty, and Meretseger	ND	X	X	X	X
KV 4: Ramesses XI	Isis, Nephthys, and king adoring sun disk on lintel; king's names on jamb	King and Re-Horakhty, king, Amen-Re-Horakhty, and Western goddess	ND	ND	ND	ND	X

* ND indicates that the chamber was not decorated; X indicates that the tomb does not possess this feature.

Table 11.3 Chart Showing Distribution of Scenes in the Rear Sections of Nineteenth and Twentieth Dynasty Kings' Tombs*

Tomb	Corridors G and H	Antechamber I	Sarcophagus Chamber J	Annex(es)	Rear Multi-Chamber Complex and/or Second Sarcophagus Chamber J2
KV 16	X	X	Book of Gates hours 3, 4 and divine scenes	Osiris, ram-headed Anubis, serpent goddess Nesret in rear annex (Jb)	X
KV 17	Opening of the Mouth	Deities	Book of Gates hours 2-3, 5 (front), Amduat hours 1-3 (rear); divine scenes and souls of Pe and Nekhen on pillars; astronomical ceiling over rear half of chamber	Book of Gates 4th hour (Ja); Amduat hours 6-8, djed-pillar and tyet-knot on walls, divine scenes and king performing rituals on pillars, funerary objects on benches (Jb); Book of the Heavenly Cow (Je); Anubis performing Opening of the Mouth on Osiris, sons of Horus in "Osiris niche"	X

Table 11.3 Continued

Tomb	Corridors G and H	Antechamber I	Sarcophagus Chamber J	Annex(es)	Rear Multi-Chamber Complex and/or Second Sarcophagus Chamber J2
KV 7	Opening of the Mouth	BD 125 and divine scenes	Book of Gates hours 2–3 (front), Amduat hours 1–2, 5, and inventory scenes (rear); divine scenes (with male deities), djed-pillars, souls of Pe and Nekhen on pillar faces; astronomical ceiling	Book of Gates 4th hour (Ja); Amduat 12th hour (Jb); Amduat hours 6–7, divine scenes on pillars (Jc); Book of Gates 5th hour, judgment hall of Osiris, abridged Amduat (Jd); Isis, Nephthys, and funerary objects (Jdd); BD 110 (Jddd); Amduat 8th hour and rock-cut Osiris figure (Je); Book of the Heavenly Cow (Jf)	X
KV 8	Opening of the Mouth	BD 125; divine scenes; king as Iunmutef; corridor I theme undetermined	Book of Gates hours 9–12, Book of Caverns closing scene, Book of the Earth closing scene, excerpts from Book of the Earth part A; divine scenes on pillars; astronomical ceiling	Rock-cut Osiris statue (Ja); decoration undetermined (Jb–Jd)	X

(continued)

Table 11.3 *Continued*

Tomb	Corridors G and H	Antechamber I	Sarcophagus Chamber J	Annex(es)	Rear Multi-Chamber Complex and/or Second Sarcophagus Chamber J2
KV 10	ND	X	X	X	X
KV 15	X	X	Rows of deities, mummiform figures from Book of Gates 6th hour; Nut on ceiling	X	X
KV 47	ND	ND	ND	X	X
KV 14	Opening of the Mouth ritual; BD 151 motifs and deities in lateral annex Ga	Tausret offering to deities	Book of Gates hours 9–12, Book of Caverns closing scene, Book of the Earth closing scene, excerpts from Book of the Earth part A; inventory scenes around sarcophagus emplacement; divine scenes on piers; astronomical ceiling	ND	Amduat hours 6–9 (K1, L); Book of Gates hours 9, 12, traces of deity on one pier, astronomical ceiling (J2); Opening of the Mouth (K2)

Table 11.3 Continued

Tomb	Corridors G and H	Antechamber I	Sarcophagus Chamber J	Annex(es)	Rear Multi-Chamber Complex and/or Second Sarcophagus Chamber J2
KV 11	Opening of the Mouth in Corridor G; enshrined deities in Chamber H	Deities: Imsety, Horus, Thoth, Anubis, and Atum	Book of Gates, Book of the Earth, deities in shrines above annex doorways; divine scenes on pillars; astronomical ceiling	BD 148 (Ja); ten figures of Osiris and two jackal standards (Jb); Book of the Heavenly Cow (Jc); BD 110 (Jd)	Enshrined deities (K1, K2); damaged decoration (L)
KV 2	X	BD 123, 124, 125, and 127 (text only)	Book of Gates hours 2–4; Books of Day and Night on ceiling	X	Book of Caverns text in central corridor; enshrined deities and food offerings on side recesses; shabtis in lateral annexes; goddesses performing *nyny* ritual, funerary furniture in rear chamber
KV 9	Amduat hours 1–3, 6–8 in Corridor G; Amduat hours 4–5, 8–11 in Corridor H	BD 124–127, 129, Maat hymn; ceiling decorated with paintings of king in day and night barks	Entire Book of the Earth on walls; Books of Day and Night on ceiling; divine scenes on pillars	Book of Gates 12th hour on rear wall, decans on lateral walls of rear annex (K)	X

(continued)

Table 11.3 *Continued*

Tomb	Corridors G and H	Antechamber I	Sarcophagus Chamber J	Annex(es)	Rear Multi-Chamber Complex and/or Second Sarcophagus Chamber J2
KV 1	X	X	Book of the Earth, pendant figures of Weret-hekau, pendant figures of king; Books of Day and Night combined with astronomical ceiling	Deceased before Osiris on lateral walls; pig and monkey from Book of Gates 6th hour, representation of food offerings, *djed*-pillars on rear wall; eight deities on ceiling	X
KV 6	X	X	Book of Caverns divisions 5,6, Book of the Earth, king in day and night barks, awakening of Osiris; Books of Day and Night on ceiling	X	X
KV 18	X	X	X	X	X
KV 4	ND	X	ND	X	X

* ND indicates that the chamber was not decorated; X indicates that the tomb does not possess this feature.

decoration, executed entirely in paint, was limited to the sarcophagus chamber and its rear annex (Hornung 2001a, 192–193). As with Horemheb's sarcophagus chamber, scenes from the Book of Gates are employed, though only on the side walls, the third hour on the right and the fourth hour on the left. The front and rear walls were decorated with scenes of Ramesses I interacting with deities. Among these are back-to-back, enthroned figures of Osiris and the solar deity Atum-Re-Khepri in the center of the rear wall, which evokes the crucial interaction of Osiris and sun god in the netherworld, a precondition for postmortem regeneration and rebirth; it also recalls the judgment of Osiris scene on the rear wall of Horemheb's sarcophagus chamber. On the rear wall of the annex, an excerpt from the Book of Gates' fourth hour depicts the enshrined Osiris, a ram-headed form of Anubis, and the serpent goddess Nesret (Piankoff 1957, 198, pl. 9B).

RAMESSIDE ROYAL TOMBS: SETI I
AND THE RAMESSIDE TEMPLATE

When Seti I cut and decorated KV 17, he redefined what a king's tomb should be. The netherworld cosmography expressed by its plan and program was enlarged and made more complex (Tables 11.2 and 11.3). While Eighteenth Dynasty kings' tombs had a maximum of four decorated chambers, those of Ramesside kings were decorated throughout, giving the impression of a vast netherworld landscape.

The differences between Ramesside kings' tomb programs and those of their predecessors are due not only to the more elaborate decoration, but also to changes in thematic emphases. The decoration reflects an increased (and increasing) "solarization" of funerary beliefs, manifested in the detailed depiction of Re's (and the deceased king's) netherworld journey. There was also a corresponding thematic reorganization into a predominantly solar "upper" half from the tomb's entrance to the columned hall, and a largely Osirian themed "lower" half from the rear wall of the columned hall downward (Wilkinson 1994, 84; 1995, 79). Some scenes previously used in Eighteenth Dynasty kings' tombs, such as the Litany of Re, were relocated and repositioned according to this new template, while newer afterlife books, such as the Book of Gates, the Book of the Heavenly Cow, and the Ritual of the Opening of the Mouth sequence, were added to the decorative repertoire (Hornung 1991, 11; 1990, 29–30, 208–210).

These thematic changes also shifted the ideal, symbolic orientation of the central axis from south-north in the Eighteenth Dynasty to east-west in the Ramesside period (Wilkinson 1995, 75–76; 1994, 84). Thus, no matter where each tomb is located or what its real, geographic orientation may be, the tomb entrance is symbolic east, the rear is symbolic west, left walls are symbolic south, and right walls are symbolic north.

Ramesside kings' tombs—up to and including that of Ramesses III—follow Seti I's template closely, though every king introduced variations in plan and program. After Seti I, the layout and iconography of some scenes changed, and the repertoire of appropriate funerary literature expanded further to include vignettes and text from the Book of the Dead (Leblanc 2001, 214–215; 1998, 24, 29; 1997, 12) and new Ramesside funerary books, such as the Book of Caverns, the Books of the Day and Night, and the Book of the Earth (Hornung 1990, 30–31, 208–210).

Of the earlier Ramesside tombs, only that of the female pharaoh Tausret, KV 14, significantly and deliberately deviates from the Seti I template. Though KV 14's plan utilizes the same sequence of corridors and chambers as KV 17 from the entrance to the first sarcophagus chamber, these chambers are smaller and decorated with a combination of "kingly," "modified kingly," and "non-kingly" scenes (McCarthy 2008, 83–85). These architectural and programmatic differences were determined by—and tailored to—Tausret's afterlife needs as both a woman and a royal individual who had been a queen (of Seti II), became co-regent (of Siptah), then assumed the full mantle of kingship, all while her tomb was being cut and decorated (McCarthy 2008, 104; Altenmüller 2003, 109; 2001, 228; 1994, 38).

Later Ramesside kings' tombs, from that of Ramesses IV, KV 2, to that of Ramesses XI, KV 4, are smaller and less architecturally complex than previous Ramesside kings' tombs, with fewer corridors and chambers. Though Seti I's template still influenced tomb plans and the thematic organization of their programs, solar themes increasingly dominated the subject matter of Twentieth Dynasty programs, leading to the expanded use of solar-oriented afterlife books such as the Book of Caverns, the Book of the Earth, "enigmatic compositions," and depictions of the solar deity taking on roles and functions earlier reserved for Osiris (Abitz 1992, 168, 173, 176, 180, 182; Wilkinson 1995, 79; 1994, 85).

Entrance Doorway (A)

From Ramesses II (KV 7) to Ramesses XI (KV 4), the entrance doorway was decorated with a lintel scene depicting the (usually kneeling) goddesses Isis (left) and Nephthys (right) flanking and adoring a central, yellow, morning sun-disk, which encircles two aspects of the solar deity: the ram-headed, nocturnal/chthonic Atum and the reborn morning sun represented by the scarab beetle, Khepri (Hornung 1990, 208; Wilkinson 1995, 76). This lintel scene effectively summarizes the solar deity's/deceased king's successful netherworld journey and consequent rebirth. Moreover, Isis and Nephthys evoke Osiris' crucial interaction with the sun-god in the netherworld. The composition of this scene remained constant until Ramesses VII (KV 1), Ramesses IX (KV 6), Ramesses X (KV 18), and Ramesses XI (KV 4) each added two pendant figures of themselves to the lintel scene, so that the kings' images flank the solar disk, while Isis stands behind the left figure of the king, and Nephthys stands behind the right (Hornung et al. 1990, pl. 98).

Except for Tausret's tomb, the thicknesses of every entrance doorway from Ramesses II's tomb to that of Ramesses III were decorated with pendant figures of the goddess Maat protecting the king's cartouche with her outstretched wings. Later Ramesside tombs, beginning with that of Ramesses IV, have thicknesses inscribed with the king's names and titles (e.g., Hornung et al. 1990, pl. 17).

First Corridor (B) Part I: Introductory Scenes

The first corridor was always decorated with a Litany of Re "frontispiece" or an equivalent divine scene on the left wall, near the entrance. This scene depicts the king, typically wearing an *Atf*-crown, before the sun god Re-Horakhty, who stands and holds to the king's nose a long staff topped with the hieroglyphs for "life," "stability," and "dominion." From KV 17 to KV 2, each frontispiece, save for that in Tausret's tomb, includes another solar motif, on the left wall behind Re-Horakhty, showing Atum and Khepri inside a sun-disk, as on the lintel. However, this disk is situated between—and notionally dispelling—chaotic animals representing darkness (Hornung 1990, 75–76; 1999, 140–141, 145; Hornung et al. 1990, pl. 19).

The appearance of the introductory Litany of Re scene remained constant until the late Nineteenth Dynasty, when significant formal/iconographic variations were introduced. KV 14's first corridor has a "modified kingly" version of the frontispiece, in which Tausret wears the regalia of a queen before Re-Horakhty. Moreover, the "life," "stability," and "dominion" hieroglyphs were omitted or deliberately erased from Re's staff, thereby lessening the statement of Tausret's kingly authority (McCarthy, 2008, 95–96).

In other tombs, a second male deity occasionally stands behind Re-Horakhty, while a similarly composed, corresponding divine scene appears at the beginning of the right wall. This occurs in Seti II's tomb, KV 15, where Nefertum stands behind Ra-Horakhty on the left wall, and Re-Horakhty and Sokar are shown together on the right wall. Ramesses V/VI's tomb, KV 9, also has pendant divine scenes, which pair Ra-Horakhty with Osiris on both left and right walls (Piankoff and Rambova 1954, pls. 6–7, 36–37; Abitz 1989, 58–61).

The pendant scenes in Ramesses VII's tomb, KV 1, are formal variants depicting the king offering to enthroned gods rather than standing deities, and each scene is set inside a golden shrine. The king censes and offers food to the solar Re-Horakhty-Atum-Khepri on the left wall and to his chthonic counterpart Ptah-Sokar-Osiris on the right (Hornung et al. 1990, pls. 100, 109).

The last three Twentieth Dynasty tombs possess introductory scenes with marked iconographic similarities, including nearly identical right walls. Ramesses IX's tomb, KV 6, like that of Ramesses V/VI, KV 9, depicts the king before Re-Horakhty and Osiris on the left wall, while the right wall shows the king offering to the divine dyad of Amen-Re-Horakhty, depicted with a human body and four rams' heads, and Meretseger, the goddess of the Theban necropoleis. Ramesses X's tomb, KV 18, depicts the king before Re-Horakhty on the left wall and before the quadruple ram-headed Amen-Re-Horakhty and Meretseger on the right. The pendant scenes in the first corridor of Ramesses XI's unfinished tomb, KV 4, are like those in KV 18, but with a Western goddess (whose name is destroyed) behind Amen-Re-Horakhty on the right wall. In both KV 18 and KV 4, there is no further decoration.

First Corridor (B) Part II

From Seti I to Ramesses IV, except for KV 14, the rest of the first corridor was adorned with Litany of Re text (Hornung 1990, 208; Hornung et al. 1990, pls. 19–25). Tausret's first corridor program comprises eight divine scenes showing Tausret, twice accompanied by a king, offering to deities (Altenmüller 2003, 117, 127, Abb. 6; 1985, 12; 1983, 38–39; McCarthy 2008, 95–97).

Later Ramesside kings typically decorate their first corridors with the beginning sections of the Book of Gates (left wall), the Book of Caverns (right wall), and/or divine scenes. Ramesses V/VI's tomb, from the first corridor to the columned hall, utilizes the entire Book of Gates on the left half of the tomb and the entire Book of Caverns on the right half. These funerary books are ordered sequentially, beginning with the prologue and first three hours of the Book of Gates on the left wall and the Book of Caverns' first division on the right (Piankoff and Rambova 1954, pls. 7–11, 37–41). In Ramesses VII's tomb, the left wall is decorated with sections of the Book of Gates' first two hours, followed by a divine scene showing Iunmutef purifying Osiris-Ramesses VII. The Book of Caverns' first division appears on the right wall, followed by another scene of Iunmutef purifying the Osiris king (Hornung et al. 1990, pls. 101–108). In Ramesses IX's tomb, the left wall is decorated with sections of the Litany of Re and Iunmutef purifying the Osiris king, while the Book of Caverns' first division appears on the right.

Second Corridor (C)

From Seti I to Ramesses III, C was programmatically divided into two sections. The front half is typically adorned with images of the sun god's seventy-five forms from the Litany of Re, while the rear half has pendant motifs from BD 151 depicting a reclining Anubis jackal and the kneeling goddesses Isis (left wall) and Nephthys (right wall) (Hornung 1991, 15–16).

However, five kings introduced additional texts, motifs, pictorial substitutions, or formal variations. Seti I's second corridor includes text from the Amduat's third hour in the rear half (Hornung 1991, 15; 1995, 70), while Seti II similarly incorporates text from the Amduat's second hour on the left wall of the corridor's rear half and the third hour on the right. In Siptah's tomb, KV 47, additional BD 151 motifs are employed on both walls in the corridor's lower half (Davis 1908, 15). Tausret's tomb has divine scenes at the corridor's beginning, while the rest is decorated with vignettes from BD 145 (McCarthy 2008, 97). In Ramesses III's tomb, the Litany of Re deities face into the tomb, though in all other tombs they face toward the entrance.

Significant programmatic changes occur after Ramesses III. The entire second corridor in Ramesses IV's tomb, KV 2, is decorated with the Litany of the Re and the sun god's seventy-five forms (Hornung et al. 1990, pls. 30–39), but BD 151 motifs were omitted, which is consistent with the increasing solarization of Twentieth Dynasty kings' tomb programs. Ramesses V/VI's second corridor utilizes the Book of the Gates' fourth, fifth, and sixth hours on the left wall (Piankoff and Rambova 1954, pls. 42–48) and the Book of Caverns' second division and beginning of the third on the right (Piankoff and Rambova 1954, pls. 12–17). The left wall scenes in Ramesses IX's second corridor are organized into two registers: the upper depicts the Litany of Re deities, part of the Amduat's second hour, and BD 126; the lower register shows the king followed by Hathor, BD 125 text, and the king adoring Khonsu-Neferhotep-Shu. The latter scene represents the king's apotheosis and corresponds to the Osiris shrine scene in the pillared hall of previous Ramesside kings' tomb; it also exemplifies the sun god's assumption of a role formerly held by Osiris (Abitz 1992, 166–167, 176, 180). The right wall is decorated with a ram-headed deity and the Book of Caverns' second, third, and fourth divisions, continuing the sequence of scenes begun on the first corridor's right wall.

Third Corridor (D)

The third corridor (D), in nearly every tomb from Seti I to Siptah, was decorated with the Amduat's fourth hour on the left wall and the fifth hour on the right wall (Hornung 1991, 16–17; 1990, 208–210). Afterward, Tausret's third corridor was decorated with BD 145 vignettes substituting for the kingly Amduat scenes (McCarthy 2008, 97–98). Ramesses III's tomb employs the Amduat scenes from the Seti I template, but they were displaced slightly from their usual location due to difficulties encountered while KV 11 was being cut. An anomalous third chamber (D1) was excavated around a collision with KV 10 and is decorated with divine scenes. The Amduat's fourth and fifth hours were then employed in the following corridor (D2), which resumes on a jogged axis.

In Ramesses IV's tomb, the third corridor is decorated with the Book of Caverns' first and second divisions on the left and right walls, respectively (Hornung et al. 1990, pls. 44–50). In Ramesses V/VI's tomb, the Book of Gates' seventh and eighth hours appear on the left wall, while the right wall is adorned with the Book of Caverns' third, fourth, and the beginning of the fifth division (Piankoff and Rambova 1954, pls. 19–23, 49–53). In Ramesses IX's third corridor, the Amduat's second and third hours are laid out on the left wall. The right wall is decorated with a scene showing the king offering a figure of Maat to Ptah, followed by enigmatic compositions known only from this tomb.

Well-Room (E)

In the tombs of Seti I and Ramesses II, the well-room chamber (E) employs a series of divine scenes showing the king interacting with deities (Hornung 1990, 208–210; 1991, 17–18). Ramesses II, uniquely, decorated his well-shaft with the Amduat's twelfth hour on the left wall and sixth hour on the right wall (Hornung 1999, 28; Leblanc 2001, 215).

Subsequent well-room programs are dominated by deities and employ fewer kings' images. Such well-rooms appear in the tombs of Merenptah, Tausret, and Ramesses III and bear marked similarities to each other, with Merenptah's apparently influencing the decoration of the later two. They have pendant entry wall scenes depicting either the king with Osiris (KV 8) or two pendant Osiris figures (KV 14, KV 11); processions of deities on both side walls, always including the four sons of Horus and funerary goddesses; and pendant images of Anubis and Iunmutef (KV 8) or two Iunmutef figures (KV 14, KV 11) on the rear wall. Seti II's well-room program similarly focuses on deities, though it comprises images of divine and funerary statues painted in the yellow "monochrome" style to imitate gold (Hornung 1990, 180–181; Thomas 1966, 112).

Ramesses V/VI's well-room differs significantly from those of earlier Ramesside kings: it is decorated with the Book of Gates' ninth and tenth hours on the left wall (Piankoff and Rambova 1954, pls. 54–57) and the Book of Caverns' fifth division on the right (Piankoff and Rambova 1954, pls. 24–28a). However, Ramesses IX's well-room, though largely undecorated, has two pendant images of Iunmutef on the rear wall, as in the well-rooms of Tausret and Ramesses III.

Pillared Hall (F)

Pillared hall F, particularly its rear wall, is usually the symbolic midpoint of kings' tombs (Abitz 1992, 166–167, 176, 180; Wilkinson 1995, 79; 1994, 84). Most, from KV 17 to KV 11, are decorated with the Book of Gates' fifth hour on the left half, its sixth hour on the right, and an Osiris shrine scene at the center of the rear wall. In addition, there are typically four pillars with a divine scene on each face. Those from Seti I to Merenptah each show the king with one deity, but all later pillars have only one figure on each face. Tausret's F is adorned with BD 145 vignettes substituting for the Book of Gates, a modified Osiris shrine scene on the rear wall, and no pillars (Hornung 1999, 55–56; 1990, 208–210; McCarthy 2008, 92–93, 99–101).

Of the later Ramesside tombs, only that of Ramesses V/VI has a decorated pillared hall, and its program concludes the Book of Gates and Book of Caverns sequence begun in KV 9's first corridor. The left half is decorated with the Book of Gates' eleventh and twelfth hours, while the Book of Caverns' sixth division appears on the right half and on three faces of the rear, right pillar. The Osiris shrine scene is at the center of the rear wall (Piankoff and Rambova 1954, pls. 30–34, 35, 57a–62, 69–69a).

The Osiris shrine scene represents the apotheosis of the king and marks the transition between the solar-themed upper chambers and the Osirian, chthonic-themed lower part (Abitz 1992, 166–167, 176, 180; Wilkinson 1995, 79; 1994, 84). This scene first appears in KV 17, and it depicts the king and Horus offering to the enthroned Osiris, while Hathor of the West stands behind Osiris (Hornung 1991, 18–19).

The next extant Osiris shrine scene appears in KV 8 and was significantly revised. Merenptah's Osiris shrine scene is centered on the rear wall, directly above the (now-central) doorway to corridor G. The figures of Hathor and Horus were omitted, narrowing the focus to the king's relationship with Osiris. The scene depicts two standing, back-to-back, enshrined figures of Osiris at the center, while one figure of the king offers to and/or adores each Osiris image. Unlike KV 17, the king is outside the shrine. This revised Osiris shrine scene became canonical, appearing for the last time in Ramesses V/VI's tomb.

However, formal/iconographic variations occur in the tombs of Tausret and Ramesses V/VI, but for different reasons. Tausret has a "modified kingly" version, in which Horus and Anubis mediate between the central figures of Osiris and the figures of Tausret. These variations communicate Tausret's less than fully "kingly" status at the time of decoration (McCarthy 2008, 99–101). By contrast, Ramesses V/VI's Osiris shrine scene reflects the increased thematic emphasis on the solar deity and the consequent "solarization" of Osiris apparent in Twentieth Dynasty kings' tombs, as each of the two back-to-back Osiris figures has a sun-disk above his head and wears a solar bark pectoral (Piankoff and Rambova 1954, pl. 35; Abitz 1992, 176).

Pillared Hall Annex (Fa) and Side-Chamber (Faa)

Only the tombs of Seti I and Ramesses III possess a decorated pillared hall annex (Fa). That in KV 17 is adorned with the Amduat's ninth, tenth, and eleventh hours, and its two pillars are decorated with divine scenes (Hornung 1991, 19, 20). KV 11's Fa, which lacks pillars, has the Book of Gates' seventh hour on its side and rear walls. The entry wall is adorned with divine scenes depicting the king with Horus, Osiris, and Thoth. Merenptah's pillared hall annex is undecorated, but it possesses a side chamber (Faa) depicting Osiris-Ramesses II in the company of other funerary deities.

Corridors G and H

During the Nineteenth Dynasty, G and H were usually decorated with the sequence of scenes from the Ritual of the Opening of the Mouth (Hornung 1991, 20–21; 1990, 208–210). The upper register depicts the statue ritual sequence; the lower comprises contiguous vertical columns of offering litany texts and offering lists. However, in the tombs of Merenptah and Ramesses III, only G is decorated with the Opening of the

Mouth. Merenptah's tomb has no corridor H, and Ramesses III's corridor G is followed by a rectangular chamber H decorated with images of enshrined deities.

Ramesses V/VI's tomb is the only late Ramesside tomb having decorated corridors G and H. As in most Nineteenth Dynasty kings' tombs, they are programmatically linked together, but they are decorated with Amduat hours one through eleven. The sequence begins on the left wall of corridor G with the first three hours; continues on the left wall of H with the fourth and fifth hours; resumes on the right wall of G with the sixth, seventh, and eighth hours; and ends on the right wall of H with the eighth through eleventh hours (Piankoff and Rambova 1954, pls. 74–100; Abitz 1989, 98–110).

Antechamber (I)

The antechamber (I) shows the king offering to and receiving favors from various deities in the tombs of Seti I, Tausret, and Ramesses III. Ramesses II and Merenptah likewise employed divine scenes, but both also added BD 125, Ramesses II on the rear wall of his antechamber and Merenptah on the entire left half of his.

The later Ramesside kings with decorated antechambers, Ramesses IV and Ramesses V/VI, eschewed divine scenes in favor of "text heavy" programs that use selections from Book of the Dead 123–129. Ramesses IV's antechamber is adorned entirely with text from BD 123, 124, 127, and 125 on the left wall and from BD 125 on the right (Hornung et al. 1990, 80–82, pls. 54–57). Ramesses V/VI's antechamber is decorated with BD 125 and 124 on the left half of the chamber, and BD 126, BD 127, BD 129, and a hymn to the goddess Maat on the right half (Abitz 1989, 110–116).

Sarcophagus Chamber (J)

Ramesside kings' sarcophagus chambers exhibit greater decorative variation than any others, but all follow the same basic pattern: the walls are adorned with sections from one or more afterlife books, and any pillars are typically decorated with divine scenes or, more rarely, with amuletic motifs, images of Iunmutef, and the souls of Pe and Nekhen. There were two major ceiling types. The completed tombs from Seti I to Ramesses III had astronomical ceilings, while those of Ramesses IV and later adopted the Books of the Day and Night. However, Ramesses VII's sarcophagus chamber ceiling combined these two types (Hornung 1990, 78–79, 86, 100–101, 208, 210; Hornung et al. 1990, pls. 68–75, pl. 10).

The sarcophagus chambers of Seti I and Ramesses II are similarly decorated with two or three of the Book of Gates' first five hours in the front half of the chamber and three of the Amduat's first five hours in the rear half. Seti I's sarcophagus chamber is decorated with the Book of Gates' second, third, and fifth hours and the Amduat's first three hours. The pillars are decorated with scenes depicting the king with male deities, images of Iunmutef, and images of the souls of Pe and Nekhen (Hornung 1991, 208–212). In

Ramesses II's sarcophagus chamber, the Book of Gates' second and third hours adorn the front half, and the Amduat's first, second, and fifth hours are in the rear half, along with "inventory" scenes of funerary objects on the rear wall. The inward-facing sides of the pillars bear images of *djed*-pillars (Hornung 1990, 61); the rest have the usual divine scenes.

Merenptah's sarcophagus chamber utilizes a new decorative scheme incorporating the more solar-oriented Book of Caverns and Book of the Earth in place of the Amduat. This program was copied by Tausret for J1 and J2 and by Ramesses III for J. The decorative scheme comprises selections from the last quarter of the Book of Gates—the ninth, tenth, eleventh, and/or twelfth hours—on the entry walls/front half of the chamber (the ninth hour on the right half of the entry wall, the tenth hour on the left half); the Book of Caverns' closing scenes on the right wall; the closing scenes from both the Book of the Earth and the Book of Gates on the left wall; and extracts from Book of the Earth part A on both. Book of the Earth excerpts also appear on Merenptah's rear wall.

Tausret and Ramesses III have decorative elements unique to their tombs. The walls surrounding Tausret's sarcophagus emplacement in J1 possess dado-level "inventory" scenes, and Ramesses III's has six "guardian deity" scenes that appear on the inner thicknesses of the entrance doorway and above each of the four annex doorways (Abitz 1986, 84–86).

The makeshift sarcophagus chamber in Seti II's unfinished tomb has a simple program tailored to the chamber's small size. It is decorated entirely in paint with rows of standing deities, representing followers of Re and Horus, and mummiform figures from the sixth hour of the Book of Gates. The ceiling is decorated with a single figure of the winged goddess Nut, clothed in a red sheath dress and pictorially distinct from the nude Nut figures in the later Book of the Day and Book of the Night.

Ramesses IV's entire sarcophagus chamber is decorated with scenes from the first quarter of the Book of Gates. The second and third hours are shown on the left, and the fourth hour appears on the right (Hornung et al. 1990, pls. 60–67). This use of the Book of Gates recalls that in the three earliest Ramesside kings' tombs, which employ some of these same scenes on the lateral walls (KV 16) or the front halves of their sarcophagus chambers (KV 17, KV 7).

Ramesses V/VI's J is decorated with the entire Book of the Earth on the walls and images of the king and deities on the faces of the four piers (Abitz 1989, 116–142; 1992, 169). Ramesses VII's sarcophagus chamber is likewise adorned with the Book of the Earth: the first through eighth divisions appear on the left lateral wall, the ninth through seventeenth on the right wall. In addition, the entry wall is decorated with pendant images of the goddesses Werethekau (left half) and Sekhmet-Bastet-Werethekau (right half), while the rear wall has pendant images of the king (Hornung et al. 1990, pls. 115–120).

Ramesses IX's tomb is the last New Kingdom pharaohs' tomb with a decorated sarcophagus chamber. The left half of the entry wall and left wall have extracts from the Book of Caverns' fifth and sixth divisions; the right wall is adorned with the Book of Caverns and Book of the Earth; and the rear wall has scenes representing the king and solar deity in the day and night barks on the cosmographically appropriate upper register, with Osiris awakening below (Abitz 1992, 173, 175, 183; 1990, 31–32).

Sarcophagus Chamber Annexes/Rear Complexes

The earlier sarcophagus chambers of Seti I, Ramesses II, Merenptah, Tausret, and Ramesses III all possess four annexes, and with the exception of Merenptah's tomb, each has at least one rear multichambered complex behind J. Not every annex was decorated, but the repertoire used in these chambers comprises divine scenes (KV 17, KV 7, KV 11); the Book of Gates' fourth, fifth, and sixth hours (KV 17, KV 7); the Amduat's sixth, seventh, eighth (KV 17, KV 17, KV 14), ninth (KV 14), and twelfth (KV 7) hours; BD 110 (KV 7, KV 11) and BD 148 (KV 11); the Book of the Heavenly Cow (KV 17, KV 7, KV 11); and the Opening of the Mouth (KV 14). There is usually a niche/annex dedicated to Osiris and decorated with two-dimensional images (KV 17, KV 7, KV 11), a rock-cut Osiris statue (KV 7, KV 8), or both (KV 7).

In KV 17 and KV 7, the Book of Gates nearly always appear in side chambers at the front of J, while the Amduat appears in chambers at the rear, following the pattern in J itself. In both KV 17 and KV 7, the Book of Gates' fourth hour is featured in the front left annex (Ja), while the Amduat's sixth, seventh, eighth, and twelfth hours appear in side chambers at the rear (Jb in KV 17; Jb, Jc, and Je in KV 7). The use of the Book of Gates' fifth hour and "judgment hall of Osiris" scene in one of KV 7's rear annexes (Jd) is the only exception to this pattern.

Book of the Dead chapters 110 and 148 adorn J side chambers in the tombs of Ramesses II and Ramesses III. BD 110 appears in Jd or Jddd in both KV 7 and KV 11, while BD 148 appears in Ja in KV 11.

The Book of the Heavenly Cow appears in the tombs of Seti I, Ramesses II, and Ramesses III (Hornung 1999, 148), where it always adorns a side chamber expressly reserved for it on the sarcophagus chamber's right side. In KV 17 and KV 7, it is featured in Je in KV 17, Jf in KV 7, and Jc in KV 11.

Neither of Tausret's two sarcophagus chambers has decorated side chambers, but the second J complex (K1, L J2, J2a-d, K2), directly behind the first sarcophagus chamber (J1), comprises two adjoining corridors (K1, L) decorated with the Amduat's sixth through ninth hours. The left walls of K1 and L feature the sixth and seventh hours, respectively, while the right walls are decorated with the ninth and eighth. The second sarcophagus chamber's rear corridor (K2) is decorated with traces of the Opening of the Mouth ritual, the only time this corpus of vignettes appears outside corridors G and H.

Ramesses III's tomb has a triple-chambered rear complex (K1, K2, L) behind the sarcophagus chamber. The only extant decoration, in the first two chambers (K1, K2), comprises images of enshrined deities.

The side chambers dedicated to Osiris, with the exception of those in Ramesses II's tomb, occur on J's left side. The "Osiris niche" in Seti I's tomb is located near the rear corner of the left wall and features Anubis performing the Opening of the Mouth ritual on the enshrined Osiris-Khentyiamentiu (Hornung 1991, 227–228). Ramesses II's tomb possesses two Osirian themed annexes: Jd, on the right half of J, includes the judgment of Osiris scene from the Book of Gates; Je contains a rock-cut statue of Osiris and the Amduat's eighth hour. Merenptah's Ja also houses a rock-cut Osiris statue. Ramesses III's Jb features ten images of Osiris and two jackal standards.

In the more architecturally and programmatically streamlined late Ramesside tombs of Ramesses IV, Ramesses V/VI, and Ramesses VII, there is only one decorated rear chamber or one multichambered complex. Each is decorated with an excerpt from the Book of Caverns (KV 2), the Amduat (KV 9), or the Book of Gates (KV 1). Though there are differences between the programs, offering themes, particularly of food, are shared by two tombs (KV 2, KV 6).

Ramesses IV's sarcophagus chamber has a rear shabti complex (Romer 1981, 280; Černý 1973, 30–31) featuring shabti images in its two side chambers and a central corridor with wall text from the Book of Caverns, scenes of enshrined deities and food offerings, representations of funerary furniture, and goddesses performing the *nyny* ritual (Hornung et al. 1990, pls. 76–88). Ramesses V/VI's rear annex is decorated with the Amduat's twelfth hour and personified decans (Piankoff and Rambova 1954, pls. 122–126), which, appropriately, evokes the rebirth of the sun god and also concludes the sequence of Amduat scenes in G and H. Ramesses VII's rear chamber depicts the king offering to Osiris on both side walls; the rear wall has a central niche with an apotropaic motif from the Book of Gates' sixth hour above it, food offerings below, and an anthropomorphic *djed*-pillar on either side (Hornung et al. 1990, pls. 126–129).

Bibliography

Abitz, F. 1986. *Ramses III. In Den Gräbern Seiner Söhne.* Orbis Biblicus et Orientalis 72. Freiburg and Göttingen.

Abitz, F. 1989. *Baugeschichte und Dekoration des Grabes Rameses' VI.* Orbis Biblicus et Orientalis 89. Freiburg and Göttingen.

Abitz, F. 1990. "Der Bauablauf und Die Dekorationen des Grabes Ramesses' IX." *Studien zur Altägyptischen Kultur* 17: 1–40.

Abitz, F. 1992. "The Structure and Decoration of the Tomb of Ramesses IX." In *After Tutankhamun: Research and Excavation in the Royal Necropolis at Thebes,* edited by C. N. Reeves, 165–185. London and New York.

Altenmüller, H. 1994. "Zweiter Vorbericht über die Arbeiten des Archäologischen Instituts der Universität Hamburg am Grab des Bay (KV 13) im Tal der Könige von Theben." *Studien zur Altägyptischen Kultur* 21: 15–36.

Altenmüller, H. 2001. "The Tomb of Tausret and Setnakht." In *The Treasures of the Valley of the Kings: Tombs and Temples of the Theban West Bank in Luxor,* edited by K. Weeks, 222–231. Cairo: The American University in Cairo Press.

Altenmüller, H. 2003. 'Tausrets Weg zum Königtum Metamorphosen einer Königin." In *Das Königtum der Ramessidenzeit Voraussetzungen—Verwirklichung—Vermächtnis Akten des 3. Symposiums zur ägyptischen Königsideologie in Bonn 7.–9. 6. 2001,* edited by R. Gundlach and U. Rößler-Köhler, 109–128. Wiesbaden.

Barta, W. 1974. "Zur Stundenordnung des Amduat." *Bibliotheca Orientalis* 31: 197–201.

Černý, J. 1973. *The Valley of the Kings: Fragments d'une manuscrit inachevé*. Cairo.

Davis, T. M. 1908. *The Tomb of Siphtah: The Monkey Tomb and the Gold Tomb*. London.

Graves-Brown, C., ed. 2008. *Sex and Gender in Ancient Egypt: "Don Your Wig for a Joyful Hour"*. Swansea.

Gundlach, R., and U. Rößler-Köhler, eds. 2003. *Das Königtum der Ramessidenzeit Voraussetzungen—Verwirklichung—Vermächtnis Akten des 3. Symposiums zur ägyptischen Königsideologie in Bonn 7.–9. 6. 2001*. Wiesbaden.

Hornung, E. 1971. *Das Grab des Haremhab im Tal der Könige*. Bern.

Hornung, E. 1990. *The Valley of the Kings: Horizon of Eternity*. New York.

Hornung, E. 1991. *The Tomb of Pharaoh Seti I/Das Grab Sethos' I*. Zurich and Munich.

Hornung, E. 1995. "Studies on the Decoration of the Tomb of Seti I." In *Valley of the Sun Kings: New Explorations in the Tombs of the Pharaohs*, edited by R. H. Wilkinson, 70–73. Tucson, AZ.

Hornung, E. 1999. *The Ancient Egyptian Books of the Afterlife*. Translated by D. Lorton. Ithaca, NY and London.

Hornung, E. 2001a. "The Tomb of Ramesses I." In *The Treasures of the Valley of the Kings: Tombs and Temples of the Theban West Bank in Luxor*, edited by K. R. Weeks, 190–193. Cairo.

Hornung, E. 2001b. "The Tomb of Thutmosis III." In *The Treasures of the Valley of the Kings: Tombs and Temples of the Theban West Bank in Luxor*, edited by K. R. Weeks, 136–139. Cairo.

Hornung, E., et al. 1990. *Zwei Ramessidische Königsgräber: Rameses IV. und Rameses VII*. Mainz.

Leblanc, C. 1997. "The Tomb of Ramesses II and Remains of his Funerary Treasure." *Journal of Egyptian Archaeology* 10: 11–13.

Leblanc, C. 1998. "Les récentes découvertes dans la tombe de Ramsès II." *Bulletin de la Société Française d'Égyptologie* 141: 20–35.

Leblanc, C. 2001. "The Tomb of Ramesses II." In *The Treasures of the Valley of the Kings: Tombs and Temples of the Theban West Bank in Luxor*, edited by K. R. Weeks, 212–217. Cairo.

Martin, G. T. 1974. *The Royal Tomb at El-'Amarna. Vol. 1, The Objects: The Rock Tombs at El-'Amarna*. Part 7.1. Egypt Exploration Society, Archaeological Survey of Egypt 35. London.

Martin, G. T. 1989. *The Royal Tomb at El-'Amarna. Vol. 2, The Rock Tombs at El-'Amarna*. Part 7.2. Egypt Exploration Society, Archaeological Survey of Egypt 39. London.

McCarthy, H. L. 2008 "Rules of Decorum and Expressions of Gender Fluidity in Tawosret's Tomb." In *Sex and Gender in Ancient Egypt: "Don Your Wig for a Joyful Hour"*, edited by C. Graves-Brown: 83–113. Swansea.

Piankoff, A. 1957. "La tombe de Ramsès I." *Bulletin de l'Institut Français d'Archéologie Orientale* 56: 189–202.

Piankoff, A. 1958. "Les peintures dans le tomb du roi Ai." *Mitteilungen des Deutschen Archäologischen Instituts Abteilung Kairo* 16: 247–251.

Piankoff, A., and N. Rambova, eds. 1954. *The Tomb of Ramesses VI*. Vols. 1 and 2. New York.

Reeves, C. N., ed. 1992. *After Tutankhamun: Research and Excavation in the Royal Necropolis at Thebes*. London and New York.

Reeves, C. N., and R. H. Wilkinson. 1996. *The Complete Valley of the Kings: Tombs and Treasures of Egypt's Greatest Pharaohs*. London.

Richter, B. A. 2008. "The Amduat and Its Relationship to the Architecture of Early 18th Dynasty Royal Burial Chambers." *Journal of the American Research Center in Egypt* 44: 73–104.

Romer, J. 1981. *Valley of the Kings*. Repr. 1988. London.

Thomas, E. 1966. *The Royal Necropoleis of Thebes*. Princeton, NJ.

Weeks, K. R., ed. 2001. *The Treasures of the Valley of the Kings: Tombs and Temples of the Theban West Bank in Luxor*. Cairo.

Wilkinson, R. H. 1993. "The Paths of Re: Symbolism in the Royal Tombs of Wadi Biban el Moluk." *Kmt* 4/3: 43-51.

Wilkinson, R. H. 1994. "Symbolic Location and Alignment in the New Kingdom Royal Tombs and their Decoration." *Journal of the American Research Center in Egypt* 31: 79–86.

Wilkinson, R. H. 1995. "Symbolic Orientation and Alignment in New Kingdom Royal Tombs." In *Valley of the Sun Kings: New Explorations in the Tombs of the Pharaohs*, edited by R. H. Wilkinson, 74–81. Tucson, AZ.

PART VI

INDIVIDUAL
KV TOMBS

CHAPTER 12

··

ROYAL TOMBS OF THE
EIGHTEENTH DYNASTY

··

CATHARINE H. ROEHRIG

TRADITIONALLY, Egyptian cemeteries were located at the edge of the Nile Valley, or on the high ground overlooking it. However, early in the New Kingdom, a ruler of the Eighteenth Dynasty chose to construct a tomb in the hidden *wadi* now called the Valley of the Kings (KV).

Eighteenth Dynasty rulers were undoubtedly influenced by the funerary preparations of earlier kings (see Ch 5). In particular, they were inspired by the Eleventh Dynasty funerary complex of Nebhepetre Mentuhotep, which includes the Bab el-Hosan, with its easily hidden entrance to a meandering corridor ending in a deep shaft.

There is an ongoing debate among Egyptologists about which ruler excavated the first tomb in the Valley of the Kings—Thutmose I or Hatshepsut—and which tomb this was—KV 38 or KV 20. Convincing arguments have been presented supporting each ruler and each tomb, but those in favor of Thutmose I and KV 38 seem the most compelling.

The essential components in any discussion of the earliest KV tomb are the KV landscape and the texts and vignettes of the Amduat found in the earliest kings' tombs, KV 38, 20, and 34. In the best-preserved example, KV 34 (Thutmose III), vignettes illustrating the fifth hour of the night show an oval-shaped cavern of Sokar beneath a shallow pyramid surmounted by a woman's head (see Figure 12.1). The southern end of the valley is dominated by a pyramidal peak, the Qurn, which was sacred to a goddess, Meretseger, and appears to correspond to the pyramid depicted in the fifth hour of the Amduat. KV 38 and 34 are at the southern end of the valley and have oval burial chambers that lie more or less beneath the Qurn. KV 20, cut into a northeast branch of the *wadi*, takes no advantage of this landscape.

In ancient times, funeral processions entered the cemetery from the north and were confronted by the Qurn at the valley's southern end. From this vantage point, KV 38 is located at the base of the cliffs directly below the peak (see Figure 12.2), whereas the locations of KV 34 and 20 are not visible. Considering the prominence of the Amduat in

FIGURE 12.1 Fifth Hour of the Amduat in KV 34.

[Photograph by Harry Burton. Courtesy of the Metropolitan Museum of Art.]

these three early tombs and the way in which the vignettes of the text and the landscape of the valley echo one another, the position of KV 38 appears to be the logical place for the founder of the cemetery to have excavated his tomb.

THE TOMB OF THUTMOSE I—KV 38

Thutmose I never claims a blood relationship with his predecessors. He appears to be establishing a new royal line, and it makes sense that he would want to found a new cemetery, away from Dra Abu el-Naga, where the Seventeenth Dynasty rulers and their immediate successors were buried (Polz 2007). The choice of the Valley of the Kings as the new cemetery appears to coincide with a decision to use the Amduat as decoration in the king's tomb.

A biographical text of the vizier Ineni states that he oversaw the excavation of the tomb of Thutmose I. Ineni describes doing this "in private, no-one seeing, no-one hearing" (*m w''w n m33 n sdm*, Dziobek 1994, 49–53). This phrase seems to make the absurd claim that Ineni created the tomb alone, but it may simply mean that Ineni was solely responsible for getting the work done (Thomas 1966, 71). Taken literally, the words perfectly describe the location of the valley, a very private place, completely hidden from public view (and hearing) behind the cliffs of western Thebes.

KV 38

FIGURE 12.2 Southern end of the Valley of the Kings, with an arrow showing the location of KV 38.

[Photograph by Emile or Henri Béchard, Courtesy of the Metropolitan Museum of Art.]

There is disagreement about the location of Thutmose I's tomb, fueled in part by evidence that the king's mummy was moved at least once, and perhaps twice, within two generations of his death. KV 38 has been a candidate since its discovery in 1899 by Victor Loret (Piacentini and Orsenigo 2004, 226–229, 242–249; Thomas 1966, 71–73). Inside the tomb was a sarcophagus inscribed with the names of Thutmose I and dedicated by "his son." A few years later, Howard Carter and Theodore M. Davis discovered another sarcophagus inscribed for Thutmose in the burial chamber of KV 20. This tomb also contained a sarcophagus recording the names and kingly titles of Thutmose's daughter, Hatshepsut. Closer examination revealed that the first sarcophagus had originally been dedicated to Hatshepsut and then reinscribed for her father. A foundation deposit at the entrance containing objects with Hatshepsut's name suggested that she had commissioned the tomb for herself and had then brought her father from his original burial place (KV 38) to help legitimize her appropriation of the throne (Davis et al. 1906).

In 1935 William C. Hayes (1935, 52–54) argued that the sarcophagus in KV 38 was not made by Thutmose II for his father, but by Thutmose III for the reburial of his grandfather. Hayes suggested that Thutmose III, not wanting his grandfather to remain in

Hatshepsut's tomb, had provided Thutmose I with a new sarcophagus and returned him to his original tomb, KV 38 (Hayes 1935, 138–140).

In 1974 John Romer (1974) suggested that Thutmose I's original tomb, and the earliest in the valley, was actually KV 20. He also theorized that KV 38 was excavated by Thutmose III for his grandfather's reburial. Since then Egyptologists have weighed in on both sides of this issue (Altenmüller 1983; Dodson 1988, 116–117; Reeves 1990, 17–18; Vandersleyen 1995), and there have been suggestions that Thutmose's original tomb is elsewhere, either around Dra Abu el-Naga or in the foothills between there and the valley (Gabolde 1987, 76–81; Polz 2007, 211–229).

The arguments in favor of KV 38 as the earliest tomb include its location (see above), its architecture, and the decoration on its burial chamber walls. The tomb has a simple plan of five elements (see Figure 12.3): a steep entrance with no overhang protecting the doorway (A), a sloping corridor that curves markedly to the left (B), and an asymmetrical room (F) with a steep stairway in the floor leading into an oval-shaped burial chamber (J). The sarcophagus was located at the far end of this room, perpendicular to the tomb's axis, its foot end facing a small side chamber (Ja). In J, Loret noted one pillar, shown slightly off center in the earliest published plan of the tomb (Baedeker 1929, 314). No trace of this pillar remained when the tomb was measured by the Theban Mapping Project in 1980, and its position was estimated. The room is large enough to have more than one support for the ceiling, and it is possible that there were originally two pillars,

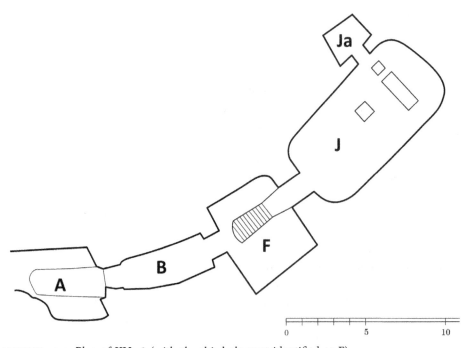

FIGURE 12.3 Plan of KV 38 (with the third element identified as F).

[Theban Mapping Project plan, modified by the author.]

relatively close together and slightly off axis to the left, as in KV 34. Even tombs carved into good quality limestone often have pillars damaged by movement in adjoining layers of expansive shale, so a second pillar might have disappeared by Loret's time.

The letter designations for the architectural elements in KV tombs were assigned by Elizabeth Thomas (1966, 274–276), who recognized that specific rooms along the axis of the royal tombs were usually repeated from one generation to the next, and that discussion would be easier if each of these elements had a unique identifier. Her designations are used here, with a few exceptions. The first occurs in KV 38, where the third element was called chamber C by Thomas. I now believe this room is the first instance of chamber F. Beginning with the tomb of Thutmose III, F is a pillared hall with a stairway leading to the next element. In tombs with an axis offset to the left, the staircase is in the far left corner; in KV 20, with an axis offset to the right, the staircase is in the far right corner of what I call F (TMP J1). Chamber/stairway C in Eighteenth Dynasty tombs is more of a steep stairway, with niches on either side (Preys 2011, 330–332). In KV 34 these niches are quite deep, and one must step up slightly from the staircase to access them. In later tombs, the niches become shallower and farther removed from the stairway.

The third element in KV 38 is a room with a stairway cut into the floor, not a stairway with niches. Although the stairwell is not in the far left corner, it begins about a meter from the entrance on the left side of the room, reinforcing the left curve of the tomb's axis. For these reasons, I have labeled it F in Figure 12.3 and refer to it as such below. But however one identifies this room in KV 38, all five of the elements in the plan are repeated in every completed king's tomb through the middle of the Nineteenth Dynasty, when the identification of Ja becomes problematic (Roehrig 2007).

The cutting of KV 38 is crude, as one might expect of the earliest tomb in the cemetery (Johnson 1992, 70–71). Erosion may account for some of this, especially in A, but evidence for the stairs in F suggests that they were never precisely carved (Carter MSS.i.G.58 on the Griffith Institute website shows this more accurately than the TMP plan). The oval shape of the burial chamber is well formed, with the walls and ceiling once covered with plaster and decorated. The ceiling was painted with stars, and there are traces of a *kheker*-frieze on the upper edge of the southwest wall. Two fragments of plaster inscribed with Amduat texts were recovered by Loret (Daressy 1902, 304; CG 24990 C), and additional fragments found a century later by Mohamed El-Bialy (Mauric-Barberio 2001, 330–332) confirm that the walls of J were decorated with these texts. Judging from the chamber's size and shape, the texts had vignettes similar to those in KV 34, where the fifth hour (Figure 12.1) shows the oval cavern of Sokar below a pyramid, echoing the physical position of KV 38 (with its oval-shaped chamber) beneath the Qurn.

Romer's argument against KV 38 as Thutmose I's original tomb was based on his view that the oval-shaped burial chamber was an innovation of Thutmose III, so tombs with this feature must have been commissioned by this king (Romer 1974; 1975, 346–347). However, one can as easily argue that the oval chamber was created by Thutmose I and copied by his grandson. Romer (1975, n.87) points out that the proportions of J in the two tombs are quite different.

KV 38 is much simpler than KV 34 and lacks chamber E, the well, which was introduced by Thutmose III. The omission of this significant symbolic element seems odd if KV 38 was the work of Thutmose III. The small tomb appears insignificant when compared to KV 34, a more fully realized form of a king's tomb, and one must ask why Thutmose III would create such a deficient sepulcher for his illustrious ancestor. If, however, KV 38 is understood as the first royal tomb excavated in a new cemetery, at a time when funerary practices were being reformulated—a tomb created as part of its natural surroundings and as a vehicle for the texts on its burial chamber walls—then it becomes an impressive, innovative funerary monument that serves as a prototype for the gradual development of the king's sepulcher in the New Kingdom.

THE TOMB OF THUTMOSE II—NOT KNOWN

The location of the tomb of Thutmose II is still debated. No burial equipment inscribed with his name is known, and the identity of his mummy has been questioned (Gabolde 1987, 73–75), so his tomb may still be undiscovered. However, several KV tombs have been suggested. KV 32 was used for a queen's burial (see Bickel, this volume) and was probably designed as such (Preys 2011; Reeves 2003; Roehrig 2010). KV 39, cleared between 1989 and 1994, has an entirely different plan from that postulated by Thomas (Thomas 1966, 73–75, 85). The entrance has the steepness of early Eighteenth Dynasty tombs, but the doorway is eroded and retains no feature that could date it more precisely (Rose 2000, fig. 25). Judging from the plan (Rose 2000, fig. 1) and my own visit to the tomb, the design was altered two and perhaps three times, and its use as the primary burial place for an Eighteenth Dynasty king appears unlikely.

KV 42 has often been identified as a tomb for Thutmose II; however, its entrance had foundation deposits recording the name of Merytre-Hatshepsut, principal wife of Thutmose III, suggesting it was intended for her. Marianne Eaton-Krauss (1999a, 2012) has discussed the tomb and the strongly held opinions about who initiated it and for whom. For me, the foundation deposits, the tomb's plan, the right angle turn of the axis, and the precise carving of the walls indicate that it was created by Thutmose III for his principal queen (Roehrig 2006). The foundation deposits are significant, as few KV tombs have inscribed deposits. The tomb was never used for a royal burial, so it seems unlikely that the deposits are secondary. As no royal name was inscribed on the tomb's walls, or on the sarcophagus inside, why would it be necessary to establish a new owner?

THE TOMB OF HATSHEPSUT—KV 20

KV 20 was not completely explored until 1906, when Carter cleared it for Davis (Davis et al. 1906). The foundation deposit at the entrance convinced Carter that the tomb was

Hatshesput's; later, Romer (1974) suggested that Thutmose I had actually cut the tomb from A through J1. Romer theorized that when Hatshepsut took on the role of king, she added a second burial chamber (J2) and placed the foundation deposit at the tomb's entrance. He based his theory on a comparison of J1 to J2 using Carter's plan (Davis et al. 1906, 76), on which J1 appears substantially larger than J2, suggesting to Romer that J2 was a later addition.

Although Carter's plan gives a reasonable impression of the tomb's size and shape, the measurements are not accurate. Looking at the TMP plan, it is clear that none of the rooms (C1, C2, J1, J2, and J2a–c) is as symmetrical as Carter's plan indicates. In a visit to KV 20 some years ago, I noted a corner of sorts at the far left of J1, not the broad curve on the TMP plan. However, even without this correction, the floor space of J1 is not significantly larger than J2. In addition, Romer's comparison of the modular measurements of J2 with those used in the temples at Deir el-Bahri is incorrect.

As noted above, KV 20 was probably the second tomb in the valley, as it takes no advantage of the landscape. The kings of the Eighteenth Dynasty placed their tombs in separate branches of the *wadi*, usually as far from their predecessor as possible. In the case of Hatshepsut, choosing the northeast branch also brought her closer to Deir el-Bahri, which was one of her principal building sites. It was also a place sacred to the goddess Hathor, a deity associated with female royalty.

The tomb's plan is odd among the royal tombs in the valley. Most noticeably, it curves twice to the right instead of shifting its axis to the left, like most kings' tombs. The three steep stairways inside the tomb (TMP C1, C2, and J1) accentuate this repeated right shift, as does the position of the burial chamber (J2). Romer (1976) studied earlier Theban tombs that make an axial shift to the right, beginning with Hatshepsut's cliff tomb, cut while she was still queen. He concludes that the sharp right angle axial shift in the cliff tomb might have been the inspiration for the right angle shift in Eighteenth Dynasty kings' tombs. Oddly, he does not argue, as I would, that the axial shift to the right in Hatshepsut's cliff tomb, coupled with a similar feature in several other early queens' tombs, supports the idea that KV 20, with its continual shift to the right, was the sole responsibility of Hatshepsut (a female king), not a joint project with her father.

When compared with other Eighteenth Dynasty kings' tombs, KV 20 has other anomalies. The entrance is followed by two steeply sloping corridors which I would call B1 and B2 (TMP B and C1). These are reasonably well carved, and both corridors, like others in the tomb, have shallow stairs along the left side, while the right side is smooth. The curving corridor B2 (TMP C1) leads to the first stairway C (also marked C1 on the TMP plan). This space is more of a stairway with niches than a room with a stairwell in its floor, and I would call this the first occurrence of C in a royal tomb.

C1 is followed by two more sloping corridors and a second stairway C (C2). This doubling of tomb elements may indicate that Hatshepsut intended from the outset to create a double tomb for herself and another king. However, it may simply reflect that there was, as yet, no tradition dictating the plan for the royal tomb. C2 is followed by a very long, sloping corridor (TMP D2) that curves right before entering a large chamber. This is J1 on the TMP plan, but I would identify it as chamber F because of the stairwell in the far right corner. The room is large enough to have at least one pillar supporting the ceiling, but Carter found no evidence for pillars.

The stairwell in F leads to corridor G, which opens into burial chamber J (TMP J2), a room with three pillars and three side rooms. The two sarcophagi were found on either side of the pillars near the far end of the room and appear to have been oriented with their foot ends facing two of the subsidiary rooms, which probably served the function of Ja in other tombs. The third subsidiary room once suggested to me that Thutmose II was also buried in this tomb, but nothing belonging to this king was found, so the third room may simply have been for storage.

The idiosyncrasies in KV 20 probably stem from two circumstances: it was excavated early in the cemetery's history, before any rules governed the design of the king's tomb, and it was created for a female king who had an interest in associating herself with her male predecessors, both in the Eighteenth Dynasty and earlier. As the crow flies, the entrance of KV 20 is between the temples of Hatshepsut and Nebhepetre Mentuhotep at Deir el-Bahri. Although Hatshepsut's temple may have been initiated by either her father or her husband, what stands today is entirely hers. Creative though Hatshepsut was, it is unlikely that she was the first king to build a tomb in the valley. She and her architects were greatly inspired by the funerary complex of Mentuhotep, whose tomb is physically part of the complex. It is difficult to imagine why Hatshepsut would have separated her own tomb from her temple, placing it behind the cliffs of Deir el-Bahri, unless the valley had already been established as a cemetery by her father.

The Tomb of Thutmose III—KV 34

KV 34 was discovered by Loret in 1898 (Loret 1898; Piacentini and Orsenigo 2004, 3–52, 154–164). Ownership of the tomb is certain, as the burial chamber contained the king's sarcophagus, and his name was in texts on the walls of two rooms. The tomb lies in a cleft at the end of the southeast branch of the *wadi*, establishing this as Thutmose's particular section of the cemetery. KV 34 takes advantage of the natural landscape, with the pyramidal Qurn visible as one approaches the tomb through the main valley. It is not as well positioned as KV 38 in this respect, but it is the next best site.

The tomb may have been started soon after Thutmose came to the throne. The asymmetrical configuration of elements A–D is reminiscent of the free-form cutting of KV 38, but the carving of chambers E, F, and J is quite precise. This suggests that work was interrupted for some time—perhaps when Hatshepsut became coruler and began her own tomb. As there was still no set design for the royal tomb, it is interesting to see which elements KV 34 shares with KV 38 and 20, and which appear for the first time, becoming integral parts of later New Kingdom royal tombs.

KV 34 begins with the typical steep staircase (A) and a doorway cut directly into the cliff face with no protective overhang. The steps are uneven and meet the doorway at an angle, continuing into the sloping corridor B. The steep stairway of C begins halfway through gate C, and the deep niches on either side are asymmetrical and slightly higher than the nearest step. The right jamb of gate C has been removed, the uneven stairs in C are broken, and the door lintel of gate D has been cut away, all probably to facilitate entry of large funerary furniture. Such modifications occur in nearly every royal tomb from Thutmose III to Merenptah, suggesting that the tomb designers and the sarcophagus makers did not communicate.

Corridor D curves slightly to the right and leads to a rectangular chamber E, a new addition. In Eighteenth Dynasty royal tombs, the gate between D and E was always blocked with a combination of stones, bricks, and plaster after the king's burial. A different method was used in KV 34. At the end of corridor D the floor was leveled and the angle of the ceiling changed to create a lintel above gate E (Roehrig 2006, 239–240). These alterations allowed the installation of a wooden door. Judging from the initial slope of the ceiling, it originally joined the top of gate E, leaving no lintel, and the floor sloped gradually from the beginning to the end of D. This suggests that the door was not part of the original plan. A door does not occur here again until Ramesses II.

KV 34 is the first tomb to have chamber E—the so-called well—along its main axis, but not the first royal tomb at Thebes. At the beginning of the Eighteenth Dynasty, two royal tombs included the feature: AN B above Dra Abu el-Naga and TT 358 at Deir el-Bahri. There is also a shaft at the end of the Bab el-Hosan in the funerary complex of Nebhepetre Mentuhotep of the Eleventh Dynasty. Chamber E becomes an integral part of completed royal tombs through the end of the Twentieth Dynasty, though there is no shaft after Ramesses III. It probably served a ceremonial function or was symbolic of some portion of the netherworld, such as the tomb of Sokar/Osiris (see Weeks, chapter 8). In KV 34 the upper part of E was partially decorated: the ceiling with stars and the walls with a *kheker*-frieze at the top. The cutting of the walls and corners is more precise than in A–D, and this continues through the burial chamber, suggesting that E–J were excavated at a later date, perhaps after workmen had completed Hatshepsut's tomb.

Beyond E is a large, asymmetrical chamber with two pillars (F). Although the corners are not square, the cutting of the walls and pillars is precise. In his detailed study of KV 34, Romer (1975, 325) argues that the unfinished southeast corner and the asymmetrical shape of F are indications of haste. However, the unfinished corner may be an outcropping of flint left in place by the tomb's excavators, and the asymmetry may be due to errors in surveying around the pillars (Romer 1975, 328 suggests surveying errors to account for idiosyncrasies in chamber J).

Chamber F in KV 34 may take its inspiration from F in KV 20 (TMP J1). Each room has a stairway cut into the far corner that leads to the burial chamber (left corner in KV 34, with its axis shift to the left; right corner in KV 20, with its axis shift to the right).

In KV 34 the F ceiling was painted with stars; the pillars were marked with grids, but left undecorated; and the walls were laid out with rectangles enclosing the images and names of underworld figures in the Amduat. This decoration closely links chamber F to the burial chamber, where the full version of the Amduat appears. Eric Hornung has suggested that F acts symbolically as a second burial chamber, reflecting the duality often seen in Egyptian royal funerary architecture (1999, 27).

In the F stairwell, only the first eight steps are preserved. The lower ones were cut away in ancient times and replaced with built steps that fill only half the stairwell. The left jamb of gate F and the lintel of gate J were also partially cut away. These modifications were needed to bring the sarcophagus into the tomb. At a later date, gate J was fitted with a wooden door (Roehrig 2006, 242).

The F stairway leads directly into burial chamber J, without the intervening corridor G of KV 20. The room is a wide oval, with two pillars placed off axis to the left and four storage rooms. The corners of these rooms are not square, but the walls are well dressed, and each room had a single-leaf wooden door. Similar doors were installed on the side rooms of chamber J through the end of the Eighteenth Dynasty (Roehrig 1995). Sunk into the floor at the far end of the chamber is a plinth supporting the sarcophagus. This is oriented perpendicular to the room's axis, with its foot end to the right facing one of the side rooms, which I would label Ja (TMP Jc).

The walls, ceiling, and pillars of J were carefully prepared for decoration (Romer 1974, 331–332). The ceiling is painted with stars; the pillars present figures from the Litany of Re and the abbreviated text of the Amduat; and the curving walls are treated like a huge, unrolled papyrus recording the complete texts and vignettes of the Amduat. The deities and denizens of the underworld have been painted with a graceful elegance and the texts with a confident fluidity that makes chamber J in KV 34 one of the most memorable spaces in the valley.

In ancient Egyptian, what we now call the Amduat ("What is in the Underworld") is entitled the "Writings of the Hidden Chamber" (Piankoff 1954, 230–318), and in the introductions to the twelve hours of the night, the text specifies where each hour should appear in this hidden room. In KV 34, an attempt was made to paint the hours on the designated walls: hours 1–4 are on what is understood as the west wall; 5–6 on the south wall (see Figure 12.1); 7–8 on the north wall; and 9–12 on the east. The oval shape of the room allows a fluid interpretation of where one cardinal point ends and the next begins. Thus, the burial chamber becomes the hidden chamber in the netherworld. The fourth hour of the night frames the entrance into J. On the left side is a map of the sun's course, with the route ending at the door jamb (Roehrig 2006, fig. 10). This juxtaposition suggests that the architecture of the tomb, with its three steep staircases separated by corridors and chambers, symbolizes the sun's pathway. The odd spacing of the side chambers and the positions of the pillars also may have been intended to work with the decoration on the walls (Roehrig 2006, 242–246).

THE TOMB OF AMENHOTEP II—KV 35

Loret discovered KV 35 in 1898 in the southwest branch of the *wadi* (Loret 1998, 98–112; Piacentini and Orsenigo 2004, XLVI–LVI, 51–150, 164–172). The tomb contained objects from the robbed burial of Amenhotep II, including a sarcophagus with the king's mummy. KV 35 also had been used as a cache for the mummies of other kings, royal family members, and nonroyal individuals.

Between entrance A and pillared hall F, the plan builds on that of KV 34. The entrance is difficult to evaluate today, as a modern concrete structure obscures any details that might remain. An early plan drawn by Emile Baraize suggests that there was no protective overhang (Piacentini and Orsenigo 2004, 164), which seems likely, but there is no evidence for the staircase he reconstructs here (Baraize frequently evens out measurements in his plans). The cutting of B-J is quite precise (similar to E-J in KV 34). The stairs in C are poorly preserved, but they appear to starts at the beginning of gate C and end at gate D. The C niches are relatively symmetrical and shallower than in KV 34.

The well chamber E is rectangular, with decoration similar to KV 34, but the well itself is deeper, and there is a room, Ea, excavated at the bottom on the right. Any problems the Egyptians had surveying around pillars in KV 34 were solved by Amenhotep's time, and F in KV 35 appears perfectly rectangular, with two pillars in the center, but the room is undecorated. As in KV 34, the tomb changes axis to the left, with a staircase in the far left corner. However, in KV 35 this shift is almost exactly 90 degrees, and the rest of the tomb becomes markedly different from KV 34.

The staircase in F leads to a corridor G, last seen in Hatshepsut's tomb. At the end of this gradually sloping corridor, the floor has been leveled in front of gate J, and other alterations have been made to facilitate the installation of a wooden door that was not part of the original plan (Roehrig 1995, 86–87). The burial chamber is entirely different from J in KV 34. Instead of being oval, it is rectangular. Entering the room, one walks between two rows of three pillars and down a stairway into a crypt, where the sarcophagus has been set perpendicular to the room's axis with the foot end to the left, opposite one of four side rooms, Ja (TMP Jb). The crypt also has four magical niches, two carved in the walls on each side of the sarcophagus (Roth and Roehrig 2002).

Although the Amduat is still the principal decoration in the burial chamber, the hours are not placed on the correct walls, but appear in order around the room. Pillars are now decorated with figures of the king interacting with various deities. The changes in J, the omission of decoration in F, the addition of Ea, and the reintroduction of G suggest that the Egyptians' understanding of the royal tomb was evolving.

The Tomb of Thutmose IV—KV 43/KV 22

KV 43 was discovered by Carter and Davis in 1903 in the northeast branch of the valley (Carter and Newberry 1904). Foundation deposits and burial equipment recorded the name of Thutmose IV. The tomb's plan follows KV 35 from A to G with slightly larger dimensions. Modern construction obscures what may remain of the badly eroded entrance A. The earliest plan (Carter and Newberry 1904, xxviii) shows a steep stairway and no protective overhang. The door jambs and stairs inside the tomb were removed in ancient times to make way for the large sarcophagus, but profiles of the steps in C and H

indicate that they were evenly cut. Corridor B leads to stairway C, which has high, shallow niches. The stairs start at the beginning of gate C and end at gate D. Chamber E is
almost perfectly square, with a chamber, Ea, at the bottom in the far wall. The decoration
in E is similar to KV 34 and 35.

The tomb's axis turns 90 degrees to the left in F, and a broad stairwell in the far left
corner leads to G. Here, Thutmose added two elements to the axis: stairway H with high,
shallow niches (reminiscent of C), and antechamber I. These two additions completed
the plan of the royal tomb, with ten chambers and corridors along the axis between
A and J.

Chamber I has stars on the ceiling, and two walls (left and straight ahead) are painted
with figures of the king and various deities (cf. pillars in KV 35). The gate leading to J is
at the far end of the left wall, shifting the tomb's axis another 90 degrees left. The decoration on either side of gate J is more carefully painted than the *kheker*-frieze across the
lintel, suggesting that the wall paintings had been finished before the gate was sealed and
painted over. Gate J has a thick, compound jamb with pivot holes for a wooden door.
This door is now part of architectural design, not an afterthought as in KV 35 and 34
(Roehrig 1995).

The burial chamber is similar to KV 35, but smaller. The huge sarcophagus is oriented with its foot to the left, opposite chamber Ja (TMP Jc). It seems that, at this
time, the Egyptians understood Ja to be on the east side of the burial chamber and
the mummy, rising up, would face this room, and presumably the rising sun (see KV
34, 35, 38). The crypt has seven magical niches laid out in red paint. Four of these are
reasonably well finished (Roth and Roehrig 2002, 124). J is undecorated, but lumps
of mud plaster in symmetrical rows on the walls suggest that decoration was about
to begin.

THE TOMB OF AMENHOTEP III—WV 22

WV 22, in the western branch of the larger KV *wadi* system, was superficially explored
by Davis and partially cleared by Carter and Lord Carnarvon (Thomas 1966, 83–87).
Since 1989, Waseda University has been working in the tomb (Yoshimura 2008).

WV 22 contained burial equipment of Amenhotep III, who also decorated the walls
in E, I, and J. However, Carter discovered foundation deposits with cartouche plaques
recording the names of Thutmose IV. For Carter, this indicated that Thutmose had initiated the tomb for his son while Amenhotep was crown prince (Romer 1981, 240, agreed).
Other scholars have suggested that Thutmose abandoned work on KV 43; began excavating WV 22 as a new tomb for himself; died when the tomb was only partially completed; and was buried in his original tomb, KV 43 (Eaton-Krauss 1999b, 334; Yoshimura
2008, 261–262). However, the WV 22 foundation deposits might indicate something else
entirely. It is curious that only the cartouche plaques are inscribed, unlike the deposits
of KV 43, where numerous objects recorded Thutmose IV's throne name, Menkheperre.

In Carter's list of objects from the deposits, he records the name on one group of plaques (no. 50) as Menkheperre, the throne name of Thutmose III (Carter, H. Notebook D, 2). Perhaps this was an error on Carter's part, but I suggest that Amenhotep III initiated WV 22 and included cartouche plaques in the foundation deposits as a way of honoring his father (and perhaps his great-grandfather).

WV 22 is in the West Valley of the Kings, a location that carries on the tradition of a king laying claim to his own section of the cemetery by placing his tomb some distance from that of his predecessor. A natural pyramid in the area may have influenced the tomb's placement (Yoshimura 2008, 245). The steep entrance A is cut into a hillside instead of beneath cliffs and, for the first time, the doorway, gate B, has a protective overhang, a feature associated with this type of entrance in later KV tombs. As in KV 43, there are ten elements along the axis from A to J, but the corridors are 20 percent wider, and the burial chamber is larger (contrary to Romer 1981). Other differences include a compound door jamb on gate B, which usually signals a wooden door, but here the soffit slopes, precluding a door. The ceiling in C slopes, making the shallow niches triangular in profile, and E has a single, unfinished chamber, Ea, cut at the bottom of the shaft, directly below corridor D.

WV 22 makes the standard 90 degree left turn in F, but G and H have no gate separating them, and H has no niches. Gate J has a compound jamb with pivot holes for a door and enters J off axis, effectively causing a second axial shift of 90 degrees to the right. In the crypt at the end of J, the sarcophagus lies perpendicular to the room's axis, with its foot facing chamber Ja (TMP Jd). There are five magical niches in the crypt, two on each side of the sarcophagus and one at the head end. There is also one niche in each of six doorways that enter/exit J (Yoshimura 2008, 255).

J originally had four side chambers and a suite of rooms probably intended for Amenhotep's principal wife, Tiye (TMP Jc-Jcc). The main room (Jc) has one pillar, and the side chamber (Jcc) probably functioned as Ja for the queen's mummy. A second suite of rooms was created by modifying one of the four side chambers (TMP Jb-Jbb), probably for Amenhhotep's eldest daughter, Sitamun, whom he married late in his reign (Yoshimura 2008, 256). These queens' suites are an innovation of Amenhotep III, whose principal wife was a prominent figure during his reign.

Interestingly, the decoration in chambers E and I includes representations of the *ka* of Thutmose IV accompanying his son while Amenhotep III interacts with various deities. No other king's tomb in the valley has a representation of the owner's father (the only thing similar is Hatshepsut's double burial with Thutmose I in KV 20). This inclusion of Thutmose IV in the tomb's decoration is undoubtedly related to the presence of the king's cartouche plaques in the foundation deposits. Betsy Bryan (1991, 194–195) suggests that Amenhotep is acknowledging his father's involvement in founding KV 22, which is logical if Thutmose did, in fact, initiate work on the tomb. However, it is also possible that Amenhotep chose to enlist his father's aid in the journey to the afterlife by naming Thutmose in the foundation deposits and representing him on the tomb walls.

The Tomb of Amenhotep IV/ Akhenaten—WV 23? and/or the Royal Tomb at Amarna

Amenhotep IV (later Akhenaten) may have started a tomb at the far end of the West Valley. The first three elements of WV 23 are similar to WV 22. Entrance A is cut into the hillside and has a pronounced overhang; gate B has a compound jamb with sloping soffit; stairway C has a sloping ceiling and triangular niches. But WV 23 was not completed. Instead, Akhenaten excavated a modified version of a KV tomb in the Royal *Wadi* at Amarna (Martin 1989, pls. 11A–12). The entrance faces due east with no protective overhang. Steep stairs in A have a central ramp, a feature repeated in C, but not again until the Ramesside period. C is truncated, with a sloping ceiling and only vestigial niches near the entrance. C leads directly into E, which is less than 4 meters deep. Chamber F (Martin's E) has two pillars to the left of the entrance. A depression in the shallow crypt suggests the sarcophagus was parallel to the axis. The small, high room in the far right wall of F appears to be a version of Ja rather than an aborted change of axis to the right. Mark Lehner's elevation drawing shows that the sun's rays could have reached F. This would explain the truncated form of C and the omission of D. Akhenaten may have intended to continue the tomb along a straight axis, allowing sunlight to penetrate as far as possible. However, his sarcophagus was not placed in direct sunlight even in the present form of the tomb (Eaton-Krauss 1999b, 334; Reeves and Wilkinson 1996, 119).

Off the right side of B, a series of corridors snakes left, and a suite of rooms off the right side of C suggests a queens' suite similar to those in WV 22.

The Tomb of Tutankhamun—KV 62

Before his early death, Tutankhamun probably initiated one of the two unfinished royal tombs in the West Valley (WV 23 or 25), or KV 57 in the main valley—but there is no evidence to prove which might have been his intended tomb. Ultimately, the king was interred in a small, nonroyal corridor tomb that was adapted for a royal burial. Discovered in 1922 by Carter and Carnarvon (Carter and Mace 1923–1933), KV 62 is the most famous tomb in the valley. The entrance is steep, with a protective overhang that suggests it dates no earlier than WV 22. Corridor B leads to an antechamber (I) with a small annex room (Ia). Burial chamber J is off the right end of I, effectively shifting the tomb's axis to the right. The floor of J was excavated into a crypt where the sarcophagus lies parallel to the tomb's original axis. The sarcophagus foot faces side chamber Ja (the Treasury). Four magical niches, their contents in place, were found in J, one in each wall. A fifth was carved into a wall of antechamber I. The decoration in J only suggests the

Amduat, with the apes on the west wall. The other walls show Tutankhamun interacting with deities, and the Opening of the Mouth ceremony performed by Ay, his elderly successor.

Perhaps during Tutankhamun's reign, at least some of the royal burials at Amarna were transferred to Thebes and reburied in another small, corridor tomb opposite KV 62. KV 55 was discovered in 1907 by Davis and Edward R. Ayerton. The entrance has a deeper overhang than KV 62, and the corridor is nearly 33 percent wider, suggesting that the tomb was excavated later (perhaps contemporary with KV 57). The floor of J was excavated into a crypt, and the unfinished side chamber probably acted as Ja, but no magical niches were cut into the walls. Equipment of several royal burials was found in the tomb.

THE TOMB OF AY—KV 23

Ay was a high official in the reigns of Akhenaten and Tutankhamun. His tomb, KV 23, was discovered by Giovanni Belzoni in 1816 (Thomas 1966, 90–92) and completely cleared in 1972 by Otto Schaden (1977, 226–253). Whether Ay excavated KV 23 himself or appropriated an unfinished tomb is impossible to determine. A–E are similar to WV 22, but in stairway C a substantial overhang precedes the doorway into D, a feature only found again in KV 57 (see below). There was no shaft in E, which leads to a rectangular room probably intended to be chamber F, but adapted as burial chamber J when the king died. Modifications included the addition of side room Ja and four magical niches, one in each wall of J.

Reeves and Wilkinson (1996, 129) note a "characteristic post-Amarna straightening of the axis," but details suggest an intended, and unusual, axial shift to the right. The doorway exiting E (gate J in this tomb) is at the right side of the far wall instead of the left side, as in WV 22 and other tombs with an axial shift to the left. J extends to the right of this door, effectively shifting the axis 90 degrees right. The decoration in J is similar in style to KV 62, but Ay has a hunting scene, something usually found in officials' tombs.

With the tomb of Ay's successor, Horemheb (see ch 13), significant changes began the transformation of the tombs of the following dynasty.

BIBLIOGRAPHY

Altenmüller, H. 1983. "Bemerkungen zu den Königsgräbern des neuen Reiches." *Studien zur Altägyptischen Kultur* 10: 25–61.

Baedeker, K. 1929. *Egypt and Sûdân: A Handbook for Travellers*. London and New York.

Bryan, B. M. 1991. *The Reign of Thutmose IV*. Baltimore and London.

Carter, H. Notebook D, 2, Griffith Institute Archive I.J.386.4.

Carter, H., and A. C. Mace. 1923–1933. *The Tomb of Tutankhamen: Discovered by the Earl of Carnarvon and Howard Carter*, 3 vols. London and New York.

Carter, H., and P. Newberry. 1904. *The Tomb of Thoutmôsis IV*. Vol. 1 of *Mr. Theodore M. Davis' Excavations: Bibân el Molûk*. Westminster.

Daressy, G. 1902. *Fouilles de la Vallée des Rois (1898–1899). Catalogue général des antiquités égyptiennes du musée du Caire*, nos. 61001–61044. Cairo.

Davis, T. M. 1912. *The Tombs of Harmhabi and Touatânkhamanou.* Vol. 7 of *Theodore M. Davis' Excavations: Bibân el Molûk.* London.

Davis, T. M., E. Naville, and H. Carter. 1906. *The Tomb of Hâtshopsîtû.* Vol. 2 of *Theodore M. Davis' Excavations: Bibân el Molûk.* London.

Dodson, A. M. 1988. "The Tombs of the Kings of the Early Eighteenth Dynasty at Thebes." *Zeitschrift für Ägyptische Sprache* 115: 110–123.

Dorman, P. F., and B. M. Bryan, eds. 2007. *Sacred Spaces and Sacred Function in Ancient Thebes.* Studies in Ancient Oriental Civilizations no. 61. Chicago.

Dziobek, E. 1994. *Die Gräber des Vizirs User-Amun Theben Nr. 61 und 131.* Mainz.

Eaton-Krauss, M. 1999a. "The Fate of Sennefer and Senetnay at Karnak Temple and in the Valley of the Kings." *Journal of Egyptian Archaeology* 85: 113–129.

Eaton-Krauss, M. 1999b. "Book Review of Reeves and Wilkinson 1997." *Bibliotheca Orientalis* 56: 330–338.

Eaton-Krauss, M. 2012. "Who commissioned KV 42 and for whom?" *Göttinger Miszellen* 234: 53–60.

El-Bialy, M. 1999. "Récentes recherches effectuées dans la tombe no. 42 de la Vallée des Rois." *Memnonia X*: 161–178, pls. XLIII–XLVII.

Engel, E.-M., U. Hartung, and V. Mueller, eds. 2008. *Zeichen aus dem Sand: Streiflichter aus Ägyptens Geschichte zu Ehren von Günter Dreyer, Menes V.* Wiesbaden.

Gabolde, L. 1987. "La Chronologie du règne de Thoutmosis II, ses conséquences sur la datation des momies royales et leurs répercussions sur l'histoire du développement de la Vallée des rois." *Studien zur Altägyptischen Kultur* 14: 61–81, pls. 2–3.

Hawass, Z., and S. Ikram, eds. 2010. *Studies in Honour of Kent R. Weeks.* Supplément aux Annales du Service des Antiquités de L'Egypte, Cahier 41. Cairo.

Hayes, W. C. 1935. *Royal Sarcophagi of the XVIII Dynasty.* Princeton, NJ.

Hornung, E. 1999. *The Ancient Egyptian Books of the Afterlife.* Ithaca, NY and London.

Johnson, G. B. 1992. "'No One Seeing, No One Hearing,' KV Prototombs 38 and 20: The First Royal Tombs in the Valley of the Kings." *Kmt* 3 (4): 64–81.

Kline, E., and D. O'Connor, eds. 2006. *Thutmose III: A New Biography.* Ann Arbor, MI.

Loret, V. 1898. "Le tombeau de Thoutmès III à Biban el-Molouk." *Bulletin de l'Institut d'Égypte* (3 série) 9: 91–112.

Martin, G. T. 1989. *The Royal Tomb at El-'Amarna II, the Reliefs, Inscriptions, and Architecture: The Rock Tombs of El-'Amarna, Part VII.* Archaeological Survey of Egypt, Thirty-Ninth Memoir. London.

Mauric-Barberio, F. 2001. "Le Premier exemplaire du Livre de l'Amdouat." *Bulletin de l'Institut Français d'Archéologie Orientale* 101: 315–350.

Piacentini, P., and C. Orsenigo, eds. 2004. *La Valle Dei Re Riscoperta: I giornali di scavo di Victor Loret (1909–1899) e altri inediti.* Milan.

Piankoff, A. 1954. *The Tomb of Ramesses VI.* Bolingen Series XL:1. New York.

Polz, D. 2007. *Der Beginn des Neuen Reiches: Zur Vorgeschichte einer Zeitenwende.* Sonderschift (Deutsches Archäologisches Institut. Abteilung Kairo) 31. Berlin.

Polz, D. 2008. "Mentuhotep, Hatschepsut und das Tal der König—eine Skizze." In *Zeichen aus dem Sand: Streiflichter aus Ägyptens Geschichte zu Ehren von Günter Dreyer, Menes V*, edited by E.-M. Engel, U. Hartung, and V. Mueller, 525–533. Wiesbaden.

Preys, R. 2011. "Les tombes non-royales de la Vallée des Rois." *Studien zur Altägyptischen Kultur* 40: 315–338.

Reeves, C. N. 1990. *Valley of the Kings: The Decline of a Royal Necropolis*. London and New York.

Reeves, C. N. 2003. "On Some Queens' Tombs of the Eighteenth Dynasty." In *The Theban Necropolis: Past, Present and Future*, edited by N. Strudwick and J. H. Taylor, 69–73. London.

Reeves, N., and R. H. Wilkinson. 1996. *The Complete Valley of the Kings: Tombs and Treasures of Egypt's Greatest Pharaohs*. London.

Roehrig, C. H. 1991. "Some Thoughts on the Occupant of Tomb 42 in the Valley of the Kings." Paper presented at the Sixth International Congress of Egyptologists, Turin.

Roehrig, C. H. 1995. "Gates to the Underworld: the Appearance of Wooden Doors in the Royal Tombs of the Valley of the Kings." In *Valley of the Sun Kings: New Explorations in the Tombs of the Pharaohs*, edited by R. H. Wilkinson, 82–107. Tucson, AZ.

Roehrig, C. H. 2006. "The Building Activities of Thutmose III in the Valley of the Kings." In *Thutmose III: A New Biography*, edited by E. Kline and D. O'Connor, 238–259, figs. 6.1–6.19. Ann Arbor, MI.

Roehrig, C. H. 2007. "Chamber Ja in Royal Tombs in the Valley of the Kings." In *Sacred Spaces and Sacred Function in Ancient Thebes*, edited by P. F. Dorman and B. M. Bryan, 117–138. Chicago.

Roehrig, C. H. 2010. "Some Thoughts on Queens Tombs in the Valley of the Kings." In *Studies in Honour of Kent R. Weeks*, edited by Z. Hawass and s. Ikram, 181–195. Cairo.

Romer, J. 1974. "Tuthmosis I and the Bibân el-Molûk: Some Problems of Attribution." *Journal of Egyptian Archaeology* 60: 119–133.

Romer, J. 1975. "The Tomb of Tuthmosis III." *Mitteilungen des Deutschen Archäologischen Instituts, Abteilung Kairo* 31: 315–351.

Romer, J. 1976. "Royal Tombs of the Early Eighteenth Dynasty." *Mitteilungen des Deutschen Archäologischen Instituts, Abteilung Kairo* 32: 191–206.

Romer, J. 1981. *The Valley of the Kings*. New York.

Rose, J. 2000. *Tomb KV 39 in the Valley of the Kings: A Double Archaeological Enigma*. Bristol.

Roth, A. M., and C. H. Roehrig. 2002. "Magical Bricks and the Bricks of Birth." *Journal of Egyptian Archaeology* 88: 121–139.

Schaden, O. J. 1977. "The God's Father Aye." PhD diss., University of Michigan (University Microfilms Iinternational 78-9739).

Strudwick, N., and J. H. Taylor, eds. 2003. *The Theban Necropolis: Past, Present and Future*. London.

Thomas, E. 1966. *The Royal Necropoleis of Thebes*. Princeton, NJ.

Vandersleyen, C. 1995. "Who Was the First King in the Valley of the Kings?" In *Valley of the Sun Kings: New Explorations in the Tombs of the Pharaohs*, edited by R. H. Wilkinson, 22–24. Tucson, AZ.

Weeks, K. R., ed. 2000. *Atlas of the Valley of the Kings*. Cairo.

Wente, E. F. 1982. "Mysticism in Pharaonic Egypt?" *Journal of Near Eastern Studies* 41: 161–179.

Wilkinson, R. H., ed. 1995. *Valley of the Sun Kings: New Explorations in the Tombs of the Pharaohs*. Tucson, AZ.

Yoshimura, S., ed. 2008. *Research in the Western Valley of the Kings [of] Egypt: The Tomb of Amenophis III (KV 22)*. English Summary 237–278. Tokyo.

CHAPTER 13

ROYAL TOMBS OF THE NINETEENTH DYNASTY

HARTWIG ALTENMÜLLER

INTRODUCTION

THE Valley of Kings, called "the Great Field" in ancient Egyptian writings (Meeks 1998, 343, 78.3739; Ventura 1986, 184–186), divides into east and west branches, the first of which accommodates the royal tombs of the Nineteenth and Twentieth Dynasties. In fact, even the early kings of the Eighteenth Dynasty laid out their tombs in hidden places in this eastern branch. When keeping the site of a tomb secret did not prove to be a guarantee of the safety of the royal burial—the first tomb robberies already occurred during the Eighteenth Dynasty—increased security measures were instituted in the Nineteenth Dynasty, including intensive surveillance of the burial sites to protect the tombs from robberies (see ch 29). The tombs of the Nineteenth Dynasty were thus more openly positioned in the middle of the eastern branch of the valley. At the same time, the newly installed security system, which became effective during the rule of Ramesses II, allowed for the display of the royal tombs, which now, for the first time, featured monumental tomb fronts.

The tomb's basic structure was also influenced by the royal tombs of the Amarna era. The first king who had himself entombed in the east branch of the Valley of the Kings after the time of Amarna was Horemheb. This king, who had risen from the elite of the old Egyptian military to royalty at the end of the Eighteenth Dynasty, abandoned his "private tomb" in Saqqara near Memphis and ordered the construction of a legitimate royal tomb in the Valley of the Kings. His royal tomb marks an intermediate stage between royal tombs of the Eighteenth and Nineteenth Dynasties, wherein the layout, although traditional in some ways, already exhibits characteristics of royal tombs of the Nineteenth Dynasty.

The Royal Tombs from Horemheb
to Tausret

Horemheb Djeserkheprure: KV 57—Reign, 1319–1292 B.C.E.; Length of Tomb, 127.88 m/419.55 ft.

It is doubtless significant that Horemheb had his own tomb cut at a spot close to the tomb of Amenhotep II (KV 35) in the Eastern Valley of the Valley of the Kings, and not, as his predecessors Aye (KV 23) and Amenhotep III (KV 22) had done, in the Western Valley. In designing his tomb, however, Horemheb was left with little leeway, since the order of the corridors and chambers of the royal tomb were substantially established. Every chamber had an individual symbolic significance (see chs 8 and 20).

Generally, this significance involved one of two major themes. The first concerns the deeds of the king in the realm of the gods. The king is depicted before the gods, worshiping them and offering them sacrifices. The other theme concerns the depiction of the world beyond the threshold of death, where the sun god resides during the night. This netherworld, which is divided into different chambers traversed by the sun god in his boat during the nocturnal hours, is described in great detail in texts and pictures. Therefore, designing the tomb involved not only planning the number and size of the chambers, but also, from a symbolic perspective, the question of how the king reaches the gods and where in the netherworld he meets the sungod (Hornung 1971).

The king's symbolic journey to the netherworld took place on the tomb axis. During the Amarna period, the axis was spirally bent, but Horemheb opted for a straight tomb axis, which he skillfully divided into two parts, creating the illusion of a bent axis. The first part of the tomb axis leads from the entrance (A) down to the well chamber (E), while the second part of the tomb axis, which is slightly shifted to the left, resumes the axial path in the lower area of the tomb from the pillared hall (F) to the sarcophagus chamber (J).

In decorating his tomb, as was common in the pre-Amarna era, Horemheb confined himself to the three focal parts of the monument—the so called well chamber (E), the vestibule of the sarcophagus chamber (I), and the actual sarcophagus chamber (J) with its adjoining chambers. However, in contrast to the pre-Amarna era, for the first time the decoration was molded in the form of painted relief and not as simple paintings as in former tombs. All the depictions feature either a painted relief or display, or, in their partly unfinished state, the preparation for the affixing of a relief and its subsequent painting.

As in earlier times, the king is depicted worshiping the gods in the well chamber and the vestibule to the sarcophagus chamber. In the transcendent world, the king steps in front of selected deities associated with the afterlife, among them Anubis, Isis, Horus, Hathor, and Osiris (James 2001, 183–186). As in earlier tombs, the sarcophagus chamber is the place where the depiction of the sun god's netherworld journey through the twelve hours of the night is located. As opposed to what was done in the Eighteenth Dynasty, however, the so called Amduat no longer unwinds as a large papyrus scroll on the walls of the sarcophagus hall. Instead, the newly created Book of Gates depicts the sun god's journey through the chambers of the netherworld during the twelve nocturnal hours, the first six of which are depicted in the sarcophagus chamber. It therefore remains unclear whether depictions of the other six hours were to be located elsewhere in the tomb or on items of the tomb equipment. The box-shaped sarcophagus is of traditional design. The corners of the sarcophagus are decorated with the winged protective deities Isis, Nephthys, Selkis and Neith.

Ramesses I Nebpehtyre: KV 16—Reign, 1292–1291 B.C.E.; Length of Tomb, 49.34 m/161.87 ft.

The tomb of Horemheb's successor, and the first king of the Nineteenth Dynasty proper, is unconventional. The differences are explainable by the age of Ramesses I at the time of his accession to the throne and the fact that his planners, foreseeing the short expected life span of the ruler, refrained from building a large royal tomb. KV16 thus represents a "synopsis" of a royal tomb, exhibiting all that was considered essential in the layout and decoration of a royal funerary monument of the post-Amarna era. It consists of three entrance corridors, (A) to (C), with a width of two times five cubits (2.62 m/8.59 ft. × 2.62m/8.59 ft.) (see Table 13.1) and the sarcophagus chamber (J), which remained without pillars.

   In the sarcophagus chamber, the only decorated chamber in the tomb, we find the whole spectrum of possible decorations of a royal tomb. Instead of painted relief, uncarved paintings are used. On the lateral walls, only excerpts from the third and fourth hours of the Book of Gates, which are representative of the commonly used pictures of the royal netherworld books, are used—and in this case, depicted in vibrant colors. Due to shortage of space, however, the pictures depict only a two-part register structure instead of the common three-part register structure (Piankoff 1957, 189–200).

   The back wall of the sarcophagus chamber shows innovative accentuations by depicting the enthroned Osiris and the beetle-headed sun god back to back in an unconventional divine scene. On the right, Ramesses I is led to the enthroned Osiris by Harsiese, Atum, and Neith; on the left, Ramesses I dedicates four chests of clothing to the sun god. The king himself, half kneeling, is included among the exultant "jackal-headed spirits of Buto and the falcon-headed spirits of Hierakonpolis" (Hornung 2001a, 190–193) in front of the sun god.

Seti I Menmaatre: KV 17—Reign, 1290–1279 B.C.E.; Length of Tomb, 137.19 m/450.09 ft.

The approximately eleven-year reign of Seti I Menmaatre (Hornung et al. 2006, 210–211) sufficed to create the most magnificent royal tomb in the Valley of the Kings

Table 13.1 Length of Reign* and Measurements of the Royal Tombs in the Valley of the Kings at Thebes**

Name of King	Reign (b.c.e.)	Length of Reign	Length of Tomb	Cross Section of Height and Width of Corridor D	Cross Section of Height and Width of Gate E
Horemheb (KV 57)	1319–1292	ca. 29 years	127.88 m	D: 2.62 × 2.63 m	E: 2.37 × 2.04 m
Ramesses I (KV 16)	1292–1291	ca. 1½ years	49.34 m	B: 2.63 × 2.61 m	J: 2.74 × 2.06 m
Seti I (KV 17)	1290–1279	ca. 11 years	137.19 m	D: 2.78 × 2.61 m	E: 2.39 × 2.08 m
Ramesses II (KV 7)	1279–1213	66 years	168.05 m	D: 2.54 × 2.60 m	E: 2.30 × 2.03 m
Merenptah (KV 8)	1213–1203	ca. 10 years	164.86 m	D: 3.49 × 2.64 m	E: 3.42 × 2.11 m
Amenmesse (KV 10)	1202–1200	3 years	105.34 m	C: 3. 15 × 2.66 m	E: 2.87 × 2.10 m
Seti II (KV 15)	1202–1198	ca. 6 years	88.65 m	D: 3.34 × 2.80 m	E: 2.95 × 2.25 m
Siptah (KV 47)	1197–1193	ca. 6 years	124.93 m	D: 3.36 × 2.59 m	E: 2.79 × 2.08 m
Tausret (KV14)	1192–1191	ca. 2 years	158.41 m	D: 2.61 × 2.11 m	E: 2.34 × 1.87 m
			length of the back part: ca. 35 m	L: 2.95 × 2.40 m	L: 2.84 × 2.07 m
Setnakht (KV 14)	1190–1188	4 years	–	–	–

* Hornung (2006, 493)
** http://www.thebanmappingproject.com/sites/

and to decorate it with painted reliefs from the entrance to the chambers beyond the sarcophagus chamber. The tomb was discovered by Giovanni Battista Belzoni in 1817 and ranks among the most significant royal tombs of the New Kingdom today (Hornung 1991).

In its main features, the architecture of the tomb is oriented toward the design of the tomb of Horemheb. As in KV 57, the tomb is designed with an essentially straight axis. It is slightly shifted to the left in the pillared hall (F) and continues parallel to the upper tomb axis down to the sarcophagus chamber. According to the plan prevailing since Amenhotep II (KV 35), the sarcophagus chamber has two parts. It consists of a front part with six pillars and a deepened back chamber that is lateral to the front part. In this back part of the sarcophagus chamber a barrel vault with a depiction of the night sky arches over the sarcophagus. Entirely new, however, is that a number of side chambers depart from the upper pillared hall (F) and the lower sarcophagus chamber (J) (Hornung 2001b, 194–211).

Unlike tombs of the Eighteenth Dynasty and that of Horemheb, decorations are no longer limited to the main chambers of the tomb, among them the well chamber

(E), the vestibule to the sarcophagus chamber (I), and the sarcophagus chamber (J). Instead, all corridors and chambers of the tomb from the entrance to the smallest adjoining chambers of the sarcophagus hall are now decorated. Even the ceiling of the corridor features decorations and is construed as the starry sky. Vultures with spread wings fly over this sky, protecting the imaginary descent of the king into his tomb.

The increase in the number of chambers leads to a tremendous expansion of wall surface, providing an unprecedented potential for the extended use of texts and pictures. The two central themes, already addressed in Horemheb's tomb (the king standing before deities, worshiping them and offering sacrifices; the sun god's journey through the netherworld), dominate the tomb decoration here as well. For the first time, a virtually inexhaustible compendium of religious and ritual texts is introduced to the decoration of the royal monument and infuses the tomb.

There is, however, a vital difference from the decoration of earlier times. The great funerary texts, most importantly the Book of Gates and the Amduat, no longer unwind as monumental papyrus scrolls on the wall, but are separated into individual parts, and these individual parts are affixed as set pieces at different places in the tomb. Consequently, the different hours of the Book of Gates are distributed throughout the different chambers of the tomb. The Book of Gates is depicted in the upper pillared hall (F), in the sarcophagus chamber (J) and in one of the side chambers of the sarcophagus chamber (Jd). It is furthermore displayed in its entity on the sarcophagus of the king (Hornung 1979a, 1984a). The depictions of the Amduat are distributed similarly. Like the Book of Gates, the Amduat is broken down into parts and displayed in different chambers, namely in the second and third corridors, (C) and (D), of the upper area of the tomb and in the side chambers of the upper pillared hall (Fa) as well as the sarcophagus chamber (J, Jb) (Hornung 1963, 1987, 1992).

Other funerary "books" and texts are also used. Among the more traditional texts is the Book of Praying to Re in the West, which had already been used under Thutmose III in KV 34. It consists of seventy-five appeals to the different guises of the sun god and is recorded in the first corridors of the tomb, (B) and (D) (Hornung 1975, 1976). In addition, the Book of the Heavenly Cow is incorporated in the inventory of texts. It addresses the dispute between the sun god and the humans who have sinned against him. Except for a few additions, changes, and other minor adjustments, the representation and text program, established under Seti I, remains mandatory for the subsequent royal hypogea and is attested in almost all tombs of the Nineteenth Dynasty (see Table 13.2).

Ramesses II Usermaatre Setepenre: KV 7—Reign, 1279–1213 B.C.E.; Length of Tomb, 168.05 m/551.34 ft.

The rock-cut tomb of Ramesses II on the northern slope of the Valley of the Kings has suffered from numerous tomb robberies and flooding since antiquity. The tomb,

Table 13.2 Decoration of the Royal Tombs of the Nineteenth Dynasty*

Name of King	Entryway A	Corridor B	Corridor C	Corridor D	Well Chamber E	Pillared Chamber F	Corridor G-H	Chamber I	Burial Chamber J and Side Chambers
Horemheb (KV 57)	none	none	none	None	King before deities	none	None	King before deities	Book of Gates
Ramesses I (KV 16)	none	none	none	–	–	–	–	–	King before a deity, Book of Gates
Seti I (KV 17)	none	Litany of Ra	Litany of Ra, Amduat	Amduat	King before deities	Book of Gates, shrine of Osiris	Opening of the mouth	King before deities	Book of Gates, Amduat, Divine Cow
Ramesses II (KV 7)	Sun and horizon	Litany of Ra	Litany of Ra, Amduat	Amduat	King before deities	Book of Gates, Shrine of Osiris	Opening of the mouth	Book of the Dead 125	Book of gates. Amduat, Divine Cow, Book of the Dead 110
Merenptah (KV 8)	Sun and horizon	Litany of Ra	Litany of Ra, Amduat	Amduat	King before deities	Book of Gates, shrine of Osiris	Opening of the mouth	Book of the Dead, king before deities	Book of Gates, Book of Aker, creation of the solar disk
Amenmesse (KV 10)	none (?)	Litany of Ra	Litany of Ra	None	Takhat and deities	Baketwerel and gods	None	–	–
Seti II (KV 15)	Sun and horizon	Litany of Ra	Litany of Ra, Amduat	Amduat		Book of gates, Shrine of Osiris	Book of gates Sarcophagus.	–	–
Siptah (KV 47)	Sun and horizon	Litany of Ra	Litany of Ra, Amduat	Amduat	none	none	None [Amduat at the end of H]	–	none
Tausret/ Setnakht (KV14), front part	Sun and horizon	Queen before deities	Book of the Dead 145	Book of the Dead 145	gods	Book of the Dead 145, shrine of Osiris	Opening of the mouth	Queen before deities	Book of Gates, Book of Aker, creation of the solar disk
Tausret/ Setnakht (KV 14), back part							Corridor K2 and L: Amduat	–	Book of Gates

* Hornung (1982b, 219); Weeks (2013)

somewhat exposed in antiquity and even displaying graffiti from this time, was partially excavated around 1817 on behalf of H. Salt. Only since 1993 has it been examined scientifically. Despite the poor state of preservation, the architecture and something of the decorations (which are of exceptional beauty) can be determined (Leblanc 2010).

The tomb's architecture differs from that of the Seti I tomb in several aspects. The tomb was the first in the Valley of the Kings with an open front. Above the tomb's entrance is the programmatic scene of the yellow sun disk, resting on the horizon, worshiped by Isis on the right and Nephthys on the left.

The tomb axis is bent. This, however, did not mean a reversion to the design of pre-Amarna times, when the bent axis was fixed in the design of royal tombs. The planned straight axis struck layers of marly soil. Continued cutting into limestone was only possible by means of bending the axis to the right, instead of continuing with the straight axis. The most significant innovation, however, is the new conception of the sarcophagus chamber. During earlier times, it was common to separate the sarcophagus chamber into a lower part with the sarcophagus and an upper part with three pillars on each side of the tomb axis. Ramesses II replaced this plan with a three-part division lateral to the tomb axis. Now a lowered center nave with an arching ceiling bounded by four pillars on each side contained the sarcophagus. All subsequent royal tombs up to the Twentieth Dynasty followed this newly created model of a sarcophagus chamber lateral to the tomb axis as introduced by Ramesses II. The sides of the pillars facing the sarcophagus were decorated with figures of deities watching over the sarcophagus and the mummy of the king.

Only minimal remainders of the wall decoration are preserved (Leblanc 1998, 2001). The representations can nevertheless be reconstructed through comparison with depictions in other tombs, especially from that of Seti I (KV 17) (Leblanc 2010). The comparison shows that numerous new texts, especially from the Book of the Dead, were added to the decoration. Among them are the Negative Confession from chapter 125 as well as spells about the Field of Offerings from chapter 110 of the Book of the Dead (Hornung 1979b).

One particularity only accredited to Ramesses II is the affixing of elements of the twelfth hour of the Amduat in the deeper part of the well chamber, which in its upper part is usually simply decorated with scenes of deities (Abitz 1974, 60–61).

Merenptah Baenre: KV 8—Reign, 1213–1203 B.C.E.; Length of Tomb, 164.86 m/540.87 ft.

Graffiti from Greco-Roman times provide evidence that this tomb was accessible until late antiquity, and European travelers made mention of it in reports from the seventeenth century. The tomb was recorded by Champollion, Lepsius, and Lefébure, and Carter cleared the lower part of the monument from debris in 1903–1904. It is currently being investigated by a French Mission of the Louvre (Barbotin and Guichard 2009).

The tomb of Merenptah is unusual because its entrance is not located at the bottom of the valley, but rather slightly higher on the mountain slope (Brock 2001). In comparison to other tombs, such as the tomb of his father Ramesses II (KV 7), the front of Merenptah's tomb is of monumental design, and its dimensions are large compared to the inner corridors. For the first time, the corridors are not constructed with a square cross section of 5 by 5 cubits (2.62 m/8.59 ft. × 2.62 m/8.59 ft.) in width and height, but instead were intended as an upended rectangle cross section of 6.5 cubits in height and 5 cubits in width (3.49 m/11.45 ft. × 2.64 m/8.66 ft.) (see Table 13.1).

Merenptah returns to the straight tomb axis and straightens it even further by eradicating the slight shift of the axis in the upper pillared hall (F). Since the back part of the well chamber was not bricked up since the time of Ramesses II, but simply sealed off with doors, the tomb axis now descended in a straight line into the earth. It led directly to the sarcophagus chamber after it had crossed through a vestibule (H) between the fourth and fifth corridors of the lower tomb area, in which chapter 125 of the Book of the Dead was recorded. The three-aisled sarcophagus chamber, as in the tomb of Ramesses II, is situated perpendicular to the axis and consists of a lowered central section between four pairs of pillars on each side.

Originally the sarcophagus ensemble consisted of four sarcophagi that were nested into each other (Sourouzian 1989, 180–184). The outer sarcophagus, of gigantic dimensions (4.10 m/13.45 ft. × 2.20 m/7.21 ft.), was too large to pass through the tomb's doors, which therefore had to be cut back from their original 2.10 m/6.89 ft. width to the full corridor width. The removed door lintels were then put back into place once the sarcophagus had been positioned (Brock 1992).

Under the rule of Merenptah, the shift from raised to sunk relief took place. The magnificent image at the entrance showing the king worshipping the sun god was still created in the style of raised relief, while the remaining parts of the tomb were decorated with more easily accomplished sunk relief. The decoration of the tomb was influenced by the example of the tomb of Seti I. The walls of the first two corridors are covered with texts and pictures of the Litany of Re, the third corridor (D) is decorated with scenes from the Amduat, and the well chamber shows the king worshipping different gods.

As in the tomb of Seti I, the images in the upper pillared hall, taken from the Book of Gates, also include the Osiris scene (Abitz 1984, 18–19). In the adjoining descending corridors, now interrupted by chamber H with decorations from the Book of the Dead, images of the mouth opening ritual, which had been depicted since Seti I, are located.

The decoration of the three-aisled sarcophagus chamber is mostly destroyed. Nevertheless, the remains indicate that the walls behind the pillars were decorated with texts from the Book of Gates, while the front walls on the left and the right of the central section carried scenes from two new funerary texts. On the left is a segment from the so-called Book of Caverns, which is concerned with the course of the sun, and on the right a passage from the Book of the Earth describing the resurrection of Osiris and the journey of the sun boat through the body of the earth god Aker (Hornung 1981). The same decorations are later found on the tomb walls of Tausret's (KV 14) and Ramesses' III tombs (KV 11).

Amenmesse Menmire: KV 10—Reign, 1202–1200 B.C.E., Likely as Anti-king to Seti II; Length of Tomb, 105 m/344.48 ft.

Apparently, the tomb of Amenmesse was still generally accessible in Greco-Roman times, as visitors' inscriptions of the time prove. Little is known about Amenmesse, but the deliberate destruction of the tomb relief shows that posterity judged him to be illegitimate. However, it remains unclear whether Amenmesse ruled before Seti II, or, as is perhaps more likely, ruled as an anti-king into the reign of Seti II (Beckerath 1994, 70–73; Hornung et al. 2006, 212–213).

The ground plan is modeled after the tomb of Merenptah (KV8), but the corridors, which are without stairs, only show slight descent. For the first time, the well chamber (E) is without a well. The end of the tomb is situated in the lowered second corridor (H) after a descent. The tomb itself is unfinished (Schaden and Ertman 1994, 1998, 2004).

The decoration of the tomb was oriented toward the iconographic program of Merenptah (KV 8), but all reliefs were subsequently hacked out. Most likely during the Twentieth Dynasty, the well chamber and the pillared hall were whitewashed and newly painted and the monument turned into a queen's tomb. Traces of a "king's mother," Takhat, survived in chamber E (Brock 2003), and remains of a decoration for the "Great royal wife/spouse" Baketwerel are located in the pillared hall (F). However, the historical identification of these two royal women is not yet secure.

Seti II Userkheprerure: KV 15—Reign, 1202–1198 B.C.E.; Length of Tomb, 88.65 m/290.85 ft.

The tomb of Seti II is located at the west end of the Eastern Valley of the Kings in a slightly elevated position. Numerous visitors have left their inscriptions in the surrounding area and the tomb itself since antiquity. The construction of the tomb was suspended for a while during the first years of Seti's II reign (Dodson 1999), and this suspension is tied to the interregnum of Amenmesse. It remains unsure if this is the reason that the name cartouches of the king were removed in the first construction phase and later reinserted during the second phase.

The tomb's corridor proceeds almost horizontally. For the first time, the corridor is elevated to 3.60 m/11.81 ft. and broadened to 2.80 m/9.18 ft., creating a monumental appearance for the tomb. Stairs in the corridor are abandoned now, and the well chamber (E) is left without the well. A descent with stairs leads from the pillared hall (F) to corridor G, which holds the sarcophagus of the king as a replacement for the sarcophagus chamber.

The iconographic program of the tomb is traditional, being guided by that of Merenptah's tomb. The decorations remained incomplete, though. The entrance area of the first corridor (B) is decorated with a sunk relief, while the rest of the chambers, which were most likely finished and decorated after the interregnum, partly contain tracings, and partly sunk reliefs and paintings.

A completely new iconographic program can be found on the walls of the well chamber (E), where figurines are depicted such as those that were included in the treasure of Tutankhamun's tomb and which, in some cases in older royal tombs, were part of the real funerary assemblage (Abitz 1979). The images of the king riding a panther, or on a boat while harpooning a hippopotamus, are noteworthy (Abitz 1979, 16–17). Presumably these images, belonging to the complex of "figurines in shrines," were a replacement for real funerary objects (Abitz 1979).

Siptah Akhenre: KV 47—Reign, 1197–1193 B.C.E.; Length of Tomb, 124.93 m/409.87 ft.

The tomb of Siptah, located to the north, but in close proximity to that of his father, Seti II (KV 15), was discovered by Ayrton in 1905 and has been the subject of scientific recording by the Basel project, "MISR: Mission Siptah—Ramesses XX," since 1999. With a length of almost 125 m/410 ft., it is among the longest tombs in the Valley of the Kings (see Table 13.1).

Its ground plan matches the classic type of royal tomb of the Nineteenth Dynasty. (Davis 1908). The stairs of the corridors were largely abandoned, the only rock-cut steps being at the tomb's entrance (A) and at the descent from the first pillared hall (F) to the chambers of the lower tomb area. The well chamber (E) remained without a well.

The tomb only differs from the traditional ground plan in one detail. Between the corridor (H) and the sarcophagus chamber (J) in the lower tomb areas, a short corridor (J1a) has been inserted. The existence of this corridor is easily explainable. It is the beginning of an initially planned, but abandoned, sarcophagus chamber. The abandoning of the site of the sarcophagus chamber at this spot in the tomb was necessary because of a collision with KV 32. The new sarcophagus chamber (J), with a single row of four pillars, was relocated further within the tomb. The sarcophagus of the king remains there today.

Only the upper tomb area is decorated with sunk relief; the lower tomb area is without images. However, on the walls of the lower corridor (J1a) traces of decorated plaster survived, suggesting that the former decorations must have been far more extensive than what is preserved today. It remains unclear why the cartouches of the king had been erased and later reinserted (Aldred 1963; Schneider 2003).

Tausret Satre-Meritamun: KV 14—Royal Spouse of Seti II (1202–1198 B.C.E.), Later Ruling Queen (1192–1191 B.C.E.); Length of Tomb, 158.41 m/519.71 ft.

During his reign, Seti II granted his wife Tausret the unconventional privilege of a burial in the Valley of the Kings. The queen's tomb, only slightly north of his tomb, is unique as a successful combination of the styles of a queen's and a king's tomb. Based on an ostracon, the start of the construction can be dated to the second year of the reign of Seti II, and it lasted for eleven years, until the death of Tausret. Work in the tomb was in abeyance for a while during the interregnum of Amenmesse (Altenmüller 1992, 159; Hornung et al. 2006, 213). The main phase of construction dates to the time of Siptah (1197—1193 B.C.E.).

After the death of Siptah, who was succeeded by Tausret, the queen's tomb was restructured as a king's tomb. This shift emphasizes the ascent of Tausret from royal spouse to pharaoh. Consequently, two different phases are mirrored in the construction itself and the decoration. Following the death of Setnakht (1190–1187 B.C.E.), the body of Tausret was removed from the tomb when Ramesses III had the tomb renovated for his father (Altenmüller 1992). Greek graffiti in the third corridor (D) indicate that the tomb was accessible during Greco-Roman times. The first plans of the tomb were already drawn in the seventeenth century.

The First Version of the Tomb

KV 14 follows the model of the classic royal tomb (Altenmüller 2001). The similarities to and differences from a traditional royal tomb of the Nineteenth Dynasty become apparent in a direct comparison with the ground plan of the approximately contemporaneous rock tomb of King Siptah (KV 47). While the corridors and chambers in the tomb of Queen Tausret are in the same order as the chambers of a king's tomb, the measurements of the chambers lag substantially behind those of a kingly tomb (see Table 13.1).

This becomes especially apparent when looking at the anterior sarcophagus chamber (J1), which matches the sarcophagus chamber of a king's tomb in all essential points. It is lateral to the tomb axis and has a three-aisled structure. The central nave, which once held the sarcophagus of the royal spouse, is lowered, is equipped with an arched ceiling, and has four pillars on each side. However, the measurements are vastly different from those of a king's tomb. The square sarcophagus chamber (10.57m/ 34.67 ft. × 10.57 m/34.67 ft.) is significantly smaller than its equivalent in a king's tomb. The pillars are slimmer as well. The anterior row consists of square pillars with a diameter of approximately 0.65 m/2.13 ft. The pillars of the back row have a rectangular shape with an edge length between 0.61 m/2.00 ft. and 0.94 m/3.08 ft. All measures lag behind the royal edge length of 2 by 2 cubits (1.10 m/3.60 ft. × 1.10 m/3.60 ft.) (see Table 13.1).

The decoration of the queen's tomb, just as the architecture of the first phase, also constitutes a mixture of aspects of a queen's and a king's tomb. The rigorously upheld taboo

against queen's tombs being decorated as king's tombs is distinctly infringed. Royal elements are the images of the winged goddess Maat on a basket, resting on the heraldic
plants of upper and lower Egypt; the ritual of the mouth opening depicted in the first
corridors of the lower tomb area, (G) and (H); as well as the decorations of the sarcophagus chamber: the back wall with the ninth and tenth hours of the Book of Gates, the
barrel-vaulted ceiling in the lowered part of the sarcophagus chamber decorated with
astronomic depictions, the left and right gable ends of the chamber as in Merenptah's
tomb (KV 8) with the images from the Book of Caverns on the left and the Book of the
Earth on the right (Hornung 1981).

The Second Version of the Tomb

When Siptah died, most likely during the sixth year of his reign, he was succeeded by
Tausret. She assumed a throne name, Tausret Setepetenmut Satre Meritamun (Gardiner
1958; Altenmüller 2012), and had the tomb extended according to royal standards. After
an initial failed attempt at the reconstruction of the sarcophagus chamber with royal
measures (attempted in K1 directly behind the already existing sarcophagus chamber, J1), the tomb was extended to the west by two corridors utilizing royal measures.
The two corridors lead to a lateral sarcophagus chamber (J2) with royal measurements
(13.31 × 12.63 m). The decoration of this part of the tomb took place at around the same
time as the expansion. Due to Tausret's short kingly reign of only two or possibly three
years (Wilkinson 2012, 97–98), it remained incomplete. The rear part of the corridors
(K2 and L) includes the depiction of the Amduat on the plaster covered walls, which due
to the time restrictions, were not fully painted. As was the initial sarcophagus chamber
from before her enthronement, the new sarcophagus chamber was decorated with texts
from the Book of Gates, though again due to time restrictions, these were executed only
in initial tracing.

The Third Version of the Tomb

The queen's destiny after her death is unknown. It is known, though, that when Ramesses
III had the queen's tomb renovated after his father's death, all cartouches with the name
of the queen were destroyed and replaced with the name of Setnakht, and all images of
Tausret were painted over and partly replaced by images of Setnakht or large-scale cartouches of that king (Altenmüller 2012).

KV 11, the tomb originally planned for Setnakht and already partially hewn, was
abandoned, and Ramesses III had the sarcophagus of Setnakht conveyed from there to
Tausret's tomb. Similar to what occurred in the tomb of Merenptah (KV 8), the door
frames of Tausret's tomb had to be modified to allow the larger sarcophagus to be
installed. The doorways were, however, never restored.

The Queen's Sarcophagi

The two sarcophagus chambers in the tomb of queen Tausret (J1 and J2) were fully finished during the queen's lifetime. One sarcophagus made of granite was provided for
each of them. The first sarcophagus was meant for the anterior sarcophagus chamber

(J1). In terms of its design and the iconographic program, it was a typical queen's sarcophagus of the Nineteenth and Twentieth Dynasties (Brock 2003). After the queen's enthronement, it was to be replaced by a second royal sarcophagus for the rear sarcophagus chamber (J2), which was, however, never finished.

Both sarcophagi were found in the neighboring tomb KV 13, intended for the "secretary of the treasury of the realm" Bay. It seems that, like the tomb itself, the sarcophagi of Tausret fell victim to the usurpation of Ramesses III. Before Ramesses had his father's sarcophagus transferred from KV 11 to KV 14, he had both of Tausret's sarcophagi moved to Bay's tomb. Tausret's queenly sarcophagus was renovated for his son, prince Amunherkhepeshef, and the second sarcophagus, meant for the reigning Tausret and unfortunately unfinished, was dedicated to another of Ramesses' III sons, prince Mentuherkhepeshef (Altenmüller 2012, 86).

Bay: KV 13

The tomb of Bay, north of Tausret's tomb, was constructed around the same time as that monument, so presumably under the reign of Seti II. The measurements of the corridors and chambers are identical with the ones in Tausret's tomb (Altenmüller 1989). When Bay was sentenced to death as an enemy of the state during the fifth year of Siptah (Grandet 2000, 339–342), construction of the tomb was ceased. The unfinished tomb remained unused for a long time. Eventually, Ramesses III had the tomb renovated after the death of Setnakht, utilizing it for the burial of two of his sons. Prince Amunherkhepeshef was buried in Tausret's queenly sarcophagus, prince Mentherkhepeshef in Tausret's kingly sarcophagus. Both sarcophagi were discovered among alluvial flooding debris at the same place where Ramesses III had them positioned. They remain in the tomb (Altenmüller 1994).

Summary

The development of the royal tombs of the Nineteenth Dynasty can be summarized as follows. As in the Eighteenth Dynasty, every king of the Nineteenth Dynasty appointed a construction supervisor immediately after his enthronement. The construction supervisor was responsible for the planning and construction of the royal tomb, as well as the erection of an appertaining funerary temple. Oversight of the planning of the tomb was the task of the vizier, who periodically traveled to Thebes to watch over the construction (Hornung 1978, 66; Černý 1973, 15–22).

Following tradition, the royal tomb was hallowed. The design of a royal tomb therefore allowed for little leeway. The order of the chambers was guided by the tomb axis. While the royal tombs of the Eighteenth Dynasty traditionally followed a bent axis, Thutmose IV and Amenhotep III introduced a doubly bent tomb axis. This doubly bent axis was abandoned by Horemheb (KV 57). Henceforth, a straight tomb axis was utilized for the royal tombs of the Nineteenth and Twentieth Dynasties.

While the tomb axis under Horemheb was divided into two parts and slightly shifted to the left in the pillared hall (F), it was straightened by Merenptah (KV 8). Starting with that king, the tomb axis descended directly from the entrance to the sarcophagus chamber (Abitz 1989).

Chamber planning was constrained by the symbolic meaning given the individual chambers, and the order and types of chambers were mostly established. An excellent example is the so-called well chamber (E) (Abitz 1974). Originally, the well likely had a purely pragmatic purpose and was supposed to protect the tomb from flooding. Early on, however, it also gained religious meaning. From early times, it was one of the few chambers that were decorated.

The images in all tombs show the recurring theme of the king's admission to the world of the gods, before whom the king is depicted worshiping and bringing sacrifices. Similarly, the king makes contact with the gods in the sarcophagus chamber and also in the images on the pillars of the tomb. This theme constitutes one major element of the royal tombs in the New Kingdom, and through the increasing number of gods depicted, emphasizes the importance of the realm of the gods for the late king (Abitz 1984).

The second major theme in the royal tombs of the New Kingdom is the description of the netherworld, with the example of the sun god's journey through the night, recurring during the twelve hours of night day after day. While the sun god's journey through the night was described in the Amduat with its original title "Book of what is in the Underworld" in earlier times, the Nineteenth Dynasty introduced the similarly structured Book of Gates for the decoration of the royal tombs. This book describes the sun god's journey through the netherworld during the night as well. The netherworld is similarly structured into twelve areas, corresponding to the twelve hours of the sun god's journey through the night in the Amduat. The first king to use the Book of Gates instead of the Amduat for decorating the sarcophagus chamber was Horemheb. His successor, Ramesses, I divided the Book of Gates into parts and integrated the third and fourth hours of the Book of Gates as set pieces into the divine scenes in his sarcophagus chamber. The crucial step, however, was taken by Seti I, who decorated all the chambers of his tomb, from beginning to end. The iconographic and text program was considerably expanded by this increase in utilized wall space. From the time of Seti I, virtual libraries of funerary "books" were inscribed in royal tombs, among them the texts of the Litany of Re in the West, the Book of Gates, and the Amduat (Hornung 1984b). Newly added was the Book of the Heavenly Cow (Hornung 1982a), which explained why the gods live privileged in heaven and the netherworld, and why mankind lives on earth. From the time of Ramesses II (KV 7), texts of the Book of the Dead were also incorporated into the textual program of the royal tombs (Hornung 1979b). The distribution of the funerary texts and the newly incorporated religious texts on the walls of the tomb followed an opaque pattern. The funerary texts no longer unwind on a gigantic papyrus scroll, but are depicted as individual chapters at different places of the tomb, without traceable cohesion.

The decoration of tombs of the Nineteenth Dynasty was in the form of painted reliefs. The transition from painting to reliefs occurred under Horemheb (KV 57). Ramesses I (KV 16) employed paintings one last time, but most likely this was only due to his short reign one and a half years, which did not leave enough time for elaborate reliefs. As can be concluded from the partially unfinished relief in Horemheb's tomb (Hornung 1971), the pictures were first sketched out and then carved out of the stone. Afterward, the created relief was covered in a fine layer of plaster and then painted (Černý 1973, 12–13).

The differences in the colored hieroglyphs can be explained by the background of the image, either blue or a golden yellow, and that accordingly different colors were chosen for the hieroglyphs.

The tomb of Seti I (KV 17) is completely covered in raised relief; only the astronomical ceiling of the sarcophagus chamber is painted. The transition from raised to sunk relief took place under Merenptah (KV 8). However, the caesura is not a severe one, since Merenptah still had some scenes close to the entrance of his tome carved in raised relief. A similar mixture of high relief and bas relief can be found in the tombs of Amenmesse (KV 10) and Seti II (KV 15). Only Siptah used sunk relief exclusively.

BIBLIOGRAPHY

Abitz, Friedrich 1974. *Die religiöse Bedeutung der sogenannten Grabräuberschächte in den ägyptischen Königsgräbern der 18. bis 20. Dynastie.* Ägyptologische Abhandlungen 26. Wiesbaden: Harrassowitz.

Abitz, Friedrich 1979. *Statuetten in Schreinen als Grabbeigaben in den ägyptischen Königsgräbern der 18. und 19. Dynastie.* Ägyptologische Abhandlungen 35. Wiesbaden: Harrassowitz.

Abitz, Friedrich 1984. *König und Gott: die Götterszenen in den ägyptischen Königsgräbern von Thutmosis IV. bis Ramses III.* Ägyptologische Abhandlungen 40. Wiesbaden: Harrassowitz.

Abitz, Friedrich 1989. Die Entwicklung der Grabachsen in den Königsgräbern im Tal der Könige. *Mitteilungen des Deutschen Archäologischen Instituts, Abteilung Kairo* 45: 1–25.

Aldred, Cyril 1963. "The Parentage of King Siptaḥ." *Journal of Egyptian Archaeology* 49: 41–48.

Altenmüller, Hartwig 1989. "Untersuchungen zum Grab des Bai (KV 13) im Tal der Könige von Theben." *Göttinger Miszellen* 107: 43–54

Altenmüller, Hartwig 1992. Bemerkungen zu den neu gefundenen Daten im Grab der Königin Twosre (KV 14) im Tal der Könige von Theben. In Reeves, C. N. (ed.), *After Tut'ankhamūn: research and excavation in the Royal Necropolis at Thebes,* 141–164. London: Kegan Paul.

Altenmüller, Hartwig 1994. Dritter Vorbericht über die Arbeiten des Archäologischen Instituts der Universität Hamburg am Grab des Bay (KV 13) im Tal der Könige von Theben. *Studien zur Altägyptischen Kultur* 21, 1–18.

Altenmüller, Hartwig 2001. In Weeks, Kent R. (ed.), *The treasures of the Valley of the Kings: tombs and temples of the Theban West Bank in Luxor.* Photographs by Araldo De Luca, 222–231. Cairo: American University in Cairo Press.

Altenmüller, Hartwig 2012. A queen in the Valley of Kings: the tomb of Tausret. In Wilkinson, Richard H. (ed.), *Tausret: forgotten queen and pharaoh of Egypt,* 67–91. Oxford: Oxford University Press

Barbotin, Christophe and Sylvie Guichard 2009. Fouilles du Musée du Louvre dans la tombe de Merenptah—KV.8 (2008). *Memnonia* 20: 175–182.

Beckerath, Jürgen von 1994. *Chronologie des ägyptischen Neuen Reiches*. Hildesheimer Ägyptologische Beiträge 39. Hildesheim: Gerstenberg.

Brock, Edwin C. 1992. The tomb of Merenptaḥ and its sarcophagi. In Reeves, C. N. (ed.), *After Tutʿankhamūn: research and excavation in the Royal Necropolis at Thebes*, 122–140. London: Kegan Paul.

Brock, Edwin C. 2001. The Tomb Merenptah. In Weeks, Kent R. (ed.), *The treasures of the Valley of the Kings: tombs and temples of the Theban West Bank in Luxor*. Photographs by Araldo De Luca, 222–231. Cairo: American University in Cairo Press.

Brock, Edwin C. 2003. The sarcophagus lid of Queen Takhat. In Hawass, Zahi and Lyla Pinch Brock (eds), *Egyptology at the dawn of the twenty-first century: proceedings of the Eighth International Congress of Egyptologists, Cairo, 2000*, 1, 97–102. Cairo; New York: American University in Cairo Press.

Černý, Jaroslav 1973. *The Valley of the Kings: fragments d'un manuscrit inachevé*. Bibliothèque d'étude 61. Le Caire: Institut français d'archéologie orientale.

Davis, Theodore M. (ed.) 1908. *The tomb of Siptah; the monkey tomb and the gold tomb*. Theodore M. Davis' excavations: Bibân el Molûk. London: Constable.

Dodson, Aidan 1999. The decorative phases of the tomb of Sethos II and their historical implications. *Journal of Egyptian Archaeology* 85: 131–142.

Gardiner, Alan 1958. "Only One King Siptaḥ and Twosre Not His Wife." *Journal of Egyptian Archaeology* 44: 12–22.

Grandet, Pierre 2000. L'exécution du chancelier Bay: O. IFAO 1864. *Bulletin de l'Institut Français d'Archéologie Orientale* 100: 339–345.

Hornung, Erik 1963. *Das Amduat: die Schrift des verborgenen Raumes. Teil 1 und 2*. Ägyptologische Abhandlungen 7. Wiesbaden: Harrassowitz.

Hornung, Erik 1971. *Das Grab des Haremhab im Tal der Könige*. Bern: Francke.

Hornung, Erik 1975. *Das Buch der Anbetung des Re im Westen (Sonnenlitanei): nach den Versionen des Neuen Reiches. Teil 1: Text*. Aegyptiaca Helvetica 2. Genève: Éditions de Belles Lettres. Autographiert von Andreas Brodbeck.

Hornung, Erik 1976. *Das Buch der Anbetung des Re im Westen (Sonnenlitanei): nach den Versionen des Neuen Reiches. Teil 2: Übersetzung und Kommentar*. Aegyptiaca Helvetica 3. Genève: Éditions de Belles-Lettres.

Hornung, Erik 1978. Struktur und Entwicklung der Gräber im Tal der Könige. *Zeitschrift für ägyptische Sprache und Altertumskunde* 105: 59–66.

Hornung, Erik 1979a. *Das Buch von den Pforten des Jenseits: nach den Versionen des Neuen Reiches. Teil 1: Text*. Aegyptiaca Helvetica 7. Genève: Éditions de Belles-Lettres. Unter Mitarbeit von Andreas Brodbeck und Elisabeth Staehelin. Text autographiert von Andreas Brodbeck.

Hornung, Erik 1979b. Das Totenbuch der Ägypter. Eingeleitet, übersetzt und erläutert. Die Bibliothek der alten Welt. Reihe der Alten Orient. Zürich; München: Artemis.

Hornung, Erik 1981. Zu den Schlussszenen der Unterweltsbücher. *Mitteilungen des Deutschen Archäologischen Instituts, Abteilung Kairo* 37: 217–226.

Hornung, Erik 1982. *Der ägyptische Mythos von der Himmelskuh: eine Ätiologie des Unvollkommenen*. Orbis Biblicus et Orientalis 46. Freiburg Schweiz; Göttingen: Universitätsverlag; Vandenhoeck & Ruprecht.

Hornung, Erik 1982. *Tal der Könige: die Ruhestätte der Pharaonen*. Zürich; München: Artemis.

Hornung, Erik 1984a. *Das Buch von den Pforten des Jenseits: nach den Versionen des Neuen Reiches. Teil 2: Übersetzung und Kommentar.* Aegyptiaca Helvetica 8. Genève: Éditions de Belles-Lettres. Unter Mitarbeit von Andreas Brodbeck und Elisabeth Staehelin.

Hornung, Erik 1984b. Ägyptische Unterweltsbücher. Eingeleitet, übersetzt und erläutert. Die Bibliothek der Alten Welt. Reihe der Alte Orient. Zürich und München, Artemis Verlag.

Hornung, Erik 1987. *Texte zum Amduat. Teil 1: Kurzfassung und Langfassung, 1. bis 3. Stunde.* Aegyptiaca Helvetica 13. Genève: Éditions de Belles-Lettres. Autographiert von Lotty Spycher.

Hornung, Erik 1991. The tomb of Pharaoh Seti I. Photographs by Henry Burton. Zürich: Artemis.

Hornung, Erik 1992. *Texte zum Amduat. Teil 2: Langfassung, 4. bis 8. Stunde.* Aegyptiaca Helvetica 14. Genève: Éditions Médecine et Hygiène. Autographiert von Barbara Lüscher.

Hornung, Erik 2001a. The Tomb of Ramses I. In Weeks, Kent R. (ed.), *The treasures of the Valley of the Kings: tombs and temples of the Theban West Bank in Luxor.* Photographs by Araldo De Luca, 190–193. Cairo: American University in Cairo Press.

Hornung, Erik 2001b. The Tomb of Seti. In Weeks, Kent R. (ed.), *The treasures of the Valley of the Kings: tombs and temples of the Theban West Bank in Luxor.* Photographs by Araldo De Luca, 194–211. Cairo: American University in Cairo Press.

Hornung, Erik, Rolf Krauss, and David A. Warburton (eds) 2006. *Ancient Egyptian chronology.* Handbuch der Orientalistik, erste Abteilung: Der Nahe und Mittlere Osten 83. Leiden: Brill.

James, T.G.H. 2001. The Tomb of Horemheb. In Weeks, Kent R. (ed.), *The treasures of the Valley of the Kings: tombs and temples of the Theban West Bank in Luxor.* Photographs by Araldo De Luca, 174–189. Cairo: American University in Cairo Press.

Leblanc, Christian 1998. Les récentes découvertes dans la tombe de Ramsès II. *Bulletin de la Société Française d'Égyptologie* 141: 20–35.

Leblanc, Christian 2001. The Tomb of Ramesses II. In Weeks, Kent R. (ed.), *The treasures of the Valley of the Kings: tombs and temples of the Theban West Bank in Luxor.* Photographs by Araldo De Luca, 212–217. Cairo: American University in Cairo Press.

Leblanc, Christian 2010. The tomb of Ramesses II (KV 7): from its archaeological excavation to the identification of its iconographical program. *Mitteilungen des Deutschen Archäologischen Instituts, Abteilung Kairo* 66: 161–174.

Meeks, Dimitri 1998. Année lexicographique. Égypte ancienne. Tome 3 (1978). 2eme édition, Paris, Cybele.

Piankoff, Alexandre 1957. La tombe de Ramsès Ier. *Bulletin de l'Institut Français d'Archéologie Orientale* 56: 189–200.

Schaden, Otto J. 1994. Some observations on the tomb of Amenmesse (KV-10). In Bryan, Betsy M. and David Lorton (eds), *Essays in Egyptology in honor of Hans Goedicke,* 243–254. San Antonio: Van Siclen Books

Schaden, Otto J. and Earl Ertman 1998. The tomb of Amenmesse (KV 10): the first season. *Annales du Service des Antiquités de l'Égypte* 73: 116–155.

Schaden, Otto J. 2004. KV-10: Amenmesse 2000. *Annales du Service des Antiquités de l'Égypte* 78: 129–147.

Schneider, Thomas 2003. Siptah und Beja: Neubeurteilung einer historischen Konstellation. *Zeitschrift für ägyptische Sprache und Altertumskunde* 130: 134–146.

Sourouzian, Hourig 1989. *Les monuments du roi Merenptah.* Sonderschrift, Deutsches Archäologisches Institut, Abteilung Kairo 22. Mainz: Zabern.

Ventura, Raphael 1986. *Living in a city of the dead: a selection of topographical and administrative terms in the documents of the Theban necropolis.* Orbis Biblicus et Orientalis 69. Freiburg (Schweiz); Göttingen: Universitätsverlag; Vandenhoeck & Ruprecht.

Weeks, Kent R. 2001. *The treasures of the Valley of the Kings: tombs and temples of the Theban West Bank in Luxor.* Photographs by Araldo De Luca. Cairo: American University in Cairo Press.

Weeks, Kent (ed.) 2003. *Atlas of the Valley of the Kings.* Publications of the Theban Mapping Project 3. Cairo; London: American University in Cairo Press; Eurospan.

Wilkinson, Richard H. (ed.) 2012. *Tausret: forgotten queen and pharaoh of Egypt.* Oxford: Oxford University Press.

CHAPTER 14

ROYAL TOMBS OF THE TWENTIETH DYNASTY

AIDAN DODSON

THE founder of the Twentieth Dynasty, Sethnakhte, began his intended tomb, KV 11 (Porter and Moss 1964, 518–526; Thomas 1966, 125–127; Marciniak 1983, 295–305; 1982, 37–43), in the central area of the Valley of the Kings, some way from the tombs of his immediate predecessors, but directly adjacent to Amenmesse's KV 10. Its outer corridors adopted the same minimal angles of descent introduced by Seti II and followed by Siptah, and that would be a feature of all remaining kings' tombs to be constructed in the Valley of the Kings.

Although a pair of unique cow-headed pilasters flanked the very entrance, decoration otherwise began in a conventional manner, with the customary solar disk and kneeling goddesses on the lintel, and scenes showing the king's greeting to the netherworld by Ra-Horakhty at the beginning of corridor B. The rest of this corridor and the following C were adorned with the Litany of Ra and the usual subsidiary figures, but the element beyond was carved with figures of the king before deities, rather than the usual Amduat. However, this seems not to have been a theological statement, but a result of a constructional incident that led to a large vestibule (D) being created at this point in the tomb.

This was the outcome of the cutting of the nascent corridor D being interrupted by its collision (at Da) with room Faa of KV 10 (cf. p. 118). As a result, the axis of the tomb had to be shifted to the right to allow construction to continue, creating the aforementioned rectangular vestibule. Decoration of this room had been completed as far as the doorjambs of the entrance to corridor Db before Sethnakhte's death, as is indicated by the presence of his cartouches there, but stonecutting must have proceeded considerably further by then, perhaps as far as the upper pillared hall (F); the drafting of portions of the decoration may also have extended significantly in that direction. The floor of Db was constructed with a negative slope, presumably to ensure a safe clearance between it and the ceilings of KV 10.

However, although the tomb was reasonably advanced, with D large enough to have, if necessary, accommodated a burial at the king's death, Tausret's unused KV 14 seems to have represented a more attractive alternative. It was thus appropriated for Sethnakhte's burial, albeit in some haste, presumably during the period of embalmment. Thus, whereas the figures of the queen in corridor B were extensively re-cut to change them to representations of Sethnakhte, most of the remaining figures of Tausret were simply covered with plaster and just Sethnakhte's names and titles drawn in black on the unpainted plaster. Only occasionally was the king's actual figure sketched in outline. The names on the sarcophagus used for his burial seem to be secondary, but it is uncertain whether the sarcophagus had originally been Tausret's kingly piece or had been taken over from, perhaps, Amenmesse.

KV 11 itself was continued in the name of the new king, Ramesses III, the extant cartouches of Sethnakhte being surcharged by those of his son. In addition, a series of side chambers were added opening off of corridors B and C, resulting in the destruction of some extant elements of the Litany of Re, with substitute texts added to the doorjambs of the new rooms. These were decorated with images of food production, boats, craftsmen, and musicians of kinds that are otherwise unknown in the Valley.

In contrast, corridor Db was conventionally adorned with the Amduat, well room E with images of deities and upper hall F with the Book of Gates and the shrine of Osiris, as had been case since the time of Seti I. Similarly, the Opening of the Mouth once again featured in corridor G, before giving access to a pair of antechambers (H and I) adorned with images of divinities. Beyond lay the burial chamber, with the central transverse crypt of the type introduced under Ramesses II, but with the sarcophagus placed along, rather than across th e axis—a feature continued in later Twentieth Dynasty tombs (cf. Wilkinson 1995, 79–81). Although the majority of the decoration was taken from the Book of Gates (Andrzejewski 1962), the room also contained scenes from the Book of the Earth (or Aker), previously found in Merenptah's KV 8 (cf. pp. 207–208). Its side chambers contained a variety of decorative elements, including depictions of the Fields of Iaru (Jd) and the Book of the Divine Cow (Jc). Various further elements were placed on the walls of the small rooms directly beyond the burial chamber.

As completed, KV 11 represents a logical enlargement of the tomb-type instigated by Ramesses II and Merenptah, with the exception of the aforementioned side chambers in the outer corridors. However, the tomb of Ramesses III was to be the last royal tomb in the Valley of the Kings to be fully completed and decorated in accordance with this design, the following sepulchre, Ramesses IV's KV 2 (Porter and Moss 1964, 497–500; Thomas 1966, 127–129; Hornung 1990), having its design significantly truncated, a phenomenon found to a greater or lesser degree in all subsequent royal tombs there.

The tomb was started with the apparent intention of surpassing KV 11 in size, the corridors of KV 2 being nearly 20 percent wider than those laid out under Sethnakhte: the corridor width established for KV 2 would then become the standard through to the end of royal tomb building in the Valley of the Kings. However, the burial chamber of KV 2 would ultimately occupy the space where one would normally have found the four-pillared upper hall, and be a modest square room, rather than the monumental pillared rectangular hall of the post-Ramesses II "standard" design.

Nevertheless, this seems to have been something more than a simple hurried finishing-off of the tomb following the king's premature death, as was the case with, for example, Seti II's KV 15 (cf. pp. 208–209), as the rooms beyond the burial chamber indicate that no substantive progress can have been made toward any descent below the embryonic upper pillared hall when the plan was changed. Accordingly, it would appear that a conscious decision to truncate the plan of the tomb was made at before any major work had been done beyond well room E. The burial chamber was given a flat roof at the same level as that room, but additional height was provided by the construction of an unbroken slope that runs from the middle of corridor D into the first part of burial chamber. Corridor D is also unusual in that its central section was vaulted, something not found in any other tomb in the Valley. As for the reasons for this truncation, it may be noted that the initiation of the tomb had been delayed into the king's second regnal year (Peden 1994, 44–45); the relatively advanced age of the king may also have suggested some recasting of the design as time went by, in spite of a bolstering of Deir el-Medina manpower soon after the beginning of work (Peden 1994, 45–46).

The decoration of the tomb begins as usual with the king, Ra-Horakhty (although for once only on the left wall) and the Litany of Ra, but introduces the new Book of Caverns to the repertoire in the third corridor. The Amduat and the Opening of the Mouth are, however, omitted, although the loss of the former may have been for reasons of space rather than for any conceptual reasons, as it reappears in the tombs of Ramesses VI and IX. The burial chamber walls are occupied by the Book of Gates, with the ceiling providing the only Valley of the Kings example of the Book of Nut, otherwise found only in the Osirion at Abydos, in the Saite tomb of Mutirdis (TT 410) and a Roman papyrus (cf. pp. 320–321). Increasing haste by the decorators can be detected in the fact that most of the burial chamber and the rooms beyond are adorned in paint only, rather than painted relief.

The burial chamber of KV 2 is dominated by a gigantic granite sarcophagus, placed along the axis of the room, and was accompanied by a set of similarly outsize canopic jars (pp. 256–257, 270–271). That the sarcophagus was once surrounded by a series of shrines is indicated by a detailed plan of the tomb on papyrus (pTurin 1885ro—Carter and Gardiner 1917 cf. ch9). Although an accurate document, it does not appear to have been a working blueprint, and its purpose remains obscure.

The other side of the same papyrus (Hornung 1988, 138–142) preserves details of the measurements of the outer corridors of KV 9, the next tomb to be begun in the Valley (Porter and Moss 1964, 511–518; Thomas 1966, 129–130). Its original intended occupant was Ramesses V, and the data in the papyrus extend as far as the well-room (E), which is also the deepest part of the tomb in which that king's cartouches can be detected. That work had actually reached just beyond the upper pillared hall (F) before Ramesses V's death in his Year 4 is shown by an ostracon dated to that year (oCairo CG25269—cf. Abitz 1989, 40–41, 45). It is unclear where Ramesses V was actually buried, as KV 9 would be continued as the sepulcher of his successor, Ramesses VI, with no architectural provision for a second interment. That it took some time to make alternative provisions is indicated by the fact that Ramesses V's actual interment did not take place until Year 2 of Ramesses VI (oCairo 25254—cf. Peden 2001, 83–88). This burial presumably occurred somewhere in the Valley of the Kings, given that Ramesses V's mummy was later cached in KV 35.

Although the outer part of the tomb had been entirely decorated by Ramesses V, it appears that his plaster was removed and decoration begun anew in parallel with the resumed cutting of inner part of KV 9 by Ramesses VI (Abitz 1989, 40–45). The plan for this continuation of the tomb was apparently recast on a considerably enhanced scale during Ramesses VI's Year 2/3, when work was restarted on the tomb (Ventura 1988, 137–156), with the final decorative scheme (Piankoff 1954) deviating greatly from earlier standards (cf. Abitz 1989, 172–186).

Thus, although the decoration of corridor B was as usual begun with the king's reception by Ra-Horakhty, the latter was now accompanied by Osiris, and the usual Litany of Ra and extracts from the Amduat in corridors B through D were replaced by a combination of the Book of Gates and the Book of Caverns. In addition, astronomical ceilings, previously specific to the burial hall, were employed from the very entrance as far as the upper pillared hall, being supplemented in corridor D and the room E by the Book of the Night. Room E also loses its time-hallowed scenes of the king and divinities in favor of more of the Gates/Caverns mix, which also extends into the upper pillared hall. In corridors G and H, the Opening of the Mouth tableaux found in this part of a tomb down to the time of Ramesses III were replaced by the returning Amduat, the ceilings being adorned with the Books of the Day and the Night and a set of cryptographic texts (Darnell 2004, 163–275) that continue into the antechamber (I). That room's walls were covered with a mixture of the Book of the Dead and images of the king and the gods. Finally, the walls of the burial hall were entirely devoted to the first extant full version of the Book of the Earth, its ceiling to the Books of the Day and Night. This comprehensive revision of the mythological environment of the tomb has been interpreted as a demotion of Osirian conceptions in favor of those centering on Ra and Amun (cf. Bács 1992), although it is interesting in that many of these changes are reversed under Ramesses IX.

During its construction, KV 9's axis, at the end of corridor H, intersected that of the anonymous Eighteenth Dynasty KV 12 (Abitz 1989, 28–31). This required a slope to be incorporated into the floor of this corridor, to permit the antechamber and the burial chamber to be cut comfortably below the floor of KV 12. The breach having been sealed, it received magical protection through a unique vignette that sealed it via the fire of the sun god (Hornung 1988, 45–51).

The burial chamber is structurally incomplete, the rear row of columns not having been released from the matrix, and the rearmost parts of the chamber never begun (Abitz 1989, 34–35), although almost all its surfaces are fully decorated. Thus, like the tomb of Ramesses IV, the plan appears to have undergone an intentional truncation, rather than an emergency one occasioned by the premature demise of the king. Substantive quarrying may have been terminated in Year 6, nearly two years before Ramesses' death, when most of the copper tools used by the Deir el-Medina workforce were withdrawn (pTurin 1879*vo*, II:7–22—cf. Amer 1985, 69–70). As in the immediately preceding tombs, the sarcophagus (p. 257) lay on the axis of the chamber.

The tomb seems to have been entered by robbers within two decades of the interment, perhaps via KV 12, as some shabtis of Ramesses VI were found outside the entrance of that tomb, where they had doubtless been discarded by the robbers (cf. Reeves 1990, 130–31). This penetration is probably to be dated to Year 9 of Ramesses IX by a graffito on the ceiling of the burial chamber, perhaps written by those responsible for resealing the breach from KV 12 (Barwick 2011, 24–30: this is likely to be the robbery that resulted in the trial recorded in pLiverpool M11186 [pMayer B]).

The locations of KV 9 and KV 2 are rather different from most earlier tombs, as they were cut into prominent tongues of rock overlooking the main path through the center of the Valley, in marked contrast to the inconspicuous locations chosen for the earliest tombs there (cf. Figure 14.1). The development of entrances that were not easily susceptible to obliteration had begun during the Nineteenth Dynasty as a concomitant to the extension of decoration to the very entrance of tombs (Roehrig 1995, 98–99), and by the latter part of the Twentieth Dynasty it is possible that "pylons" of rubble were arranged to flank gateway entrances that lay several meters above the contemporary ground level. A similar location was chosen for Ramesses VII's KV 1 (Porter and Moss 1964, 495–497; Thomas 1966, 130–131; Hornung 1990; 1999, 109; Brock 1995), although to find such a spot the entrance to the tomb would have to lie some way back from the main axis of the Valley and a significant distance northeast of its core area.

Although begun on the same scale as the tombs of Ramesses VII's immediate predecessors, the plan of that king's KV 1 was even more attenuated than KV 2, comprising only an entrance corridor, a burial chamber and a small room and niche beyond.

FIGURE 14.1 The Valley of the Kings, showing the locations of the tombs of the kings of the Twentieth Dynasty, including the positions of the tombs of Ramesses IV (KV 2), VI (KV 9), and VII (KV 1) in prominent tongues of rock, contrasting with the less prominent positions of the tombs of Ramesses X (KV 18) and XI (KV 4).

[Aidan Dodson]

Unfortunately, no documentary material survives to account for the degree of trun-cation of the plan, given that Ramesses VII's reign equaled in length the tenures of Ramesses IV and VI, both of whom achieved significantly more in the time available.

On the other hand, the decoration is complete, and shows a number of changes in detail from earlier tombs. In particular, the king becomes an active player in the scenes at the entrance, making offerings to the greeting deity, who is now seated, rather than standing, as found in preceding sepulchers. In addition, while the left-hand god is, as usual, Ra-Horakhty, on the right he is Ptah-Sokar-Osiris, each tableau also now being enclosed in a shrine. Beyond, the left wall has the first part of the Book of Gates, the right the first part of the Book of Caverns, both clearly intended to invoke the remainders of these compositions, excluded for lack of space. In the burial chamber beyond, the lower right wall is occupied by scenes from the Book of the Earth, but the remainder of the side walls contain images that are not apparently taken directly from any identifiable "book." While the vaulted ceiling of the burial chamber is astronomical, the outer corri-dor reverts to pre-Ramesses VI pattern, in that it is adorned with images of vultures with outstretched wings.

In addition to his representations at the entrance, the king also appears in the corridor just before the entrance to the burial chamber, on its end wall, flanking the door into the inner chamber, and on the side walls of that room. In the first case, he is shown as Osiris, receiving the ministrations of *Iwn-mwt.f* (the latter's first appearance since the Nineteenth Dynasty), in the second in a solar form and in the third offering to Osiris. The sarcophagus in KV 1 takes a new form, with a rock-cut coffer and very high lid, apparently also incorporating locations for the canopic jars (see pp. 257, 271).

No tomb is known for Ramesses VIII, nor has any of his funerary equipment ever come to light. It has been suggested that KV 19 (Porter and Moss 1964, 546; Thomas 1966, 151–152), begun for a prince Setherkhepeshef who may have been Ramesses VIII before his accession, might have been continued as Ramesses VIII's kingly sepulcher, but clearly was not used as such, as it was finally decorated for prince Mentuherkhepeshef C, son of Ramesses IX. Given Ramesses VIII's very short reign—perhaps a year at most—it is likely that the construction of any new monumental tomb will have progressed mini-mally, at best. Assuming that he was indeed buried at Thebes, rather than in the north, it would seem probable that he was buried in a small tomb that may have been so utterly plundered as to now be unidentifiable—or may, just possibly, remain undiscovered.

Any new beginning made in the name of Ramesses VIII would probably have been continued for Ramesses IX as his KV 6 (Porter and Moss 1964, 501–505; Thomas 1966, 131–132; Abitz 1990). The tomb is once again in the central area, occupying the last prom-inent tongue of rock in the Valley, although perhaps a problematic site on the grounds of the numerous tombs already in the area, given that Ramesses VII had implicitly eschewed it in favor of the remote site actually used for KV 1.

Although the king was to rule for some two decades, progress in the construction of this tomb seems to have been slow or intermittent. The design was once again intention-ally attenuated as compared to the "standard" plan: although the descent from the upper pillared hall was achieved, a much-reduced burial chamber was constructed directly beyond, without any intervening corridors and chambers. This form can be seen in a surviving ancient plan of the tomb (oLuxor [ex-Cairo] CG25184—Rossi, 2001).

There was in addition a clear discontinuity in the decorative process in and beyond the second corridor (C—Figure 14.2), with the third corridor, well room, and burial chamber (D, E, and J) adorned with work purely in paint or in lower quality relief. This combination of techniques is rather curious, as their use is intermixed on the same wall. It has been argued that this later phase of work is to be dated to the period following the king's death (Abitz 1990, 2–6), although it is also possible that it could be attributed to a hiatus in the construction process, followed by a need to expedite work, perhaps owing to the king's poor health. It is also clear that work in the Valley was also hampered by ongoing bandit attacks from the western desert, a problem that would endure for some time and apparently contributed to the ultimate retirement of the Deir el-Medina community to the safer environs of Medinet Habu (Barwick 2011, 3–5).

FIGURE 14.2 Corridors C and D of the tomb of Ramesses IX (KV 6).

[Martin Davies]

As far as the actual composition of the decoration of KV 6 is concerned, the tableaux of the king before the sun god at the entrance are enshrined in the manner introduced by Ramesses VII. However, the gods are now again standing, and while on the left we find Ra-Horakhty (accompanied by Osiris, following the example of KV 9), on the right is the quadruple-ram-headed Amun-Ra-Horakhty, supported by the Goddess of the West.

Beyond, the Litany of Ra is reintroduced into the first two corridors and the Amduat into the third, supplemented by images of the king and the gods and a "enigmatic" composition (Darnell 2004, 276–373), although the Litany is now accompanied by elements from the Book of Caverns and the Book of the Dead. In the burial chamber, we find a combination of vignettes from the Books of Caverns, the Earth, and the Amduat on the walls and the Book of the Night on the ceiling. The mix and choice of elements from the various funerary compositions within the tomb of Ramesses IX is unique and includes some texts and scenes that are not found elsewhere.

Architecturally, KV 6 reintroduces side rooms into the first corridor, although these seem never to have been finished or decorated. In its truncated form, the burial chamber is relatively small, but seems to have been dominated by a large sarcophagus installation, the exact form of which is uncertain, as nothing remains apart from a two-level cutting in the floor (cf. p. 257). The tomb of Ramesses IX appears to have been the last royal tomb in the Valley of the Kings to be employed for a primary burial: his is also the latest New Kingdom pharaoh's mummy to have been found in a royal cache (Forbes 1998, 646–647; Nail 2009, 194–196).

KV 18, the tomb of Ramesses X (Porter and Moss 1964, 545; Thomas 1966, 132; Jenni 2000), is located adjacent to the much earlier tombs of Ramesses I and Seti I, a site unlike the prominent positions employed by the preceding kings and probably reflecting the increasingly limited number of sites appropriate for the large Ramesside tombs left in the Valley. All three years of Ramesses X's reign are covered in documents relating to the Deir el-Medina construction teams (Schneider 2000) and they reveal that during Year 3 only one working day in five actually saw work on the royal tomb, including interruptions caused the incursion of foreign bandits, following on from previous incidents attested under Ramesses IX.

Such conditions were clearly not conducive to royal tomb construction, and the state of Ramesses X's sepulcher when work was discontinued reflects this. Only the entrance to the tomb, the first corridor and a small fragment of the second had been cut, while decoration was limited to the entrance lintel and the initial tableaux on each wall of the first corridor—of which only the outer lintel was ever finished. The tableaux employed the same distribution of deities as the tomb of Ramesses IX, but with an additional figure of the king directly inside the entrance to the tomb. Beyond, the only extant traces are of a solar disk on the right, something that is without parallel in this position. It is thus unclear whether the tomb will have followed KV 6 in placing the Litany of Re in its outer corridor, or the rather different scheme to be found in the succeeding tomb of Ramesses XI.

There is no indication of the tomb having been made ready for even an improvised interment, and thus it is unclear where the king was buried. It has been suggested that he could have been laid to rest in the royal residence city of Per-Ramesses in the northeastern Delta (Schneider 2000, 104–108), but it is also possible that had been interred in a modest location at Thebes. In any case, his posthumous fate (and perhaps even demise) may have been influenced by potentially tumultuous state of the country at the end of his reign (cf. Dodson 2012, 8–9, 14).

The final royal tomb to be constructed in the Valley was KV 4, the intended sepulchre of Ramesses XI (Porter and Moss 1964, 501; Thomas 1966, 132–133; Ciccarello and Romer [1979]). Unlike many of the immediately preceding tombs, KV 4 seems not to have undergone any significant truncation of its plan, having a large four-pillared burial chamber at the end of a set of corridors that are the widest and highest found in any royal tomb, continuing a new trend of enlargement also found in KV 18. On the other hand, the inner rooms were by no means complete, with a number of elements only partly released from the rock matrix.

Compared with KV 9, the previous tomb to approach structural completion, the upper pillared hall (F) is rectangular rather than square, with the longest dimension along the axis of the tomb, resulting in a deeper stairway leading down toward the burial chamber. The latter diverges even further from previous post-Ramesses II practice, abandoning the usual pattern of eight square pillars in favor of four rectangular piers. In addition, a deep rectangular pit in the center of the hall replaced the sunken crypt, standard since the time of Amenhotep II. Unfortunately, although foundation deposits of Ramesses XI were found at the corners of the pit (Ciccarello and Romer [1979]), the exact intended mode of burial is unknown as the tomb was never occupied by the king, the shaft being found containing debris apparently from the restoration/recycling of earlier funerary equipment during the Twenty-first Dynasty, together with an intrusive burial of the mid-Twenty-second Dynasty (Ciccarello and Romer [1979], 2–5; Reeves 1990, 121–123).

Although the cutting of the tomb was complete in the outer corridors (Figure 14.3— contrasting with the unfinished state of the pillared halls), decoration had been hardly begun, being restricted to red-ink sketches in the first corridor. These indicate a development of the arrangement of material glimpsed in KV 18. On the left wall, the king is shown twice, the second time before a raptor-headed Amun-Re-Horkahty. On the right wall, the king is first shown alone and then within a shrine before quadruple-ram-headed Amun-Ra-Horakhty, supported by the Goddess of the West, who has a unique epithet associating her with the "Place of Smiting" (Brooklyn Museum Theban Expedition 1979, 22). Beyond her figure is a solar disk, perhaps intended to introduce the Litany of Re, no traces of which, however, survive.

As in the case of Ramesses X, there is no indication of where the eleventh Ramesses was finally interred. However, it appears that Panedjem I had briefly contemplated taking over KV 4 for his own, as on the left-hand wall of KV 4, just beyond the point where the last isketch for Ramesses XI's decoration had been applied, the raptor-headed figure of Amun-Re-Horakhty was duplicated, together with the accompanying text containing

FIGURE 14.3 The outer corridors of the tomb of Ramesses XI (KV 4).

[Aidan Dodson]

the god's speech, albeit amended by the substitution of Panedjem's names for those of Ramesses XI (Brooklyn Museum Theban Expedition [1979], 18–19; Ciccarello [1979]; Jansen-Winkeln 2007, 21[28]; Dodson 2012, 49–50). This can be dated to the very soon after Pinedjem transitioned from being High Priest of Amun to King, as he here followed Herihor in using "High Priest of Amun" as his prenomen, rather than his definitive Khakheperre. However, this new phase of decoration was, like Ramesses' original work, left as a simple ink-sketch and the tomb never occupied by Panedjem, whose original place of interment remains unknown (cf. Dodson 2012, 50, 62–64).

With this final abandonment of KV 4 as a royal sepulcher, the kingly burial ground moved away from the Valley, being located at San el-Hagar (Tanis) for much of the Third Intermediate Period (cf. Lull 2002). Although the tombs there were built structures sunk into the soil of typical Delta type, and far smaller than any pharaoh's tomb in the Valley of the Kings, their decoration represented a direct outgrowth of Twentieth Dynasty schemes. This is particularly the case in the tombs of Osorkon II (NRT-I) and

Shoshenq III (NRT-V), which adopted the Books of the Earth, the Day, and the Night, all particularly prominent in Ramesses VI's KV 9, together with the time-hallowed Amduat (Lull 2002, 102–115, 135–150). On the other hand, in addition to sections of the Book of the Dead used in Ramesside royal tombs, those featuring the judgment of the dead—the weighing of the heart and the Negative Confession—also appear in the Twenty-second Dynasty tombs (Lull 2002, 89–92, 150–151), marking a fundamental change in the conception of the dead king, from a divine being joining the gods to something more human, requiring the judgment of the gods before being allowed to come into their company. In some ways this represents the antithesis of the phenomenon of the appropriation (or reappropriation—cf. Dziobek 1994, 42–47) of the Amduat by private individuals from the Twenty-first Dynasty onwards (Aston 2009, 308, 311–315), with a range of formerly royal underworld books or elements thereof finding their way into papyri and onto sarcophagi and tomb walls through the Late Period (cf. Hornung 1999, 56, 96, 113, 116, 123), providing the most lasting legacy of the Twentieth Dynasty tombs in the Valley of the Kings.

BIBLIOGRAPHY

Abitz, F. 1989 *Baugeschichte und Dekoration des Grabes Ramses' VI*. Freiburg and Göttingen.

Abitz, F. 1990. "Der Bauablauf und die Dekorationen des Grabes Ramesses' IX." *Studien zur altägyptichen Kultur* 17: 1–40.

Aldred, C. 1979. "More Light on the Ramesside Tomb Robberies." In *Glimpses of Ancient Egypt*, edited by J. Ruffle, G. A. Gaballa and K. A. Kitche, 96–99. Warminster.

Amer, A. A. A. 1985. "Reflections on the Reign of Ramesses VI." *Journal of Egyptian Archaeology* 71: 66–70.

Andrzejewski. 1962. "Le Livre des portes dans la salle du sarcophage du tombeau de Ramsès III." *Annales du Service des Antiquités de l'Égypte* 57: 1–6.

Aston, D.A. 2009. *Burial Assemblages of Dynasty 21-25: Chronology – Typology – Developments*. Vienna.

Bács, T. A. 1992. "Amun-Ra-Harakhti in the Late Ramesside Royal Tombs." In *The intellectual heritage of Egypt: studies presented to László Kákosy by friends and colleagues on the occasion of his 60th birthday*, edited by U. Luft, 43–53. Budapest.

Barwick, M. 2011. *The Twilight of Ramesside Egypt: Studies on the History of Egypt at the End of the Ramesside Period*. Warsaw.

Brock, E. C. 1995. "The Clearance of the Tomb of Ramesses VII." In Wilkinson, 47–67.

Brooklyn Museum Theban Expedition. 1979. *Theban Royal Tomb Project: A Report of the First Two Seasons*. San Francisco.

Carter, H. and A.H. Gardiner. 1917. "The Tomb of Ramesses IV and the Turin Plan of a Royal Tomb." *Journal of Egyptian Archaeology* 4: 130–158.

Ciccarello, M. 1979. *The Graffito of Pinutem I in the Tomb of Ramesses XI*. San Francisco.

Ciccarello, M. and J. Romer. 1979. *A Preliminary Report of the Recent Work in the Tombs of Ramesses X and XI in the Valley of the Kings*. San Francisco.

Darnell, John C. 2004. *The Enigmatic Netherworld Books of the Solar-Osirian Unity: Cryptographic Compositions in the Tombs of Tutankhamun, Ramesses VI and Ramesses IX*. Freiburg and Göttingen.

Dodson, A. 2012. *Afterglow of Empire: Egypt from the fall of the New Kingdom to the Saite Renaissance*. Cairo.

Dziobek, E. 1994. *Die Gräber des Vezirs User-Amun: Theben Nr, 61 und 131*. Mainz.

Forbes, D. C. 1998. *Tombs, Treasures, Mummies: Seven Great Discoveries of Egyptian Archaeology*. Sevastopol & Santa Fe.

Hornung, E. 1988. "Zum Schutzbild im Grabe Ramses' VI." In *Funerary Symbols and Religion. Essays dedicated to Professor M.S.H.G. Heerma van Voss on the occasion of his retirement from the Chair of the History of Ancient Religions at the University of Amsterdam*, edited by J. H. Kamstra, H. Milde and K. Wagtendonk, 45–51. Kampen.

Hornung, E. 1988. "Zum Turiner Grabplan." In *Pyramid Studies and Other Essays Presented to I. E. S. Edwards*, edited by J. Baines, T. G. H. James, A. Leahy, and A. F. Shore, 138–142. London.

Hornung, E. 1990. *Zwei Ramessidische Königsgräber: Ramses IV. und Ramses VII*. Mainz.

Hornung, E. 1999. *The Ancient Egyptian Books of the Afterlife*, trans. by D. Lorton. Ithaca.

Jansen–Winkeln, K. 2007. *Inschriften der Spätzeit*, I: *Die 21. Dynastie*. Wiesbaden.

Jenni, H., ed. 2000. *Das Grab Ramses' X (KV18)*. Basel.

Lull, J. 2002. *Las tumbas reales egipcias del Tercer Período Intermedio (dinastías XXI – XXV): Tradición y cambios*. Oxford.

Marciniak, M. 1982. "Réparations anciennes dans le tombeau de Ramsès III (no. 11) dans la Vallée des Rois." *Africana Bulletin* 31: 37–43.

Marciniak, M. 1983. "Deux campagnes épigraphiques au tombeau de Ramsès III dans la Vallée des Rois (no 11)." *Études et Travaux* 12: 295–305.

Nail, N. 2009. "Appendix 3: Ramesses IX." In *Refugees for Eternity: The Royal Mummies of Thebes*, IV: *Identifying the Royal Mummies*, edited by D. Bickerstaffe, 194–196. N.p.

Peden, A. J. 1994. *The Reign of Ramesses IV*. Warminster.

Peden, A. J. 2001. "Where Did Ramesses VI Bury his Nephew?" *Göttinger Miszellen* 181: 83–88.

Piankoff, A. 1954. *The Tomb of Ramesses VI*. New York.

Porter, B. and R. L. B. Moss. 1964. *Topographical Bibliography of Ancient Egyptian Hieroglyphic Texts, Reliefs and Paintings, I/2: Royal Tombs and Smaller Cemeteries*, 2nd ed. Oxford.

Reeves, C. N. 1990. *Valley of the Kings: The Decline of a Royal Necropolis*. London.

Roehrig, C. 1995. "Gates to the Underworld: The Appearance of Wooden Doors in the Royal Tombs in the Valley of the Kings." In *Valley of the Sun Kings: New Explorations in the Tombs of the Pharaohs*, edited by R.H. Wilkinson, 82–104. Tucson.

Rossi, C. 2001. "The plan of a royal tomb on O. Cairo 25184." *Göttinger Miszellen* 184: 45–53.

Schneider, T. 2000. "Ramses X.: Person und Geschichte." In Jenni, 81–108.

Thomas, E. 1966. *The Royal Necropoleis of Thebes*, I: *The Major Cemeteries*. Princeton.

Ventura, R. 1988. "The Largest Project for a Royal Tomb in the Valley of the Kings." *Journal of Egyptian Archaeology* 74: 137–156.

Wilkinson, R. H. 1995. "Symbolic Orientation and Alignment in New Kingdom Royal Tombs." In *Valley of the Sun Kings: New Explorations in the Tombs of the Pharaohs* edited by R. H. Wilkinson, 74–81. Tucson.

CHAPTER 15

··

OTHER TOMBS

Queens and Commoners in KV

··

SUSANNE BICKEL

MORE than half of the tombs in the Valley of the Kings (KV) were not designed for kings. The valley also served—at certain periods—as a necropolis for people other than pharaohs. Regarding these "other tombs," many research questions remain open. Because these nonroyal tombs are almost systematically undecorated and sometimes even rather crude, they have been the focus of very little scholarly attention until recently. They form, however, a most interesting and specific group of sepulchers, not only within the KV, but within the entire Theban necropolis. Although they share certain common features, their architecture shows a great typological variety. The social spectrum of tomb owners seems restricted to royal family and the kings' intimate entourage.

The fact that the royal necropolis also housed burial places for nonroyal individuals comes as no surprise. Since the Old Kingdom the tombs of members of the royal family, as well as of certain officials, were located in the vicinity of the sepulcher of the king with whom they lived. This geographical proximity must have been of conceptual relevance for both the king and his entourage. With the retreat of the royal tombs to the remote and highly secluded Valley of the Kings, only a very few commoners were given the privilege of a burial close to the king. Instead, the connection of elite burials and the king was redirected around the royal funerary temple complexes in the plain of western Thebes. A majority of Eighteenth and Nineteenth Dynasty officials' tombs are located close to or in visual correspondence with the temple of the king they served.

NUMBER AND LOCATION

··

Since spring 2012 the Valley of the Kings counts sixty-four numbered tombs (for the latest discovery, see Bickel and Paulin-Grothe 2012); some twenty additional pits or tomb commencements (designated with letters) were generally not used for burials (with the probable exception of tomb A; Reeves and Wilkinson 1996). Among the sixty-four tombs identified so far, twenty-four were designed for a pharaoh (the two disputed cases, KV 38 and KV 42, were in all probability intended as royal tombs; Eaton-Krauss 2012; Roehrig 2006; also a probable royal project is KV 25). Some thirty-eight sepulchers were designed for nonroyal individuals (including KV 62, eventually used for Tutankhamun). Three tombs contained mainly animal remains (KV 50–52), although they were probably intended for humans (Thomas 1966). Two of the numbered "tombs" clearly served as deposits (KV 54, KV 63) and not as burial places, although KV 63 might have been conceived as such (Schaden 2009). The Valley of the Kings was therefore much more often used for the burial of nonroyal individuals than for pharaohs, even more so as many of these "other tombs" served for the interment of several people. A very cautious estimation suggests that at least seventy-five to one hundred individuals other than pharaohs were carried to rest in a tomb in the KV, not taking into account the burials of royal sons in the Ramesside period. This would amount to almost one nonroyal burial per year during the reigns of Thutmosis III to Amenhotep III. With one nonroyal tomb initiated every three to four years during this same time span, the Valley of the Kings appears to have been a fairly busy space. Whether this constant activity and relative "crowdedness" of the valley were the reason Amenhotep III decided to withdraw to a new area remains a moot question.

The large majority of nonroyal tombs cluster in the areas and side valleys south of the central path; only a few lie north of the path and in the Western Valley. According to the earlier tradition, which placed a pharaoh's pyramid or tomb in the center of the burials of his family and entourage, one would expect a similar constellation in the KV. It is indeed probable that the tombs of Hatshepsut, Thutmosis III, Amenhotep II, and Thutmosis IV—each located at the end of a side valley—served as focal points for the installation of nonroyal tombs belonging to people from their families or entourages (Preys 2011). Our very incomplete knowledge of tomb ownership does not allow a systematic assessment of this assumption. In the sidevalley below the sepulcher of Thutmosis III nonroyal tombs spread from his reign down to the later years of Amenhotep III, several tombs having therefor no direct geographical relation to the pharaoh under whom they were commissioned.

CHRONOLOGY

As research is still ongoing, not all nonroyal tombs can be securely dated so far. It is, however, clear that the majority date from the pre-Amarna Eighteenth Dynasty, the reigns of Hatshepsut to Amenhotep III (1479–1353 B.C.E.). Only a few tombs are precisely dated through known ownership; others can be given an approximate date based on small finds and pottery (Aston et al. 2000) or set into a loose chronology according to their shape and typology (suggestions by Preys 2011). KV 55 and KV 62 were prepared before or during the Amarna period, clearly intended as nonroyal burial places, but finally used for a king of the Amarna period, probably Akhenaton (Reeves and Wilkinson 1996; Gabolde 2009), and for Tutankhamun.

In the Ramesside period, only five nonroyal tombs were prepared in the valley: KV 5, KV 3, and KV 19 for royal sons; KV 14 for a queen; and KV 13 for a commoner. From the late Eighteenth Dynasty onward, the Valley of the Kings became, with very few exceptions, an exclusively royal necropolis. This evolution induced—for the first time in Egyptian history—a clear-cut separation between the pharaohs and their family members, who were mostly laid to rest farther south in the Valley of the Queens. It has to remain an open question whether gender considerations were involved in this evolution. Whereas female family members seem to have been predominant in the nonroyal tombs of the Eighteenth Dynasty, the Ramesside period accommodated almost exclusively royal sons in this necropolis, burying women as well as certain individual sons in the Valley of the Queens.

OWNERS

Nowhere was tomb ownership less spontaneous than in the Valley of the Kings. The possession of a burial place in this area must always have been officially granted by the king or the court. The location of the tomb as well as its architectural shape were carefully planed according to fixed conventions and regulations. The "other tombs" were administrated by the same authorities as the pharaohs', as is shown by the use of the same official necropolis seal employed to close royal and nonroyal burial chambers. It also seems most probable that the same tomb builders were responsible for the preparation of royal and nonroyal sepulchers, although the investment of time and care differed sensibly between the two groups.

Only a minority of nonroyal tombs have an identified ownership. The individuals buried in the valley can be classified in three groups: queens, royal family members (princesses, princes, parents-in-law, etc.), and officials. The strategies of selection of the individuals who were granted a burial in the valley remain most indistinct. For the members of their families and probably even some of their queens, the kings of the Eighteenth Dynasty could decide whether to have them interred either in a tomb close to their own or in one of the other necropolises: in the Valley of the Queens, in one of its adjacent *wadis*, or in the area of Deir el-Bahri. From the reign of Amenhotep II onward, yet another possibility was burying family members inside the royal tombs (Dodson 2003). They were interred in side chambers in the tomb of Amenhotep II (KV 35, son Websenu and a female) and of Thutmosis IV (KV 43, son Amenemhet and daughter Tanetamun). Amenhotep III (WV 22) had separate additional burial chambers prepared within his own tomb for the burial of queen Tiye and his daughter Satamun. This practice raises the question of the sequence of interments and the possibility (or not) of reopening a royal burial chamber, a question that is still debated with respect to the burial of queen Tiye.

Queens

Much discussion has been devoted to the identification of queens' tombs in the valley (Reeves 2003; Roehrig 2010). In the perspective of tradition, major royal wives and queen mothers would indeed be the principal candidates for a burial in the immediate vicinity of the pharaohs. However, only very limited positive information is available. The only certain identification of a queen's tomb so far was made in 2001 by the team from Basel University (Jenni et al. n.d.), when the reinvestigation of KV 32 revealed funerary material of queen Tiaa, wife of Amenhotep II and mother of Thutmosis IV. Some of these objects match fragments found in the tomb of Siptah (KV 47), which were washed by rain floods through the accidental breakthrough between the two tombs. The interment of queen Tiaa just below the sepulcher of Thutmosis III raises the question of whether KV 32 could have been originally intended for a queen of his own entourage (Roehrig 2006; Preys 2011).

One of the principal queens of Thutmosis III, Merytre-Hatshepsut, is attested in the valley through a foundation deposit found next to KV 42. No trace of her interment was found, however, inside the tomb, the shape and partial decoration of which rather point to an intended royal burial (Eaton-Krauss 2012).

The identification of possible queens' sepulchers is based mainly on architectural typology (see below), on the location, and sometimes on finds.

Its conspicuous situation directly beside the tomb of Thutmosis III would seem to predestine KV 33 for a particularly prestigious owner, presumably a queen. The clearing of the tomb in 2012–2013 revealed a well-cut burial chamber, the eastern part of which shows a lowered floor, and two side rooms. No conclusive finds were made to indicate the tomb's owner; alabaster fragments, pottery, and human remains—still to be analyzed—suggest an occupation in the mid-Eighteenth Dynasty (Bickel and Paulin-Grothe 2012, 2009-2014). Typology and location could also designate KV 37—situated in the *wadi* just beneath the tomb of Thutmosis III—as a queen's tomb.

Its position in the side valley leading to the tomb of Thutmosis IV and its architectural characteristics have led to the assumption that KV 21 belonged to women of his entourage. Two female mummies are reported to have been found by Belzoni in 1817. It has to be noted that the frequent assertion that female mummies with a bent left and a straight right arm were necessarily queens cannot yet be substantiated.

Location and shape suggest that KV 49, close to the tomb of Amenhotep II, might have been intended for a queen. In account of its architecture, KV 56 has also been tentatively identified as an unfinished queen's tomb (Reeves 2003).

KV 39, located outside the actual valley far above the tomb of Thutmosis III and in the area of the path leading to the workmen's "station de repos," is still insufficiently known (Rose 2000). The first phase of its complex building history could typologically resemble a queens' tomb (Aston 2013).

The much debated KV 55 might have been intended for a queen of the entourage of Amenhotep III. Despite the presence of her shrine, it is uncertain whether Tiye was ever buried here. The tomb eventually accommodated a king, presumably Akhenaton (Reeves and Wilkinson 1996; Gabolde 2009).

Only very exceptionally were royal women buried in the valley during the Ramesside period. Textual evidence might indicate the interment of Isisnofret, a queen of Ramesses II, within the valley (Lakomy 2008). KV 14 was begun as a nonroyal tomb intended for queen Tausret and only later reworked as a royal sepulcher (Altenmüller 2003).

The usurpation of KV 10, built for Amenmesse, by two queens of the Twentieth Dynasty called Takhat and Baketwerel seems to be an exceptional phenomenon.

Royal Family

Next to queens, other members of the royal family were also granted a burial in the valley. They seem to have been buried regularly in groups together in one tomb. The most famous tomb of this category is KV 46, where Amenhotep III had his parents-in-law Yuya and Thuya interred with luxurious funerary equipment. This tomb was discovered in 1905 in a fairly intact state.

In the large tomb structure KV 40, more than thirty individuals from the royal court of Thutmosis IV and Amenhotep III were buried over a certain time span. Inscriptions on jars containing embalming refuse reveal the identity of twelve hitherto unknown princesses and at least four princes as well as some ladies of foreign origin and a number of females without title. Some princesses belong to an institution called "the house of the royal children" (Bickel and Paulin-Grothe 2014).

Only some of the royal family members of the Eighteenth Dynasty were, however, given a burial place in the Valley of the Kings: some sixty tombs of this period are located in the Valley of the Queens (Leblanc 1989), and a few additional ones are in the adjacent valleys.

The interment of male members of the royal family in one common tomb with numerous individual burial chambers seems to have been a new feature of the Ramesside period. KV 5, created for the sons of Ramesses II, is here the most impressive example, followed by a more modest project under Ramesses III, KV 3.

In the Twentieth Dynasty KV 13, originally prepared for the chancellor Bay, was used for two princes, Amunherkhepeshef, son of Ramesses III, and Montuherkhepeshef, son of Ramesses VI (Altenmüller 2009).

Toward the end of the Twentieth Dynasty, KV 19, probably originally intended for a king, was decorated for a royal son in the manner of the corresponding tombs in the Valley of the Queens. The first princely beneficiary eventually became pharaoh Ramesses VIII, so that the tomb was attributed to Montuherkhepeshef, son of Ramesses IX.

Commoners

People from outside the royal family seem to have been admitted in the valley right from the beginning of its occupation. One of the first private individuals to have been buried here was Hatshepsut's wet nurse Satra-In, found in KV 60, situated just underneath the entrance of Hatshepsut's tomb. Recent research also revealed the coffin of a singer called Ty within this tomb (Ryan 2010).

The best-known commoner is Maiherperi, thanks to the fact that his tomb, KV 36, was found with abundant funerary equipment, although it was plundered in antiquity. This man, probably of Nubian origin, was a "child of the royal nursery" and "royal fan-barer"; his name "the lion on the battlefield," might be a sobriquet he received during a military campaign, perhaps in the company of one of the Eighteenth Dynasty kings. It is still uncertain to which king he was connected.

A few officials of the Eighteenth Dynasty were probably interred in the valley, although they all possess a richly decorated burial chapel in the Theban necropolis (Dorman 1995). This phenomenon points to the utmost symbolic value of the location and indicates that the attribution of even a modest shaft tomb in the king's vicinity was the sign of a rarely accorded and significant social distinction.

KV 48 contained a body, parts of a coffin, and pottery, as well as shabti figurines and magical bricks inscribed in the name of Amenemopet, called Pairy, who was mayor of Thebes and vizier under Amenhotep II. The burial was obviously much disturbed and the find situation poorly documented, but the material seems sufficient to consider that Amenemopet was buried here in the immediate neighborhood of the pharaoh he served. TT 29 in Sheikh Abdel Gurna is his burial chapel.

The case of Amenemopet's cousin (Laboury 2007), the mayor of Thebes Sennefer, and his wife Senetnay, the wet nurse of Amenhotep II, is more complicated. They are often mentioned in connection with KV 42, where a set of canopic vases inscribed for Senetnay was found together with other pieces of funerary furniture and coffins (Eaton-Krauss 1999). Limestone imitation vessels with the names of Sennefer and Senetnay were found outside KV 42 as well as in KV 32. The canopic jars seem to indicate that Senetnay was indeed buried somewhere in the Valley of the Kings, though most probably not in KV 42, where the material might have been brought during the Twenty-first Dynasty. Her original burial place is unknown, and the question of whether Sennefer was also interred here remains open. Their burial chapel and decorated burial chamber ("the tomb of the vines") are TT 96 in Sheikh Abdel Gurna. Among the material found in KV 42 was also an offering table inscribed in the name of a "royal adornment" called Baketre, of whom canopic jars were found in the valley.

KV 45 was reused in the Twenty-second Dynasty by two individuals, but fragments of canopic jars indicate that the original occupant was the "overseer of fields of Amun" Userhat. His decorated tomb TT 56 in Sheikh Abdel Gurna shows that he was active during the reign of Amenhotep III, that he was also a "child of the royal nursery," and that his wife and his daughter wore the title "royal adornment." As the recent reinvestigation of KV 45 revealed the remains of four individuals (Ryan 1994), it is possible that Userhat was interred here together with his wife.

From these fragmentary indications it can be deduced that the rank in the administrative hierarchy of an official was probably less decisive for the attribution of a tomb in the valley than his relationship to the king and the court.

Most women attested in the Valley of the Kings, who were neither royal wives nor daughters, bore the titles of royal wet nurse and/or "royal adornment," two activities that introduced them into the intimacy of the royal harem and conferred a high social status on them (Fekri 2003). Men were connected with the royal family as children of the royal nursery, which indicates that they were brought up together with the future king. Their titles show that these people belonged to the innermost circle around queens and especially around the young or future king. It is certainly this personal closeness that motivated the kings to assign a burial place next to their own to these selected individuals.

During the Ramesside period the chancellor Bay was the only official who planned to be interred in the valley, in KV 13. As he was disgraced at the end of his career, he was certainly never buried here; his tomb was reused by two later princes (Altenmüller 2009).

The very intense activity undertaken during the Twenty-first Dynasty to retrieve all valuables and reusable objects did not spare the nonroyal tombs. Only a few of the nonroyal mummies, however, were redeposited together with the bodies of the pharaohs in caches. Most of them were left behind in a looted state.

ARCHITECTURE

Every tomb in the Valley of the Kings is different. The royal sepulchers show a clear evolution, with constant innovations and expansions of the preceding model (Hornung 1990). Such a development is more difficult to observe among the nonroyal tombs, partly because of our difficulties in placing them firmly in a chronological order. Despite the continual evolution of the royal tombs and the variety of shapes of the nonroyal sepulchers, the two categories clearly follow a separate canon from the beginning. Although most nonroyal tombs date to the time between Hatshepsut and Amenhotep III, none of them shows a bent axis, nor do they present a well. Only three of the "other tombs" have a pillar, albeit of more modest size than the royal ones.

All the tombs are subterranean; there are no structures that would have remained visible once the burial was closed and the entrance refilled with the loose material of stones and sand from the desert surface. This particularity markedly distinguishes nonroyal tombs in the valley from those in other parts of the Theban necropolis, where the aspect of visibility seems to have been central (see below).

There are two major groups to be distinguished with regard to the tomb entrance: the subterranean part can be accessed either via a flight of steps or through a vertical shaft.

Tombs with Stairs

Eleven nonroyal tombs present an access with stairs (KV 5, 12, 21, 32, 33, 37, 39, 46, 49, 55, 60), as well as KV 62, of nonroyal design, eventually used for Tutankhamun. Three tombs stand out because they have a central pillar in the burial chamber (KV 12, 21, 32), although these pillars have nonroyal dimensions (Hornung 1978). The presence of a pillar was sometimes deemed a distinctive feature of queens' tombs (Reeves 2003). It is possible that tombs accessed by stairs were in general intended for people of very high status. Hatshepsut's wet nurse Satra-In and the singer Ty are the only individuals from outside the royal family known to be buried in a tomb with stairs; however, the steps leading to KV 60 (probably the oldest nonroyal tomb) are extremely steep and the interior very rough and irregular.

Most tombs of this category have a corridor; some even possess a second flight of stairs and a second corridor—features reminiscent of royal tombs. These tombs always have a single burial chamber, although some were used for several interments (e.g., KV 46, Yuya and Thuya, and KV 21). The list in Table 15.1 organizes the nonroyal tombs with a stepped entrance according to their architectural complexity, which does not necessarily imply a chronological order. KV 21 and KV 32 show particularly elaborate interior structures. KV 12 and KV 39 seem to have gained a higher architectural complexity through later extensions (KV 12: Thomas 1966, 148; Reeves and Wilkinson 1996, 109; KV 39: Rose 2000; Aston 2013).

With the notable exception of KV 37, which has perfectly horizontal interior structures, all corridors have a marked slope of 20–25 degrees.

KV 5 is one of the most extravagant subterranean structures ever conceived in ancient Egypt. It is possible, however, that it originally was an Eighteenth Dynasty nonroyal tomb, accessible over a flight of steps leading into two successive rooms (Weeks 2006, 21). Under Ramesses II it was turned into a huge complex—still not entirely explored—with a large pillared hall and at least six long corridors at various levels, which opened into more than 150 chambers. It was destined for royal sons; four princes are attested by name to have been buried here, and many more were probably interred, their remains having vanished due to the infiltration of rainwater.

A similar, though more modest, project was started under Ramesses III to accommodate one or several of his sons. KV 3 has a stepped entrance, two corridors leading to a hall with four pillars, and five chambers.

The custom of individual nonroyal burials in the valley having been abandoned for over a century, the tomb prepared for the chancellor Bay (KV 13), and later the one made for prince Montuherkhepeshef (KV 19 unfinished and possibly originally of royal design) have no typology of their own, but follow the scheme of contemporaneous royal sepulchers in a somewhat simplified way. They have a flat entrance, sloping slightly downward, and a sequence of corridors.

Shaft Tombs

The majority of nonroyal tombs are accessible through a vertical shaft. The dimensions of the perimeter are fairly standard, with a width of 1.2–1.5 meters and a length varying

Table 15.1 Architectural Complexity of Nonroyal Tombs with Stepped Entrance

KV 33	Stairs	Chamber + annexes			
KV 12	Stairs	Chamber + pillar later extensions?			
KV 60	Stairs	Corridor + annex	Chamber		
KV 37	Stairs	Corridor	Chamber		
KV 49	Stairs	Corridor	Chamber		
KV 55	Entrance + stairs	Corridor	Chamber + annex		
KV 62	Stairs	Corridor	Chamber + annexes		
KV 39	Stairs	Corridor	Chamber later extensions?		
KV 46	Stairs	Corridor	Stairs	Chamber	
KV 21	Stairs	Corridor	Stairs	Corridor	Chamber + pillar annex
KV 32	Stairs	Corridor	Stairs	Corridor	Chamber + pillar annex

from 1.5 to 3 meters. This size allowed a man to descend without a ladder, little footholds being sometimes still visible in the lateral walls. These dimensions also allowed the maneuvering of a wooden coffin. The depth of the shafts varies significantly, although it is impossible to know for what reasons (geology, social status?). Many shafts have a depth of 3 to 6 meters, the shaft of the still unexplored KV 29 is about 9 meters deep, and the enigmatic unfinished KV 41 has a profundity of over 11 meters.

The shaft tombs can be subdivided into two types: those with a single subterranean chamber and those with several rooms. A few examples show a corridor between the bottom of the shaft and the burial chamber(s). The burial chambers of the shaft tombs have no annexes. Where several rooms exist, they are all of larger size and seem to have served as burial chambers in their own right.

The single chamber type is quite frequent: KV 24, 28, 36, 44, 45, 48, 50, 51, 52, 53, 56, 58, 59, 61, 63, and 64 have only one room, generally of rather modest size. It has been suggested (Reeves 2003) that the unfinished KV 56 was planned to receive a central pillar, which would have made it the only shaft tomb with a pillar.

KV 26 has a short corridor leading to a single chamber. KV 30 and KV 40 have a corridor and five and four chambers, respectively, which all seem to be part of the original design. KV 27 has four and KV 31 three chambers. The additional chambers are always distributed around a central room. These larger tombs were probably prepared from the outset to receive multiple burials.

It is noteworthy that the shaft tombs of the Valley of the Kings are typologically quite different from contemporary shaft tombs in the Valley of the Queens, supposedly designed for the same very limited segment of society (Leblanc 1989).

DISTINCTIVE FEATURES

The major distinctive feature of nonroyal tombs in the Valley of the Kings is the systematic absence of decoration (Ryan 1992). The only exceptions are the tombs from the Ramesside period—KV 5 (for sons of Ramses II), KV 13 (Bay), KV 3 (for sons of Ramesses III), and KV 19 (Montuherkhepeshef)—which show wall decoration comparable to contemporary tombs in the Valley of the Queens.

All the Eighteenth Dynasty sepulchers have walls that are absolutely bare of inscriptions or iconographic elements. Also, there are no structures above ground. It is obvious that this is an intentional and even a conceptual aspect and has nothing to do with a possible unfinished state of the tombs or inferior quality of carving. There is no evident reason for this feature, which had important consequences and stands in marked contrast to the contemporaneous tomb-chapels of the nobles with their lavish wall decoration. It has to be noticed, however, that the Eighteenth Dynasty tombs in the Valley of the Queens are also systematically undecorated and anonymous.

In our understanding of ancient Egyptian funerary conceptions, the permanence on earth of an individual's name and image would be an essential factor for the person's survival in the other world. Wall decoration in the tomb-chapels also served as the representation of the deceased's social sphere, both in terms of social environment and social status. The absence of all types of visual and nominal remembrance and visibility after death also implied the lack of statuary or funerary stelae in the royal necropolis. It seems as though the social distinction of a burial in this prestigious area also implied the impossibility of visualizing and commemorating not only this distinction, but even the person's existence.

Conceptually related to the maintenance of memory, the presentation of the funerary cult was also a prerequisite for an individual's survival after death. This cult was necessarily linked to a specific space and related to some kind of markers of memory.

In analyzing the nobles' tombs on the Theban west bank, current research emphasizes the importance of maintaining the deceased's memory not only through a regular cult but also through his or her integration into the various religious activities and feasts staged in the area.

Where did the funerary cult for the nonroyal individuals buried in the Valley of the Kings take place? How and where could their descendants maintain their memory, nourish their *ba*-soul, and celebrate an encounter with the deceased during the religious feasts?

Queens might have been integrated into the cult of their husbands in the royal funerary temples, although no specific structures are known to visualize their existence (with the possible exception of the chapel next to the Ramesseum). Royal sons were depicted in their father's temple from the Ramesside period onward. Those Eighteenth Dynasty officials who possessed a decorated tomb-chapel on the Theban west bank did indeed have the best of both worlds: their corps in the most sacred area next to the pharaoh and a cult structure that guaranteed their enduring social integration.

It is still unknown where people like Yuya and Thuya would be commemorated, or whether and where somebody could present an offering to Maiherperi. Cult statues in divine temples might have been a possible substitute, although we would then perhaps expect to find many more statues of members of the royal family.

There appears to have been a specific funerary concept for queens, members of the royal family, and those rare individuals related not by blood but by ties of personal closeness with the king. This concept also implied a canon of tomb shape, perhaps tomb location, and the renouncement of all tomb decoration and exterior markers of memory. Another prohibition seems to have applied to stone sarcophagi, which are systematically absent from nonroyal tombs in the Valley of the Kings.

ARCHAEOLOGY AND RESEARCH

Scholarly interest in the nonroyal tombs is fairly recent. Because of their lack of wall decoration and significant funerary material, they were almost systematically dismissed by the explorers and archaeologists of the nineteenth and early twentieth centuries. However, many tombs were already visible (and probably accessible), and their location was indicated on the early sketches and maps of John Gardner Wilkinson, James Burton, Robert Hay, and later Eugène Lefébure (Reeves and Wilkinson 1996). Certain tombs were probably visited by robbers during the nineteenth century; the heavy looting and fire that can be observed in KV 40 is only one clear example (Bickel and Paulin-Grothe 2011–2014).

It was only with the discovery of Maiherperi by the team of Victor Loret in 1899 (Gabolde 2007) that a nonroyal tomb was scientifically documented, although mainly for its funerary equipment. The same holds true for the tomb of Yuya and Thuya, found in 1905 by James Quibell. In subsequent years Edward Ayrton, Harold Jones, and Howard Carter accessed and numbered several tombs, but only very cursorily referred to them in reports or in publications of royal tombs. It is only toward the end of the twentieth and at the beginning of the twenty-first centuries that scholarly interest in undecorated tombs resumed, with the Pacific Lutheran University Valley of the Kings Project (Ryan 1994, 2010; Aston et al. 2000), the work conducted under the direction of Zahi Hawass (rediscovery of KV 53), and the ongoing research of the University of Basel Kings' Valley Project (discovery of KV 64, rediscovery of KV 59, and first documentation of KV 29, 31, 33, and 40; Bickel and Paulin-Grothe 2009–2014, 2012; Bickel 2013; Bickel and Paulin-Grothe 2014; www.kv64.ch).

BIBLIOGRAPHY

Aston, D. 2013. "TT 320 and the ḳзy of Queen Inhapi—A Reconsideration Based on Ceramic Evidence." *Göttinger Miszellen* 236: 7–20.

Aston, D., B. Aston, and D. P. Ryan 2000. "Pottery from Tombs in the Valley of the Kings KV 21, 27, 28, 44, 45 and 60." *Cahiers de la Céramique égyptienne* 6: 11–38.

Altenmüller, H. 2003. "Bemerkungen zu den neu gefundenen Daten im Grab der Königin Twosre (KV 14) im Tal der Könige von Theben." In *After Tutankhamun, Research and Excavation in the Royal Necropolis at Thebes*, edited by N. Reeves, 141–164. London & New York: Kegan Paul International.

Altenmüller, H. 2009. "Prinz und Pharao—Amunherchopeschef und Ramses VI." In *Die ihr vorbeigehen werdet . . . Gedenkschrift für Sayed Tawfik Ahmed, Sonderschrift Deutsches Archöologisches Institut Abteilung Kairo* 16, Berlin, edited by U. Rößler-Köhler and T. Tawfik, 5–16. Berlin and New York: de Gruyter.

Bickel S. 2013. "Ein neues Grab im Tal der Könige." *Antike Welt* 1: 75–82.

Bickel, S., and E. Paulin-Grothe. 2009–2014. "Preliminary Reports." http://aegyptologie.uni-bas.ch/forschung/projekte/university-of-basel-kings-valley-project/ (accessed February 28, 2014).

Bickel, S., and E. Paulin-Grothe. 2012. "The Valley of the Kings: Two Burials in KV 64." *Egyptian Archaeology* 41: 36–40.

Bickel, S., and E. Paulin-Grothe. 2014. "Princesses and Princes in the Kings' Valley." *Egyptian Archaeology* 45: 21–24.

Dodson A. 2003. "The Burial of Members of the Royal Family during the Eighteenth Dynasty." In *Egyptology at the Dawn of the 21st Century*, edited by Z. Hawass and L. Pinch-Brock, 2:187–193. Cairo: American University Press Cairo.

Dorman, P. 1995. "Two Tombs and One Owner." In *Thebanische Beamtennekropolen: neue Perspektiven archäologischer Forschung*, Studien zur Archäologie und Geschichte Altägyptens 12, Heidelberg, edited by J. Assmann, 141–154.

Eaton-Krauss, M. 1999. "The Fate of Sennefer and Senetnay at Karnak Temple and in the Valley of the Kings." *Journal of Egyptian Archaeology* 85: 113–129.

Eaton-Krauss, M. 2012. "Who Commissioned KV 42 and for Whom?" *Göttinger Miszellen* 234: 53–60.

Fekri, M. M. 2003. "Une nouvelle enquête sur les tombes civiles et anonymes de la Vallée des Rois." In *Egyptology at the Dawn of the Twenty-First Century*, edited by Z. Hawass and L. Pinch-Brock, 1:180–184. Cairo: American University Press.

Gabolde, L. 2007. "Sur quelques tombeaux mineurs de la Vallée des Rois découverts par V. Loret." In *Proceedings of the Ninth International Congress of Egyptologists*, Orientalia Lovaniensia Analecta 150, Leuven, edited by J.-C. Goyon and C. Cardin, 749–762. Leuven: Peeters Publishers.

Gabolde, M. 2009. "Under a Deep Blue Starry Sky." In *Causing His Name to Live: Studies in Egyptian Epigraphy and History in Memory of William J. Murnane*, Culture and History of the Ancient Near East 37, Leiden, edited by P. Brand and L. Cooper, 109–120. Leiden: Brill Academic Publishers.

Hornung, E. 1978. "Struktur und Entwicklung der Gräber im Tal der Könige." *Zeitschrift für Ägyptische Sprache und Altertumskunde* 105: 59–66.

Hornung, E. 1990. *The Valley of the Kings: Horizon of Eternity*. New York: Timken.

Jenni, H. et al. n.d. "MISR: Mission Siptah—Ramses X.: Das Grab der Tiaa (KV 32)." http://aegyptologie.unibas.ch/forschung/projekte/misr-mission-siptah-ramses-x/koenigin-tiaa/ (accessed January 4, 2013).

Laboury, D. 2007. "Sennefer et Aménémopé: Une affaire de famille." *Égypte, Afrique & Orient* 45: 43–52.

Lakomy, K. C. 2008. *Cairo Ostracon J. 72460: Eine Untersuchung zur königlichen Bestattungstradition im Tal der Könige zu Beginn der Ramessidenzeit.* GM Beihefte 4. Göttingen.

Leblanc, C. 1989. "Architecture et évolution chronologique des tombes de la Vallée des Reines." *Bulletin de l'Institut Français d'Archéologie Orientale* 89: 227–247.

Preys, R. 2011. "Les tombes non-royales de la Vallée des Rois." *Studien zur Altägyptischen Kultur* 40: 315–338.

Reeves, N. 2003. "On Some Queens' Tombs of the Eighteenth Dynasty." In *The Theban Necropolis, Past, Present and Future*, edited by N. Strudwick and J. Taylor, 69–73. London: British Museum Press.

Reeves, N., and R. H. Wilkinson. 1996. *The Complete Valley of the Kings: Tombs and Treasures of Egypt's Great Pharaohs.* Cairo: American University Press.

Roehrig, C. H. 2006. "The Building Activities of Thutmoses III in the Valley of the Kings." In *Thutmoses III. A New Biography*, edited by E. H. Cline and D. O'Connor, 238–259. Ann Arbor: University of Michigan Press.

Roehrig, C. H. 2010. "Some Thoughts on Queen's Tombs in the Valley of the Kings." In *Thebes and Beyond, Studies in Honour of Kent R. Weeks*, Supplément aux Annales du Service des Antiquités de l'Égypte, Cahier 41, Cairo, edited by Z. Hawass and S. Ikram, 181–195.

Rose, J. 2000. *Tomb KV 39 in the Valley of the Kings: A Double Archaeological Enigma.* Bristol: Western Academic & Specialist Press.

Ryan, D. P. 1992. "Some Observations Concerning Uninscribed Tombs in the Valley of the Kings." In *After Tutankhamun, Research and Excavation in the Royal Necropolis at Thebes*, edited by N. Reeves, 21–27. London & New York: Kegan Paul International.

Ryan D. P. 1994. "Exploring the Valley of the Kings." *Archaeology* 47 (1): 54–59.

Ryan, D. P. 2010. "Pacific Lutheran University Valley of the Kings Project: Work conducted during the 2007 Field Season." *Annales du Service des Antiquités de l'Égypte* 84: 383–389.

Schaden O. 2009. "KV 63. Origins of the Discovery." In *Das geheimnisvolle Grab 63*, edited by E. Dziobek, M. Höveler-Müller, and C. E. Loeben, 62–65. Rahden: Verlag Marie Leidorf.

Thomas, E. 1966. *The Royal Necropoleis of Thebes.* Princeton, NJ.

University of Basel Kings' Valley Project. www.kv64.ch (accessed February 28, 2014).

Weeks, K. R. 2005. *The Theban Mapping Project: Atlas of the Valley of the Kings.* Cairo, New York: American University in Cairo Press. (Also available at www.thebanmappingproject.com.)

Weeks, K. R. 2006. *KV 5: A Preliminary Report on the Excavation of the Tomb of the Sons of Rameses II in the Valley of the Kings.* Cairo: American University Press.

PART VII

....

CONTENTS OF ROYAL KV TOMBS

....

CHAPTER 16

··

SARCOPHAGI

··

AIDAN DODSON

THE sarcophagus, the distinctive rectangular outer box used to hold the body (and other containers) in Egyptian burials, first appeared in the Old Kingdom. The earliest example dates to the time of Djoser. Hardstone sarcophagi are known from the reign of Khufu, and culminate in Thirteenth Dynasty examples, which had grown to become monolithic integrated burial chambers/sarcophagi/canopic chests (Dodson 1987).

During the Seventeenth Dynasty, the only evidence we have for royal sarcophagi is the rock-cut coffer, still attached to the bedrock, that held the coffin of Nubkheperre Intef (VI) when discovered by local plunderers at Dra Abu'l-Naga at Thebes-West in 1827 (Athanasi 1836, x–xi). No sarcophagi are known for the first kings of the Eighteenth Dynasty, Ahmose I and Amenhotep I, although there remain major issues regarding the identification of their burial places (see pp. 67–68).

Typologically, the earliest New Kingdom royal sarcophagi are one made for Hatshepsut as regent and found in her tomb in the Wadi Siqqa Taqa el-Zeide (Cairo JE47032, Porter and Moss 1960–1964, 591) and an unfinished and uninscribed example found in KV 42 in the Valley of the Kings, a tomb that has been attributed to both Thutmose II and Queen Meryetre Hatshepsut (see p. 188; for references to all Valley of the Kings sarcophagi, see Table 16.1, below); in favor of Thutmose II is the fact that no simple queen-consort is known to have had a stone sarcophagus until much later in the dynasty. Both of these are simple rectangular boxes of yellow quartzite, with the brief text- and *wadjet*-eyes-based decoration of the Hatshepsut piece closely following that of wooden coffins of the Middle Kingdom (cf. Grajetzki 2005), with the exception of the placement of a cartouche on the upper surface of the lid, together with a figure of Nut.

Of the same form and material (painted red, as were all subsequent sarcophagi of quartzite) was the first of the sarcophagi manufactured for Hatshepsut subsequent to her assumption of full pharaonic names and titles. The original decoration of this piece is uncertain, as it was soon redecorated for the reburial of Thutmose I in her own burial chamber in KV 20 (see pp. 188–90), a process that involved the removal and recarving of all the outside decoration. This scheme placed images of the four sons of Horus at the ends of the long side-walls, with Anubis-Imywet and -Khentysehnetjer in the center,

Table 16.1 Sarcophagi from the Valley of the Kings

Tomb	Owner	Current Location	Material	Comment	Bibliography
KV 42	Thutmose II or Meryetre-Hatshepsut?	In situ	Quartzite	Rectangular; ownership of tomb is debated	Porter and Moss 1960–64, 559; Hornung 1975; Dodson 1988, 120–122
KV 20	Thutmose I ex-Hatshepsut	Boston MFA 04.278	Quartzite	Rectangular; re-carved	Porter and Moss 1960–64, 547; Manuelian and Loeben 1993a;1993b
KV 20	Hatshepsut	Cairo JE37678 = 52459	Quartzite	Cartouche-form	Porter and Moss 1960–64, 547
KV 34	Thutmose III	In situ	Quartzite	Cartouche-form	Porter and Moss 1960–64, 553
KV 38	Thutmose I	Cairo JE52344	Quartzite	Cartouche-form; manufactured under Thutmose III	Porter and Moss 1960–64, 557
KV 36	Maihirpri	Cairo CG24001	Wood	Rectangular	Porter and Moss 1960–64, 557
KV 35	Amenhotep II	In situ	Quartzite	Cartouche-form	Porter and Moss 1960–64, 554
KV 43	Thutmose IV	In situ	Quartzite	Cartouche-form	Porter and Moss 1960–64, 553
WV 22	Amenhotep III	In situ	Granite	Cartouche-form; coffer lost	Porter and Moss 1960–64, 549
KV 46	Yuya	Cairo CG51001	Wood	Rectangular	Porter and Moss 1960–64, 562
KV 46	Tjuiu	Cairo CG51005	Wood	Rectangular	Porter and Moss 1960–64, 563

Table 16.1 *Continued*

Tomb	Owner	Current Location	Material	Comment	Bibliography
KV 62	Tutankhamun	In situ	Quartzite/granite	Rectangular	Porter and Moss 1960–64, 572; Eaton-Krauss 1993
WV 23	Aye	In situ, ex-Cairo JE72131	Granite	Rectangular	Porter and Moss 1960–64, 551; Schaden 1984, 48–54; Reeves 1990, 71
KV 57	Horemheb	In situ	Granite	Rectangular	Porter and Moss 1960–64, 569
KV 16	Ramesses I	In situ	Granite	Cartouche-form	Porter and Moss 1960–64, 535
KV 8	Merenptah (inner)	Cairo JE 87297	Granite	Rectangular; usurped by Pasebkhanut I for his burial in Tanis NRT-III	Montet 1951, 111–125; Sourouzian 1989, 182–183; Brock 1992, 127–128
KV 8	Merenptah (mid)	In situ	Granite	Cartouche-form; coffer fragmentary	Porter and Moss 1960–64, 509; Sourouzian 1989, 181–182; Brock 1992, 126–127
KV 8	Merenptah (outer)	In situ	Granite	Rectangular; coffer fragmentary	Porter and Moss 1960–64, 509; Assmann 1972a; 1972b; Sourouzian 1989, 180–181; Brock 1992, 125–126
KV 15	Seti II	In situ + Louvre E6205	Granite	Rectangular; coffer lost	Porter and Moss 1960–64, 533

(*continued*)

Table 16.1 *Continued*

Tomb	Owner	Current Location	Material	Comment	Bibliography
KV 47	Siptah	In situ	Granite	Cartouche-form	Porter and Moss 1960–64, 565
KV 14	Sethnakhte, ex-Tausret?	In situ	Granite	Cartouche-form; coffer fragmentary	Porter and Moss 1960–64, 532
KV 11	Ramesses III	Louvre D1 = N337 + Fitzwilliam E.1.1823	Granite	Cartouche-form	Porter and Moss 1960–64: 526
KV2	Ramesses IV	In situ	Granite	Cartouche-form	Porter and Moss 1960–64, 500; Hornung 1990, 120–127
KV9	Ramesses VI	In situ	Greywacke	Cartouche-form; fragmentary	Brock 2010
KV1	Ramesses VII	In situ	Granite	Rectangular, rock-cut coffer	Porter and Moss 1960–64, 496; Hornung 1990, 128–131; Brock 1996, 47–51

plus a panel on the left-proper side with a pair of *wadjet*-eyes, and on the right-proper by a panel of text. A kneeling figure of Nephthys was inscribed on the head-end and one of Isis on the foot, while on the top of the lid were once again a cartouche and a figure of Nut, but with more extensive accompanying texts. The texts on the sarcophagus as a whole were essentially derived from the Book of the Dead and the Pyramid Texts, which remained the main source for sarcophagus inscriptions down to the beginning of the Nineteenth Dynasty.

Essentially the same images were added to the formerly-plain interior of the sarcophagus when it was reworked for Thutmose I. The decoration at the head and foot of the interior was partly removed when it was found that the outer coffin of Thutmose I (Cairo CG61025, later usurped by Panedjem I, Porter and Moss 1960–1964, 662; Manuelian and Loeben 1993b, 127–128) was too large to fit. No trace of any original sarcophagus of Thutmose I has ever come to light, and thus it might have been of wood (which may also have been the case for any sarcophagi of Ahmose I and Amenhotep I).

For her own ultimate burial in KV 20, Hatshepsut manufactured a new sarcophagus of the same basic decorative type, but somewhat larger and given the plan of a cartouche, with a rounded head-end and flat foot-end. Inside, the side-walls were left unadorned, with Nephthys at the head and foot, and Nut on both the floor of the coffer and the underside of the lid, the king thus being encapsulated between images of the sky goddess. An almost identical sarcophagus, but with both the head- and foot-ends rounded to avoid the royal cartouche shape, was manufactured for Hatshepsut's close associate Senenmut (New York MMA 31.3.95, Porter and Moss 1960–1964, 141): stone sarcophagi for persons other than kings are rare during the New Kingdom (although stone anthropoid coffins became fairly common during the late Eighteenth/early Nineteenth Dynasties), further emphasizing Senenmut's exceptional status in having such an item.

The basic design established by Hatshepsut's final sarcophagus was continued for all kingly sarcophagi manufactured down to the accession of Akhenaten. Two were made under the auspices of Thutmose III—one for the king himself and one in KV 34 for the further reburial of Thutmose I from KV 20 to KV 38 (cf. pp. 184–87). That made for Thutmose I was the somewhat larger of the two, having been designed to contain the already-existing outer coffin of the king. However, they were otherwise all but identical, deleting the images of the goddesses inside the head and foot found in Hatshepsut's final sarcophagus, but retaining the embracing figures of Nut under the lid and on the floor of the coffer. The sarcophagus of Thutmose III preserves remains of polychrome painting of its texts and divine images; since later sarcophagi were also painted thus, it is likely that the pieces of Hatshepsut and Thutmose I were also originally so adorned.

Interior decoration was entirely dropped from the sarcophagus of Amenhotep II (Figure 16.1), as were the text on the opposite side from the *wadjet*-eye panel, the carved cartouche on the upper surface of the lid, and the latter's figure of Nut. The coffer was also a third taller than that of Thutmose III, marking the beginning of a trend for significant increases in size of sarcophagi from one reign to the next. The heightening of Amenhotep II's monument may have been linked with the reconfiguration of the burial chamber first seen in KV 35 (see p. 193), with a sunken crypt at the end housing the sarcophagus, perhaps surrounded by nested shrines, as found in the tomb of Tutankhamun and marked on an ancient plan of the tomb of Ramesses IV (see p. 220).

The aforementioned progressive expansion of sarcophagus size was applied to all dimensions under Thutmose IV, whose sarcophagus coffer was 22 percent longer, 60 percent wider, and 28 percent taller than that of his father. The decoration of Thutmose IV's sarcophagus in KV 43 marks a revision of the scheme first established by Hatshepsut, in that the *wadjet*-eyes were moved to the head-end of the left-proper side, thus bringing the divine figures together, with the Four Sons of Horus and the two Anubi further joined by figures of Sokar and Horus close to the foot-ends of the long sides (on the left- and right-proper, respectively). The figure of Nut on the upper surface of the lid was also reinstated.

Although the lid of the sarcophagus of Amenhotep III survives in his WV 22, the coffer is missing, presumably taken out during the recycling of material from royal tombs during the Twenty-first Dynasty that also resulted in the removal of some or all of the sarcophagi of Merenptah (see below, p. 254). Amenhotep III's lid diverges

FIGURE 16.1 Sarcophagus of Amenhotep II in KV 35, typical of the type of cartouche-form used for kings during the middle of the Eighteenth Dynasty.

[Martin Davies.]

from immediately preceding royal sarcophagi in being of granite, a material also used in the succeeding reign. It also once again has decoration on its underside, including a small figure of Nut, who is, however, excluded from the upper surface, which only bears texts. The lid is 3 meters long—the same as that of Thutmose IV—but slightly narrower, marking a halt in the continual enlargement of the royal sarcophagus.

The lid of Amenhotep III marks the end of the first phase of royal sarcophagus development—that of cartouche-form containers, protected by Nut and the male deities of the funeral. Private practice for all aspects of the enclosure of the dead had diverged from royal custom early in the dynasty, when the *rishi*-coffin had been dropped by private individuals—but retained for kings' burials until the Twenty-first Dynasty—in favor of first a predominantly white scheme, and then a bichrome one of a black ground with yellow or gilded texts and divine images, which lasted until the end of the Eighteenth Dynasty (Dodson 1998, 2000). In the Valley of the Kings, the tombs of Maihirpri (KV 36) and Yuya and Tjuiu (KV 46, pp. 234, 235) both preserved such "black" outfits, including wooden sarcophagi. That of Maihirpri was a simple box, with a vaulted lid with end-boards typifying a *pr-nw* shrine: decoration comprised Nephthys and Isis on the head and foot, with a *wadjet*-eye, the Four Sons of Horus, the two Anubi, and a human-headed figure (Geb?) on the long sides. In the cases of Yuya and Tjuiu, a cavetto-cornice and torus-moulding were added to upper margins of the coffer and, while Yuya's lid followed that of Maihirpri in being of *pr-nw* form, that of Tjuiu adopted the *pr-wr* form—a rounded head-end and a flat surface sloping toward the foot. Decoratively, Tjuiu followed Maihirpri (but omitting the *wadjet*-eyes), but Yuya

supplemented the Four Sons of Horus and the two Anubi with an image of Thoth at both
ends of each long side.

It was this rectangular form that was adopted by Akhenaten and the remaining
kings of the Eighteenth Dynasty, with the addition of protective female figures enfolding the corners, a concept probably derived from the new kind of kingly canopic chest
adopted from the reign of Amenhotep II onward (see pp. 263–64, below). On the sarcophagus of Akhenaten himself (Cairo TR 3/3/70/2 et al., Martin 1974, 13–30; Raven 1994,
16–18), installed in his tomb at Amarna, the protective figures at the corners were those
of the king's principal wife, Nefertiti, rather than the four tutelary goddesses found on
the canopic prototypes. The decoration of this now-fragmentary monument was built
around the typical Aten sun disks, with descending rays centered on each of the four
exterior faces and the flat upper surface of the lid. The lid also had a cavetto-cornice
and torus-moulding incorporated into its edges, again following canopic practice, and
contrasting with most sarcophagi of this form, which had this adornment incorporated
into the coffer. The sun-disk icon also featured in the decoration of the sarcophagus of
Akhenaten's mother Tiye (Raven 1994; Brock 1996; Gabolde 1998, 134–136), but supplemented by adoring figures.

For the next kingly sarcophagus to be manufactured, the corner figures returned
to the status given to them in the canopic prototypes: the four tutelary goddesses,
Isis, Nephthys, Neith, and Selqet. In its final form, this sarcophagus housed the body
of Tutankhamun but also showed signs of extensive rework: while the corner figures
always represented the goddesses, the wings they ultimately sported had been added,
and a large proportion of the original texts had been removed and replaced. It is unclear
whether this change took place following the renaming of the king from Tutankhaten to
-amun, or as the result of the coffer's appropriation from an earlier ruler. If the latter, the
original owner will most likely have been Neferneferuaten, for whom the canopic coffinettes (cf. p. 268, below) and a significant number of other items used for Tutankhamun's
burial had first been manufactured.

Apart from the winged corner-goddesses, the ultimate decoration of the
sarcophagus-coffer was fairly simple, with a frieze of *djed* and *tjet*-signs around its lower
margin and a *wadjet*-eye at the head-end of each long side. Texts ran around the upper margin, with brief columns of text on the long sides and more extensive ones on the head-end.
It reverted to painted quartzite for its material, but the lid found with it was both made of
granite and of inferior workmanship. It is uncertain whether this was the result of a late
replacement of a (damaged?) quartzite original lid or was always intended to contrast with
the coffer. In this connection, one might note that the sarcophagus of Akhenaten and its lid
were made of different colors of granite and different surface treatment. Tutankhamun's lid
was of *pr-wr* design, its decoration restricted to a winged sun disk at the head-end and a few
bands of text. It had been broken in half and repaired in ancient times, perhaps at the time
it was discovered that the feet of the coffin of the king's outer coffin were too high to allow
the sarcophagus lid to be put in place, resulting in emergency carpentry work.

The granite sarcophagus of Aye (WV 23, Figure 16.2) marks a continuation of the
same basic design, albeit with a flat-ended arched lid in place of Tutankhamun's *per-wer*.
The decoration of the coffer is also more elaborate, with a winged sun disk dominating

FIGURE 16.2 Sarcophagus of Ay in WV 23, an example of the type of rectangular type used during the last part of the Eighteenth Dynasty.

[Aidan Dodson.]

the long sides of the coffer and almost all vertical surfaces covered with texts; on the other hand, the *djed/tjet* frieze was replaced by a plain zone. Another area of difference was that the wings of the corner goddesses were angled downward, rather than placed horizontally as had been the case on Tutankhamun's sarcophagus. The lid was simply adorned, with a central column of text and a pair of *wadjet*-eyes at the head-ends of both long sides.

The final sarcophagus in this rectangular tradition was that of Horemheb (KV 57). Compared with that of Aye, the key areas of difference on the coffer were the deletion of the winged sun disks and the addition of the Four Sons of Horus and the two Anubi on the long sides—the Four Sons partly obscured by the goddesses' wings—and the placement of a "palace-façade" frieze around the bottom. The lid also differed in having end-boards added, making it the roof of a *pr-nw* shrine.

Although Horemheb's sarcophagus marked the end of the use of "shrine-form" sarcophagi for kings, they would continue in use (in wood) for private individuals, albeit without corner goddesses (e.g., Sennedjem and Khonsu [TT 1], Porter and Moss 1960–1964, 4–5). However, Ramesses I (KV 16) reverted to the old cartouche-form conception for his sarcophagus. It was, however, never finished, its coffer decoration being only in paint, a significant amount of which has now been lost. Kneeling figures of Isis and Nephthys—for the first time on a royal sarcophagus depicted with wings—occupied the head- and foot-ends, surrounded by texts, while the long sides had the Four Sons of Horus, the two Anubi, and at the foot-ends, images of Thoth, complemented by a *wadjet*-eye panel at the head-end of the left-proper side. Thoth here makes his first appearance on a king's sarcophagus, although he had been common on private sarcophagi and coffins for some time (e.g., Yuya's). The lid was of an unusual form, only slightly bigger than the cavity in the coffer, and rounded in all directions, but did actually have its texts carved.

In size, the "corner-goddess" group of sarcophagi are somewhat smaller than the massive monuments of Thutmose IV and Amenhotep III, although that of Aye is exceptionally long compared with those of Tutankhamun and Horemheb. That of Ramesses I is of similar size to these two, although of wholly different form. Curiously, however, no traces of stone sarcophagi have ever come to light in the tombs of Seti I and Ramesses II, particularly as such containers were reintroduced for queens under the latter king (Habachi 1974). Given that all other royal tombs of the period have preserved at very least some fragments of stone sarcophagi, it seems thus all but certain that neither king had one. This was almost certainly connected with the introduction under Seti I of a large (bigger than the sarcophagus of Ramesses I) calcite outer anthropoid coffin for apparently the first time (Sir John Soane's Museum, Porter and Moss 1960–1964, 543). Fragments of such coffins have been found for a number of kings, including Ramesses II (Leblanc 1997, 12), Merenptah (British Museum EA49739 et al., Porter and Moss 1960–64, 509; Sourouzian 1989, 183–184; Brock 1992, 136–137), Siptah (Metropolitan Museum of Art 14.6.375 et al., Porter and Moss 1960–1964, 565; Hayes 1959, 356), and Ramesses III (unpublished), while a similar container, in greywacke, was adopted by Ramesses VI (in situ in KV9, Brock 2010). While from Merenptah onward they were enclosed in stone sarcophagi, those of Seti I and Ramesses II may have stood without such a covering, although all but certainly enclosed within the kind of nested shrines already noted as employed by Tutankhamun and Ramesses IV. It is also possible that a sarcophagus was employed, but was made of wood and perhaps resembled contemporary private pieces (e.g., those from TT 1; see above).

Relatively naked as the coffins of Seti I and Ramesses II may have been in their tombs, the reign of Merenptah saw a reaction that produced the most extensive sarcophagus installation of any Egyptian king. No fewer than three granite sarcophagi bear his name, and although there have been suggestions that the smallest of them might have been employed in a cenotaph (see references in Brock 1992, 139–140, n.12), it seems most likely that they were nested within each other to shelter the calcite and other coffins that held Merenptah's mummy when it was interred in KV 8. The coffer of the innermost sarcophagus was the same size as the earliest Eighteenth Dynasty examples and had been made while Merenptah was still crown prince to Ramesses II. It was of rectangular form, with a paneled motif around its lower margin reminiscent of—but by no means identical to—that seen on Middle Kingdom sarcophagi of the reigns of Senwosret III and Amenemhat III (Arnold 2002, 36–37). Above the paneling the sides and ends of the coffer were carved with various underworld demons, with extracts from the Book of Gates appearing inside, while the floor was adorned with a wide range of ritual items, the latter reminiscent of the object friezes found in some Middle Kingdom coffins. In all these features the piece has little in common with kings' sarcophagi. When Merenptah became king, the coffer was equipped with a fresh lid of a new type featuring a recumbent figure of him in the round on top and one of Nut—also in the round—on the concave undersurface. Both of these features occur here in this form for the first time, although the presence of a "flat" figure of Nut under a sarcophagus or coffin lid goes back much further, as already noted. The whole sarcophagus was later usurped by Pasebkhanut I of the Twenty-first Dynasty, and all but one of Merenptah's names was replaced by those of the new owner, who was then buried in it in tomb NRT-III at Tanis.

The extraction of this sarcophagus from KV 8 was probably the immediate cause of the demolition of the coffers of the two larger sarcophagi manufactured for Merenptah, although the salvage of their thick granite floors (no traces of which survive in the tomb) for reuse, perhaps as stelae, was clearly also a factor. The middle sarcophagus was of cartouche-form and 15 percent longer than any Eighteenth Dynasty piece. Like the inner lid, it was topped by a recumbent figure of the king, although in this case wearing a *nemes* rather than tripartite headdress and differently posed, and flanked by protective deities. A kneeling and winged figure of Isis was carved on the foot-end, with Nephthys at the head-end and an image of Nut on the underside, distorted by the need to provide adequate clearance for the image on top of the lid of the inner sarcophagus. The sides of the lid bear the beginning of the Book of Gates, which was also found on the exterior of the very fragmentary remains of the coffer, which also had the Amduat on its interior.

The outer sarcophagus was rectangular, over 4 meters long, without any figure on the lid. Instead it had extensive texts on its upper surface, with a scene of Osiris and supporting deities toward the foot. The sides of the lid were decorated with extracts from the Book of Gates and the Amduat, together with other vignettes, and it had a figure of Nut carved on the underside, together with further extracts from the Gates. Sufficient fragments of the coffer survive to show that it was decorated with a combination of elements from the Book of Gates and the Amduat; these were reassembled within a restoration of the whole coffer in its original location in the burial chamber of KV 8 in 2011–2012.

A broken sarcophagus lid very similar in size and design to Merenptah's innermost one remains within Seti II's KV 15, although no sign of the coffer remains. The head-end is also missing, including with the head of the recumbent figure of the king, but the head from the figure of Nut on the underside is now in the Louvre Museum. Given the small size of the lid, it is likely that a larger outer case was planned, but perforce omitted from the burial due to the restricted size of the improvised burial chamber in KV 15 (cf. p. 209). It is possible that this outer sarcophagus was eventually used for Ramesses III, as the design of that found in his tomb has features more similar to those of the middle sarcophagus of Merenptah than those of Ramesses's immediate predecessors and successors (Dodson 1986; Mojsov 1991–1992; see further below, p. 256).

The sarcophagi used for the burials of Siptah and Sethnakhte in KV 47 and KV 14, respectively, are very similar in design to one another, with the coffer sides having an upper register of alternating *kheker*- and recumbent-jackal motifs and a palace-façade motif around the lower margin. On that of Siptah (see Figure 16.3), there survives a

FIGURE 16.3 Sarcophagus of Siptah in KV 47, a typical example of the kind of royal sarcophagus in use from the middle of the Nineteenth Dynasty to the middle of the Twentieth Dynasty.

[Francis Dzikowski.] [TMP photo 15607.]

middle register of vertical columns of texts and a lower one of various denizens of the underworld, derived from a number of the books of the underworld found in Ramesside royal tombs (cf. Manassa 2007, 13–14); these areas are lost from Sethnakhte's fragmentary (but restored in recent years) coffer. The head and foot of the coffer of Siptah have standing winged figures of Nephthys and Isis, although traces of only the former survive on Sethnakhte's. Both kings' lids have a recumbent figure of the king upon them, holding crossed scepters, wearing an *atef*-crown and flanked by Isis (left-proper) and Nephthys (right-proper), supported by snake-bodied beings, a snake and crocodile. The edges of the lids are undecorated, with a pair of cartouches flanked by Nephthys and Isis on the foot-ends; underneath the lid of Sethnakhte—the situation in the case of Siptah appears to be unrecorded—is an image of Isis in two-dimensional sunk relief, rather than the expected Nut. This change is perpetuated on the lid of Ramesses III.

The royal names on the sarcophagi of both Siptah and Sethnakhte are carved over erased previous cartouches. In the case of Siptah's sarcophagus, this ties in with the erasure and reinstatement of his cartouches on the walls of the tomb—perhaps erased by Tausret and replaced by Sethnakhte. In the case of the sarcophagus used by Sethnakhte, it is possible that it had been made for Tausret as king and was taken over at the same time as the rest of her tomb for Sethnakhte (but cf. pp. 211–12; other potential prior owners could be Seti II or Amenmesse).

Although there are, unlike in the case of these two monuments, no signs of altered cartouches on the sarcophagus of Ramesses III, as has been noted above, there are suspicions about his original ownership of both the lid and coffer. The decorative scheme of the exterior of the coffer has kneeling winged images of Nephthys and Isis on the head- and foot-ends, with the long sides adorned with the seventh and eighth hours of the Book of Amduat, contrasting with the *kheker*-jackal-frieze-topped scheme found not only on the coffers of Siptah and Sethnakhe, but *also* on that of Ramesses III's successor, Ramesses IV (for which see just below). The Amduat had previously been used (with the similar voyage-of-the sun-god-based Book of Gates) as the principal decorative source for the outer two sarcophagi of Merenptah, while another similarity is that the scepters on the Ramesses III recumbent figure are held vertically—as is the case on the middle and sarcophagus lid of Merenptah—contrasting with their crossing on those of Siptah and Sethnakhte and a somewhat different arrangement seen on that of Ramesses IV. Since the vertical arrangement of scepters is also to be found on the lid of Seti II's extant (inner) sarcophagus, there is a temptation to see the Ramesses III sarcophagus as intended as Seti II's outer case. Since royal names only appear on the head- and foot-ends of the coffer, no changes to the main decoration will have been needed. Internally, the coffer of this sarcophagus is (apart from the inner coffer of Merenptah) the only one to be decorated since the earlier Eighteenth Dynasty. The interiors of the head- and foot-ends received extracts from the Book of Gates, but the long sides were adorned with the *kheker*-jackal-frieze scheme found on the exteriors of preceding and succeeding coffers.

Apart from the arrangement of the scepters (and the omission of cartouches on either side of the king's head), the recumbent figure and supporting figures on the upper surface of the lid were identical to those on the sarcophagi of Siptah and Sethnakhte, with the exception of the relative orientation of the images of Isis and Nephthys, with Isis on the proper-left and Nephthys on the right, which reverses the situation found on the lids of Siptah and Sethnakhte (and also of Ramesses IV). The sides of the lid differ from those of the preceding pair in being decorated with texts and a snake, but the underside once again bears an image of Isis. Stone sarcophagi with recumbent figures were also used for the burials of some sons of Ramesses III, although all are fragmentary (e.g., Ramesses C, in situ in QV 53, Nelson and Janot 1993; Khaemwaset E, Turin S.5216, Porter and Moss 1960–1964, 755); other sons simply had anthropoid stone coffins (e.g., Amenherkhepeshef B, in situ in QV 55).

The three late Nineteenth/early Twentieth Dynasty sarcophagi were similar in size to that of Thutmose IV, but while Sethnakhte's is larger than that of Siptah, reflecting the trend toward larger size with time seen in almost all manifestations of funerary productions, that of Ramesses III is rather smaller than either, again suggesting that it may be the earliest of the three. However, that of Ramesses IV in KV 2 was significantly larger in all dimensions, with 25 percent more volume than the sarcophagus of Sethnakhte, this additional size allowing the interior to have a coffin-emplacement occupying the lower half of the coffer. Decoratively, the long sides followed the pattern of the coffers of Siptah and Sethnakhte, but the ends abandoned the time-hallowed goddesses in favor of an extension of the long-side decoration and a single column of text at the head and a vignette derived from the Book of the Earth at the foot. The lid again followed the imme- diately preceding monuments in its design, although the now-damaged state of the upper half of the recumbent figure makes some details difficult to verify, but its seems to have held its scepters in a manner different from any of them.

No lid survives from the sarcophagus in KV 9—perhaps begun, like the tomb, for Ramesses V, but in any case ultimately used for Ramesses VI (see pp. 220–21). The coffer—partly broken up, most probably with a view to recycling during the early Third Intermediate Period—was never finished and never received carved decoration, but was roughly the same size as that of Ramesses IV and was probably intended to be very simi- lar to it. However, rather than the integral coffin-emplacement seen in that piece, a gran- ite anthropoid coffin was provided, now restored from fragments.

An entirely new approach to sheltering the royal mummy was taken for Ramesses VII in KV 1. Rather than utilizing a freestanding coffer, a shallow cutting was made in the floor of the burial chamber to receive the lower edges of a very deep, hollow lid, with an inner deeper cutting for the coffin. Two cylindrical cuttings were made on each long side of the outer cut, apparently to receive the canopic jars (see further p. 271).

The lid covered roughly the same area as that of the sarcophagus of Ramesses III and was nearly 1.5 meters high; it was left fairly rough and decorated primarily in paint. The head-end was adorned by a kneeling, winged figure of Nephthys, flanked by a pair of winged cobras, the foot-end by a *djed*-pillar and a pair of *tjet*-signs. The long sides bore principally the Four Sons of Horus, protected by Isis and Nephthys (right-proper) and Neith and Selqet (left-proper), the latter accompanied by a recumbent jackal adjacent to the head-end. Thus, not only was the concept of the shelter for the mummy fundamen- tally changed, but the decoration of that shelter likewise, perhaps reflecting some of the ongoing theological change that can be seen in the tombs of the later Twentieth Dynasty (see pp. 223–26). It is interesting, however, to see the return of the Four Sons of Horus, last seen substantively on the sarcophagus of Ramesses I.

It is possible that a similar installation, but on more than twice the scale, was con- templated in the tomb of Ramesses IX (KV 6). It once again has a two-level cutting in the burial chamber, but no trace of any cover has ever been found; this would have been even larger than the vast outer sarcophagus lid of Merenptah.

The tomb of Ramesses X (KV 18) was abandoned long before any burial installation could have been begun. The sepulcher constructed for Ramesses XI (KV 4) had a deep shaft cut in the center of its burial chamber, which was presumably intended to hold the king's body. However, as the shaft and surrounding floor of the burial chamber were never fully finished, it is wholly uncertain whether any kind of stone sarcophagus was to have been placed at the bottom of the shaft or even if a hardstone cover was contem- plated for the shaft; any such item would have been of similar size to the one mooted for the much shallower cut in KV 6.

The evolution of the royal sarcophagus terminates temporarily at this point, all extant sarcophagi used by following kings down to the middle of the Twenty-second Dynasty being reused pieces. As already noted, Pasebkhanut I was interred in the former inner sarcophagus of Merenptah, while Middle Kingdom pieces were appropriated for both Amenemopet and Takelot I, before Osorkon II and Shoshenq III apparently resumed original royal sarcophagus manufacture (cf. Montet 1960, 73–76).

BIBLIOGRAPHY

Arnold, Dieter. 2002. *The Pyramid Complex of Senwosret III at Dahshur: Architectural Studies.* New York.

Assmann, J. 1972a. "Die Inschrift auf dem äußeren Sarkophagdeckel des Merenptah." *Mitteilungen des Deutschen Archäologischen Instituts, Kairo* 28: 47–73.

Assmann, J. 1972b. "Neith spricht als Mutter und Sarg (Interpretation und metrische Analyse der Sargdeckelinschrift des Merenptah)." *Mitteilungen des Deutschen Archäologischen Instituts, Kairo* 28: 115–139.

Athanasi, Giovanni d'. 1836. *A Brief Account of the Researches and Discoveries in Upper Egypt made under the Direction of Henry Salt.* London.

Brock, E. C. 1992. "The Tomb of Merenptah and its Sarcophagi." In *After Tut'ankhamūn: Research and Excavation in the Royal Necropolis at Thebes*, edited by C. N. Reeves, 122–140. London.

Brock, E. C. 1995. "The Clearance of the Tomb of Ramesses VII." In *Valley of the Sun Kings: New Explorations in the Tombs of the Pharaohs; Papers from the University of Arizona International Conference on the Valley of the Kings*, edited by R. H. Wilkinson, 47–67. Tucson, AZ.

Brock, E. C. 1996. "The Sarcophagus of Queen Tiy." *Journal of the Society for the Study of Egyptian Antiquities* 26: 8–21.

Brock, E. C. 2003. "The Sarcophagus Lid of Queen Takhat." In *Egyptology at the Dawn of the Twenty-first Century: Proceedings of the Eighth International Congress of Egyptologists, Cairo, 2000*, edited by Z. Hawass and L. Pinch Brock, I, 97–102. Cairo.

Brock, E. C. 2010. "Contribution of the Sarcophagus of Ramesses VI: Piecing Together a Three-dimensional Puzzle." In *Preserving Egypt's Cultural Heritage: The Conservation Work of the American Research Center in Egypt*, edited by R. Danforth, 63–67. San Antonio, TX and Cairo.

Danforth, R., ed. 2010. *Preserving Egypt's Cultural Heritage: The Conservation Work of the American Research Center in Egypt.* San Antonio, TX and Cairo.

Demarée, R., and A. Egberts, eds. 2000. *Deir el-Medina in the Third Millennium AD.* Leiden.

Dodson, A. 1986. "Was the Sarcophagus of Ramesses III Begun for Sethos II?" *Journal of Egyptian Archaeology* 72: 196–198.

Dodson, A. 1987. "The Tombs of the Kings of the Thirteenth Dynasty in the Memphite Necropolis." *Zeitschrift für Ägyptische Sprache und Altertumskunde* 114: 36–45.

Dodson, A. 1988. "The Tombs of the Kings of the Early Eighteenth Dynasty at Thebes." *Zeitschrift für Ägyptische Sprache und Altertumskunde* 115: 110–123.

Dodson, A. 1998. "On the Burial of Maihirpri and Certain Coffins of the Eighteenth Dynasty." In *Proceedings of the 7th International Congress of Egyptologists*, edited by C. Eyre, 331–338. Louvain.

Dodson, A. 2000. "The Late Eighteenth Necropolis at Deir el-Medina and the Earliest 'Yellow' Coffin of the New Kingdom." In *Deir el-Medina in the Third Millennium AD*, edited by R. Demarée and A. Egberts, 89–100. Leiden.

Donadoni Roveri, A. M. 1969. *I sarcofagi egizi dalle origine alla fine dell'Antico Regno.* Rome.

Eaton-Krauss, M. 1993. *The Sarcophagus in the Tomb of Tutankhamun.* Oxford.

Eyre, C., ed. 1998. *Proceedings of the 7th International Congress of Egyptologists*. Louvain.

Gabolde, M. 1998. *D'Akhenaton à Toutânkhamon*. Lyon.

Grajetzki, W. 2005. "The Coffin of the 'King's Daughter' Neferuptah and the Sarcophagus of the 'Great King's Wife' Hatshepsut." *Göttinger Miszellen* 205: 55–65.

Habachi, L. 1974. "Lids of the Outer Sarcophagi of Merytamen and Nefertari, Wives of Ramesses II." In *Festschrift zum 150 jährigen Bestehen des Berliner Ägyptischen Museums*, edited by G. Poethke, U. Luft, and S. Wenig, 105–112. Berlin.

Hayes, W. C. 1935. *Royal Sarcophagi of the XVIII Dynasty*. Princeton, NJ.

Hayes, W. C. 1959. *The Scepter of Egypt: A Background to the Study of the Egyptian Antiquities on the Metropolitan Museum of Art*, II. New York.

Hornung, E. 1975. "Das Grab Thutmosis' II." *Revue d'Égyptologie* 27: 125–131.

Hornung, E. 1990. *Zwei Ramessidische Königsgräber: Ramses IV. und Ramses VII*. Mainz.

Leblanc, C. 1997. "The Tomb of Ramesses II and Remains of His Funerary Treasure." *Egyptian Archaeology* 10: 11–13.

Manassa, C. 2007. *The Late Egyptian Underworld: Sarcophagi and Related Texts from the Nectanebid Period*. Wiesbaden.

Manuelian, P. Der, and C. E. Loeben. 1993a. "From Daughter to Father: The Recarved Egyptian Sarcophagus of Queen Hatshepsut and King Thutmose I." *Journal of the Museum of Fine Arts Boston* 5: 24–61.

Manuelian, P. Der, and C. E. Loeben. 1993b. "New Light on the Recarved Sarcophagus of Hatshepsut and Thutmose I in the Museum of Fine Arts." *Journal of Egyptian Archaeology* 79: 121–155.

Martin, G. T. 1974. *The Royal Tomb at El-'Amarna*, I: *The Objects*. London.

Montet, P. 1951. *La nécropole de Tanis*, II: *Les constructions et le tombeau de Psousennès à Tanis*. Paris.

Montet, P. 1960. *La nécropole de Tanis*, III: *Les constructions et le tombeau de Chéchanq III à Tanis*. Paris.

Mojsov, B. 1991–1992. "A Royal Sarcophagus Reattributed." *Bulletin of the Egyptological Seminar* 11: 47–55.

Nelson, M., and F. Janot. 1993. "Une 'gisante' renaissant de ses cendres." *Bulletin de l'Institut Français d'Archéologie Orientale* 93: 371–378.

Porter, B., and R. L. B. Moss. 1960–1964. *Topographical Bibliography of Ancient Egyptian Hieroglyphic Texts, Reliefs and Paintings*, I: *The Theban Necropolis*. 2nd ed. Oxford.

Porter, B., and R. L. B. Moss. 1974–1981. *Topographical Bibliography of Ancient Egyptian Hieroglyphic Texts, Reliefs and Paintings*, III: *Memphis*. 2nd ed. by J. Málek. Oxford.

Raven, M. J. 1994. "A Sarcophagus for Queen Tiy and other Fragments from the Royal Tomb at el-Amarna." *Oudheidkundige mededelingen uit het Rijksmuseum van Oudheden* 74: 7–20.

Reeves, C. N. 1990. *Valley of the Kings: The Decline of a Royal Necropolis*. London.

Schaden, O. J. 1984. "Clearance of the Tomb of King Ay (WV 23)." *Journal of the American Research Center in Egypt* 21: 39–65.

Sourouzian, H. 1989. *Les monuments du roi Merenptah*. Mainz.

CHAPTER 17

....

CANOPICS

....

AIDAN DODSON

THE basic pattern for canopic equipment had been established by the early Middle Kingdom. This comprised a canopic chest of the same material and design concept as the sarcophagus or outer coffin, containing a quartet of canopic jars, each bearing a human-headed stopper. Any texts on the chest and the jars focused on the Four Sons of Horus, Imseti (guardian of the liver), Hapy (lungs), Duamutef (intestines), and Qebehsenuef (stomach), and their respective protective goddesses, Isis, Nephthys, Neith, and Selqet, with an evolution of a basic formulaic structure that would provide the basis for canopic texts until the Twenty-fifth Dynasty (Sethe 1934, 1*–2* [Typus I–VII]).

Although three kingly canopic chests of the Seventeenth Dynasty are extant (Berlin ÄM 1175 [Djehuty]; Louvre N.491 = E 2538 [Sekhemre-wepmaat Inyotef]; Leiden AH.216 [Sobekemsaf II]—Dodson 1994, 37–47, 118[24–26]), nothing is known of those of Ahmose I and Amenhotep I and, although a canopic chest survives bearing the name of Thutmose I, it was found in KV 38 alongside a sarcophagus that had been made for his reburial under Thutmose III (see ch 16), and should certainly be similarly dated. Accordingly, the earliest known New Kingdom royal canopic is the chest of Hatshepsut (Figure 17.1.1—Cairo JE30872—Dodson 1994, 118, 154–155[27]).

It was found in KV 20 directly east of the south end of her sarcophagus—a standard position during the Old Kingdom (Dodson 1994, 9, figure 1) and on occasion during the Middle Kingdom (Dodson 1994, 25, 27, 35–36). Made of quartzite, thus matching Hatshepsut's sarcophagi (pp. 245, 248–249), the chest has an interior that was once divided into four by a set of cross-boards, and adorned externally with a cavetto cornice and torus molding. In the latter aspect, the chest represents a move away from pre–New Kingdom chests, which are simple cubic boxes, usually with a vaulted lid with raised end pieces (the pr-nw shrine-form). Instead, the cavetto cornice of Hatshepsut's chest implies that its lost lid would have been of the sloping pr-wr shrine-form henceforth used for most later canopic chests (and some sarcophagi: see pp. 250–253). On the other hand, in contrast to the Seventeenth Dynasty royal chests that had each side adorned with a recumbent jackal, Hatshepsut's chest lacked any images, decoration being restricted to incised texts. These follow the general concepts established in the Middle Kingdom, but

1. Hatshepsut (Cairo JE 38072).
2. Thutmose I (Cairo JE 36416).
3. Amenhotep II (Cairo CG 5029).
4. Tutankhamun (Cairo JE 60687).
5. Horemheb (Cairo TR $\frac{9|12}{22|1-14}$).
6. Ramesses II (British Mus. EA 49740).

FIGURE 17.1 Canopic chests and fragments. [Aidan Dodson]

differently arranged, and with wholly new introductory material, which speaks of the dead king being "carried" by the Four Sons of Horus. On the other hand, the key elements all continue to emphasize the king's honor before the four genii and protection by the tutelary goddesses.

In marked contrast are the texts on the chest made for Thutmose I (Figure 17.1.2—Cairo JE36416—Dodson 1994, 119, 156–157[28]). These exceptionally fail to mention the Four Sons of Horus at all, while the speeches of the tutelary goddesses (of whom Selqet

FIGURE 17.2 The canopic chest, a canopic jar, and a mask from a visceral bundle of Tjuiu, from KV 46 (Cairo CG51013, JE94244A & JE95244).

[R. B. Partridge.]

is missing) are of non-canopic type. A range of other deities also feature in the texts, including Geb, The Western Necropolis, Re, The Beautiful West, and Anubis-tepdjuef, as does "the *nsw-bity*"—the latter clearly Thutmose III dedicating the chest to his grandfather. Curiously, the only extant parallels to many of these texts (none of which are even implicitly "canopic") appear to be on the canopic chest of Yuya (Cairo CG51012—Porter and Moss 1964, 562), made a century later. Intriguingly, these parallels even include the "*nsw-bity*" speech (in Yuya's case presumably by Yuya's son-on-law, Amenhotep III, as donor of his Valley of the Kings tomb and funerary equipment).

In contrast to the "Old Kingdom" position of Hatshepsut's chest, that of Thutmose was found lying at the foot end of the sarcophagus (Piacentini and Orsenigo 2004, 228–229[94]), as had generally been the case in Middle Kingdom pyramids (Dodson 1994, 28–33). In form, the whole aspect of the chest is much "lighter" than that of Hatshepsut's rather squat monument; the treatment of the cornice is also far more refined, while the fine carving of a knob, intended to secure the (lost) lid is unique for New Kingdom stone chests, although a usual feature of wooden examples.

The form of the interior differs significantly from earlier chests, being reminiscent of a four-leafed clover, shaped to embrace the perimeter of the four jars that once lay within. Given the anomalous nature of the texts on the chest, one would presume that more traditional canopic texts will have been inscribed upon the king's canopic jars (although the parallel texts of Yuya were accompanied by blank jars). Unfortunately, no definite traces of Thutmose I's jars are known,[1] with only one lid extant (Cairo JE33862 = CG24975—Dodson 1994, 119[28a1]; Lilyquist 1993, 112). This is in the form of a human head, with a summary headdress of non-royal form, but with the remains of an inserted uraeus on its brow.

It is to be assumed that the rest of the king's set of lids followed those of Ahmes-Nefertiry, wife of Ahmose I (Cairo JE26255—Lilyquist 1993, 111–112), in being uniformly human headed. However, during the Eighteenth Dynasty, the iconography of the Four Sons of Horus changes from all being human-headed to having individualized visages: Imseti remains human, but Hapy now acquires an ape head, Duamutef affects that of a canid, and Qebehsenuef that of a raptor. Although all known kingly lids remain human headed into the Ramesside Period, differentiated heads are all but universal in private usage by the time of Ramesses II.

No trace of canopic equipment was found in Thutmose III's KV 34, but given the close similarity between the his sarcophagus and that which he had made for Thutmose I (p. 249), it is probable that their canopic chests were all but identical as well (cf. Hayes 1935, 13). As for the fate of Thutmose III's chest, one wonders whether it was removed during the Late Period (cf. Reeves 1990, 24): that the tomb was accessible at this time is indicated by the fact that the decoration of the sarcophagus of one Hapymen (BM EA 23—Porter and Moss 1934, 72) is a copy of that of the king's (Hayes 1935, 153 n.42).

The changes in the form and furnishings of the royal tomb introduced in Amenhotep II's KV 35 (pp. 193, 278) included a complete recasting of the canopic equipment. Whereas Hatshepsut and Thutmose I had simple boxes matching their sarcophagi in material, Amenhotep II's artisans produced a wholly fresh design that not only replaced quartzite with calcite but also united the chest and jar in a single unit and gave concrete expression to the canopic formulae in which the four tutelary goddesses are enjoined to "embrace... that which is in them" (Sethe 1934, 2*–8* [Typus VI–XII]). Interestingly, the texts on the chest return to just such canopic norms, contrasting strongly with the anomalous texts placed on the chest made for Thutmose I in the previous reign.

Thus, on Amenhotep II's chest we find the four goddesses shown in raised relief, bent around the corners of the chest, their arms outstretched (Figure 17.1.3—Cairo CG5029—Dodson 1994, 119, 158–159[29]). The two sides of the chest that include the goddesses' visages also carry small figures of the Four Sons of Horus in sunk relief. Such representations of these genii are common on private canopic chests but are not again found on extant royal chests until the time of Seti I.

Innovation continues inside the chest, where the arrangements inside Thutmose I's are taken further by carving the canopic jars as one with the box. Such an approach has a Middle Kingdom parallel (Cairo CG4029—Reisner 1967, 32–33), but seems otherwise to be new. Each of these "jars" was stopped by a lid in the form of the king's head, wearing a *nms*-headdress. This contrasts with earlier kings' extant canopic lids—the aforementioned example of Thutmose I and those of Mentuhotep II (BM EA47628 and Museum of Staten Island 58.3.2—Dodson 1994, 111–112[9/1–2]), Senwosret I (Cairo JE25400 = CG4001–4—Dodson 1994, 112[10/1–4]) and Hor (Cairo JE30954 = CG4019–22—Dodson 1994, 115–116[18b1–4]).—which had "non-royal" coiffures, with the implication that they were intended to represent the Four Sons of Horus, rather than the king himself. The switch to the *nms* by Amenhotep II, combined with his other funereal innovations, suggests a reconceptualizing of the royal canopic heads, one that endures until at least the end of Eighteenth Dynasty. Nothing of the main lid of Amenhotep II's chest seems to survive: to judge from contemporary private and later chests it is likely to have been of *pr-wr* form. Although the principal fragments of the smashed chest were actually found near the head-end of the sarcophagus (Piacentini and Orsenigo 2004, 100, 101, 102),[2] one would have assumed that, like the chest of Thutmose I and later royal examples, the chest had been placed directly beyond the foot of the sarcophagus.

Amenhotep II's wife Tiaa is the first royal lady of the Eighteenth Dynasty known to have owned a stone canopic chest (all known earlier royal family canopics of the New Kingdom are simplejars—Porter and Moss 1964, 769–770.) Its calcite fragments have been recovered from KV 32 (her own tomb: see Jenni 2001, 2) and KV 47 (into which they had been swept by flood-water: MMA 14.6.347 and others—Aldred 1963, 41–42, pl. vii[2]; Dodson 1994, 72–73, both misattributing them to the mother of Siptah). The fragments show that it took the same basic internal form as that of the king. Externally, it appears to have featured pairs of tutelary goddesses, back to back, on the front, with similarly disposed Sons of Horus on the sides, accompanied by brief speeches of protection.

The chests of Tiaa's kingly son and grandson, Thutmose IV (Cairo CG46041—Dodson 1994, 120[30]) and Amenhotep III (WV22),[3] were both also reduced to fragments, but appear to have been broadly similar to that of Amenhotep II. Apart from the fact that most fragments were found in the crypt of the burial chamber of Thutmose IV's KV 43, nothing is known of the precise former location of Thutmose's chest. However, just beyond the foot end of the former location of Amenhotep III's sarcophagus is an irregular cutting roughly 1.5 m square and 1.2–1.3 m deep. It thus seems likely that the chest was originally sunk into the floor, an arrangement also seen subsequently under—at least—Horemheb and Ramesses II, and also has Middle Kingdom parallels (e.g., Beni Hasan tomb 186—Dodson 1994, pl. va).

Most private burials in the Valley have been irretrievably robbed, but the tombs of Maihirpri (KV 36) and Yuya and Thuya (KV 46) preserved most of their contents, including their canopics. These appear to have been largely typical of "high-end" private examples of their time, with *pr-wr*-form blackened wooden chests—incorporating gilded texts and images—containing separate jars, in these cases all human-headed. Although differing in detail, the chests of Maihirpri (Cairo CG24005—Porter and Moss 1964, 557), Yuya (Cairo CG51012—Porter and Moss 1964, 562) and Thuya (Figure 17.2.—Cairo CG51013 = JE95237—Porter and Moss 1964, 563; Wiese and Brodbeck 2004, 184–185[28]) all have the tutelary goddesses on their fronts and backs, with the Four Sons of the Horus on their sides. Interestingly, the latter are in all cases human-headed, contrasting with the position on, for example, the sarcophagi of Maihirpri (Cairo CG24001—Porter and Moss 1964, 557) and Yuya (Cairo CG51001—Porter and Moss 1964, 562). The jars from the two tombs (Cairo CG24006a–d, CG51014–21—Porter and Moss 1964, 557, 563; Wiese and Brodbeck 2004, 186–187[29a–b]) are in all cases simple (those of Yuya being uninscribed), although the actual canopic bundles of Thuya additionally bore gilded cartonnage masks (Cairo JE95244—Wiese and Brodbeck 2004, 186–187[29c]). Simple human-headed jars also feature in the broadly contemporary interments of junior members of the royal family found in KV 35 and KV 43 (Cairo CG5031, CG46036–40; MFA 03.1129ab, 03.1130ab—Lilyquist 1993, 112, 115–116), as well as later in KV 5 (Brock and Walschaerts 2006, 104–111). Jar-texts (where they exist) are wholly conventional in their formulations, although the presence of deviant chest texts in Yuya's outfit has already been noted: one can only speculate how this may link with the complete lack of texts on his jars.

Although the burial of Akhenaten took place outside the Valley of the Kings, in Amarna tomb 26, his canopic equipment (Cairo JE59454, &c—Dodson 1994, 121, 159[32]) followed the basic concepts introduced under Amenhotep II, albeit adjusted in accordance with the Aten-religion. Thus, although protective figures still enclosed the corners of his chest, these were now those of the Aten, in his early, avian form as a solar raptor, suggesting the chest's manufacture early in the reign (cf. Aldred 1959, 22–24). Unfortunately, none of the extant fragments include the king's names, making it a moot point as to whether the chest might even have been made while the king was yet Amenhotep IV: certainly the raptor form of the Aten had ceased to be his principal icon prior to the king's change of name to Akhenaten. The only surviving texts are actually the earlier didactic cartouche names of the Aten, although the scale of loss means that other texts may originally have been present. The human-headed compartment lids (Cairo CG18492, JE59388, 59443–5, &c—Dodson 1994, 121–122, 159[32a1–3]) are interesting in that they incorporate protective falcons on either side of the royal head, and very short hair-coverings—or even the blue crown—rather than the *nms* headdress found on other extant royal lids. Texts on them are limited to the cartouches of the Aten.

A glimpse at the canopics manufactured for lesser royalty under Akhenaten is provided by the jars from KV 55 (Cairo JE39637; MMA 07.226.1+30.8.54—Dodson 1994: 122–123[33/1–4]), originally made for the king's junior wife Kiya, but later adapted for the reburial of a king whose identity (Akhenaten or Smenkhkare) remains a matter for debate. Their stoppers bear what appears to be a female head, while the original inscription simply combined the name and titles of Kiya with those of the Aten and Akhenaten in a manner that seems to have been standard on a range of Kiya's monuments (Krauss 1986). This will presumably also have been the case on a fragment of another queenly jar of the period (BM EA9558—Reeves 1994, 198–199).

The intact tomb of Tutankhamun (KV 62) provides us with our single example of a complete New Kingdom kingly canopic outfit. Rather than being placed in the burial chamber itself, it was installed in a chamber beyond the foot of the sarcophagus, although this is almost certainly a function of the size of the tomb appropriated for the king's interment. On the other hand, the outfit is significantly more elaborate than suggested by extant remains from earlier tombs, as the chest itself (Figure 17.1.4) was enclosed in a gilded wooden shrine, protected by three-dimensional images of the tutelary goddesses, and itself sheltered by a gilded canopy (Cairo JE60686—Dodson 1994, 123–124, 160–165[34, 34a], pl. xxiii, xxiva; in preparation, [19–20]).

Both items are of the now-canonical *pr-wr* form for canopic chests, with the addition of friezes of uraei around their roofs. The relief decoration of the shrine itself is based on pairings on each side of a goddess facing and a male deity. Curiously, these are not in all cases the usual combinations of tutelary goddess and canopic genius. Thus, whereas the front and right side have the normal pairings of Isis/Imseti and Nephthys/Hapy, on the back the female figure is accompanied by texts of Ptah-Sokar-Osiris. "Her" unequivocally male companion is referred to as Qebehsenuef, but one accompanying text names Atum. On the left hand side of the shrine, the goddess is unequivocally Neith and the genius Duamutef, but one of his texts again names another deity, in this case Geb.

The shrine and canopy were set upon a large sled, equipped with the aforementioned figurines the four tutelary goddesses. They were fitted facing the shrine, their arms outstretched in an attitude of protection, similar to that adopted by the figures on the corners of the post–Amenhotep II canopic chest. Three of the four sockets were marked with a goddess's name, clearly as a guide to assembly, with the intention that each statuette should correspond to the female deity on the relevant side of the shrine (with Selqet guarding the anomalous Ptah–Sokar–Osiris/Qebehsenuef/Atum combination), but in the event the figures of Selqet and Nephthys were inadvertently swapped over.

Within the shrine lay the canopic chest itself (Cairo JE60687—Dodson 1994, 124, 166–167[34b–c]); in preparation, [20–24]), mounted on a gilded sled, and in form a straightforward development of the type established under Amenhotep II (Figure 17.1.4). As compared with that chest, however, there are a number of significant changes in the decoration, perhaps most importantly the elimination of images of the Four Sons of Horus. In the texts, a curious point is that whereas, as normal, Isis is teamed with Imseti, and Nephthys with Hapy, the other pairings in the chest texts are Neith/Qebehsenuef and Selqet/Duamutef, which recur later on the canopic chest of Horemheb.

Features apparently unique to Tutankhamun's in the extant series of calcite chests are the winged sun discs that appear at the top of the front and back faces of the box, paralleling the use of this motif on the slightly later sarcophagus of Ay (see pp. 251–252). The lower part of the box is also decorated with a gilded frieze of *ḏd* and *tit* symbols—a feature also found on Akhenaten's chest, but not apparently on any other known chest.

Tutankhamun's chest is the only one of the royal calcite examples in which the form of the interior is fully intact, and shows the cross divisions of wooden chests faithfully represented, while the cylindrical compartments have raised rims, giving the impression of jars. It has been suggested that the faces of the stoppers from the compartments are sufficiently unlike other depictions of Tutankhamun to hint that they, like various other items from Tutankhamun's burial outfit (cf. p. 251), were taken over from an earlier king (Vandersleyen 1992), but there is no direct indication that they, nor that the chest itself were appropriated pieces.

The actual visceral bundles were housed in a set of four solid gold miniature coffins, inlaid with glass (Figure 17.3—Cairo JE60688-61—Dodson 1994, 124–125, 168–169 [34c1a–34c4a], pl. xxvi; in preparation [25–28]). No such items are known from other royal burials, but given their material they are likely to have been primary targets for thieves—and a more-than-adequate explanation for the utter destruction of all other calcite chests. The concept of canopic coffinettes is also found in private burials of the mid/late New Kingdom (e.g. those of Sennedjem, from Theban Tomb 1, Cairo JE27218 = CG4249-51—Mahmoud Abd el-Qadir 2011, 17, 42, DVD 146–152[99–102]) and is found in a royal burial as late as the Twenty-second Dynasty (those of Shoshenq IIa, from Tanis NRT-III, Cairo JE72159-62—Dodson 1994, 132–134, 178–179[45/1a–4a]).

Those of Tutankhamun had originally been made for the female king Neferneferuaten (for the reading of the palimpsest cartouches, see Gabolde 2009, 118, figures 9 and 10; on Neferneferuaten's identity, cf. Dodson 2009, 34–52) and conform to the glass-inlaid stylized *rishi* design distinctive of the Amarna Period (cf. the fragmentary coffin(s) of Amenhotep III, that from KV55 and the middle coffin of Tutankhamun). They bear a single inlaid column of text down the front of the lid, each comprising a conventional invocation of tutelary goddesses as protectoresses of their usual Son of Horus. The goddesses are depicted in relief on the inside of the lids, accompanied by texts, respectively, of Geb (Isis), Re (Nephthys), Re (Neith), and Shu (Selqet). The insides of the four troughs each bear a chapter from the Book of the Dead, respectively chapters 1, 134, 130, and 136A.

Nothing survives from the canopic equipment of Ay, but any chest may have been placed at the foot of the sarcophagus, not only on the basis of previous practice, but also though the presence of a painting of the Four Sons of Horus above the entrance to the small chamber (Fa) that lay directly west of this putative location. In contrast, numerous fragments of the chest of Horemheb (Figure 17.1.5) were found in his tomb, KV57 (Cairo TR 9/12/22/1-14+JE46809+46826+55369—Dodson 1994, 126, 170–171[35, 35a1–4]).

FIGURE 17.3 Canopic coffinette, originally made for Neferneferuaten and usurped for Tutankhamun, from KV62 Cairo JE60690.

[R. B. Partridge]

The chest is more elongated in overall form than any previous example, continuing a trend begun with that made for Thutmose I: height: base-length ratios move from 0.62:1 under Hatshepsut to 1.35:1 by the time of Horemheb. Compared with Tutankhamun's chest, that of Horemheb loses the winged sun discs, but the goddesses enfolding the corners are elaborated by the addition of wings to their outstretched arms, a motif also seen on the sarcophagi of Tutankhamun, Ay and Horemheb (see pp. 251–253). The goddesses also lose the insignia found upon the heads of Tutankhamun's examples and, in addition, the *ḏd/tit* motif around the lower margin is replaced by a stylized palace façade, which is also to be found on the later chests of Ramesses II and Siptah.

The surviving texts on Horemheb's chest are fragmentary, but certainly covered a greater proportion of the surface than in earlier cases. As in the case of Tutankhamun, there are some eccentricities in the pairing of goddesses and Sons of Horus, something that also occurs on Horemheb's sarcophagus. We find Neith "correctly" with Duamutef, in contrast to his pairing with Selqet on Tutankhamun's box, but Isis may be coupled with Qebehsenuef on the same side and Nephthys with Imseti, although the fragmentary state of the piece makes reconstructions on occasion problematic. It appears that Horemheb's canopic installation may have resembled that of Amenhotep III, as a large pit lay just beyond the foot of the sarcophagus (Davis 1912, 59, pl. lxvi). Like the pit in WV 22, it is rather irregular, with maximum dimensions to be estimated at ca. 125 cm long by 110 cm broad; no information is available regarding its depth.

There is yet another gap in the kingly record covering the next reign, that of Ramesses I, but from the tomb of Seti I (KV 17) was recovered a fragment of the corner of a calcite canopic chest, with two more pieces found in a secondary deposit in KV 18 (Sir John Soane's Museum, London, X74 and at Luxor—Dodson 1994, 126, 172–173[36], pl. xxixb; Jenni 2000, 67–71). Insofar as it can be reconstructed from these fragments, it bore a winged goddess on each corner, with inward-facing images of the Four Sons of Horus on the sides. The latter had last definitely seen on a royal chest back in the days of Amenhotep II.

The canopic chest of Ramesses II is also represented only by fragments (Figure 17.1.6—BM EA49740 and found in KV 7—Dodson 1994, 126–127, 172–173[37], pl. xxxa; Leblanc 1996, 195, pl. liiiB, liv; 1997a, 160, pl. xlii; 1997b, 12–13). Although its basic design remains in accordance with earlier kings' examples, with "integral" jars and protective goddesses on the corners, the latter differ in having their feathers inlaid in glass, rather than simply carved in relief and highlighted merely with solid pigment. The chest's former installation in the burial chamber of KV 7 is interesting. Like Amenhotep III and Horemheb, Ramesses II seems to have placed his chest in a pit in the floor of the crypt of his burial chamber, but in this case it had a lower section, closed off by a limestone trapdoor, under the probable emplacement for the chest itself. It has been suggested that this once contained a set of four faience jars, bearing the names of the king, that are now in the Louvre (E.11094—Porter and Moss 1964, 507; Kanawaty 1995), although it now appears that their current contents date to the Third Intermediate and Ptolemaic Periods (Charrié-Duhaut et al. 2007, 957–967).

Four fragments are known of the canopic chest of Merenptah, from KV 8 (Brock, in Dodson 1994, 127[38]). These include the heads of figures of Duamutef and Imseti, accompanied by the protective texts of Neith and Isis, demonstrating that, as on the chest of Seti I, the Four Sons of Horus were a major feature of the decoration. However, the old arrangement of goddesses on the corners seems now to have been abandoned, the four associated female deities apparently being depicted on the faces at right angles to those bearing the Sons of Horus, as had been the case on private chests since the middle of the Eighteenth Dynasty (cf. Figure 17.2).

Although nothing survives canopically from the tombs of Seti II and Amenmesse, a significant proportion of the chest of Siptah has been recovered (MMA 14.6.3.375—Brock and Dodson in Dodson 1994, 127, 172–173[39], pl. xxxb; Dodson 2010, 109, figure 104). It continued the tradition seen since the time of Horemheb in having a panelled lower margin but, like that of Merenptah, the corners lack the embrace of the tutelary goddesses, a feature apparently now definitively abandoned. Siptah's lid was of *pr-wr* form, with the undulating body of a snake along its sides; some feathered pieces possibly derive a kneeling goddess, as seen on the lid of Tutankhamun's chest. However, what can be seen of the underside of Siptah's lid suggests that it was not hollowed out after the manner of earlier chests, making portrait stoppers unlikely to have been present.

The progress of royal canopic practice directly after the reign of Siptah is obscure, as nothing belonging to Tausret, Sethnakhte or Ramesses III has been identified. On the other hand, a conventional canopic jar of Ramesses IV survives (Berlin ÄM 8424—Dodson 1996, 11–17), indicating fundamental changes in royal canopic practice in the interim. First, there is the very fact that it is a separate jar, indicating that the "integral" chests employed by kings since Amenhotep II were no more. Interestingly, while the depiction of the mummy of Siptah on its bier in KV 47 has nothing shown underneath, the similar vignette in Tausret's KV 14 shows a set of canopic jars beneath the bier: could this suggest that the reversion back to separate jars happened directly after Siptah's death?

Second, there is the size of Ramesses IV's surviving jar: it is no less than 54 cm tall, making it among the largest of all canopic jars made for a human being, which rarely exceed 30–40 cm in height (although Apis bulls' jars [Dodson 1999, 59–75] could be up to 75 cm high). Indeed, it was probably owing to its exceptional size that it was later reused as a measuring jar, with a notation of volume added below its original texts. Such a size may have been intended to parallel the great increase in the dimensions of the royal sarcophagi of the early Twentieth Dynasty, that of Ramesses IV having some 150% greater volume than that of Siptah (cf. pp. 256–257). The original panel of text on the jar is very simple, with the double cartouches of the king flanked by a pair of identical invocations of Imseti. There is no reference to Isis or any other tutelary goddess.

No trace of any canopic chest is known, and it has been suggested that Ramesses IV's jars were placed in the innermost chamber of KV 2, as its the north wall includes a scene showing four differentially headed canopic jars under a funerary couch (Carter and Gardiner 1917, 140, 143; Hornung 1990, pl. 87–88). However, this would place the internal organs facing the head of the corpse, against their time-honored orientation opposite its feet.

Another possibility is that Ramesses IV's jars stood close alongside his sarcophagus, two on each of the long sides. This is suggested by the situation in Ramesses VII's KV 1, where the sarcophagus-cut (see p. 257) has a pair of semicylindrical niches carved in the long sides of each side of its upper pit, approximately 35 cm in width and 50 cm deep—ideally sized to hold canopic jars of the size provided for Ramesses IV. Canopic associations are further supported by the fact that the decoration of Ramesses VII's sarcophagus lid includes prominent depictions of the Four Sons of Horus, flanked on each side by two of the tutelary goddesses, Isis and Nephthys on one side, Selqet and Neith on the other (Brock 1995, 51; Hornung 1990, pl. 130–32). Interestingly, although the placement of canopic at the foot of the mummy is found again in the Third Intermediate Period (e.g., in Tanis NRT-III—Dodson 1994, 80–82), locating the jars separately along its flanks may be seen again in a Theban royal tomb of the mid-Third Intermediate Period (Horsieset in Medinet Habu tomb 1—Hölscher 1954, 8–10).

The installations of Ramesses IV and VII represent the latest certain canopic material known from burials in the Valley of the Kings. Some calcite fragments in Ramesses VI's tomb (KV 9) are of uncertain import (Dodson 1996, 14 n.24), with nothing recorded from the burial of Ramesses IX in KV 6. The tombs of Ramesses X and XI (KV 18 and KV 4) were never finished and thus will never have housed canopic equipment.

The reversion to separate canopic jars in kingly burials is seen to be continued in the Third Intermediate Period royal tombs at Tanis, Medinet Habu, El-Kurru, and Nuri, where vases (with differentiated heads where these elements survive) are found throughout (Dodson 1994, 126–142, 172–183[41–43, 45–57]; separate jars are also attested for Wahibre in the Twenty-sixth Dynasty (Dodson 1994, 14[58]). However, there is one exception: the canopic chest of Shoshenq I (Berlin ÄM11000—Dodson 1994, 131[44]) is an "integral" calcite chest of Eighteenth/Nineteenth Dynasty concept, albeit with detail differences. So different is it from the equipment of his predecessors and successors that one can only assume it was actually intended as a simulacrum of a royal chest of the New Kingdom: intriguingly, of course, it was after Shoshenq I's Year 11 (Reeves 1990, 191–192) that the last of the Valley of the Kings royal mummies were removed to the cache in TT320...

NOTES

1. Cairo CG24976 (Porter and Moss 1964, 559; Piacentini and Orsenigo 2004, 226–227[90]) shows no true indication of being from a canopic.
2. Reeves 1990, 193 had previously placed the main pieces at the foot, through a misinterpretation of Loret's grid-system (lost at his time of writing).
3. Apparently removed to KV 4 by Howard Carter, catalogued there by John Romer as RXI.1979.#186 (Dodson 1994: 120[30], 127–128[40]).

BIBLIOGRAPHY

Aldred, C. 1959. "The Beginning of the El-'Amārna Period." *Journal of Egyptian Archaeology* 45: 19–33.

Aldred, C. 1963. "The Parentage of King Siptaḥ." *Journal of Egyptian Archaeology* 49: 41–48.

Brock, E. C. 1995. "The Clearance of the Tomb of Ramesses VII." In *Valley of the Sun Kings: New Explorations in the Tombs of the Pharaohs*, edited by R. H. Wilkinson, 47–67. Tucson.

Brock, E. C. and N. Walschaerts. 2006. "Inscribed Objects." In *KV 5: A Preliminary Report*, edited by K. R. Weeks, rev. ed., 95–117. Cairo.

Carter, H. and A. H. Gardiner. 1917. "The Tomb of Ramesses IV and the Turin Plan of a Royal Tomb." *Journal of Egyptian Archaeology* 4: 130–158.

Charrié-Duhaut, A., J. Connan, N. Rouquette, P. Adam, C. Barbotin, M.-F. de Rozières, A. Tchapla, and P. Albrecht. 2007. "The Canopic Jars of Rameses II: Real Use Revealed by Molecular Study of Organic Residues." *Journal of Archaeological Science* 34: 957–967.

Davis, T. M. 1912. *The Tombs of Harmhabi and Touatânkhamanou*. Westminster.

Dodson, A. 1994. *The Canopic Equipment of the Kings of Egypt*, with contributions by O. J. Schaden, E. C. Brock and M. Collier. London.

Dodson, A. 1996. "A Canopic Jar of Ramesses IV and the Royal Canopic Equipment of the Ramesside Period." *Göttinger Miszellen* 152: 11–17.

Dodson, A. 1999. "The Canopic Equipment from the Serapeum of Memphis." In *Studies on Ancient Egypt in Honour of H.S. Smith*, edited by A. Leahy and W. J. Tait, 59–75. London.

Dodson, A. 2009. *Amarna Sunset: Nefertiti, Tutankhamun, Ay, Horemheb and the Egyptian Counter-Reformation*. Cairo.

Dodson, A. 2010. *Poisoned Legacy: the Fall of the Nineteenth Egyptian Dynasty*. Cairo.

Dodson, A. (in preparation). *The Coffins and Related Equipment from the Tomb of Tutankhamun*.

Gabolde, M. 2009. "Under a Deep Blue Starry Sky." In *Causing His Name to Live: Studies in Egyptian Epigraphy and History in Memory of William J. Murnane*, edited by P. Brand and L. Cooper, 109–120. Leiden.

Hayes, W. C. 1935. *Royal Sarcophagi of the XVIII Dynasty*. Princeton.

Hölscher, U. 1954. *The Excavation of Medinet Habu, V: Post-Ramessid Remains*. Chicago.

Hornung, E. 1990. *Zwei Ramessidische Königsgräber: Ramses IV. und Ramses VII*. Mainz.

Jenni, H., ed. 2000. *Das Grab Ramses' X (KV18)*. Basel.

Jenni, H. 2001. "MISR: Mission Siptah - Ramses X. Drei königliche Gräber und eine Ansammlung von Arbeiterhütten im Tal der Könige (Luxor)." *Archaeologie-online* 20.8. Retrieved from: http://www.archaeologie-online.de/magazin/thema/neues-aus-dem-alten-aegypten/misr-mission-siptah-ramses-x/.

Kanawaty, M. 1995. "Les vases bleues de Ramsès II." *Memnonia* 6: 175–190.

Krauss, R. 1986. "Kija - ursprüngliche Besitzerin der Kanopen aus KV55." *Mitteilungen des Deutschen Archäologischen Instituts, Abteilung Kairo* 42: 67–80.

Leblanc, C. 1996. "Trois campaignes de fouille dans la tombe de Ramsès II. KV.7 - Vallée des Rois - 1993/1994/1995." *Memnonia* 7: 185–211.

Leblanc, C. 1997a. "Quatrième campagne de fouille dans la tombe de Ramsès II [KV7] - 1996–1997." *Memnonia* 8: 151–172.

Leblanc, C. 1997b. "The Tomb of Ramesses II and remains of his Funerary Treasure." *Egyptian Archaeology* 10: 11–13.

Lilyquist, C. 1993. "Some Dynasty 18 Canopic Jars from Royal Burials in the Cairo Museum." *Journal of the American Research Center in Egypt* 30: 111–116.

Mahmoud Abd el-Qadir, A. 2011. *Catalogue of Funerary Objects from the Tomb of the Servant in the Place of Truth Sennedjem*, edited by S. Donnat. Cairo.

Piacentini, P. and C. Orsenigo. (2004.) *La Valle dei Re Riscoperta: I giornali di scavo di Victor Loret (1898–1899) e altri inediti*. Milan.

Porter, B. and R. L. B. Moss. 1934. *Topographical Bibliography of Ancient Egyptian Hieroglyphic Texts, Reliefs and Paintings*, IV: *Lower and Middle Egypt*. Oxford.

Porter, B. and R. L. B. Moss. 1964. *Topographical Bibliography of Ancient Egyptian Hieroglyphic Texts, Reliefs and Paintings*, I/2 : *Royal Tombs and Smaller Cemeteries*, 2nd ed. Oxford.

Reeves, C. N. 1990. *Valley of the Kings: The decline of a royal necropolis*. London: Kegan Paul International.

Reeves, C. N. 1994. "A fragment of the canopic jar of an Amarna queen." *Revue d'Égyptologie* 45: 198–199.

Reisner, G. A. 1967. *Canopics*. Cairo.

Sethe, H. (1934). "Zur Geschichte der Einbalsamierung bei den Ägyptern und einiger damit verbundener Bräuche." *Sitzungberichte der Preußischen Akademie der Wissenschaften zu Berlin: philosophische-historiestiche Klasse* 1934: 211–239.

Vandersleyen, C. 1992. "Royal Figures from Tut'ankhamūn's Tomb: Their Historical Usefulness." In *After Tut'ankhamūn: Research and Excavation in the Valley of the Kings*, edited by C. N. Reeves, 76–84. London.

Wiese, A. and A. Brodbeck, eds. 2004. *Tutankhamun, the Golden Beyond: Tomb Treasures from the Valley of the Kings*. Basel.

CHAPTER 18

....

OTHER TOMB GOODS

....

CAMPBELL PRICE

THE royal tombs in the Valley of the Kings were intended, alongside their other functions, to contain objects that the deceased king might require for his journey to—and existence in—the afterlife. The almost intact tomb of Tutankhamun (KV 62) provides the most complete picture of a royal burial assemblage. Two-dimensional images of some of the same categories of objects occur in the tombs of Seti II (KV 15), Tausret (KV 14), and Ramesses III (KV 11) and IV (KV 2). Fragments of many more items survive from tombs throughout the valley. This evidence can be used to evaluate the expected components of royal burial equipment.

Widespread tomb robbery obscures our understanding of the valley's original holdings. The material value of royal funerary goods was well known to those who built and furnished the tombs. Ostraca provide documentary evidence of furnishing grave goods: checklists found near KV 9, presumably of objects introduced into the tomb (Reeves 1990b, 117 and n.33); records of the stocking of the tomb of Merenptah from his years 7–8 (Černý 1935, 2, 2*–3*); and notes regarding funerary equipment that was brought to the tomb of Ramesses III on the fourth day one month, while the funeral itself took place on the twenty-fourth day (Černý 1975, 607). Having been filled, tombs were susceptible to looting soon after an interment. The late Ramesside Tomb Robbery papyri are a rare and important testament to this activity (Peet 1930). Papyrus Salt 124, for example, records the accusations made against the notorious workman Paneb regarding his thefts from the tomb of Seti II (Černý 1929, 245).

Many different types of objects are attested from royal tombs, although any discussion necessarily centers on examples from the tomb of Tutankhamun. This chapter reviews the main categories, their attestations, and some of their potential implications for our understanding of the New Kingdom royal afterlife.

STATUES OF THE KING

Wooden sculptures representing the king, often coated with black resin, were a key element of New Kingdom royal burial equipment from the valley (Forbes 1995b, 110–127). Two types may be distinguished: life-size (or slightly larger) standing statues, likely made as a pair, and smaller images showing the king in different poses.

The two best preserved examples, of Tutankhamun, have resin-painted flesh and clothing and jewelry covered in gold leaf. These closely correspond in height to the stature of the king in life—known from his physical remains—so can truly be called "life-size" (Carter 1927, 157–158). The closest parallels to Tutankhamun's statues come from the tomb of Ramesses I (KV 16). Giovanni Belzoni describes their discovery in the burial chamber; there was

> in a corner a statue standing erect, six feet six inches high, and beautifully cut out of sycamore-wood: it is nearly perfect except the nose. . . in the chamber on our right hand we found another statue like the first, but not perfect. No doubt they had once been placed one on each side of the sarcophagus, holding a lamp or some offering in their hands, one hand being stretched out in the proper posture for this, and the other hanging down
>
> (1822, 229–230)

Two similar, though less well-preserved, statues come from the tomb of Horemheb (Davis 1912, 101–102, pl. 79). Like those of Ramesses I, these are somewhat over life-size in scale. One other statue of this type originates from the tomb of Ramesses IX, and is roughly life-size. All of these are resin-coated and seem to have originally been partly gilded. Earlier parallels are difficult to identify. The presence of this statue type at the beginning of the Eighteenth Dynasty is perhaps attested in KV 20, the tomb of Hatshepsut/Thutmose I. The excavators note "a part of the face and foot of a large wooden statue covered with bitumen" (Davis 1906, 80) but do not include further description of these among the tomb's "important pieces." Amenhotep II was provided with a resin-coated example in the same pose as later statues but only eighty centimeters in height (Daressy 1902, 155 and pl. 31) and fragments of images on the same scale come from the tombs of Thutmose III (Daressy 1902, 281–282) and IV (Davis 1904, 11–15). Parts including "two left ears and two right feet" for "lifesize wooden statues" were found in the cache tomb WV 25 (Schaden 1979, 165), but perhaps washed in from the neighboring tomb of Aye (WV 23) (Reeves 1990b, 42). Taken together, this evidence suggests that such royal images increased in scale over time.

In Tutankhamun's pair, one wears the *nemes* headdress and the other a *khat* bag-wig. The same head coverings also occur on the pair of statues from the tomb of Ramesses I, although other statues are insufficiently preserved to know if this pattern was standard. Tutankhamun's pair have been interpreted as guardians for the burial chamber (Carter

1927, 39, 41), representations of the king himself and his *Ka*-spirit (James 2000, 174–175), or the king as ruler of both night and day (Manniche 2010, 110).

The *khat*-wearing statue of Tutankhamun has a text on the kilt apron labeling it as: "The Perfect God... the royal Ka-spirit of the Horakhty, the Osiris... Nebkheperura, justified" (Edwards 1972, cat. no. 1). This favors the interpretation of the statue(s) as a home for the royal *Ka*-spirit (Bell 1985, 256). The supposed function of these sculptures as "guardians" may be secondary (Edwards 1972, cat. no. 1), deriving from the seemingly threatening maces they hold and especially the over-life-size scale of the Horemheb and Ramesses I examples. It is interesting to note, however, the designation in a Ramesside ostracon of the end of the "Fourth Passage"—the area before the "Chariot Hall" and burial chamber—as "the room of the two door keepers" (Černý 1973, 28). It is tempting to imagine this as the intended position—whether created, used, or not—for the pair of royal statues.

Another group of royal statues on a smaller scale and in more varied poses may fulfill a different function. Tutankhamun's tomb contained seven such statuettes (Carter 1933, 54–56; Edwards 1972, cat. nos. 26–28). In two the king wears the Red Crown and is shown on a papyrus skiff in the act of harpooning; in another pair he wears the White Crown and strides atop a panther. A further three show him standing with crook and flail in Red (twice) and White (once) Crowns.

Corresponding images of the king appear in the well-room (E) of the tomb of Seti II (KV 15) (see Figure 18.1), implying the concept of a standard "set." The only difference in these representations is that Seti strides atop a lion rather than a panther (Hornung 1990, 180). Remains of similar statuettes are attested from other tombs. For example, panthers with mortises for the attachment of a striding royal image occur in the tombs of Amenhotep II (Daressy 1902, 160–161), Thutmose IV (Davis 1904, 15), and Horemheb (Davis 1912, 103).

STATUES OF THE GODS

Three-dimensional depictions of deities and divine animals are among the few New Kingdom tomb goods attested only for royalty. Tutankhamun's tomb contained twenty-eight such statuettes, most identified by yellow, painted inscriptions on their bases. Many were shrouded in linen (often reused royal garments), garlanded with small floral wreaths, and housed in twenty-two black, resin-painted shrines (Carter 1933, 51–54; Abitz 1979). Again, two-dimensional parallels occur in the well-room of KV 15, which includes images of enshrined divinities (Hornung 1990, 180–181). Close correspondences are the two figures of the youthful, sistrum-carrying god Ihy, which are matched by two resin-coated statuettes from Tutankhamun's tomb (James 2000, 146–147) and an almost identical figure in Amenhotep II's burial (Daressy 1902, 157).

Conversely, while Tutankhamun only had one figure of the recumbent jackal god Anubis (Carter 1933, 33), two appear in Seti II's tomb, and heads of several jackal statues

FIGURE 18.1 Two-dimensional images of royal and divine statues, similar to three-dimensional examples found elsewhere in the valley. Well-room (E) of the tomb of Seti II (KV 15)

[Photograph by Aidan Dodson]

were found in the tomb of Horemheb (Davis 1912, 104). Turtle- and gazelle-headed statuettes, unattested in KV 62, are known from the tombs of Horemheb and Ramesses I (Davis 1912, 102–105; Russmann 2001, 160–161). These and other apotropaic deities are represented on the walls of Ramesside royal tombs (Waitkus 1987, 51–82), and on post–New Kingdom coffins (Taylor 2010, 198–203). Some wooden images of deities had a hollow section for the insertion of papyri (Reeves 1985, 39–45). Belzoni (1822, 235) describes encountering several for this purpose in the tomb of Seti I, and a papyrus copy of the Amduat was found inside a mummiform statuette in the tomb of Amenhotep II (Daressy 1902, 184–189). Due to poor preservation, the modern impression of papyri as a purely private tomb object may, therefore, be misleading.

In the tomb of Ramesses IV (KV 2), the corridor beyond the burial chamber (K) has a recessed ledge decorated with images of the gods in shrines, along with piles of offerings. In the Turin papyrus plan of the tomb, this space is designated "the resting place of the gods" (Carter and Gardiner 1917, 142–143), and it may have been here that shrines housing divine statuettes were placed. Carter and Gardiner (1917, 143) suggest that "in this way the king could acquit himself of his religious duties in his renewed existence after death," an interpretation complementary to the images' apotropaic function.

SHABTIS

Shabti figurines—substitutes or servants for the deceased—were a common feature of private burials from the early Middle Kingdom until the Ptolemaic period (Schneider 1977, I:2–31), and one known for royalty only from the New Kingdom onward.

The first known royal shabti represents Ahmose I, now in the British Museum, and presumably originates from his as-yet-unlocated Theban tomb. The earliest attested royal shabti from the valley is a fragmentary example of Hatshepsut now in The Hague (Reeves and Wilkinson 1996, 93). Amenhotep II had at least eighty-eight examples, mostly of blue faience, empty-handed or holding an *ankh* (Daressy 1902, 85–104). The thirty-odd known shabtis of Thutmose IV (KV 43) were the first to be equipped with agricultural tools (Davis 1904, 45–57), explicitly adopting the role of servants.

The range of sizes, materials, and regalia increased with the shabtis of Amenhotep III (Bovot 2003, 36–71). Hard stones and wood were favored materials, and one example is sixty-seven centimeters tall (Ziegler and Bovot 2006, 102). The same diversity is seen in Tutankhamun's 413 examples, which presumably represent a complete set (Carter 1933, 81–83; James 2000, 110–127). Most of Tutankhamun's shabtis do not hold tools, but his tomb contained 1,866 model implements (Carter 1933, 82). Similar provision of extra equipment is evident in the tombs of Thutmose IV (Davis 1904, 56–57) and Horemheb (KV 57) (Martin 2008, 156), the latter without any evidence for the shabti figures themselves.

Six of Tutankhamun's shabtis were dedicated by high-ranking courtiers, the treasurer Maya (one) and the general Minnakht (five) (Carter 1933, 83–86; Edwards 1972, cat. no. 11). Poor preservation of inscribed material from elsewhere obscures how typical such donations to the royal funeral equipment would have been. While the short-lived

Tutankhamun's assemblage was perhaps more hastily prepared than usual, prestige may have accrued to donors of such objects at any time.

The assemblage of Seti I must originally have represented the most extensive provision of royal shabtis, with over 1,000 known examples in wood, faience, steatite, and alabaster (Bovot 1998, 37–42; Jenni 2000, 66–67), varying in quality of craftsmanship. In his account of the 1817 discovery of Seti's tomb (KV 17), Giovanni Belzoni described "scattered in various places, an immense quantity of small wooden figures of mummies six or eight inches long, and covered with asphaltum to preserve them. There were some other figures of fine earth baked, coloured blue, and strongly varnished" (1822, 235). Some of Seti's wooden examples have since been identified as juniper wood (Hepper 2000, 166) (see Figure 18.2).

In contrast, relatively few shabtis of Ramesses II are known (Taylor 1992, 198). This probably reflects the problems of differential preservation from one reign to another rather than a drastic change in provision. At least one bronze shabti of Ramesses II is known, and several for Ramesses III (Clayton 1972, 167–175). These may represent the few remaining specimens in a material particularly prone to reuse. A new shabti type, common to both kings and nonroyals, appeared toward the end of the Ramesside period. Known as "peg" or "*contours perdus*" shabtis (Weill 1921–1922, 437), after their crude modeling, these figurines are attested for Ramesses VI, VII, IX, X, and XI (Aubert and Aubert 1974, 117–120). They are usually made of travertine, often carry brief inked inscriptions, and sometimes have had green wax applied to their surface.

In the Turin papyrus plan of the tomb of Ramesses IV, the corridor beyond the burial chamber (K) is referred to as the "shabti place" (Carter and Gardiner 1917, 140–141; Černý 1973, 30). Two small chambers leading off this space (Ka, Kc) are, uniquely, decorated with scenes of forty mummiform figures of the king, labeled with the same texts as are found on the actual shabti figures of Ramesses IV (Schneider 1977, 265–266 and fig. 38). These rooms are plausible as the original or intended location for the king's shabtis. The location of other extant shabti assemblages is suggestive of organized placement. Belzoni describes a concentration of Seti's shabtis in the "Apis Room," or pillared room beyond the burial chamber (Clayton 1972, 170; Bovot 2003, 80–81), and all but one of Thutmose IV's shabtis were found in a single room off the burial chamber (Jd) (Davis 1904, 45–52). Tutankhamun's shabtis were distributed between the annexe and treasury (Reeves 1990a, 136–139), likely due to lack of space.

MODELS

Tutankhamun was provided with a model quern and a granary (Carter 1933, 62–64), as well as a flotilla of model boats (Carter 1933, 56–61; Jones 1990). Fragments survive to indicate similar boats in the tombs of Thutmose III (Daressy 1902, 295–298),

FIGURE 18.2 One of many hundreds of wooden shabtis of Seti I, now in collections around the world. The Manchester Museum, Accession Number 13906.

[Photograph by Glenn Janes.]

Amenhotep II (Daressy 1902, 239–277), and Horemheb (Davis 1912, 106). While such tomb models are a well-attested component of private tombs in the late Old and Middle Kingdoms, they had largely gone out of fashion by the New Kingdom (Hornung 1990, 170). The intact, contemporary burials of Yuya and Tjuiu (Davis 1907) and Maihirpri (Daressy 1902, 1–62) contain none of these models. Royal burials seem therefore to have anticipated additional eventualities for the pharaoh's afterlife by retaining very ancient concepts in the inexpensive form of models, even when these might have been considered outmoded or unnecessary in the burials of nonroyals.

FURNITURE

Furniture was a standard component of elite New Kingdom burials (e.g., Davis 1907, pls. 33–42) and is likely to have once been well-represented in royal tombs. Tutankhamun's furniture contained many items recognizable from private contexts, but also pieces that appear unique to royalty, such as three animal-headed couches or beds. The purpose of these is most likely funerary, as suggested by their inscriptions, form, and elaborate decoration (Carter 1923, 112–116; Beinlich 2006, 17–31). Only telltale fragments survive to indicate the original presence of such couches in other tombs: the trefoil glass inlays from a cow-headed couch in the tomb of Horemheb (Martin 2008, 156) and fragmentary alabaster teeth from a hippo-headed couch in the tomb of Aye (Schaden 1984, 54). Two-dimensional representations of similar couches were recorded by Belzoni in the tomb of Seti I (Hornung 1990, 182) and recur in room Kb in the tomb of Ramesses IV, indicating their expected presence in a royal tomb assemblage.

KV 62 also contained four beds of more conventional design, and a fifth folding or "camp" bed (Carter 1933, 110–111), along with eight headrests (Reeves 1990a, 180–183). Tutankhamun was also provided with a group of thirty-one "thrones," chairs, and footstools (Eaton-Krauss 2008), several suited in scale to a child. Remains of panels from the side of a similar, full-size chair were found in the tomb of Thutmose IV (Davis 1904, 20–21).

WEAPONS

Whether for anticipated combat or ritual/ceremonial use, KV 62 contained a range of weaponry, including archery equipment (McLeod 1970, 1982), slingshots, throwsticks, boomerangs, clubs, swords, daggers, and body armor (Reeves 1990a, 174–177). There were eight shields buried with Tutankhamun, four for practical, defensive use and four likely to be figurative and designed for use as standards (Nibbi 2003, 170–181; 2006, 66–71).

The room immediately preceding the burial chamber could be referred to as the "Chariot Hall," perhaps designating the equipment it contained (Černý 1973, 29). Tutankhamun was buried with six chariots, entirely or partly dismantled (Carter 1927, 54–63; Littauer and Crouwel 1985). Fragments belonging to chariots occur in the tombs of Amenhotep II (Daressy 1902, 70–71), Thutmose IV (Davis 1904, 24–38), Amenhotep III (Reeves and Wilkinson 1996, 114), and Aye (Reeves 1981, 11–19). Papyrus Salt 124 also mentions chariots in the tomb of Seti II (Černý 1929, 245), attesting the inclusion of this item in royal tombs well into the Ramesside period. The presence of a chariot in the tomb of Yuya and Tjuiu (Davis 1907, 35–36) shows the vehicle not to have been unique to royalty.

CLOTHING, JEWELRY, AND COSMETICS

Aside from Tutankhamun's extensive—though quite poorly preserved—wardrobe and some tapestry-woven scraps from the tomb of Thutmose IV (Davis 1904, 143–144), nothing survives of the clothing buried with New Kingdom royals in the valley. An unprovenanced "girdle" of Ramesses III, now in World Museum Liverpool (Bienkowski and Tooley 1995, 46), may be another exceptional survival of the least robust of a royal tomb's contents.

Tutankhamun's remaining textiles were largely woven from fine linens and included garments, gloves, and footwear (Crowfoot and Davies 1941, 113-130; Vogelsang-Eastwood 1999; Veldmeijer 2011). Some items bear inked inscriptions indicating that they belonged to "His Majesty LPH! when he was a boy" (Černý 1965, 57). These cannot have been for the "use" of an adult in the afterlife, but rather represent a collection of used goods. Perhaps clothing was kept simply because it had come into contact with the divine person of the king; it is interesting to note that some garments were reused to wrap statues of the king and deities. A truncated wooden image of the king that Carter (1923, 120) termed a "mannequin"—perhaps for use in fitting the king's garments—has so far not received a convincing alternative classification (James 2000, 191).

Unsurprisingly, jewelry was among the items most immediately susceptible to theft; even Tutankhamun's tomb lacks an unknown amount. There had been, however, a concern to record the contents of boxes (Černý 1965) and Carter believed (1923, 136) that this might allow a full reconstruction of what was stolen. References in such dockets to a "funerary procession" emphasize the use of jewelry in burial rituals and may imply the creation of specific items for this purpose (Černý 1965, 58; Wilkinson 1984, 335–345). Amenhotep II's burial contained a fragment of a wooden box with hieratic inscription detailing contents of silver (Daressy 1902, 173), providing a tantalizing clue to what existed in less well-preserved royal tombs.

Although Tutankhamun was buried with scepters and a diadem (Reeves 1990a, 153–154), there was a notable lack of headgear that might be interpreted as a "crown." Possibly this is indicative of the value of such items or may suggest their absence from tomb goods. Crowns could have been transferable in nature, passing to successive rulers in the manner of more modern royal regalia. It is notable, however, that before the reign of Merenptah the pharaoh is very rarely shown in tomb (as opposed to temple) wall decoration with a crown other than a simple headcloth (Hornung 1990, 169).

Cosmetic equipment is attested from the earliest burials, and physical appearance was a central concern to Egyptian expectations about the afterlife. Tutankhamun was provided with a range of cosmetic objects, including mirrors and containers for eye makeup, although his shaving equipment is known only from a docket on a box (Reeves 1990a, 158–159). Remarkably few of these objects survive from other tombs, indicating their immediate value to robbers. A gilded wooden model of a bag inscribed with the name of Ramesses II and the word "*mesdemet*" (black eye paint) (Ziegler 2002, 485) may be a rare survival from that king's tomb.

FOOD AND DRINK

One of the key contents of burials from predynastic times onward were provisions of food and drink. This is most often evidenced—and magically ensured—by the presence of storage vessels. Remains of stone vases, bowls, and jars are found in the earliest valley tombs, such as KV 20 (Davis 1906, 80), showing the continuity of this traditional concern. Evidence of storage vessels, in both stone and pottery, is a feature of many other tombs (e.g., El-Khouli et al. 1993; Aston et al. 1998, 137–214). Fragments of mud seals, such as those in the tomb of Amenhotep II (Daressy 1902, 277–279), indicate the original presence of now-lost amphorae.

An inked hieratic inscription on a broken pottery vessel from the tomb of Aye (WV 23) makes the origin and function of this vessel's contents clear: "The storehouse of pharaoh LPH! on the left side. Pressed meat for the Bull (= the king) which was made as cargo for the Neshmet-boat" (Schaden 1984, 55 and fig. 28). The deceased king was thus supplied with sustenance—albeit necessarily limited—for his travels to and journeys within the afterlife. Here is another good illustration of tomb goods as additional insurance. It may be presumed that the royal mortuary cult would supply an ongoing source of nourishment for the king's *Ka*-spirit, but backup supplies were nevertheless important.

The tomb of Tutankhamun contained a range of wine amphorae, labeled in hieratic with a range of vintages, and vessels were identified as containing nuts, fruit, honey, oils, and fats (Černý 1965, 1–7). Meat was provided in the form of victual mummies, consisting of joints of meat or whole birds wrapped in bandages and placed in wooden containers. The majority of packages of this type come from Theban royal tombs (Ikram 2000, 660), and Tutankhamun had forty-eight examples (Reeves 1990a, 206). Also included in KV 62 were over one hundred baskets, mostly containing foodstuffs (Reeves 1990a, 204). Baked bread was supplied along with raw grain in Tutankhamun's tomb, and grain had also been found in "great quantities. . . reduced to chaff" in the tomb of Thutmose IV (Davis 1904, x). Scenes of food preparation occur in a small chamber (Ba) in the tomb of Ramesses III (KV 11), but these are exceptional. Floral remains are hardly attested, so the flowers found in Tutankhamun's tomb provide valuable insight into these fragile goods (Hepper 1990).

RITUAL OBJECTS

Everything that went into the royal tomb was placed with the intention of ensuring the king's successful afterlife, but in some cases ritualized uses appear more pronounced than practical functions. Significant in this category are the so-called Osiris beds—wooden frames in the distinctive outline of the god Osiris, filled with Nile mud and sown with grains of barley. Such a bed is known from the tomb of Yuya and Tjuiu (Davis 1907, 45), and examples are attested in the tombs of Tutankhamun (Carter 1933, 61) and Horemheb (Davis 1912, 105 and pl. 88).

The small golden shrine of Tutankhamun (Eaton-Krauss and Graefe 1985), which presumably once contained a cult statuette, is significant because it may imply the transfer of ritual furniture used in a palace context into the royal tomb (Robins 2010, 207–231). Faience models, often in miniature, of objects such as libation vessels, amuletic signs, lotus buds, papyrus rolls, and serpent heads, survive in profusion from the tomb of Amenhotep II (Daressy 1902, 118–126) and of Thutmose IV (Davis 1904, 56–134). Their multiplicity seemingly ensured their effectiveness. Tutankhamun's provision of these "token" objects was more modest, being limited to sixty-seven small vessels in faience (Reeves 1990a, 200–201). Some of Tutankhamun's cups contained natron and resin (Carter 1927, 32), suggesting a link with rituals such as mummification.

Tutankhamun's burial chamber—and presumably those of other royal tombs—contained perhaps the most potent ritual objects, although these often appear the most obscure to modern eyes. Among these were two gilded Anubis emblems or "fetishes" representing an animal skin attached to a pole (Edwards 1972, cat. 24), a resin-varnished pylon, and wooden oars arranged around the outer shrine (Carter 1927, 32). These objects make reference to a number of mythic afterlife possibilities and ritual duties of the king. Most widely attested in this category are four "magic bricks," which were a feature of several valley tombs. These four amuletic objects (a mummiform figure, a jackal, a *djed*-pillar, and a torch), mounted on bricks, are attested as early as Thutmose III, and niches are provided for them in burial chambers from Thutmose IV through to (at least) Merenptah. Chapter 151 of the Book of the Dead explains the bricks' protective purpose—"to repel the enemy of Osiris (the deceased), in whatever form he may come"—and calls for them to be "covered up" within the burial chamber (Thomas 1964, 71–72), ensuring their effectiveness while attempting to keep them hidden.

OTHER OBJECTS

Tutankhamun's tomb contained a series of other objects that do not easily fit into the previously defined categories and which are without clear parallels from other royal tombs. The king was provided with writing equipment (Carter 1933, 79–81; Reeves 1990a, 166–167), implying royal literacy, and perhaps also the necessity of writing in the afterlife. There were also practical objects should the king require them, including chisels, knives, measuring rods, fire-making equipment, and oil lamps (Reeves 1990a, 194–196). The tomb also contained the frame from a portable canopy, to protect the king from the sun (Reeves 1990a, 187); eight fans (Carter 1933, 132–133); and some 130 sticks and staves

(Reeves 1990a, 178–179). The inscription on one example, "a reed which His Majesty cut with his own hand" (Carter 1927, 35–36), is the best indication that such objects were employed during the king's lifetime.

There were four complete gaming boards in KV 62 (Edwards 1972, cat. no. 18; Tait 1982) along with musical instruments including sistra, clappers, and trumpets (Manniche 1976). Although often viewed as items for pleasure and entertainment (Reeves 1990a, 160–165), these items equally carry ritual significance—with music-making a key component of temple cult and gaming being shown in some New Kingdom tomb scenes and Book of the Dead papyri.

The tomb of Tutankhamun contained a number of objects bearing the names of earlier Eighteenth Dynasty royals. Carter (1933, 87) described some of these as "heirlooms," although many may simply have been "odds and ends" used to supplement a hastily gathered burial assemblage (Reeves 1990a, 168–169; cf. Jeffreys 2003, 208–210). Perhaps the most personal mementos are a scribal palette, with "used" pigments (Edwards 1972, cat. no. 19), belonging to Princess Meritaten (Tutankhamun's half-sister), and a lock of hair, contained within four miniature coffins—the innermost identifying the king's grandmother Queen Tiye, to whom the lock presumably belonged (Reeves 1990a, 168–169).

AFTERWORD

During the Twenty-first Dynasty clearance and reburial of royal mummies from the Valley of the Kings, very few tomb goods other than coffins accompanied their owners (Reeves 1990b, 183–224). Given the quantity of fragmentary tomb goods found in tombs throughout the valley and in spite of modern pillaging of the caches, it seems that most items were simply abandoned (Taylor 1992, 190).

The adaptation and reuse of a shabti of Ramesses II as a Ptah-Sokar-Osiris figure within the DB 320 cache is therefore significant. This may represent practical expediency to create an object for that king's reburial (Aston 1991, 95–96) or a more general appreciation of the continuing power of such royal funerary objects (Taylor 1992, 190–199). A bronze brazier of Ramesses II found in the Tanis tomb of Psusennes I (Yoyotte 1988, 43) may also have originated from the valley and suggests the value of objects with this provenance for Third Intermediate Period royal burials.

The process of collecting together the mummies from desecrated royal tombs, and the gathering of what few valuables remained, would have given the agents of Pinudjem I the chance to examine—and collect—the funerary provisions of centuries before. It is notable that the deep blue glaze of faience Thutmoside shabtis seems to have gone out of fashion in the later Ramesside period, but was revived in the early Third Intermediate Period, perhaps in imitation of earlier funerary figurines—many of which are likely still to have been in situ. Indeed, compared to other royal tomb contents, shabtis survive into modern times in relative abundance. This is because of their often large number and generally low intrinsic value for ancient robbers, in contrast to many other objects buried in the tombs. Their portability and attractiveness, especially if recognized as depicting royal persons, accounts for shabtis' early modern saleability as tourist souvenirs. These circumstances have resulted in royal shabtis being the most widely distributed objects of any type from the Valley of the Kings, although there are surely many objects with a vague or unknown provenance that originate from the valley.

CONCLUSIONS

Through a combination of their physical forms, the imagery and texts employed in their decoration, "ritual" or "practical" objects could promote and affirm a successful rebirth for the deceased king as it was conceptualized during the New Kingdom. The range of goods attested from tombs in the Valley of the Kings shows strong parallels from one tomb to another, suggesting an ideal "set" of objects. As Carter noted (1933, 36) of Tutankhamun, "however strange, however extensive, this funerary outfit may be, it doubtless belonged to a more or less organised system for the common good of the dead. . . . This association of equipment. . . had been created to achieve unknown ends."

Such large assemblages of objects allowed for a variety of possibilities and offered the means for protection, regeneration, and practical survival after death. It is notable that the contents of royal burials overlap extensively with those of private individuals, and few objects can be identified as distinctively royal. New Kingdom kings and their subjects shared the same concerns. The main limiting factor to the scale of funerary provision seems to have been material wealth. It is worth acknowledging, however, the apparent contradictions in royal preparations for the afterlife. It is difficult to imagine that the king would actually *need* an army of shabtis, were he to spend eternity in the company of deities. Presumably he was unlikely to be obliged to work in the Fields of Iaru? Likewise, did Tutankhamun really require child-sized clothing or furniture?

The question must remain of how typical Tutankhamun's provisions actually were. The royal move from Amarna, and the relatively young age at which the king died, further obscure this. Do Tutankhamun's objects reflect a lack of time to decorate this small sepulcher extensively (Jeffreys 2003, 208)? Or, as Carter (1933, 37) suggests, did representations in the round give way to wall scenes? Images of objects from the walls of some Ramesside royal tombs seem likely to have reinforced rather than simply replaced the presence of physical objects within these burials. According to the scheme of magical insurance, representation affirmed the presence of an object should it be destroyed or damaged. Other kings may have had the same types of material, only in greater volumes, built up over longer reigns. These do not survive, so we are left to extrapolate from Tutankhamun's treasures.

BIBLIOGRAPHY

Abitz, F. 1979. *Statuetten in Schreinen als Grabbeigaban in den ägyptischen Königsgräbern der 18. und 19. Dynastie.* Wiesbaden: Harrassowitz.

Aston, D. 1991. "Two Osiris Figures of the Third Intermediate Period." *Journal of Egyptian Archaeology* 77: 95–107.

Aston, D., B. Aston, and E. Brock. 1998. "Pottery from the Valley of the Kings: Tombs of Merenptah, Ramesses III, Ramesses IV, Ramesses VI and Ramesses VII." *Ägypten und Levante* 8: 137–214.

Aubert, J. F., and L. Aubert. 1974. *Statuettes Égyptiennes: Chaouabtis, ouchebtis.* Paris: Adrien Maisonneuve.

Beinlich, H. 2006. "Zwischen Tod und Grab." *Studien zur Altägyptischen Kultur* 34: 17–31.

Bell, L. 1985. "Luxor Temple and the Cult of the Royal Ka." *Journal of Near Eastern Studies* 44: 251–294.

Belzoni, G. 1822. *Narrative of the Operations and Recent Discoveries in Egypt and Nubia.* 2nd ed. London: John Murray.

Bienkowski, P., and A. Tooley. 1995. *Gifts of The Nile: Ancient Egyptian Arts and Crafts in Liverpool Museum.* London: Her Majesty's Stationery Office.

Bovot, J.-L. 1998. "Sethy Ier: Le pharaon aux mille et un chaouabtis." *Egypte: Afrique et Orient* 11: 37–42.

Bovot, J.-L. 2003. *Les serviteurs funéraires royaux et princiers de l'Ancienne Égypte.* Paris: Réunion des musées nationaux.

Carter, H. 1923. *The Tomb of Tut.ankh.Amen I: Search, Discovery and Clearance of the Antechamber.* London: Cassell.

Carter, H. 1927. *The Tomb of Tut.ankh.Amen II: The Burial Chamber.* London: Cassell.

Carter, H. 1933. *The Tomb of Tut.ankh.Amen III: The Annex and Treasury.* London: Cassell.

Carter, H., and A. Gardiner. 1917. "The Tomb of Ramesses IV and the Turin Plan of a Royal Tomb." *Journal of Egyptian Archaeology* 4: 130–158.

Černý, J. 1929. "Papyrus Salt 124 (Brit. Mus. 10055)." *Journal of Egyptian Archaeology* 15: 243–258.

Černý, J. 1935. *Catalogue général des antiquités égyptiennes du Musée du Caire.* Nos. 25501–25832, *Ostraca hieratiques.* Cairo: Institut Français d'Archéologie Orientale du Caire.

Černý, J. 1965. *Hieratic Inscriptions from the Tomb of Tutankhamen.* Oxford: Griffith Institute.

Černý, J. 1973. *The Valley of the Kings: fragments d'un manuscrit inachevé.* Cairo: Institut Français d'Archéologie Orientale du Caire.

Černý, J. 1975. "Egypt from the Death of Ramesses III to the End of the Twenty-First Dynasty" in *The Cambridge Ancient History.* Vol. 2, Pt. 2, *The Middle East and the Aegean Region, c. 1380–1000 BC,* 3rd ed., edited by I. E. S. Edwards et al., 606–657. Cambridge: Cambridge University Press.

Clayton, P. 1972. "Royal Bronze Shawabti Figures." *Journal of Egyptian Archaeology* 58: 167–175.

Crowfoot, G.M. and N. de Garis Davis. 1941. "The tunic of Tut'ankhamūn." *Journal of Egyptian Archaeology* 27: 113–130.

Daressy, G. 1902. *Catalogue des antiquités égyptiennes du Musée du Caire.* Nos. 24001–24990, *Fouilles de la Vallée des Rois (1898–1899).* Cairo: Institut Français d'Archéologie Orientale du Caire.

Davis, T. 1904. *The Tomb of Thoutmôsis IV.* London: Archibald Constable.

Davis, T. 1906. *The Tomb of Hâtshopsîtû.* London: Archibald Constable.

Davis, T. 1907. *The Tomb of Iouiya and Touiyou.* London: Archibald Constable.

Davis, T. 1912. *The Tombs of Harmhabi and Touatânkhamanou*. London: Archibald Constable.

Eaton-Krauss, M. 2008. *The Thrones, Chairs, Stools, and Footstools from the Tomb of Tutankhamun*. Oxford: Griffith Institute.

Eaton-Krauss, M., and E. Graefe. 1985. *The Small Golden Shrine from the Tomb of Tutankhamun*. Oxford: Griffith Institute.

Edwards, I. E. S. 1972. *Treasures of Tutankhamen*. London: Thames and Hudson.

Edwards, I. E. S., C. J. Gadd, N. G. L. Hammond, and E. Sollberger. 1975. *The Cambridge Ancient History*. Vol. 2, Pt. 2, *The Middle East and the Aegean Region, c. 1380–1000 BC*. 3rd ed. Cambridge: Cambridge University Press.

El-Khouli, A., R. Holthoer, C. Hope, and O. Kaper. 1993. *Stone Vessels, Pottery, and Sealings from the Tomb of Tutankhamun*. Oxford: Griffith Institute.

Forbes, D., ed. 1995a. *Amarna Letters: Essays on Ancient Egypt c. 1390–1310 BC*. Vol. III. San Francisco: KMT Publications.

Forbes, D. 1995b. "Ritual Figures in KV 62: Prototypes and Correspondences." In *Amarna Letters: Essays on Ancient Egypt c. 1390–1310 BC*, edited by D. Forbes, III, 110–127. San Francisco: KMT Publications.

Hawass, Z., and J. Houser Wegner, eds. 2010. *Millions of Jubilees: Studies in Honor of David P. Silverman*. Vol. 2. Cairo: Supreme Council of Antiquities.

Hepper, F. N. 1990. *Pharaoh's Flowers: The Botanical Treasures of Tutankhamen*. London: Her Majesty's Stationery Office.

Hepper, F. N. 2000. "Amelia Edward's Sethos I Shabti." *Journal of Egyptian Archaeology* 86: 165–166.

Hornung, E. 1990. *Valley of the Kings: Horizon of Eternity*. New York: Timken.

Ikram, S. 2000. "Meat Processing." In *Ancient Egyptian Materials and Technology*, edited by P. Nicholson and I. Shaw, 656–672. Cambridge: Cambridge University Press.

James, T. G. H. 2000. *Tutankhamen: The Eternal Splendour of the Boy Pharaoh*. London and New York: Tauris Parke.

Jeffreys, D. 2003. "All in the family? Heirlooms in ancient Egypt." In: *'Never had the like occurred': Egypt's view of its past*, edited by J. Tait, 197–211. London: UCL Press.

Jenni, H. 2000. *Das Grab Ramses' X. (KV 18)*. Basel: Schwabe & Co.

Jones, D. 1990. *Model Boats from the Tomb of Tutankhamen*. Oxford: Griffith Institute.

Kousoulis, P., ed. 2008. *Tenth International Congress of Egyptologists: Abstracts of Papers*. Rhodes: University of the Aegean.

Littauer, M. A. & J. H. Crouwel. 1985. *Chariots and related equipment from the tomb of Tut'ankhamun*. Oxford: Griffith Institute

Manniche, L. 1976. *Musical Instruments from the Tomb of Tutankhamen*. Oxford: Griffith Institute.

Manniche, L. 2010. *The Akhenaten Colossi of Karnak*. Cairo: American University in Cairo Press.

Martin, G. T. 2008. "Re-excavating KV 57 (Horemheb) in the Valley of the Kings." In *Tenth International Congress of Egyptologists: Abstracts of Papers*, edited by P. Kousoulis, 155–156. Rhodes: University of the Aegean.

McLeod, W. 1970. *Composite Bows from the Tomb of Tutankhamen*. Oxford: Griffith Institute.

McLeod, W. 1982. *Self Bows and Other Archery Tackle from the Tomb of Tutankhamen*. Oxford: Griffith Institute.

Nibbi, A. 2003. "Some Remarks on the Ancient Egyptian Shield." *Zeitschrift für ägyptische Sprache und Altertumskunde* 130: 170–181.

Nibbi, A. 2006. "The Four Ceremonial Shields from the Tomb of Tutankhamun." *Zeitschrift für Ägyptische Sprache und Altertumskunde* 133: 66–71.

Nicholson, P., and I. Shaw, eds. 2000. *Ancient Egyptian Materials and Technology.* Cambridge: Cambridge University Press.

Peet, T. E. 1930. *The Great Tomb Robberies of the Twentieth Egyptian Dynasty.* Oxford: Clarendon Press.

Reeves, N. 1981. "A State Chariot from the Tomb of Ay?" *Göttinger Miszellen* 46: 11–19.

Reeves, N. 1985. "Tutankhamen and His Papyri." *Göttinger Miszellen* 88: 39–45.

Reeves, N. 1990a. *The Complete Tutankhamen.* London: Thames and Hudson.

Reeves, N. 1990b. *Valley of the Kings: The Decline of a Royal Necropolis.* London: Kegan Paul.

Reeves, N., ed. 1992. *After Tut'ankhamun: Research and Excavation in the Royal Necropolis at Thebes.* London: Kegan Paul.

Reeves, N., and R. H. Wilkinson. 1996. *The Complete Valley of the Kings.* London: Thames and Hudson.

Robins, G. 2010. "The Small Golden Shrine of Tutankhamen: An Interpretation." In *Millions of Jubilees: Studies in Honor of David P. Silverman,* edited by Z. Hawass and J. Houser Wegner, 2: 207–231. Cairo: Supreme Council of Antiquities.

Russmann, E., ed. 2001. *Eternal Egypt: Masterworks of Ancient Art from the British Museum.* Berkeley and Los Angeles: University of California Press.

Schaden, O. 1984. "Clearance of the Tomb of King Ay (WV-23)." *Journal of the American Research Center in Egypt* 21: 39–64.

Schneider, H. 1977. *Shabtis: An Introduction to the History of Ancient Egyptian Funerary Statuettes.* 3 vols. Leiden: Rijksmuseum van Oudheden.

Tait, W. J. 1982. *Game Boxes and Accessories from the Tomb of Tutankhamun.* Oxford: Griffith Institute.

Taylor, J. H. 1992. "Aspects of the History of the Valley of the Kings in the Third Intermediate Period." In *After Tut'ankhamun: Research and Excavation in the Royal Necropolis at Thebes,* edited by N. Reeves, 186–206. London: Kegan Paul.

Taylor, J. H. 2010. *Journey through the Afterlife. Ancient Egyptian Book of the Dead.* London: British Museum Press.

Thomas, E. 1964. "The Four Niches and Amuletic Figures in Theban Royal Tombs." *Journal of the American Research Center in Egypt* 3: 71–78.

Veldmeijer, A. 2011. *Tutankhamun's Footwear: Studies of Ancient Egyptian Footwear.* Leiden: Sidestone Press.

Vogelsang-Eastwood, G. 1999. *Tutankhamen's Wardrobe: Garments from the Tomb of Tutankhamen.* Rotterdam: Barjesteh van Waalwijk van Doorn.

Waitkus, W. 1987. "Zur Deutung einiger apotropäischer Götter in den Gräbern im Tal der Königinnen und im Grabe Ramses III." *Göttinger Miszellen* 99: 51–82.

Weill, R. 1921–1922. "Quelques types de figurines funéraires des XIXe et XXe dynasties" *Monuments Piot* 25: 419–438.

Wilkinson, A. 1984. "Jewellery for a Procession in the Bed-Chamber in the Tomb of Tut'ankhamun." *Bulletin de l'Institut Français d'Archéologie Orientale* 84: 335–345.

Yoyotte, J. 1988. *Gold of the Pharaohs.* Edinburgh: City of Edinburgh Museums and Art Galleries.

Ziegler, C. 2002. *The Pharaohs.* London: Thames and Hudson.

Ziegler, C. and J.-L. Bovot. 2006. *L'art égyptien.* Paris: Larousse.

PART VIII

....

GETTING TO THE AFTERLIFE

....

CHAPTER 19

....

MORTUARY RITUAL IN THE VALLEY OF THE KINGS

....

ALEXANDRA VON LIEVEN

It is almost certain that the Valley of the Kings was a place of intense ritual activity, both before and after the burial of a king. Unfortunately, however, our knowledge of these rituals is very limited because of the lack of preserved textual evidence. Moreover, possible material evidence might have been destroyed without adequate documentation in the early excavations and sadly may still be destroyed by attempts at "restoration" for the sake of tourism and similar efforts. Thus one needs to draw on a wide array of external sources in order to arrive at an idea of the likely range of rituals that once took place in the valley. Therefore, it should be made clear from the outset that this chapter relies heavily on contemporary material from the private sphere, and even from other, mostly later, periods. The proposals made therefore can only be tentative at best.

Utilizing comparison with temples as well as with the earlier Coffin Texts of the Middle Kingdom, it is to be expected that the foundation of a new tomb would be marked by a ritual that likely consisted of symbolic acts of delimitating and consecrating the ground. As the ritual for building a tomb is only known from a few private Middle Kingdom coffins (CT spells 115–119, von Lieven in preparation), and it differs markedly from the ritual for founding a temple (el-Adly 1981), it is clear that one may not simply project one or the other onto a royal tomb of the New Kingdom. It would be interesting to know whether the finished tomb also had to be ritually activated. For temples, it is known that they got an Opening of the Mouth ceremony, like a statue (Quack 2015, 147). As temples could be personified, it is likely that this ritual was indeed performed on a statue of the personified temple. Tombs, on the contrary, do not seem to appear personified as do, for example, mortuary temples. Rather, a king's tomb is typically called his "horizon of eternity," thus having almost cosmic qualities. Whether it assumed these qualities via ritual or via its very nature as part of the rocky landscape of the western mountains into which it was built (cf. the hieroglyph for horizon!) must remain open. Of course, these options are not mutually exclusive.

The most important rituals were certainly the mortuary rituals after a king's death. Again, it remains unclear which of them took actually place in the valley and which would already have happened in other places before transferring the corpse to the KV. One would expect that there might already be at the place of death some specialist, a doctor or priest (which of course was the same for some medical offices), who would perform some act to ascertain the king's death. That there were veritable treatises detailing different causes of death, and that they were part of the professional knowledge of the embalmer, has recently been demonstrated (Fischer-Elfert 2013). The text in question seems not to deal with the king but with nonroyal people, yet there is no reason why the same scrutiny should not have been applied to a royal corpse as well. The interesting question is of course what the deeper purpose of this procedure was. As the evidence is mounting that the Egyptians actually had some, however vague, ideas about hygiene and the prevention of infections, it is possible that there were also special precautions taken concerning burial depending on the reason for death. Whether they would also have been valid for kings is of course another question. If so, it would have been interesting to know whether the treatment of Ramesses V varied in any significant way from that of the other kings, as his mummy shows possible indications of smallpox.

Where the actual mummification took place must remain open. For obvious reasons, it must have been a secluded place. On the other hand, the climate of Egypt made it advisable to have the embalming workshops not too far away from the settlement where the death occurred. As the Valley of the Kings would often still have been busy with workers trying to finish the royal tomb as much as possible, probably even during the seventy days of mummification, it seems unlikely that the royal embalming workshop would have been within the Valley of the Kings itself. It might have been either in another valley on the west of the Nile or even on the east, perhaps related to some temple.

A possible glimpse into the proceedings themselves is offered by the embalming ritual as preserved in several papyri from the Roman period (Sauneron 1952; Reeves 1985; Töpfer 2015). However, because of the gap in time as well as the fact that again this ritual is known only from nonroyal contexts, there is no guarantee that royal mummification in the New Kingdom worked similarly.

Once the preparation of the body as a mummy was finished, both the mummy itself and the refuse of the mummification process were made ready for burial. In a great procession, the mummy, the canopic chest, and other objects were led to the tomb. While from private tombs there is ample evidence for this (Settgast 1963), for kings almost nothing is known, as royal tombs usually lack any decoration of this type. However, in the tomb of Tutankhamun, atypical in many respects anyway, there is a scene showing the king's mummy being dragged to the tomb by the "nine friends." As the decoration there is much abbreviated, it is unclear whether this was meant to imply that really only very few persons were present at a royal funeral in contrast to a private one. While this would fit modern expectations of secrecy and security measures taken, it is questionable whether this modern view has any validity.

The most important part of this stage was the ritual of Opening of the Mouth (Otto 1960) for the mummy, or perhaps rather for the anthropoid coffin in which it was by that time enclosed. The mummy itself most likely had already received a first Opening of the Mouth ritual upon completion of the embalming process. This is the only ritual that is rather well documented, with evidence even coming from some royal tombs of the period. As in some private Book of the Dead papyri the ritual is shown being performed right in front of the tomb, one may assume this was also the case in the Valley of the Kings. After that, the mummy within its coffins was laid to rest in the tomb. Again from the private context, it is clear that the whole family was present at this act, and that it was the occasion for the widow to say farewell to her husband. In the tomb of Tutankhamun, Ankhesenamun is not shown in this context, but we see an idealized image of his successor, Aye, acting in a priestly role. He performs the Opening of the Mouth on the dead king, who is represented wearing the Atef crown, being already identified with Osiris. That the Opening of the Mouth on a king was performed by his successor was likely the rule, although normally the crown prince would have been a bodily son of the deceased king. It is also to be expected that the whole court administration and nobility would have attended the royal funeral, while in the private case it was colleagues and friends.

That not only the mummy, but also the waste from the mummification, were buried with respect is clear from the finds of several deposits of such waste. The most famous cases of such deposits are the one belonging to Tutankhamun (Winlock 1941; Allen 2003) and the one recently found in KV 63 (Schaden 2008), where unfortunately it is not known to which burial this belongs. Interestingly, both deposits also contained remains from the celebrations outside the tomb by those who had escorted the mummy—for example, a number of flower collars. From this evidence it is clear that a sort of banquet followed the actual burial, the remains of which were buried as well. That the mummification waste also received an Opening of the Mouth ceremony cannot be proven for the New Kingdom deposits, but it is made likely by the comparative evidence of the Embalming Manual of the Apis Bull, again attested only from the late Ptolemaic period (Vos 1993; Quack 1997–1998). There it is clearly stated that the mummification waste, in this case including even the contents of the bull's anus, is the recipient of elaborate rituals, namely the recitation of nine sacred books. Some of them are protective rituals; one is also called Opening of the Mouth. Finally, the mummification refuse is buried.

Despite the gap in time and the fact that a king is not a sacred bull, the attested mummification deposits of the New Kingdom (for other examples see Eaton-Krauss 2008) speak in favor of somewhat similar ideas being at work already. Clearly, in both cases the underlying idea is that everything that either came in contact with the body during mummification or was even a product of that body had to be treated with respect and deposed of in a tomb, not on a simple rubbish heap (von Lieven 2011). That the pharaoh and the sacred bulls actually were thought to be comparable is proven by the phrase "the Apis, the Mnevis and Pharaoh, the three gods" and the like in some late sources—interestingly always in the context of particularly splendid burial practices for human beings, which should be performed in a way similar to the burial rites for the sacred animals (Quack 2006, 118–123).

While one can get a fairly clear idea about the treatment of the mummy, it is difficult to know what other rites would have been conducted in the tomb during the funeral. For example, the four magical bricks within the sarcophagus chamber (Roth and Roehrig 2002; Theis 2015) had to be placed there and were most likely consecrated to make them efficient. While this could already have happened long before the actual funeral, other rites connected with the grave goods could not. Taking again the evidence from depictions of private tombs and Books of the Dead of New Kingdom date, it is to be assumed that the grave goods were part of the funeral procession, following the mummy and the shrine containing the canopic jars. The tomb of Tutankhamun is unfortunately rather atypical in its architecture, and because of its date at the close of the Amarna period, it is also problematic as a paradigm for the periods before and after. Nevertheless, enough pictorial and archaeological evidence remains to ascertain that at least a good deal of the material found there was also present in other royal tombs of the New Kingdom. Apparently the placement of objects was not random, but followed a fixed plan. For the divine statues in shrines or for the royal guardian statues flanking the entrance of the sarcophagus chamber, it is very likely that their setting up was accompanied by some ritual spell. At least, they will also have received an abbreviated Opening of the Mouth ritual, although, again, that could already have happened at an earlier time, in the workshop where they were produced. On the other hand, they only assumed their imagined "task" on being installed within the tomb, thus making it likely that a ritual act would also have been performed then.

Similarly, the placement of other parts of the equipment, such as, for example, the oars around the king's sarcophagus (Carter nos. 182–192), were likely not performed silently. After all, spells for such objects, including, for example, the oars of the four directions of the sky, are even part of the Book of the Dead, as in BD spell 148, where they are depicted. Oars of the solar barque are also mentioned in BD spells 58, 122, and some versions of 136. Moreover, in front of the canopic shrine of Tutankhamun, in the treasury, stood a wooden head of the celestial cow (Carter no. 264), and between the shrine and the cow's head were arranged three calcite "tazze," bowls on a stand, the two outer ones of which were closed by lids (Carter no. 265). These bowls contained a mixture of natron powder, salt, and soda sulphate. Thus, they assured the ritual purity of the place.

The entrance of the treasury was guarded by the famous figure of Anubis sitting majestically on top of another shrine. Between the two carrying poles of the Anubis shrine, right on the room's threshold, there was placed a reed torch inserted into a sun-dried brick (Carter no. 263, Beinlich and Saleh 1989, 97). The brick had a hieroglyphic inscription, in which the torch itself speaks and declares that it is there for the protection of the king: "The hidden(?), who repels the one who repels him as torch of the desert. I have set the desert (*smi.t*) aflame, I have redirected the way. I am as protection for Osiris king (Nebkheperure)|, the lord of eternity and everlastingness." Interestingly, the top of the torch was gilded, so it could not actually be used, yet the gold at the same time suggested a permanent flame emanating from the torch. That the ensemble was not just set out like this and abandoned, but rather had to be ritually activated, is indicated by a tiny detail that has been documented thanks to Carter's keen observation. He noted that on the ground beside the torch there were some grains of charcoal. This is a likely indication that a vessel containing real fire was used to symbolically "light" the torch for eternity. Interestingly, the text on the brick is clearly a short excerpt of a version of BD spell 151, the spell related to the four magical bricks (Lüscher 1998). In the full text of this spell as found on the slightly older Book of the Dead papyrus of Yuya, it is stipulated that the spell be recited over a brick of fresh clay. A torch should be lighted and be planted into the brick. While this brick should be placed in a niche in the south wall, which was not done with the torch here, the continuation speaks about the brick to be placed in the east wall, facing west. A figure of Anubis, again of clay, should sit on this brick. It is perhaps not entirely circumstantial that the torch and brick were found just at the feet of the Anubis on the shrine, who guards the door in the east wall of the sarcophagus hall, himself facing west. Although it is impossible to always know the exact procedures, these arrangements are clear signs of several ritual acts being celebrated within the tomb.

Also, the tomb of Tutankhamun contained a certain number of objects dedicated to him either by female members of his family or by high officials. They might have been connected with a ceremony of farewell and mourning, but it is not clear when exactly they were donated. Neither is it known whether the flower wreath wrought around the uraeus and vulture on the brow of the outermost anthropoid coffin was a "last greeting" of the widow, as Carter assumed, mere decoration, or had a more profound ritual function. That the flower decoration with its associations of life and pleasant scent was in general important is at least corroborated by the royal mummies that were reburied during the Twenty-first Dynasty. All of them were heavily decked with blue lotus flowers, which supposedly were still fragrant upon their discovery in the late nineteenth century.

From analogy with private funerals (Werbrouck 1938; Lüddeckens 1943), it is also to be expected that a large number of—mainly female—mourners were present. Some of them might even have been professionals, but apart from them, it is likely that the whole royal harem and also the temple songstresses from the Theban temples would have been involved. Whether they were allowed to actually follow the funeral into the valley or had to stay back at some point, possibly even on the eastern shore of the Nile, is of course unclear. Again, private Books of the Dead seem to indicate the presence of mourners right in front of the tomb, although it is always difficult to extrapolate reality from ancient Egyptian pictorial conventions. That high-ranking male officials could also express intense mourning at the death of their king is demonstrated nicely by an inscription from the Twenty-second Dynasty in the royal tombs at Tanis. At the entrance of the tomb of Osorkon II there is a depiction of a man strewing his head with earth and an accompanying text with a heart-rending lament about the king's death: "I weep for you without restriction, I do not tire of searching for your face, my heart is overflowing with pain if it remembers your goodness" (Montet 1947, 71–73, pls. XXII–XXIII). The speaker is a general of the troops of Upper and Lower Egypt.

After closing the tomb, there might have been further rites to assure its future inviolability. While some of the rituals described were probably celebrated similarly for all the royal burials that took place there during the New Kingdom (e.g., the Opening of the Mouth for the mummy), there was also certainly an aspect of changing concepts.

While the evolution of the general architecture and the decoration of the tombs is obvious, it is unfortunately unclear whether this implies also ritual changes. However, there
is one clear architectural change that definitely reflects a change in ritual as well. During
the Eighteenth Dynasty, tombs were not accessible any more after the burial. The
entrances were walled up and the plaster on the wall sealed with the seal of the necropolis. Thus, the tombs were hidden from view, a fact that accounts for the preservation
of Tutankhamun's grave. In contrast, from the time of Ramesses II onward, the tombs
in the valley had wooden doors, not just inside—some before had them already—but
actually also at their entrance (Roehrig 1995). This implies that they were intended to
be accessible, at least for a certain period of time. If this assumption is correct, the only
reason can have been to provide the possibility for ritual acts to be done there regularly.
A likely time for such activity would have been the Beautiful Feast of the Valley (Schott
1952; Seyfried 2013). From private tombs it is known that this feast consisted of a visit of
the god Amun-Re from Karnak on the western shore, where he spent the night within
the ruling king's memorial temple. The populace visited the tombs of their deceased relatives, offering to them and to the gods and celebrating together with the dead. Usually
it is assumed that the king participated via his memorial temple only. However, there
is good reason to assume that from the early Ramesside period onward, rites were also
celebrated at the royal tombs. As the evidence for private activity comes almost exclusively from the wall decoration of said tombs, it is no wonder that there are no clearer
indications for royal tombs, which, as already stated, had a completely different type of
decoration. It has also been proposed that the doors might have been opened to let the
sun shine into the tomb. As for the Feast of the Valley, a similar focus on the sun is obvious from some private tomb inscriptions, a fact that ties in well.

  Another aspect, apart from changes occurring over the half millennium that the
valley was used as a royal necropolis, is whether there would have been special rituals depending on special circumstances connected with the individual king concerned.
A case in which this might have become relevant is that of Ramesses III, who was murdered in a harem conspiracy designed to bring his son Pentaweret to the throne. As
has recently been shown (Hawass et al. 2012), the cut in his throat, which killed him,
had been secured post-mortem by a plaque with an *udjat* eye, similar to the one always
used to close the evisceration cut in the flank of the body. This physical evidence on the
mummy is augmented by the textual evidence from pHarris I (Grandet 1994), written
under Ramesses IV, but styled as a speech of Ramesses III from the beyond. It demonstrates that it was deemed necessary to show the gods and the population as well that the
king had actually been a rightful king despite his sorry fate. Of course, it could be mere
chance that we possess this papyrus for just this king, and there might have been similar
ones for other kings. On the other hand, it seems to make perfect sense that just for a
king who had died in a way contrary to royal ideology, his successor felt the need to provide this posthumous account of his father's reign. After all, the murderer was also his
brother, so the legitimate nature of Ramesses IV's rule was ultimately at stake. While it is
impossible to know whether this would have had any bearing on mortuary ritual, it can
at least not be excluded. After all, a king murdered by a relative hungry for power would

have fit the Osirian model in the most perfect way, and his funeral rites could potentially have capitalized on this.

As there were not only royal tombs in the valley but also burials of high-ranking officials or royal relatives like Yuya and Thuya, mortuary ritual within the valley will also have varied according to its recipients. For the nonroyal occupants, however, it is most likely that their funerals were not much different from those of nonroyal persons buried elsewhere in the Theban necropolis. There might have been access restrictions for the family members and other acquaintances, though, as there were apparently restrictions concerning the decoration of the walls for nonroyal tombs in the Valley of the Kings.

BIBLIOGRAPHY

el-Adly, S. Abd el-Azim. 1981. *Das Gründungs- und Weiheritual des ägyptischen Tempels von der frühgeschichtlichen Zeit bis zum Ende des Neuen Reiches.* Tübingen.

Allen, S. J. 2003. "Tutankhamun's Embalming Cache Reconsidered." In *Egyptology at the Dawn of the Twenty-first Century: Proceedings of the Eighth International Congress of Egyptologists, Cairo 2000; 1 Archaeology,* edited by Z. Hawass and L. Pinch-Brock, 23–29. Cairo.

Backes, B., and J. Dieleman, eds. 2015. *Liturgical Texts for Osiris and the Deceased in Late Period Egypt: Collected Papers of the Colloquia at New York (ISAW), 6 May 2011, and Freudenstadt, 18–21 July 2012.* Studien zur spätägyptischen Religion. Wiesbaden.

Beinlich, H., and M. Saleh. 1989. *Corpus der Hieroglyphischen Inschriften aus dem Grab des Tutanchamun.* Oxford.

Dorman, P. F., and B. M. Bryan, eds. 2007. *Sacred Space and Sacred Function in Ancient Thebes.* Studies in Ancient Oriental Civilization 61. Chicago.

Eaton-Krauss, M. 2008. "Embalming-Caches." *Journal of Egyptian Archaeology* 94: 288–293.

Fischer-Elfert, H.-W. 2013. "Anfang eines *iry.w*-Traktats des *wti*-Umwicklers inclusive einer post-mortalen Thanatologie (Pap. UCL 32781 verso)." *Chronique d'Égypte* 88: 15–34.

Fischer-Elfert, H.-W., and K. Zibelius-Chen, eds. 2006. *"Von reichlich ägyptischem Verstande": Festschrift für Waltraud Guglielmi.* Philippika 11. Wiesbaden.

Grandet, P. 1994. *Le papyrus Harris I (BM 9999).* Bibliothèque d'Étude 109. Cairo.

Hawass, Z., and L. Pinch-Brock, eds. 2003. *Egyptology at the Dawn of the Twenty-first Century: Proceedings of the Eighth International Congress of Egyptologists, Cairo 2000; 1 Archaeology.* Cairo.

Hawass, Z., C. M. Pusch, A. R. Zink, et al. 2012. "Revisiting the Harem Conspiracy and Death of Ramesses III: Anthropological, Forensic, Radiological, and Genetic Study." *British Medical Journal* 345. doi: http://dx.doi.org/10.1136/bmj.e8268.

Lüddeckens, E. 1943. *Untersuchungen über religiösen Gehalt, Sprache und Form der ägyptischen Totenklagen.* Mitteilungen des Deutschen Instituts für Ägyptische Altertumskunde in Kairo 11. Berlin.

Lüscher, B. 1998. *Untersuchungen zu Totenbuch Spruch 151.* Studien zum Altägyptischen Totenbuch 2. Wiesbaden.

Montet, P. 1947. *Les constructions et le tombeau d'Osorkon II à Tanis.* Paris.

Otto, E. 1960. *Das ägyptische Mundöffnungsritual.* Ägyptologische Abhandlungen 3. Wiesbaden.

Quack, J. F. 1997–1998. "Beiträge zum Verständnis des Apisrituals." *Enchoria* 24: 43–53.

Quack, J. F. 2006. "Das Grab am Tempeldromos. Neue Deutungen zu einem spätzeitlichen Grabtyp." In *Von reichlich ägyptischem Verstande*, edited by H.-W. Fischer-Elfert and K. Zibelius-Chen, 113–132. Wiesbaden.

Quack, J. F. 2015. "Das Mundöffnungsritual als Tempeltext und Funerärtext." In *Liturgical Texts for Osiris and the Deceased in Late Period Egypt*, edited by B. Backes and J. Dieleman, 145–149. Wiesbaden.

Reeves, C. N. 1985. "Fragments of an Embalming-Ritual Papyrus in the Oriental Museum Durham." *Revue d'Égyptologie* 36: 121–124.

Roehrig, C. H. 1995. "Gates to the Underworld: The Appearance of Wooden Doors in the Royal Tombs in the Valley of the Kings." In *Valley of the Sun Kings: New Explorations in the Tombs of the Pharaohs*, edited by R. H. Wilkinson, 82–107. Tucson, AZ.

Roehrig, C. H. 2007. "Chamber Ja in Royal Tombs in the Valley of the Kings." In *Sacred Space and Sacred Function in Ancient Thebes*, edited by P. F.Dorman and B. M. Bryan, 117–138. Chicago.

Roth, A. M., and C. H. Roehrig. 2002. "Magical Bricks and the Bricks of Birth." *Journal of Egyptian Archaeology* 88: 121–139.

Sauneron, S. 1952. *Rituel de l'embaumement*. Cairo.

Schaden, O. J. 2008. "The Amenmesse Project, Season of 2006." *Annales du Service des Antiquités de l'Égypte* 82: 231–260.

Schott, S. 1952. *Das schöne Fest vom Wüstentale: Festbräuche einer Totenstadt*. Abhandlungen der geistes- und sozialwissenschaftlichen Klasse, Akademie der Wissenschaften und der Literatur Mainz 11. Wiesbaden.

Settgast, J. 1963. *Untersuchungen zu altägyptischen Bestattungsdarstellungen*. Abhandlungen des Deutschen Archäologischen Instituts Kairo 3. Glückstadt, Hamburg, and New York.

Seyfried, K.-J. 2013. *Bemerkungen und Quellen zum ḥ3b nfr n jnt, dem "Schönen Fest des Tales" in Theben*. Göttinger Miszellen Beihefte 13. Göttingen.

Theis, Ch. 2015. "Wenn Archäologie und Philologie nicht harmonieren. Magische Ziegel, ihre Nischen und Totenbuchspruch 151d -g." *Zeitschrift für ägyptische Sprache und Altertumskunde* 142: 85–95.

Töpfer, Susanne 2015. *Das Balsamierungsritual: eine (Neu-)Edition der Textkomposition Balsamierungsritual (pBoulaq 3, pLouvre 5158, pDurham 1983.11 + pSt. Petersburg 18128)*. Studien zur spätägyptischen Religion 13. Wiesbaden.

von Lieven, A. 2011. "'Where There Is Dirt, There Is System.' Zur Ambiguität der Bewertung von körperlichen Ausscheidungen in der ägyptischen Kultur." *Studien zur altägyptischen Kultur* 40: 287–300.

von Lieven, A. (In preparation). *Die nichtfunerären Ursprünge ausgewählter Sprüche der sogenannten Sargtexte*.

Vos, R. L. 1993. *The Apis Embalming Ritual*. Orientalia Lovaniensia Analecta 50. Leuven.

Werbrouck, M. 1938. *Les pleureuses dans l'Égypte ancienne*. Brussels.

Wiebach, S. 1986. "Die Begegnung von Lebenden und Verstorbenen im Rahmen des thebanischen Talfestes." *Studien zur altägyptischen Kultur* 13: 263–291.

Wilkinson, R. H., ed. 1995. *Valley of the Sun Kings: New Explorations in the Tombs of the Pharaohs; Papers from the University of Arizona International Conference on the Valley of the Kings*. Tucson, AZ.

Winlock, H. E. 1941. "Materials Used at the Embalming of King Tut-ankh-amun." The Metropolitan Museum of Art Papers no. 10. New York. http://www.griffith.ox.ac.uk/tut-ankhamundiscovery.html.

CHAPTER 20

SYMBOLIC ASPECTS
OF ROYAL TOMBS

RICHARD H. WILKINSON

It is unknown to what extent symbolism played a role in the production of the earliest tombs in the Valley of the Kings (KV), but it is clear that as time progressed symbolic considerations were involved in many aspects of the funerary monuments of the New Kingdom. Even by the mid-Eighteenth Dynasty, five aspects of funerary symbolism are found in the royal tombs—symbolism of location, orientation, decoration, text and designation (nomenclature of the parts of the tomb). These five aspects are surveyed individually in this chapter, though it is unavoidable that some overlap between the various aspects occurs utilizing this approach—for example, between the symbolism of location and orientation, and that of orientation and decoration.

SYMBOLISM OF LOCATION

The ancient Egyptians clearly accorded special significance to certain areas that they viewed as sacred or symbolic locations of religious and mythical importance. Often these areas were determined or delimited by topographic and other physical characteristics. Symbolic significance could thus be associated with a royal tomb in terms of its *absolute* placement within an area regarded as sacred or symbolically important. On the other hand, symbolic locational significance could also be associated with the *relative* placement of architectural features, representational motifs, or funerary assemblage artifacts within the tomb itself.

Absolute Location

The dichotomous geography of Egypt as bisected by the Nile Valley made its mark in the symbolic importance attached to east and west from earliest times. For the Egyptians the west was, of course, equated with the setting sun and thus the afterlife. As a result, the royal necropoleis of ancient Thebes were situated on the west bank of the Nile in an area that, from the perspective of the city of Thebes itself, on the east bank, lay between two mountainous protrusions of the Theben massif that formed the shape of the *3ḫt* or "horizon" glyph used by the Egyptians as a symbol of the interface between the world of the living and that of the afterlife (Wilkinson 1994a, 159, 167). That this was not coincidental is seen in multiple references in text and representation to the afterlife and the tomb as an "*3ḫt*" (see, e.g., Roberson 2007).

At the center of this geographic *3ḫt*, the pyramidal shape of the highest peak—known today as *el-Gurn* ("the Horn"), and in ancient times as *t3 dhnt* ("the Peak")—was doubtless not lost on the Egyptians as a perfect symbolic focus for a royal necropolis, and many of the kings' tombs were cut in the cliffs and *wadi* floors at its base. It is true, as several writers have noted, that little effort was made by the tombs' architects to enter the mountain from the ritually correct northern side (as with a true pyramid); and the tombs themselves were certainly not connected with, or even directly oriented toward, the monarchs' royal temples on the western side of the Nile as one might expect if the analogy of a pyramidal burial complex was being actively developed (Wilkinson 1994b, 79). But the actual pyramid form of the royal burial was already being superseded by the time the Valley of the Kings was first utilized, so a close parallel to that model was unnecessary. Nevertheless, the pyramidal shape of this mountain is so striking that it does seem likely, given the grouping of tombs cut around it, that a general funerary symbolism was recognized for this location when the royal necropolis was instituted.

In any event, once established, the area of the Valley of the Kings took on its own symbolic importance as *t3 st ʿ3t*, the great place, and other symbolic factors seem to have come into play at the more immediate level of the individual monuments. Tombs were often cut directly beneath, or in line of vision with, *3ḫt*-shaped notches in the cliff walls of the royal valley, and this was sometimes quite possibly for symbolic context. In many cases the original intent was clearly to position the tomb beneath a waterfall area so that in time, with inevitable rain runoff from the heights behind and above the cliffs, the tombs would be covered and effectively hidden with waterborne debris. But this positioning is also true of a number of royal tombs cut into rock spurs at some distance from the cliff faces. A vignette from the Book of the Dead of Neferubenef that shows a tomb having its roof in the form of an *3ḫt* with the disk of the sun positioned directly upon it illustrates this idea within the context of funerary mythology (Hornung 1979, 184; Wilkinson 1994a, 158, 167); and the fact that a private tomb could be visualized and depicted as an *3ḫt* indicates that the Egyptians could have positioned certain royal tombs with this factor in mind, and that the "search" (*gmgm*) conducted for a suitable site for the royal tomb may have included such symbolic considerations.

Relative Location

The aspect of symbolic relative placement in the art and architecture of the royal tombs may be clearly demonstrated in many specific instances, though these often overlap with the aspect of the orientation of the tomb and its constituent parts and are considered below.

Symbolism of Orientation

Tomb Alignment

The external relative alignment of a given tomb is difficult to assess for a number of reasons. Orientation might be judged by the alignment of the entrance to a tomb, the alignment of its passages up to the first pillared hall, the alignment of those passages beyond the first pillared hall in tombs with bent axes, or the alignment of the burial chamber. To these possibilities the alignment of the sarcophagus itself must also be added (Abitz 1989; Wilkinson 1994b, 80–83, 1995b, 75–81). A number of scholars have considered the orientation of specific tombs using one or more of these criteria of alignment, but the search for consistent orientation toward external structures or points has not been successful. In the case of Hatshepsut's tomb (KV 20), the tomb entrance does aim approximately toward the queen's mortuary temple at Deir el-Bahri, but this case appears to be exceptional and cannot be shown to be replicated in clear parallel examples.

In terms of alignment to the cardinal points, there is an added difficulty in that we must also consider whether the Egyptians might have utilized approximations of the cardinal points based on observation of sunrise and sunset positions of the sun, stellar observation, or approximation based on "local north" in that the Nile River flows roughly south to north in the area of Thebes, but at an angle of some 30 degrees east of "true" (stellar) north.

If specific alignments were utilized, it is possible, of course, that some tombs could have been aligned according to one of these methods of direction finding, some with another. The entrances to the tombs of Horemheb and Siptah, for example, are oriented fairly precisely (though in opposite directions) on a true north–south axis, while that of Thutmose IV seems to be aligned just as precisely with local north. But even if we accept the general range of direction lying between true cardinal north and local north as determined by the Nile, it appears that the alignment of tomb entrances and passages in the Valley of the Kings follows no consistent pattern. Despite the ancient Egyptian's evident preoccupation with the cardinal directions in much of their pyramid and temple architecture then, most of the royal tombs in the Valley of the Kings appear to be situated according to the local topography and ostensibly, at least, do not appear to be aligned to the actual cardinal points. This is not to say, however, that the Egyptians did not carry over their interest in cardinal symbolism to the planning and decoration of these tombs.

The Burial Chamber and Sarcophagus

Given the clear importance of the solar elements of the Egyptian funerary books and the solar symbolism found in the decoration of the Nineteenth and Twentieth Dynasty tombs, it has often been claimed that the rounded shape of the burial chambers of the earlier tombs of the Eighteenth Dynasty (e.g., KV 34, the tomb of Thutmose III) was consciously chosen by the Egyptians to be symbolic of the solar cycle, but no texts directly confirm this. Likewise, the curving, somewhat circular plans of many of the earlier tombs in the royal valley could perhaps have been intended to reflect the cyclical path of the sun, but once again we have no definitive proof of this. In fact, while the tombs of Thutmose I (KV 38) and Hatshepsut (KV 20) do curve in this manner, other early tombs, such as those of Thutmose II (KV 40), Thutmose III (KV 34), and Thutmose IV (KV 43) are of a much more angular design, although these could be said to also follow a stylized "circular" plan overall.

It is also possible that some kind of directional pattern may occur in the alignment of KV sarcophagus chambers, though the only pattern that the present writer has been able to determine (Wilkinson 1994b) is that many Eighteenth Dynasty tombs were constructed with either the burial chamber or the head of the sarcophagus aligned toward the north (i.e., somewhere in the range between true and local north). In the Nineteenth and Twentieth Dynasty tombs, the actual orientation of the burial chamber shows no such tendency—though regardless of actual orientation, by this time the entrance to each tomb was already regarded as being symbolically in the south and the burial chamber in the north. This is because the nocturnal path of the sun was regarded as having its zenith in the north, just as the daytime sun is at its highest in the south each day. The niches cut into the sides of the entrance passages of the tombs from the time of Thutmose III were thus named for the gods of the east and west. Beginning in the Nineteenth Dynasty, however, and continuing throughout the Twentieth, we find the development of what appears to be a second symbolic orientation based upon a different view of the path of the sun, and one which was much more frequently and consistently applied (Wilkinson 1995a, b). In this new scheme the major axis of the tomb seems to have been viewed not as running south to north, but as representing the sun's east–west (and its returning west–east) journey, as will be seen when tomb decoration is considered.

It may not be coincidental, therefore, that beginning with the Twentieth Dynasty we find the reorientation of the royal sarcophagus along the lines of the main axis of the tomb rather than at right angles to the axis as in earlier tombs (Wilkinson 1995b, 79–80). The sarcophagus (or the pit that eventually replaces it) was consistently positioned from this time with the head to the tomb's far end, so that the king's head was now always symbolically aligned to the west, with the monarch looking toward the east, according to the symbolic east–west orientation of the tomb which was clearly primary by this time (as may be seen, for example, in the sarcophagus chamber of Ramesses IV). It should also be noted that this change also had the general effect of repositioning the representations of Isis and Nephthys that had been placed on the royal sarcophagus since the early Eighteenth Dynasty. These images flanked the figure of the king on the sarcophagus lid in the Nineteenth Dynasty, and with the realignment of the sarcophagus that took place in the Twentieth Dynasty, the two images were now brought into alignment with the overall east-to-west symbolic orientation of the tomb. This is only one example of the interplay between orientational and decorative symbolism that is examined in more detail in the next section.

Symbolism of Designation

The symbolism examined so far is further reflected in some of the designations given by the ancient Egyptians to the parts of the royal tomb. This terminology is examined in detail in chapter 8 and is discussed only briefly here. It must be stressed, however, that our knowledge of the ancient names for the various parts of the royal tomb is based on a number of sources, but primarily on an annotated papyrus-drawn plan of the tomb of Ramesses IV (KV 2) and a limestone ostracon bearing a plan of Ramesses IX (KV 6). This terminology comes, therefore, mainly from the Nineteenth and Twentieth Dynasties, so earlier terminology could possibly have been different, but at least by the Nineteenth Dynasty the names applied to certain parts of the tomb had clear symbolic references.

The entryway passage (passage A) which, in the Ramesside era, was open to the sky and termed "the god's passage of the way of Shu" (or the air) led into "the passage of Re/ the sun" or "the first god's passage of the sun's path" (passage B), and "the second god's passage. . ." (passage C)—doubtless symbolically following the concept of the diurnal/ nocturnal journey of the sun as well as being areas into which sunlight could physically penetrate when the tomb's doors were opened. Solar-related representations dominate these passages.

The second "passage of the sun" (C) regularly contained two wall recesses called "the niches in which the gods of the east and west rest." Although this name might appear to refer to various deities, the images painted in the niches beginning with KV 17 actually depict only various forms of the sun god as found in the Litany of Re, and it seems likely that the "gods" after which the niches were named may have simply been various morning and evening forms of the sun god himself. In any event, the nomenclature applied to the entrance sections of the royal tomb from the Nineteenth Dynasty intimated aspects of the solar cycle and the nocturnal journey of the sun under the earth and correlates with the directional symbolism already discussed. The names of other sections of the royal tomb, such as the burial chamber or "House of Gold," may have also had symbolic aspects, but if so these meanings are not clear, and the names often seem to refer simply to the objects associated with the various chambers and rooms within the subterranean tomb.

Symbolism of Text

For the ancient Egyptians, writing and representation were often the same thing because the hieroglyphic images used for writing also formed the basis of much of larger representational "art," so that it might be said that the Egyptians "wrote with pictures and painted with words" (Wilkinson 1994a, 148–169). Although this is a simplification, its basic truth underlies the fact that the funerary texts and the depictions that accompany them in the royal tombs (see chapter 21) were largely inseparable in meaning and purpose. Nevertheless, for the sake of convenience and clarity, text and image are considered separately here.

The Books of the Netherworld

From the very beginnings of tomb decoration in the Valley of the Kings the concept of the path of the sun throughout its cycle is clearly delineated in the registers of the royal funerary "books," such as the Amduat and the Book of Gates that were painted on the tomb walls (Abitz 1984; Hornung 1999). Although these works were limited to the burial chambers of the earlier Eighteenth Dynasty monuments, the extension of the decorative program that occurs in the Nineteenth Dynasty meant that the textual motif of the netherworld solar path was carried to other parts of the tomb and manifested in a number of ways, primarily in terms of location, orientation, and content.

The employment of the Egyptian funerary books within the royal tombs was clearly done with orientational symbolic considerations in mind. As Erik Hornung has written, "The documents of the draftsmen usually noted that certain divisions of the Books of the Netherworld should be oriented according to predefined cardinal directions to ensure that the tomb conform as faithfully as possible to the vision of the Netherworld" (Hornung 1990, 41). For example, the cavern of Sokar in the fifth hour of the Amduat and the throne of Osiris in the sixth hour of the Book of Gates are both often positioned so as to be situated on the northern side of the early tombs—in the direction ascribed to these locales in Egyptian mythology. This same orientational concern underlies the specific directional notations that appear in tombs such as that of Horemheb (KV 57), and it is evident that orientation and alignment did play an important, though not always fully understood, role in the deployment of the texts inscribed in the royal necropolis.

In the tombs of the later dynasties of the New Kingdom a different kind of orientational symbolism may be found (Wilkinson 1994b, 1995b). As a general rule, we find a pattern in that the funerary texts that were inscribed in the entrance passages of the Nineteenth Dynasty royal monuments lead down into the tomb on both walls. Here, the hieroglyphs seem to face outward on both parietal surfaces in order that a clear progression into the tomb be maintained. In the Twentieth Dynasty, this orientation changes; whereas the texts on the left-hand wall (as one enters the tomb) may continue to read into the monument, those inscribed on the right-hand wall often face the other direction and read out of the tomb. The effect of this change is obvious and provides a pattern of progression into the tomb on the left wall and return on the right side—and thus follows what will also be seen in the representational elements as a pattern most probably indicative of the journey of the sun as it symbolically descends into the netherworld, travels through the burial chamber, and then emerges from the tomb in renewed ascendance.

The symbolic content of the funerary texts themselves is a vast subject that has been examined by a number of scholars and cannot be detailed here. However, the specific significance of many of these texts for understanding the Egyptian conception of the netherworld path of the sun has been concisely summarized by Suzanne Onstine (1995) and may also be seen in examination of the interplay between symbolism of the funerary texts and representations.

SYMBOLISM OF DECORATION

Certain representations and decorative motifs within the royal tombs were clearly positioned so as to be oriented toward their symbolically associated cardinal points, especially, as noted earlier, beginning in the Nineteenth Dynasty when we find the development of what appears to be a symbolic decorative orientation with the major axis of the tomb viewed as representing the path of the sun's east–west journey.

The Path of the Sun

This pattern is seen in a number of solar-related iconographic images that appear or are repositioned at this time, and although these images have often been viewed as merely decorative elements, they are discrete iconographic devices not found in the vignettes for the traditional Netherworld Books and seem to have functioned as markers showing symbolic alignment. The most obvious of these elements is the solar disk containing the images of Khepri and Atum that appears for the first time above the entrance to the tomb of Ramesses II and was then routinely placed in this location in each subsequent tomb (Figure 20.1). Here, outside the tomb (and sometimes in the first passages) the disk is painted yellow, the color of the daytime sun, whereas within the tomb—at points along the ceilings or walls—the same image is painted red, indicating the sun's evening and nighttime appearance and thus reinforcing the idea of its progression along the tomb's axis.

The use of royal cartouches as symbolic equivalents to solar disks along the ceilings of passages in the royal tombs—uniting the person of the king with the sun—is well understood. The equivalency of the two images is established in parallels of shape, color (the cartouches are invariably yellow or red), location in the tomb, and the original solar significance of the cartouche itself. So there can be no real doubt as to the solar significance of the cartouche when it is used repeatedly along the ceilings of the tombs, often alternating with the solar disk itself or with the flying vulture (another solar/royal image) and forming part of a continuous visual thread delineating the descending path of the

FIGURE 20.1 Motif of the solar disk with its morning and evening forms, flanked by the deities Isis and Nephthys, entering the underworld. Entrance to the tomb of Merenptah, KV 8.

(Photograph by Richard H. Wilkinson)

sun. The parallel use of cartouches and solar disks is not only an important aspect of symbolic programmatic interaction in itself, but also is instructive in terms of suggesting the solar equivalency of other elements such as the various forms of yellow bands placed along the entrance corridors of the royal monuments, as will be seen.

While various solar-related images follow this east-to-west path, other iconographic elements stress the north–south orientation of the side walls. From the first occurrence of the sun disk being used in this way, the goddesses Isis and Nephthys, who were symbolically associated with the south and north respectively, were shown flanking the disk as though indicating the intersecting south–north axis at the sides of the sun as it passes from east to west. These two goddesses are also shown at points along the entrance passages, Isis on the left (or symbolic south) and Nephthys on the right (or symbolic north) walls—as in the tomb of Seti I where they appear on their respective sides of the entrance corridors and even dominating the symbolic north and south sides of that king's burial chamber. At the entrance to Seti's sarcophagus hall the deities Nekhbet and Wadjet are also depicted in serpent guise above the lily and the papyrus—the heraldic plants of Upper and Lower Egypt—on their respective (left and right) sides of the doors.

Beginning with the tomb of Ramesses II, another device of this kind is found in the two opposing figures of the seated goddess Maat that were carved and painted on the jambs of the tomb entrance, and supported on the left (or symbolic south) wall by a large lily plant and on the right (or symbolic north) by a large papyrus clump. This device became standard in succeeding monuments, and in the tomb of Tausret and Sethnakht it is also repeated along the sides of the passages at further threshold points within the tomb. Thus, in addition to the east–west path of the sun being clearly delineated on the lintels and ceilings of the Ramesside tombs, the side walls are also given iconographic elements with obvious connotations of north and south so that a consistent fourfold symbolic orientation is set up within the tomb regardless of its actual cardinal alignment.

Another aspect of the symbolic orientation of the royal tomb that seems to have taken place in the 19th Dynasty is the logical division of the tomb into a front, entrance, half (symbolically to the east) and the back half (symbolically to the west), giving precedence to the sun god Re in the front half and to Osiris, "Foremost of the Westerners," in the back. This conscious division may be clearly seen in the fact that from the time of Seti I, the king is shown at the entrance to the royal tomb greeting the sun god Re-Horakhty as a frontispiece to the Litany of Re, which was now moved from the depths of the tomb where it was originally painted and placed in the first corridors. At precisely the same time that the Litany of Re was moved to the front of the tomb, the large so-called "Osiris shrine" with its juxtaposed images of the underworld god was also placed at the dividing halfway point of the tomb—on the far wall of the first pillared hall, directly above the steps into the lower reaches (see Figure 20.2). In the lower, back half of the tomb the sun god continues to appear, of course, but his images are usually much smaller than those of Osiris and other chthonic deities (sometimes, as will be seen below, to specifically show the diminishing nature of the dying sun god—Figure 20.3). Both Friedrich Abitz and Erik Hornung have stressed this division of the tomb into two halves, and Hornung has also noted the precedence given to female deities in the upper half of the tomb and male deities in the lower half (Hornung 1990). This realization in no way contradicts the respective stress on Re and Osiris in the two halves of the tomb, however, as most of the female deities are sky- and sun-related goddesses and the male deities chthonic ones, so that the two explanations are actually complementary.

FIGURE 20.2 The "Osiris Shrine" depicted on the rear wall of the first pillared hall of many tombs marks the inner, lower half of the tomb as the realm of the netherworld deity. Out of sight, at left, deities pull the rope that hauls the barque of the sun god traveling down into the underworld realm. Tomb of Ramesses III, KV 11.

(Photograph by Richard H. Wilkinson)

FIGURE 20.3 The diminishing "Flesh of Re" shown much smaller than the deities around him as he approaches the Osiris shrine and enters, as it were, the realm of Osiris himself. First pillared Hall, Tomb of Merenptah, KV 8.

(Photograph by Richard H. Wilkinson)

Somewhat less obvious are the previously mentioned narrow yellow bands that often run along the tops of the walls (Wilkinson 1995a, Plate VIIIa) in corridors without the broad ceiling band and often alternate with the latter in such a way as to provide an unbroken path from the tomb entrance to the well room where the bands always terminate. This terminus is hardly coincidental, as it is here that the major solar images are replaced by chthonic ones in the Nineteenth Dynasty tombs. Sometimes, rows of yellow cartouches painted on the ceilings connect passages with yellow ceiling or wall bands and seem to function in the same manner, so that in a given tomb the image/corridor progression might be: corridor A: yellow wall bands, corridor B: center yellow band, corridor C: ceiling row of yellow cartouches—giving an unbroken path of one type of solar symbol or another. It is important to note, however, that multiple elements are usually not utilized within the same passages, which would appear to suggest the symbolic equivalency of the various elements in representing the continuity of the path of the sun.

In the Twentieth Dynasty we see a strengthening, throughout the tomb, of the direct association of the deceased king with the sun god. In the tomb of Ramesses IV, for instance, the king's cartouches are inscribed along the ceilings of the halls leading into the burial chamber, surrounded by the stars of the heavens. Thus the king's names follow the path of the sun and clearly identify him with the solar journey, with the cartouches containing the king's names being the equivalent of the solar disks also found on the tomb ceilings and on the architraves of the Egyptian temple (Wilkinson 1995a, Plate VIIIb). The journey to and from the west is also reflected in another Ramesside motif in which the king is shown, facing opposite directions, in the juxtaposed evening and morning barques of the sun god. Although the two barques appear randomly on the side walls of earlier tombs, they are now centrally positioned along the tomb's axis—as in the tomb of Ramesses VI, and that of Ramesses IX where the motif appears at the center or visual turning point of the rear wall of the sarcophagus hall. At this point, scenes in several later tombs depict the sun god being reborn or beginning his outward journey (Figure 20.4).

So, the conception of the solar journey, or at least its expression within the royal tombs, changes as time progresses. In the Nineteenth Dynasty old decorative elements were relocated and new ones produced that specifically showed the path of the sun through the entrance passages and halls of the tomb in symbolic descent into the netherworld. From this time the inner half of the tomb, beginning with the first pillared hall—or its threshold, the well room—is viewed as the heart of the underworld and is clearly under the control of the god Osiris and associated chthonic deities. In the Twentieth Dynasty the decorative program utilized in the royal tombs changes again so that the walls of the entrance passages appear to show in many details not only the descent of the sun into the netherworld, but also its subsequent return in a complete nocturnal solar cycle.

FIGURE 20.4 The rebirth of the sun god. Rear wall of burial chamber of the tomb of Ramesses V/VI, KV 9.

(Photograph by Richard H. Wilkinson)

The Sun God and the Chthonic Deities

While the aspects considered in the preceding section are all elements showing the directional path of the sun through the tomb in its role as a model of the netherworld, other aspects of the decoration deal with the nature of the sun god and the changes that occur to the deity in the course of his cyclic journey. Perhaps most important among these aspects are the relative sizes accorded the sun god and the netherworld deities in symbolically key locations, and the gesture symbolism incorporated within specific representational scenes. Both of these aspects carry considerable force, from the perspective of Egyptian art, in defining state of being and relational status.

Rather than being wholly arbitrary, as is often assumed, the relative size of the images of deities within the royal tombs is an important aspect of the monuments' programmatic decorative symbolism. Although absolute size is naturally determined by factors such as location and available register size, relative size within given registers or areas of representation is usually carefully controlled and is sometimes the single most salient aspect of symbolic significance. An obvious example may be found in the generalization that in the tombs of the Nineteenth Dynasty the figure of the sun god tends to be shown larger in the upper, entrance, part of the tomb and smaller in the lower part—with the figure of Osiris tending to be shown correspondingly larger in the lower reaches of the tomb. In the Twentieth Dynasty—as in the example of the tomb of Ramesses VII mentioned previously—this pattern is abrogated by the cyclic or returning nature of the decorative program, and the figures of Osiris and other chthonic deities may be shown just as large as those of the sun god in both parts of the tomb.

Less noticeable, yet just as important, a number of compositionally specific adjustments of relative scale may be seen to have been used in key areas within the tombs. This is especially clear in liminal and other transitional areas such as the well shaft and first pillared hall, which form the main dividing point between the realms of Re and Osiris in the Nineteenth Dynasty royal tomb. In the first pillared hall of the tomb of Seti I, the figure of the sun god is shown at a smaller scale than that used for the attendant figures who pull the solar barque along. This simple device gives a very real impression of the diminishing power of the solar deity as he enters the depths of the underworld realm, in effect suffering loss of power and metaphorically experiencing the extremes of age and the death that must occur before rebirth. In later tombs the visual analogy is made yet clearer. In Merenptah's tomb, for example, the same figure of the "flesh" of the sun god, shown traveling through the underworld in the divine solar barque, is depicted as entering Osiris' realm on the outer wall of the first pillared hall where the god is as large as the deities in his retinue (Wilkinson 1995a, Plate IXa). Yet on the inner wall of the same hall, opposite this image and adjacent to the stairway leading into the tomb's lower half, the same figure of the sun god is shown much smaller than the deities around him as he approaches the Osiris shrine and enters, as it were, the realm of Osiris himself (Figure 20.3 and Wilkinson 1995a, Plate IXb).

Examples of this kind of relative sizing may be found in different locations in other tombs with the size of the sun god always tied in some way to the conceptualization of the sun's journey. In KV 18, the tomb of Tausret/Sethnakht—which, despite its decorational complexity based on the monument's usurpation (see ch 23), shows many aspects of transition into the cyclic style of the Twentieth Dynasty—the passage immediately before the final burial chamber contains similar scenes from the Book of the Amduat on each of its side walls. On the left-hand wall—facing into the burial chamber—the figure of Re is somewhat smaller than those of his attendants in the barque. On the right-hand wall, where the solar barque is shown emerging as it were from the burial chamber, the figure of Re is now larger than those of his fellow deities, as though the god has been renewed in the depths of the netherworld and is now emerging from the tomb in a revitalized, and hence larger, form.

The same status interrelationship seen in the relative sizes of the sun god and Osiris in the two halves of the Nineteenth Dynasty tombs may also be seen in the gesture symbolism associated with representations of the two deities. This aspect of symbolic interaction has been touched upon by several commentators in terms of individual scenes but has not always been systematically studied in terms of the sun god's journey through the tomb as netherworld. Suzanne Onstine has noted that in the first five tableaus of the Book of Caverns, Re makes a gesture of submission (in the form of hands extended at waist level with palms turned down) to the gods in the following of Osiris (Onstine 1995). Just as in the area of relative size, we find that although Re appears ubiquitous in the Nineteenth Dynasty funerary books—and is of course of great importance in them all—the relationship of the sun god with Osiris and the netherworld is still essentially one of respect and submission. Re must indeed submit himself to the underworld and acknowledge its power over him in order to be rejuvenated and reborn. There is some level of reciprocation involved, but the details of the reciprocation are instructive. Onstine has stressed that figures of Osiris never make submissive gestures to Re (although in certain scenes Re makes the gesture of submission to Osiris and Osiris makes a gesture of adoration in return), while those in the following of the netherworld god do make gestures of submission to Re, as they are dependent on the sun god to be awakened by his light.

The location of some of the major images of the sun god relative to those of Osiris also shows what is occurring at the various points of the sun's journey through the tomb as netherworld. In KV 9, the tomb of Ramesses VI, a large image of solar rebirth is enshrined at the very back of the tomb—at the precise halfway point between the incoming and declining images of the sun god and the outgoing, rejuvenated images. The parallel between this niche's focal location and the similarly placed Osiris niches found in some of the earlier tombs is instructive.

SYMBOLISM IN THE VALLEY OF THE KINGS

While the foregoing brief survey shows that the symbolism found in the planning and design of the royal tombs of the Valley of the Kings was given expression in a number

of different ways, all of these aspects of symbolism were utilized to underscore two fundamental concepts of Egyptian afterlife ideology: the path of the sun through the netherworld (with the inclusion of the deceased king on that path being a natural corollary
of that same great theme) and the interaction of the sun god/king with Osiris and other
netherworld deities. This is not to say that other minor themes did not exist in the funerary texts and representations painted within the tombs, but that symbolism, where it is
found, invariably is tied to the *Grundthema* of the path of the sun or that of the sun/king
and the netherworld deities.

In most of the earlier royal tombs only the burial chambers and some other points
are decorated, and both symbolic themes are found in the same areas. However, in
the later hypogea both the tombs and the decorated areas within them were expanded
and solar symbolism takes precedence in the outer sections of the tomb, with the
netherworld-related symbolism being expressed more fully in the lower reaches, the
burial chamber, sarcophagus and various items of the funerary assemblage. The division
is not a hard and fast one, and elements from both themes may be found in the other
theme-focused areas of the tombs. Nevertheless, the dichotomy is generally true and
underscores both the reality and importance of the two great symbolic themes found in
the Valley of the Kings.

Bibliography

Abitz, F. 1984. *König und Gott: Die Götterszenen in den ägyptischen Königsgräbern von
Thutmosis IV. bis Ramses III*. Ägyptologische Abhandlungen 40.Wiesbaden.

Abitz, F. 1989. "Die Entwicklung der grabachsen in den Königsgräbern im Tal der Könige."
Mitteilungen des Deutschen Archäologischen Instituts, Abteilung Kairo 45: 1–25.

Abitz, F. 1995. *Pharao als Gott in den Unterweltsbüchern des Neuen Reiches*. Orbis Biblicus et
Orientalis 146. Freiburg and Gottingen.

Creasman, P. P., ed. 2013. *Archaeological Research in the Valley of the Kings and Ancient
Thebes: Papers Presented in Honor of Richard H. Wilkinson*, Wilkinson Egyptology Series
1. Tucson.

Hornung, E. 1979. *Das Totenbuch der Ägypter*. Zurich and Munich.

Hornung, E. 1990. *The Valley of the Kings: Horizon of Eternity*. New York.

Hornung, E. 1999. *The Ancient Egyptian Books of the Afterlife*. Ithaca.

Kroenke, K. R. (2013). "The Motif Alignment Project." In Creasman, 27–38.

Onstine, S. 1995 [1999]. "The Relationship between Osiris and Re in the Book of Caverns."
Journal of the Society of the Study of Egyptian Antiquities XXV: 66–77.

Redford, D., ed. 2001. *The Oxford Encyclopedia of Ancient Egypt*. Oxford.

Roberson, J. A. 2007. *The Book of the Earth: A Study of Ancient Egyptian Symbol-Systems and
the Evolution of New Kingdom Cosmographic Models*. Philadelphia.

Wilkinson, R. H. 1993. "The Paths of Re: Symbolism in the Royal Tombs of Wadi Biban El
Moluk." *Kmt* 4(3): 41–52.

Wilkinson, R. H. 1994a. *Symbol and Magic in Egyptian Art*. London and New York.

Wilkinson, R. H. 1994b. "Symbolic Location and Alignment in New Kingdom Royal Tombs
and their Decoration." *Journal of the American Research Center in Egypt* XXXI: 79–86.

Wilkinson, R. H. 1995a [1999]. "The Motif of the Path of the Sun in Ramesside Royal Tombs: An Outline of Recent Research." *Journal of the Society of the Study of Egyptian Antiquities* XXV: 78–84, pl. VIII–X.

Wilkinson, R. H. 1995b. "Symbolic Orientation and Alignment in New Kingdom Royal Tombs." In Wilkinson, 74–81.

Wilkinson, R. H., ed. (1995c). *Valley of the Sun Kings: New Explorations in the Tombs of the Pharaohs.* Tucson.

Wilkinson, R. H. 2001. "Symbols." In Redford, 329–335.

CHAPTER 21

THE ROYAL
FUNERARY BOOKS
The Subject Matter of Scenes and Texts

JOSHUA A. ROBERSON

INTRODUCTION

THE so-called funerary books employed in the Valley of the Kings constitute one of the most distinctive and complex corpora of religious literature known from ancient Egypt. Their scenes and texts represent the zenith of Egyptian speculation on the nature of the divine world. As such, they belong to the realm of cosmology and build upon mythological traditions that stretch back to the earliest religious literature. However, the New Kingdom books rely much more heavily on the use of illustrations, cataloging in ever-increasing detail the landscape and inhabitants of the beyond. These compositions may be divided into three broad categories: the Book of the Dead; etiological treatises; and the cosmographic Books of the Underworld and Sky.

The various books under consideration have been preserved almost exclusively as monumentalized inscriptions and paintings on the walls and ceilings of tombs, as well as sarcophagi and, rarely, other burial equipment. Evidence for master copies, written presumably on papyrus for storage and editing in temple scriptoria, may be deduced from explicit indications of "gaps" (*gm wš*, lit., "found missing") in the monumental record (e.g., Hornung 1963–1967, 2:18); the use of cursive, "stick figure" illustrations in some early monuments (e.g., KV 34), which imitate the style found on papyri; texts written occasionally in cursive hieroglyphs or full hieratic (e.g., KV 34, KV 6); as well as hieroglyphic inscriptions that include apparent errors from the hieratic and intrusive hieratic groups (e.g., KV 9; see Roberson 2012, 74–83). However, with the exception of the Book of the Dead, no papyrus copies of any funerary books are known prior to the Twenty-First Dynasty and the abandonment of the Valley of the Kings as a royal burial site.

The designation of the various cosmological books as "funerary" is also somewhat problematic. Some texts and scenes, such as spell 151 from the Book of the Dead and the tableau depicting the Awakening of Osiris, refer explicitly to the funerary rites. However, the relationship of most other cosmological books to actual rituals culminating in burial is far from certain. Complicating this picture is a series of passages from one of the earliest attested cosmographic books, the Amduat, that refer explicitly to use by the living, while they are "upon the earth" (*tp t3*). Such clues might be interpreted as evidence for an otherwise scarcely attested mystical tradition within the Egyptian priestly sphere, which was then adapted to funerary use (Wente 1982). In any event, it was the literate priests, working probably from the temple scriptorium known as the "House of Life" (*pr ʿnḫ*), who composed, edited, updated, and preserved the various books (see Gardiner 1938). In fact, many of the supposedly "funerary" books, including the Book of Nut, Book of the Night, Book of the Earth, Book of Caverns, and the Awakening of Osiris, are attested first in the Osireion, a ritual tomb for the god Osiris at Abydos, begun by Seti I. That monument necessarily evokes the funerary sphere, in celebration of the death and burial of the god. However, the Osireion—with all of its innovative religious texts—was constructed as an adjunct to the great temple of Seti I, as one of many stops along the processional route, within the broader cult landscape of Abydos. Along that same route, the Litany of the Sun also appears, in the adjacent temple of Ramesses II (Hornung 1975–1976, 2:13). Thus, while we may speak confidently of both "temple" and "mortuary" contexts for many of the books under consideration, the qualification of those works as specifically "funerary" must be viewed with due caution. Most importantly, we must recognize that the broader cosmological corpus probably reflects multiple traditions, multiple stages of composition, and multiple audiences or beneficiaries, depending on context: living and dead; divine and mortal; priestly, royal, and private.

THE BOOK OF THE DEAD

The Book of the Dead (BD; ed. Naville 1886; Allen 1974; Quirke 2013), known to the Egyptians as "Utterances for Going forth by Day" (*r3.w n.w prt m hrw*), was a collection of at least 192 magical spells that functioned something like a traveler's visa for the afterlife, permitting passage from one region to the next, with a minimum of resistance from guardians at the borders. The BD corpus represents a direct continuation from the mortuary literature of the Middle Kingdom (Coffin Texts) and Old Kingdom (Pyramid Texts), with many spells or parts of spells attested in one or both of the earlier corpora. In contrast to the etiological and cosmographic traditions discussed below, the spells of the BD rely less on descriptions of the divine world itself, focusing instead on the magical assistance and knowledge necessary to pass successfully through its trials (Hornung 1999, 17).

The earliest attested BD spells occur on the Seventeenth Dynasty coffins of queen Montuhotep and prince Herunefer, at Thebes (Parkinson and Quirke 1992, 48). Private use of BD material becomes common by the early to mid-Eighteenth Dynasty, in the reign of Thutmose III (Hornung 1999, 13). The earliest known use of material from the BD corpus in a royal tomb is spell 168, employed as an independent composition (see below, Spell of Twelve Caverns) on a papyrus from the tomb of Amenhotep II (KV 35). Spells from the BD also appear on the gilded shrines surrounding the sarcophagus of Tutankhamun (KV 62). These occurrences suggest strongly that other kings from the Eighteenth Dynasty might also have employed BD spells on burial equipment that has not survived.

Selections from the BD corpus first appear on the walls of a royal tomb in the late Eighteenth Dynasty sarcophagus chamber of Aye, indicative perhaps of that king's originally nonroyal status. In the Ramesside period, from the reign of Merenptah and later, BD spells appear sporadically on the walls of various king's tombs (see Table 21.1). From

Table 21.1 Occurrences of Book of the Dead Spells in the Valley of the Kings

BD 1	Dyn. 18: Tutankhamun (KV 62, first and second gilded shrines).
BD 17	Dyn. 18: Tutankhamun (KV 62, second and fourth gilded shrine).
BD 26	Dyn. 18: Tutankhamun (KV 62, second gilded shrine).
BD 27	Dyn. 18: Tutankhamun (KV 62, second gilded shrine).
BD 29	Dyn. 18: Tutankhamun (KV 62, second gilded shrine).
BD 110	Dyn. 20: Ramesses III (KV 11).
BD 123	Dyn. 20: Ramesses IV (KV 2). Prince Montuherkhepeshef (KV 19).
BD 124	Dyn. 20: Ramesses IV (KV 2). Ramesses VI (KV 9).
BD 125	Dyn. 19: Merenptah (KV 8).
	Dyn. 20: Ramesses IV (KV 2). Ramesses VI (KV 9).
BD 126	Dyn. 20: Ramesses VI (KV 9).
BD 127	Dyn. 20: Ramesses IV (KV 2). Ramesses VI (KV 9).
BD 129	Dyn. 20: Ramesses VI (KV 9).
BD 130	Dyn. 18: Ay (KV 23).
BD 134	Dyn. 18: Tutankhamun (KV 62, first gilded shrine).
BD 139	Dyn. 20: Prince Montuherkhepeshef (KV 19).
BD 141	Dyn. 18: Tutankhamun (KV 62, first gilded shrine). Ay (KV 23).
BD 142	Dyn. 18: Tutankhamun (KV 62, first gilded shrine). Ay (KV 23).
BD 144	Dyn. 18: Ay (KV 23).
BD 145	Dyn. 19: Tausret (KV 14). Chancellor Bay (KV 13).
BD 146:	Dyn. 19: Tausret (KV 14)
BD 148	Dyn. 18: Tutankhamun (KV 62, third gilded shrine).
	Dyn. 20: Ramesses III (KV 11).
BD 151	Dyn. 19: Merenptah (KV 8). Siptah (KV 47), Tawosret (KV 14).
	Dyn. 20: Ramesses III (KV 11).
BD 168	*Dyn. 18: Amenhotep II (KV 35) See "Spell of Twelve Caverns," below.*

this same period, the number of illustrations, in both royal and private contexts, also increased dramatically. It is possible that this change was conditioned by the richly illustrated cosmographic books (see below), which began to appear frequently alongside BD material in the royal tombs at that time.

The individual BD spells were assembled on an ad hoc basis, with no canonical selection or order and no single source including all known spells. Of the 192 spells, only 23 are attested in the Valley of the Kings and most of these do not occur more than once. The most frequently encountered spell, with four exemplars, is BD 151. The text and vignette depict the Osirian funeral, wherein the mummy of the deceased lies upon his bier, tended by Anubis, Isis, and Nephthys, with the four sons of Horus, who guard the canopic equipment and viscera (see ch 17), arranged around the corners of the funeral hall. BD 125, one of the most popular spells from private contexts, is also attested reasonably well in the royal sphere, with three exemplars from the Valley of the Kings. In this spell, the heart of the deceased is weighed in the Judgment Hall of Osiris, a theme that appears also in the cosmographic Book of Gates. In the BD version, the principal text consists of the "negative confession," a litany of ritually impure acts that the deceased swears not to have committed, followed by an interrogation in which the deceased supplies a series of stock responses, which demonstrate correct knowledge of the divine world.

ETIOLOGICAL COMPOSITIONS

The three compositions grouped broadly here under the rubric of "etiology" focus on the mythological explanation of celestial phenomena. Their content and context overlap significantly with the cosmological tradition discussed below. Ultimately, the difference between the two groups may be merely a question of textual or iconographic primacy. In the etiological tradition, the illustrations generally lack the complexity and diversity of their cosmographic counterparts and could even be omitted altogether, in some cases.

The Litany of the Sun

The earliest attested etiological book (see Table 21.2), which modern scholars designate the Litany of the Sun (ed. Hornung 1975–1976), was known to the ancient Egyptians as the "Book of Adoring Re (i.e. the Sun) in the West and Adoring the United One (i.e. Re-Osiris) in the West" (*mḏꜣ.t n.t dwꜣ Rꜥ m jmnt.t dwꜣ dmd m jmnt.t*). The book opens with the "Great Litany," enumerating, through text and image, the seventy-five "transformations" (*ḫpr.w*) of the sun god. The Great Litany is followed by a series of nine additional hymns in praise of the deity. Special emphasis is placed on the union of the sun god with the god of the dead, Osiris—a theme that is of central importance to many of the cosmographic books, as well as the Book of the Dead.

Table 21.2 Occurrences of Etiological Books in the Valley of the Kings

Litany of the Sun	Dyn. 18: Thutmose III (KV 34; burial shroud).
	Dyn. 19: Seti I (KV 17). Ramesses II (KV 7). Merenptah (KV 8).
	    Amenmesse (KV 10). Seti II (KV 15). Siptah (KV 47).
	Dyn. 20: Ramesses III (KV 11). Ramesses IV (KV 2). Ramesses IX (KV 6).
	    Ramesses X (KV 18, opening tableau).

Heavenly Cow	Dyn. 18: Tutankhamun (KV 63, first gilded shrine). Dyn. 19: Seti I (KV 17). Ramesses II (KV 7). Dyn. 20: Ramesses III (KV 11). Ramesses VI (KV 9).
Nut	Dyn. 20: Ramesses IV (KV 2).

The Litany of the Sun occurs first in the tomb of Thutmose III (KV 34), on the pillars in the sarcophagus hall as well as on the king's mummy shroud, recovered from the royal burial cache at Deir el-Bahri (Hornung 1975–1976, 2:10). The Litany becomes common from the Ramesside period, occurring frequently in the first and second corridors of the royal tombs, in conjunction usually with a programmatic, opening tableau depicting the three principal, solar transformations: morning (Khepri, as a scarab), day (Re, as a disk), and night (Atum, as a ram-headed man).

Book of the Heavenly Cow

The modern designation of the Book of the Heavenly Cow (ancient title unknown; ed. Hornung 1982) refers to its principal illustration, which depicts the vault of the sky as a great cow, whose belly is lined with stars, upon which sail the twin barques of the sun. The body and legs of the cow are supported by the personification of light and empty space, Shu, and a group of eight additional gods, identified as "infinite ones who are" (*ḥḥ.w ntj.w*). Two additional illustrations, depicting the personifications of solar and Osirian time (*nḥḥ* and *ḏ.t*, respectively), together with the king as supports of the sky, appear in the Ramesside versions. A lengthy mythological text accompanies these images and explains how the current ordered cosmos arose, following the near-destruction of humankind at the hands of the sun god.

Book of Nut

The Book of Nut (ancient title unknown; ed. von Lieven 2007) is attested sporadically from the Nineteenth Dynasty through the Roman period, although astronomical dates and other internal evidence suggest that portions of the text might date to the Middle Kingdom or earlier (von Lieven 2007, 223, 251–254). The Book of Nut occurs only once in the Valley of the Kings, in the tomb of Ramesses IV (KV 2), where it serves as the diurnal counterpart to the Book of the Night, on the ceiling of the burial chamber. The book's modern designation refers to its principal vignette, which depicts the sky as the arched body of the goddess Nut. The air god, Shu, elevates the body of Nut, recalling the disposition of the former god in the Book of the Heavenly Cow. The sun, in the form of a winged disk, enters the mouth of the sky goddess in the west and emerges from between her legs, as a winged scarab, in the east. Texts enumerate the regions of the sky that the sun traverses and account for the passage of time, as reckoned by the thirty-six decan star groups. An extended, mythological treatise, appended to the main vignette in some versions (omitted in the KV), links the Book of Nut to the etiological tradition. On the other hand, as an anthropomorphized diagram of the celestial region, the Book of Nut overlaps iconographically, thematically, and functionally with the Books of the Night and Day, discussed below. Unlike the two latter books, however, the Book of Nut does not include illustrations of the solar barque, the multifarious inhabitants of the Duat, or the Damned.

THE COSMOGRAPHIC BOOKS OF THE UNDERWORLD AND SKY

The Books of the Underworld and Sky quantify the geography and inhabitants of the divine world, or Duat (*dw3.t*), through which the sun god travels, region by region, with varying degrees of systematization. As schematic diagrams of the Egyptians' conceptual universe, the Books of the Underworld and Sky belong to the realm of cosmography. Unlike the Book of the Dead and the etiological treatises, the cosmographic books place much greater emphasis on their figural components, which are generally more complex, both internally and in their contextual relationship to surrounding scenes. In some cases, the illustrations even supersede most or all of the original annotations, as seen, for example, in the programmatic use of the concluding image from the Book of Caverns in the tombs of Merenptah (KV 8), Tausret (KV 14), and Ramesses III (KV 11), or in the abbreviated Books of the Night and Day employed in the tomb of Ramesses IX (KV 6).

The designation that the ancient Egyptians applied most frequently to individual books in this genre was "the Book of That which is in the Duat" (*t3 md3.t n.t jmj(.t) dw3.t*). Nine books from this tradition are attested in the Valley of the Kings. These compositions include, in order of earliest occurrence, the so-called Amduat; the Spell of Twelve Caverns; the Book of the Solar-Osirian Unity; the Book of Gates, the Book of Caverns; the Book of the Earth; the Books of the Night and Day; and the Awakening of Osiris and the Transit of the Solar Barques.

Cosmological books were employed in the Valley of the Kings to magically activate the tomb as a functioning, three-dimensional model of the divine world. This realm was identified broadly as the Duat (*dw3.t*), divided into "upper" (*ḥrj.t*) and "lower" (*ẖrj.t*) regions, the limits of which were defined by the diurnal and nocturnal course of the sun through the sky (east to west by day, west to east by night) and by the course of the stars (north and south). The Duat included both the visible heavens and a hidden region that was conceived simultaneously as inside the visible sky and beneath the earth, as a literal underworld. The interface between the visible and hidden realms was a sort of horizon, known as the Akhet (*3ḥ.t*). Most of the cosmographic books conclude with a representation of this interface as a great, semicircular border, which served also as a concise summary of the entire solar journey (Hornung 1981).

The Twelve-hour Cosmographic Tradition

The cosmographic Books of the Underworld and Sky fall into two broad groups, based on the way in which their texts and illustrations partition the various regions of the divine world. The earliest attested tradition approaches this problem from the perspective of solar time, dividing the Duat into twelve sections that correspond to the regions traversed in sequence by the sun god, through each of the twelve hours of the night or day. In this tradition, the sun appears most often as a ram-headed (nocturnal) or falcon-headed (diurnal) man inside the solar barque, accompanied by various gods. The specific crew of the barque varies from book to book, hour by hour, adapting to face the ever-changing topography and dangers of the solar journey. The barque itself also transforms from its evening form (*mskt.t*) to its morning form (*mᶜnḏ.t*), as the sun god travels from night to day and back again. The twelve-hour compositions typically divide the individual regions or hours into three horizontal registers, while the Book of the Day employs a unique system of five registers throughout. In all cases, the middle register represents the path traveled by the sun, over water or land, while the upper and lower registers correspond to the "two shores" (*jdb.wy*) that flank the sun's path on the left and right.

Book of Amduat

The so-called Book of Amduat (ed. Hornung 1963–1967, 1987–1994; Warburton, Hornung, and Abt 2007) derives its modern designation from the general nomenclature for the cosmographic genre, as a book of "That which is in the Duat." However, the ancient Egyptians referred to this book specifically by the title *sš nj ᶜ.t jmnt.t*, "Writing for the Hidden Chamber." The "chamber" in question refers to the physical sarcophagus hall, in which the earliest known copies were inscribed, as well as to a mythological locale in the depths of the underworld, where the sun god unites with the god of the dead, Osiris. The title sequence goes on to stress the importance of knowledge (*rḫ*) concerning the transformations of the sun, the forms and attributes of the gods and various spirits, the topography of the divine world, and the gates that divide the hours. In some tombs, a "short version" of the text was appended as a sort of coda to the main composition. In the reign of Tutankhamun and later, select hours from the Amduat were employed frequently in place of the whole book (see Table 21.3).

The Amduat is the earliest attested underworld book, appearing first in the early Eighteenth Dynasty, under Hatshepsut (KV 20). However, mounting evidence from royal tomb architecture and private magical iconography suggests that certain hours and episodes might have existed in some form already from the mid- to late Twelfth Dynasty (Rößler-Köhler 1999; Gestermann 1999; Wegner 2009; Roberson 2009). The Amduat is also the most widely attested and, arguably, most influential cosmographic book. Thus, all of the subsequent Books of the Underworld and Sky include select localities, beings, and themes present already in this earliest "Writing for the Hidden Chamber."

The central theme of the Amduat is the sun's death at sunset and the ensuing nocturnal journey from the western horizon toward his ultimate rebirth at sunrise, in the east. As the sun enters the underworld, he assumes the guise of Re-Atum, whose ram's head puns on the homophonous Egyptian words for "ram" and "soul" (*b3*). In addition to the sun god, the usual crew aboard the solar barque consists of nine deities: "Opener of Ways" (*wp w3.wt*), "Flesh" (*jwf*), "Vigilance" (*nhs*), "Perception" (*sj3*), "Speech" (*ḥw*), "Lady of the Barque" (*nb.t wj3*), "Controller of the Barque" (*ḥrp wj3*), "Bull of Ma'at" (*k3 m3ꜥ.t*), and "Horus who praises" (*ḥrw ḥknw*). Additional deities supplement this basic crew in select hours, for example, Nephthys (hour 2), Isis (hours 2 and 7), and "Elder Magic" (*ḥk3 šmsw*, hour 7). From the seventh hour onward, the sun god is encircled also

Table 21.3 Occurrences of the Book of *Amduat* in the Valley of the Kings

Dyn. 18	Thutmose I / Hatshepsut (KV 38 / 20: <u>complete?</u>). Thutmose III (KV 34: <u>complete</u> + "short version"). Amenhotep II (KV 35: <u>complete</u> + "short version"). Amenhotep III (KV 22: <u>complete</u> + "short version"). Tutankhamun (KV 62: <u>Hour 1</u>; third gilded shrine). Ay (KV 23: <u>Hour 1</u>).
Dyn. 19	Seti I (KV 17: <u>Hours 1–7, 9–11</u> + "short version"). Ramesses II (KV 7: <u>Hours 1–2, 4–8, 12</u> + "short version"). Merneptah (KV 8: <u>Hours 3–5, 10–11</u>; sarcophagi: <u>Hours 2–3, 5, 7–8, 11</u>). Amenmesse (KV 10: <u>Hours 4–5</u>). Seti II (KV 15: <u>Hours 2–5</u>). Siptah (KV 47: <u>Hours 4–5+</u>).
Dyn. 20	Setnakht (KV 14: <u>Hours 6–9</u>). Ramesses III (KV 11: <u>Hours 4–5</u>; sarcophagus: <u>Hours 7–8</u>). Ramesses IV (KV 2: <u>Hours 6, 9</u>). Ramesses VI (KV 9: <u>Hours 1–11</u>). Ramesses IX (KV 6: <u>Hours 2–3</u>).

by the protective serpent Mehen (*mḥn*, the "coiled one; encircler"). In hours 1, 5, 6, and 12, the solar barque encounters various scarab figures, alluding to the "transformation" (*ḫpr*) of the sun generally, while anticipating his ultimate rebirth in the morning, as Khepry (*ḫpry*).

The nocturnal solar journey, as depicted in the Amduat, unfolds in three distinct phases. After its initial entry in the first hour, the solar barque travels through hours 2 and 3 along a great waterway in the middle register, past files of praising deities who inhabit a bountiful marshland known as Wernes (*wrns*). The second phase of the journey begins in hour 4, where the waterway yields to the desert wasteland of Rosetau (*r₃-sṯꜣw*, the "gateway of dragging") and the solar barque transforms into a serpent, which must be towed by means of ropes across the sandy expanse. The sun's path then plunges down a precipitous, sloping corridor that evokes the physical architecture of the royal tomb itself. In the fifth hour, the boat is hauled across a great, pyramidal hill that conceals the "secret path of the Land of Sokar" (*w₃.t št₃.t n.t t₃ skr*), a liminal zone so profound that even the sun dares not enter. Beneath the god Sokar in the lower register, the waters of chaos (*nnw*) churn at the border of the ordered cosmos. In the final phase of the journey (hours 6–12), the solar barque resumes its normal form as it sails toward the moment of sunrise. This phase commences from the sun's union with Osiris in the sixth hour. This consummate reaffirmation of the divine order results, on the one hand, in the joyous salutations of the properly equipped and justified spirits (hours 8, and 9) and the blessed Drowned (hour 10), and in the punishment of the Damned and slaughter of the archfiend Apep (hours 7, 11, and 12), on the other. In the twelfth hour, immediately prior to sunrise, the solar barque is hauled through the body of a great serpent, from tail to head, reversing the course of time (Hornung 1999, 41), such that the gods "enter. . . as venerated ones" (i.e., deceased; *ꜥq=sn . . . m jm₃ḥy.w*) but "emerge as solar children, daily" (*pr=sn m ḥwnw.w Rꜥ rꜥ nb*).

Spell of Twelve Caverns

The Spell of Twelve Caverns (ed. Piankoff and Jacquet-Gordon 1974), also known as the "Book of *Quererets*" (from *qrr.wt*, "caverns"), must be distinguished from the so-called Book of Caverns, discussed below. The former composition was known in antiquity as the "Spell [to enable] the Osiris so-and-so (i.e., the deceased) to enter." The spell consists of four basic elements: one or more images of the deceased, including names and titles; an introductory text identifying the respective caverns, twelve in number; representations of the various deities inhabiting each cavern and their names; and an offering text (Piankoff and Jacquet-Gordon 1974, 44–45). The Spell of Twelve Caverns was employed both as an independent book and in conjunction with the Book of the Dead, as spell 168, according to the modern numbering system. Only one example has been discovered so far in the Valley of the Kings, from the Eighteenth Dynasty tomb of

Amenhotep II (KV 35), on a papyrus inscribed for the king and placed inside a wooden statue.

Book of Gates

No ancient title referring specifically or exclusively to the Book of Gates (Hornung 1979–1980; Zeidler 1999; Hornung and Abt 2014) has been found. The modern designation refers to the twelve "gates" or "portals" (*sbḫ.wt*) that separate the various regions of the Duat. These portals appear as towering doors that span the height of all three registers. A gigantic serpent rises up from the bottom of the door leaf, balancing on its tail, while the head peers threateningly over the top of the gate itself. Starting from the second hour, each of the gates is protected also by a pair of crenelated fortifications, surmounted by fire-spitting cobras and surrounded by files of mummiform deities. The function of the gates is to bar access into and out of the divine world, thereby ensuring that all beings—living, dead, divine, justified, and damned—remain in their correct places. Of course, the sun god passes unhindered through each of these barriers. The Book of Gates extends this privilege to the justified deceased, as both companion and hypostasis of the solar creator (see Table 21.4).

The Book of Gates represents a clear development from the earlier Amduat tradition, overlapping significantly with that work in its presentation of the sun god's twelve-hour journey through the underworld. Thus, even the twelve, eponymous gates were mentioned already in the earlier book, although the names of the individual portals vary, and the towering gates themselves were not yet illustrated. Other themes, such as the ubiquitous jubilation in response to the solar presence, the union of Re and Osiris (hour 6), the provisioning of the blessed dead (hours 2–4), the punishment of the damned (hours 2, 5, 7, and 9) and Apep (hours 3, 5, 6, 10, and 11), and the sun's emergence from

Table 21.4 Occurrences of the Book of Gates in the Valley of the Kings (Hour numbers following Hornung 1979–80)

Dyn. 18	Horemheb (KV 57: Hours 2–6).
Dyn. 19	Ramesses I (KV 16: Hours 3–4). Seti I (KV 17: Hours 2–3, 5–6; sarcophagus: complete). Ramesses II (KV 7: Hours 2–5; sarcophagus: Hours 8, 9, 11, concluding image). Merenptah (KV 8: Hours 3–6, 9, concluding image; sarcophagi: Hours 1–3). Amenmesse (KV 10: Hours 5–6). Tausret (KV 14: Hours 9–11).
Dyn. 20	Setnakht (KV 14: Hours 9, 12). Ramesses III (KV 11: Hours 5–7+; sarcophagus: opening scene). Ramesses IV (KV 2: Hours 2–4). Ramesses VI (KV 9: complete). Ramesses VII (KV 1: Hours 1–2).

the curved horizon at dawn (hour 12), all echo episodes from the Amduat. However, the specific sequences of events, the identities of the participants, and iconographic details vary considerably.

One of the most obvious departures from the Amduat tradition is the considerably diminished crew of the solar boat, which includes only Sia and Heka, the personified divine faculties of "Perception" and "Magic," respectively. Also, whereas the Amduat depicts the ram-headed sun god standing either inside a shrine or encircled by the serpent Mehen, the Book of Gates combines these features. Here, the serpent wraps its body in great, spiral coils around the solar shrine, a striking evocation of the creature's identity as the "encircler" or "coiled one" (*mḥn*). Another major departure from the Amduat is the omission of the Cavern of Sokar from the fifth hour and the insertion of a unique version of the Judgment Hall of Osiris, expanding on themes present already in spell 125 from the Book of the Dead. In addition, the Book of Gates omits the Amduat's instructions for the spiral distribution of scenes around the points of the compass (see ch 12), opting instead for a simple linear progression through the twelve hours of the night.

Books of the Night and Day

Like the Book of Nut, the Book of the Night (Roulin 1996) and Book of the Day (Müller-Roth 2008) employ representations of the sky goddess Nut as their principal illustration. For this reason, modern scholars often group these three books together as "Books of the Sky," in contrast to the various "Books of the Underworld" (Hornung 1999, 112). However, unlike the Nut book, the Books of the Night and Day also include register systems illustrating the sun's path (three registers in the former book, five in the latter), as well as illustrations and descriptions of the solar barque and its crew, the twelvefold division of the celestial regions by hour, the gates that divide these regions, and the punishment of the Damned (see Table 21.5).

Table 21.5 Occurrences of the Books of the Night and Day in the Valley of the Kings

Dyn. 19	Night	Merenptah (KV8).
Dyn. 20	Night	Ramesses IV (KV 2). Ramesses VI (KV 9). Ramesses IX (KV 6, vignette only).
	Day	Ramesses VI (KV 9). Ramesses IX (KV 6, vignette only).

The Bipartite Cosmographic Tradition

The bipartite cosmographic tradition includes a variety of compositions that depart from the twelvefold, hourly division of the divine world in favor of a more general division into two, generally symmetrical sections. Another trend evident in most of the bipartite books is the frequent omission of the solar barque and its crew. In its place, the ram-headed sun god often stands directly on the register line, accompanied in many cases by a red (i.e., nocturnal) solar disk. Occasionally, the god stands inside the disk itself, as a somewhat more "naturalistic" variation on the barque motif. It may be significant that this new emphasis on the solar disk occurs first in the Books of the Solar-Osirian Unity from the tomb of Tutankhamun, immediately following the icono-clastic interlude of Akhenaten.

Books of the Solar-Osirian Unity

The so-called Books of the Solar-Osirian Unity (BSOU; ed. Darnell 2004), identified in antiquity by the generic designation of "Amduat" (Darnell 2004, 38), are united by their shared emphasis on the nocturnal union of the sun god and Osiris. As a result of this union, the composite deity Re-Osiris emerges as a gigantic, register- and cosmos-spanning figure, whose head reaches the "upper region" (*ḥry.t*) of the sky and whose feet extend to the deepest pit of the underworld, the "place of destruction" (*ḥtmy.t*), where the Damned are nullified. In each book, the giant deity dominates the composition as its largest figure, in conjunction with various concluding representa-tions depicting sunrise from the eastern horizon and the fiery destruction of the ene-mies of order. The scenes and texts also make frequent reference to the inverted entry of spirits into the netherworld and their subsequent "turning upright" (*pnꜥ*), in contrast to the Damned, who remain "upside down" (*sḥd*). Another characteristic feature of the BSOU is its use of the cryptographic script for a vast majority of texts. Cryptography is present to a greater or lesser degree in most books from the cosmographic tradition, as well as the Book of Nut, and others. However, the ubiquity of this feature in the BSOU is unparalleled, hence the frequent modern designation of these works as "Enigmatic" (Darnell 2004, 6–13; Hornung 1999, 77–78, see Table 21.6).

Table 21.6 Occurrences of the Book of the Solar-Osirian Unity in the Valley of the Kings

Dyn. 18	Tutankhamun (KV 62, second gilded shrine).
Dyn. 20	Ramesses VI (KV 9).
	Ramesses IX (KV 6).

Apart from these shared thematic and orthographic features, perhaps the most striking feature of the BSOU is their lack of standardization. Of the three versions attested in the Valley of the Kings, no two duplicate even a single scene or text in its entirety, although they do make apparent allusions to one another, as well as to other books from the cosmographic tradition (Darnell 2004, 450–453).

Book of Caverns

Similar to books from the twelve-hour tradition, the Book of Caverns (ancient title unknown; ed. Werning 2008) also exhibits an ideal, fixed layout for the various divisions of the Duat. However, unlike the former tradition, the Book of Caverns splits the underworld into halves, subdivided into three sections each, for a total of six divisions. The annotations identify these divisions as *qrr.(w)t*, or "caverns," as found already in the "Spell of Twelve Caverns," discussed above. Each of the two greater halves begins with a large figure of the sun god, who stands apart from the horizontal register system that governs the other figures, in a vertical column reminiscent of the portal-divisions from the Book of Gates. Additional "giant" figures include upright serpents in the fourth and fifth caverns (again reminiscent of the Book of Gates), and symmetrically opposed figures of the sky goddess Nut and the earth god Geb, also in the fifth cavern. In all of the caverns, the lower register is devoted primarily or entirely to the punishment of the Damned (see Table 21.7).

Many textual and iconographic elements in the Book of Caverns parallel other books from both the bipartite and twelve-hour cosmographic traditions. Thus, for example, the giant figure of Nut (division five) and the frequent appearance of gods in sarcophagi and burial mounds find close parallels in the Book of the Earth; the double-headed sphinx Aker, the encircling of the sun god by a tail-biting serpent, and a similarly encircled, ithyphallic Osiris (division three) recall similar figures from the fifth hour of the Amduat and the Book of the Earth; the use of giant, register-spanning gods is reminiscent of the giant figures in the Books of the Solar-Osirian Unity; and the curved concluding representation (division six) recalls

Table 21.7 Occurrences of the Book of Caverns in the Valley of the Kings

Dyn. 19	Merenptah (KV 8: <u>concluding image variant</u> = Book of the Earth scene 22). Tausret (KV 14: <u>as Merenptah</u>).
Dyn. 20	Ramesses III (KV 11: <u>as Merenptah</u>). Ramesses IV (KV 2: <u>Divisions 1–3</u>). Ramesses VI (KV 9: <u>complete</u>). Ramesses VII (KV1: <u>Division 1</u>). Ramesses IX (KV 6: <u>Divisions 1–4</u>).

similar images found in most of the other cosmographic books. It is possible that such parallels reflect the direct influence of one book on another. However, it is equally possible that such similarities reflect merely the use of stock imagery and phrases, in conjunction with innovative elements, (re)combined to create distinct compositions.

Books of the Earth

The so-called Books of the Earth (BE; ed. Roberson 2012), referred to also in modern scholarship as the Creation of the Solar Disk and the Book of Aker (ancient title unknown), include collections of discrete episodes from the nocturnal solar journey, arranged on an ad hoc basis, with considerable variation among the numerous sources. However, despite this general lack of systematization, a number of individual texts and scenes, as well as occasional larger groups from the BE corpus, do occur in multiple sources (see Table 21.8).

Like the other bipartite compositions, the BE divides the underworld into two major sections. In the Valley of the Kings, these two sections appear almost exclusively on the opposing sidewalls of the burial chamber, in conjunction with an image of the double sky (including the Books of the Day and Night, the Book of Nut, and "astronomical ceilings") on the ceiling above. The combination of the celestial and terrestrial images creates a striking evocation of the solar cycle: the sun sets, swallowed by the western sky, then descends through the first half of the Book of the Earth, ascending through the

Table 21.8 Occurrences of the Book of the Earth in the Valley of the Kings (scene numbers following Roberson 2012)

Dyn. 19	Merneptah (KV 8: Scenes 2, 19, 20, 22, 38, 65, 68). Siptah (KV 47 sarcophagus: Scenes 8, 12, 52, 56). Tausret (KV 14: as Merenptah).
Dyn. 20	Setnakht (KV 14 sarcophagus: Scene 56). Ramesses III (KV 11: as Merenptah + Scenes 25, 45, 55, 56, 69, 70; sarcophagus: Scenes 8, 12, 26, 41, 52, 56, 57). Ramesses IV (KV 2: Scene 2; sarcophagus: Scenes 12, 26, 41, 57, 56). Ramesses VI (KV 9: Scenes 1, 2, 3, 4, 5, 6, 7, 8, 9, 10, 13, 14, 15, 16, 17, 18, 19, 20, 24, 25, 26, 27, 28, 30, 31, 32, 33, 35, 38, 40, 43, 44, 47, 48, 49, 51, 53, 55, 56, 58, 64, 63, 66, 67, 68, 70, 72, 74, 75, 76, 77, 78; sarcophagus: as Ramesses III). Ramesses VII (KV 1: Scenes 11, 12, 21, 23, 29, 33, 34, 37, 49, 50, 59, 61, 62, 76, 79, 80). Ramesses IX (KV 6: Scenes 12, 19, 29, 36, 37, 39, 42, 46, 47, 52, 54, 60, 61, 71, 73, 75).

second half, before rising in the east to traverse the sky on the ceiling above, repeating the cycle in perpetuity.

The Awakening of Osiris and the Transit of the Solar Barques

Like many of the other works discussed above, the Awakening of Osiris and the Transit of the Solar Barques (AOTSB; ed. Roberson 2013) is attested first in the cenotaph of Seti I at Abydos, prior to its appearance in the tombs of the Valley of the Kings. The AOTSB represents the most concise exemplar from the cosmographic tradition, consisting of two complementary images, arranged one above the other. In the lower register, Horus, in the guise of the king, extends the hieroglyph for "life" (*ꜥnḫ*) toward the nose of his father, the prone, mummiform god Osiris, who is labeled as "awake" (*rs*). Surrounding these major deities, thirty-six smaller figures, including the four canopic genies, their tutelary goddesses, and a host of minor divinities, flank the central scene. Numerous scholars, such as Waitkus, Quack, and von Lieven (see Roberson 2013, 130–131, n. 610) have noted that the number of these minor gods might correspond to the thirty-six decan star groups, alluding perhaps to the hour vigil that was held on behalf of the deceased prior to final interment (see Table 21.9).

Immediately above the Awakening scene, the upper register depicts the transit of the sun, in the company of the king and the goddess Maʾat, through the visible sky. At the center of the scene, the evening barque and its crew meets the day barque, prow-to-prow. On the edge of the tableau, hieroglyphic emblems and other texts label the eastern and western horizons, in conjunction with twenty-four gods of the "northern" (*mḥ.t*) and "southern" (*rs.t*) skies. The explicit directionality of the scene defines the four quarters of the sky and the limits of the cosmos, as understood in Egyptian terms. A winged sun disk hovers at the top of the composition, emitting light in the form of "life" (*ꜥnḫ*) and "stability" (*ḏd*) hieroglyphs onto an emblem designating the "union of the Two Lands" (*sm3-t3.wy*). This last sign sits between the prows of the day- and night-barques, in the upper register, and directly above the awakened Osiris, in the register below. In this way, the AOTSB offers a compact summary of the entire cosmological genre, whereby the sun's daily circuit links and sustains the celestial and terrestrial realms, being perpetuated through the nightly union of Re and Osiris and the transmission of kingship from the latter, deceased god to the living king, as Horus.

Table 21.9 Occurrences of the Awakening of Osiris and the Transit of the Solar Barques in the Valley of the Kings

Dyn. 20	Ramesses VI (KV 9).
	Ramesses IX (KV 6).

BIBLIOGRAPHY

Abitz, F. 1995. *Pharao als Gott in den Unterweltsbüchern des Neuen Reiches*. Orbis Biblicus et Orientalis 146. Freiburg and Göttingen.

Allen, T. G. 1974. *The Book of the Dead or Going Forth by Day: Ideas of the Ancient Egyptians Concerning the Hereafter as Expressed in Their Own Terms*. Studies in Ancient Oriental Civilization 37. Chicago.

Barta, W. 1985. *Die Bedeutung der Jenseitsbücher für den verstorbenen König*. Münchner ägyptologische Studien 42. Munich, Berlin.

Barta, W. 1994. *Komparative Untersuchungen zu vier Unterweltsbüchern*. Münchener Ägyptologische Untersuchungen 1. Frankfurt, Bern, New York, Paris.

Darnell, J. 2004. *The Enigmatic Netherworld Books of the Solar Osirian Unity: Cryptographic Compositions in the Tombs of Tutankhamun, Ramesses VI and Ramesses IX*. Orbis Biblicus et Orientalis 198. Freiburg and Göttingen.

Gardiner, A. H. 1938. "The House of Life." *Journal of Egyptian Archaeology* 24: 157–179.

Gestermann, L. 1999. "Königliche Vorstellungen zu Grab und Jenseits im Mittleren Reich, Teil II: Osirisgräber des Mittleren Reiches in königlichen Kontext: Amduat, 6. Stunde." In *Das frühe ägyptische Königtum: Akten des 2. Symposiums zur ägyptischen Königsideologie in Wien*, edited by R. Gundlach and W. Seipel, 97–110. Wiesbaden.

Gundlach, R., and W. Seipel, eds. 1999. *Das frühe ägyptische Königtum: Akten des 2. Symposiums zur ägyptischen Königsideologie in Wien*. Wiesbaden.

Hornung, E. 1963–1967. *Das Amduat: Die Schrift des Verborgenen Raumes*. 3 vols. Wiesbaden.

Hornung, E. 1975–1976. *Das Buch der Anbetung des Re im Westen (Sonnenlitanei): Nach den Versionen des Neuen Reiches*. 2 vols. Aegyptiaca Helvetica 2–3. Geneva.

Hornung, E. 1979–1980. *Das Buch von den Pforten des Jenseits*. 2 vols. Aegyptiaca Helvetica 7–8. Geneva.

Hornung, E. 1981. "Zu den Schlusszenen der Unterweltsbücher." *Mitteilungen des Deutschen Archäologischen Instituts, Abteilung Kairo* 37: 217–226.

Hornung, E. 1982. *Der ägyptische Mythos von der Himmelskuh: Eine Ätiologie des Unvollkommenen*. Orbis Biblicus et Orientalis 46. Freiburg and Göttingen.

Hornung, E. 1987–1994. *Texte zum Amduat*. 3 vols. Aegyptiaca Helvetica 13–15. Geneva.

Hornung, E. 1999. *The Ancient Egyptian Books of the Afterlife*. Translated from the German by D. Lorton. Ithaca, NY and London.

Hornung, E., and T. Abt. 2014. *The Egyptian Book of Gates*. Zurich.

Lloyd, A. B., ed. 1992. *Studies in Pharaonic Religion and Society in Honour of J. Gwyn Griffiths*. London.

Müller-Roth, M. 2008. *Das Buch vom Tage*. Orbis Biblicus et Orientalis 236. Freiburg and Göttingen.

Naville, E. 1886. *Das aegyptische Todtenbuch der XVIII. bis XX Dynastie aus verschiedenen Urkunden zusammengestellt*. Berlin.

Parkinson, R., and S. Quirke. 1992. "The Coffin of Prince Herunefer and the Early History of the Book of the Dead." In *Studies in Pharaonic Religion and Society in Honour of J. Gwyn Griffiths*, edited by A. B. Lloyd, 37–51. London.

Piankoff, A., and H. Jacquet-Gordon. 1974. *The Wandering of the Soul*. Bollingen Series XL 6. Princeton, NJ.

Quirke, S. 2013. *Going out in Daylight—prt m hrw: The Ancient Egyptian Book of the Dead; Translations, Sources, Meanings*. GHP Egyptology 20. London.

Roberson, J. 2009. "The Early History of 'New Kingdom' Netherworld Iconography: A Late Middle Kingdom Apotropaic Wand Reconsidered." In *Archaism and Innovation: Studies in the Culture of Middle Kingdom Egypt*, edited by D. P. Silverman, W. K. Simpson, and J. Wegner, 427–445. New Haven, CT and Philadelphia.

Roberson, J. 2012. *The Ancient Egyptian Books of the Earth*. Wilbour Studies in Egypt and Ancient Western Asia 1. Atlanta, GA.

Roberson, J. 2013. *The Awakening of Osiris and the Transit of the Solar Barques: Royal Apotheosis in a Most Concise Book of the Underworld and Sky*, Orbis Biblicus et Orientalis 262. Freiburg and Göttingen.

Rößler-Köhler, U. 1999. "Königliche Vorstellungen zu Grab und Jenseits im Mittleren Reich, Teil I: Ein 'Gottesbegräbnis' des Mittleren Reiches in königlichem Kontext: Amduat 4. und 5. Stunde." In *Das frühe ägyptische Königtum: Akten des 2. Symposiums zur ägyptischen Königsideologie in Wien*, edited by R. Gundlach and W. Seipel, 73–96. Wiesbaden.

Roulin, G. 1996. *La Livre de la Nuit: Une composition égyptienne de l'au-delà*. 2 vols. Orbis Biblicus et Orientalis 147. Freiburg and Göttingen.

Silverman, D. P., W. K. Simpson, and J. Wegner, eds. 2009. *Archaism and Innovation: Studies in the Culture of Middle Kingdom Egypt*. New Haven, CT and Philadelphia.

von Lieven, A. 2007. *Grundriss des Laufes der Sterne: Das sogenannte Nutbuch*. 2 vols. The Carlsberg Papyri 8. Copenhagen.

Warburton, D., E. Hornung, and T. Abt. 2007. *The Egyptian Amduat: The Book of the Hidden Chamber*. Zurich.

Wegner, J. 2009. "The Tomb of Senwosret III at Abydos and Considerations on the Development of the Royal Amduat-Tomb." In *Archaism and Innovation: Studies in the Culture of Middle Kingdom Egypt*, edited by D. P. Silverman, W. K. Simpson, and J. Wegner, 103–169. New Haven, CT and Philadelphia.

Wiebach-Koepke, S. 2007. *Sonnenlauf und kosmische Regeneration: Zur Systematik der Lebensprozesse in den Unterweltsbüchern*. Ägypten und altes Testament 71. Wiesbaden.

Wente, E. 1982. "Mysticism in Pharaonic Egypt?" *Journal of Near Eastern Studies* 41: 161–179.

Werning, D. 2008. *Das Höhlenbuch. Textkritische Edition und Textgrammatik*. 2 vols. Göttinger Orientforschungen 48. Wiesbaden.

Zeidler, J. 1999. *Pfortenbuchstudien*. 2 vols. Göttinger Orientforschungen 36. Wiesbaden.

PART IX

DESTRUCTION, DESECRATION, AND REUSE

CHAPTER 22

DAMNATIO MEMORIAE IN THE VALLEY OF THE KINGS

RICHARD H. WILKINSON

ALTHOUGH the literal meaning of the Latin phrase *damnatio memoriae* does not extend beyond "condemnation of memory," the goal of the phenomenon, where it is applied, is to erase all records and sometimes the tangible works of an individual from history. This is usually the result of either criminal or heretical acts of the individual attacked or the desire of the individual's successors to discount the targeted individual's legitimacy and to enhance their own legitimation at the personal or dynastic level.

The monuments of an individual thus sanctioned by *damnatio* were natural targets for varying degrees of destruction—from total destruction at worst, to selective destruction or, where usurpation[1] was involved, the careful reattribution of the monuments through replacement of the individual's names, titles, or images. In the Valley of the Kings (KV), although the phenomenon is not a common one, the results of *damnatio* are apparent in a number of royal tombs known to have suffered this kind of treatment. The phenomenon has received little study except in terms of the subjects of *damnatio*, however (Hari 1984), and there is less clear evidence for it in the KV than might be expected. In some cases, the destruction may not be officially and fully perpetrated—a situation in which the phrase *de facto damnatio memoriae* is sometimes used; but the known examples in the KV do seem to have been conducted officially, although not always thoroughly.

While a complete enacting of *damnatio* would theoretically remove all traces of an individual and render the subject invisible to later viewers, no such level of destruction appears to have been enacted within the KV, though this may not have been for the want of trying. On the other hand, *damnatio* was sometimes selectively applied. For example, although the names and images of Hatshepsut as king were widely destroyed after her reign, depictions of her as queen were unharmed (Dorman 2005, 267). Even when images and names of individual rulers were quite thoroughly hacked away, the Egyptians usually avoided desecration of adjacent divine images and texts, or of other non-proscribed persons, so the total destruction of a proscribed tomb is not known in the KV. Even in what appear to be systematically effaced monuments, the destruction is invariably incomplete. For example, the Egyptians seem to have felt that the consistent erasure of cartouches in long running texts was less important than those accompanying a representation of the proscribed individual (Reeves 1990, 87, n. 136).

There is thus a range of damage involved in the known examples of *damnatio* in the KV. In some cases the desecration is obvious, but in other cases it is uncertain exactly to what degree, or even if, *damnatio* was involved. This range of possibilities and the resultant uncertainties may be seen in a brief survey of some of the relevant tombs.

TOMBS HISTORICALLY ASSOCIATED
WITH *DAMNATIO*

The following tombs,[2] listed in chronological order, represent monuments where some degree of *damnatio* occurred or may have occurred. In some cases (such as KV 20—the tomb of Hatshepsut, and KV 10—the tomb of Amenmesse) the possibility is mentioned only because it has been put forward in the published literature on the KV, although the actual situation may be more complex or uncertain than has been believed. Even including tombs where *damnatio* "may have occurred," the total number of affected monuments is only seven—representing a scant 11 percent of the total number of tombs in the royal valley.

KV 20—Hatshepsut: Although the kingly monuments of Hatshepsut suffered desecration some years after her death, the destruction seems to have been limited to some degree and does not seem to have been extended to her tomb, KV 20. However, although there is no evidence that the tomb of Hatshepsut ever suffered desecration (Dorman 2005, 267), such action may not have been necessary beyond the removal of the queen's body, both because the tomb was not in public view and because KV 20 was undecorated. This situation also raises the question to what degree *damnatio* would be visible in an undecorated tomb. One would expect that at least the tomb goods might be destroyed or removed, but in tombs that were anciently—and sometimes frequently—plundered or vandalized, this might not always be clear.

KV 55—Amarna Era: The uncertainties still surrounding the history of this tomb and its erstwhile Amarna era owner/s make analysis in the context of *damnatio* difficult if not impossible. Yet it is clear that the cartouches removed from some of the objects found within KV 55 are the result of some type of removal of evidence of ownership (Reeves 1990, 44). Once again we are limited by the total lack of parietal inscriptions and the evidence that their effacement would supply.

KV 23—Ay: The tomb of Ay remains the clearest example we have of what might be termed normative *damnatio* and as such it is considered in detail in the next section. But even in this monument the desecration was not entirely total—some of the cartouches on the sarcophagus were not erased, though that may have been the unintended result of destruction effected against the tomb before the official *damnatio* was carried out (Wilkinson 2011).

KV 10—**Amenmesse:** The tomb of Amenmesse was long believed to reveal *damnatio* in the destruction of the representations in the outer corridors, but it is now realized that this is not necessarily the case in that the intrusive burials that led to the tomb's redecoration were of a considerably later date (Reeves 1990, 104 and 113, n. 33). Nevertheless, the memory of "the Enemy" Amenmesse was certainly attacked, though the nature of the evidence makes it difficult to know if some form of destruction of his tomb inscriptions and representations preceded the redecoration associated with the later burials.

KV 13—**Bay:** Although a number of publicly visible monuments depicting the Chancellor Bay were left untouched, some level of *damnatio* was evidently enacted on this individual who was executed for apparently overstepping his position during the reign of Siptah. Certainly, Bay's tomb in the royal valley was not fully completed, and extant inscriptions were erased at some point (Reeves 1990, 133).

KV 47—**Siptah:** Possibly because he was a son of Amenmesse (so, *inter alia*, Aldred 1963, 45, though see Lesko 1966, 31), this king clearly suffered a *damnatio*, and his name was omitted from later records. The evidence of his tomb is difficult to assess, however, as Siptah's names were erased from KV 47 at some point—as they were also from the tomb of Tausret—and replaced with those of Seti II, though in some locations in the tomb of Siptah the king's names were replaced in paint.

KV 14—**Tausret and Sethnakht:** This is another monument that was long considered to have suffered *damnatio* on the images of the female ruler Tausret. However, Hartwig Altenmüller's careful work in this tomb has shown that the situation is not as simple as previously believed (Altenmüller 2012). It is now clear that the extensive changes made to the decoration of KV 14 were not accomplished until after the death of Sethnakht, when it was decided to bury him in Tausret's tomb rather than the one which was in preparation, but not fully ready, for him (KV 11). Only at this point, when the tomb was rededicated to Sethnakht by his son Ramesses III, were the names and images of Tausret apparently removed and replaced by names and depictions of Sethnakht. Nevertheless, the images of Seti II were left in the tomb so that Sethnakht was historically connected to the earlier king without linkage through the intervening Siptah and Tausret. As such, an element of *damnatio* was present, and it is clear that a number of the statues and monuments of Tausret were reinscribed or destroyed and that she was omitted from later king lists.

CASE STUDY: KV 23—THE TOMB OF AY

The clearest example of *damnatio* in a royal tomb in the Valley of the Kings is found in KV 23, the tomb of Ay, and this tomb is closely considered in this chapter as it represents our primary evidence for many aspects of the phenomenon.

Although many details of KV 23's origin and intended ownership are unclear, the tomb was certainly decorated for Ay, the erstwhile servant of Akhenaten and successor to Tutankhamun. A sarcophagus inscribed for Ay was installed in the tomb, and there is some evidence that the burial chamber was also stocked with burial goods, making it likely that Ay was interred there. At some time after the tomb was prepared for Ay, however, the monument was subjected to an extensive *damnatio memoriae* that was likely carried out by the king's immediate successor, Horemheb. The effects of the *damnatio* consisted of the erasure of Ay's names and images—and those of his queen, Tiy—throughout the burial chamber (the only decorated area of the tomb) along with damage to certain other elements of the decoration (Schaden 2000). Although the effacement executed in this tomb represents the clearest case of *damnatio* extant in the royal valley, it has unfortunately received little analysis until only recently, and the primary evidence was itself damaged to the extent of severely limiting any further study when the tomb was prepared for tourism (Wilkinson 2011, 130 n. 10, 131, 146 n. 25).

Although *damnatio*-related damage might be expected to have been leveled only at the names and images of the king, the *damnatio* enacted against Ay's tomb consisted of the infliction of damage on four aspects of its decoration: the names of the king and his queen, the depictions of the king and queen, delimited damage to some of the deities, and two images of the royal *ka* (Figures 22.1 and 22.2). The names of the king and queen were carefully excised from every area of the burial chamber decoration—both from within running columns of texts and from name labels accompanying their

FIGURE 22.1 The king and the royal *ka* before the goddess Nut, southern section of the west wall of the tomb of Ay.

(Photograph by Richard H. Wilkinson)

FIGURE 22.2 The king and royal *ka* before the goddess Hathor, northern section of the west wall of the tomb of Ay.

(Photograph by Richard H. Wilkinson)

representations. The king's names were also erased from his sarcophagus except for a few exceptions that may be adequately explained (Wilkinson 2011, 134), yet the *serekh* names of Ay were untouched in the banners above the heads of both royal *ka* figures depicted in the tomb. Likewise, all the depictions of Ay and the single image of Tiy that had been painted in the king's burial chamber were attacked and heavily damaged, although erasures of these images were rarely, if ever, complete, in the sense that some areas of the king's body were often ignored. This may have been due to the necessary time and work that total erasure of all the body surface areas would have involved, though, as will be seen, it is perhaps more likely due to an understanding that only certain key areas of the royal figures needed to be destroyed for their symbolic destruction to be totally effective. Because it represents our single clearest example of *damnatio* in the KV, the destruction carried out in this tomb is examined in detail.

Symbolic Aspects of Destruction

When the damaged areas of plaster in KV 23 were carefully examined in a recent study (Wilkinson 2011), it was possible to differentiate between areas of natural plaster fall (some patches doubtless having fallen as a result of the pounding on the tomb's walls in the process of chiseling away nearby names and images) and areas that had actually been damaged by consciously applied chisel cuts. This fact revealed a number of aspects of the symbolic dimension of the *damnatio* leveled against various elements of the tomb decoration.

Figures of the King

Differentiation between the two types of plaster damage (fallen/cut) in the tomb of Ay showed that in most cases the face (though often not the whole head) of the king was hacked away, as was at least a good section of the shoulders and upper torso, along with the lower arms. The lower torso was often untouched, though a section of the lower abdomen through the upper thighs was invariably attacked. The lower legs were often undamaged. Damage to these three areas of the representations of Ay varied to only a small extent (as discussed later) and was unmistakably clear in terms of the specific areas of focused destruction. This pattern doubtless reflects a threefold desire:

1. To delete the nose (and hence the breath of life)—a focused point of destruction known from usurped private tombs, though in the case of royal images there was probably also a desire to remove the personal appearance of the individual;
2. To delete the heart (as this was viewed by the Egyptians as the receptacle of the spirit);
3. To remove the genital area (and hence, symbolically, the power of procreation).

Images of Gods

Although images of the gods were rarely the targets of destruction in Egypt (beyond, of course, in the purge of Amun's names and images conducted by Akhenaten), we do find evidence of *damnatio* affecting divine images in the tomb of Ay as the result of what might be termed "collateral *damnatio*," in which images of gods are not the subjects of the condemnation, but are nonetheless affected by it—even beyond accidental damage.

In the tomb of Ay, the figure of the goddess Nut depicted near the center of the rear wall of the burial chamber bears damage that appears to be deliberate and that must be considered carefully. The representation of the goddess is intact except for two small sections of lightly cut plaster—one at each wrist (Figure 22.3). This unusual cutting of a deity may best be explained in that the goddess is shown performing an invocation gesture as she welcomes the king into the afterlife. The figure may be seen as a rebus—the streams of refreshing water that pour from her hands are depicted in the form of the hieroglyph *n* (representing water), which may be read prepositionally as "to," along with the figure of the goddess herself, which acts as the subject "I," the whole rebus reading

FIGURE 22.3 The goddess Nut with cuts at wrists, southern section of the west wall of the tomb of Ay.

(Photograph by Richard H. Wilkinson)

n.i n.i "[come] to me, [come] to me." But the king is denied the goddess's invocation and blessing by means of the small cuts that symbolically sever her hands and the blessing they impart. It is interesting that the cuts were actually made to the wrists of the goddess and that the water hieroglyphs were not simply excised, though it may have been felt that the goddess's gesture would still have remained and that it too needed to be nullified. On the other hand, in the nearby representation of a goddess holding an *ankh* to the king's nose (Figure 22.2), only the *ankh* itself is hacked away and the figure of the goddess remains virtually untouched, though this difference in approach may be explained (as we will see in the following section).

   Damage also seems to have been incurred by the figure of the seated Osiris on this same wall, as the god and the king were shown in direct proximity with the king embracing the mummiform deity. But in this case, it is clear that the figure of the deity was simply damaged collaterally in areas around the destroyed depiction of the king. Nevertheless, the fact that the images of the gods could—and apparently did—receive damage or minor excision, as seen in the images of Nut and Osiris, has direct relevance to another class of figure depicted in the tomb of Ay—that of the royal *ka*.

The Royal *Ka*

Although all of the representations of Ay as king in KV 23 were heavily damaged, usually across a great part of the body, the two figures representing his royal *ka* were treated differently. Both figures received a focused area of damage on the region of the lower abdomen (plaster fall makes this area of damage look larger than it was on one of the figures). One *ka* figure was damaged in a focused area of the chest, while the other received only very slight damage there. One figure was damaged in the area of the face while the face of the other figure was untouched (cf. Figures 22.1 and 22.2). This lack of thorough damage coverage may have been due to an understanding of the wider identity of the royal *ka*, for according to Egyptian kingship ideology the royal *ka* included not only the *ka* of the deceased king, but also those of his cumulative ancestors. Thus Ay's *ka* figures may have been left largely undamaged out of respect for the royal ancestors fused within them.

But there is a difficulty here. It is not easy to ascertain why even small sections of the *ka* figures were cut if the figures were viewed as protected by virtue of the royal ancestors they also represented. Logically, only two possibilities would seem to present themselves. First, it is possible that the workmen began to cut the figures in error and were quickly stopped by a supervising scribe or official. This might explain the limited nature of the damage to the *ka* figures, though it is difficult to believe that the workmen would not have been instructed in regards to these figures before starting work, and no attempt was made to repair the cut areas. The second possibility is that there was symbolic meaning behind the limited cutting of the *ka* figures. The small, purposefully cut area located on the chest at the level of the heart in both figures is of particular interest in this regard. The shape of the larger chest cut is, in fact, roughly similar to that of the heart hieroglyph. Interestingly, the destroyed figure of the king to the right of the *ka* figure with this heart-shaped cut bears similar damage (Figure 22.1). Although this adjacent image of the king was much more thoroughly hacked across the chest area, it is possible to see a very similarly shaped cut in the same area of the king's chest. Was this the first symbolically important cut—to the all–important heart—that was made to figures singled out for *damnatio*?

In any event, it seems likely that the "heart cuts" made on the two *ka* figures were intentional, and it is possible that they may have represented the symbolic removal of Ay from the composite royal *ka*. The difference in the size and nature of the two heart cuts can easily be accounted for by virtue of different cutting styles of two different workmen, and the damage to the figures adjacent to the two *ka* figures does in fact indicate the activity of different workmen. It is unclear, however, why only one of the two *ka* figures received damage to the face, unless this too is seen as a result of the different styles of individual workmen or that the damage to the one *ka*'s face was contrary to instruction and stopped by a supervising official.

Thus, although they exhibit some differences in the manner of cutting, both *ka* figures were cut at the abdomen and at the heart, and one at the face—precisely the areas attacked in the depictions of the king, though in a much more controlled manner and to a more limited extent perhaps commensurate with the understanding of the composite nature of the royal *ka*. In any event, it seems clear that the damage to the royal *ka* figures indicates a level of controlled or directed desecration being involved in the execution of the *damnatio* beyond a simple hacking away of condemned representations. This fact has obvious implications for our understanding of how *damnatio* was carried out and underscores the value of further study of the details of the destruction.

DECONSTRUCTING DESTRUCTION

Careful analysis of the destroyed representations within the tomb of Ay reveals different degrees and styles of erasure within the general pattern of destruction. The marsh scenes on the east wall of the burial chamber provide a clear example. Exactly the same profile of destruction (and the same chisel width gauged by measured individual cuts in the plaster) that was found in the damage to the royal figures is seen in individual cartouche groups in the area. Cartouches that were roughly excised are associated with depictions of the king that were likewise equally roughly excised—with evidence of the same chisel width cuts and increased incidence of plaster fall. On the other hand, cartouches excised in a more controlled manner are associated with more carefully damaged royal figures that also show decreased incidence of plaster fall and cuts of identical chisel width. The different damage profiles of destroyed royal names and images found in individual sections of walls throughout the burial chamber thus clearly represent the work of different individuals working alongside each other.

Apart from the officials who would have been present to direct the work, the *damnatio* enacted against the names and images of Ay seems to have been carried out by at least four and possibly five workmen. This may be ascertained through the recognition of some four styles of destruction in different parts of the burial chamber and at least four different widths of chisel cuts utilized in the work and associated with the respective styles. Each distinct width of chisel cut doubtless represents an individual workman. Because excision was made only in the relatively soft decorated plaster layer of the tomb walls and the underlying limestone was not cut, it is unlikely that new chisels would have been needed before the work of *damnatio* was completed. This supposition is probably confirmed by the fact that cursory examination of the cuts made in all the tomb's figures did not reveal any noticeable change of blade width within a single figure.

It is also apparent that all of the workmen carrying out the *damnatio* in KV 23 were right–handed and all but one were probably of average height for ancient Egypt. The workmen's right-handedness may be seen in the fact that a right-handed person holds a chisel in the left hand and canted slightly to the right so that it may be more easily struck by the hammer or mallet held in the right hand. As a result, the right side corner of the chisel cut is invariably deeper than the left side. In addition, the right-leaning angle of the chisel means that it will sometimes glance off the wall as it is hit and produce side-slippage cuts away from the area actually being attacked, as may be seen in several areas of the tomb.

In a similar manner, the likelihood that the workmen were of average height can be inferred from the fact that chisel cuts are made directly into a wall surface at about shoulder height (where a chisel is held for optimum control and ease of usage), but will be angled upward in those cuts made above shoulder height and downward in cuts made below that same level.

The workmen assigned the destruction of Ay's names and images had to have stood on some structure or object to reach the depictions and texts, as these are at a good height above the floor surface of the tomb. If they squatted or knelt on the supporting object, the range of chisel cut angles would be at that lower level while if, or when, they stood on the supporting object, there would be a correspondingly higher chisel cut range. But whatever the height of the object a workman squats or stands upon, the fact that an individual utilizing a hammer and chisel indicates his approximate shoulder height in the straight cuts made in the wall surface means that the greater the range between the straight cuts made at shoulder height and the uppermost angled cuts on a given section of the wall, then the longer the arms and greater the relative height of the workman must have been. In the tomb of Ay this simple fact indicates that one workman who worked on a section of the western wall of the burial chamber (that of the king wearing the white crown) was apparently much taller than the others. Probably not coincidentally, the apparent work of that larger individual exhibits deeper than average cutting and more plaster fall.

The analysis of the destruction enacted in KV 23 also indicates that the whole *damnatio* was probably effected quickly and doubtless within a single day. Because the destroyed areas were selective and multiple workmen were involved in the destruction, there is no reason why a long period of work would have been needed. Even a small team of around four or five workmen—as posited earlier—would not need many hours to complete the job. It is likely, in fact, that the crew performing this work was encouraged to work quickly in order to complete the symbolic erasure of the king and to reclose the condemned tomb.

Much can be assessed, therefore, through analysis of the pattern of destruction in KV 23. We can be reasonably sure of details such as the number of individuals that carried out the work, know something of the individual workmen's physical characteristics, and even ascertain something of the individual "styles" utilized by these workmen in the process of destruction. This last aspect is an important one as it shows that the destruction of Ay's names and images was conducted within a range of possibilities and that many specific details were not mandated. Despite a number of uncertainties, through careful study of the mechanics of the destruction we can also recover some elements of the ideology which apparently guided the specifics of the *damnatio*—as may be seen in the case of the royal *ka* figures.

The example of KV 23 has been considered in some detail here as its microhistory (Magnússon, 2006) demonstrates how many aspects of the enacting of a *damnatio* might be understood in a given tomb, and that the deconstruction of this damage is the most profitable viewpoint we have available to us on how the practice of this phenomenon was carried out.

QUESTIONS REMAINING REGARDING *DAMNATIO*

The facts outlined in the preceding paragraphs regarding the destruction enacted in KV 23, the best example we have of *damnatio* in the Valley of the Kings, demonstrate that much can be seen and inferred from the careful study of an individual instance of *damnatio*-inflicted damage if it is examined closely. A number of questions regarding the practice of *damnatio* have been answered by study of this tomb, yet if it had been possible to conduct a full formal study of KV 23 before it was prepared for tourism and much of the evidence lost, many more questions could have been asked and perhaps answered. For example, were more skillful workmen (judged by cutting style) assigned to more ideologically important images? Is there any significance to where the heaviest cutting strikes occurred within given images? And so forth. In any event, although most of the primary evidence of the destruction enacted in KV 23 is now inaccessible, the tomb still represents a clear example of what the proscription of an individual interred in the royal valley entailed.

At the broader level, many other questions remain to be answered regarding the phenomenon of *damnatio* in ancient Egypt. For example, was the process primarily grounded in religious belief—did the monarchial and administrative machinery that commissioned and effected the destruction truly wish to root out every aspect of the targeted king's being at the theological level, or was the primary aim of *damnatio* usually a more delimited political one, a public communication of the condemned's disgrace made at the establishment of a new regime? Both motives could have been present in any given instance, but to what degree? The evidence of KV 23 certainly indicates that religious concerns were heavily involved, yet this tomb shows that even depictions of the gods could be subject to damage in order for a *damnatio* to be completely executed.

Another question that we cannot yet answer is to what extent were the details of how *damnatio* was carried out controlled by a central vision? We do not know if, or to what extent, there was an established and detailed procedure regarding how a tomb that had been singled out for *damnatio* should be desecrated. Clearly the king's names and images were primary targets of destruction, but were the instructions for carrying out this damage precise regarding the parts of the king's figure to be specifically or more heavily attacked? The above consideration of the royal figures in the tomb of Ay might well support that possibility.

KV 23 also provides a clear reminder that the *damnatio* enacted against a king's names and images in a royal tomb (or, of course, any other monument) is as much a part of the monument's history as its construction or its utilization for its intended purpose.

Notes

1. *Damnatio* and usurpation are separate yet frequently related phenomena. However, not all usurpation involves *damnatio* and not all *damnatio* involves usurpation. In fact, in the royal tombs of the Valley of the Kings the two phenomena rarely, if ever, coincided and so they are examined separately in this volume.
2. Background bibliography for each of the monuments referenced in this list of tombs may be found in Porter and Moss (1960), Thomas (1966), Reeves and Wilkinson (1996), Weeks (2003), and on the website of the Theban Mapping Project, http://www.thebanmapping-project.com/.

Bibliography

Aldred, C. 1963. "The Parentage of King Siptah." *Journal of Egyptian Archaeology* 49: 43.

Altenmüller, H. 2012. "A Queen in a Valley of Kings: The Tomb of Tausret." In Wilkinson, 67–91.

Bergman, J., J. F. Borghouts and C. Brunon, eds. 1984. *Mélanges Adolphe Gutbub*. Montpellier.

Dorman, P. F. 2005. "The Proscription of Hapshepsut. " In Roehrig, 267–269.

Hari, R. 1984. "La 'damnatio memoriae' amarnienne." In Bergman, Borghouts and Brunon, 95–102.

Lesko, L. H. 1966. "A Little More Evidence for the End of the Nineteenth Dynasty." *Journal of the American Research Center in Egypt* 5: 31.

Magnússon, S. G. 2006. "Social History as 'Sites of Memory'? The Institutionalization of History: Microhistory and the Grand Narrative." *Journal of Social History* 39(1): 892–913.

Porter, B. and R. Moss. 1960. *Topographical Bibliography of Ancient Egyptian Hieroglyphic Texts, Reliefs and Paintings. Vol. I, Part 2: The Theban Necropolis. Royal Tombs and Smaller Cemeteries*. Oxford.

Reeves, C. N. 1990. *Valley of the Kings: The Decline of a Royal Necropolis*. London and New York.

Reeves, C. N. and R. H. Wilkinson. 1996. *The Complete Valley of the Kings*. London.

Roehrig, C. H., ed. 2005. *Hapshepsut: From Queen to Pharaoh*. New York.

Schaden, O. 2000. "Paintings in the Tomb of Ay (WV–23) and the Western Valley of the Kings Project." *Amarna Letters* 4: 88–111.

Thomas, E. 1966. *Royal Necropoleis of Thebes*. Princeton.

Weeks, K. R., ed. (2003 ed.). *Atlas of the Valley of the Kings*. Cairo.

Wilkinson, R. H. 2011. "Controlled Damage: The Mechanics and Microhistory of the *damnatio memoriae* Carried out in KV-23, the Tomb of Ay. " *Journal of Egyptian History* 4: 129–147.

Wilkinson, R. H., ed. 2012. *Tausret: Forgotten Queen and Pharaoh of Egypt*. Oxford.

CHAPTER 23

....

USURPATION AND REUSE OF ROYAL TOMBS

....

RICHARD H. WILKINSON

WHILE the term usurpation is often found in Egyptological literature applying to the seizure of the royal throne, the term applies equally to the appropriation and reuse of royal monuments (Capart 1932; Helck 1986; Murnane 1994; Brand 2010) and specifically, in this chapter, to the reuse of tombs in the Valley of the Kings (KV).

Although tombs in the royal valley were appropriated and reused at various times in later history, the focus here is primarily on the usurpations enacted while the KV was in use as a royal necropolis, during the New Kingdom (NK), and to a much lesser extent those later appropriations involving the officially sanctioned use of NK tombs.

Even within these narrowed parameters, the phenomenon is more complex than it might appear on the surface, and in its broader definition of the "encroachment, infringement, trespass, or seizure" of physical things, usurpation may involve different degrees of taking possession and reuse of an extant tomb and, in some cases, its tomb goods. In the context of royal burials, usurpation may be said to be complete when the tomb was entirely taken over from its original owner.[1] In this case the original burial assemblage was usually removed, and the tomb's representational program was often modified to some extent to depict and name the new occupant of the tomb. Usurpation may also be partial when the original burial and/or at least part of the tomb's representational program were not removed, and the monument was effectively shared.

Many other variables of usurpation involving the agent, specific timing, and method of appropriation may be discerned in the archaeological record of the KV, and these aspects of the phenomenon are considered individually in this chapter.

Usurped and Reused Tombs in the Valley of the Kings

A brief survey of the most important royally usurped tombs in the KV[2] reveals a number of things regarding aspects of reuse ranging from the frequency of usurpation to the apparent reasons associated with the individual appropriations. In some cases the reuse is certain, as with KV 14 (Figure 23.1), though in others it is probable, though not certain, as with KV 15 (Figure 23.2).

Eighteenth Dynasty

KV 20—Thutmose I/Hatshepsut: One of the earliest tombs in the KV, tomb 20 is now believed to have been cut for Thutmose I and later taken over by Hatshepsut, who extended the tomb to also include her own burial along with that of her father.

   KV 42—Meryetra–Hatshepsut/Sennefer et al: A tomb originally prepared for this wife of Thutmose III appears not to have been used for her, but was taken over during

FIGURE 23.1 Certain reuse: A double scene originally showing Tausret led before Osiris by Horus and Anubis in the first hall of the queen's tomb, KV 14. The queen's images were deleted (at both sides of the scene) and the cartouches of her successor, Sethnakht, inscribed in their place (partly visible along the right side of this photograph).

(Photograph by Richard H. Wilkinson)

FIGURE 23.2 Uncertain reuse: Although it was clearly decorated for Seti II, the history of KV 15 is uncertain and it is not known if it was actually reused. It is clear that a number of Seti's names were erased at some point, followed by their later recarving, indicating that reuse was perhaps at least intended.

(Photograph by Richard H. Wilkinson)

the reign of her son Amenhotep II for use by Sennefer, the mayor of Thebes; his wife Senetnay; and another woman, Baketra – unless items from their burials were cached there later.

KV 35—**Amenhotep II/various royal mummies:** Prepared in the Eighteenth Dynasty for the burials of Amenhotep II, his son Websenu, and apparently his mother Meryetra–Hatshepsut, this tomb was reused during the Twenty-first Dynasty for the caching of the mummies of Thutmose IV, Amenhotep III, Merenptah, Seti II, Siptah, Ramesses IV, Ramesses V, Ramesses VI, the anonymous "Elder Woman," and one other mummy, perhaps that of Sethnakht.

KV 5—**?/Sons of Ramesses II:** Originally a small tomb of apparently Eighteenth Dynasty date (based on architectural aspects of entryway A, Chambers 1 and 2, and part of pillared Chamber 3), KV 5 was appropriated by Ramesses II and massively enlarged in several phases of development to receive the burials of at least 6 and possibly as many as 20 of his sons (Weeks 2000).

KV 62—Ay?/Tutankhamun: The tomb of Tutankhamun is not of royal design, and it may have been hastily taken over for his burial when the young king died and the tomb that was being prepared for him (apparently KV 23 in the western branch of the royal valley) was not yet complete. If this scenario is correct, KV 62 was originally a private tomb—very possibly being prepared for the "god's father" Ay.

KV 23—Tutankhamun/Ay: If KV 62 was originally being prepared for Tutankhamun's servant and eventual successor Ay, the appropriation of that tomb for Tutankhamun's burial would have naturally led to Ay's use of KV 23, the incomplete tomb apparently intended for Tutankhamun.

Nineteenth Dynasty

KV 10—Amenmesse/Takhat and Baketwerel: Although there is yet no concrete evidence that the Nineteenth Dynasty usurper Amenmesse was buried in KV 10, the tomb was certainly prepared for him. It was evidently used later by the king's daughter and great royal wife Takhat. There is also indication of another queen, Baketwerel, though no evidence that she was interred in the tomb. These royal women were originally assumed to have been the wife and mother of Amenmesse, but it is now realized that they more probably date to the Twentieth Dynasty and were related to Ramesses IX.

KV 15—Seti II /?: Although clearly decorated for Seti II, the history of this tomb is uncertain and it is not known if it was actually reused, although it is clear that a number of Seti's names were erased at some point, followed by their later recarving. If Amenmesse ruled concurrently with and in opposition to Seti II, rather than prior to Seti's reign, it is possible that Amenmesse removed the names of Seti, though Amenmesse evidently had prepared KV 10 for himself. Otherwise, Seti's names may have been removed during the reign of Siptah (who also had his own tomb), and then later restored by Tausret; or some other scenario of which we are not aware may have applied.

KV 47—Siptah/Third Intermediate Period burial?: This tomb was used for the burial of Siptah, and possibly also for that of his mother, Tia'a, a minor wife of Seti II. The cartouches of the king were erased at some point, and then later restored in paint, though when these events occurred is not known for sure. The tomb may have been reused, however, as bones of an intrusive burial (perhaps dating to the Third Intermediate Period) were found in the sarcophagus

KV 13—Bay/Amenherkhepeshef and Mentuherkhepeshef: Originally cut for Bay, chancellor under Siptah toward the end of the Nineteenth Dynasty, this tomb was reused for the burials of princes Amenherkhepeshef and Mentuherkhepeshef during the reign of Ramesses III (Reeves 1990, 133), or perhaps more likely, following Dodson (2010, 99, 159 n. 62), Amenherkepeshef the son of Ramesses VI.

KV 14—Tausret/Sethnakht: Completed for Tausret, this extensive tomb was usurped by Ramesses III for the burial of his father, Sethnakht. The texts and decorative program utilized by Tausret were adjusted for Sethnakht, and her sarcophagi (as king and as queen) were used for other burials. KV 14 provides the most detailed evidence of usurpation of any tomb in the royal valley (Altenmüller 2012).

Twentieth Dynasty

KV 11—Sethnakht/Ramesses III: Approximately the first third of this tomb—the entrance, corridors B and C, and the first chamber—originally bore the names of Sethnakht but were reinscribed for that king's son Ramesses III, for whom the remainder of the tomb was decorated. It seems clear that the tomb was not ready to receive Sethnakht as intended at that king's death and he was therefore buried in the usurped tomb of Tausret.

KV 9—Ramesses V/Ramesses VI: Ramesses V apparently started the construction of this tomb (the entrance and corridors 1–5), which was completed by Ramesses VI, who decorated the added sections with his own name and images while usurping the cartouches and representations of Ramesses V in the first five corridors. It is not known if the usurpation of this tomb was total or partial—whether Ramesses VI removed the body of Ramesses V, or if he inserted his own burial effectively to share the tomb with his predecessor (Reeves 1990, 117).

KV 19—Ramesses Setherkhepeshef/Ramesses Mentuherkhepeshef: It is believed that KV 19 was originally intended for Prince Ramesses Setherkhepeshef, who became Ramesses VIII. Although the tomb was never completed, KV 19 was later appropriated for Prince Ramesses Mentuherkhepeshef, a son of Ramesses IX, for whom it was decorated. This tomb also received a number of intrusive burials in the Twenty-second Dynasty.

KV 4—Ramesses XI/Pinedjem I (?): The last tomb cut in the Valley of the Kings, KV 4, was constructed for Ramesses XI but was not used for the king's interment. However, although Pinedjem I added his cartouche to the tomb's decoration in the Twenty-first Dynasty, he did not use KV 4 for his own burial. John Romer has suggested that the tomb may have been used by Pinedjem as a refurbishing workshop to deal with material from the tombs of Hatshepsut (KV 20), Thutmose I (KV 38), and Thutmose III (KV 34) (Reeves 1990, 123).

Beyond the royal usurpations listed in the preceding text, other tombs in the KV were affected by appropriation, such as the many which received intrusive burials during the Twenty-second Dynasty or later (see next section). Many of these cases are poorly documented, but a great number of appropriations from the later periods were clearly not of an "official" nature and are essentially beyond the scope of this study. It should also be remembered that in some cases tombs may have been reused in later periods as well as during the NK, but poor preservation of the evidence makes it difficult to tell what exactly occurred when. Examples of these cases are generally avoided in this discussion to concentrate on clear patterns of usurpation discernible in tombs with generally well understood histories.

However, even the 15 tombs listed earlier—of which we have a fairly clear under-standing of the reuse involved—represent some 24 percent or almost one in four of the known tombs in the KV—showing that a significant number of usurpations and reuses occurred relative to the total number of tombs cut in the valley's history. This ratio is increased if the non-royal tombs within the KV are discounted as they were not usually candidates for royal appropriation, though in some cases non-royal elite tombs were reused for such burials.

The Timing of Appropriation

Although the appropriation of existing tombs could occur at any time, four major peri-ods of usurpation activity may be discerned:

1. Within the New Kingdom itself when most of the tombs were first cut and some were appropriated under royal order
2. In the Third Intermediate Period, especially during the Twenty-second Dynasty and shortly thereafter when non–royal individuals were interred in a number of the existing tombs (e.g., KV 19, KV 22, KV 24, KV 25, KV 34, KV 44, KV 45, and KV 47)
3. During the Greco–Roman era, when at least 10 royal tombs were visited and per-haps utilized in some ways as may be seen by the thousands of extant graffiti from this period
4. Finally, in the Byzantine era when a number of open tombs were reused in various ways, sometimes as dwellings for Christian hermits (KV 1, KV 2, KV 4, KV 8, KV 9, KV 15) and evidently even as a religious shrine or chapel (KV 3).

Even within the NK the appropriation and reuse of royal tombs occurred at widely different times. Some tombs were apparently appropriated for reuse before they were even completed for their intended owner. Others were evidently reused not long after an original interment took place, while yet others were not reused until much later in the NK. Clearly, no particular length of time needed to pass before a tomb was considered "available" and an appropriate target for appropriation, though rapid reuse is usually associated with situations where the original owner of a royal tomb had lost favor due to religious or dynastic transition. Beyond this, ascertaining frequency patterns in the tim-ing of appropriations is difficult, largely because relatively few monuments are involved in the total corpus of appropriated KV tombs.

The simple breakdown, by dynasty, of the reused tombs surveyed above is as fol-lows: Eighteenth Dynasty: six tombs; Nineteenth Dynasty: five tombs; Twentieth Dynasty: four tombs. This breakdown of tombs by dynasty is not particularly instruc-tive other than indicating that tombs of all periods were taken over, with kings appro-priating the tombs (and, on occasion, even the temples of millions of years) of earlier rulers according to need, and that the process of tomb usurpation was fairly constant. It is more instructive to consider the specific circumstances in which royally sanctioned usurpations occurred.

Within the three dynasties represented in the KV, the usurpation of funerary monuments is particularly common in some periods. Periods of political uncertainty and instability were natural times for this occurrence, and the immediate post-Amarna period provides a clear example. Just as the tomb used for the burial of Tutankhamun (KV 62) was apparently requisitioned by Ay from an elite but non-ruling individual who had been granted burial within the KV, Ay then usurped Tutankhamun's intended tomb (KV 23) for his own use, and Horemheb, in turn, usurped Ay's royal temple.

In situations like these we see a period of general political flux and instability with the resultant hurried need for an available tomb being the underlying causal factor influencing usurpation. Such instances of appropriation enacted soon after the transfer of power that occurred between individual reigns and between dynasties represent the most frequent timing of royal usurpation. But usurpation also took place at other times and for other reasons, as may be seen by considering the aspect of agency in appropriation.

Agents of Appropriation

The most common instigators of officially sanctioned appropriation among the usurpers of the tombs surveyed above were the new rulers (or those who buried them) who, by reason of age or other factor, needed a quickly prepared tomb if they were to obtain burial within the royal necropolis. Some of these rulers were the direct successors of monarchs who had been discredited for religious or political reasons such as dynastic change. In those cases the appropriation of the recent ruler's tomb may have been part of the overall program of negation of the earlier monarch's memory even if an actual *damnatio* (see ch 20) was not involved. The example of KV 23, the tomb of Ay, shows that reuse of the tomb of a religiously proscribed ruler was unlikely to occur. However, the tombs of rulers who had simply lost favor as part of the dynamic of dynastic change would be very likely candidates for usurpation by the successors of those monarchs.

Usurpation of tombs by pharaohs who had ample time to prepare funerary monuments was much less frequent, though sometimes this occurred when other considerations were involved—such as the reuse of KV 20 by Hatshepsut to link herself to the burial of her father, Thutmose I. Also infrequent but equally important for a full understanding of the phenomenon of tomb reuse, what might be termed "reflexive–reuse" or "owner–reuse" could occur with the change in status of the individual for whom a tomb was being prepared. In these cases, previously established plans for the monument had to be completely changed to reflect the new status of the tomb owner, and for the ancient Egyptians this was far more complex than the simple enlargement or embellishment of a monument which had already been begun. It necessitated instead the transformation of the monument to an entirely new type of tomb as reflected both in its new architectural and decorative programs—with the physical proportions and representational motifs of private or royal–related tombs being abandoned in favor of royal canons and motifs.

This phenomenon may possibly have occurred in several royal tombs, but a definite and clear example is seen in KV 14, the tomb of Tausret. The work of Hartwig Altenmüller in this tomb has shown that Tausret repeatedly changed the architectural elements and decorative programs utilized in her monument as time passed and her political role changed—with the tomb first reflecting her role as the queen of Seti II, then as regent for Siptah, and finally as ruling pharaoh (Altenmüller 2012, 80). In this way, the development of KV 14, exhibiting the changed status of Tausret, stands as a well-documented example of "owner–reuse." In its later history this tomb also reflects clear evidence of the more usual appropriation by another ruler. Although it was long believed that Sethnakht took over Tausret's monument and expanded it to almost double its size for his own burial, Altenmüller's careful work has shown that the tomb was actually completed in its fullest extent for Tausret and only later taken over by Ramesses III to be used for the burial of his father, Sethnakht, when that king died before his own tomb (KV 11) was completed.

The history of this later usurpation is instructive. When KV 14 was rededicated to Sethnakht, all of Tausret's images were covered over and replaced with images or the names of Sethnakht (Figure 23.1). However, images of Tausret's husband, Seti II, with whom Tausret appeared in some of her scenes, were untouched. As Altenmüller has written, "[Ramesses III] was thus able to place his father Sethnakht in the direct line of succession to Seti II and bypass. . . what were now viewed as the "empty years" connected with Siptah and Tausret at the end of the 19th Dynasty" (Altenmüller 2012, 80).

This example clearly demonstrates that the usurpation of a royal tomb could be based on a political agenda that involved an interaction with the usurped monument beyond its simple redecoration. In this case, the agent of appropriation utilized selected elements of the extant decoration to link the new occupant of the tomb to an acceptably orthodox predecessor.

However, it is interesting to consider who the intended audience of this linkage might be. The reused monument would naturally be closed on the burial of its intended occupant and would not be visible to a human audience beyond that point. It is perhaps likely, therefore, that this type of linkage for legitimization or other purposes was primarily for the eyes of the gods, and if this were the case then other aspects of the appropriation of tombs could also have had theological or at least symbolic significance. It is also interesting in this regard that even in instances of dynastic change such as that which lay behind the usurpation of Tausret's tomb, we have no evidence of any kind of proclamation of appropriation having been made; and usurpation seems usually to have been enacted quietly, if not covertly. With earlier tombs this could have been a matter of general secrecy regarding the location of the tomb, but by the Twentieth Dynasty this was hardly the case, as tombs were no longer being hidden as they had been earlier.

REASONS FOR APPROPRIATION

Although during most of the NK each new occupant of the Horus throne of Egypt would theoretically cut his/her own tomb within the KV, the preceding discussion shows clearly that many did not. There appear to have been a number of reasons for the appropriation of extant royal tombs. Several of these reasons have been considered already: the need for an available tomb when there was not enough time or resources available to construct a new one; the taking over of an extant tomb owing to the loss of favor of its owner; and even the "reuse" of a tomb for the same owner under new circumstances where a larger and different type of tomb was required subsequent to changes in the owner's status or social/political role. A number of other reasons exist for usurpation of royal tombs, and together with those already discussed, these may be tabulated as follows:

1. **When a planned or in-progress tomb was not ready for its occupant, another tomb might be appropriated.** The example of KV 62, the tomb of Tutankhamun, has already been considered for this category—a clearly private tomb taken over when the young king's intended monument (apparently KV 23) was not complete enough for use.
2. **The taking over of the tomb of an individual who had lost favor or the right to KV burial.** KV 14, the tomb of Tausret, reused by Ramesses III for the burial of his father, has been examined above as the clearest example of usurpation as part of a program of discrediting or *damnatio*.
3. **"Owner reuse" of a tomb due to a change in the owner's status.** The tomb of Tausret also qualifies as an example of this in the new dimensions and new decoration utilized in the modification of KV 14 as the queen rose in power and a higher status tomb was needed.
4. **Lack of suitable sites in a chosen area of the KV—especially in the center of the valley.** Although we do not know if this was a sole or even a contributing factor in the appropriation of tombs, it seems likely that it may have been involved in the reuse of some monuments—such as KV 11, the tomb finished by Ramesses III, and some others in the Ramesside era.
5. **Simple availability of a previously initiated but unused tomb.** KV 19, the tomb intended for Prince Ramesses Setherkhepeshef and later appropriated for Prince Ramesses Mentuherkhepeshef, is an example of this.
6. **A tomb is appropriated for status by association.** KV 10, the tomb of Amenmesse, is an example of the reuse of a king's tomb for the later burial of one and perhaps two queens. It is probable that such burials of non-regnant elites in royal tombs were allowed as a gift of enhanced status through direct association with the royal necropolis.

7. **A tomb is appropriated but shared for legitimization or status by means of polit-ical or relational ties.** KV 20—originally the tomb of Thutmose I and also used by Hatshepsut for her own burial—appears to be a prime example of this type of tomb reuse.

8. **Usurpation of a tomb for the safekeeping of other royal mummies.** The offi-cial caching of royal mummies which were deposited in KV 35, the tomb of Amenhotep II, and other tombs, provide obvious examples of this.

9. **A tomb is appropriated for non–burial use.** Tombs could be officially taken over and used for purposes other than for interments, as may have been the case with KV 4, originally intended for Ramesses XI, which appears to have been used as a workshop. Later in history, of course, many of the known tombs were taken over by early Christians and others for use as shelters and places of religious use.

Other reasons for the usurpation of royal tombs could have existed, but it seems prob-able that the ones enumerated here were the primary ones. Naturally, more than one of these reasons for appropriation could have been involved in individual cases of usurpa-tion, and the fact that several reasons might be involved in a given instance underscore why tomb reuse was doubtless attractive as an alternative to the standard practice of having a new tomb cut.

The Extent of Work Applied
to Appropriated Tombs

It is clear that the usurpation of royal tombs was often not simply the taking over of a tomb with minimal further involvement for the purpose of limiting either expense or work. Within the parameters dictated by the reasons for tomb reuse listed above, many variations occurred. Incompletely cut tombs could be taken over and finished for their new owner, or simply reused in their incomplete state. Fully cut but undecorated tombs could be left undecorated or decorated for the usurper. Completely cut and decorated tombs could be redecorated and, in some cases, extended with new sections.

Careful redecoration of the usurped tomb was indeed frequent. Although sometimes only selected images or texts were changed or added, in other cases reused tombs were considerably expanded or their complete decorative program was removed and redone. For example, as noted in point 6 above, KV 10, the tomb of Amenmesse, was originally decorated for that king with raised and sunk relief extending as far as its pillared hall. All of this decoration was later erased—not simply covered—and replaced with scenes painted on plaster for the queens Takhat and Baketwerel. This kind of extensive redeco-ration, if not outright "remodeling," for non-regnal elites militates against the idea of tomb reuse being based simply on the use of an available and convenient burial space. Such extensive work suggests, in fact, the involvement of other factors such as status gifting as the primary reason for such appropriations. Even in cases of tomb reuse for ruling monarchs, what might appear lesser work was often doubtless the result of time constraints. When KV 14, the tomb of Tausret, was rededicated for the burial of Sethnakht, although some images of the queen were simply covered over with plaster on which the names of Sethnakht were inscribed, in other instances the queen's images were carefully replaced by representations of the king, and the simple name replacement instances were almost certainly the result of the need for quick conversion of the tomb, perhaps accomplished within the period of embalmment for Sethnakht.

The careful reworking of a funerary monument could also apply to the major element of the burial assemblage, the sarcophagus. When the tomb of Tausret (KV 14) was rededicated by Ramesses III for Sethnakht, the latter was buried in a sarcophagus that had been altered for him. It is unclear whether this was Tausret's kingly sarcophagus, or whether that is represented by an unfinished example that was relocated into the tomb of Bay (KV 13) along with her first sarcophagus, made for her as the "Great Royal Wife" of Seti II. That unfinished sarcophagus was reused for Ramesses III's son Mentuherkopeshef, while Tausret's queenly sarcophagus was reused for a prince Amenherkhepeshef, variously identified as another son of Ramesses III or as a son of Ramesses VI. In any event, the careful re-cutting and reuse of royal sarcophagi was certainly an integral part of the usurpation of some royal tombs.

Usurpation of a royal monument may thus often be seen to have involved just as careful attention to the preparation of the tomb and its decorative program as that employed in freshly cut tombs, and although usurpations are sometimes characterized as instances of "hasty" reuse in the Egyptological literature, there are few indications that the officially sanctioned appropriation of earlier funerary monuments was normally treated any less seriously or with less care than that afforded new tombs. The relatively lesser quality of decoration in some usurped tombs was doubtless the result of a need for great haste, the economic conditions behind later burials, or the lesser status of the individuals interred in reused monuments. In usurped tombs where these factors were not issues, redecoration was often near the same quality as that applied originally.

CONCLUSIONS

The officially appropriated tombs briefly surveyed in this chapter show that although usurpation sometimes involved the negative aspect of the taking over and reuse of the tomb of an individual who had fallen from official favor, conversely, reuse could occur for the purpose of obtaining status through association with a respected earlier individual. In other cases, appropriations may have been based on the purely neutral need for an available tomb under short time constraints, but considering the amount of work often involved in the actual reuse of many tombs it seems likely that other reasons or benefits of appropriation were often involved.

The phenomenon of tomb reuse was also more prevalent than might be expected, and the fact that almost one out of every four tombs in the Valley of the Kings was appropriated for reuse clearly demonstrates that the practice of usurpation and reuse was an important aspect of the royal valley's history. The phenomenon is deserving, therefore, of further study, and certain questions are particularly pressing if we are to understand fully the underlying causes and effects of tomb usurpation and reuse.

NOTES

1. *Damnatio* and usurpation are separate yet frequently related phenomena. However, not all usurpation involves *damnatio* and not all *damnatio* involves usurpation. In fact, in the royal tombs of the Valley of the Kings the two phenomena rarely, if ever, coincided, and so they are examined separately in this volume.
2. In addition to the citations for specific points referenced in this list of tombs, background bibliography for each of the monuments may be found in Reeves and Wilkinson (1996), Weeks (2003), and on the website of the Theban Mapping Project, http://www.theban-mappingproject.com/.

BIBLIOGRAPHY

Altenmüller, H. 2012. "A Queen in a Valley of Kings: The Tomb of Tausret." In Wilkinson, 67–91.
Brand, P. 2010. "Usurpation of Monuments." In Wendrich, online.
Brock, E. 1992. "The Tomb of Merenptah and its Sarcophagi." In Reeves, 122–140.
Brock, E. 2013. "Some Observations on the Valley of the Kings in the Twentieth Dynasty." In Creasman, 101–122.
Capart, J. 1932. "L'usurpation des monuments dans l'antiquité égyptienne." In Gobeaux-Thonet, 57–66.
Creasman, P. P., ed. 2013. *Archaeological Research in the Valley of the Kings and Ancient Thebes: Papers Presented in Honor of Richard H. Wilkinson*, Wilkinson Egyptology Series 1. Tucson.
Dodson, A. 2010. *Poisoned Legacy: The Fall of the Nineteenth Egyptian Dynasty*. Cairo.
Gobeaux-Thonet, J., ed. 1932. *Mélanges de philologie orientale publiés à l'occasion du Xe anniversaire de la création de l'Institut supérieur d'histoire et de littératures orientales de l'Université de Liège*. Louvain.
Helck, W. 1986. "Usurpierung." In Helck and Westendorf, cols. 905–906.
Helck, W. and W. Westendorf, eds. 1986. *Lexikon der Ägyptologie*. Wiesbaden.
Murnane, W. 1994. "Egyptian Monuments and Historical Memory: New Light on the Ancients' 'Uses of the Past' from the Great Hypostyle Hall at Karnak." *KMT* 5(3): 15–24, 88.
Porter, B. and R. Moss. 1960. *Topographical Bibliography of Ancient Egyptian Hieroglyphic Texts, Reliefs and Paintings*. Vol. I, Part 2: *The Theban Necropolis. Royal Tombs and Smaller Cemeteries*. Oxford.
Reeves, N. C., ed. 1992. *After Tut'ankhamun: Research and Excavation in the Royal Necropolis at Thebes*, Studies in Egyptology. London and New York.

Reeves, N. C., ed. 1990. *Valley of the Kings: The Decline of a Royal Necropolis*. London and New York.

Reeves, C. N. and R. H. Wilkinson. 1996. *The Complete Valley of the Kings: Tombs and Treasures of Egypt's Greatest Pharaohs*. London.

Thomas, Elizabeth. 1966. *Royal Necropoleis of Thebes*. Princeton.

Weeks, K. R., ed. 2000. *KV5: A Preliminary Report on the Excavation of the Tomb of the Sons of Ramesses II in the Valley of the Kings*. Cairo.

Weeks, K. R., ed. (2003 ed.). *Atlas of the Valley of the Kings*. Cairo.

Wendrich, W., ed. 2010. *UCLA Encyclopedia of Egyptology*. Online: http://digital2.library.ucla.edu/viewItem.do?ark=21198/zz0025h6fh.

Wilkinson, R. H., ed. 2012. *Tausret: Forgotten Queen and Pharaoh of Egypt*. Oxford.

....

CHAPTER 24

INTRUSIVE BURIALS
AND CACHES

JOHN H. TAYLOR

FOLLOWING the construction of the tomb of Ramesses XI, which was never completed, no further royal burials took place in the Valley of the Kings. The cutting of new tombs ceased, and over the next 140 years many of the existing burials of kings and other royal personages were dismantled. This process, carried out under the authority of the Theban administration, involved the restoration of mummies that had been despoiled by robbers and their reburial in collective tombs ("caches"), some of which were located within the valley, while others lay beyond its boundaries in other parts of the Theban necropolis. Most of the grave goods that had escaped the hands of robbers were evidently appropriated by the representatives of the state, and some of them were recycled. A by-product of these operations was the recovery of knowledge of the past in the form of royal funerary texts, which were used to revitalize contemporary mortuary practices. Following the final closure of the caches of royal mummies, some of the tombs in the valley that had been vacated were reused for the burials of private individuals from the Twenty-second to the Twenty-sixth Dynasties, after which access to the tombs for this purpose seems to have ceased.

THE DISMANTLING OF THE NEW KINGDOM
ROYAL BURIALS

The alteration in the treatment of the royal necropolis reflects more far-reaching changes that affected Egypt at the end of the New Kingdom. For centuries the principal seat of royal authority had been located in the Eastern Delta, though the pharaohs were still brought to Thebes for burial. At the beginning of the Twenty-first Dynasty the country became politically divided. The line of kings who succeeded Ramesses XI was based at Tanis, and they chose to break with tradition by constructing their tombs there, within the precinct of the temple of Amun (Lull 2002, 17–162). Upper Egypt was controlled by a succession of army commanders who also functioned as high priests of Amun at Karnak. Although nominally acknowledging the authority of the king in Tanis, it was they who had immediate jurisdiction over the Theban necropolis. It was these men—principally the high priests and generals-in-chief Piankh, Herihor, and Pinedjem I—who authorized and initiated the reorganization of the burials in the Valley of the Kings.

The immediate motivations for this new policy were the endemic threat of robbery and the weakness of the state economy. Minor thefts had occurred in the valley during the Eighteenth Dynasty, but these had been made good by the necropolis administration; they left a written record of their visit to the tomb of Thutmose IV and hastily tidied up Tutankhamun's antechamber before resealing the blocked entrance, which robbers had breached (Reeves 1990, 233, 275). More serious outbreaks of plundering in the reigns of Ramesses IX–XI coincided with a general atmosphere of insecurity at Thebes, where bands of roving Libyans posed a recurrent threat. This situation perhaps persuaded the necropolis authorities that long-term protection of all the tombs could not be maintained (Taylor 1992, 186). This was also a period in which the resources of the state were under considerable strain, manifested by high grain prices and food shortages, a loss of revenue from the Nubian goldmines and Near Eastern trading partners, and a significant reduction in royal building projects (Jansen-Winkeln 1995, 76). It would therefore have been a logical step for the authorities to strip the royal burials of their valuables, rendering them less attractive to robbers and simultaneously releasing large reserves of precious commodities, which could be directed back into the magazines of the state (Reeves 1990, 276–278; Jansen-Winkeln 1995, 66–67).

The evidence for the process that followed comes chiefly from the surviving mummies of kings and other members of the New Kingdom royal families, which were found in the late nineteenth century in the caches where they had been secreted. Punctiliously dated hieratic dockets on their wrappings and coffins record their identities and the stages in their restoration and transfer from tomb to tomb (Reeves 1990, 225–243). Notes written on the walls of some of the tombs in the valley complement these data, as do many graffiti carved on the rocks of the necropolis by the officials involved in the operations. The dockets that accompanied the bodies are of two main types—one ("Type A") that simply records the name of the deceased, and a second ("Type B") that describes under various terms the treatment they had received. Prominent among these treatments are *ḳrs* ("burial"), *wḥm ḳrs* ("repetition of burial"), and *rdt Wsr* ("Osirification," probably referring to rewrapping the corpse in the required form of Osiris) (Reeves 1990, 225–231). These longer texts often also record the transfer of a mummy from one place of burial to another.

The records usually note that these interventions had been carried out on the instructions of the incumbent Theban high priest. Any disturbance to or transfer of a king's burial evidently required the sanction of the highest authority. A precedent existed in the removal of the bodies of the Amarna royal family from their tombs for reinterment in the Valley of the Kings under Tutankhamun (Reeves 1990, 276), but it is probable that nothing on the scale of the Twenty-first Dynasty reburials had ever been attempted at Thebes. On at least one occasion during the procedure the goddess Mut was approached—probably by means of an oracle—to give divine sanction to such a momentous undertaking (Reeves 1990, 237–238; Taylor 1992, 187).

The actual work was carried out by the officials in charge of the Theban west bank, the most prominent of whom in the early Twenty-first Dynasty was the scribe of the necropolis, Butehamun. His name occurs in many inspection graffiti throughout the necropolis, and he is mentioned in some of the dockets as having performed various specific duties, including the "Osirification" of Ramesses III (Reeves 1990, 235). The inclusion of named figures of several members of the New Kingdom royal families in the paintings on Butehamun's coffins (Turin, Museo Egizio 2236–2237: Niwinski 2004, 21–47, Tav. I-VII) and some unusual official titles in the inscriptions may be a reflection of the role he played in restoring their burials (Jansen-Winkeln 1995, 73–74).

THE CREATION OF THE CACHES

The operations focused principally on the tombs located within the Valley of the Kings, but royal sepulchers of the late Second Intermediate Period and early Eighteenth Dynasty in other parts of the Theban necropolis were also entered. The pyramids of Seventeenth Dynasty kings at Dra Abu el-Naga had been specifically targeted by thieves in the reign of Ramesses IX, and it appears that some of these sepulchers were now officially emptied. A few of the mummies, such as those of King Kamose and a queen Ahhotep, were reburied at Dra Abu el-Naga itself, while others eventually found their way to the great Deir el-Bahri cache, TT 320 (described below). The tombs of all of the following rulers were also entered: Seqenenra; Ahmose I; Amenhotep I; Thutmose I, II and III; Amenhotep II; Thutmose IV; Amenhotep III; Horemheb; Ramesses I; Seti I; Ramesses II; Merenptah; Seti II; Siptah; Tausret and Setnakht; Ramesses III–VI; and Ramesses IX. Besides these, the mummies of several queens and royal children of the Seventeenth and Eighteenth Dynasties were also restored and reburied. The tombs that held the burials and associated embalming residues of the Amarna royal family—that of Tutankhamun and KV 54, KV 55, and KV 63—were conspicuously excluded from this process, perhaps on account of the "tainted" character of those rulers in the eyes of later generations.

The royal remains underwent several different types of treatment. Some mummies were simply rewrapped and laid to rest again in their original tombs. In many instances the mummies were transferred to other tombs and gathered together in groups, constituting "caches." Some of these caches were later reopened to admit more bodies, and ultimately the largest assemblage was transferred to the tomb now known as the Royal Cache at Deir el-Bahri (TT 320).

Most of the restoration and transport dockets name the officials responsible for the activity recorded, together with a year-date, but usually do not specify to which ruler the date refers. Although this has led scholars to formulate different reconstructions of the sequence of events, the long-term pattern is in general clear. The inscriptional evidence indicates that the process began during the phase of transitional government known as the *whm mswt*, or "renaissance," at the end of the Twentieth Dynasty. In a letter on papyrus (British Museum EA 10375), dated in year 10 of this era, Piankh, the army commander and virtual ruler of Upper Egypt, ordered Butehamun to "uncover a tomb among the tombs of the ancestors and preserve its seal until I return" (Reeves 1990, 277; Reeves and Wilkinson 1996, 204–205). This has been interpreted to mean that Piankh intended to appropriate the valuables from a royal tomb, perhaps to provide funds for his ongoing military campaigning in Nubia (Reeves 1990, 277; Jansen-Winkeln 1995, 66–69). The immediate sequel of his order is unknown, but many graffiti written by Butehamun and his colleagues in and around the Valley of the Kings indicate that an extensive survey was carried out at around this time, evidently to identify the locations of old tombs and to assess their condition (Jansen-Winkeln 1995, 69–71; Reeves and Wilkinson 1996, 205).

Under the generals and high priests Herihor and Pinedjem I, in the first third of the Twenty-first Dynasty, numerous dockets and inscriptions record restorations of mummies and the transfer of some to new resting places. A graffito in the tomb of Horemheb (KV 57) refers to activity carried out there in a year 6 by Butehamun. The text, only partly legible when it was copied by Sir Alan Gardiner, may have recorded an in situ restoration of Horemheb's burial (Reeves 1990, 77–79). The shattered remains of at least four mummies, found when the tomb was discovered in 1908, perhaps indicate that a small cache was assembled there, only to be subsequently plundered. Among the bodies may have been that of Horemheb himself (and perhaps also that of Aye, who is otherwise unaccounted for among the surviving royal mummies) (Reeves and Wilkinson 1996, 204).

Further restorations of mummies are attested under Pinedjem I, both during his pontificate as high priest and subsequently in his years as king. All of the dockets are dated by regnal years, which can be attributed to the reigns of the Tanite rulers Smendes I and Psusennes I, but it is clear that Pinedjem exercised the immediate authority in arranging these restorations, since he is regularly named in the texts. As high priest he ordered the restorations of the mummies of Amenhotep I and Thutmose II in a year 6, of Amenhotep III in a year 12 or 13, of Ramesses III in a year 13, and of Ramesses II in a year 15. During Pinedjem's kingship, princess Ahmose-Sitkamose was restored in a year 7, and Ahmose I and his son prince Siamun in a year 8 (Reeves 1990, 234–236; Jansen-Winkeln 2007, 21–23; Dodson 2012, 42–43, 61–62).

The grouping of mummies together also continued under Pinedjem. Seti I, having been rewrapped on the orders of Herihor and laid to rest again in his own tomb, was later joined by his father, Ramesses I, and his son, Ramesses II. KV 17 thus became another cache, although, unlike the mummies secreted in the tomb of Horemheb, the occupants of this communal burial place were later to be evacuated. Perhaps around the same time (although proof of the date is lacking) two other major caches were established. One of these was in the tomb of Amenhotep II (KV 35). Amenhotep's mummy was provided with a crude anthropoid coffin and replaced in his sarcophagus, while four unidentified mummies were accommodated nearby: in side chamber Jc two females and a boy, all stripped and without coffins, and in the antechamber an adult male who had been placed in the hull of a funerary boat. Tightly packed into side chamber Jb were the bodies of eight kings (Thutmose IV, Amenhotep III, Merenptah, Seti II, Siptah, and Ramesses IV, V, and VI) and an unidentified female lying in the coffin lid of Setnakht. It has been suggested that Setnakht himself might have been identified as the unnamed body on the antechamber boat (Reeves 1990, 192–199).

Dockets indicate that another group of mummies was secreted in the tomb of the early Eighteenth Dynasty queen Ahmose-Inhapi (or Tenthapi). The location of this sepulcher is uncertain, although it was evidently situated outside the main valley; the tombs WN A and KV 39 have both been suggested as the place in question (Reeves 1990, 190; Rose 2000, 144–148; Aston 2013, 15–16). The mummy of Amenhotep I had certainly been taken to the tomb of Inhapi before year 10 of the Tanite king Siamun, at which time the mummies of Ramesses I, Seti I, and Ramesses II were added to this group, after being removed from the tomb of Seti I. The Inhapi cache probably received other royal corpses before its contents were transferred to TT 320.

The restorations and transfers that were carried out during the time of Pinedjem I were not confined to the Valley of the Kings. The burial of the early Eighteenth Dynasty queen Merytamun at Deir el-Bahri (TT 358) was restored in a year 19, the royal mummy being relieved of its jewelry and carefully rewrapped, while the coffins were painstakingly stripped of gilding and valuable inlays, before being painted and returned to their owner (Winlock 1932; Jansen-Winkeln 1995, 71–72).

There appears then to have been a hiatus of perhaps as much as sixty years in these activities, until the reign of Siamun, when another phase of transfers took place. In year 5 of this reign the first recorded burials were made in the tomb that was to become known as the Royal Cache, TT 320. This sepulcher, located at the base of the cliffs on the south side of the bay of Deir el-Bahri, is a shaft-tomb with three corridors leading to a burial chamber. The date of its cutting has been debated, but its location and design, together with ceramic and other material found there, and probably from the original burial, indicate that it was made for a queen of the late Seventeenth or early Eighteenth Dynasties (Aston 2013, 10–13). In the reign of Siamun it was taken over as the family burial place of the high priest of Amun Pinedjem II. Graffiti located at the bottom of its entrance shaft recorded the burials of Pinedjem's wife Neskhons in year 5 of Siamun's reign and of the high priest himself in year 10 (Reeves 1990, 237, 239). Their mummies were joined subsequently by those of Pinedjem's other wife, Istemkheb, his daughter Nesitanebisheru, and his probable son-in-law Djedptahiuefankh.

To this tomb also were brought numerous earlier mummies of royal personages. The chronology of their introduction into the cache is open to debate, since the dockets on the coffins and wrappings of most of them do not record their final deposition, and uncertainty exists about the positioning of the coffins within the tomb's chamber and passages at the time of discovery (Aston 2013, 13–14). Ultimately, in addition to the members of Pinedjem II's family, mentioned above, the "Royal Cache" contained the remains of the following individuals: from the late Seventeenth and early Eighteenth Dynasties, the kings Seqenenra, Ahmose I, Amenhotep I, Thutmose II and III, the queens Ahmose-Inhapi, Ahmose-Sitkamose, Ahmose-Henutempet, Ahmose-Merytamun, and Ahmose-Nefertari, princes Siamun and Ahmose-Sipair, and princesses Sitamun and Ahmose-Henuttemehu, and the nurse Rai; from the Nineteenth Dynasty, kings Seti I and Ramesses II; from the Twentieth Dynasty, kings Ramesses III and Ramesses IX; and from the early Twenty-first Dynasty, Nodjmet, Pinedjem I, his wife Henuttawy, Pinedjem's daughter Maatkara, his son Masaharta, and the latter's probable wife Tayuherit. There were also six unidentified mummies, among whom were perhaps Queen Tetishery and Ramesses I (whose burial shroud and coffin, respectively, were also recovered from the cache).

The only coffins whose position in the tomb can be reliably established are those that were nearest to the entrance. These included the coffin of the nurse Rai (inside which was the mummy of Queen Inhapi) and that of Seti I, which had previously been housed in Inhapi's own tomb. Their location close to the entrance of TT 320 strongly suggests that they were among the last bodies to be brought into the cache—either directly from the tomb of Inhapi or perhaps via some intermediary resting place (Reeves 1990, 185–192). The date of this final transfer is unknown, but it may have occurred as late as the reign of Shoshenq I, first ruler of the Twenty-second Dynasty. The interment of Djedptahiuefankh in or after Shoshenq's year 11 was the last occasion on which the cache is known to have been opened before its modern discovery; some of the New Kingdom royal mummies may have been brought into TT 320 at that time.

RESTORATION AND APPROPRIATION

TT 320 was officially cleared in 1881, and the cache in KV 35 was discovered in 1898. Most of the royal mummies from these two deposits were unwrapped in the late nineteenth and early twentieth centuries C.E., revealing the treatments they had been subjected to first by robbers and later by the necropolis officials. Many had suffered damage, varying in extent from the breaking off of hands and feet to extensive dismemberment and deliberate mutilation. Not all of this rough treatment seems to have been caused by thieves, since there were signs that the reburial commission had removed the wrappings from some mummies very crudely, by cutting them open from head to foot with edged tools. Prior to rewrapping, the broken body parts were reassembled, although in some cases only a rough approximation of the body shape could be made. The corpse of Ramesses VI was so badly damaged that the fragments had to be tied to a wooden board, and part of another body was inadvertently included.

The bodies were rewrapped with linen. Some of the cloths used bear ink inscriptions indicating that they had been made for use in Theban temples (Reeves and Wilkinson 1996, 203). A docket on the mummy of Ramesses IX reveals that, in this instance at least, the rewrapping was carried out at Medinet Habu, the administrative center for the Theban west bank at the time (Reeves and Wilkinson 1996, 171, 206). Other mummies were perhaps rewrapped in their own tombs, as had been done for Queen Merytamun. The linen used to wrap the body of Ramesses III was brought from Medinet Habu for the purpose; graffiti in the small tomb KV 49, located close to the sepulcher of Ramesses III, mention the bringing of linen there by Butehamun and others, perhaps in connection with the in situ refurbishment of this king's mummy (Reeves and Wilkinson 1996, 206). At the completion of the operation most of the mummies were labeled with dockets written in ink on the outer wrappings, recording their names. These notes appear on the whole to be reliable, although doubts were cast on some of the identifications following an X-ray survey of the mummies in the 1970s, since estimates of age at death and craniofacial morphology appeared to be at variance with expectations based on historical sources (Reeves and Wilkinson 1996, 202–204). The fact that some mummies were left without labels by the restorers suggests that identifications were recorded only where these were considered as certain.

The almost total lack of objects within the wrappings of the mummies that have been unwrapped or X-rayed since their modern discovery indicates that most items of value, if not already taken by robbers, were removed by the officials in charge of the restorations. Rare exceptions include beads and bracelets on the mummies of Amenhotep I and Thutmose III, and a *wḏȝt*-eye amulet on the left arm of Seti I that was detected by X-rays (Reeves and Wilkinson 1996, 99, 204).

Although stripped of virtually all other burial goods, most of the royal mummies reached their final resting place inside an anthropoid coffin. These not only facilitated transportation of the often fragile remains; the coffin was the single most important item of funerary equipment from the ritual viewpoint, conferring magical protection and resurrection on its occupant. Royal coffins of the New Kingdom were richly adorned with gold leaf and often with inlays of precious materials on their surfaces. They were therefore a prime target for thieves and for the official appropriators of valuables. Some of the mummies found in the caches still retained their original coffins, but these had been meticulously stripped of their gold coverings and had been "restored" through the application of yellow paint as a magically viable symbolic substitute for gilding. On the coffin of Seqenenra gold leaf had even been left untouched where it adorned elements of strong religious significance (such as the uraeus, the falcon-headed collar terminals, the vulture of Nekhbet, and the name of the god Ptah-Sokar), a clear indication that this was not the work of robbers but of persons who retained a measure of respect for the dead (Taylor 1992, 187–188). Careful "restoration" by repainting was performed on the coffins of Queen Merytamun under Pinedjem I, providing a clue to the date at which this type of treatment was being undertaken. Other coffins were more roughly handled. The surface of that of Thutmose III, retrieved from TT 320, had been crudely hacked with adzes to remove its gilding (see Figure 24.1). Its dimensions suggest that it originally housed an innermost coffin, perhaps of solid gold like that of Tutankhamun; not surprisingly, all trace of such immensely valuable objects had disappeared. Chippings and shavings of wood from the surfaces of royal coffins, found

FIGURE 24.1 Coffin of Thutmose III, stripped of its original gilded and inlaid surface, from TT 320. Cairo Museum CG 61014.

[From G. Daressy, *Cercueils des Cachettes Royales*, Cairo 1909, pl. XIV.]

among debris in the tomb of Ramesses XI (KV 4), indicate that at least some of this activity took place there (Reeves 1990, 123).

Mummies that had been deprived of their original coffins altogether were placed in substitute receptacles for reburial. Most of these were recycled private coffins, ranging in date from the early Eighteenth to the mid-Twenty-first Dynasties (Daressy 1909, 1–39, 217–226, pls. I–XXIV, LXI–LXIV). Many of them were of surprisingly poor workmanship. On those used for Amenhotep I and Thutmose II, formal bands of inscription were adapted to incorporate the names of the new owners, but in other cases the original decorated surface was left unaltered or imperfectly concealed beneath a layer of paint, the identities of the occupants being hastily written in ink.

Of the rich burial equipment with which the royal tombs had originally been stocked, scarcely anything was salvaged to accompany the mummies into the caches. How much had escaped robbers, to be confiscated by the restorers, is unknown. The items that they left behind in the tombs of Thutmose III, Amenhotep II, Thutmose IV, Amenhotep III, Horemheb, Ramesses I, Seti I, Ramesses IX, and others evidently represent classes of object held to be of little interest or value after any precious materials had been extracted. These included wooden statuary, shabtis, model boats, canopic containers, stone vessels, weapons, horse harness, and the body of a chariot.

Recycling of Objects from the Royal Tombs

The evidence of the royal mummies appears to reflect a deliberate "decommissioning" of the burials, carried out systematically, and the treatment of some of the coffins indicates that a key motivation was the retrieval of valuable materials for reuse. While much of the precious metal may have been melted down, some of the objects taken were adapted and put to use in the burials of the contemporary rulers. The lid of a coffin that had belonged to Thutmose I was appropriated and reinscribed for Pinedjem I, who by the end of his career had adopted royal titles. The lid was richly refurbished with extensive gilding and inlays, as was another New Kingdom coffin, of an unknown owner, which was refashioned for Pinedjem's wife Henuttawy (Daressy 1909, 50–66, pls. XXVIII–XXXV). While the use of older coffins may have been driven in part by economic factors, ideological reasons could also have played an influential role, since Pinedjem I sought to make a direct association with the Thutmosid royal family, possibly to support his own pretensions to kingship (Taylor 1992, 191, 198; Dodson 2012, 50–52).

The royal necropolis of the Twenty-first Dynasty at Tanis contained numerous objects of earlier date, which had been provided for the burials of kings and members of their court. It is possible, though proof is lacking, that some of these objects had been "liberated" from the Valley of the Kings during the decommissioning process. The most substantial of them is a red granite sarcophagus, originally made for Merenptah, which was reinscribed for King Psusennes I. A heart scarab amulet bearing the name of a king Usermaatra (Ramesses II or III?) was found on the mummy of the army commander Wendjebauendjed (Taylor 1992, 205, n. 56), while a gold ritual vessel of Ahmose I and several items of jewelry in New Kingdom style, also found at Tanis, have been proposed as possible "refugees" from earlier royal burials (Reeves and Wilkinson 1996, 206).

Although many funerary statuettes were abandoned in the royal tombs, some were transformed into burial goods for private individuals. The most striking instance of this is a wooden shabti of Ramesses II, which was adapted into an Osiris figure of late Twenty-first to early Twenty-second Dynasty type by removing the uraeus, reshaping the *nemes* headdress into a tripartite wig, and adding twin feathers and a sun disk. The figure was then mounted on a rectangular plinth and coated with black varnish. Although this outer layer (now flaked away) concealed the inscriptions that identified the original owner of the shabti, the association with Ramesses II may have been regarded as contributing to the magical potency of the statue (Taylor 1992, 198–200, pls. 20, 21, 24; Reeves and Wilkinson 1996, 206).

The opening of tombs and the unwrapping of mummies would undoubtedly have brought to light funerary texts that had been previously the prerogative of kings. Some of these were copied and incorporated into the steadily evolving body of mortuary literature and iconography that was in use at Thebes in the Twenty-first Dynasty. A Book of the Dead spell (166 according to the supplementary numbering by Willem Pleyte) is described in its rubric as "the book that was found at the neck of the mummy of King Usermaatra Setep[enra] [Ramesses II] in the necropolis" (Taylor 1992, 199; Reeves and Wilkinson 1996, 206). Copies of the spell with this gloss occur in several of the papyri of the Twenty-first Dynasty that were found with mummies of priests of Amun in the collective tomb known as the Bab el-Gasus. As with the shabti of Ramesses II, the royal provenance of the spell may have been valued as highly as its content. The funerary texts and images on the walls of the kings' tombs appear also to have been studied and copied, and adapted for use in nonroyal burials. The version of the Amduat painted in the tomb of Amenhotep II has been identified as the direct source for extracts from this composition that were used on coffins and papyri in the late Twenty-first and early Twenty-second Dynasties (Niwinski 1989, 178–179, 234–235; Reeves and Wilkinson 1996, 206), while images on other Twenty-second Dynasty coffins seem to have been inspired by scenes in the tomb of Ramesses IX.

INTRUSIVE BURIALS IN THE VALLEY OF THE KINGS

During the stage-by-stage process of restoration and transfer of royal mummies, which continued throughout the Twenty-first Dynasty, it appears that the Valley of the Kings was "out of bounds" to nonroyal burials. Within a short time of the final closure of the Deir el-Bahri cache in the reign of Shoshenq I, this situation changed, and during the Twenty-second Dynasty several of the now-empty tombs were used for the interment of private individuals.

Some of these burials survived intact and in good condition, notably one found by Howard Carter in 1901 in KV 44 and another by the University of Basel expedition in

2012 in KV 64 (Carter 1901; Bickel and Paulin-Grothe 2012). Many others were destroyed by later plundering or by the infiltration of rainwater into the tombs, but the stylistic features of the fragmentary coffins that have been recovered (most distinctively the use of inner cases made of cartonnage) allow most of this burial activity to be dated to the Twenty-second Dynasty.

Although undatable human remains have been found in tombs in all parts of the valley, those that can be attributed to the Third Intermediate Period are mainly located in the extremities of the necropolis. Two mummies were interred in the tomb of Thutmose III, in the cleft at the valley's southern end, and the recently discovered KV 64 lies close by. Well-dated Twenty-second Dynasty burials were found in KV 44 and 45, and remains of another were recovered from KV 4 in the same eastern part of the valley. The tomb of Mentuherkhepeshef (KV 19) contained several mummies when it was found by Giovanni Belzoni, and although these are now lost, a contemporary reference to a fragment of painted cartonnage from the tomb also suggests a Twenty-second Dynasty date (Taylor 1992, 200). The Western Valley seems also to have received intrusive burials in WV 24 and 25. The badly broken fragments that have been retrieved by excavation point to interments in the Third Intermediate Period in WV 24 (Schaden 1991), while painted coffins containing eight mummies (one of which had apparently been rewrapped) were reportedly found by Belzoni in WV 25 in 1817. These were subsequently broken up or lost, but fragments recovered during a re-clearance in 1972 suggest that some of these also dated to the Twenty-second Dynasty (Schaden 1979).

The Twenty-second Dynasty witnessed significant changes in the patterns of use of the Theban necropolis, most notably the opening of the Ramesseum temple enclosure for use as a burial ground (in line with the custom of locating high-status tombs within temple precincts, already pioneered at Tanis). A lifting of restrictions on the use of the Valley of the Kings may have taken place within the context of this restructuring of Theban cemeteries. It is noteworthy that persons buried at the Ramesseum—and subsequently within other temple enclosures, such as those at Medinet Habu and Deir el-Bahri—appear from their titles and elaborate funerary outfits to have belonged to the higher strata of Theban society, whereas those interred in the Valley of the Kings were evidently of lower rank. Those who can be identified from the coffin inscriptions were Merenkhonsu, a doorkeeper of the domain of Amun (KV 45), a Lady of the House named Tenkerer, a "singer" Iufaa and an unnamed chantress (KV 44), and a chantress of Amun-Ra named Nehemesbast (KV 64) (Ryan 1992; Carter 1901; Bickel and Paulin-Grothe 2012). Two persons buried in KV 34 were perhaps of still lower status, on the evidence of the very simple character of their undecorated and uninscribed coffins. Apart from crude shabtis in KV 45 and a small wooden stela placed next to the coffin in KV 64, grave goods with these burials were limited to floral garlands (reported by Carter in KV 44). The tombs in which they lay had not even been thoroughly cleared of the remains of earlier burials, and the presence of bees' nests inside KV 44 indicated that the tomb had stood open for some time before the final occupants were placed inside.

The last attested phase of burial in the valley dates to the Twenty-sixth Dynasty. Fragments of coffins of this date (one with the name Padihorresnet) were recovered from the "well" of the tomb of Amenhotep III in the Western branch (Taylor 1992, 200, 206). It has been suggested that the tomb of Thutmose III was also entered once again at this period. The rather indirect evidence for this comes from the sarcophagus of Hapimen (British Museum EA 23), the decoration of which appears to have been specifically inspired by the iconography of the king's sarcophagus (Hayes 1935, 153–154; Reeves 1990, 24; Reeves and Wilkinson 1996, 99).

The complete absence of evidence for burials in the valley in the Ptolemaic and Roman periods is striking, as almost all other areas of the Theban necropolis were intensively used during those centuries (Strudwick 2003, 184; Riggs 2003, 189). Among the explanations that have been put forward for this are the valley's inconveniently remote location and a reluctance to intrude upon the perceived sanctity of the former royal cemetery. Perhaps more significant is the fact that the spot had by that time already become a tourist attraction, as the Greek and Latin graffiti left by visitors on the walls of some of the tombs testify.

BIBLIOGRAPHY

Aston, D. A. 2013. "TT 320 and the qAy of Queen Inhapi: A Reconsideration based on Ceramic Evidence." *Göttinger Miszellen* 236: 7–20.

Bickel, S., and E. Paulin-Grothe. 2012. "The Valley of the Kings: Two Burials in KV 64." *Egyptian Archaeology* 41: 36–40.

Carter, H. 1901. "Report on Tomb-pit Opened on the 26th January 1901, in the Valley of the Tombs of the Kings, between No. 4 and No. 28." *Annales du Service des Antiquites de l'Egypte* 2: 144–145, pl. I–II.

Daressy, G. 1909. *Catalogue General des Antiquites Egyptiennes du Musee du Cairo: Nos. 61001–61044, Cercueils des Cachettes Royales*. Cairo, Institut Francais d'Archeologie Orientale.

Dodson, A. 2012. *Afterglow of Empire: Egypt from the Fall of the New Kingdom to the Saite Renaissance*. Cairo and New York: American University in Cairo Press.

Graefe, E., and G. Belova, eds. 2010. *The Royal Cache TT 320: A Re-examination*. Cairo: Supreme Council of Antiquities Press.

Hayes, W. C. 1935. *Royal Sarcophagi of the XVIII Dynasty*. Princeton, NJ: Princeton University Press.

Jansen-Winkeln, K. 1995. "Die Plünderung der Königsgräber des Neuen Reiches." *Zeitschrift für Ägyptische Sprache und Altertumskunde* 122: 62–78.

Jansen-Winkeln, K. 2007. *Inschriften der Spätzeit. I: Die 21. Dynastie*. Wiesbaden: Harrassowitz Verlag.

Lull, J. 2002. *Las tumbas reales egipcias del Tercer Periodo Intermedio (dinastias XXI–XXV)*. British Archaeological Reports International Series 1045. Oxford: Archaeopress.

Niwinski, A. 1989. *Studies on the Illustrated Theban Funerary Papyri of the 11th and 10th centuries B.C.* Orbis Biblicus et Orientalis 86. Freiburg and Göttingen: Universitätsverlag Freiburg & Vandenhoeck & Ruprecht Göttingen.

Niwinski, A. 2004. *Catalogo del Museo Egizio di Torino. Serie Seconda – Collezioni, IX. Sarcofagi della XXI Dinastia (CGT 10101–10122)*. Turin: Ministero per I Beni e le Attivita Culturali – Soprintendenza al Museo delle Antichita Egizie.

Reeves, C. N. 1990. *Valley of the Kings: The Decline of a Royal Necropolis*. London and New York: Kegan Paul International.

Reeves, C. N., ed. 1992. *After Tutankhamun: Research and Excavation in the Royal Necropolis at Thebes*. London and New York: Kegan Paul International.

Reeves, C. N., and R. H. Wilkinson. 1996. *The Complete Valley of the Kings: Tombs and Treasures of Egypt's Greatest Pharaohs*. London: Thames and Hudson.

Riggs, C. 2003. "The Egyptian Funerary Tradition at Thebes in the Roman Period." In *The Theban Necropolis: Past, Present and Future*, edited by N. Strudwick and J. H. Taylor, 189–201. London: British Museum Press.

Rose, J. 2000. *Tomb KV39 in the Valley of the Kings: A Double Archaeological Enigma*. Bristol: Western Academic and Specialist Press.

Ryan, D. P. 1992. "The Valley Again." *Kmt* 3 (1): 44–47, 69.

Schaden, O. J. 1979. "Preliminary Report on the Re-clearance of Tomb 25 in the Western Valley of the Kings." *Annales du Service des Antiquites de l'Egypte* 63: 161–168, pls. I–VII.

Schaden, O. J. 1991. "Preliminary Report on Clearance of WV 24 in an Effort to Determine its Relationship to Royal Tombs 23 and 25." *Kmt* 2 (3): 53–61.

Strudwick, N. 2003. "Some Aspects of the Archaeology of the Theban Necropolis in the Ptolemaic and Roman Periods." In *The Theban Necropolis: Past, Present and Future*, edited by N. Strudwick and J. H. Taylor, 167–188. London: British Museum Press.

Strudwick, N., and J. H. Taylor, eds. 2003. *The Theban Necropolis: Past, Present and Future*. London: British Museum Press.

Taylor, J. H. 1992. "Aspects of the History of the Valley of the Kings in the Third Intermediate Period." In *After Tutankhamun: Research and Excavation in the Royal Necropolis at Thebes*, edited by C. N. Reeves, 186–206. London and New York: Kegan Paul International.

Winlock, H. E. 1932. *The Tomb of Queen Meryet-Amun at Thebes*. New York: Metropolitan Museum of Art.

PART X

HUMAN REMAINS FROM THE KV AND THEIR STUDY

CHAPTER 25

EARLY STUDY AND THE UNWRAPPING OF MUMMIES

ROSALIE DAVID

THE human remains discovered in the Valley of the Kings, belonging to kings and queens and, more rarely, to their offspring and other family members, provide an unparalleled opportunity to study various aspects of the royal families of the New Kingdom (Eighteenth to Twentieth Dynasties). Some studies have sought biological evidence in order to identify or confirm familial relationships and to promote speculation about individual degrees of kinship within the royal family. Although this approach does not always produce definitive answers (see ch 26), the additional insight it provides is especially important, because identification based solely on archaeological and historical data can sometimes be misleading.

Biological evidence can also supply information about an individual's gender, lifestyle, diet, pathological conditions, age at death, and sometimes cause of demise, while physical examination of the body and any associated artifacts can increase knowledge about mummification techniques during the New Kingdom. In general, data from mummies have augmented information about health patterns, history, and religious and funerary customs during this period.

SOURCE MATERIAL FOR SCIENTIFIC STUDIES

Human remains from the Valley of the Kings come from caches, individual tomb groups, or mummies no longer associated with their original find-spots. A breakdown in necropolis security toward the end of the New Kingdom led to the plunder of many tombs, but the mummies, although sometimes badly damaged and separated from their original coffins, often survived. During an inspection of all known tombs in this area, the priests of the Twenty-first and Twenty-second Dynasties transferred these royal survivors to official centers where they were repaired, rewrapped, and provided with (often new) coffins, prior to reburial. The hieratic notes that the priests attached to coffins and bandages provided the names of individuals and details of their rewrapping and reburial, but in some cases this information is probably inaccurate, which has resulted in misidentification of some royal mummies. At first, the rewrapped mummies were reburied in various tombs throughout the necropolis where they could be better protected, but eventually most were transferred to one of the royal caches. Two caches have been identified so far, located in a large tomb (DB 320) at Deir el-Bahri and in the tomb of Amenhotep II (KV 35); however, other caches may await discovery.

The existence of the first royal cache in DB 320 was announced in 1881, although it had been discovered some ten years earlier by the Abd el-Rassul family. The elder brother of the family, reassured that he would be immune from punishment, finally provided the authorities with details of the tomb's location. On their first visit, the officials found an assemblage of funerary artifacts and a cache of over forty royal mummies, which contained members of the royal family of the Twenty-first Dynasty, moved there for safekeeping, and an earlier group of New Kingdom royalty, probably transferred at the same time. These included Seqenenre; Ahmose I; Amenhotep I; Thutmose I, II, and III; Seti I; Ramesses II, III and IX; and several queens and princesses (Brugsch and Maspero 1881).

Fear that local villagers might seize the treasure prompted the officials to empty the tomb. The contents were cleared within two days and moved to Luxor, but since no record was kept of the location of the mummies and artifacts within the tomb, researchers later found it difficult to identify some of the bodies. Finally, on July 14, 1881, the mummies were transported by river to Cairo and installed in the Boulaq Museum (Maspero 1887).

In 1891 the Abd el-Rassul family reported the discovery of a second cache at Deir el-Bahri, which contained coffins, funerary objects, and the mummies of 150 high priests and priestesses of Amun, transported from their own burial sites for safekeeping (Daressy 1900). These were also transferred to Cairo and later subjected to scientific studies.

In 1898, Victor Loret, director of the Egyptian Antiquities Service, discovered a second royal cache in the tomb of Amenhotep II (KV35) (Loret 1899). The tomb had been plundered in antiquity, but the king's mummy remained in the burial chamber in its original coffin and sarcophagus (Daressy 1902, 62–279); another single, unidentified mummy was found in the antechamber. The side chambers accommodated two groups of mummies. Chamber C housed three uncoffined bodies: a young boy wearing the "Sidelock of Youth" and two females (the "Elder Lady" and "Younger Woman"), all perhaps brought there either when Amenhotep II was interred, or later in the Eighteenth Dynasty, or even after the arrival of the mummies in Chamber B.

Loret discovered a group of thirteen mummies in Chamber B. Initially, he believed they were relatives of Amenhotep II, but inscriptions on the coffins of eight of these bodies identified them as Thutmose IV, Amenhotep III, Merenptah, Seti II, Siptah, and Ramesses IV, V, and VI. A ninth coffined mummy may have belonged to the female ruler Tausret. According to inscriptions on the bandages, priests of the Twenty-first Dynasty, acting on a royal edict, had transferred this group of royal mummies to KV 35 at the same time as the first cache was deposited in the Deir el-Bahri tomb. In due course, all identifiable mummies from KV 35 were moved to Cairo, but the three unidentified bodies in Chamber C remained in situ. Amenhotep II's body was also left at the tomb in its own sarcophagus, but tomb-robbing eventually prompted the authorities to move the mummy to Cairo.

In 1907 Ayrton (working on behalf of T. M. Davis) discovered KV 55, a small, uninscribed, and undecorated tomb that contained an assemblage sometimes known as the "Amarna cache." The burial included a poorly preserved, almost skeletal mummy, housed in a gilded, inlaid wooden coffin. Among the funerary goods were panels from a gilded wooden shrine designed to protect the sarcophagus of Queen Tiye; the name of Akhenaten, originally inscribed on the panels, had been erased. Other items carried the names of Amenhotep III, Tutankhamun, Sitamun, and Kiya. Originally, this assemblage may have been housed in the royal tomb or other tombs at Amarna, but it was perhaps moved to KV 55 when Amarna was abandoned and the royal burials returned to Thebes.

Ownership of the funerary objects in this tomb has been disputed; the coffin, for example, has been variously attributed to Tiye, Akhenaten, or Smenkhkare, and the identity of the mummy remains uncertain. Davis believed that the mummy, identified by a preliminary examination as female, belonged to Tiye, and that she was the owner of this tomb.

Only two almost intact tombs have been discovered in the Valley of the Kings; although robbed in antiquity, these still contained the mummies of their owners and impressive funerary assemblages. Tomb KV 46, excavated by Quibell and Weigall in 1905, belonged to Yuya and Thuya, commoners granted the honor of burial in the valley because they were the parents of Queen Tiye. This high quality burial tomb contained the owners' two well-preserved mummies, Thuya's viscera stored in canopic jars, and some magnificent funerary equipment.

The most famous tomb in the valley (KV 62), discovered by Carter in 1922 (Carter and Mace 1923, 1927, 1933), contained the mummy and largely intact burial assemblage of Tutankhamun, as well as two female fetuses, probably the offspring of the king and his wife, Ankhesenamun (Derry 1933).

KV 5, a tomb first noted by James Burton in 1825, was rediscovered by Weeks in 1989 (Weeks 1998; see also www.kv5.com). Subsequent excavation and study have confirmed an earlier theory (Thomas 1966) that KV 5 was the "Tomb of the Royal Children" mentioned in the Turin Papyrus, where some of Ramesses II's sons were buried. The skeletal remains of four adult males have been discovered so far, and further biological evidence will doubtless appear as remaining chambers of this vast tomb are excavated (see Figure 25.1).

On opening KV 60 in 1903, Carter discovered two badly damaged female mummies. When Ayrton re-entered the tomb in 1906, he dispatched one body (attributed to Sitre-In, the wet nurse of Hatshepsut) to Cairo, but the second mummy remained in the burial chamber. The sealed tomb was rediscovered in 1989 (Ryan 1989), and a new examination of the mummy revealed an obese, middle-aged woman with worn teeth and long, reddish-gold hair, whose right hand was placed across the chest in a position sometimes found in queens' mummies. These findings led Ryan (1990) to propose that the mummy belonged to Hatshepsut, an attribution suggested some years earlier by Thomas (1966), drawing on information given in Carter's brief notes about the tomb and the mummy.

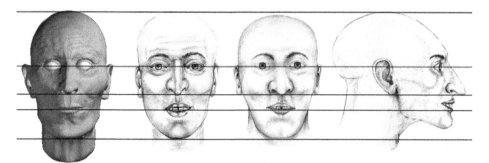

Ramesses II

FIGURE 25.1 Comparison of the facial reconstructions of individuals from Tomb KV 5 and Ramesses II. Faces 2 and 3 show consistent proportions with those of Ramesses II, perhaps indicating that these men were the king's sons. However, the horizontal proportions of Face 3 are significantly different from the other faces, so it is probably less likely that the owner was closely related to Ramesses II.

[Professor Caroline Wilkinson, University of Dundee, Scotland.]

Ryan has relocated and reopened many smaller tombs in the Valley of the Kings and found unidentified, possibly royal, mummies, including two female bodies in Tomb KV 21 (originally uncovered by Belzoni in 1817) and human remains in KV 44 (a tomb first discovered by Carter in 1901). Human skeletal material from at least nine individuals has also been retrieved from Rose's re-excavation of KV 39 (originally explored by Macarios and Andraos in 1900) (Rose 2000).

Although most New Kingdom rulers can be identified with the mummies discovered in caches and tombs in the Valley of the Kings, the current location of some royal mummies remains uncertain. This has prompted speculation that one mummy, brought from Egypt in the nineteenth century and donated to the Niagara Falls Museum in the United States, might be the missing body of Ramesses I. Scientific tests carried out on the mummy persuaded researchers that it probably was the mummy of a pharaoh, and a supposedly close resemblance to the mummies of Seti I and Ramesses II led to its tentative identification as Ramesses I. On this assumption, the body was returned to Egypt in 2003 and placed on display in the Luxor Museum. However, this identification is not universally accepted, and some Egyptologists doubt that the mummy came from a royal cache or tomb (Bickerstaffe 2009, 112–120).

DIAGNOSTIC AND INVESTIGATIVE TECHNIQUES

In recent years researchers have added new diagnostic tools to the various methods used by early investigators to examine mummies. From the Renaissance onward, museums, learned societies, and private collectors in Europe acquired mummies, and from the sixteenth century, some bodies were unwrapped and autopsied on frivolous social occasions. No academic record of these unwrappings has survived, but a few early investigators performed multidisciplinary, scientific studies and published their results. The most notable of these "unrollings" were carried out in London by the surgeon T. J. Pettigrew (1791–1865) and the physician A. B. Granville (1783–1872), while in 1825 a multidisciplinary team at the Leeds Philosophical and Literary Society performed an exemplary autopsy on the mummy of a priest.

The early projects concentrated on unwrapping and dissection, followed by an anatomical examination of the general state of the body. Although destructive and irreversible, autopsy optimizes the chances of gaining information and provides the best opportunity for sample collection, and therefore, even in the 1970s and 1980s, several teams still chose this as their preliminary method of investigation.

Endoscopy—a virtually nondestructive method of investigation and sample collection—was introduced in the 1970s, when one team carried out an endoscopic examination of the mummies of Ramesses II, Merenptah, and Ramesses V (Manialawi et al. 1978). Some early projects used flexible (medical) endoscopes, but the rigid (industrial) version was found to be more effective in penetrating hard, inflexible tissue (Tapp et al. 1984). Endoscopy and radiography are often used in conjunction so that optimum areas within the mummy can be pinpointed for tissue sampling.

Radiography, discovered in 1896, provided an early nondestructive method of examination, which was soon employed to examine Egyptological specimens (Böni et al. 2004), including the mummy of Thutmose IV (see below). Later, comprehensive radiographic surveys of mummy collections were undertaken by Moodie, Gray, Harris, and Wente (see ch 26), and there have been other, more recent studies at Manchester and Leiden. Paleoimaging has also made a significant contribution to studies of individual mummies. The most significant advance, computed tomography (CT), developed for clinical use in the 1970s, was soon adopted for mummy studies and has now become a standard procedure in many investigations.

There have been studies of the dentitions of individual mummies, as well as surveys of oral health and disease in specific population groups (Harris 1989; Harris and Wente 1980, 328–345). Where dry skulls are available for handling and visual examination, researchers can gain valuable experience in identifying pathological and nonpathological conditions. However, radiography and CT scanning are used to study mummified or wrapped heads. These can often supply useful information about a particular dentition, but where dental details are obscured by a funerary mask or hard facial tissue around the mouth, better results can be achieved by using specialized equipment (the orthopantomograph), which provides a panoramic view of the teeth.

Paleohistology, an important aspect of paleopathology (the study of disease occurrence in ancient populations), makes a particularly significant contribution to research on mummified remains. Although this technique was first promoted in Egypt by Fouquet in 1889, it is Ruffer, a bacteriologist working in Cairo in the early twentieth century, who is the acknowledged pioneer in this field (Ruffer 1911). His main contribution was the development of an agent (Ruffer's Solution) to rehydrate ancient tissues prior to the application of contemporary histological techniques (Ruffer 1921). This has facilitated all subsequent paleohistological studies, as well as providing the basis for more recent developments in rehydrating and processing ancient tissues.

Electron microscopy and immunohistochemistry have added new dimensions to this area of study (Lewin 1967). The specialized stains used in immunohistochemistry increase the likelihood of identifying cell constituents in tissue, while the greater magnification offered by electron microscopy provides a much better resolution of a sample's detailed structure.

Analysis of ancient DNA (aDNA) offers the possibility of identifying genetic markers in ancient populations, which may help to determine their origin, composition, and migration patterns. However, before DNA techniques were introduced to Egyptology in the 1980s (Pääbo 1985), paleoserology (the study of blood groups in ancient human remains) offered opportunities to trace ancient kinship patterns and population movements. Early studies of blood groups in Egyptian mummies (Boyd and Boyd 1934) led to limited technical success with the serological micromethod (SMM) and the inhibition agglutination test (IAT). However, because of the considerable technical challenges of this method, the results were never entirely convincing, and this persuaded researchers to choose aDNA analysis as the preferred option for population studies.

In recent years, mummy studies have adopted new investigative techniques (some are discussed in ch 26). In addition to aDNA analysis (Zink and Nerlich 2003), researchers now employ advanced paleoimaging methods, scientific facial reconstruction, and immunological diagnostic tools (Deelder et al. 1990; Rutherford 2008), as well as instrumental analyses, which include studies of materials used in mummification (Buckley and Evershed 2001) that build on Lucas's pioneering work (Lucas and Harris 1962).

SCIENTIFIC STUDIES OF MUMMIES FROM THE VALLEY OF THE KINGS

Many scientific studies have been carried out on mummies found in the Valley of the Kings. These include surveys of the large collections from the caches, multidisciplinary investigations of bodies believed to have familial associations (particularly the Amarna group), and multidisciplinary studies of individual mummies.

In the 1880s, following Brugsch's initial attempts to unwrap the mummies of Thutmose III, Ahmose-Nefertari, and Ramesses II (Brugsch and Maspero 1881), Maspero initiated the first large-scale project to unwrap and partially autopsy the royal mummies from the two royal caches (Maspero 1889). His team included Fouquet, a doctor of medicine, and Mathey, a chemist; he also invited the anatomist Elliot Smith (see Figure 25.2) to examine all available royal mummies and produce a report on their anatomical and pathological features.

FIGURE 25.2 Portrait of Sir Grafton Elliot Smith, who left Cairo to take up a post as professor of anatomy at the University of Manchester, England (1909–1919). During this period, he wrote his pioneering work, *The Royal Mummies* (1912), which describes the anatomical studies he undertook while in Egypt.

[Reproduced by courtesy of the University Librarian and Director, The John Rylands Library, The University of Manchester.]

However, in many cases this was impossible without damaging the mummies, and Smith proposed the recently invented technique radiography as a means of overcoming this problem. Maspero was apparently unwilling to authorize its use, and Smith's vision was only realized many years later when a complete radiographic survey of the royal mummies was undertaken by the Michigan-Alexandria team (Harris and Wente 1980) (see ch 26).

Smith was only permitted to radiograph the mummy of Thutmose IV, which had been unwrapped several months earlier. In 1903, accompanied by Howard Carter, he took the body to a private nursing home (the only place in Cairo where such facilities were available); X-rays of the mummy taken by Dr. Khayrat revealed the condition of the epiphyses and enabled the king's age at death to be established.

Although early studies provided only limited information about age at death and disease patterns, access to a large collection of royal and nonroyal mummies gave Smith the opportunity to study the evolution of mummification techniques in the New Kingdom. His discoveries were published in two pioneering works (Smith 1912; Smith and Dawson 1924). Other studies also provided information (Daressy 1902), including the investigation of the cache of priests and priestesses discovered at Deir el-Bahri (Daressy and Smith 1903).

Although these early autopsies were undertaken at great speed, and valuable and irreplaceable evidence was undoubtedly lost, they nevertheless represent significant, pioneering ventures that underpin all later research on this unique material.

Mummies associated with the Amarna royal family have also provided a rich resource for research into individual identifications, disease occurrence, lifestyle, cause of death, and mummification procedures. There have been four major investigations of the mummy of Tutankhamun. Derry performed the first autopsy in 1923 (briefly summarized in Derry 1927, with publication of the scientific report appearing much later in Leek 1972, 11–20). Derry concluded that the shape of Tutankhamun's skull matched that of the mummy found in KV 55—a similarity confirmed by craniofacial morphology studies undertaken as part of a multidisciplinary project in 1968 (Harrison 1973). This research team also demonstrated that the men had shared the same relatively rare blood group (A2 with the antigens MN present) (Connolly 1969), indicating that they had a close genetic relationship within the family, perhaps as brothers or father and son.

In recent years, two major studies of Tutankhamun's mummy have been undertaken by the Egyptian Antiquities Service. Evidence of a broken leg first emerged when the body was CT scanned in 2005. Opinion was divided as to whether this had occurred ante-mortem or post-mortem, but some researchers claimed that the injury had resulted in complications that caused the king's death (Hawass et al. 2009). The study does not support earlier speculation that Tutankhamun may have been murdered, a theory that arose from Harrison's observation (1971), based on the 1968 radiographs, that the king's death may have resulted from a brain hemorrhage caused by a blow to the head.

A more detailed analysis of the CT scans has since provided evidence of a left club foot, diseased bones in the right foot, and a cleft palate, and DNA studies have been undertaken to search for genetic evidence of disease organisms and to compare Tutankhamun's DNA profile with those of eleven other mummies (Hawass et al. 2010). This investigation has proposed that malaria, exacerbated by an inbred, sickly constitution, was the cause of the king's death. However, the results have been disputed, and the cause of death remains unconfirmed; other suggestions include hereditary metabolic bone disease, an accident, or an encounter with a wild animal.

Derry was the first to examine the two female fetuses found in Tutankhamun's tomb (Carter and Mace 1923, 1927, 1933, 3:167–169). A later radiological and serological assessment of one of the fetuses, undertaken to determine its relationship to Tutankhamun and other family members, reported multiple congenital conditions, including Sprengel's deformity, spinal dysraphism, and scoliosis (Harrison et al. 1979). However, CT scans have not subsequently confirmed the presence of the most serious of these anomalies (Hawass and Saleem 2011). Chamberlain (2001) speculated that the fetuses were twins, the difference in their size and development explained by a twin-to-twin transfusion syndrome, and a recent study of ancestry in the Amarna family has indicated that the fetuses were probably the offspring of Tutankhamun (Hawass et al. 2010).

The mummies found in KV 55 and KV 35 have been the subject of much speculation, and although there is no definitive evidence, many studies propose that they all belong to the Amarna royal family. Even after Smith established that the body in KV 55 (originally reported as female) was male, debate has continued about its age at death and identity. Suggestions include Akhenaten, Smenkhkare, or another unknown royal prince (Derry 1931; Harrison 1966; Connolly et al. 1976), although marked similarities between this body and the mummy of Tutankhamun would suggest that their owners were closely related.

The identity of the two female bodies in KV 35 has also been the subject of intense discussion. Initially, the mummy of the Elder Lady was attributed to Hatshepsut on account of its physical similarity to those of Thutmose II and III. However, craniofacial studies have since demonstrated a close match between the Elder Lady and the firmly identified mummy of Thuya (mother of Tiye), suggesting that the Elder Lady might be Queen Tiye (Harris et al. 1978).

To clarify the situation, electron scanning tests were carried out on strands of hair taken from the Elder Lady and from a lock enclosed in a coffinette found in Tutankhamun's tomb that bears Tiye's name. A comparison of these results has demonstrated that the samples are very similar, but some researchers do not regard this as a conclusive outcome (Germer 1984). Attempted identification of the mummy of the Younger Woman has generated even greater controversy, with widespread criticism of Fletcher's proposal (2004) that the body might belong to Nefertiti.

Most recently, a major study, based on evidence from CT scans and DNA analysis, has addressed identities and genetic relationships within the Amarna royal family (Hawass et al. 2010). The conclusions include the identifications of the Younger Woman (perhaps Akhenaten's secondary wife, Kiya) as the mother of Tutankhamun, and Yuya and Thuya as the parents of the Elder Lady, thus confirming that the Elder Lady is Queen Tiye. This research, which introduces some controversial perspectives based on DNA evidence from the mummies, has generated considerable discussion (Marchant 2011; see also K. Phizackerley's blog "DNA Shows the KV55 Mummy Probably Not Akhenaten," http://www.kv64.info/2010/03/dna-shows-that-kv55-mummy-probably-not.html, March 2, 2010).

There have also been biological studies of individual mummies. When the mummy of Seqenenre-Tao II, unwrapped by Maspero's team in 1886, was examined by Smith, he noted five skull wounds and the poorly preserved condition of the body. This led him to suggest that the king had died in battle, attacked by two or more assailants armed with an axe, a spear, and arrows; he had died instantly or soon after the attack, and was cursorily mummified on the battlefield. A more recent theory suggests that he may have been murdered while he slept, while an X-ray analysis has demonstrated evidence of new bone growth around one of the skull perforations, probably indicating that the king survived for a few months before death (Fleming and Fishman 1980).

A Discovery Channel documentary, *Secrets of Egypt's Lost Queen* (July 15, 2007), related how CT scans and DNA analysis have confirmed the tentative identification that one of the mummies found in KV 60 was Queen Hatshepsut (see above). A molar tooth with a missing root was found inside a box inscribed with Hatshepsut's name, which was recovered from the Deir el-Bahri cache. CT scans were used to match this tooth with the root of a missing molar found in situ in the mummy's dentition. Researchers claimed that this evidence proved the mummy's association with Hatshepsut, a result apparently confirmed by DNA tests.

The poorly preserved mummy of Ramesses II, partly unwrapped by Maspero in 1886 in front of a celebrated audience, was taken to France in 1976 for conservation treatment, which involved irradiation with gamma rays. At the same time, the mummy underwent extensive, noninvasive investigations. Although CT scanning and destructive sampling techniques were not permitted, the project produced some interesting results, including the discovery that the king had suffered from severe dental problems, arthritis, ankylosing spondylitis, and advanced atherosclerosis but had survived into his nineties (Balout and Roubet 1985). Studies also showed that, although his white hair had been colored with a yellow dye at the time of his death, its original natural pigmentation was auburn.

The mummy of his son, Merenptah, was unwrapped by Smith in 1907 (Smith 1907a). Histological examination of a piece of his aorta, sent to the Royal College of Surgeons in London, revealed evidence of atheroma, which probably indicates that the king had suffered from atherosclerosis (Shattock 1909).

A shortening of the left leg and gross deformity of the ankle observed in the mummy of Siptah have been variously attributed to club foot, poliomyelitis, a congenital abnormality, cerebral palsy, or even a post-mortem artifact. The condition was first diagnosed as *talipes equino-varus* (club foot) when Smith unwrapped the mummy in 1905 (Smith 1907b). However, subsequent radiological studies have described the condition as an overall shortening of the left leg and a deformed foot (Harris and Wente 1980) and have indicated that the king may have suffered from a neuromuscular disease in childhood. A possible diagnosis of poliomyelitis remains uncertain because the disease does not occur in isolation, but evidence of similar deformities is lacking in other mummies.

The Judicial Papyrus (Egyptian Museum, Turin) recounts that Ramesses III met a violent death during a power struggle in the royal harem. Recent CT scans of the mummy lend some support to this account, since they reveal the presence of a deep cut (probably made with a sharp knife) in the king's throat (Hawass et al. 2012).

When Smith unwrapped Ramesses V in 1905 (Smith 1907b), smallpox was tentatively identified as the cause of cutaneous vesicles observed on the face, neck, chest, and lower abdomen of the mummy. It was possible to test this diagnosis in 1979, when researchers were permitted to remove minute skin samples from the mummy. However, although particles in one of the scabs examined looked like the smallpox virus, this identification could not be confirmed because the radioimmune test for smallpox produced a negative result (Lewin 1982). Eventually, application of the more sensitive immunoprecipitation test confirmed the presence of smallpox, a disease that may have affected other members of the royal family (Strouhal 1996).

PROBLEMS AND POSSIBILITIES

Mummy research faces a variety of problems. For example, the dockets attached to royal mummies probably do not provide correct identifications of the owners, while paleoimaging techniques sometimes produce personal data about a ruler's identification and age at death that are at variance with historical records. DNA studies also produce technical challenges, including contamination of samples and the low survival rate of aDNA in the post-mortem environment (Zink and Nerlich 2003).

Pseudo-pathology raises other issues. For example, radiographic evidence of alkaptonuria (ochronosis) was frequently noted in mummies, although it is a very rare disease in modern patients. This apparent discrepancy was only resolved when analysis of the "evidence"—a radiopaque crystalline material found in the intervertebral space—demonstrated that this material was a product of mummification and not attributable to disease (Wallgren et al. 1986). Paleopathologists should also be aware of the impact of taphonomic effects on archaeological remains so that they avoid misinterpretation of pseudo-pathological, post-mortem changes as examples of ante-mortem disease.

Despite these difficulties, newly discovered material, as well as the many mummies that still await modern investigation, will continue to provide a unique and ample resource for future biological studies. Technical advances in traditional diagnostic methods and access to new techniques as they become available will enhance the capabilities of investigators of the future.

Until now, many scientific studies have focused on attempts to identify individual mummies and clarify familial relationships, but this approach has often produced confusing and frustrating results. Disease diagnosis is arguably a less controversial route and may offer the best opportunities for future research. A comprehensive assessment of the diseases, diet, and lifestyle of the Egyptian rulers, and a comparative study of evidence from other groups in ancient Egyptian or contemporary societies, would make a major contribution to the history of disease and medicine.

As well as the more traditional diagnostic methods of anatomy, paleoimaging, paleohistology, and electron microscopy, future research could involve stable isotope ratio studies and immunological, molecular, and trace element analyses. In addition, a Mummy Tissue Bank could be established in Egypt to hold a comprehensive collection of samples from the Valley of the Kings and elsewhere; this would provide a unique research resource, removing the need to return to the mummy on each occasion to obtain new samples.

BIBLIOGRAPHY

Balout, L., and C. Roubet, eds. 1985. *La Momie de Ramsès II (1976–1977): Contribution Scientifique a l'Égyptologie*. Paris: Éditions Récherche sur les Civilisations.

Bickerstaffe, D. 2009. *Refugees for Eternity: The Royal Mummies of Thebes*. Pt. 4, *Identifying the Royal Mummies*. Chippenham.

Böni, T., F. J. Rühli, and R. K. Chhem. 2004. "History of Paleoradiology: Early Published Literature, 1896–1921." *Journal of the Canadian Association of Radiology* 55 (4): 211–217.

Boyd, W. C., and L. G. Boyd. 1934. "An Attempt to Determine the Blood Groups of Mummies." *Proceedings of the Society for Experimental Biology and Medicine* 31: 671–672.

Brugsch, É., and G. Maspero. 1881. *La trouvaille de Deir-el-Bahari*. Cairo.

Buckley, S. A., and R. P. Evershed. 2001. "Organic Chemistry of Embalming Agents in Pharaonic and Graeco-Roman Mummies." *Nature* 413: 837–841.

Carter, H., and A. C. Mace. 1923, 1927, 1933. *The Tomb of Tut-ankh-Amen Discovered by the Late Earl of Carnarvon and Howard Carter*. 3 vol. London. (Repr. 1963, New York).

Chamberlain, G. 2001. "Two Babies That Could Have Changed World History." *Historian* 72: 6–10.

Connolly, R. C. 1969. "Kinship of Smenkhkare and Tutankhamen Affirmed by Serological Micromethod: Microdetermination of Blood Group Substances in Ancient Human Tissue." *Nature* 224 (October): 325.

Connolly, R. C., R. G. Harrison, and S. Ahmed. 1976. "Serological Evidence for the Parentage of Tut'ankhamūn and Smenkhkarē." *Journal of Egyptian Archaeology* 62: 184–186.

Daressy, G. 1900. "Les sépultures des prêtres d'Ammon à Deir el-Bahari." *Annales du Service des Antiquités de l'Égypte* 1: 141–148.

Daressy, G. 1902. *Fouilles de la Vallée des Rois 1898–1899: Catalogue Général des Antiquités Égyptiennes du Musée du Caire, Nos. 24001–24990*. Cairo.

Daressy, G., and G. E. Smith. 1903. "Ouverture des momies provenant de la seconde trouvaille de Deir el-Bahri: I. Procès-verbeaux des 12 Mai et 16 Juin 1903; II. Report on the Four Mummies." *Annales du Service des Antiquités de l'Égypte* 4: 150–160.

David, A. R., ed. 1986. *Science in Egyptology*. Manchester.

David, A. R., ed. 2008. *Egyptian Mummies and Modern Science*. Cambridge.

David, R., and E. Tapp, eds. 1984. *Evidence Embalmed*. Manchester.

Deelder, A. M., R. L. Miller, N. De Jonge, and F. W. Krijger. 1990. "Detection of Schistosome Antigens in Mummies." *Lancet* 335: 724–725.

Derry, D. E. 1927. "Appendix I: Report upon the Examination of Tut-Ankh-Amen's Mummy." In *The Tomb of Tut-ankh-Amen Discovered by the Late Earl of Carnarvon and Howard Carter*, edited by H. Carter and A. C. Mace, 2:143–161. London.

Derry, D. E. 1931. "Note on the Skeleton Hitherto Believed to be that of Akhenaten." *Annales du Service des Antiquités de l'Égypte* 31: 115–119.

Derry, D. E. 1933. "Report upon the two Human Foetuses discovered in the Tomb of Tutankhamen." In *The Tomb of Tut-ankh-Amen Discovered by the Late Earl of Carnarvon and Howard Carter*, edited by H. Carter and A. C. Mace, 2:167–169. London.

Fleming, S., and B. Fishman. 1980. *The Egyptian Mummy: Secrets and Science*, 21. University Museum Handbook 1. Philadelphia.

Fletcher, J. 2004. *The Search for Nefertiti: The True Story of a Remarkable Discovery*. London.

Germer, R. 1984. "Die Angebliche Mumie de Teye: Probleme Interdisziplinaren Arbeiten." *Studien zur Altägyptischen Kultur* 11: 85–90.

Harris, J. E. 1989. "The Nubian People of the Nile Valley: Past and Present." *Paleopathology Newsletter* 67: 9–13.

Harris, J. E., and E. F. Wente, eds. 1980. *An X-ray Atlas of the Royal Mummies.* Chicago.

Harris, J. E., E. F. Wente, C. F. Cox, I. El Nawawy, C. J. Kowalski, A. T. Storey, W. R. Russell, P. V. Ponitz, and G. F. Walker. 1978. "Mummy of the 'Elder Lady' in the Tomb of Amenhotep II: Egyptian Museum Catalogue Number 61070." *Science* 200 (June 9): 1149–1151.

Harrison, R. G. 1966. "An Anatomical Examination of the Pharaonic Remains Purported to Be Akhenaten." *Journal of Egyptian Archaeology* 52: 95–119.

Harrison, R. G. 1971. "Post Mortem on Two Pharaohs: Was Tutankhamun's Skull Fractured?" *Buried History* 4: 114–129.

Harrison, R. G. 1973. "Tutankhamun Post-Mortem." *Lancet* 1: 259.

Harrison, R. G., R. C. Connolly, S. Ahmed, A. B. Abdalla, and M. el-Ghawaby. 1979. "A Mummified Foetus from the Tomb of Tutankhamun." *Antiquity* 53: 19–21.

Hawass, Z., Y. Z. Gad, S. Ismail, R. Khairat, D. Fathalla, N. Hasan, A. Ahmed, H. Elleithy, M. Ball, F. Gaballa, S. Wasef, M. Fateen, H. Amer, P. Gostner, A. Selim, A. Zink, and C. M. Pusch. 2010. "Ancestry and Pathology in King Tutankhamun's Family." *Journal of the American Medical Association* 303 (7, February 17): 638–647.

Hawass, Z., S. Ismail, A. Selim, S. Saleem, D. Fathalla, S. Wasef, A. Z. Gad, R. Saad, S. Fares, H. Amer, P. Gostner, Y. Z. Gad, C. M. Pusch, and A. R. Zink. 2012. "Revisiting the Harem Conspiracy and Death of Ramesses III: Anthropological, Forensic, Radiological and Genetic Study." *British Medical Journal* (Clinical Research edition) 345 (1): e8268.

Hawass, Z., and S. N. Saleem. 2011. "Mummified Daughters of King Tutankhamun: Archeologic and CT Studies." *American Journal of Roentgenology* (November): W829–W836.

Hawass, Z., M. Shafik, F. Rühli, A. Selim, E. El Sheikh, S. Abdel Fatah, H. Amer, F. Gaballa, A. Gamal Eldin, E. Egarter-Vigl, and P. Gostner. 2009. "Computed Tomographic Evaluation of King Tutankhamun, ca. 1300 BC." *Annales du Service des Antiquités de l'Égypte* 81: 159–174.

Leek, F. F. 1972. *The Human Remains from the Tomb of Tutankhamun.* Tutankhamun's Tomb Series V. Oxford.

Lewin, P. K. 1967. "Paleo-electron Microscopy of Mummified Tissue." *Nature* 213: 416–417.

Lewin, P. K. 1982. "Ramses V: Smallpox Victim?" Paper presented at the 9th Annual Meeting of the Paleopathology Association, Toledo, USA. Abstract in *Paleopathology Newsletter* 36 (supplement): 10.

Loret, V. 1899. "Les tombeau d'Aménophis II et la cachette royale de Biban el-Molouk." *Bulletin de l'Institut Égyptien* 3 (9): 98–112.

Lucas, A., and J. R. Harris. 1962. *Ancient Egyptian Materials and Industries.* 4th ed., rev. London.

Manialawi, M., R. Meligy, and M. Bucaille. 1978. "Endoscopic Examination of Egyptian Mummies." *Endoscopy* 10 (3): 191–194.

Marchant, J. 2011. "Curse of Pharaoh's DNA." *Nature* 472 (April 28): 404–405.

Maspero, G. 1887. "Les momies royales de Déir el-Bahari." *Mémoires de la Mission Archéologique Française au Caire* (Paris) 1: 511–787.

Maspero, G., ed. 1889. *Les Momies Royales de Déir el-Bahari.* Cairo.

Moodie, R. L., ed. 1921. *Studies in the Paleopathology of Egypt.* Chicago.

Pääbo, S. 1985. "Molecular Cloning of Ancient Egyptian Mummy DNA." *Nature* 314: 644–645.

Rose, J. 2000. *Tomb KV39 in the Valley of the Kings: A Double Archaeological Enigma.* Bristol.

Ruffer, M. A. 1911. "Histological Studies on Egyptian Mummies." *Mémoires de l'Institut de l'Égypte* 6 (3): 644–645.

Ruffer, M. A. 1921. "Pathological Notes on the Royal Mummies of the Cairo Museum." In *Studies in the Paleopathology of Egypt*, edited by R. L. Moodie, 166–178. Chicago.

Rutherford, P. 2008. "The Use of Immunocytochemistry to Diagnose Disease in Mummies." In *Egyptian Mummies and Modern Science*, edited by A. R. David, 99–115. Cambridge.

Ryan, D. 1989. "The Pacific Lutheran University Valley of the Kings Project: A Synopsis of the First (1989) Season." *Newsletter of the American Research Center in Egypt* 146: 8–10.

Ryan, D. 1990. "Who Is Buried in KV60? A Field Report." *KMT: A Modern Journal of Ancient Egypt* 1 (1, Spring): 34–39, 53–54, 58.

Shattock, S. G. 1909. "Microscopic Sections of the Aorta of King Merneptah." *Lancet* 1: 318.

Smith, G. E. 1907a. "Report on the Unwrapping of the Mummy of Meneptah." *Annales du Service des Antiquités de l'Égypte* 8: 108–112.

Smith, G. E. 1907b. "Report on the Unrolling of the Mummies of the Kings Siptah, Seti II, Ramses IV, Ramses V and Ramses VI." *Bulletin de l'Institut Égyptien* 5th series, 1: 45–67.

Smith, G. E. 1912. *The Royal Mummies: Catalogue Général des Antiquités Égyptiennes du Musée du Caire, Nos. 61051–61100*. Cairo.

Smith, G. E., and W. R. Dawson. 1924. *Egyptian Mummies*. London.

Strouhal, E. 1996. "Traces of Smallpox Epidemic in the Family of Ramses V of the Egyptian 20th Dynasty." *Anthropologie* 34: 315–319.

Tapp, E., P. Stanworth, and K. Wildsmith. 1984. "The Endoscope in Mummy Research." In *Evidence Embalmed*, edited by R. David and E. Tapp, 65–77. Manchester.

Thomas, E. 1966. *The Royal Necropoleis of Thebes*. Princeton.

Wallgren, J. E., R. Caple, and A. C. Aufderheide. 1986. "Contributions of Nuclear Magnetic Resonance to the Question of Alkaptonuria (Ochronosis) in an Egyptian Mummy." In *Science in Egyptology*, edited by A. R. David: 321–327. Manchester.

Weeks, K. R. 1998. *The Lost Tomb: The Greatest Discovery at the Valley of the Kings since Tutankhamun*. London.

Zink, A., and A. Nerlich. 2003. "Molecular Analyses of the Pharaohs: Feasibility of Molecular Studies in Ancient Egyptian Material." *American Journal of Physical Anthropology* 121: 109–111.

CHAPTER 26

....

MODERN BIOMEDICAL
STUDIES

....

ROSALIE DAVID AND RYAN METCALFE

INTRODUCTION

....

EGYPTOLOGY has benefited from a long relationship with various scientific disciplines, including a number of medical and medically related fields. Some of these have been adopted very swiftly, such as the use of radiography by Petrie (1898) within two years of the discovery of X-rays by Roentgen. Others have been pioneering, such as the development of paleohistological methods for the microscopic investigation of mummified material by Ruffer (1909) or the use of Egyptian mummies for one of the first ancient DNA studies (Pääbo 1985). These tools enable data to be gathered that would otherwise be impossible or excessively destructive to obtain and add greatly to our understanding of life and death in ancient Egypt.

These data are highly diverse, and although there is some overlap in what can be determined through their use, the different methods have both benefits and costs. Radiology is nondestructive, allowing osteological analysis without having to autopsy or even unwrap a mummy, but it is somewhat limited for identifying infectious diseases, for example. DNA analysis offers the chance to find evidence of diseases that may not be detected using osteological techniques, but it requires tissue samples that will be destroyed during the process, and its application to Egyptology is hounded by controversy (see ch 27 for more details).

These methods have been employed in many areas of archaeology, but their adoption in Egyptology has been limited by the restrictions imposed on the movement of material out of the country for analysis (Marchant 2011a). This, combined with the limited availability of facilities for the analysis of ancient material inside Egypt, has until recently forced a concentration on material from museums and other collections, except where techniques could be performed in situ. However, funding from National Geographic and the Discovery Channel has allowed the Supreme Council of Antiquities to gain access to a CT scanner and to build and furnish ancient DNA laboratories inside Egypt. This has at long last allowed the royal mummies from the Valley of the Kings to be investigated using these extraordinarily powerful methods.

PALEOIMAGING OF EGYPTIAN MUMMIES

Imaging methods play an important role in diagnosing disease and providing archaeological and historical information about mummified remains. Radiography, one of the earliest scientific techniques applied to the investigation of mummies (see ch 25), has formed the basis for more recent studies that utilize a variety of imaging methods.

In 1965, mindful of the loss of archaeological evidence that would result from the planned flooding of Lake Nasser, the Egyptian authorities invited the Universities of Michigan and Alexandria (Egypt) to radiograph the skulls of the ancient Nubians who once populated the vicinity of the Second Cataract on the Nile. Other material from the excavated cemeteries of Gebel Adda was added to this study, providing a substantial resource for research into a subject area—craniofacial variation—that was of particular interest to the Michigan expedition.

X-ray cephalometry was developed for clinical use by B. H. Broadbent in 1931, to provide a method of visualizing and accurately quantifying the craniofacial skeleton (Wente and Harris 1992). Since this technique could be readily applied to ancient human remains (whether skeletal material or intact mummies with remaining soft tissue and bandages), a special version of the X-ray cephalometer was developed for undertaking a field survey of the Nubian skulls; this was lightweight, was readily portable, and did not require an external power supply.

Subsequently, this technique was employed when the Department of Egyptian Antiquities invited the Michigan-Alexandria team to undertake a complete X-ray survey of the royal mummies in the Egyptian Museum, Cairo (Harris and Weeks 1973). Commencing in 1967, the project eventually obtained full-body X-rays of the museum's entire royal collection, and also of its nonroyal mummies from the Middle Kingdom to the Greco-Roman period. Not only did the researchers gain information about the health and age at death of the royal mummies, but they also gathered data that enabled craniofacial similarities between individual mummies in this collection to be traced and comparisons to be made between this group and any other (Egyptian, non-Egyptian, living, or dead) (Harris and Wente 1980, 346–379).

This radiographic survey included lateral and frontal views of the head, thorax, pelvis, and lower limbs of each individual and provided the basis for a major reference work, *An X-ray Atlas of the Royal Mummies* (Harris and Wente 1980). To obtain data for the cephalometric studies, carefully aligned X-rays of the heads were taken, and then outlines of the skulls were drawn on a computer. On each skull, 177 anatomical points were precisely located, and the measurements between these points on one head were compared with those on another, enabling the researchers to demonstrate greater craniofacial similarity between some skulls than others; it could then be argued that individuals with similar craniofacial morphology were likely to belong to particular family groups.

In his anatomical study of the royal mummies (1912), Smith had already noted that some individuals seemed to share a strong family resemblance. He also concluded that, in some cases, the anatomical evidence derived from individual mummies (often only tentatively identified as particular rulers) did not always match the historical information known about the length of their reigns. The statistical comparisons based on the cephalometric X-rays of the royal mummies now provided an opportunity to revisit Smith's comments. However, only limited confirmation was forthcoming; one study in particular, Harris and Hussein (1991), which used the cephalometric data to quantify the discrepancies that Smith had noticed, decided that although generally supportive of Smith's findings, the new evidence was not conclusive.

However, in general the X-rays indicated that the accepted identification of some of the mummies in the royal collection was suspect (the ancient priests had probably mislabeled these individuals in the course of rewrapping the mummies and transporting them to new burial locations), and that, indeed, the identity of every individual could reasonably be questioned. Nevertheless, some identifications and ages at death based on the biological data appear to be at variance with historical evidence available for individual reigns. These issues may have arisen because, in the calculations of age at death, no allowance was made for the probable delayed skeletal maturation of ancient Egyptians compared with modern Western populations (Bickerstaffe 2009, 67–75). Even in early studies, Smith (1912, 25 and 40) commented that the models of skeletal development derived from studies of modern Western populations cannot necessarily be applied to the ancient Egyptians. Some support for this is provided by more recent research, which compares data from modern Nubian schoolchildren and their American counterparts (Harris et al. 1970; Verlinich et al. 1977). This has indicated that in Nubian children there may be a delay of one or two years in dental and skeletal maturation and the onset of puberty. Thus, if American assessment standards are used, the age of a Nubian child might be wrongly identified as eleven instead of twelve or thirteen. It has been argued that similar discrepancies and inaccuracies may exist when Western standards are used to pinpoint the ages of ancient Egyptians.

Some have therefore argued that radiological evidence is not accurate enough to be used as a starting point for establishing a chronology, and that no historical or chronological statement, based solely on the biological evidence of age at death of an individual, can be considered valid. Indeed, Robins (1981) has proposed that, in any conflict of evidence presented by biological or archaeological/historical sources, the latter should have priority. At the very least, such studies demonstrate that science cannot always provide definitive answers, and they emphasize the need for an interdisciplinary approach.

Evidence of disease in the royal collection has proved less controversial. Dental studies in particular, based on examination of the lateral and anterior-posterior cephalometric X-rays and limited observation of each individual dentition, have provided useful information (Harris and Wente 1980, 328–345). They confirm that, although caries was insignificant, most individuals suffered from periodontal disease and attrition; also, that the skulls in this collection are heterogeneous, with considerable variation in dental profile and occurrence of malocclusion.

The most significant development in paleoimaging has been the introduction of computed tomography (CT), a technique devised for clinical practice by Sir Godfrey Hounsfield in 1972 (Adams and Alsop 2008, 25–26). Early CT studies on mummies were undertaken by Harwood-Nash (1979), Notman (1986), and Isherwood and Hart (1992). Although CT scanning now is such an important tool in the nondestructive examination of mummies, and has, to some extent, superseded the use of radiography, both systems have their advantages and disadvantages and continue to make a valid contribution. Radiography remains the simplest noninvasive diagnostic tool, and most projects will first employ this method to survey a mummy and identify any pathology or associated archaeological artefacts. Where there is no access to sophisticated hospital equipment (especially during field studies), researchers must rely on radiography.

One famous multidisciplinary project, with access to the hospital equipment and expertise required for computed tomography, still had to rely on radiography. The mummy of Ramesses II was taken to Paris in 1976 to undergo conservation and scientific investigations, but permission was not granted to move the body to a CT facility. Instead, a complete radiographic study of the mummy was undertaken, and further details were provided by chromodensitography and xeroradiography (a method invented by the American physicist C. F. Carlson in 1937, which rapidly produces images on paper that are precise and demonstrate excellent contrast) (Balout and Roubet 1985).

In 2005 an extensive, ongoing scientific program was inaugurated by the Supreme Council of Egyptian Antiquities in Cairo (Hawass 2004–2005). To date, the project has started to CT scan the royal mummies of the New Kingdom. This has provided extensive data about individual mummies, enabling researchers to revisit and revise earlier theories that were based on anatomical investigations or plain radiography. This research addresses disease, age at death, cause of death, and familial relationships (Janot 2008) and includes new studies of Tutankhamun (Harer 2011, 2012; Hawass et al. 2009; Marchant 2011b); the two fetuses from Tutankhamun's tomb (Hawass and Saleem 2011; Hellier and Connolly 2009); the bodies from KV 35 and KV 55 (Hawass et al. 2010); the mummy, possibly identified as Hatshepsut, from KV 60 (Hawass 2007); and the mummy of Ramesses III (Hawass et al. 2012). These studies have provided fascinating information, such as evidence that Ramesses III may have been murdered during the harem conspiracy by having his throat cut down to the bone (Hawass et al. 2012), and that Tutankhamun suffered from a range of medical problems, including a cleft palate, club foot, and both a missing bone and necrosis of other bones in his left foot (Hawass et al. 2010). The numerous problems with his feet are forwarded as an explanation for the number of canes found in the tomb and the depictions of Tutankhamun sitting while hunting, for example, but there has been some doubt cast on their veracity (Gamble 2010).

The latest developments in CT technology create images that enable researchers to undertake a "virtual flight" through the inside of a mummy, without damaging the body. This method was used for the radiological study of the supposed mummy of Ramesses

I undertaken by Emory University, Atlanta. The British Museum, London, has produced pioneering work in this field, with the development of a technique that combines the latest noninvasive imaging technology with leading-edge computer graphics. This has enabled researchers to perform a "virtual unwrapping and autopsy" of the mummy of the priest Nesperennub, allowing the complete body to be investigated interactively and any feature inside or outside the body to be revealed and scrutinized in detail (Taylor 2004). The technology clearly has considerable potential for future studies.

RECONSTRUCTING ANCIENT EGYPTIAN FACES

Techniques that use CT data and graphic software now play an important role in reconstructing the images of ancient faces. Facial reconstruction involves a process by which an individual's appearance is re-created by relating the skeletal structure to the overlying soft tissue (Wilkinson 2008, 162). These scientific representations provide the opportunity to visualize the appearance of individuals; they depict details derived from the CT data of the mummified tissue as well as the skeleton and make available information that would otherwise remain inaccessible in wrapped mummies. The technique enables researchers to seek out evidence of any family likeness by comparing individual reconstructions from several mummies and to compare the features visible in ancient faces with those seen in contemporary populations in Egypt and elsewhere. The methods employed to reconstruct ancient faces can, to some extent, be validated; the same techniques are also widely employed in the investigation of modern forensic identifications, and this provides an opportunity to assess their accuracy.

Pioneering developments in reconstructing the faces of ancient Egyptians have been pursued at The University of Manchester, England, since the 1970s. The earliest techniques were manual and required direct access to the skull; a cast of the skull was made, and this formed the basis for building up the reconstruction in sculptors' clay (Neave 1979). In more recent times, with the increasing application of computed tomography to mummified remains, it has been possible to develop noninvasive techniques that use cross-sectional data, created by CT scanning, to produce a three-dimensional digital model of the skull (Wilkinson 2005). The development and use of various sophisticated systems for computerized facial reconstruction continue to produce increasingly convincing results (Wilkinson 2003, 2004).

Some facial reconstructions of individual royal mummies have been produced, such as Tutankhamun (Gatliff 2001; Handwerk 2005) and Ramesses II (Wilkinson 2008, 170). An important study, based on the evidence of the skulls, has attempted to ascertain if the human remains discovered in KV 5 in the Valley of the Kings could have belonged to relatives of Ramesses II (Wilkinson 2008, 175–177). Rediscovered by Weeks in 1987, KV 5 is one of the largest tombs ever found in Egypt and has been identified as the burial place of several sons of Ramesses II (Weeks 2006). The skulls of four adult males were discovered in the tomb, but due to their physical condition, only three were available for assessment; there was limited access even to these skulls, and their incomplete and fragile physical condition meant that only photographic evidence could be gathered for the project.

Two-dimensional facial reconstructions were made from these skulls, and these were then compared with the mummy and facial reconstruction of Ramesses II. It was noted that all the faces had similar features: a long narrow face, long nose, and prominent cheek bones. The long vertical distances between the nose and the mouth and the mouth and the chin were a particularly remarkable feature of Ramesses II's face, and the same vertical proportions were visible in two of the skulls from KV 5; however, the third had very different proportions. The researcher concluded that the similarity between the facial proportions and morphology of two of the KV 5 skulls and that of Ramesses II possibly suggest that these skulls should be attributed to his sons; the third one, however, which was significantly different from the other faces, is less likely to have had a direct relationship to Ramesses II.

To some extent, therefore, these results help to support the identification of KV 5 as the burial place of Ramesses II's sons. However, researchers in this field emphasize that although facial reconstruction can demonstrate similarity between individuals in terms of their morphology, proportions, and facial features, it cannot be used to positively identify a genetic relationship (Wilkinson 2008, 176). Nevertheless, although caution is required in interpreting any results derived from facial reconstruction, developments and improvements continue to ensure that this nondestructive methodology has considerable potential for Egyptological research.

MOLECULAR METHODS

Since its development in the mid-1980s, ancient DNA (aDNA) analysis has had a transformative effect on archaeology (Pääbo 1985). The underlying principle, the comparison of the differences in DNA sequences within and between species, is relatively simple, but this allows the technique to be applied to a huge range of research questions. The basis of the vast majority of ancient DNA analysis is the polymerase chain reaction (PCR). This method allows the damaged, fragmented, and scant remnants of DNA within ancient samples to be faithfully copied many millions of times over to produce sufficient quantities for detection and sequencing. The method can be tailored to more or less specific targets, allowing researchers to look at as broad a target as bacteria in general (e.g., Ubaldi et al. 1998) or as specific a target as the six-letter difference in code between the human male and female versions of a single gene (Mannucci et al. 1994).

One quite common use of aDNA is in paleopathology. Traditional methods rely on the identification of lesions and modification to the bones, a process that is much aided in Egyptology by the use of medical imaging techniques to peer through the various layers of wrappings and soft tissues that may be found on mummies. Though success-fully used for a very long time, such methods do have their limitations. It can take some time for the lesions that are characteristic of tuberculosis to appear, for example, so reliance on these alone will make it difficult to spot those cases in which the sufferer died too swiftly for his or her skeleton to be affected (Wright and Yoder 2003). Other diseases, such as malaria and schistosomiasis, do not affect the skeleton directly, but may do so by causing anemia, which in turn may result in osteological changes. These changes are specific only to anemia rather than the underlying condition, which makes distinction, and hence diagnosis, difficult.

It is in these unclear cases that aDNA has the most promise, as it allows minuscule traces of a bacterium or parasite to be spotted. That is not to say that it is infallible, of course. The sheer power of PCR may be its biggest drawback, as it makes the method very vulnerable to contamination, which can lead to false positive results. False negatives may also arise, typically when samples are simply too degraded to be successfully analyzed. Further problems may become apparent if disease-causing organisms reside only in particular tissues, making those organs vitally important for the detection of such diseases. There are even questions about the survival of DNA in ancient Egyptian remains, which some claim to be impossible due to the climate of the area (more detail on this can be found in ch 27). A genetic approach to paleopathology is therefore best viewed as an additional tool in the archaeologist's box, rather than as a universally applicable method that can answer all questions asked of it.

Recent research into the family tree of Tutankhamun (described in ch 27) included a genetic component that was extended to include the identification of a number of pathogenic organisms, both parasitic and bacterial (Hawass et al. 2010). The diseases investigated were bubonic plague, tuberculosis, leprosy, leishmaniasis, and malaria. Of these, the only methodology described in detail was that used for malaria, as all the others returned negative results. Of the sixteen mummies investigated, four tested positive for the parasite that causes malaria: Tutankhamun, his great-grandparents Yuya and Thuya, and the body that may be Thutmose I, though that identification is considered doubtful (Harris and Hussein 1991). Each of these cases appears to be of the most severe form of malaria (malaria tropica), and in addition it appears that Tutankhamun and Yuya suffered multiple infections. These results were all supported by the use of multiple DNA targets with verification at a separate laboratory, increasing the confidence that this represents a genuine result. In Tutankhamun's case, this diagnosis was indicated as being a possible factor in his death, with various other conditions and injuries weakening his immune system sufficiently for malaria to prove fatal. However, in contrast, it has been suggested that his age at death indicates instead that he had partial immunity due to sickle cell disease. This hypothesis is bolstered by the advanced age at death of Yuya and Thuya, and sickle cell disease may also explain the necrotic damage seen in Tutankhamun's left foot (Timmann and Meyer 2010).

This illustrates a very important point: for all that ancient DNA can help to spot diseases that might otherwise be missed in human remains, it is extremely difficult to use by itself to assign a cause of death. Unless additional information is available, such a genetic diagnosis should be used carefully, as people suffering from potentially fatal diseases may still meet their end through other means, such as accident or violence. One of the authors of the study has stated that it will be impossible to prove that death was due to malaria (Butler 2010), thereby adding this to an already well-populated list of theories, including accident and murder (see, e.g., Counsell 2008), that has yet to produce a solid answer.

In addition to infectious diseases, a wide range of other diseases have been associated with the Amarna royal family thanks to their unusual appearance in statues and other depictions. One list of possible diseases includes Marfan syndrome, Frohlich syndrome, Klinefelter syndrome, androgen insensitivity syndrome, a combination of aromatase excess syndrome and sagittal craniosynostosis, and a hitherto-unknown variant of Antley-Bixler syndrome (Braverman et al. 2009). Other suggestions have included an adrenal tumor (Weller 1972) and familial epilepsy (Ashrafian 2012), the latter paper including a useful and comprehensive listing of the various theories that have been presented. Biomedical methods may be able to help narrow this range, as although the diagnosis of genetic diseases would typically require the preservation of nuclear DNA, which is unusual in ancient remains, Hawass et al. (2010) reported a surprisingly high level of preservation for five generations of Tutankhamun's family. Other methods that might be appropriate may be significantly harder to perform. For example, while tumors can be identified in mummified material (e.g., Strouhal and Němečková 2004), the removal of the brain during mummification would make diagnosis of Frohlich syndrome impossible, as it is related to a tumor of the hypothalamus. Similarly, the diagnosis of a previously unknown genetic disease would be very difficult to accomplish with ancient remains (Gad et al. 2010).

In addition to the experimental difficulties that confirmation of these diseases may face, another common factor between them is that their diagnosis is based largely or wholly on the artistic record rather than the physical remains. These do not appear to show unusual physiques, though damage and decay do limit this assessment somewhat (Hawass et al. 2010). However, as the recent identification of the body from KV 55 as Akhenaten is the subject of some debate (see ch 27), it is unlikely that this argument is anywhere near closure.

Other Biomedical Tools

Although genetic analysis has been used with some success and not a little controversy, other methods that have been more rarely used can inform us about health and disease. Two that are especially relevant to mummified remains have the same basic principle—that tissues and their components can be differentially stained to make them visible and identifiable using a microscope—but the methods used are quite different.

The first of these, histology, has been a valuable tool in Egyptology for just over a century. Although it is rather less commonly used than many of the other techniques that have been borrowed from the sciences, it still has an important, basic role to play in support of other methods (Denton 2008). The essence of the method is that tissue samples are rehydrated to restore as much as possible of their premummification appearance, then they are embedded in a supporting medium such as wax or resin that enables them to be cut very thinly—typically around 5 micrometers, or approximately 1/20th the thickness of a human hair. Once mounted onto glass slides, these thin sections may be stained with one of a multitudinous array of methods, ranging from simple oversight stains to very specific stains that pick out individual tissue types or classes of molecule (see, e.g., Kiernan 2008 for more information).

Once stained, it is possible to judge the state of preservation of the tissue, which is of great importance for molecular analyses such as aDNA testing, as there is a link between the microscopic appearance of tissue and the success of aDNA extraction (Haynes et al. 2002). There is the added benefit, if the tissue is well preserved, of being able to identify the tissue type with confidence. As indicated above, for some tests a specific organ may be needed, and it can be extremely difficult to distinguish ancient tissues with the naked eye. There is, for example, a case of a supposed human mummified liver sample that was histologically determined as being plant matter (Denton 2008, 77). Although extreme, this example does indicate the usefulness of histology as a supporting tool for the examination of samples before embarking on lengthy molecular biological analysis.

A related method, immunohistochemistry, follows much the same preparation route as histology, and samples prepared for one may be used for the other, thus reducing the demand for tissue. The main differences are in the final stage, wherein tissue components are rendered visible. Rather than dyes and stains, immunohistochemistry uses antibodies to identify and bind onto chosen molecules in the tissue with a very high level of specificity. This binding site is then labeled using one of a wide range of markers.

Typically, immunohistochemistry is used to search for proteins within tissue sections, which makes it potentially very useful for studying parasitic diseases such as schistosomiasis (Rutherford 2008). The nature of the method makes it particularly appropriate for such applications, because not only can it reveal whether or not the eggs and worms of a parasite are present, but because it is based on microscopic examination of the tissue, it also can show their morphology, which provides a useful double check for the results. Despite this, immunohistochemistry does not appear to be widely used, possibly because it is less sensitive than aDNA, as there is no amplification process that is analogous to PCR.

CONCLUSIONS

After many years of reliance on material stored outside Egypt and on methods such as plain X-rays that can be carried out using easily portable equipment, significant investment in archaeological science facilities in Egypt has allowed biomedical techniques common in other areas to be used on the royal mummies from the Valley of the Kings.

Although the focus to date has been on familial relationships and the identification of high profile figures whose mummies had not been identified, pathologies and cause of death have also been investigated, and the use of medical imaging has allowed the reproduction of some of the royal mummies' faces as they would have appeared in life.

Although these methods are able to provide useful data on a wide range of diseases and trauma, they must be used with care and typically are best used in concert rather than individually. However, when they are used appropriately, and the data are interpreted carefully, they can offer insights that other methods simply cannot offer.

BIBLIOGRAPHY

Adams, J., and C. W. Alsop. 2008. "Imaging in Egyptian Mummies." In *Egyptian Mummies and Modern Science*, edited by R. David, 21–42. Cambridge.

Ashrafian, H. 2012. "Familial Epilepsy in the Pharaohs of Ancient Egypt's Eighteenth Dynasty." *Epilepsy and Behaviour* 25: 23–31.

Balout, L., and C. Roubet, eds. 1985. *La Momie de Ramsès II (1976–1977): Contribution Scientifique a l'Égyptologie*. Éditions Récherche sur les Civilisations. Paris.

Bickerstaffe, D. 2009. *Refugees for Eternity: The Royal Mummies of Thebes*. Pt. 4, *Identifying the Royal Mummies*. Chippenham.

Braverman, I. M., D. B. Redford, and P. A. Mackowiak. 2009. "Akhenaten and the Strange Physiques of Egypt's 18th Dynasty." *Annals of Internal Medicine* 150: 556–560.

Butler, D. 2010. "King Tut's Death Explained?" *Nature*, February 16. http://www.nature.com/news/2010/100216/full/news.2010.75.html.

David, R., ed. 1986. *Science in Egyptology*. Manchester.

David, R., ed. 2008. *Egyptian Mummies and Modern Science*. Cambridge.

David, R., and E. Tapp, eds. 1992. *The Mummy's Tale*. London.

Denton, J. 2008. "Slices of Mummy: A Histologist's Perspective." In *Egyptian Mummies and Modern Science*, edited by R. David, 71–82. Cambridge.

Gad, Y. Z., A. Selim, and C. M. Pusch. 2010. "King Tutankhamun's Family and Demise." *Journal of the American Medical Association* 303: 2473–2475.

Gamble, J. G. 2010. "King Tutankhamun's Family and Demise." *Journal of the American Medical Association* 303: 2472.

Gatliff, B. P. 2001. "Facial Reconstruction of Tut Ankh Amun (1980)." In *Forensic Art and Illustration*, edited by K. T. Taylor, 466–467. Boca Raton.

Handwerk, B. 2005. "King Tut's New Face: Behind the Forensic Reconstruction." *National Geographic Magazine*, May 11.

Harer, W. B. 2011. "New Evidence for King Tutankhamun's Death: His Bizarre Embalming." *Journal of Egyptian Archaeology* 97: 228–233.

Harer, W. B. 2012. "Was Tutankhamun Killed by a Hippo?" *Ancient Egypt* 12 (6, June/July): 50–54.

Harris, J. E., and K. R. Weeks. 1973. *X-raying the Pharaohs*. New York.

Harris, J. E., and E. F. Wente, eds. 1980. *An X-ray Atlas of the Royal Mummies*. Chicago.

Harris, J. E., and F. Hussein. 1991. "The Identification of the Eighteenth Dynasty Royal Mummies: A Biological Perspective." *International Journal of Osteoarchaeology* 1: 235–239.

Harris, J. E., P. V. Ponitz, and M. S. Loufty. 1970. "Orthodontic's Contribution to UNESCO's Campaign to Save the Monuments of Nubia: A 1970 Field Report." *American Journal of Orthodontics* 58 (6): 578–596.

Harwood-Nash, C. D. 1979. "Computed Tomography of Ancient Egyptian Mummies." *Journal of Computer Assisted Tomography* 3 (6): 768–773.

Hawass, Z. 2004–2005. "The EMP: Egyptian Mummy Project." *Kmt* 15 (4, Winter): 34.

Hawass, Z. 2007. "The Scientific Search for Hatshepsut's Mummy." *Kmt* 18 (3, Autumn): 20–25.

Hawass, Z., Y. Z. Gad, S. Ismail, R. Khairat, D. Fathalla, N. Hasan, A. Ahmed, H. Elleithy, M. Ball, F. Gaballa, S. Wasef, M. Fateen, H. Amer, P. Gostner, A. Selim, A. Zink, and C. M. Pusch. 2010. "Ancestry and Pathology in King Tutankhamun's Family." *Journal of the American Medical Association* 303 (7, February 17): 638–647.

Hawass, Z., S. Ismail, A. Selim, S. Saleem, D. Fathalla, S. Wasef, A. Z. Gad, R. Saad, S. Fares, H. Amer, P. Gostner, Y. Z. Gad, C. M. Pusch, and A. R. Zink. 2012. "Revisiting the Harem Conspiracy and Death of Ramesses III: Anthropological, Forensic, Radiological and Genetic Study." *British Medical Journal* (Clinical Research ed.) 345 (1): e8268.

Hawass, Z., and S. N. Saleem. 2011. "Mummified Daughters of King Tutankhamun: Archeologic and CT Studies." *American Journal of Roentgenology* (November): W829–W836.

Hawass, Z., M. Shafik, F. Rühli, A. Selim, E. El Sheikh, S. Abdel Fatah, H. Amer, F. Gaballa, A. Gamal Eldin, E. Egarter-Vigl, and P. Gostner. 2009. "Computed Tomographic Evaluation of King Tutankhamun, ca. 1300 BC." *Annales du Service des Antiquités de l'Egypte* 81: 159–174.

Haynes, S., J. B. Searle, A. Bretman, and K. M. Dobney. 2002. "Bone Preservation and Ancient DNA: The Application of Screening Methods for Predicting DNA Survival." *Journal of Archaeological Science* 29: 585–592.

Hellier, C. A., and R. C. Connolly. 2009. "A Re-assessment of the Larger Fetus Found in Tutankhamen's Tomb." *Antiquity* 83: 165–173.

Isherwood, I., and C. W. Hart. 1992. "The Radiological Investigation." In *The Mummy's Tale*, edited by R. David and E. Tapp, 100–116. London.

Janot, F. 2008. *The Royal Mummies: Immortality in Ancient Egypt.* Vercelli.

Kiernan, J. A. 2008. *Histological and Histochemical Methods: Theory and Practice.* Banbury.

Mannucci, A., K. M. Sullivan, P. L. Ivanov, and P. Gill. 1994. "Forensic Application of a Rapid and Quantitative DNA Sex Test by Amplification of the X-Y Homologous Gene Amelogenin." *International Journal of Legal Medicine* 106: 190–193.

Marchant, J. 2011a. "Spring Comes to Ancient Egypt." *Nature* 479: 464–467.

Marchant, J. 2011b. "Death on the Nile." *New Scientist* 2795: 42–44.

Neave, R. 1979. "Reconstruction of the Heads of Three Ancient Egyptian Mummies." *Journal of Audiovisual Medicine* 2 (4): 156–164.

Notman, D. N. H. 1986. "Ancient Scannings: Computed Tomography of Egyptian Mummies." In *Science in Egyptology*, edited by R. David, 251–320. Manchester.

Pääbo, S. 1985. "Molecular Cloning of Ancient Egyptian Mummy DNA." *Nature* 314: 644–645.

Petrie, W. M. F. 1898. *Deshasheh.* London.

Reeves, C. N., ed. 1992. *After Tutankhamun: Research and Excavation in the Royal Necropolis at Thebes.* London and New York.

Robins, G. 1981. "The Value of the Estimated Ages of the Royal Mummies at Death as Historical Evidence." *Goettinger Miszellen* 45: 63–68.

Ruffer, M. A. 1909. "Preliminary Note on the Histology of Egytian Mummies." *British Medical Journal* 1 (2521): 1005.

Rutherford, P. 2008. "The Use of Immunocytochemistry to Diagnose Disease in Mummies." In *Egyptian Mummies and Modern Science*, edited by R. David, 71–82. Cambridge.

Smith, G. E. 1912. *The Royal Mummies: Catalogue Général des Antiquités Égyptiennes du Musée du Caire, Nos. 61051–61100.* Cairo.

Strouhal, E., and A. Němečková. 2004. "Paleopathological Find of a Sacral Neurilemmoma from Ancient Egypt." *American Journal of Physical Anthropology* 125: 320–328.

Taylor, J. H. 2004. *Mummy: The Inside Story*. London.

Taylor, K. T., ed. 2001. *Forensic Art and Illustration*. Boca Raton, LA.

Timmann, C., and C. G. Meyer. 2010. "King Tutankhamun's Family and Demise." *Journal of the American Medical Association* 303: 2473.

Ubaldi, M., S. Luciani, I. Marota, G. Fornaciari, R. J. Cano, and F. Rollo. 1998. "Sequence Analysis of Bacterial DNA in the Colon of an Andean Mummy." *American Journal of Physical Anthrology* 107: 285–295.

Verlinich, D. M., J. E. Harris, and C. J. Kowalski. 1977. "Skeletal Maturation in the Egyptian Nubian." *Journal of Dental Research Special Issue B* 56: B75.

Weeks, K. R., ed. 2006. *KV5: A Preliminary Report on the Excavation of the Tomb of the Sons of Ramesses II in the Valley of the Kings*. Cairo.

Weller, M. 1972. "Tutankhamun: An Adrenal Tumour?" *The Lancet* 300:1312.

Wente, E. F., and J. E. Harris. 1992. "Royal Mummies of the Eighteenth Dynasty. A Biologic and Egyptological Approach." In *After Tutankhamun: Research and Excavation in the Royal Necropolis at Thebes*, edited by C. N. Reeves, 2–20. London and New York.

Wilkinson, C. M. 2003. "Virtual Sculpture as a Method of Computerized Facial Reconstruction." *Proceedings of the 1st International Conference on Reconstruction of Soft Tissue Parts, Potsdam, Germany*: 59–63.

Wilkinson, C. M. 2004. *Forensic Facial Reconstruction*. Cambridge.

Wilkinson, C. M. 2005. "Computerised Facial Reconstruction: A Review of Current Systems." *Journal of Forensic Science, Medicine and Pathology* 1 (3): 173–177.

Wilkinson, C. M. 2008. "The Facial Reconstruction of Ancient Egyptians." In *Egyptian Mummies and Modern Science*, edited by R. David, 162–178. Cambridge.

Wright, L. E., and C. J. Yoder. 2003. "Recent Progress in Bioarchaeology: Approaches to the Osteological Paradox." *Journal of Archaeological Research* 11: 43–70.

....

CHAPTER 27

RECENT IDENTITY AND RELATIONSHIP STUDIES, INCLUDING X-RAYS AND DNA

....

RYAN METCALFE

INTRODUCTION

....

As the Valley of the Kings is home to so many of the greatest and most famous of Ancient Egypt's sons and daughters, it is not surprising that a great deal of effort is spent on trying to match the names of missing royalty to the unidentified bodies found in individual tombs and caches throughout the valley. Although this is by no means a simple task, many have tried. The results are rarely if ever accepted without a great deal of discussion, argument, or controversy. Even those that were moved to caches by priests and given dockets bearing their names have been viewed with suspicion, but it has been suggested that the ancient labels be accepted unless there is good reason not to (Reeves and Wilkinson 1996, 202–204). For those awaiting identification, matters are more complex. Medical and forensic tools can provide a huge quantity of data to help with this process, but they are only another piece of the puzzle—a DNA sequence may be unique to an individual, but his or her name is not encoded among the genes, and a CT scan will not reveal a person's name written through his or her bones like a stick of rock.

Radiology and genetics have played a major role in several studies aiming to rediscover the names of unidentified mummies in the last ten years, accompanied by much publicity and excitement. It is unfortunate, however, that the primary sources for a number of these studies are press releases and documentaries. Documentaries may see many repeats, and increasingly may be found in online repositories, but if the theories they present fall out of favor, they can become very hard to find. Similarly, press releases may not be archived once their purpose is fulfilled. Both sources are aimed at educating and informing a wide section of the public rather than a small number of experienced researchers and academics. This means that much of the information a specialist would require, whether an Egyptologist or a scientist, is not presented, making a detailed review rather difficult. Though they are not a substitute for a journal article, monograph, or other scholarly work, these sources can be an interesting and valuable complement to a scholarly publication.

Nefertiti Found and Lost?

In 2003, it was reported that the mummy of the Younger Lady in KV 35 (KV 35 YL) had been identified as Nefertiti by Joann Fletcher. Rather than publishing the results in a peer-reviewed journal or writing a monograph, this discovery was announced in a press release and accompanied by a documentary. By the time the underpinning research was published in a book (Fletcher 2004), there had been a great deal of debate and argument over not just the identification of the mummy, but also the manner in which it had been made public.

By releasing the discovery directly to the public without first discussing it with the Supreme Council of Antiquities (SCA), Fletcher and the rest of her team were declared to be in breach of a bond made between The University of York and the Egyptian authorities, leading to Dr. Zahi Hawass (then head of the SCA) declaring that she should be prevented from working in Egypt (see, e.g., Hawass 2005). Though this may be seen as a rather extreme reaction, and the ban has since been lifted, it is a clear example of the depth of feeling and sense of controversy that the research produced.

The evidence provided in favor of this identification was presented and assessed by Dr. Susan James shortly after the press release (James 2003). In summary, the arguments in favor of KV 35 YL being Nefertiti are the presence of a "Nubian-style" wig of the sort supposedly favored by royal women of the Eighteenth Dynasty; a double ear piercing that was thought to be unique to Nefertiti and one of her daughters; indications that the mummy habitually wore a tight-fitting brow band; and the identification of a disarticulated right arm, which showed signs of being flexed into a position signifying royalty, as belonging to the mummy in question. Each of these points was, however, contradicted in turn—there is no evidence the wig was associated with the Younger Lady beyond simple proximity in the tomb, for example, and even if it were, it was not a style unique to Nefertiti. Double ear piercings were similarly not as uncommon as indicated, and brow bands were likely to be far from rare (James 2003, 26–27).

The detached right arm is particularly interesting, as two were found in the tomb, only one of which is consistent with the flexed position associated with royal women. The other, straight arm was determined to be too long to be that of the Younger Lady. The flexed arm, thought to be a better match to the still attached left arm, cannot however be taken as solid evidence of the owner's royalty, as the "royal" convention was for the left arm to be bent, not the right. Perhaps more problematically, this position is not as exclusive as it was indicated to be, as it is also seen on depictions of nonroyal women (Mertz 2003). Furthermore, it was even suggested by Hawass that the body was actually that of a man (CNN 2003).

Unfortunately, although these criticisms were raised very swiftly after the first airing of the documentary and publication of the press releases, they were not addressed in the accompanying book that was published the following year. There are of course many possible reasons for this, including simply the time required to turn a manuscript into a publication, so very little weight can be placed on this omission.

Nefertiti, Still Missing?

The question of Nefertiti's identity was raised once more in 2007, though frustratingly it was again announced primarily through the media, with one of the main sources of information currently available being a television documentary (Quilici 2007a). The Elder and Younger Ladies from KV 35 were again investigated, along with the mummy from KV 55, but this time the team had the advantage of a CT scanner as a primary analytical tool. The results, though far from conclusive, are certainly interesting.

The mummy from KV 55 was swiftly ruled out as a contender once it was determined to be male, confirming a much earlier analysis (Elliot-Smith 1910) that was already far from controversial. The age at death and similarities between this body and that of Tutankhamun, such as skull shape and a cleft palate, were used to tentatively identify the body as that of Akhenaten (Quilici 2007a). However, the subsequent press release (SCA 2007a) tones this conclusion down somewhat, saying that further investigation would be required before a firm decision could be made. This is neither the first nor the last time that the identity of this mummy has been brought into question, and more detail on this appears below.

The Elder Lady was determined to be between forty and sixty years old at death, based on a number of degenerative osteological indicators. This, combined with the bent left arm, led to the suggestion that this body may be that of Queen Tiye—a suggestion that had been made in the past based on analysis of the hair of this mummy and a lock found in a miniature coffin that bore her name, in Tutankhamun's tomb (Harris et al. 1978). That analysis has been disputed, but the new findings remain consistent with that identity. Again, further work was urged before a solid conclusion could be drawn (SCA 2007a).

Finally, the re-examination of the Younger Lady produced very different results than the 2003 study, but the body was shown to be female despite earlier claims to the contrary (e.g., CNN 2003). The detached, bent forearm that was so pivotal to the earlier identification of this body as Nefertiti was this time judged not to belong to the Younger Lady, with the straight arm suggested as the better match in terms of both length and bone density, in direct contradiction to Fletcher's findings. Other interesting findings on this mummy include similarities in skull morphology to Tutankhamun, taken as evidence that this mummy may be that of his mother and leading to a tentative suggestion that this may not be Nefertiti, but possibly Kiya, one of Akhenaten's other wives.

Although an excellent indicator of the power of CT scanning in the examination of mummified remains, the lack of any firm conclusions from this research is an indicator of its limitations. In this case, for example, all the evidence that was collected was refutative or indicative rather than confirmatory. It takes a very unusual set of circumstances for radiological evidence to be able to positively identify a mummy.

Hatshepsut's Tooth

Such a set of circumstances came to light very shortly after the SCA's investigation of the bodies in KV 35 and KV 55. The focus this time was another famous and influential royal woman, Hatshepsut, though again we are forced to rely mainly on media coverage for information.

As before, CT scanning played a major role in the hunt for Hatshepsut's body. A number of candidate mummies were gathered together for scanning, including both bodies found within KV 60—one had previously been identified as Sitre-In and moved to the Cairo Museum; the other was unnamed and had remained in the tomb. Two other unidentified female mummies were also included, though the sources disagree somewhat over where these came from. Some refer to them as Unknown Women A and B from tomb TT 320 (Quilici 2007b; SCA 2007b), while other sources refer to them as Unknown Woman A from TT 320 and Unknown Woman D from KV 35 (Hawass 2007; Taher 2007). The mummies of Thutmose I, II, and III were also CT scanned, but there appears to be some disagreement over the role this played in the attempt to identify Hatshepsut. The documentary film refers to using the CT scans to build a composite Thutmosid face to compare to the putative Hatshepsuts as well as indicating any possible "common features" that she may have shared with them (Quilici 2007b). The press release is rather less verbose, merely mentioning that they were scanned (SCA 2007b), while Hawass's own account of the research is silent on the matter (Hawass 2007).

Although somewhat confusing and contradictory, this situation has had little effect on the end results of the project, as the two mummies from TT 320 and/or KV 35 were ruled out as candidates on the basis of age at death or the nonroyal position of their arms, leaving only those from KV 60. In order to provide more data for the analysis, a DNA laboratory specifically for investigating mummies was founded as part of the documentary, with bone samples from both KV 60 mummies, Hatshepsut's father Thutmose I, and her maternal grandmother Ahmose Nefertari taken in an attempt to provide a genetic comparison. Initial results were highly promising, with surprisingly good DNA preservation reported (Applied Biosystems 2007). This was not, however, what provided the information that prompted the announcement of Hatshepsut's rediscovery.

A small box, labeled with her name, had been discovered during the excavation of TT 320. This box was thought to contain some preserved viscera that could act as a confidently provenanced source of Hatshepsut's DNA for comparison to the mummies, but it proved impossible to open, as it was sealed with resin. When the box was CT scanned, a tooth missing a root was seen among the other contents. This corresponded to a broken-off root seen in the maxilla of the unidentified body from KV 60. Comparison of the density of the two parts and their size provided compelling enough evidence for a public announcement that the body left behind by Carter in KV 60 was in fact Hatshepsut (SCA 2007b).

It is unfortunate to say the least that the research has not to date been published in detail, as the data that are available have been released piecemeal and without peer review. This prevents the independent analysis of the radiological data that is so vitally important to the identification of this mummy. Genetic confirmation is also impossible, as DNA results have yet to be released at the time of writing. The interpretation of these results may be difficult, as there are questions about the identification of Thutmose I's mummy (Harris and Hussien 1991) and uncertainty over the relationship between Ahmose Nefertari and Hatshepsut, but if the initial assessment of the level of preservation was correct, then the prospects are significant.

TUTANKHAMUN'S FAMILY TREE

Though the projects discussed above have produced a great deal of debate and argument, they are overshadowed by what may be one of the most ambitious mummy study projects in recent years and the fantastic quantity of discussion that it catalyzed (Hawass et al. 2010).

Building on the methodology adopted in the hunt for Hatshepsut, the SCA used their new DNA laboratory and CT scanner to try to reconstruct the ancestry of Tutankhamun, which has long been the subject of uncertainty. Many previous attempts have been made using a range of methods both archaeological and forensic, but none can provide the level of detail that DNA analysis is capable of. The blood group testing of Tutankhamun and the body in KV 55, for example, produced results that were consistent with but not proof of a relationship between the two (Harrison et al. 1969). In addition to identifying unknown mummies and elucidating one of the most famous and confusing family trees in Egyptology, the genetic and radiological data were also used to investigate disease, trauma, and congenital abnormalities in the mummies, which are described in more detail in chapter 26.

ANCIENT EGYPTIAN DNA

The analysis of ancient DNA (aDNA) was pivotal to the investigation of Tutankhamun and his family, and although a young discipline compared to Egyptology, it is a maturing field that can trace its origins back to the mid-1980s (Higuchi et al. 1984; Pääbo 1985). Early research suggested that DNA may be preserved over millions of years, though many of the examples of extreme preservation have since been shown to be due to contamination or experimental artifact. The limit is now accepted to be on the order of tens or hundreds of thousands of years—still more than sufficient to cover the history of pharaonic Egypt.

However, for such an important molecule, DNA is surprisingly delicate and easily damaged. This chemical vulnerability is a necessary part of its structure, as without it the repair and reproduction of DNA would be extremely difficult. Unfortunately, the repair mechanisms that keep it intact and working during an organism's life stop working upon death, allowing chemical and physical damage to build up, with heat and water greatly accelerating the rate of damage. The effect of this can range from producing misleading results to entirely preventing analysis. There are several precautions that should be taken as standard when working with aDNA, such as using labs specific to ancient samples and having independent laboratories try to reproduce the results.

Although there are a multitude of different targets for the analysis of ancient animal and human DNA, there is a significant choice that needs to be made when devising the experiment. Animals have two genomes; the vast majority of their DNA is stored in the cell nucleus and is inherited equally from both parents, with only one copy of this nuclear DNA per cell. There is also a much smaller genome stored within the chemical power plants of the cell, the mitochondria. There can be many hundreds or thousands of these in each cell, so although there is less information stored within each one, there is a great statistical advantage to their study, as there is a higher chance that some will survive. However, this small genome is inherited solely from the mother, so it cannot provide any information on the paternal lineage of the subject.

The use of aDNA analysis on Egyptian remains and artifacts is somewhat controversial, thanks mainly to the high temperature of the country. A paper published in 2002 tested the half-life of DNA preservation in Egypt using papyrus as a proxy for mummified remains (Marota et al. 2002). The results showed that DNA would degrade to the point of being undetectable after approximately 600 years—far too short a life span to allow genetic investigation of Egyptian mummies. A series of responses to this paper appeared, with arguments about the various aspects of mummification and tomb environment that would be expected to prolong DNA preservation, but no consensus was reached, and the field of aDNA research has remained divided. A fascinating description of the state of the field can be found in an article that was prompted by the investigation into Tutankhamun's family (Marchant 2011), though there has since been a slight softening of opinion from one of the most vocal skeptics (Gilbert 2011) thanks to a carefully performed series of experiments on mummified crocodiles (Hekkala et al. 2011).

THE AMARNA FAMILY TREE: GENETIC RESULTS

The published components of the ancestry study were conducted in what appears to have been the same manner as the research into Hatshepsut described above. This approach is somewhat different from a "normal" ancient DNA project. It is usual to amplify the amount of preserved DNA using the polymerase chain reaction (PCR), a technique that can be viewed as a molecular photocopier, producing millions of copies of specifically targeted DNA sequences. These copies are then usually sequenced for more in-depth analysis, producing a large amount of data to work with. In contrast, the SCA team used a method more common to forensic or paternity testing.

Throughout the human genome, there are large areas of "junk" DNA that appear to serve little if any purpose. Within these areas, there are often short, repetitive sequences called short tandem repeats (STRs) or microsatellites. These are simply small sequences of DNA, usually between two and six base pairs in length, that are repeated several times, one after the other. Just as you inherit one-half of your nuclear genome from each parent, you also inherit one set of STRs at each location from each parent. Comparison between members of a family can show how these flow between generations, allowing a family tree to be built up. The more STRs are investigated, the clearer and more specific the information becomes (Brown 2000). These tests are not commonly applied to ancient remains, as they do not provide specific sequence data and require the preservation of nuclear DNA. As mentioned above, as each cell has only a single copy of the nuclear genome, it tends to be less well preserved and as such is harder to work with.

However, using an extremely sensitive STR analysis kit that is designed for tiny and degraded forensic samples, the team managed to obtain complete profiles for the mummies of Thuya, Yuya, Amenhotep III, and Tutankhamun, as well as the mummy from KV 55 and the Younger and Elder Ladies from KV 35—a truly phenomenal result. Partial profiles were also obtained for two mummies from KV 21 and the two fetuses thought to be Tutankhamun's children. This enabled a significant family tree to be built up, showing Tutankhamun to be the son of KV 55 and the KV 35 Younger Lady, who were also identified as siblings, and providing further evidence against the identification of KV 35 YL as Nefertiti. They in turn were the children of Amenhotep III and the KV 35 Elder Lady, prompting her identification as Tiye, the child of Yuya and Thuya (Hawass et al. 2010).

The partial profiles of the fetuses are consistent with them being the offspring of Tutankhamun, and there is a possible identification of one of the KV 21 mummies being the mother, raising the tentative identification of her as Ankhesenamun. Further confirmation of the family tree was obtained by testing of Y-chromosomal DNA, which is passed only from father to son.

With the relationships of the Amarna period rulers thus apparently resolved, and with some previously unknown mummies now identified, one big question remained that genetic analysis alone cannot answer: Who was buried in KV 55?

The Amarna Family Tree:
Radiological Findings

The body discovered in KV 55 has been subjected to a great deal of scrutiny since its discovery, partially because there has been such disagreement over the age and even the gender of the body. When it was first discovered, the body was declared by two (perhaps mercifully) unnamed surgeons to be female, an identification that, along with the presence of other finds that bore her name, prompted the publication of the excavation as "The Tomb of Queen Tîyi" (Davis 1910). The same volume, however, also contained a short note by the anatomist Grafton Elliot Smith stating his opinion that the body was that of a young man, approximately twenty-five years of age at death but with the possibility of being several years older (Elliot-Smith 1910, xxiii–xxiv). More details of how he reached this conclusion, including the contention that the body is that of Akhenaten (Khouniatonou in the report), are published in "The Royal Mummies" (Elliot-Smith 2000, 51–56). Later anatomical investigation of these remains pointed to a younger age at death, less than twenty-five years old and perhaps as young as twenty. This suggested that the body was that of Semenkhkare, supporting earlier work that had led to the same conclusion (Harrison 1966).

The age at death appears to be the key to determining the identity of this body. If the younger estimates are correct, then the body is not old enough to be that of Akhenaten and is more consistent with Semenkhkare. If an age toward the upper end of Smith's estimate is correct, then an identification as Akhenaten becomes the more plausible. With the genetic evidence pointing to this body as the father of Tutankhamun, the answer to this question carries even more importance. Using the radiological data obtained during the 2010 study, the body in KV 55 was determined to be between thirty-five and forty-five years old at death. This led the researchers to announce that this body was that of Akhenaten, finally identified after just over a century of debate.

Response and Discussion

As may be expected, the publication of this research prompted a great deal of discussion of the methodology, the results, and the interpretation of data. Among those directed at the kinship and individual identity determination aspects of the research were questions about the reliability of the genetic evidence. The question of whether DNA can even survive in pharaonic Egyptian remains was raised, along with doubts over the plausibility of achieving so great a success rate for analysis of relatively scarce nuclear DNA. The methods used to avoid contamination were also questioned, as little detail was included in the original paper beyond mention of the reproduction of the results over several samples and between two different laboratories, and the testing of laboratory staff for comparison to the ancient tissue for exclusionary purposes. It was further suggested that the recently developed "next generation" sequencing methods, which are better able to produce data from degraded samples, should have been used, and that nonhuman remains associated with the mummies should also have been tested, as these would be more easily tested for the presence of human contamination than human remains would be (Lorenzen and Willerslev 2010).

The project members' response to this included evidence of the successful extraction of DNA from a number of the mummies involved in the study (Gad et al. 2010).

However, given the firmly entrenched nature of the debate over the preservation of DNA in Egyptian remains, it would perhaps be surprising if this single instance would be sufficient to persuade the skeptics when a range of other such experiments claiming success have failed to do so (Zink and Nerlich 2003). The consistency of results between and within analyses was again reinforced as evidence that the results were genuine and not due to contamination. Of particular interest is the statement that "DNA isolated from Egyptian mummies was highly informative when processed with next generation sequencing" (Gad et al. 2010). Although this could be taken as being somewhat ambiguous regarding exactly *which* mummies are being referred to, the clear implication is that the mummies in question here have been tested using this method. There was no mention of this in the original paper, and no further details were offered as part of the response to Lorenzen and Willerslev. It is possible that the results had not been fully interpreted at the time the paper was written, as next generation sequencing produces vast data sets. However, they have unfortunately still yet to be released a little over three years later.

Not addressed in the response is the suggestion that insufficient testing of those who have come into contact with the bodies was carried out, and that associated nonhuman remains could be used as indicators of contamination. These suggestions appear to be quite reasonable in theory, particularly the former. Identifying and ruling out potential sources of contamination can only increase certainty in the results of an experiment. However, in the case of the royal mummies from the Valley of the Kings, it would be a vast, impossible task. These mummies have been the subject of so much interest since their discovery that they have been viewed and handled by an impossible to estimate number of people. Tracing and genetically testing everyone who has come into contact with the bodies is unfeasible, not least because the length of time since their discovery means that many will have died. The names of those involved directly in their study are not always recorded—the names of the doctors who identified KV 55 as female are not known, for example—making matters even worse.

The second suggestion, that associated nonhuman remains should be tested for evidence of human DNA, is not uncommon in the genetic analysis of ancient samples. Difficulties arise in this case not from an over abundance of handling, but from a lack. Any floral or faunal remains found in the tombs will have been subject to far less scrutiny than the human remains, so the spectrum of contaminants will be far more restricted. Regardless, such associated remains are, according to the Theban Mapping Project website's tomb inventories, not present in all tombs and so would not be representative of the sample group as a whole.

Far more specific issue was taken with the new estimation for the age at death of the KV 55 mummy. A letter by Baker (2010) points out a specific problem with the description of the methods used during this assessment: "Based on computed tomography. . . Dr. Hawass and colleagues purported an age of 35-45 years. . ., older than previously thought. Prior studies that refute this claim were dismissed and no substantiation for a much older age range was given in the text or online content."

In other words, no evidence for this new age was presented. Baker's letter lists a number of factors that other authors have provided in numerous studies that, taken together, indicate an age at death of the late teens or early twenties.

The rebuttal to this presents some information supporting the new age, "ruling out the much younger age," and suggests that the previous studies "used inaccurate and vague age estimation methods" (Gad et al. 2010). This is rather misleading, however, as the questionable method (suture closure) is but one of many that have been used previously that agree with the younger age. That there is disagreement between the various skeletal indicators should not be surprising. Smith was uncertain about the age he calculated because of exactly this disagreement, for example (Elliot-Smith 1910), and in adult skeletons it is known that there may be variations in the apparent age of different bones (Franklin 2010). However, there is no indication provided by Gad et al. (2010) that the new information is so much more accurate that the older assessments are not applicable. Indeed, part of the information provided by Baker includes a method described as being "a long favored approach" due to its "greater reliability" (Franklin 2010).

The presentation by Gad et al. (2010) of only the information that supports an age range of thirty-five to forty-five years, and the rather offhand dismissal of the more frequently quoted younger range without discussion of the relative merits of the data, do little to inspire confidence. However, a published response to a letter in a journal leaves little room for in-depth analysis, especially when the response needs to answer comments and criticisms from a number of contributors, as in this case.

Beyond the *Journal of the American Medical Association* letters pages, further questions were raised by Phizackerley (2010) regarding the identification of both Tutankhamun's mother and the mummy from KV 21, thought to be mother of his children. The original paper (Hawass et al. 2010) indicated that KV 35 YL was a previously unknown wife of Akhenaten, and that the KV 21 mummy might be Ankhesenamun, Tutankhamun's only recorded wife and a daughter of Akhenaten. Akhenaten would therefore be both paternal and maternal grandfather of the fetuses found in KV 62. However, although the fetuses only returned partial results, those obtained are inconsistent with this hypothesis at one STR locus. Phizackerley suggests that the resolution to this would be that Tutankhamun had another wife, whose name went unrecorded, as the name of his mother did. As an alternative, which does not require unknown queens, Phizackerley suggests that the family tree is simply not complete.

Almost the only clear conclusion from this study is that there is still room for much debate over the family tree of Tutankhamun. The genetic data are certainly controversial, as all ancient DNA data from Egyptian remains are, though there is the tantalizing prospect of information obtained using the next generation sequencing methods that have revolutionized the field of aDNA research (Millar et al. 2008). The accompanying documentary (Quilici 2010) that followed the project states that mitochondrial DNA analysis was carried out, which would allow for the maternal lineages of the family to be studied, but as yet no further information has been forthcoming despite the publication of this and the Y-chromosomal data having been proposed for 2011 (Marchant 2011). These data sets would add a great deal to the debate, though exactly what they would tell us cannot be guessed at. A more thorough description of the osteological investigation of KV 55 would also be useful, as it is upon this that so much of the identification rests, and the conflicting information needs to be assessed and resolved before a name can be confidently assigned.

Summary

The recent identity studies from the Valley of the Kings have been dogged by controversy and sometimes bitter argument. This is perhaps not surprising, as the simple cases have already been completed, whether through inscription, artifact, or a priest's helpful docket. Those remaining are necessarily more difficult and require the gathering of as much data as possible using a variety of archaeological and scientific methods.

Forensic and medical tools have been applied to the search and appear to be providing results far beyond most expectations. CT scanning provided the lynchpin for the identification of Hatshepsut from a broken tooth and has been used to help narrow the search for many others. DNA analysis has been used to reconstruct a multigenerational family tree for possibly the most famous pharaoh of ancient Egypt. However, the radiological data pertaining to Hatshepsut have not been subjected to peer review, and the genetic evidence that was gathered alongside has also yet to be released, making it difficult for scholars to review the evidence.

The ancestry of Tutankhamun is even more strongly contested, with a variety of charges leveled against the data collection and their interpretation. The identification of KV 55 as Akhenaten is particularly controversial, with the key factor of age at death remaining an area of major disagreement. Although the DNA results are also a source of some skepticism, there is the promise of more data to be released, including sequences obtained using massively powerful next generation methods and the mitochondrial DNA, which will allow maternal lineages to be investigated. Whether these will reinforce the published family tree or serve to further muddy the waters remains to be seen.

There is much exciting work still to be done, but the amount of criticism and even the possible political repercussions that have faced the authors of the studies presented here may make some researchers think twice. However, the high profile of the bodies found in the Valley of the Kings ensures that we can almost certainly look forward to seeing new data. What effect this will have on our understanding remains to be seen, but as new analytical methods are developed, the data will continue to improve in both quantity and reliability.

Bibliography

Applied Biosystems. 2007. "AmpFiSTR® MiniFiler™ PCR Amplification Kit Put to the Ultimate Test with Ancient Egyptian Mummy Identification Project." http://marketing.

appliedbiosystems.com/images/Product_Microsites/Minifiler1106/pdf/articles/Put_to_ the_Ultimate_Test_with_Ancient_Egyptian_Mummy_Identification_Project.pdf.

Baker, B. J. 2010. "King Tutankhamun's Family and Demise." *Journal of the American Medical Association* 303: 2471–2472.

Brown, K. 2000. "Ancient DNA Applications in Human Osteoarchaeology: Achievements, Problems and Potential." In *Human Osteology in Archaeology and Forensic Science*, edited by M. Cox and S. Mays, 455–473. London.

CNN. 2003. "Mummy Thought to Be Nefertiti May Be a Man." http://www.cnn.com/2003/ TECH/science/09/01/mummy.nefertiti.reut/.

Cox, M., and S. Mays, eds. 2000. *Human Osteology in Archaeology and Forensic Science*. London.

Davis, T. M. 1910. *The Tomb of Queen Tiyi*. London.

Elliot-Smith, G. 1910. "A Note on the Estimate of the Age Attained by the Person Whose Skeleton Was Found in the Tomb." In *The Tomb of Queen Tiyi*, edited by T. M. Davis, xxiii–xxiv. London.

Elliot-Smith, G. 2000. *The Royal Mummies*. London.

Fletcher, J. 2004. *The Search for Nefertiti*. London

Franklin, D. 2010. "Forensic Age Estimation in Human Skeletal Remains: Current Concepts and Future Directions." *Legal Medicine* 12: 1–7.

Gad, Y. A., A. Selim, and C. M. Pusch. 2010. "King Tutankhamun's Family and Demise." *Journal of the American Medical Association* 303: 2471.

Gilbert, M. T. P. 2011. "The Mummy Returns . . . and Sheds New Light on Old Questions." *Molecular Ecology* 20: 4195–4198.

Harris, J. E., E. F. Wente, C. F. Fox, I. El Nawaway, C. J. Kowalski, A. T. Storey, W. R. Russell, P. V. Ponitz, and G. F. Walker. 1978. "Mummy of the 'Elder Lady' in the Tomb of Amenhotep II: Egyptian Museum Catalog Number 61070." *Science* 200: 1149–1151.

Harris, J. E., and F. Hussien. 1991. "The Identification of the Eighteenth Dynasty Royal Mummies: A Biological Perspective." *International Journal of Osteoarchaeology* 1: 235–239.

Harrison, R. G. 1966. "An Anatomical Examination of the Pharaonic Remains Purported to be Akhenaten." *Journal of Egyptian Archaeology* 52: 95–119.

Harrison, R. G., R. C. Connolly, and A. Abdalla. 1969. "Kinship of Smenkhkare and Tutankhamun Affirmed by Serological Micromethod." *Nature* 224: 325–326.

Hawass, Z. 2005. "No Discrimination." http://web.archive.org/web/20050426164436/http:// www.zahihawass.com/wc_no_discrimination.htm.

Hawass, Z. 2007. "The Quest for Hatshepsut: Discovering the Mummy of Egypt's Greatest Female Pharaoh." http://www.drhawass.com/events/quest-hatshepsut-discovering-mu mmy-egypts-greatest-female-pharaoh.

Hawass, Z., Y. Z. Gad, S. Ismail, R. Khairat, D. Fathalla, N. Hasan, A. Ahmed, H. Elleithy, M. Ball, F. Gaballa, S. Wasef, M. Fateen, H. Amer, P. Gostner, A. Selim, A. Zink, and C. M. Pusch. 2010. "Ancestry and Pathology in King Tutankhamun's Family." *Journal of the American Medical Association* 303 (7, February 17): 638–647.

Hekkala, E., M. H. Shirley, G. Amato, J. D. Austin, S. Charter, J. Thorbjarnarson, K. A. Vliet, M. L. Houck, R. DeSalle, and M. J. Blum. 2011. "An Ancient Icon Reveals New Mysteries: Mummy DNA Resurrects a Cryptic Species within the Nile Crocodile." *Molecular Ecology* 20: 4125–4199.

Higuchi, R., B. Bowman, M. Freiberger, O. A. Ryder, and A. C. Wilson. 1984. "DNA Sequences from the Quagga, and Extinct Member of the Horse Family." *Nature* 312: 282–284.

James, S. E. 2003. "Duelling 'Nefertitis'!" *KMT* 14 (3): 22–29.

Lorenzen, E. D., and E. Willerslev. 2010. "King Tutankhamun's Family and Demise." *Journal of the American Medical Association* 303: 2471.

Marchant, J. 2011. "Curse of the Pharaoh's DNA." *Nature* 472: 404–406.

Marota, I., C. Basile, M. Ubaldi, and F. Rollo. 2002. "DNA Decay Rate in Papyri and Human Remains from Egyptian Archaeological Sites." *American Journal of Physical Anthropology* 117 (4): 310–318.

Mertz, B. 2003. "Nefertiti Maelstrom." *Kmt* 14 (4): 4.

Millar, C. D., L. Huynen, S. Subramaniian, E. Mohandesan, and D. M. Lambert. 2008. "New Developments in Ancient Genomics." *Trends in Ecology and Evolution* 23: 386–393.

Pääbo, S. 1985. "Molecular Cloning of Ancient Egyptian Mummy DNA." *Nature* 314: 644–645.

Phizackerley, K. 2010. "DNA Shows That KV55 Mummy Probably Not Akhenaten." http://www.kv64.info/2010/03/dna-shows-that-kv55-mummy-probably-not.html.

Quilici, B., dir. 2007a. *Nefertiti and the Lost Dynasty*. Silver Spring: National Geographic.

Quilici, B., dir. 2007b. *Secrets of Egypt's Lost Queen*. Silver Spring: Discovery Channel.

Quilici, B., dir. 2010. *Tutankhamun: The Mystery Revealed*. Silver Spring: Discovery Channel.

Reeves, N., and R. H. Wilkinson. 1996. *The Complete Valley of the Kings: Tombs and Treasures of Egypt's Greatest Pharaohs*. London and New York.

SCA (Supreme Council of Antiquities). 2007a. "Press Release—CT-scans of Egyptian Mummies from the Valley of the Kings." http://www.drhawass.com/blog/press-release-ct-scans-egyptian-mummies-valley-kings.

SCA (Supreme Council of Antiquities). 2007b. "Press Release—Identifying Hatshepsut's Mummy." http://www.drhawass.com/blog/press-release-identifying-hatshepsuts-mummy.

Taher, A. W. 2007. "The Mummy of Queen Hatshepsut Identified" *Ancient Egypt* 8 (2k): 10–13.

Theban Mapping Project. 2012. "Sites in the Valley of the Kings." http://www.thebanmapping-project.com/sites/.

Zink, A., and A. G. Nerlich. 2003. "Molecular Analyses of the 'Pharaos': Feasibility of Molecular Studies in Ancient Egyptian Material." *American Journal of Physical Anthropology* 121: 109–111.

PART XI

THE ADMINISTRATION OF THE KV IN DYNASTIC TIMES

CHAPTER 28

THE TEMPLES OF MILLIONS OF YEARS AT WESTERN THEBES

MARTINA ULLMANN

INTRODUCTION

WHERE was the cult dedicated to the kings buried in the Valley of the Kings performed? Usually we can observe a close spatial connection between the place of interment and installations for a funerary cult within the Egyptian culture, regardless of the royal or nonroyal nature of the dead. This was the case in the Old and Middle Kingdoms with the pyramid complexes, which combined the burial within the pyramid with the pyramid temple where the cult for the king took place.

With the choice of a rock-cut tomb in the Valley of the Kings for the royal burial in the early Eighteenth Dynasty the situation changed. The location of the Kings' Valley in the West-Theban hills was too remote to allow a proper daily cult and regular visits during festival processions. No buildings where a royal funerary cult could have been performed have been identified in the valley, and no priestly titles related to the valley as a whole or to a specific royal tomb there are known.

This leads to the question posed above: Where did the royal funerary cult take place during most of the New Kingdom? Usually the answer points to the row of royal temples in Western Thebes, which were built on the flat desert strip between the lower irrigated land to the east and the desert hills to the west, from Qurna in the north to Medinet Habu in the south. These temples are commonly interpreted as "funerary" or "memorial" temples, with their cult focused on the deceased kings (e.g., Stadelmann 1986; Gundlach 2001). One of the main reasons for this interpretation is the location of the temples in Western Thebes, that is, within the necropolis area and thus in the vicinity of the royal tombs in the Kings' Valley. The Egyptian designation for these temples as *ḥw.t n.t ḥḥ.w m rnp.wt* "house of millions of years" has therefore often been regarded as denoting an installation that was dedicated specifically to the royal funerary cult.

But the simple equation of "house of millions of years" with "funerary" or "memorial" temple and the setting up of an opposition to so-called divine temples does not work (for this and the following, see Ullmann 2002). First of all, temples of millions of years do not represent a feature that is in any way exclusive to the Theban necropolis area, as they are also documented in Eastern Thebes (within the Karnak precinct and at Luxor temple) and throughout Egypt and Nubia. Apart from the Theban area, concentrations of temples of millions of years existed at Heliopolis, Memphis, and Abydos. All of them are cult places that were especially relevant for kingship ideology. But the evidence for million year houses at places like Pi-Ramesse, Thinis, Serabit el-Khadim, and at several locations in Nubia shows that the theological concept that underlies these temples could at least in principle be transferred to any place. And it is important to note that in many cases more than one temple with this designation was erected by the same king.

Chronologically the temples of millions of years are not tied exclusively to the kings who were buried in the Valley of the Kings. The evidence runs from the reign of Amenemhat III in the late Twelfth Dynasty to the Third Intermediate Period (Scheschonq I and Osorkon II), with a late resumption of the designation at the beginning of Greek rule in Egypt under Alexander the Great at Luxor temple.

That means that topographically and chronologically there is no specific relationship between the temples referred to by the Egyptians as "houses of millions of years" on the whole and the royal tombs in the Valley of the King. But the question arises whether all or some of the temples of millions of years, which were located at Western Thebes, formed a specific group with distinct features that set it apart from other royal temples, and if so, if this might be due to a royal funerary cult.

The following discussion considers this question from various points of view: temple designation, layout, architecture, iconographic program, temple theology, priesthood, and cult.

THE NAMES OF THE WEST-THEBAN ROYAL TEMPLES

The royal temples in Western Thebes are designated as "*ḥw.t* of king N" ("house of king N"), that can be varied to "*ḥw.t-nṯr* of king N" ("god's house of king N") (for this and the following, see Ullmann 2002, 639–660). The term for "temple" may be expanded by the genitive connection *n.t ḥḥ.w m rnp.wt* ("of millions of years"). In most cases the so-called prenomen of the king—his *nswt-bjt* or "throne" name—was used for denoting his West-Theban temple, whereas the *sꜣ Rꜥ* name was usually employed for royal temples in Eastern Thebes and elsewhere in Egypt. But there are some exceptions to this rule, and it is only from Ramesses II through the end of the Ramesside period that this topographical pattern of use of the royal names is observed strictly.

This brings up the question whether the *nswt-bjt* name had a specific significance that made its use for the West-Theban royal temples especially fitting. The title *nswt-bjt* characterizes the king as keeper of the royal office upon earth; it empowers him to act as a ruler politically and within the cult. The prenomen itself sets up a relationship between the king and the sun god by its constant use of the element "R⁽ᶜ⁾". We may therefore assume that especially these aspects of the royal ideology were of importance for the theological setting in which the West-Theban royal temples were functioning.

The so-called proper or religious name of a West-Theban royal temple, like *Dsr Dsrw Jmn*, "Sacred is the Sacredness of Amun," for the temple of Hatshepsut at Deir el-Bahri, usually follows the king's name in elaborate temple designations, but it is often used as a kind of shorthand for the temple in question, for example, within priestly titles (Helck 1960, 79–81). It implies a short theological message, which may refer either to the cult topographical setting of the temple or to the cultic function of the building, or it takes the form of a religious statement that is related to either the king or a god (see Table 28.1).

Table 28.1 List of Royal Temples at Western Thebes

King	Royal temple/s in Western Thebes	Location	Proper Name of the Temple
Ahmose	not proven		
Amenhotep I/ Ahmes-Nefertari	yes	east of Dra Abu el-Naga?	most probably *Mn js.t/Mn js.wt* "Enduring is the place/ are the places"
Thutmose I	yes	north of *Ḥnk.t ꜥnḫ*?	*Ḥnm.t ꜥnḫ* "The one which is united with life"
Thutmose II	yes	north of Medinet Habu	*Šsp.t ꜥnḫ* "The one which receives life"
Hatshepsut	yes	Deir el-Bahri	*Dsr Dsrw Jmn* "Sacred is the Sacredness of Amun"
	yes (classification as royal temple not entirely certain)	unknown	*Ḥ ꜥj 3ḫ.t Jmn* "The horizon of Amun appears"
Thutmose III	yes	Deir el-Bahri	*Dsr3ḫ.t Jmn* "Sacred is the horizon of Amun"
	yes	north of Ramesseum	*Ḥnk.t ꜥnḫ* "The one which bestows life"
Amenhotep II	yes	north of Ramesseum	*Šsp.t ꜥnḫ* or alternatively *J ꜥb3ḫ.t* "The one which receives life" or "The one which unites with the horizon"

(continued)

Table 28.1 *Continued*

King	Royal temple/s in Western Thebes	Location	Proper Name of the Temple
Thutmose IV	yes	south of Ramesseum	unknown
Amenhotep III	yes	Kom el-Heitan	*Šsp.t Jmn wṯs.t nfrw=f* "The one which receives Amun and which raises his beauty"
Amenhotep IV/ Akhenaten	not proven		
Semenchkare	probably yes, but not entirely certain	unknown	unknown
Tutankhamun	probably yes, but not entirely certain	north of Medinet Habu?	unknown
Aye	yes	north of Medinet Habu	*Mn mnw* "Enduring are the monuments"
Horemheb	yes	north of Medinet Habu	unknown
Ramesses I	uncertain	unknown	unknown
Seti I	yes	Qurna	*ꜣḫ* (*Stḫj mrj.n-Ptḥ*) "Beneficial is Seti, loved by Ptah"
Ramesses II	yes	Ramesseum	*Ḥnm.t Wꜣs.t* "The one which is united with Thebes"
Merenptah	yes	northwest of Kom el-Heitan	unknown
Seti II	yes	unknown	unknown
Siptah	yes	north of Ramesseum	unknown
Tausret	yes	south of Ramesseum	[. . .] *ꜥn mj Stḫ nḫt* [. . .] ". . . beautiful like Seth the strong one. . ."
Sethnacht	not proven		
Ramesses III	yes	Medinet Habu	*Ḥnm.t nḥḥ* "The one which is united with eternity"
Ramesses IV	yes	north of Medinet Habu?	unknown
	yes (classification as royal temple not entirely certain)	Asasif	unknown
Ramesses V	yes	unknown	unknown
Ramesses VI	yes	unknown	unknown
Ramesses VII	not proven		

(continued)

Table 28.1 *Continued*

King	Royal temple/s in Western Thebes	Location	Proper Name of the Temple
Ramesses VIII	not proven		
Ramesses IX	yes	unknown	unknown
Ramesses X	not proven		
Ramesses XI	not proven		

Source: Based mainly on Helck (1960, 82–115); Haring (1997, 419–425); Ullmann (2002); and Leblanc (2010).

Compared with the religious names of royal temples in Eastern Thebes or elsewhere in Egypt, no specific grammatical or semantic pattern can be detected for the West-Theban temples, apart from the fact that if a god is mentioned, it is usually Amun, but this relates to the fact that the royal temples in Western and Eastern Thebes alike are in theology and cult closely connected to the god Amun, as the main local deity.

During Ramesside times a tendency arose to create the names of several royal temples by following a uniform pattern. In the reign of Seti I the religious names for his temples of millions of years in Karnak and in Qurna almost paralleled each other: Karnak, *3ḫ (Stḫi mri.n-Jmn)* "Beneficial is Seti, loved by Amun"; and Qurna, *3ḫ (Stḫi mri.n-Ptḥ)* "Beneficial is Seti, loved by Ptah". During the reign of Ramesses II the names of his temples in Abydos and at Western Thebes made the same kind of cult topographical statement: Abydos, *Ḥnm.t T3-wr* "The one which is united with *T3-wr*"; and Western Thebes, *Ḥnm.t W3s.t* "The one which is united with Thebes". And the name of his newly built part of the Luxor temple, which can be extended to the entire temple, varied the theme to *Ḥnm.t nḥḥ*, "The one which is united with eternity". Exactly the same name was later chosen by Ramesses III for his West-Theban royal temple. This is a clear warning against too obvious modern interpretations, like *nḥḥ* = eternity = some kind of funerary meaning. The Egyptian concept of eternity was different from the modern use of the term, and *nḥḥ* might best be described as eternal cyclic rejuvenation (Assmann 1975).

The evidence provided by the proper names of the royal temples shows clearly that the temples in Western Thebes were not treated in any way differently from royal temples elsewhere. The religious statements made within these names were not specific to Western Thebes, and no special reference to a funerary or memorial cult can be detected. The uniform name pattern of the Nineteenth Dynasty might point to a building program for the royal temples of a king conceptualized early in his reign.

Another important part of the designation of a royal temple in Western Thebes is the phrase "*m pr Jmn*" ("in the house of Amun"). In the Ramesside period "*m pr Jmn*" is frequently added after the proper name or, if this is omitted, directly after the king's name. In the Eighteenth Dynasty the use of this phrase is attested much less, but we do have evidence for it (dated to the reign of Amenhotep III), for example, for the West-Theban temple of Thutmose III called

Ḥnk.t ʿnḫ. The small number of attestations before the Nineteenth Dynasty may be due in part to the poorer documentation for the Eighteenth Dynasty and also to a growing tendency in the early Ramesside period toward a greater standardization of temple names.

The "*m pr Jmn*" phrase connects the royal temples in Western Thebes with the main temple of the local patron deity, that is, the temple of Amun at Karnak. The royal temples in other religious centers were associated with the respective main local cult in the same way: the ones in Memphis were "in the house of Ptah," the ones in Heliopolis were "in the house of Ra," and the ones in Abydos were "in the house of Osiris".Furthermore the "*m pr Jmn*" phrase is not specific to West-Theban temples. The million year houses known from Eastern Thebes were connected to the Amun cult alike, for example, the Achmenu of Thutmose III at Karnak, or the so-called triple shrine of Seti II in the forecourt of the Karnak temple, or the Luxor temple during the reign of Ramesses II.

Primarily the "*m pr* god N" phrase reflects a religious dependency; that is, the royal temple was attached to the theological system and the cult regulations of the temple of the local patron deity. Usually this was made visible by means of festival processions between the temples. Administrative and economical bonds could come along with this, too.

Sometimes a location is added to the designation of a West-Theban royal temple. It describes the topographical position of the temple, most often as being simply *ḥr jmnt.t W3s.t*, "to the west of Thebes" or as indicating its relation with the Amun temple at Karnak: *m ḫft-ḥr n Jp.t-s.wt*, "opposite of *Jp.t-s.wt*".

The most elaborate form of denoting a West-Theban royal temple thus consists of five parts and runs, for example, for the temple of Ramesses III at Medinet Habu, like this: *ḥw.t n.t ḥḥ.w m rnp.wt n nswt-bjt nb t3.wj (Wsr-M3ʿ.t-Rʿ mrj Jmn) Ḫnm.t nḥḥ m pr Jmn ḥr jmnt.t W3s.t*, "house of millions of years of the king of Upper and Lower Egypt, the lord of the Two Lands Ramesses III 'Which is united with eternity' in the temple of Amun to the west of Thebes." A wide range of combinations of the five different elements is attested. Most common were the abbreviations "*ḥw.t* of king N" and/or the proper name of the temple. There was a growing tendency toward complexity over the time.

WEST-THEBAN ROYAL TEMPLES ATTESTED DURING THE NEW KINGDOM

The tombs of the first kings of the Eighteenth Dynasty, Ahmose and Amenhotep I, are most likely to be found in Dra Abu el-Naga, the traditional burial ground of the Seventeenth Dynasty (for the tomb of the latter, see Polz 2007, 172–197). A temple of Ahmose in Western Thebes is not proven (Ullmann 2002, 17–25), and it is not certain whether some personnel of *Nb-pḥtj-Rʿ* refers to a West-Theban temple of this king (Helck 1960, 82; Haring 1997, 426). Several temples connected with Amenhotep I and Ahmes-Nefertari are attested in Western Thebes, but most of them were only set up in the Ramesside period within the context of the special veneration for these individuals in the Theban necropolis, and in most cases the exact location is disputed. The best candidate for a royal temple erected during the lifetime of Amenhotep I is the *ḥw.t Ḏsr k3 Rꜥ*, for which priests and other officials are documented from the Eighteenth to the Twentieth Dynasties (Helck 1960, 83; Haring 1997, 426–427). The location and proper name of this temple are not known with certainty, but it has been convincingly equated with the temple named *Mn js.t/Mn js.wt* and identified archaeologically with a building that was situated below the hills of Dra Abu el-Naga (Polz 2007, 104–111, 187–190).

A temple of Thutmose I called *ḥw.t ꜥ3-ḫpr-k3-Rꜥ* at Western Thebes with the proper name *Ḫnm.t ꜥnḫ* is amply attested until the late Twentieth Dynasty, but the exact location is much debated (Helck 1960, 88–91; Haring 1997, 419, 428–431). Recently an identification with a structure unearthed by Abu el-Ayun Barakat in 1970/71 about 200 m north of the Thutmose III temple called *Ḥnk.t ꜥnḫ* was proposed (Iwaszczuk 2009).

The construction of temples of millions of years in Western Thebes is proven for the majority of the kings (see Table 28.1) through the end of the Twentieth Dynasty, with the notable exception of Akhenaten (for possible reasons, see Ullmann 2002, 628).

In the reign of Thutmose III two different royal temples were erected at Western Thebes, called *Ḥnk.t ꜥnḫ* and *Ḏsr 3ḫ.t Jmn*. A block from the Asasif area with a partly destroyed inscription mentioning a house of millions of years of Hatsheput—with her name replaced by the cartouche of Thutmose II—seems to attest a second royal temple already for Hatshepsut, but the proposed identification with the textually proven temple *Ḥꜥj 3ḫ.t Jmn* (Ullmann 2002, 53–59) as well as the location and exact nature of the latter remains uncertain. If the block is indeed part of the material unearthed by Abu el-Ayun Barakat in 1970/71, then the temple referred to might instead be the royal temple of Thutmose I called *Ḫnm.t ꜥnḫ* (see above). A considerable part of its decoration seems to have been executed only during the reign of Hatshepsut (Iwaszczuk 2009, 273, 275).

During the reign of Ramesses IV three or even four temples were planned on the west bank (Ullmann 2002, 524–542; Budka 2009). The textually well proven "house of millions of years" of this king may have been located north of Medinet Habu, close to the temple of Aye/Horemheb (Ullmann 2002, 534–535; Budka 2009, 42–43). But the very large temple in the Asasif, where work started under Ramesses IV (for the latest dating, see Budka 2009: 40–41) and was continued by Ramesses V and VI, might as well have been considered a royal temple due to its presumed function within the Beautiful Festival of the Valley (Ullmann 2002, 535–536; Budka 2009, 42–44). It remains uncertain where the royal temples of the late Ramesside rulers, especially the textually proven ones of Ramesses V, VI, and IX, were located (Ullmann 2002, 548–563; Budka 2009, 43; Polz 1998, 279–281).

After the end of the Twentieth Dynasty no newly founded royal temples are attested in Western Thebes. A temple of Sheshonq I, called *ḥw.t Ḥḏ-ḫpr-Rꜥ stp.n-Rꜥ m W3s.t*, is most likely to be equated with the building activity of this king at Karnak (Ullmann 2002, 573).

Taking all the written and archaeological evidence together, we may assert that each monarch who was buried in the Valley of the Kings had at least one royal temple—sometimes even several—erected in Western Thebes. The frequency with which temples of millions of years are attested in Western Thebes is thus definitely higher than at any other place in Egypt. This may in part be due to the much better evidence within the Theban area, but it also points to the desire or even need to have a place for the royal cult established especially at Western Thebes.

TOPOGRAPHY, LAYOUT, AND FUNCTION

The royal temples on the west bank are an integrant part of the Theban ritual land-scape, which encompasses the temples at Karnak and Luxor as well as the sanctuaries at Western Thebes and the tombs there. Numerous cult buildings on both banks of the Nile were linked together theologically in manifold ways. Festival processions (Cabrol 2001) revived the underlying religious and ideological concepts at various occasions through-out the year and presented them to a broader public, thus enabling the participation of at least parts of the population for their own benefits.

The location, layout, and function of the temples of millions of years at Western Thebes can only be understood by putting them within this wider framework of a sacred area. Of primary importance is the Beautiful Festival of the Valley, which came into being in the Eleventh Dynasty, during the later reign of Mentuhotep II, when an annual bark procession between the Amun temple at Karnak and the royal temple in the valley of Deir el-Bahri was introduced. The joining of the royal cult and that of Amun in the latest building period of the Mentuhotep temple at Deir el-Bahri led to the development of the temples of millions of years in general and to the West Theban ones in particular (Arnold 1974a, 73, 78–80, 88; 1974b, 30–33; 1997, 74–76; Ullmann 2002, 674–675; 2007).

When Queen Hatshepsut in the early Eighteenth Dynasty chose a place near the Mentuhotep temple at Deir el-Bahri for her own royal temple, which clearly depends in its location and general layout (valley temple and processional way leading up to a ter-race temple) on the Eleventh Dynasty sanctuary (Arnold 1978), the Valley Festival was revived. Throughout the New Kingdom this feast played a major role within the theo-logical concept of the royal temples at Western Thebes. Apart from iconographic and inscriptional evidence, this is indicated by the east-west alignment of all royal temples at the west bank since the time of Hatshepsut, which clearly relates these sanctuaries with the main temple of Amun-Ra at Karnak.

The situation is different for the royal temples of the very early Eighteenth Dynasty. The temple below the hills of Dra Abu el-Naga, which might have served for the cult of Amenhotep I and Ahmes-Nefertari, is oriented north-south with its axis pointing toward the courts of two tombs up the hill (K93.11 and K93.12), which have been pro-posed as the burial places of Amenhotep I and Ahmes-Nefertari (Polz 2007, 172–192). The general layout of the temple—especially in its rear part—resembles other sanctu-aries of the early Eighteenth Dynasty, but the scarcity of information available does not allow a detailed functional interpretation (Polz 2007, 104–111). The temple of Thutmose I has not been thoroughly investigated till now (Iwaszczuk 2009). The one for Thutmose II is very badly preserved, though it was quite small, differs in its plan from later royal temples, and was altered by Thutmose III (Stadelmann 1979, 309).

The reign of Hatshepsut was pivotal for the evolution of the West Theban royal tem-ples and the emerging Theban ritual landscape. Numerous features that can be observed with a constant development in these temples are attested for the first time at her site at Deir el-Bahri (Arnold 1978; Stadelmann 1979). The theology and cult of Amun-Ra, together with the closely related royal ideology and the cult directed toward the divine ruler and the royal ancestors, were expressed in the layout and the iconographic program of her temple in an all-encompassing effort unseen prior to that time.

Essential features of the layout of most of the West-Theban royal temples since Hatshepsut are (Stadelmann 1979, 1986; Hölscher 1941, 22–32, pl. 2) the already mentioned east-west alignment; huge open courtyards, arranged in ascending terraces, which provide the monumental festival architecture along the processional route into the inner part of the temple; one or several columned halls for the admission of the bark processions with lateral chambers; and the westernmost part of the temple, which displays a tripartite structure. This tripartite arrangement consists of chambers for Amun-Ra (and, probably from the time of Thutmose III, chapels for Mut and Chonsu) in the center, with rooms for the royal cult and the king's ancestors in the south, and an open court (sometimes with adjoining rooms) in the north, which served as a cult place for the sun god. The rooms for the royal cult in the south display a combination of certain architectural and iconographic elements that can be traced back to the innermost part of the pyramid temples of the Old Kingdom: a vaulted ceiling, the king sitting in front of the offering table, and in the temple of Hatshepsut at Deir el-Bahri and the one of Thutmose III called *Ḥnk.t ꜥnḫ* a false door at the rear wall (Arnold 1978). It is important to note that elements of the royal ideology and the royal cult were not restricted to these rooms in the south dedicated primarily to the king's cult, but were an essential feature of all parts of the temple.

Within this distinctive tripartite structure of most of the West-Theban million year houses the cult was oriented along two different ritual axes (Karkowski 2003): in the center, a large east-west oriented temple designed for processions with the barks of Amun-Ra (and sometimes accompanying deities) and the divine king; in the south an area dedicated to the cult of the king and his royal ancestors and in the north an open court as a cult place for the sun god Ra-Horakhty-Atum. The latter two are connected by a north-south axis for the ritual manifestation of the annual circuit of the sun, as well as for the inclusion of the king, more specifically his divine reign, within the cyclic renewal of the sun god. This tripartite structure can be proven archaeologically with a constant development starting from Hatshepsut until the late Twentieth Dynasty (Stadelmann 1979, 1986; Hölscher 1941, 22–25, pl. 2).

A recurring element of the royal temples at Western Thebes is the integration of a temple palace for ritual purposes (Stadelmann 1973; Waitkus 2008, 286).

Another important feature of the Hatshepsut temple at Deir el-Bahri is the cult of Hathor, which might go back at this site to the time of Mentuhotep II (Arnold 1974a, 83–84). A small temple directly to the south was dedicated to her. The cult of Hathor was integrated in the Valley Festival, but beyond that Hathor played an important role within the concept of royal renewal (Beaux 2012). The temple *Ḥnk.t ꜥnḫ* of Thutmose III had its own Hathor chapel in the southern forecourt, but in the later royal temples this element is not regularly found.

Thutmose III had another temple of millions of years, called *Ḏsr ꜣḫ.t Jmn*, built at Deir el-Bahri. Its layout does not display the distinctive tripartite structure described above. The iconographic program seems to center around two closely connected main topics: the cult for Amun-Ra, especially in connection with the Valley Festival, and the royal cult, primarily directed toward a *Ka* statue of Thutmose III, but also including statues of his predecessors, Thutmose I and II (Ullmann 2002, 88–95; Dolinska 2010 with bibliography).

Most probably only one temple was dedicated permanently—that is, lasting beyond the death of the king—to the cult of each individual king at Western Thebes as a rule. This at least is indicated by the distribution of titles referring to the cult of an individual king (Helck 1960, 79–117). Beginning with the reign of Hatshepsut, these temples displayed the tripartite structure described above.

Due to the lack of archaeological evidence, we do not know whether the royal temples at Heliopolis and Memphis had the same or a similar structure as the one described above as distinctive for most of the West-Theban temples. The royal temples at Abydos do not exhibit exactly this kind of structure, but in the sanctuaries of Seti I and Ramesses II the rooms for the cult of the ancestors and the king are situated at least partially to the south of the main east-west-oriented ritual axis (Ullmann 2002, 246, 323; David 1981). The plan of the Akhmenu of Thutmose III at Karnak, which functioned as a house of millions of years too, differs greatly from the royal temples in Western Thebes, but structural similarities can be observed by placing rooms for chthonic rituals and the ancestors in the southern part and by installing a place for the worship of the sun god on the roof in the northern part (Ullmann 2002, 82–83; Barguet 1962, 283–340). The great speos of Ramesses II at Abu Simbel seems to have been modeled after the contemporary West-Theban royal temples (Ullmann 2013): It displays the same tripartite structure and great similarities within the decoration program. But for the other royal temples of the Eighteenth and Nineteenth Dynasties in Nubia, individual architectural and decorative programs were preferred.

ICONOGRAPHIC PROGRAM, TEMPLE THEOLOGY, AND CULT

The decoration program of the royal temples at Western Thebes, especially along the east-west main axis, clearly attests a form of the local patron deity Amun (-Ra) as the main deity (Ullmann 2002, 663). A specific form of Amun seems to have been resident in each of the West-Theban royal temples, called "Amun (-Ra) of/in temple N" (Nelson 1942; Stadelmann 1979, 320–321; Ullmann 2002, 666–667; Waitkus 2008, 180–181). He received a daily cult within these temples, as well as a festival one, when the portable statue of Amun-Ra from Karnak visited the royal temples at the west bank at least once per year during the Beautiful Festival of the Valley. The itinerary most probably included the million year house of the reigning king, the construction of which usually started very early in a reign (Ullmann 2002, 668–669), and all the other royal temples still in use, as well as the Hathor sanctuaries at Deir el-Bahri (Waitkus 2008, 182, with further references). The main purpose of these visits seems to have been the temporary merging of Amun of Karnak with his manifestation resident in each of the royal temples in order to provoke a regular regeneration for the local form of Amun (Waitkus 2008, 181–182).

In addition to Amun, the king in his divine aspects received a cult service in his temple (Ullmann 2002, 661–663). This is amply proven by the priests assigned to the cult of king N within his West-Theban royal temple (Helck 1960, 79–119; Haring 1997, 426–459). The documentation of priests and other officials also makes it very clear that as a rule the royal temples already were in use during the lifetime of a king. Within the temple decoration the royal cult is displayed regularly by the scene in which the Iunmutef priest assigns an offering to the king, or rather his divine *Ka*, sitting in front of an offering table (Rummel 2010a, 96–125; 2010b). Royal statues received daily cult in the royal temples and also as participants in festival processions, as in the case of the West-Theban temples in particular during the Valley Festival. The earliest known depiction of a processional bark for a statue of the reigning king dates to the time of Tutankhamun (Karlshausen 2009, 62–64), but a statue of the reigning king doubtless took part in the ceremonies performed during the Valley Festival since its revival in the early Eighteenth Dynasty.

Pivotal for the cult and the underlying theology of the West-Theban royal temples is the fact that the processional images of the kings were identified with the special form of Amun resident within the particular royal temple (Nelson 1942; Ullmann 2002, 666–667; Waitkus 2008, 189–197). This is proven for the Twentieth Dynasty, but was most probably already established in the early Eighteenth Dynasty. A title like "wab of Amun of *Mn-ḫpr-Rˁ* in *Ḥnk.t ˁnḫ*" (Helck 1960, 96) surely refers to this special relationship between the king and the Amun of his temple. By identifying the king in his capacity as a divine ruler—embodied in his *Ka* statue—with the Amun resident in his temple, he took part in whose annual regeneration during the Valley Festival when Amun of Karnak visited the royal temples at Western Thebes. It might even be asked if not the regeneration of the divine ruler—as the main purpose of the royal temples (see below)— by a temporary ritual merging between his statue and that of Amun of Karnak only provoked the existence of a special form of Amun within such a temple, who as a consequence then was closely related to the king.

The existence of special manifestations of Amun within royal temples is not restricted to Western Thebes, but can also be seen in other temples of millions of years, like the Akhmenu of Thutmose III at Karnak or the Luxor temple (Ullmann 2002, 667; Waitkus 2008, 204–209, 215–222). There is also evidence outside of Thebes for the temporary identification of the divine ruler with the local patron deity within his temples of millions of years during certain festivals (Ullmann 2002, 667; Waitkus 2008, 194–197, 282–285).

In addition to Amun and the king, a cult in favor of the Ennead as the ensemble of the local ancestor gods can be observed in the royal temples, be it at Western Thebes or elsewhere (Ullmann 2002, 663–664). But in the West-Theban temples the cult of the royal ancestors was of special importance. This can clearly be seen by the above-described specific tripartite structure of most of the royal temples at Western Thebes, where rooms dedicated to the cult of the royal ancestors—in most cases exemplified by either the direct predecessor or a specially important one (like Thutmose I in the Hatshepsut temple at Deir el-Bahri)—were located to the south of the east-west axis.

Other deities who were venerated regularly in the West-Theban temples were Ra-Horakhty-Atum, whose cult place is in the northern part of the temple (see above), and Osiris, often combined with Ptah and Sokar.

The iconographic program of the temples of millions of years, be it at Western Thebes or elsewhere, generally displays the living king, and the cult is directed toward the reigning divine king (Ullmann 2002, passim and esp. 661–670; Gulyás 2003; Rummel 2010a, 108–114; 2010b, 204–208). The ruler who was responsible for building the temple is usually not characterized as deceased within the decoration (e.g., by using the *mȝˁ-ḫrw* formulae), and no specific funerary rituals are depicted (not even in the rooms dedicated primarily to the royal cult), but rather renewal rituals. These are primarily the coronation of the king, allusions to the Hebsed, and the Opening of the Mouth, which is often closely connected to the king sitting in front of the offering table with the Iunmutef performing the ritual. In the temple of Seti I at Qurna the Opening of the Mouth is performed within the context of the annual visit of Amun of Karnak in the temple during the Valley Festival and is thereby closely related to the identification of the king with Amun (Waitkus 2008, 175–203; Rummel 2010a, 128–132; 2010b, 200–202). It is important to stress that the ritual of the Opening of the Mouth is not exclusively related to a funerary context at a tomb, but is equally meaningful for the regular revival of cult statues within the daily and the festival temple cult (Rummel 2010a, 142–144).

The denotation of the ruling king as "Osiris N", which is sometimes, albeit quite rarely, found in the West-Theban royal temples scenes, has to be seen within the context of royal renewal: Ritual death as the precondition for achieving a new, regenerated divine status involved a temporary association between the king and Osiris (Ullmann 2002, 669–670; Rummel 2010a, 108–114, 129–132, 143–144; 2010b, 202–208). The so-called Osiride pillar statues, which are regularly found in royal temples, are connected with the sed festival and the royal renewal as well (Leblanc 1980, 1982; Gulyás 2007).

The primary goal of the cult in the royal temples, be it at Western Thebes or elsewhere, was the regeneration of the divine king, or rather the royal power bestowed upon him by the gods (Haeny 1997; Ullmann 2002, 664–668; Rummel 2010a, 108–114; 2010b). This renewal of the divine rule of the king was fulfilled in analogy to the regeneration of the gods. The perception of Egyptian kingship as a sacred institution, with the reigning king as the earthly representative of the Great God, formed the ideological background. In the "houses of millions of years" first the rule of the living Horus king and later the one of the Osiris king should be perpetuated into eternity by endless cyclical renewal, in analogy to the daily, as well as the annual, circuit of the sun.

Several constantly recurring iconographic elements refer to this main aspect within the function of the royal temples: the king sitting in front of the offering table with the Iunmutef performing the ritual, the so-called Osiride pillar statues of the king, scenes displaying the divine parentage of the king, the writing of the king's name on the sacred persea tree, coronation scenes often combined with the presentation of palm panicles and sed festivals, *smȝ-tȝ.wi* scenes, bestowing of the lifetime of Ra and the years of Atum in combination with the celebration of the sed festival, and so forth.

The regeneration of the king's power was closely linked to his royal-divine ancestors, who legitimized his rule. This is why the presence of the Ennead as the divine ancestors in the royal temples was of importance. For the same reason, quite regularly the cult of one of the predecessors of the reigning king was integrated within the temple, especially at Western Thebes.

CONCLUSION

The main purpose of the temples of millions of years was the regular regeneration of the divine rule of the king in analogy to the renewal of the gods, in order to maintain the cosmic order. In the temples at Western Thebes this was accomplished by linking the royal ideology with the theology of Amun (-Ra) and by establishing the Beautiful Festival of the Valley. Based on this theological background and the cultic needs resulting out of it, a regular pattern for the architecture and the layout of these royal temples was developed in the early Eighteenth Dynasty, starting with Hatsheput. But the basic idea behind these temples could be realized at any place in Egypt or Nubia by connecting the royal cult with that of the local patron deity and by adapting theology and rituals to the specific features of the site. The architecture, layout, and iconographic program of these royal temples displayed many similarities to the West-Theban temples, and even the tripartite structure, which was so distinctive for these sanctuaries, could be transferred to another site, as the example of the temple of Ramesses II at Abu Simbel seems to indicate.

Priests performing the royal cult are documented especially well for most of the West-Theban royal temples ("priest of king N in temple N"), but again this is not unique for Western Thebes, as is shown, for example, by several priests of Tutankhamun connected with his temple at Faras in Nubia (Helck 1960, 152). The abundance of prosopographical material found at Thebes might easily provoke a one-sided picture in this case.

The question "Where did the royal funerary cult take place in the New Kingdom?" implies that there was indeed a special cult performed exclusively for the dead kings, but the rituals executed in the West-Theban royal temples or anywhere else are not specifically funerary in their character, and the iconography of these temples shows no special adherence to the dead king. Rather, we should assume that the cult for the dead king at that time was basically a continuation of the cult for the divine ruler, which was an intrinsic part of Egyptian religion. The continuous regeneration of the divine kingship did take place for each individual king, and it was to be carried on after his death. But there is no evidence that the actual rituals in the temples changed.

One specific feature of the royal temples in Western Thebes is that in several cases the cult for individual kings lasted longer there than anywhere else. This was most probably due to the specific importance of the theology of Amun for the royal cult during the New Kingdom, which led to better economic resources for the West-Theban royal temples. The proximity of the royal tombs in the Valley of the Kings might have stimulated further the duration of the cult, especially at Western Thebes.

BIBLIOGRAPHY

Arnold, D. 1974a. *Der Tempel des Königs Mentuhotep von Deir el-Bahari, Band I: Architektur und Deutung.* Archäologische Veröffentlichungen 8. Mainz.
Arnold, D. 1974b. *Der Tempel des Königs Mentuhotep von Deir el-Bahari, Band II: Die Wandreliefs des Sanktuars.* Archäologische Veröffentlichungen 11. Mainz.
Arnold, D. 1978. "Vom Pyramidenbezirk zum 'Haus für Millionen Jahre.'" *Mitteilungen des Deutschen Archäologischen Instituts, Abteilung Kairo* 34: 1–8, Mainz.
Arnold, D. 1997. "Royal Cult Complexes of the Old and Middle Kingdoms." In *Temples of Ancient Egypt*, edited by B. Shafer, 31–85. Ithaca, NY.
Assmann, J. 1975. *Zeit und Ewigkeit im Alten Ägypten: Ein Beitrag zur Geschichte der Ewigkeit.* Abhandlungen der Heidelberger Akademie der Wissenschaften. Heidelberg.
Barguet, P. 1962. *Le temple d'Amon-Rê à Karnak.* Recherches d'archéologie, de philology et d'histoire 21. Cairo.
Beaux, N. 2012. *La chapelle d'Hathor—Temple d'Hatchepsout à Deir el-Bahari: I. Vestibule et sanctuaires.* Mémoires publiés par les membres de l'Institut français d'archéologie orientale du Caire 129. Cairo.
Bickel, S., and A. Loprieno, eds. 2003. *Basel Egyptology Prize 1: Junior Research in Egyptian History, Archaeology, and Philology.* Basel.
Budka, J. 2009. "The Ramesside Temple in the Asasif: Observations on Its Construction and Function, Based on the Results of the Austrian Excavations." In *Ägyptologische Tempeltagung: Structuring Religion*, edited by R. Preys, 7:17–45. Wiesbaden.
Cabrol, A. 2001. *Les voies processionnelles de Thèbes.* Orientalia Lovaniensia Analecta 97. Leuven.
David, R. 1981. *A Guide to Religious Ritual at Abydos.* Warminster.
Dolińska, M. 2010. "Temple of Thutmosis III at Deir el-Bahari after 30 Years of Research." In *Ägyptologische Tempeltagung: Interconnections between Temples*, edited by M. Dolińska and H. Beinlich, 8:57–66. Wiesbaden.
Dolińska, M., and H. Beinlich, eds. 2010. *Ägyptologische Tempeltagung: Interconnections between Temples*, Vol. 8. Königtum, Staat und Gesellschaft früher Hochkulturen 3, 3. Wiesbaden.
Dorman, P., and B. Bryan, eds. 2007. *Sacred Space and Sacred Function in Ancient Thebes.* Occasional Proceedings of the Theban Workshop. Studies of Ancient Oriental Civilizations 61. Chicago.
Flossmann-Schütze, M. C., et al., eds. 2013. *Kleine Götter—grosse Götter: Festschrift für Dieter Kessler zum 65. Geburtstag.* Tuna el-Gebel 4. Vaterstetten.
Gulyás, A. 2003. "Die Erneuerungstheologie der *HH m rnpwt*-Tempel." In *Basel Egyptology Prize 1: Junior Research in Egyptian History, Archaeology, and Philology*, edited by S. Bickel and A. Loprieno, 163–172. Basel.
Gulyás, A. 2007. "The Osirid Pillars and the Renewal of Ramesses III at Karnak." *Studien zur Altägyptischen Kultur* 36: 31–48, Hamburg.
Gundlach, R. 2001. "Temples." In *The Oxford Encyclopedia of Ancient Egypt*, edited by D. Redford, 3:363–379. Oxford.

Haeny, G. 1997. "New Kingdom 'Mortuary Temples' and 'Mansions of Millions of Years.'" In *Temples of Ancient Egypt*, edited by B. Shafer, 86–126. Ithaca, NY.

Haring, B. 1997. *Divine Households: Administrative and Economic Aspects of the New Kingdom Royal Memorial Temples in Western Thebes*. Egyptologische Uitgaven 12. Leiden.

Helck, W. 1960. *Materialien zur Wirtschaftsgeschichte des Neuen Reiches (Teil I–V)*. Abhandlungen der Mainzer Akademie der Wissenschaften. Wiesbaden.

Helck, W., and W. Westendorf, eds. 1986. *Lexikon der Ägyptologie*. Wiesbaden.

Hölscher, U. 1941. *The Mortuary Temple of Ramesses III*. Pt. I, *The Excavation of Medinet Habu III*. The University of Chicago Oriental Institute Publications 54. Chicago.

Iwaszczuk, J. 2009. "The Temple of Thutmosis I Rediscovered." *Polish Archaeology in the Mediterranean* 21, 269–277, Warsaw.

Jaritz, H. 2010. "The Temple of Millions of Years of Merenptah. The Recovery of an Almost Lost Site." In *Les temples de millions d'années et le pouvoir royal à Thèbes au Nouvel Empire*, edited by C. Leblanc and G. Zaki, 147–158. Cairo.

Karkowski, J. 2003. *The Temple of Hatshepsut: The Solar Complex*. Deir el-Bahari VI. Warsaw.

Karlshausen, C. 2009. *L'iconographie de la barque processionnelle divine en Égypte au Nouvel Empire. Orientalia Lovaniensia Analecta* 182. Leuven.

Leblanc, C. 1980. "Piliers et colosses de type 'osiriaque' dans le contexte des temples de culte royal." *Bulletin de l'institut français d'archéologie orientale* 80: 69–89, Le Caire.

Leblanc, C. 1982. "Le culte rendu aux colosses 'osiriaques' durant le Nouvel Empire." Bulletin de l'institut français d'archéologie orientale 82: 295–311, Le Caire.

Leblanc, C. 2010. "Les Châteaux de millions d'années: Une redéfinition à la lumière des récentes recherches; De la vocation religieuse à la fonction politique et économique." In *Les temples de millions d'années et le pouvoir royal à Thèbes au Nouvel Empire*, edited by C. Leblanc and G. Zaki, 19–57. Cairo.

Leblanc, C., and G. Zaki, eds. 2010. *Les temples de millions d'années et le pouvoir royal à Thèbes au Nouvel Empire*. Memnonia Cahier Suppl. 2. Cairo.

Nelson, H. H. 1942. "The Identity of Amon-Re of United-with-Eternity." *Journal of Near Eastern Studies* 1: 127–155, Chicago.

Petrie, W. M. F. 1897. *Six Temples at Thebes 1896*. London.

Polz, D. 1998. "The Ramsesnakht Dynasty and the Fall of the New Kingdom: A New Monument in Thebes." *Studien zur Altägyptischen Kultur* 25: 257–293, Hamburg.

Polz, D. 2007. *Der Beginn des Neuen Reiches: Zur Vorgeschichte einer Zeitenwende*. Sonderschrift des Deutschen Archäologischen Instituts, Abteilung Kairo 31. Berlin.

Preys, R., ed. 2009. *Ägyptologische Tempeltagung: Structuring Religion*, Vol. 7. Königtum, Staat und Gesellschaft früher Hochkulturen 3, 2. Wiesbaden.

Redford, D. 2001. *The Oxford Encyclopedia of Ancient Egypt*, Vol. 3. Oxford.

Rummel, U. 2010a. *Iunmutef: Konzeption und Wirkungsbereich eines altägyptischen Gottes*. Sonderschrift des Deutschen Archäologischen Instituts, Abteilung Kairo 33. Berlin.

Rummel, U. 2010b. "Generating 'Millions of Years': Iunmutef and the Ritual Aspect of Divine Kingship." In *Les temples de millions d'années et le pouvoir royal à Thèbes au Nouvel Empire*, edited by C. Leblanc and G. Zaki, 193–208. Cairo.

Schröder, S. 2010. *Millionenjahrhaus: Zur Konzeption des Raumes der Ewigkeit im konstellativen Königtum in Sprache, Architektur und Theologie*. Wiesbaden.

Sesana, A. 2010. "Le temple d'Amenhotep II à Thèbes-ouest: du passé au présent." In *Les temples de millions d'années et le pouvoir royal à Thèbes au Nouvel Empire*, edited by C. Leblanc and G. Zaki, 73–79. Cairo.

Shafer, B., ed. 1997. *Temples of Ancient Egypt*. Ithaca, NY.

Sourouzian, H. 2010. "The Temple of Millions of Years of Amenhotep III: Past, Present, and Future Perspectives." In *Les temples de millions d'années et le pouvoir royal à Thèbes au Nouvel Empire*, edited by C. Leblanc and G. Zaki, 91–98. Cairo.

Sourouzian, H. 2011. "Investigating the Mortuary Temple of Amenhotep III." *Egyptian Archaeology* 39: 29–32, London.

Stadelmann, R. 1973. "Tempelpalast und Erscheinungsfenster in den thebanischen Totentempeln." Mitteilungen des Deutschen Archäologischen Instituts, Abteilung Kairo 29: 221–242, Mainz.

Stadelmann, R. 1979. "Totentempel und Millionenjahrhaus in Theben." Mitteilungen des Deutschen Archäologischen Instituts, Abteilung Kairo 35: 303–321, Mainz.

Stadelmann, R. 1986. "Totentempel III." In *Lexikon der Ägyptologie*, edited by W. Helck and W. Westendorf, 6:706–711. Wiesbaden.

Ullmann, M. 2002. *König für die Ewigkeit—Die Häuser der Millionen von Jahren: Eine Untersuchung zu Königskult und Tempeltypologie in Ägypten*. Ägypten und Altes Testament 51. Wiesbaden.

Ullmann, M. 2007. "Origins of Thebes as a Ritual Landscape." In *Sacred Space and Sacred Function in Ancient Thebes*, edited by P. Dorman and B. Bryan, 3–25. Chicago.

Ullmann, M. 2013. "Von Theben nach Nubien—Überlegungen zum Kultkomplex Ramses' II. in Abu Simbel." In *Kleine Götter—grosse Götter: Festschrift für Dieter Kessler zum 65. Geburtstag*, edited by M. C. Flossmann-Schütze et al., 503–524: Vaterstetten.

Waitkus, W. 2008. *Untersuchungen zu Kult und Funktion des Luxortempels*. Aegyptiaca Hamburgensia 2. Hamburg.

Wilkinson, R. H., ed. 2011. *The Temple of Tausret: The University of Arizona Egyptian Expedition Tausret Temple Project, 2004–2011*. Tucson, AZ.

CHAPTER 29

POLICING AND SITE PROTECTION, GUARD POSTS, AND ENCLOSURE WALLS

CAROLA VOGEL

FROM the moment they were sealed, the treasure-filled tombs in the Valley of the Kings became an attractive target for robbery (see ch 30). It thus must have been a major task of the Theban authorities, spearheaded by the vizier, to guarantee the safety of the royal necropolis through an effective security system. As clear as this situation may seem, it is astonishing that our knowledge of the supposed site protection is rather limited. Numerous sources contribute to the subject, but their content is very restricted. This is mainly due to their sporadic coverage for the period under discussion. Whereas textual records referring to the situation in the early and mid-Eighteenth Dynasty occur irregularly, they are more frequent for the time between the end of the Eighteenth and the beginning of the Twentieth Dynasties. Moreover, our comprehension of the entire period in question is limited by the lack of archaeological evidence. The chronological inconsistency and uneven distribution of textual and archaeological data should be kept in mind when discussing the question of how the Valley of the Kings was secured. We also must distinguish between general, long-term protective measures and individual actions necessitated by specific situations.

TOPOGRAPHICAL CONSIDERATIONS

The valley chosen to serve as the royal necropolis offered perfect conditions in terms of site protection. To some extent already naturally sheltered by its hidden location within the Theban hills, access to it was only possible via a limited number of paths, which were dictated by the topography of the area (see ch 2) and are thus the ones still in use today. Guarding these routes, and especially their entries into the valley, is the method that

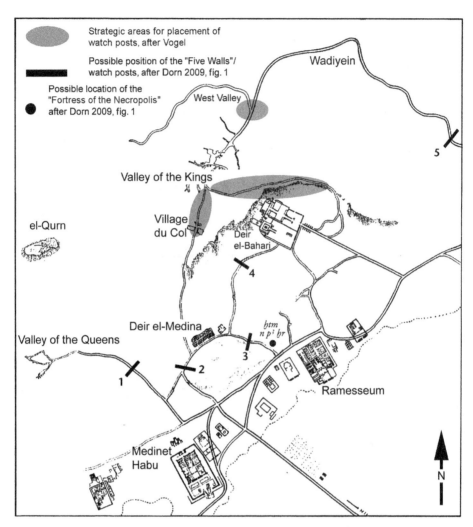

FIGURE 29.1 Western Thebes: possible positions of walls and watch posts.

[Based on Dorn 2009, fig. 1, with additions by Carola Vogel.]

would be expected to protectively fence off the interior of the valley. Hence one would imagine that a staggered security system of guards and defense installations existed, including a minimum of at least three permanent watch posts monitoring the trailheads of the three major tracks leading to the inner valley (see Figure 29.1). These roads are as follows:

> To the valley's north, the so-called Wadiyein road was the only route leading from the plains into the inner *wadi* (the modern entry). Ideally a post would have been established at the junction to the western *wadi* (where, in fact, a modern guard hut stands).

To the east, the (still popular) path via Deir el-Bahri was used for the funeral processions to the Valley of the Kings. Ideally, a post would have been located somewhere
midway on top of the cliffs and/or at the junction with the path coming from Deir
el-Medina, allowing traffic to be monitored in both directions;

To the south, the road approaching from Deir el-Medina also ran over the hills into
the valley. Any watch posts or other placements would be expected either at the
track's peak on the high ridges or at its very end before the path descended to the
inner valley.

Among these choices there is only archaeological proof to support guarding of the
last path. Situated at the northern end of the route running from the workmen's village at Deir el-Medina to the Valley of the Kings, we find the remains of a well-known
settlement, the so-called Village du Col (see Figure 29.2). Consisting of three groups
of stone-built huts named after their location (West, East, and North Group), its main
occupation phase is dated by diagnostic ceramics to the mid- and later part of the
Nineteenth Dynasty. Additional pottery, but in less significant numbers, indicates also
a mid-Eighteenth Dynasty and late New Kingdom phase (Toivari-Viitala 2012, 11–12).
The site was initially excavated in the 1930s by Bernard Bruyère (Bruyère 1939), who

FIGURE 29.2 Workmen's huts above the Valley of the Kings.

[Photograph by Carola Vogel.]

considered its function to be a "station de repos," a resting-place for workmen from the nearby Valley of the Kings who preferred to stay close to their workplace instead of walking the greater distance to their permanent homes in Deir el-Medina. Recent research by a team of the Theban Mountain Project of the Finnish Academy and the University of Helsinki, directed by Jaana Toivari-Viitala, might change this view in favor of a rather pragmatic explanation, that the settlement and its inhabitants guarded one of the most vulnerable entries to the Valley of the Kings, the intersection between the Deir el-Medina path and minor pass roads approaching from the west. The assemblages of huts lack any defenses, but the settlement might have been effective by its sheer existence and size.

POLICING AND SITE PROTECTION

By the early and mid-Eighteenth Dynasty, the safety of a royal tomb was established by its remote location in one or another of the side *wadis* that branched from the main valley and by the hiding of the tomb's entrance under rubble. A change in this custom, when later tombs were situated in the center of the valley with visible entrances, might be seen as an invitation to robbery. However, the changed tomb location might be seen as a double-edged sword: the entrances were very visible, but the same applied to possible intruders. Thus, guards must have played a prominent role in terms of both watching and protecting the tomb.

Who in particular were these men? Moreover, what do we know about their tasks and organization? These questions lead us to three groups of individuals who can be judged as the main forces involved in safeguarding tombs under construction and the entire necropolis.

The Personnel Involved

z3w/ty—Guards

Persons who worked as guards in Western Thebes are detectable by their title, *z3w/ty*. Similar to other titleholders from the policing sector (doorkeepers and Medjay; see below), they were assigned to different jurisdictions. During the time of the Nineteenth and Twentieth Dynasties we have knowledge of guards in the Place of Truth (*st nt M3ʿt*) or guards of the Lord of the Two Lands (in the Place of Truth), whereas guards of the necropolis (*p3 ẖr*) are only attested for the end of this period (Černý 2004, 149–160). Quite a few texts mention these guards without specifying their affiliation; thus if the context does not clarify this, we cannot be sure where exactly the men worked. Guards in service at the royal tomb under construction were organized in teams of two, each guard assigned to one side of the gang. Their main task was the supervision and replacement of the materials needed by the tomb workers, providing the objects to the workmen when required. For instance, we are aware of guards who replaced damaged and worn copper tools. This happened in the presence of the foremen and the scribe, who registered the event (Černý 2004, 159). As copper was a valuable material and served as currency, the guards and their superiors kept special watch on it. Thus, the complex Egyptian bureaucracy, which noted every detail of the assignment and replacement of such valuable materials, can be seen as one of the methods employed against possible thefts and corruption.

In addition to those guards working at the tomb, one would expect additional guards stationed at posts or checkpoints surrounding the Valley of the Kings in order to ensure that only authorized individuals entered the territory under their surveillance. This function was closely connected to those of the regular Medjay police, who might have been their superiors. A small hint of interaction may be derived from a Ramesside model letter, in which the Medjay Mininiuy reports about his tasks from the reign of Horemheb onward: "I served as Medjay of Western Thebes, guarding the watch posts [*inbw*] of his Great Place"(O. Toronto A. 11, recto 22; Gardiner 1913, 16h). Even if the precise meaning of the expression *inbw* remains uncertain (see discussion below), one might expect these installations to have been manned; otherwise the phrase "the *inbw* in the district are . . . safe and sound" (O. Toronto A. 11, recto 14; Gardiner 1913, 16g) would hardly make any sense.[1]

Besides their work at the tomb, guards took over various tasks, most related to their assumed personal integrity. So we know them, for example, as witnesses in private transactions and meetings of the *qnbt* (court). They also show up among other trustworthy groups of security-related personnel gathered together to conduct inspections in the Valley of the Queens, and at Deir el-Medina (Černý 2004, 160). Closely connected to the group of *iry-ꜥ3* doorkeepers, it seems that some of the *z3w/ty* guards started their careers as *iry-ꜥ3* (Černý 2004, 169).

Doorkeepers

The title doorkeeper (*iry-ꜥ3* [*n p3 ḫr*]/*iry-ꜥ3* [*n ḫtm n p3 ḫr*]) is frequently attested in the Deir el-Medina context (Černý 2004, 161–173; Goecke-Bauer 2003). The available data, so far limited to the Nineteenth and Twentieth Dynasties, shed light on the doorkeepers' duties and daily life, but offer only scant information, about a particular door they had to guard (Goecke-Bauer 2003, 64).

It has been assumed that doorkeepers worked at the tombs in the Valley of the Kings (Černý 2004, 170–171). However, none of the texts bearing evidence of doorkeepers offer proof that the door the official holders had to protect belonged to a royal tomb. Moreover, Goecke-Bauer showed that the translation of the title *iry-ꜥ3* as "doorkeeper" is misleading, as it points in the wrong direction. Persons holding this title are known to have fulfilled various tasks that a job outline would rather qualify as an Arabic "bawwab" (Goecke-Bauer 2003, 142). These men, literally the "gatekeepers," stand day and night in the corridors and lobbies of Cairo's apartment buildings and are doormen and building superintendents rolled into one.

In light of this, one should not characterize doorkeepers as proper guards standing or patroling at the door or gate to which they were assigned. Thus, this job must have been done by someone else; if not by the *z3w* "guards," then by individuals who do not appear in the textual record.

The question remains if and how the ancient doorkeepers fit into the overall site protection of Western Thebes. What were their tasks? First of all, it appears that two kinds of doorkeepers must be distinguished: the doorkeeper of the *p3 ḥr*, and the doorkeeper of the *ḥtm n p3 ḥr* (for the function and possible location of this latter building/institution, see the discussion below). It is known that both groups of titleholders delivered goods to the workmen and were sent to report to other institutions. Further tasks could be assigned to one or the other.

Doorkeepers of the *p3 ḥr* are known to have worked in teams of two, each connected with one side of the workmen's gang but not belonging to them. Some examples illustrate their multifaceted duties. A textual record names a doorkeeper accompanying a woman from Deir el-Medina to a meeting of the *qnbt* (court) outside of Deir el-Medina (O. Berlin P. 14214). From the reign of Ramesses III we learn about a doorkeeper sent by the vizier to deliver an order to the workmen (O. Berlin P. 10663). In P. BM 10053, dated to year 17 of Ramesses IX, the doorkeeper *Ḥnsw-msyw* appears among the persons responsible for bringing back the stolen and already resurfaced burial equipment (Goecke-Bauer 2003, 137).

With respect to the second group, we are aware of an unknown number of *iry-ꜥ3* stationed at the *ḥtm n p3 ḥr*, the original location of which is still a matter of debate (see below). From two lists of the Turin Strike Papyrus we learn that doorkeepers were members of the service personnel (*smdt*), and that one of their duties was to open the *ḥtm n p3 ḥr* (RAD 46, vso II.; see Goecke-Bauer 2003, 123), but this does not imply that they had to guard it themselves. Despite their responsible position, they were viewed and paid as low-ranking personnel.

The Role of the Medjay-Forces

Among the group of persons involved in policing the Valley of the Kings, the Medjay deserve special mention. During the Old Kingdom and early Middle Kingdom, the term "Medjay" was used by the Egyptians to denote Eastern Desert nomads originating from the First or Second Cataract. By the New Kingdom a shift to a secondary usage had taken place, characterizing Medjay as paramilitary troops, regardless of their ethnic identity (Liszka 2010, 2012). These units worked as highly trained police and desert scouts. How exhausting daily patrols could be for the Medjay has recently been demonstrated by the find of a unique stela from the Kurkur Oasis dating to the reign of Tutankhamun. Here, an anonymous Medjay-man, accused of the neglect of his duty, defends himself against the fortress commander, Penniut, by complaining about the inhumanly long distance of approximately 42 kilometers he has to track[2] along the "Western Wall [of the Pharaoh]": "How great are they, the four *itrw* which I make daily; five times going up [the gebel], and five times going down [the gebel], so do not let me be replaced by another" (translation from Darnell 2003, 76).

The set of tasks Medjay had to conduct in Western Thebes, including the Valley of the Kings, is well reflected in the textual record (see especially Černý 2004, 261–284) and has been convincingly reviewed only recently by Kate Liszka (2012, 370–375). Liszka showed that some of the men's duties were consistent with those of the Medjay elsewhere, while others depended on the uniqueness of the site. The major task of the Medjay was to guarantee the security of *p3 ḥr*, comprising the Valley of the Kings and institutions that supported the necropolis. Interestingly, although working in the surroundings of Deir el-Medina and the Valley of the Kings, the Medjay were not considered members of Deir el-Medina and subsequently were viewed as "those who were outside" in the official terminology of the royal necropolis. They were thought to live in the plain between the Temple of Seti I at Gurna and Medinet Habu (Liszka 2012, 372, incl. n.1578), whereas their headquarters at Deir el-Medina is considered to be at the *ḥtm* (see below).

From geographically qualifying phrases attached to some of the Medjay titles attested for the period of interest here (Eighteenth–Twentieth Dynasties), we are aware of their different areas of jurisdiction (Liszka 2012, 379–381):

> *ḥry Mḏ3yw ḥr Jmntt nlwt* Captain of the Medjay of the West of the City, *ḥry Mḏ3yw ḥr W3st* Captain of the Medjay in Thebes, *Mḏ3y n Jmntt W3st* (*z3w n3 n inbw ntJ=f st ⸢3t Pr-⸢3*) Medjay of the West of Thebes (who guards the walls/watch posts at the Great Place of Pharaoh), *Mḏ3y n Jmntt* Medjay of the West, *Mḏ3yw n Pr-nbyt* Medjay of Pernebyt (region North of Thebes?), *p3 Mḏ3y n t3 ḥwt* Medjay of the Mansion (Medinet Habu), *Mḏ3y n p3 ḥr* Medjay of the tomb, and *ḥry Mḏ3yw n p3 ḥr* Captain of the Medjay of the tomb.

Two examples might highlight the hierarchy among the Medjay. Under Thutmose IV, Nebamun—the owner of TT 90—holds the title of a *ḥry Mḏ3yw ḥr Jmntt nlwt*, "Captain of the Medjay of the West of the City"; thus he was at the least supervising the Medjay stationed on the West bank of Thebes. Liszka even considers the Greater Western Thebaid, perhaps up to Kharga Oasis (Liszka 2012, 379).

The promotion of a regular Medjay to a captain of the Medjay is attested in the previously mentioned model letter of the official Mininiuy, sent to his city prefect and vizier Khay in the reign of Ramesses II:

> The Captain of the Medjay Minimuy communicates to [his] lord, the city prefect and vizier Khay: In life, prosperity and health! This is a missive to inform my lord. A further communication [to] my lord to the effect that the Great Place (tomb) of Pharaoh, l.p.h., that is [under] my lord's authority is in excellent order, and the watch posts in its vicinity are safe and sound. . . . A further communication to my lord to the effect that I have been my lord's veteran servant since Year 7 of King Djeserkheperur[re] (Horemheb). I ran ahead of Pharaoh's horses, held the reins(?) for him, and yoked up for him. I made report to him, and he called upon my name in the presence of the Council of Thirty. Not any fault was found in me. I served as

Medjay of Western Thebes, guarding the watch posts of his Great Place. I was appointed Captain of the Medjay, being handsomely rewarded on account of the goodness of [my] conduct. Now look, the Captain of the Medjay Nakhtsobeki has been letting the Great Place of Pharaoh, l.p.h., in which I am (employed), go to ruin (?). I am informing my lord of his failings (?). He has been beating my Medjay in conducting investigations (?). "You are an old man, and I am young," so he says to me. "Put the place in order for me. You are a...," so he says to me. He appropriated my fields in the countryside. He appropriated two planted with vegetables, which belong to my lord as the vizier's share. He gave them to the Captain of the Medjay Monturekh and gave the rest to the high priest of Montu. He appropriated my grain while it was stowed in the countryside. This is a missive to inform my lord. The draftsman Sia[mon].

(Ostracon Toronto A.11, after Liszka 2012, 364)

As shown above, Medjay were in charge of distinct districts in the Theban area. They obviously supervised both Medjay in subordinate positions belonging to their jurisdiction and guard posts/defenses located in their district. The latter were subdivided into smaller areas guarded by ordinary Medjay. Moreover, the document sheds light on both the duties of Medjay in Western Thebes and the existence of watch posts in the Valley of the Kings. New evidence that might refer to an early workmen's strike from the reign of Merenptah (Pap. Berlin P. 23300a/b rt.; Fischer-Elfert 2012, esp. 51–55, 65) supports the close connection between the Medjay and the walls/watch posts. Of interest to our subject is an incomplete passage naming two well-known captains of the Medjay (Nakht-Sobeki, Ostracon Toronto A.11, Černý 2004, 267, no. 14; and Nakht-Min, Černý 2004, 267, no. 13) accompanied by an anonymous inferior who inspected "these walls/guard-posts" after mentioning a particular wall/guard post "inner [. . .] of the inner wall/guard post." The reason that the three men were sent to inspect the walls remains unclear, but the context speaks rather for an immediate reaction to a rumor about the state of the "walls" than for a regular control. Be that as it may, the qualifying term "inner" demands an "outer" feature and hence might hint at the supposed staggered defense system mentioned above. We are still missing supporting proof from the archaeological record. However, the textual record allows no other conclusion than to expect at least watch posts: small shelters from which the guards or policemen could observe their district and signal neighboring posts (compare the section below, "Guard Posts; Enclosure Walls—The Textual Record").

Besides the described tasks, additional policing responsibilities were secured for Medjay in Western Thebes: Medjay fended off intruders to the necropolis; they interrogated thieves; they inflicted punishments; they patrolled an area of unknown extent, which individuals "who were inside" were not allowed to leave without authorization; and they patrolled the surroundings of Deir el-Medina (Liszka 2012, 371–375). Moreover, they were even sent from somewhere else to support their colleagues in case of an emergency, as occurred, for example under Ramesses V (or VI) when Libyan (?) forces approached Thebes from the West:

Year 1, first month of winter, day 13. Inactive because of the enemy. Coming by the two Chiefs of the Medjay to say: "The people who are enemies have come and reached Pernebyt. . .". Now the high priest of Amen said to us, "Bring the Medjay of Per-nebyt together with those who are in the South and those of the Necropolis, and let them stand there guarding the Necropolis."

(P. Turin Cat. 2044, II, 8–12; translation after Liszka 2012, 375)

As anywhere else, the chief of the Medjay or even regular Medjay reported to the vizier. Regardless of the multitude of sources referring to Medjay in Western Thebes, we still lack evidence of their precise working conditions. Thus, for example, we still do not know if or to what extent the men served on horseback. However, given the fact that quite a few later chiefs of the Medjay started their careers connected with horses/chariotry (Liszka 2012, 343), we might consider the possibility of mounted patrols.

GUARD POSTS; (ENCLOSURE) WALLS—THE TEXTUAL RECORD

The absence of archaeological remains of features related to site protection can be somewhat compensated for investigating architectural terms and toponyms pointing to their existence. The problem with these expressions has rightly been assessed by Raphael Ventura: "Place names coined by the workmen. . . could hardly have held any meaning to outsiders" (1986, XIII). And that is precisely the problem we deal with: these terms were self-sufficient. The location and function to which they referred were familiar to the readers of the records and hardly needed any further explanation. Only a few records offer hints about the nature of these sites, and they are subsequently the ones thoroughly investigated by various scholars.

"Fortress/Administrative Outpost of the Necropolis": *p3 ḫtm (n p3 ḫr)*

An essential expression referring to a building that may have acted as a gateway or control point for Deir el-Medina and the royal necropolis is attested by the term *p3 ḫtm (n p3 ḫr)*, "Fortress/administrative outpost (of the necropolis)." Besides the geographical qualifier *n p3 ḫr* (of the necropolis), two others, namely *n dmj*, "of the village" (i.e., Deir el-Medina) or *n t3 mryt* (of the riverbank), are known. Some records simply quote a *p3 ḫtm*, and hence could refer to either place (cf. Burkard 2006, 32). McDowell favored the idea that one has to distinguish between two institutions: one close to Deir el-Medina, where the distribution of goods for the inhabitants of the village took place, and another at the riverside area, thought to have been used for the turnover of shipments (McDowell 1990, 169ff.). However, at this point the textual evidence at our disposal does not allow a final answer. Of utmost interest for our discussion is the function and location of the *p3 ḥtm n p3 ḥr*. Whereas Eyre emphasizes "that the primary role of the *ḥtm* was that of a receiving point, and neither that of an administrative office nor a guard post" (2009, 116), this need not be the case. The definition Ellen Morris established with respect to *ḥtm*-fortresses along Egypt's frontiers—might be favorable for the Theban *ḥtm* as well: "The *ḥtm*-fortress should be regarded as a military base that functioned as a seal or a gateway, allowing access to a restricted area to be carefully monitored, and, if need be, prevented. The term is most frequently utilized with respect to border-fortresses" (Morris 2005, 809). As this institution served as the head office for various groups with administrative and policing background, possessed granaries of interest to those from inside and outside, and even served as a holding place for offenders (Eyre 2009, 107, n.5), we should not underestimate its possible paramilitary function and fortified appearance.

Crucial hints referring to the whereabouts of this institution may be derived from P. Turin Cat. 1923, rto (KRI VI, 367f.). Here we learn that in order to determine the level of groundwater for deepening a well, a master builder used the distance to the *p3 ḥtm n p3 ḥr* as a cross-reference for his measurement. Even if we agree with most scholars that the well in question could have been the famous Grand-Puits next to Deir el-Medina, the exact location of the *p3 ḥtm n p3 ḥr* is still difficult to conclude from this record. This has been shown by the different interpretations of scholars using the same data. Hence the possible location of the *ḥtm* still ranges, according to various authors, from a "site within a radius of 300 m from the southwestern corner of the encompassing wall of the Ramesseum" (Ventura 1987), on top of a slightly higher spot in the plain close to the Ramesseum (Burkard 2003a, 131, fig. 2; 2006, 41, 42, fig. 2), and an assumed similar position by Dorn (Dorn 2009, fig. 1; see Figure 29.1). Finally, a location closer to Deir el-Medina was favored by Koh (2005–2006),[3] who even traced some archaeological structures as its possible remains, and a rather rough location between the Great Well and the Ramesseum was considered by Liszka (2012, 373) (see Figure 29.3).

The (Five) Walls/Guard Posts: *t3 5/inbt/n3 inbwt/t3 inb*

The term *t3 5/inbt*[4] occurs frequently in the Ramesside textual record and is usually translated as "Five Walls" or "Five Guard Posts," thought of as a borderline of unknown appearance between an inner and an outer space, which the people from Deir el-Medina periodically passed. As the "Five Walls" are described as being crossed by the workmen's crew on their way to the back of the temple of the pharaoh (Medinet Habu?) in P. Turin 1880, line above vso. Col ii-vi (Dorn 2009, 263), they were initially thought of as a sequence of five walls situated within a short distance of a few hundred meters in the upper *wadi* leading south from Deir el-Medina to the plain (e.g., Ventura 1986, fig. 1).

FIGURE 29.3 View from the west across the northern part of Deir el-Medina into the plain: the area in which the *ḫtm n p3 ḥr* "Fortress of the Necropolis" might have been located.

[Photograph by Carola Vogel.]

Paul John Frandsen disagreed with this idea, understanding them as being lined up next to each other, and proposed a more strategic location. Calling O.IFAO 1255 to attention, he imagined one "guard post" close to the causeway of Mentuhotep III and hence favored the idea that the five guard posts were situated at different spots, each of them monitoring the traffic in overlapping areas controlled by the adjacent guard posts (Frandsen 1989, 121). In light of this and further new evidence, Andreas Dorn restudied the entire material and introduced a new idea of their possible location at five strategic spots (Dorn 2009, esp. fig. 1; see Figure 29.1). Despite different approaches regarding where these "walls" were located, most scholars see the "Five Walls" and other expressions referring to these "walls" not as proper manned guard posts, but rather as attestations for some kind of "virtual" borderlines that separated the inner and outer world, and which marked the radius in which the people from Deir el-Medina were allowed to move. However, as the workmen's passing of the "(Five) Walls" is obviously judged as an illegal event or at least so unusual as to be worth mentioning, one still wonders how the access control might have been performed without appropriate posts manned by personnel from the security sector. Taking the iconographic evidence from the tomb of the captain of the Medjay, Mahu, in Amarna into account, where a watch tower is represented that surely refers to Mahu's professional background, one might expect similar posts for Western Thebes as well (cf. Liszka 2012, fig. 37; Vogel 2010, 20, 39). As the above-mentioned Ostracon Toronto A.11 and the episode on the Kurkur stela clearly showed, there were "walls/guard posts" under the surveillance of the Medjay that reported their status to the vizier. Thus, here again absence of evidence is not evidence of absence.

WHEN SECURITY FAILED—INSPECTIONS

Unfortunately, we know much more about the protection of tombs in progress (see "Excursus," below) than about the already sealed ones. The textual records provide us with particular information about "what went wrong" and "how it should have been," primarily when security failed. This is especially true when it comes to inspections that are attested under various kings. Two graffiti in KV 43 dating to year 8 of Horemheb tell us about the reburial of the owner of the tomb, Thutmosis IV (Urk. IV 2170-2171; Theban Mapping Project 15558, 15559). Whereas this and a further record from KV 62 dated shortly thereafter name no reasons that made these measures necessary, later records refer to inspections made in order to assess the extent of thefts brought to the attention of the authorities. The famous tomb robbery papyri, discussed by Ogden Goelet in chapter 30, reveal the weak points of safety measures in the troubled times of the Twentieth Dynasty. Moreover, recent studies favor the idea that reburials, ostensibly announced to prevent possible thefts and declared as piously motivated acts, could rather be explained as a welcome chance to steal valuables such as amulets from the mummies before rewrapping the bodies.

EXCURSUS: WORKMEN'S HUTS IN THE VALLEY—INCORPORATED IN SITE PROTECTION?

Besides the famous "Village du Col" a second group of architectural features should be taken into account when considering methods of policing the valley, even if their main function was different. Until recently, our knowledge of these features, namely the workmen's huts within the valley proper, relied on the known huts from the building phase of the tomb of Ramesses VI, whose clearance led to the discovery of the tomb of Tutankhamun. However, recent excavations conducted by the University of Basel MISR: Mission Siptah-Ramses X: Arbeiterhütten project revealed further evidence of various roomed entities connected to the building period of Ramesside tombs. Foremost is the huge settlement dated to the time of Ramesses IV, stretching along the *wadi* east of the later tomb of Ramesses X, which was in use by workmen over a time span of five to seven years. It seems clear that this place of habitation offered some protection for the tomb in progress—as is indicated by the workmen's presence there during the day and the night (which was of less importance as long as the funeral equipment was not in place)—and most likely for the already sealed tombs in the neighborhood (see chapter 7).

ACKNOWLEDGMENTS

I would like to express my sincere thanks to Katja Lehmann, of Phoenix, Arizona, for proofreading an earlier draft of this text.

NOTES

1. A famous example of a guard on duty is attested for the fortification of the "Walls of the Ruler" in the story of the flight of Sinuhe (R 44/45). Here, in order to avoid his discovery by the observing watchman (here: *wršy*), Sinuhe hides away behind bushes. For a discussion of the phrase in question and its existing versions, see Agam (1982).
2. Meaning of *t3tꜥ* uncertain (Darnell 2003, 80, favors "to guide").
3. Rejected by Dorn, who considers it more likely to be recent heap (Dorn 2009, 266, n.18).
4. For an attempt to answer the difficult question of how to distinguish between the different male and female expressions of *inb/t* and their possible meaning and appearances, see Monnier (2012).

BIBLIOGRAPHY

Agam, J. 1982. "Zur Wache an der 'Fürstenmauer'—Sinuhe B 19." *Göttinger Miszellen* 54: 7–10.

Bruyère, B. 1939. Rapport sur les fouilles de Deir el Médineh (1934–1935). Troisième partie, *Le village, les décharges publiques, la station de repos du col de la Vallée des Rois*, 348, 354–364, pl. XXXV. *Fouilles de l'Iinstitut français d'archéologie orientale du Caire* XVI. Cairo.

Burkard, G. 2003a. " . . . 'Die im Dunkeln sieht man nicht": Waren die Arbeiter im Tal der Könige privilegierte Gefangene?" In *Grab und Totenkult im alten Ägypten*, edited by Guksch et al., 128–146. Munich.

Burkard, G. 2003b. "'Oh, diese Mauern Pharaos!' Zur Bewegungsfreiheit der Einwohner von Deir el Medine." *Mitteilungen des Deutschen Archäologischen Instituts, Abteilung Kairo* 59: 11–39.

Burkard, G. 2006. "Das ḫtm n p3 ḫr von Deir el-Medine: Seine Funktion und die Frage der Lokalisierung." In *Living and Writing in Deir el-Medine: Socio-Historical Embodiment of Deir el-Medine Texts*, edited by A. Dorn and T. Hoffmann, 31–42. Basel.

Černý, J. 2004. *A Community of Workmen at Thebes in the Ramesside Period*. Bibliotheque de'Étude 50. Cairo.

Darnell, J. C. 2003. "A Stela of the Reign of Tutankhamun from the Region of Kurkur Oasis." *Studien zur altägyptischen Kultur* 31: 73–91.

Dorn, A. 2009. "Die Lokalisation der ,5 Mauern'/Wachposten (t3 5 inb.t/n3' inb.wt/t3 inb)." *The Journal of Egyptian Archaeology* 95: 263–268.

Dorn, A., and T. Hoffmann, eds. 2006. *Living and Writing in Deir el-Medine: Socio-Historical Embodiment of Deir el-Medine Texts*. Aegyptiaca Helvetica 19. Basel.

Eyre, C. 2009. "Again the *Ḥtm* of the Tomb: Public Space and Social Access." In *Texte, Theben, Tonfragmente—Festschrift Günter Burkard*, edited by D. Kessler et al., 107–117. Munich.

Fischer-Elfert, H.-W. 2012. "A Strike in the Reign of Merenptah? Plus the Endowment of Three Cult Statu(ett)es on Behalf of the Same Ling at Deir el-Medina (Pap. Berlin P. 23300 and P. 23301)." In *Forschung in der Papyrussammlung: Eine Festgabe für das Neue Museum*, edited by V. M. Lepper, 47–74. Berlin.

Frandsen, P. J. 1989. "A Word for 'Causeway' and the Location of 'The Five Walls'." *Journal of Egyptian Archaeology* 75: 113–124.

Gardiner, A. H. 1913. *Theban Ostraca I: Hieratic Texts*. Toronto.

Goecke-Bauer, M. 2003. "Untersuchungen zu den 'Torwächtern' von Deir el Medine." In *Woodcutters, Potters and Doorkeepers—Service Personnel of the Deir el-Medina Workmen*, edited by J. Janssen et al., 63–153. Leiden.

Guksch, H., E. Hofmann, and M. Bommas, eds. 2003. *Grab und Totenkult im alten Ägypten*. Munich.

Hawass, Z. A., and J. R. Houser Wegner, eds. 2010. *Millions of Jubilees: Studies in Honor of David P. Silverman, Vol. 1*. Annales du Service des Antiquités de l'Egypte, Supplement 39. Cairo.

Janssen, J., E. Frood., and M. Goecke-Bauer, eds. 2003. *Woodcutters, Potters and Doorkeepers—Service Personnel of the Deir el-Medina Workmen*. Egyptologische Uitgaven 17. Leiden.

Kessler, D. et al., eds. 2009. *Texte, Theben, Tonfragmente—Festschrift Günter Burkard*. Ägypten und Altes Testament 76. Munich.

Kitchen, K. A. 1983. *Ramesside Inscriptions*. Vol. VI, *Ramesses IV to XI and Contemporaries*. Monumenta Hannah Sheen dedicata 3 (KRI VI). Oxford.

Koh, A. J. 2005–2006. "Locating the *ḥtm n p3 ḫr* of the Workmen's Village at Deir el-Medina." *Journal of the American Research Center in Egypt* 42: 95–101.

Lepper, V. M., ed. 2012. *Forschung in der Papyrussammlung: Eine Festgabe für das Neue Museum*. Ägyptische und Orientalische Papyri und Handschriften des Ägyptischen Museums und Papyrussammlung Berlin, 1. Berlin.

Lesko, L. H., ed. 1994. *Pharaoh's Workers: The Villagers of Deir el Medina*. London and Ithaca, NY.

Liszka, K. 2010. " 'Medjay' (no. 188) in the Onomasticon of Amenemope." In *Millions of Jubilees: Studies in Honor of David P. Silverman*, edited by Z. A. Hawass and J. R. Houser Wegner, 315–331. Cairo.

Liszka, K. 2012. "'We Have Come to Serve Pharaoh': A Study of the Medjay and Pangrave Culture as an Ethnic Group and as Mercenaries from c. 2300 BCE until c. 1050 BCE." PhD diss., University of Pennsylvania.

McDowell, A. G. 1990. *Jurisdiction in the Workmen's Community of Deir el-Medina*. Egyptologische Uitgaven 5. Leiden.

McDowell, A. G. 1994. "Contact with the Outside World." In *Pharaoh's Workers: The Villagers of Deir el Medina*, edited by L. H. Lesko, 41–59. London and Ithaca, NY.

Monnier, F. 2012. "Quelques reflexions sur le terme 'jnb'." *Égypte nilotique et méditerranéenne* 5: 257–283.

Morris, E. F. 2005. *The Architecture of Imperialism: Military Bases and the Evolution of Foreign Policy in Egypt's New Kingdom*. Probleme der Ägyptologie 22. Leiden, Boston.

Toivari-Viitala, J., et al. 2012. "Academy of Finland and University of Helsinki: Workmen's Huts in the Theban Mountains Project." Preliminary report of the work performed during the fourth season in 2011–2012. (http://www.egyptologinenseura.fi/fieldwork/Preliminary%20 report_WHTM%20Project_fourth%20field%20season%202011-2012.pdf (accessed March 31, 2013).

Ventura, R. 1986. *Living in a City of the Dead: A Selection of Topographical and Administrative Terms in the Documents of the Theban Necropolis.* Orbis biblicus et orientalis 69. Freiburg (CH)/Göttingen.

Ventura, R. 1987. "On the Location of the Administrative Outpost of the Community of Workmen in Western Thebes." *Journal of Egyptian Archaeology* 73: 149–160.

Vogel, C. 2010. *The Fortifications of Ancient Egypt 3000–1780 BC.* Fortress 98. Oxford.

CHAPTER 30

TOMB ROBBERIES IN THE VALLEY OF THE KINGS

OGDEN GOELET

INTRODUCTION

GRAVE robbery in ancient Egypt must have existed from the moment when the Egyptian began to bury their dead with the simplest of grave goods (Phillips 1992). The history of tomb robbery is a fascinating but elusive subject—more so when royal burials were involved. Two studies in particular have provided useful information on robberies in the Valley of the Kings. The first is T. E. Peet, *The Great Tomb Robberies of the Twentieth Dynasty* (1930), the seminal study of the most important documents from this period, which, despite its title, reveals almost nothing directly about what happened to the great royal tombs in the valley, but reveals much about the environment in which the thefts occurred. As far as the valley itself was concerned, the evidence we have for robberies there is largely indirect and circumstantial. One must rely chiefly on careful observation of the archaeological evidence, which is only rarely supplemented by textual sources. This is admirably accomplished by the second, indispensable major source on royal tomb robberies, C. N. Reeves, *Valley of the Kings; The decline of a royal necropolis* (Reeves 1990b; important critique by Eaton-Krauss 1992).

SETTING THE SCENE

In order to grasp how difficult it must have been to plunder the royal tombs, we might first imagine ourselves on a tour bus today as it ascends to the Valley of the Kings. Granted, the route the bus takes today is not the same as the ancient route into the royal *wadi*, but after a modern visitor has been to the great memorial temples—the "temples of millions of years"—on the low desert of the west bank, one is immediately struck by the upward movement of the bus and the circuitousness of the route. Disembarking from the bus, one can immediately understand how inaccessible and isolated a location the valley must have been in ancient times, even for those who had legitimate business there. Even if the routes the ancient visitors took—officials, workmen, and thieves alike—were different, their trip was an arduous one. However great the perils of the physical journey may have been for ancient thieves, they had to cross even greater psychological barriers—the knowledge that they were committing a veritable sacrilege against the deceased, godlike monarchs, crimes that if they were caught might lead to a gruesome execution by impalement in this life and outright damnation in the next (Peet 1930, 27; Lorton 1977, 26–27, 33–40).

Ideally, an Egyptian burial was expected to be a permanent affair, as we can see in the frequent references to eternity in tombs. In the case of a royal burial, the expected inviolability was even greater, as shown by the absence of the "appeal to the living" in these tombs. There were to be no visitors or intrusions. One of the implicit purposes of the royal memorial temples was to provide an extra measure of safety for the royal burials in the valley by separating the tombs from the place where the royal cult was maintained. These increased security measures reflected realistic expectations of what might happen with the passage of time. The oft-repeated popular notion that special traps against violators were placed in tombs is fallacious (Abitz 1974).

General Description of the Robberies

There were four, widely spaced groups of robberies, by which we mean deliberate, illicit intrusions into the royal tombs and theft of their furnishings (Reeves 1990b, 274; Reeves and Wilkinson 1996, 191). However, in many instances thefts seem to have been followed by a variety of officially sanctioned intrusions in response, which could have consisted of simply reordering the disarray caused by the robberies or else more extensive repairs and clearances. The first group of robberies may have taken place between the reigns of Amenhotep III and Horemheb. The second group probably occurred during the last reigns of the Nineteenth Dynasty and was followed by another cluster of thefts, the third group, during the last third of Ramesses III's reign. In the final period, when the most significant intrusions took place, not every encroachment was illicit. This final phase lasted for roughly a century, beginning somewhere around the reign of Ramesses V and continuing into the Third Intermediate Period during the first "reigns" of the High Priests of Amun, who by then had become the virtually independent rulers of Upper Egypt. In particular, this discussion pays special attention to the well-documented robberies during the reigns of Ramesses IX and Ramesses XI. Although the latter events have rightfully earned the name "the Great Tomb Robberies," it is important also to consider the various types of despoliation and violation of royal tombs and other sacred property more broadly. Furthermore, the tomb robberies occurred in a broader context of civil disorders that plagued the Theban region during the transition between the Twentieth Dynasty and the Third Intermediate Period.

WHEN ROBBERIES OCCURRED

As far as the Valley of the Kings itself is concerned, we have only small scraps of specific textual information about the tomb robberies there. The official dismantling of the royal tombs and the subsequent reburial of the royal mummies that began at the end of the Twentieth Dynasty have done much to obscure the situation (Reeves 1990b, 183–282; Reeves and Wilkinson 1996, 190–207; Graefe 1999, 2003). One might say, then, that virtually all the valley tombs were in some manner "robbed," but dating any of the intrusions—illicit, official, or accidental—is often a difficult proposition, except in the rare instances when an official commission left a record of restoration work or a robbery was recorded in a papyrus (Reeves 1990b, 271). A few unintended intrusions occurred when tunneling for a new monument accidentally collided with an older tomb, as happened in the case of KV 11. What direct evidence remains comes from two general types of sources, with some minor overlaps. The first group of sources consists of archaeological evidence, primarily in the form of traces of breakage caused by the robbers and inscriptions left by those repairing such damage. Most of the second group is the official papyri recording the examination of people who had been involved in various robberies and their aftermath. The great majority of the documentary evidence is concerned with thefts from royal tombs *outside* the valley, as well as from the great temples on both the west and east banks of the river. These papyri present a rather depressing picture of a decaying regime incapable of providing safety for the living, the dead, or even the gods throughout the Theban nome and indirectly describe the lawless environment that rendered further use of the valley untenable.

Judging primarily from traces of what might be delicately termed "postinterment activity" in four tombs dating from the reign of Thutmose IV to the immediate aftermath of the Amarna period—KV 43 (Thutmose IV), KV 46 (Yuya and Thuya), WV 22 (Amenhotep III), Maiherpre (KV 36), and KV 62 (Tutankhamun)—they were robbed. A precise date for any of these intrusions would be speculative, but it seems most likely that several robberies in the valley occurred in the unsettled years at the end of the Eighteenth Dynasty. For the tombs of the monarchs of the Nineteenth and Twentieth Dynasties, dating thefts and other intrusions is yet more difficult, but with the last outbreak of pillage, the evidence points strongly to similarly unsettled conditions.

TUTANKHAMUN'S TOMB AS AN EXAMPLE
OF THEFT AND RESTORATION

By the time the first systematic, scientific examinations in the Valley of the Kings began in the nineteenth century of our era (for good overviews, see Romer 1981; Reeves and Wilkinson 1996, 48–85), most of the royal tombs had long since been extensively cleared of almost all the grave goods and other furnishings they had originally contained. To be sure, the burial chambers of some tombs still possessed the large, immovable (and empty) stone sarcophagi that had once held additional coffins and the royal mummy itself. Several of the royal mummies were discovered in three caches in the tomb of Amenhotep II (KV 35), but nearly all of the wealthy trappings that had accompanied those pharaohs at the time of their death had been removed before their reburial. Many of the other royal mummies had been secreted in a nearly inaccessible tomb high in a cliff at Deir el-Bahri, significantly a fair distance from the valley. Otherwise little royal funerary equipment was found except for occasional shabtis, vases, and other pieces of minor arts, some wooden statuary, plus a few fragments of chariots. In order to get a clearer picture of the funerary repertoire of a royal tomb, we should supplement these sparse survivals with what is depicted in the wall paintings of the so-called treasury in the tomb of Seti II (KV 15; Hornung 1982, 180–181), probably a pictorial inventory of the elaborate repertoire of golden statuary that had been once been deposited there (cf. Abitz 1979). Additional comparisons might be found in the paintings in the tomb of the mid-Eighteenth Dynasty vizier Ramose, depicting a procession of men bringing boxes containing the tomb owner's funerary equipment, befitting a member of the highest level of the elite (TT 55; Davies 1941, pls. XXV–XXVII). Except for such rare and sparse bits of data, the discovery of the largely intact tomb of Tutankhamun has been the most informative source for what a New Kingdom royal burial and its equipment might have contained.

Ironically, Tutankhamun's tomb (KV 62; for a good overview, see Reeves 1990a; for some differences of opinion, see Krauss 1986) also offers us unparalleled insights into royal tomb robbery and its mechanics. First of all, it is likely that, before the large-scale plundering of kings' tombs at the end of the Twentieth Dynasty, most previous robberies followed roughly the same pattern as the thefts in KV 62. The outbreaks of robbery in the Eighteenth Dynasty and some of the thefts of the Nineteenth Dynasty appear to have been small-scale affairs and opportunistic in nature; that is to say, the thieves may have been working in the valley at the time of the funeral or else been members attached to the burial team. A commonality that all thefts, great and small, shared was that they undoubtedly occurred when security in the Valley of the Kings had slackened considerably or was temporarily absent. As mentioned previously, it is easy to imagine that particularly good opportunities arose during periods of political confusion or dynastic changeover, such as the end of the Amarna period and its immediate aftermath. At the end of the Nineteenth and Twentieth Dynasties similar conditions occurred when the country was probably suffering from some degree of political instability and/or dynastic crisis.

Description of the Thefts in the Tomb of Tutankhamun

As Howard Carter's team was clearing out the descending staircase corridor to the tomb's blocked entrance doorway in 1923, small finds in the rubble fill already signaled that the burial might not be intact (Reeves 1990b, 80, n. 10). The most clear-cut evidence was the obvious signs that the blockage had been previously penetrated at the top left, then subsequently closed again, with the official seals of the royal necropolis administration impressed into the plastering (Reeves 1990b, 61–63). As the excavation progressed and similar resealed blockages were encountered, it became apparent that there had been two separate intrusions (and restorations). The length of the interval between the events is unknown. Since the disturbances at the site caused by the first break-in and the official response would have made the tomb's location more visible, it is likely that the interval between the thefts was not long (Reeves 1990b, 68–69). In any case, that there were two successive burglaries speaks volumes about the insufficient security measures at the end of the Eighteenth Dynasty, the most probable time of these robberies.

In comparison with the crudely destructive methods of the robberies of the Seventeenth Dynasty royal tombs that the much later Amherst-Leopold papyrus describes (Capart, Gardiner, and van der Walle 1936; Kitchen 2012, 361–378), the treatment of Tutankhamun's burial was almost benign. Even though there were still a vast number of objects left in the tomb, the looting had nevertheless been significant. Using what might be called negative evidence—that is, inferring what was likely to be included among a king's funerary furnishings and then noting what appears to be missing—we can arrive at a well-informed guess at what tomb robbers desired the most. In a similar fashion we can also infer how the tomb administration responded to the disorder the thieves had caused.

We should resist the temptation to look at the contents of Tutankhamun's tomb through the eyes of a modern museum curator or art collector. The immediate concerns of any thief would have been how to carry out the stolen goods and later dispose of them. When one considers the narrow dimensions of the tunnels and the holes through which the thieves maneuvered (Reeves 1990b, 61–69; contra Krauss 1986), size and portability undoubtedly would have had to be an important factor in choosing what to take. It is not surprising, then, that metal objects and jewelry were prime targets for theft and relatively uncommon in the tomb (compare their presence in an ancient inventory of a small private tomb; Zonhoven 1978). A bundle of cloth thrown carelessly back in the tomb was found to contain several gold rings that had either been dropped by or taken from the thieves (Reeves 1990a, 96–97). Such things as cloth, small metal vases, earrings, and bracelets can be disguised by reusing, dismantling, melting, and otherwise recycling; furthermore, they tend to be portable. Oils, unguents, and perfumes, provided that they were still reasonably fresh and stable, would be both valuable and untraceable; their absence, in fact, suggests that one of the violations of Tutankhamun's tomb occurred not long after the burial (Reeves 1990a, 95–97). Small jars containing these cosmetics were removed or emptied, but the elaborate wooden chests and boxes that held them had been left behind. After all, just the high quality of many other items in the tomb would have made them glaringly out of place in most elite households, let alone that of a thief from Egypt's vast lower class. Another practical concern was that a high percentage of things in the tomb bore the king's cartouche, the royal brand name, so to speak, rendering those objects unusable unless they were dismantled and destroyed.

Even something as seemingly innocuous as a royal shabti could be potentially fatal to an unfortunate person found possessing one. After goods had been stolen, we can only speculate about the difficulties an ancient Egyptian thief might have faced when disposing of his loot, especially if it was highly valuable. We know virtually nothing about that essential element of a criminal enterprise: the "fence," the conveyor of stolen goods.

Questions of Security and Police

Underlying the discussions of all the robberies thus far is the unspoken assumption that the security in the royal *wadi* would have been very tight. In actuality, we know little of the details of the valley's protection beyond the certainty that much was owed to its isolation. We can imagine that on a quiet night or day it would have been difficult to move silently over a rough surface littered with pebbles and loose stone chips. The sides of the *wadi* were barren and steep, offering little concealment. Most important, it was a place to which only tomb workers and a select number of necropolis officials had legitimate access. The number of people assigned to guard the valley, their identities, and where they were stationed are discussed in chapter 29 of this volume.

Tutankhamun's Tomb as an Example of Post-Robbery Restorations

Just as Tutankhamun's tomb shines invaluable light on the methods of royal tomb robbery, its largely intact state, combined with some contemporary inscriptional evidence, allows us to reconstruct the steps that the royal tomb administration might have taken in the aftermath of such a theft. The general description that follows is largely based on archaeological evidence and does not apply in all details to other robberies in the royal *wadi*, particularly those of the Twentieth Dynasty.

The first step in the restoration process, of course, would be noticing that there had been a robbery. In most instances, discovery of an intrusion might come about through regular inspections by officials of the necropolis administration (Thomas 1966, 255); these officials most likely had a good idea of the location of tombs, sometimes through location markers, so they could spot disturbed areas. In other cases, there may have been rumors of thefts, or stolen material may have been recovered, leading back to the source. Further information might be gleaned through interrogation of the suspected thieves, who would presumably suffer capital punishment in most cases.

The next step would be an inspection inside the violated tomb, followed by restorative and preventative measures. To a certain extent, a restoration was a tomb robbery in reverse. The tomb robbery papyri of the Twentieth Dynasty unfortunately do not describe initial inspections in much detail, but when entrance into the monument was not too arduous, it appears that occasionally a commission of officials would visually assess the state of the tomb and its contents, as described in Papyrus Abbott-Leopold, recto (Kitchen 2012, 361–367). However, at least in the case of those charged with the second repair and restoration of Tutankhamun's tomb, the task of a more thorough inspection inside the tomb was probably delegated to a lower level of authority, because the robbers' holes do not seem to have been much enlarged, perhaps in the name of speed and efficiency. Consequently, the men performing the second restorations probably worked under conditions only slightly better than those of the thieves before them—hardly something expected of a high-ranking official.

One can only imagine the state of disarray a team of restorers would encounter in the wreckage of a plundered burial. If the damage was not extensive, a select number of minor items would be repaired. A relative degree of order and neatness would be restored, although there are many places in Tutankhamun's tomb where things appear to have been merely repacked and stacked in careless haste. Some of the items that the thieves had strewn about hurriedly would be returned to the chests from which they had been taken. After packing, the restorers put lids back on chests and occasionally some affixed official seals (for a secondary inspection).

Finally, a violated tomb needed to be made secure once again. Broken doorways and their blockages were partially rebuilt, then plastered over. As a final measure, after the front doorway had been blocked again, the authorities attested to the tomb's integrity by impressing the official seal of the necropolis administration—normally an oval depicting nine bound prisoners surmounted by the Anubis jackal (Reeves 1990b, 61–69; Reeves 1990a, 92–94)—into the plaster layer over the doorway. The entrance passageway staircase was once more filled with rubble. This may not seem like much of a deterrent, but it was necessary to ensure that significantly more time, effort, and noise would be required for any subsequent break-in. Tutankhamun's tomb inadvertently received an additional measure of security later in the Twentieth Dynasty, when a large amount of construction debris from the nearby tomb of Ramesses V/VI (KV 9) was piled up in front of the doorway, so that all traces of Tutankhamun's tomb were obliterated—luckily, since this allowed it to escape the robberies and official stripping that so many other royal sepulchers suffered at the end of the Twentieth Dynasty, and thus it slipped into oblivion until its rediscovery by Carter.

THE POST-AMARNA ROBBERIES

Direct and indirect evidence points to a cluster of robberies that can be dated with varying certainty to the end of the Eighteenth Dynasty. The violated tombs in question were those of Amenhotep III (WV 22), the joint tomb of his in-laws Yuya and Thuya (KV 46); his father Thutmose IV (KV 43), and the enigmatic burials in KV 55. Much of what we have learned in our examination of the robbery and official restoration of Tutankhamun's tomb can be applied generally to what happened in these instances, so we need not examine these robberies in the same amount of detail. Neither the scope of the thefts nor the countermeasures of the authorities departed significantly from the pattern seen in the violation of Tutankhamun's tomb. For the most part, these four Eighteenth Dynasty tombs appear not to have been extensively robbed. More important, they escaped the thorough official clearances that occurred at the end of the Twentieth Dynasty. Thus, as in the case of Tutankhamun's tomb, they remained forgotten until their rediscovery in the early twentieth century.

In each case, the violations share the appearance of the limited and opportunistic thefts in Tutankamun's tomb. Starting from the premise that only a few people had detailed information about the royal *wadi*, particularly the location of the royal tombs, the main suspicion must fall on the necropolis workmen as the culprits or accomplices in this instance. After all, not only had these men worked in close proximity to some of the violated tombs, but they were also among the few who had legitimate business in the valley and most likely had performed the heavy manual labor of moving objects into a royal tomb.

The tomb of Thutmose IV (KV 43; Reeves 1990b, 97) contains key evidence about the most likely date for this group of robberies. Two graffiti in the tomb, one of which is dated late in the reign of Horemheb (Reeves and Wilkinson 1996, 108), the last king of the Eighteenth Dynasty, offer solid evidence of when a restoration of Thutmose IV's tomb took place. The work was conducted by a certain Maja, a well-known high official of the reign of Tutankhamun and a close associate of Horemheb, and his assistant, the scribe Djehutymose. These men almost certainly were involved with at least one of the restorations of Tutankhamun's burial (Reeves 1990b, 97), which occurred in a period characterized by the uncertainty of dynastic transition. However, the outbreak of robberies in the valley in the last years of the Eighteenth Dynasty was certainly a reflection of the contemporary political environment.

THE EARLIER RAMESSIDE TOMB ROBBERIES

From the period beginning with the advent of the Nineteenth Dynasty to the middle of the reign of Ramesses III, the number of tomb robberies may have diminished. Perhaps this was due to an important innovation in how construction and other activities in the valley were administered. Although there had long been groups of highly skilled artisans, reminiscent of a medieval guild, whose occupation was to excavate and decorate the royal tombs in the Valley of the Kings, we know little about that community before its extensive reorganization in the beginning of the Ramesside period (Valbelle 1996, 1–26). We can only speculate why the new administration decided to abandon the time-tested practice of assembling teams of specialized workers from many parts of the country to work on the royal tomb, but it is quite likely that a need to increase the security of the royal burials was a major consideration. By that time, this "company town," so to speak, had become a segregated and governmentally supported village at Deir el-Medina, with its own specialized organization and administrative structure (Černý 1973; Valbelle 1996; Bierbrier 1984). A wall surrounded the settlement (Burkard 2003a, 2003b; Ventura 1986,

120–144), but it is uncertain whether this signaled a sharp curtailment of the inhabitants' freedom of movement and association with the rest of the Theban west bank. The police force that guarded the valley itself, significantly, was not stationed in the village and maintained a largely separate administration. The men of Deir el-Medina left a vast number of documents pertaining to every aspect of their lives and work, so it is not surprising to see occasional references to robberies in the royal cemetery.

The Earlier Tomb Robberies of the Ramesside Period

Although dating any royal tomb robberies that followed the ones at the end of the Eighteenth Dynasty becomes an increasingly uncertain venture, a few intrusions can be ascribed to the part of the Ramesside period before the latter part of the Twentieth Dynasty.

The circumstances surrounding the violation of the tomb of Maiherpre (KV 36; Reeves 1990b, 140–147), a nonroyal person and a likely favorite of an early Eighteenth Dynasty monarch, appears to fit patterns of previous robberies around the last years of Horemheb's reign. When Victor Loret rediscovered Maiherpre's tomb in 1899, it was substantially intact. The negative evidence provided by missing items that one would expect to find, the state of the tomb, and the apparent restorations are comparable to what was found in Tutankhamun's tomb, but otherwise the circumstances surrounding the plundering of Maiherpre's burial are uncertain. The evidence seems to point to two robberies, the more important intrusion occurring in the middle of the Eighteenth Dynasty, followed by an accidental discovery and reordering during the Ramesside period (Reeves 1990b, 146–147).

We can affix a reliable date to an intrusion into the tomb of Ramesses II (KV 7), but as with the other robberies in the earlier part of the Twentieth Dynasty, we cannot tell much about the attempted theft itself because of the parlous state of the tomb, due largely to its later dismantling in the late Twentieth Dynasty. The so-called Strike Papyrus, now preserved in the Turin Museum, records a passing remark made in trial testimony to the effect that attempts had been made to break into the tombs of Ramesses II and that of his children (Edgerton 1951, 141). This occurred in the twenty-ninth year of the reign of Ramesses III, toward the end of a reign that was marked by considerable troubles, such as a strike of the necropolis workforce and a possibly successful assassination attempt against the king himself. As with other violations, there is an opportunistic quality to the affair. The culprit may well have been taking advantage of an unsettled atmosphere and slackened security for his break-in. Interestingly enough, the trial testimony refers to a certain Paneb's activities, which had occurred a considerable time before and which deserve special attention.

Paneb—Thefts and Accusations

Prior to the end of the Twentieth Dynasty, the most vivid description of a robbery in the valley comes from Papyrus Salt 125 in the British Museum (Černý 1929; Collier 2011;

Bierbrier 2000). The text dates to the Twentieth Dynasty during the reign of Ramesses III. It presents a lengthy list of accusations against Paneb, one of the two chief foremen of the tomb worker force since the end of the Nineteenth Dynasty. Judging from the complaints against him—several death threats against other crew members, serial adultery, and tomb robbery—he must have been a colorful character indeed. Paneb was accused of robbing the tomb of Seti II (KV 15), who ironically had been something of a patron to him. In addition, Paneb had purportedly plundered a queen's burial in the Valley of the Queens. We should be a bit cautious here, because Paneb had risen to his high position among the royal necropolis gang at the expense of Amennakht, the main witness charging him. Putting aside whether or not accusations against Paneb were true, the description of his alleged thefts nevertheless conforms to the general pattern of a royal tomb robbery gained from other sources: the likely targets for thefts, when robberies were apt to occur, and who was apt to commit crimes.

If robberies could be said to have a style or theme, the description of this supposed robbery is that of a hasty, limited, and opportunistic action that took place near the time of the king's funeral. The burial detail, significantly, would have been led by Paneb by virtue of his high position in the crew. The burial detail, as one might expect, committed the theft shortly after the funeral, alleging that they did so only because Paneb had ordered them to, but it is not believable that they did not participate willingly. As usual, the thieves focused on the usual portable or recyclable items whose origins could be readily disguised. The men obviously had a good idea of where to look, since they primarily targeted the many wooden chests among the royal funerary equipment.

The Tomb Robberies in the Late Twentieth Dynasty—Reframing the Topic

As we move to a discussion of the late Twentieth Dynasty and the final phase of robberies, there are two ways in which we must reframe the topic. First, we must first realize that phrase "tomb robberies" is inadequate to describe the situation that arose in the Valley at that time. The fate of the royal tombs took the same downward trajectory that befell the prestige and power of the ruling house. What befell the tombs cannot be treated in isolation mainly because the *wadi* itself was no longer the isolated place it had been for centuries. The chief source of information about the final group of tomb violations is a group of several papyri that were collected and studied by T. E. Peet in his seminal work, *The Great Tomb Robberies of the Twentieth Dynasty* (Peet 1930). The title is somewhat misleading since these documents were primarily concerned with tomb robberies that occurred *outside* the royal *wadi* and dealt as well with an extensive outbreak of thefts from the great temples on both banks of Thebes. It is fair to say that outside events had now spilled over into the Valley and that the robberies were the most dramatic sign of a disintegrating central administration that gave rise to a new regime.

Secondly, once we move to a discussion of the final phase of thefts in the Valley, we should also ask, what constitutes a violation of a tomb? Thus far the focus has been on unauthorized and illicit removals of grave goods or damage to the decoration, usually with the intent of personal profit or post-mortem harm to the tomb owner (Dodson 1992). The intrusions during the Eighteenth, Nineteenth, and early Twentieth Dynasties show that there were several such violations, but they were infrequent and limited, particularly given the vast expanse of time involved. The latter point is especially important, since a characteristic of all these prior robberies was that they were sporadic and had a rather opportunistic, almost amateurish character. The earlier official responses focused on repair and restoration, accompanied by a tightening of security in the Valley. At the end of the Twentieth Dynasty, the character of countermeasures changed dramatically to the extent that the term "tomb violations" might apply as well to the royal reburials and the official dismantling of the royal tombs (Graefe 1999; Graefe 2003; Jansen-Winkeln 1995), followed by reburial of the royal mummies. In these instances "reburial," would be an euphemism for a stripping of the coffins and related items. These acts were in effect a tacit, official acknowledgement that the Valley of the Kings had ceased to be secure for the burial of the royal dead.

The Political and Chronological Background of the End of the Twentieth Dynasty

The events at the end of the Twentieth Dynasty and the beginning of the Third Intermediate Period are the focus of a major historical and chronological controversy. The chief points of contention, regrettably, consist of nearly the entire corpus of evidence for the last phase of thefts: the "Tomb Robbery Papyri" and a small group of monumental inscriptions, some of which we can hardly call texts. Reduced to their essentials, the controversies center on the identity of the men who were the actual effective powers of the Theban region and their sequence in office. This was a tumultuous era of near revolts, incursions by nomadic Libyans (Haring 1992, 1993), collapse of civil authority, and widespread economic distress, followed by investigations and the eventual imposition of order (Wente 1966; Niwinski 1992; Niwinski 1995; Thijs 2003).

The interpretation of the evidence is further complicated by the introduction of an unusual dating system referring to a special era of political reformation called the *whm mswt* "Repeating of Births"—a term meaning something close to "renaissance" (Gundlach 1986; Niwinski 1996)—rather than the normal dating of events according to the regnal year of the current monarch. At the very least, the new dating system was an indication that the king had become a largely nominal, remote figure in the minds of the men whose task was to normalize conditions in the Theban region. The very use of *whm mswt* reflected the determination of the governing officials to restore order. In the rare instances during this period when documents mentioned the king's regnal year, the *whm mswt* date occurred first (Nims 1948, 159). This dating system was employed only in the area around Thebes and southward—no examples of renaissance dating can be ascribed to Middle or Lower Egypt.

Ultimately the resolution of these controversies, should a consensus be reached, will have an unquestionably great impact on our overall perceptions of the political conditions at the end of the Twentieth Dynasty and the transition into the Third Intermediate Period. Within the narrow historical context of Thebes and the Valley of the Kings, however, any revised chronology of this era will not materially change our view of the nature of the thefts themselves, nor of the atmosphere of great political and social turmoil in which they happened.

The reason for this is actually simple. From the limited perspective of the tomb and temple robberies, the major personages around whom the controversies revolve remain largely in the background of the evidence. Whether the momentary governing authority in the Theban region at any given moment was, for example, the king (Ramesses IX or Ramesses XI), the High Priest of Amun, one of the several generals (Panehsi, Piankhi, or Herihor), or someone else, that person was a distant, absent figure from the viewpoint of the documents themselves. Except perhaps for the king, those central figures in the chronological dispute are hardly mentioned at all. During the renaissance the governing powers would have been more concerned with more pressing and wide-ranging restorative measures in the Theban region and beyond. The officials who appear in the surviving documents were probably simply delegated to handle the interrogations and trials of the suspects. The men conducting the investigations—they can hardly be called trials—were very important, to be sure, but they seem to have operated at a lower level of authority.

THE TOMB ROBBERY PAPYRI

There are few aspects of Egyptian history as well documented as the various types of robberies of royal and divine property that occurred over the course of the last three reigns of the Twentieth Dynasty, beginning in the ninth regnal year of Ramesses IX and extending into years 19 and 20 of Ramesses XI. There is a large corpus of papyri connected with these events. In this case the evidence for tomb robberies becomes largely textual yet at the same time inferential. Nearly all the documents were collected by Peet in his indispensable study, *The Great Tomb-Robberies of the Twentieth Egyptian Dynasty* (1930). Since 1930 only a few additional documents have been found, such as the second part of Papyrus Abbott, which is now completed by the discovery of Papyrus Leopold II (Capart, Gardiner, and van der Walle 1936; Kitchen 2012, 361–370) and Pap. Rochester MAG 51.364.1 (Goelet 1996; Fischer-Elfert 1998, 107–108; Quack 2000). Details of the robberies emerge from the "trials" of the miscreants, which were little more than interrogations under torture (McDowell 1990, 189–200; Boochs 1989). Since the papyri were topically connected and described some of the most sensitive and embarrassing moments of the period, they may have been collected in a secure archive somewhere on the west bank, the most probable location being the fortress-like great temple of Medinet Habu.

Despite the phrase "Great Tomb-Robberies," Peet's book tells little about the fate of the great royal tombs in the royal *wadi*. Only one of the papyri treated, the rather damaged Pap. Mayer B (Peet 1920; 1930, 169, 176, pl. XXIV), mentions thefts from a king's tomb in the valley, namely that of Ramesses IX (KV 9), probably the last king to be buried in the valley. The identity of the tomb is significant, since the theft would have certainly occurred before the official dismantlement program began. The other documents in Peet's collection are concerned with robberies in the older royal cemetery at Dra Abu'l-Naga (Polz 2007, esp. 224–229) and in the Valley of the Queens, or with the pillage of a wide variety of objects from the great memorial temples on the Theban west bank. It is productive to focus on the nature of these robberies outside the royal *wadi* and what the thieves wanted.

Mayer B, the only one of the entire collection to describe a theft in the valley, conforms to the pattern of earlier robberies. The date of the papyrus is uncertain, but it is likely to have been written somewhere in the middle of Ramesses IX's reign. Although the thief's confession is not entirely clear (Kitchen 2012, 383–384), he apparently went up to Ramesses VI's tomb with a group of four other men, guided by a foreigner who also was not a crew member. The robbers were not royal necropolis workers and probably had only secondhand knowledge of the *wadi*. It took four days to break in, a remarkably long time that shows a total absence of security in the valley. Once inside the tomb, the robbers concentrated their efforts on opening chests, from which they collected numerous copper basins, ewers, and vases, yielding about one hundred *deben* or approximately 0.9 kilogram as well as thirty-five cloth garments for each thief, much wealth for an impoverished person. More goods were stolen, but the details are lost because the papyrus breaks off. This papyrus alone provides ample reasons why the valley could no longer be used for royal burials, even before the start of the renaissance.

If the events described in Pap. Mayer B seem dramatic, one can only imagine the revulsion and indignation the authorities must have felt upon hearing the confessions of the robbers who ransacked the more exposed royal tombs of the Seventeenth Dynasty in the Dra Abu'l-Naga section of the Theban necropolis and in the Valley of the Queens. As the Leopold-Amherst Papyrus records, the thieves brutally tore apart the bandages of the royal mummies in search of amulets, jewelry, precious stone inlays, and other finery wrapped in the bindings or inset into the coffins. They even hacked apart or set fire to the wooden sarcophagi, presumably to speed the collection of gold and silver foil on the coffins. The use of fire and the thoroughness of the plundering, combined with their description of their break-ins as repeated affairs, indicate that there must have been extended periods when there was little or no risk of being apprehended.

Nearly all the remaining robbery papyri were concerned with widespread depredations in the memorial temples on the west bank, yet these documents are quite pertinent to events in the valley, because these documents describe vividly the lawless environment that led to the reimposition of order during the "renaissance." Significantly, the thieves who plundered the memorial temples targeted the same types of items that attracted the attention of those who robbed Tutankhamun's tomb: many wooden chests and shrines. Other loot that figured prominently was metal vessels in gold, silver, or copper; carrying poles; and pieces of cloth. The extensive looting was done by people deprived of their occupations and income and desperate for any goods that might be traded for food and other necessities of life. The great number of people involved is quite striking, particularly since many were low-level employees of the temples. Members of the Deir el-Medina community, including the royal tomb builders, also participated. The temple thefts were undoubtedly open knowledge and demonstrated a total breakdown of societal order at Thebes.

For a brief overview of the chronological problems connected with robberies and documents from the end of the Twentieth Dynasty onward, see the pages for this volume at http://thebanmappingproject.com/resources/handbook.html.

Bibliography

Abitz, F. 1974. *Die religiöse Bedeutung der sogenannten Grabräuberschächte in den ägyptischen Königsgräbern der 18. bis 20. Dynastie.* Ägyptologische Abhandlungen 26. Wiesbaden.

Abitz, F. 1979. *Statuetten in Schreinen als Grabbeigaben in den ägyptischen Königsgräbern der 18. und 19. Dynastie.* Ägyptologische Abhandlungen 35. Wiesbaden.

Aldred, C. 1979. "More Light on the Ramesside Tomb Robberies." In *Glimpses of Egypt: Studies in Honour of H. W. Fairman,* edited by J. Ruffle et al., 92–99. Warminster.

Andreu, G., ed. 2003. *Deir el-Médineh et la Valée des Rois: La vie en Égypte au temps des pharaons du Nouvel Empire; Actes du colloque organisé par le musée du Louvre les 3 et 4 mai 2002.* Paris.

Assmann, J., and E. Blumenthal, eds. 1999. *Literatur und Politik im pharaonischen und ptolemäischen Ägypten.* Bibliothèque d'Étude 127. Cairo.

Beckerath, J. von. 1984. "Drei Thronbesteigungsdaten der XX. Dynastie." *Göttinger Miszellen* 79: 7–9.

Beckerath, J. von. 1995. "Zur Chronologie der XXI. Dynastie." In *Gedenkschrift für Wilfried Barta,* edited by D. Kessler and R. Schultz, 49–55. Frankurt.

Beckerath, J. von. 1997. "Zur Datierung des Grabraüberpapyrus Brit.Mus. 10054." *Göttinger Miszellen* 159: 5–9.

Bierbrier, M. L. 1972. "A Second High Priest Ramessesnakht?" *Journal of Egyptian Archaeology* 58: 195–199.

Bierbrier, M. L. 1975. "The Length of the Reign of Ramesses X." *Journal of Egyptian Archaeology* 61: 251.

Bierbrier, M. L. 1984. *The Tomb-Builders of the Pharaohs.* New York.

Bierbrier, M. L. 2000. "Paneb rehabilitated?" In *Deir el-Medina in the Third Millenium AD: A Tribute to Jac. J. Janssen,* edited by R. J. Demarée and A. Egberts, 51–54. Leiden.

Bonhême, M.-A. 1978. "Hérihor fut-il effectivement roi?" *Bulletin de l'Institut français d'archéologie orientale* 79: 267–283.

Boochs, W. 1989. "Das altägyptische Strafverfahren bei Straftaten von besonderem staatlichem Interesse." *Göttinger Miszellen* 109: 21–26.

Broekman, G. P. F., et al., eds. 2009. *The Libyan Period in Egypt Historical and Cultural Studies into the 21st–24th Dynasties; Proceedings of a Conference at Leiden University, 24–25 October 2007.* Egyptologische Uitgaven 23. Leiden.

Burkard, G. 2003a. "'. . . die im Dunkeln sieht man nicht': Waren die Arbeiter im Tal der Könige privilegierte Gefangene?" In *Grab und Totenkult im Alten Ägypten*, edited by H. Guksch, E. Hofmann, and M. Bommas, 128–146. Munich.

Burkard, G. 2003b. "'Oh, diese Mauern Pharaos!' Zur Bewegungsfreiheit der Einwohner von Deir el Medine." *Mitteilungen des Deutschen Archäologischen Instituts, Abteilung Kairo* 59: 11–39.

Capart, J., A. H. Gardiner, and B. van der Walle. 1936. "New Light on the Ramesside Tomb-Robberies." *Journal of Egyptian Archaeology* 22: 169–193.

Černý, J. 1929. "Papyrus Salt 124 (Brit. Mus. 10055)." *Journal of Egyptian Archaeology* 15: 243–258.

Černý, J. 1973. *The Valley of the Kings: Fragments d'un manuscrit inachevé*. Bibliothèque d'Étude 61. Cairo.

Collier, M. 2011. "More on Late Nineteenth Dynasty Ostraca Dates, and Remarks on Paneb." In *Ramesside Studies in Honour of K. A. Kitchen*, edited by M. Collier and S. Snape, 111–122. Bolton.

Collier, M., A. Dodson, and G. Hamernik. 2010. "P. BM EA 10052, Anthony Harris, and Queen Tyti." *Journal of Egyptian Archaeology* 96: 242–247.

Collier, M., and S. Snape, eds. 2011. *Ramesside Studies in Honour of K. A. Kitchen*. Bolton.

Creasman, P. P., ed. 2013. *Archaeological Research in the Valley of the Kings and Ancient Thebes: Papers Presented in Honor of Richard H. Wilkinson*. Wilkinson Egyptology Series 1. Tucson, AZ.

Davies, N. de G. 1941. *The Tomb of the Vizier Ramose*. Mond Excavations at Thebes I. London.

Demarée, R. J. 2003. "Quelques textes de la fin de la XXe et du début de la XXIe dynastie." In *Deir el-Médineh et la Valée des Rois: La vie en Égypte au temps des pharaons du Nouvel Empire; Actes du colloque organisé par le musée du Louvre les 3 et 4 mai 2002*, edited by G. Andreu, 235–251. Paris.

Demarée, R. J., and A. Egberts, eds. 1992. *Village Voices: Proceedings of the Symposium Texts from Deir el-Medîna and Their Interpretation*. Leiden.

Demarée, R. J., and A. Egberts, eds. 2000. *Deir el-Medina in the Third Millennium AD: A Tribute to Jac. J. Janssen*. Leiden.

Demarée, R. J., and D. Valbelle. 2011. *Les registres de recensement du village de Deir el-Medineh (Le "Stato Civile")*. Louvain.

Demidoff, G. 2000. "Pour une revision de la chronologie de la fin de l'époque ramesside." *Göttinger Miszellen* 177: 91–101.

Demidoff, G. 2008. "Hérihor-Piankhy, Piankhy-Hérihor. Retour sur une controverse." In *Mélanges offerts à François Neveu par ses amis, élèves et collègues à l'occasion de son soixante-cinquizième anniversaire*, edited by C. Gallois et al., 99–111. Cairo.

Dodson, A. 1987. "The Takhats and Some Other Royal Ladies of the Ramesside Period." *Journal of Egyptian Archaeology* 73: 224–229.

Dodson, A. 1992. "Death after Death in the Valley of the Kings." In *Death and Taxes in the Ancient Near East*, edited by S. E. Orel, 53–59. Lewiston, NY and Queenston, ON.

Dorn, A. 2009. "Die Lokalisation der '5 Mauern' / Wachposten (*t3 5 jnb.t / n3 jnb.wt / t3 jnb*)." *Journal of Egyptian Archaeology* 95: 263–268.

Eaton-Krauss, M. 1992. "[Review of] C.N. Reeves, *Valley of the Kings: The Decline of a Royal Necropolis*". *Bibliotheca Orientalis* 49: 706–717.

Edgerton, W.F. 1951, "The Strikes in Ramses III's Twenty-ninth Year." *Journal of Near Eastern Studies* 10: 137–145.

Edwards, I. E. S. 1982. "The Bankes Papyri I and II." *Journal of Egyptian Archaeology* 68: 126–133.

Egberts, A. 1991. "The Chronology of *The Report of Wenamun*." *Journal of Egyptian Archaeology* 77: 57–67.

Egberts, A. 1997. "Piankh, Herihor, Djutmose and Butehamun: A Fresh Look at O. Cairo CG 25744 and 25745." *Göttinger Miszellen* 160: 23–25.

Egberts, A. 1998. "Hard Times: The Chronology of 'The Report of Wenamun' Revised." *Zeitschrift für Ägyptische Sprache und Altertumskunde* 125: 93–108.

Eichler, S. 1990. "Untersuchungen zu den Wasserträgern von Deir-el-Medineh I." *Studien zur altägyptischen Kultur* 17: 135–175.

Epigraphic Survey. 1979. *Scenes of King Herihor in the Court with Translations of Texts: The Temple of Khonsu 1 (Plates 1–110). Oriental Institute Publications 100.* Chicago.

Epigraphic Survey. 1981. *Scenes and Inscriptions in the Court and the First Hypostyle Hall with Translations of Texts and Glossary for Volumes 1 and 2: The Temple of Khonsu 2 (Plates 111–207). Oriental Institute Publications 103.* Chicago.

Eyre, C. J. 1999. "Irony in the Story of Wenamun: The Politics of Religion in the 21st Dynasty." In *Literatur und Politik im pharaonischen und ptolemäischen Ägypten*, edited by J. Assmann and E. Blumenthal, 235–252. Cairo.

Fischer-Elfert, H.-W. 1998. "Legenda Hieratika—I." *Göttinger Miszellen* 165: 106–112.

Gallois, C. et al., eds. 2008. *Mélanges offerts à François Neveu par ses amis, élèves et collègues à l'occasion de son soixante-cinquinzième anniversaire.* Bibliothèque d'Étude 145. Cairo.

Gamer-Wallert, I., and W. Helck, eds. 1992. *Gebengaben: Festschrift für Emma Brunner-Traut.* Tübingen.

Gasse, A. 2012. "Panakhtemipet et ses complices (à propos du Papyrus BM EA 10054, ro 2, 1–5)." *Journal of Egyptian Archaeology* 87: 81–92.

Goecke-Bauer, M. 2003. "Untersuchungen zu den 'Torwächtern' von Deir el-Medine." In *Woodcutters, Potters and Doorkeepers: Service Personnel of the Deir El-Medina Workmen*, edited by J. J. Janssen, E. Frood, and M. Goecke-Bauer, 63–153. Leiden.

Goelet, O. 1996. "A New 'Robbery' Papyrus: Rochester MAG 51.346.1." *Journal of Egyptian Archaeology* 82: 107–127.

Goldberg, J. 2000. "Was Piankh the Son of Herihor After All?" *Göttinger Miszellen* 174: 49–58.

Graefe, E. 1997. "Zur Datierung des Grabräuberpapyrus Brit.Mus.10054." *Göttinger Miszellen* 159: 5–9.

Graefe, E. 1999. "Über die Goldmenge des Alten Ägypten und die Beraubung der thebanischen Königsgräber." *Zeitschrift für Ägyptische Sprache und Altertumskunde* 126: 19–40.

Graefe, E. 2003. "The Royal Cache and the Tomb Robberies." In *The Theban Necropolis: Past, Present and Future*, edited by N. Strudwick and J. H. Taylor, 74–82. London.

Guksch, H., E. Hofmann, and M. Bommas, eds. 2003. *Grab und Totenkult im Alten Ägypten.* Munich.

Gundlach, R. 1986. "Wiederholung der Geburt." *Lexikon der Ägyptologie* VI: 1261–1264.

Gundlach, R. 1994."Das Königtum des Herihor: Zum Umbruch in der ägyptischen Königsideologie am Beginn der 3. Zwischenzeit." In *Aspekte spätägyptische Kultur: Festschrift für Erich Winter zum 65. Geburtstag*, edited by M. Minas and J. Ziedler, 133–138. Trier.

Hari, R. 1982. "Un monument du grand-prêtre Herihor." *Bulletin de la Société d'égyptologie de Genève* 7: 39–46.

Haring, B. J. J. 1992. "Libyans in the Late Twentieth Dynasty." In *Village Voices: Proceedings of the Symposium Texts from Deir el-Medîna and Their Interpretation*, edited by R. J. Demarée and A. Egberts, 71–80. Leiden.

Haring, B. J. J. 1993. "Libyans in the Theban Region, 20th Dynasty." In *Sisto Congresso Internationale di Egittologia*, 159–165. Atti II. Torino.

Helck, W. 1964. "Feiertage und Arbeitstage in der Ramessidenzeit." *Journal of the Economic and Social History of the Orient* 7: 136–166.

Helck, W. 1990. "Drei Ramessidische Daten." *Studien zur altägyptischen Kultur* 17: 205–214.

Hornung, E. 1982. *Tal der Könige: Die Ruhestätte der Pharaonen*. Zürich.

Hornung, E. 1990. *The Valley of the Kings: Horizon of Eternity*. Translated by D. Warburton. New York.

Jansen-Winkeln, K. 1992. "Das Ende des Neuen Reiches." *Zeitschrift für Ägyptische Sprache und Altertumskunde* 119: 22–37.

Jansen-Winkeln, K. 1994. "Der Schreiber Buteamun." *Göttinger Miszellen* 159: 35–40.

Jansen-Winkeln, K. 1995. "Die Plünderung der Königsgräber des Neuen Reiches." *Zeitschrift für Ägyptische Sprache und Altertumskunde* 112: 62–78.

Jansen-Winkeln, K. 1997. "Die Begründer der 21. Dynastie." *Göttinger Miszellen* 157: 49–74.

Janssen, J. J. 1992. "A New Kingdom Settlement: The Verso of Pap. BM. 10068." *Altorientalische Forschungen* 19: 8–23.

Janssen, J. J., E. Frood, and M. Goecke-Bauer, eds. 2003. *Woodcutters, Potters and Doorkeepers: Service Personnel of the Deir El-Medina Workmen*. Egyptologische Uitgaven 17. Leiden.

Jenni, H., ed. 2000. *Das Grab Ramses' X. (KV 18)*. Aegyptiaca Helvetica 16. Basel.

Kessler, D., and R. Schultz, eds. 1995. *Gedenkschrift für Wilfried Barta*. MÄU 4. Frankurt.

Kitchen, K. A. 1982. "The Twentieth Dynasty Revisited." *Journal of Egyptian Archaeology* 68: 116–125.

Kitchen, K. A. 1984. "Family Relationships of Ramesses IX and the Late Twentieth Dynasty." *Studien zur altägyptischen Kultur* 11: 127–134.

Kitchen, K. A. 2009. "The Third Intermediate Period in Egypt: An Overview of Fact & Fiction." In *The Libyan Period in Egypt: Historical and Cultural Studies into the 21st–24th Dynasties; Proceedings of a Conference at Leiden University, 24–25 October 2007*, edited by G. P. F. Broekman et al., 161–201. Leiden.

Kitchen, K. A. 2012. *Ramesside Inscriptions Translated & Annotated. Translations VI, Ramesses IV to XI, & Contemporaries*. Oxford.

Krauss, R. 1986. "Zum archäologischen Befund im thebanischen Königsgrab Nr. 62." *Mitteilungen der Deutschen Orientgesellschaft* 118: 165–181.

Lorton, D. 1977. "The Treatment of Criminals in Ancient Egypt." *Journal of the Economic and Social History of the Orient* 20: 2–64.

McDowell, A. G. 1990. "Cases Handled by Neither Oracle nor ḵnbt." In *Jurisdiction in the Workmen's Community of Deir el-Medîna*, edited by A. G. McDowell, 187–234. Leiden.

McDowell, A. G., ed. 1990. *Jurisdiction in the Workmen's Community of Deir el-Medîna*. Egyptologische Uitgaven 5. Leiden.

Minas, M., and J. Ziedler, eds. 1994. *Aspekte spätägyptische Kultur: Festschrift für Erich Winter zum 65. Geburtstag*. Aegyptiaca Treverensia 7. Trier.

Nims, C. F. 1948. "An Oracle Dated in the Repeating of Births." *Journal of Near Eastern Studies* 7: 157–162.

Niwinski, A. 1992. "Bürgerkrieg, militärischer Staatsreich und Ausnamezustand in Ägypten unter Ramses XI: Ein Versuch neuer Interpretation der alten Quellen." In *Gebengaben: Festschrift für Emma Brunner-Traut*, edited by I. Gamer-Wallert and W. Helck, 235–262. Tübingen.

Niwinski, A. 1995. "Le passage de la XXe à XXIIe dynastie: Chronologie et histoire politique." *Bulletin de l'Institut français d'archéologie orientale* 95: 329–360.

Niwinski, A. 1996. "Les périodes *whm mswt* dans l'histoire de l'Égypte: Un essai comparatif." *Bulletin de la Société française d'égyptologie* 136: 5–26.

Orel, S. E., ed. 1992. *Death and Taxes in the Ancient Near East*. Lewiston, NY and Queenston, ON.

Peet, T. E. 1920. *The Mayer Papyri A & B*. London.

Peet, T. E. 1930. *The Great Tomb-Robberies of the Twentieth Egyptian Dynasty*. 2 vols. Oxford.

Phillips, J. 1992. "Tomb-robbers and Their Booty in Ancient Egypt." In *Death and Taxes in the Ancient Near East*, edited by S. E. Orel, 157–192. Lewiston, NY and Queenston, ON.

Polz, D. 1998. "The Ramsesnakht Dynasty and the Fall of the New Kingdom: A New Monument in Thebes." *Studien zur altägyptischen Kultur* 25: 257–293.

Polz, D. 2007. *Der Beginn des Neuen Reiches: Zur Vorgeschichte einer Zeitwende. Sonderschrift des Deutschen Archäologischen Instituts, Abteilung Kairo* 31. Berlin.

Quack, J. F. 2000. "Eine Revision im Tempel von Karnak (Neuanalyse von Papyrus Rochester MAG 51.346.1)." *Studien zur altägyptischen Kultur* 28: 219–232.

Reeves, C. N. 1990a. *The Complete Tutankhamun: The King. The Tomb. The Royal Treasure*. New York.

Reeves, C. N. 1990b. *Valley of the Kings: The decline of a royal necropolis*. London and New York.

Reeves, C. N., ed. 1992. *After Tutʿankhamun: Research and Excavation in the Royal Necropolis in Thebes*. London.

Reeves, C. N., and R. H. Wilkinson. 1996. *The Complete Valley of the Kings: Tombs and Treasures of Egypt's Greatest Pharaohs*. London and New York.

Ritner, R. K. 2009. *The Libyan Anarchy: Inscriptions from Egypt's Third Intermediate Period*. SBL Writings from the Ancient World 21. Atlanta, GA.

Romer, J. 1981. *Valley of the Kings*. New York.

Rössler-Köhler, U. 1998. "Pianch—Nedjmet—Anchefenmut—eine Kleinigkeit." *Göttinger Miszellen* 167: 7–8.

Ruffle, J., et al., eds. 1979. *Glimpses of Egypt: Studies in Honour of H. W. Fairman*. Warminster.

Schneider, T. 2000. "Ramses X.: Person und Geschichte." In *Das Grab Ramses' X. (KV 18)*, edited by H. Jenni, 81–108. Basel.

Strudwick, N. 2013. "Ancient Robbery in Theban Tombs." In *Archaeological Research in the Valley of the Kings and Ancient Thebes: Papers Presented in Honor of Richard H. Wilkinson*, edited by P. P. Creasman, 333–352. Tucson, AZ.

Strudwick, N., and J. H. Taylor, eds. 2003. *The Theban Necropolis: Past, Present and Future*. London.

Taylor, J. H. 1992. "Aspects of the History of the Valley of the Kings in the Third Intermediate Period." In *After Tutʿankhamun: Research and Excavation in the Royal Necropolis in Thebes*, edited by C. N. Reeves, 186–206. London.

Thijs, A. 1998a. "Reconsidering the End of the Twentieth Dynasty, Part I: The Fisherman Pnenkhtemope and the Date of BM 10054." *Göttinger Miszellen* 167: 95–108.

Thijs, A. 1998b. "Two Books for One Lady: The Mother of Herihor Rediscovered." *Göttinger Miszellen* 163: 101–110.

Thijs, A. 1999a. "Reconsidering the End of the Twentieth Dynasty, Part II." *Göttinger Miszellen* 170: 83–99.

Thijs, A. 1999b. "Reconsidering the End of the Twentieth Dynasty, Part III: Some Hitherto Unrecognized Documents from the *whm mswt*." *Göttinger Miszellen* 173: 175–191.

Thijs, A. 2000a. "'Please Tell Amon to Bring Me Back from Yar': Dhutmose's Visits Back to Nubia." *Göttinger Miszellen* 177: 63–70.

Thijs, A. 2000b. "Reconsidering the End of the Twentieth Dynasty, Part IV: The Harshire-Family as a Test for the Shorter Chronology." *Göttinger Miszellen* 175: 99–103.

Thijs, A. 2000c. "Reconsidering the End of the Twentieth Dynasty, Part V: pAmbras as an Advocate of a Shorter Chronology." *Göttinger Miszellen* 179: 69–83.

Thijs, A. 2001. "Reconsidering the End of the Twentieth Dynasty, Part VII: The History of the Viziers and the Politics of Menmare." *Göttinger Miszellen* 184: 65–73.

Thijs, A. 2003. "The Troubled Careers of Amenhotep and Panehsi: The High Priest of Amun and the Viceroy of Kush under the Last Ramessides." *Studien zur altägyptischen Kultur* 31: 289–306.

Thijs, A. 2005. "In Search of King Herihor and the Penultimate Ruler of the 20th Dynasty." *Zeitschrift für Ägyptische Sprache und Altertumskunde* 132: 73–91.

Thijs, A. 2010. "The Lunar Eclipse of Takelot II and the Chronology of the Libyan Period." *Zeitschrift für Ägyptische Sprache und Altertumskunde* 137: 171–190.

Thijs, A. 2011a. "Introducing the Banishment Stele into the 20th Dynasty." *Zeitschrift für Ägyptische Sprache und Altertumskunde* 138: 163–181.

Thijs, A. 2011b. "Reconsidering the End of the Twentieth Dynasty, Part VI: Some Minor Adjustments and Observations Concerning the Chronology of the Last Ramessides and the *wḥm mswt* ." *Göttinger Miszellen* 181: 95–103.

Thomas, E. 1966. *The Royal Necropoleis of Thebes*. Princeton, NJ.

Valbelle, D. 1996. *"Les ouvriers de la tombe": Deir el-Médineh à l'époque ramesside*. Bibliothèque d'Étude 96. Cairo.

Ventura, R. 1986. *Living in a City of the Dead: A Selection of Topographical and Administrative Terms in the Documents of the Theban Necropolis*. Orbis biblicus et orientalis 69. Göttingen.

Wente, E. F. 1966. "The Suppression of the High Priest Amenhotep." *Journal of Near Eastern Studies* 25: 73–87.

Winlock, H. E., and Dorothea Arnold. 2010. *Tutankhamun's Funeral*. New York.

Zonhoven, L. 1978. "The Inspection of a Tomb at Deir El-Medina (O. Wien Aeg. 1)." *Journal of Egyptian Archaeology* 65: 89–98.

PART XII

THE KV FROM THE END OF THE NEW KINGDOM TO THE LATE TWENTIETH CENTURY

....

CHAPTER 31

LATE DYNASTIC, GRECO–ROMAN, AND CHRISTIAN TIMES

Post–New Kingdom Graffiti

....

FILIP COPPENS

THE VALLEY OF THE KINGS IN THE THIRD INTERMEDIATE PERIOD AND THE LATE PERIOD

....

THE end of the New Kingdom and the subsequent Third Intermediate Period saw considerable changes in Egyptian society caused by the decline of centralized power (and subsequent fragmentation of the state), growing incursions of foreign populations into Egypt, and worsening economic conditions as a result of a reduction in revenue from abroad. While the north of the country was controlled from Tanis by the kings of the Twenty-first Dynasty, starting with Smendes, a line of generals doubling as high priests of Amun ruled the south from Thebes (Ńiwinski 2007).

The last major chapter in the history of the Valley of the Kings as a burial ground was written in the course of the Third Intermediate Period. A spate of tomb robberies occurred during the Ramesside period, particularly during the reigns of Ramesses IX and Ramesses XI, followed by the dismantling of the no longer secure tombs and the reburial of numerous kings and several other members of the royal family between the very end of the New Kingdom and the early Twenty-second Dynasty. This activity was not necessarily prompted by pious sentiments; rather, it was the frail financial situation of the state that appears to have led to the dismantling of royal burials, coffins being stripped of precious materials and some of the burial equipment appropriated to be reused by the new rulers to increase their prestige. The majority of the dismantled burials were eventually cached in DB 320 and KV 35 in the course of the Twenty-first and early Twenty-second Dynasty (Reeves 1990, 181–268; Ñiwinski 2005; Taylor in this volume).

After the final closure of DB 320 shortly after the eleventh year of Sheshonq I, the royal wadi functioned for several centuries as a private burial ground. Simple burials of individuals of lower rank have been discovered in the tombs of kings Thutmose III (KV 34), Amenhotep III (WV 22), Siptah (KV 47), and Ramesses XI (KV 4); in the tomb of prince Montuherkhepeshef (KV 19) and in tombs KV 44 and 45 (Userhet); and WV 24 and 25. Numerous other tombs in the royal wadi also contained unidentified human remains that cannot at present be dated with any degree of certainty (Taylor 1992, 200–202). Fragments of wooden coffins discovered in the tomb of Amenhotep III and dated to the seventh century BC represent the last use of the valley as a cemetery for almost a millennium (Kondo 1992, 51–52).

During the Late Period the valley was still occasionally visited, but at present not a single interment can be indisputably ascribed to this era (Aston 2003). A quarry inscription bearing the cartouches of Haibra Apries (Twenty-sixth Dynasty), found near the entrance to the royal wadi, suggests activity in or near the valley at this time (Gauthier 1908, 141; Petrie 1909, 15, pl. LVI). This is confirmed by two Demotic ostraca recovered from the tiny wadi in front of the tombs of Seti I (KV 17) and Ramesses I (KV 16) and dated to the late Twenty-sixth or early Twenty-seventh Dynasty (Cruz-Uribe and Vinson 2005–2006). The design and some of the texts of the sarcophagus of Hapmen (EA 23), dated to the Twenty-sixth Dynasty or later and found in the mosque of Ibn Tulun in Cairo, are almost exact copies of those on the sarcophagus from the tomb of Thutmose III (KV 34), suggesting that either the design survived until the Late Period or someone made a copy of it in the tomb in later times (Hayes 1935, 153–154; Reeves 1990, 24).

The reason for the apparent absence of burials in the royal wadi during the Late Period and throughout Ptolemaic and Roman times remains a subject of speculation. Administrative impediments and respect for the last resting place of the kings might have played a role, but the main reason was perhaps more prosaic: in comparison with many other cemeteries in use on the West Bank, the royal wadi might have been considered simply too remote and difficult to access (Riggs 2003, 189; Strudwick 2003, 184).

THE VALLEY OF THE KINGS
IN GRECO–ROMAN TIMES

Over the course of the first millennium BC the Theban region gradually saw the powerful politician, the wealthy merchant and the influential priest disappear, but it did attract a species of a different kind—the tourist. Numerous travelers journeyed up the Nile to feast their eyes on the sacred city of Thebes and to satisfy their curiosity. Already in Ptolemaic times Thebes received its fair share of visitors, but especially during the first three centuries of Roman rule the region witnessed a large influx of tourists from all layers of the society and from all over the ancient world (Bataille 1951, 348–352; Bataille 1952, 153–179; Łajtar 2012, 183–185; Rutherford 2012, 705–709). The small sanctuary dedicated to Amenhotep, son of Hapu, and Imhotep on the third terrace of the temple of Hatshepsut at Deir el-Bahri was frequented especially by the sick hoping to regain their health (Łajtar 2006). The two sites that topped the list of places to visit when in Thebes were associated with Memnon, the son of the goddess of the dawn Eos: the statues of Amenhotep III, known as the Colossi of Memnon (Bernand and Bernand 1960), and the tomb of Ramesses V/VI (KV 9) in the Valley of the Kings which was identified with Memnon's last resting place.

The Sources

The tomb of Ramesses VI received the most attention in Greco–Roman times, but it was certainly not the only visitor destination in the valley. Classical authors who recorded their visit to the Valley of the Kings mentioned the existence of more than 40 tombs, of which a dozen were still accessible. The Greek historian Diodorus Siculus in the first book of his *Library of History* (I.46.7–8) mentions: "Now the priests said that in their records they find forty–seven tombs of kings; but down to the time of Ptolemy son of Lagos, they say, only fifteen remained, most of which had been destroyed at the time we visited those regions, in the one hundred and eightieth Olympiad [i.e., 60–56 BC]. Not only do the priests of Egypt give these facts from their records, but many also of the Greeks who visited Thebes in the time of Ptolemy son of Lagos and composed histories of Egypt, one of whom was Hecataeus [of Abdera], agree with what we have said." Strabo, who visited the Theban region in the company of one of the first prefects of Roman Egypt, Aelius Gallus, a generation later mentions in the eighth volume of his *Geography* (17.1.46) the existence of about 40 rock-cut tombs. Other authors referring to the tombs of the kings include Aelian (*De natura Animalium* VI, 43 and XVI, 15) and Heliodoros of Emesa (*Aethiopica*, I, 6 and II, 27). Following a mention in the *Description of Greece* (I.42.3) of Pausanias, the rock-cut tombs characterized by long sloping corridors and small chambers were referred to as *syringai* based on their resemblance to the pan or shepherd's flute (*syrinx*).

The primary evidence of tourism in the Valley of the Kings takes the form of thousands of incised, carved, and scratched inscriptions (graffiti) and brush and ink written texts (dipinti) left behind by the tourists in the royal tombs. These short texts were already observed by early visitors to the valley, including Richard Pococke, Jean-François Champollion, and John Gardner Wilkinson. These and other graffiti and dipinti were gathered for the first time by Jean Antoine Letronne (1848, 255–316 and pls. 23–30), but only in the early 1860s a serious attempt was made by C. Wescher, a member of the mission of Emmanuel de Rougé, to collate all Greek graffiti and dipinti. His efforts resulted in about 900 Greek texts being copied, but never published. In the late 1880s Gaston Maspero assigned two scholars the task of collating and studying all the graffiti and dipinti. Georges Bénédite, in charge of the Demotic graffiti and dipinti, copied but, like Wescher before, never published the fruits of his labour. Jules Baillet, on the other hand, gathered more than 2100 Greek and some Latin and Coptic inscriptions in 1888–1889, collated his material in 1913–1914 (Baillet 1920, 107–109), and published it. The multivolume result remains to the present day the main and nearly only source available for the study of the graffiti and dipinti (Baillet 1920–6 = *I. Syringes* 1–2126). A number of individual Greek and Coptic graffiti and dipinti have been restudied in recent years, illustrating that one should proceed with caution when using Baillet's copies and his general analysis and interpretation (Bataille 1952, 169; Speidel 1974). The published material is known to contain misreading (e.g., Tod 1925) and ghost names (e.g., Martin 1991, 357–358), while the dating of the graffiti and dipinti (e.g., Winnicki 1987 on re-dating several graffiti of the army commander Dryton, dated to the Roman period by Baillet, to the second century BC) and the interpretation of the origin of their writers (e.g., Baillet 1952, 170–171; Martin 1991, 358–359 on the Egyptian origin of Baillet's Scythian visitors) has been proven faulty. A new collation and detailed analysis of the graffiti and dipinti is urgently needed (e.g. Łukaszewicz 1999 on KV 9) that should be combined with a detailed study (especially prosopographical and palaeographical) of comparative material acquired from other sites since the publication of Baillet's study.

Only a dozen of in excess of 250 Demotic graffiti and dipinti known from the tombs in the royal wadi have thus far been published and analyzed (Winnicki 1987, 1995b; Vinson 2006), but a comprehensive publication of all Demotic material is currently being prepared by Eugene Cruz-Uribe, Jacqueline Jay, and Steve Vinson (Vinson 2010–2011: 131).

Visitors to the Valley of the Kings

Who were the people that visited the royal tombs, where did they come from, and when did they journey to Thebes? The currently available sources allow us to paint only a general picture of the visitors drawn to the Valley of the Kings in Greco–Roman times (Baillet 1920–1926, i–cxiv; Bataille 1952, 167–179). At least 10 royal tombs appear to have been open to the public in the main (eastern) valley at the time, while not a single visitor's graffito or dipinto attests the presence of tourists in the western valley. The rock-cut sepulchres all date to the Ramesside period and are, with the exception of the tomb of Seti II (KV 15), all located at the entrance or in the first section of the royal wadi. All tombs are characterized by large entrances followed by a succession of long, gently sloping corridors that make them relatively easy to access. A total of 2105 Greek; more than 250 Demotic; and several Latin, Cypriot, Lycian, and Phoenician graffiti and dipinti were left behind on the walls of the tombs of Ramesses II (KV 7), Merenptah (KV 8), Amenmesse (KV 10), Seti II (KV 15), Ramesses III (KV 11), Ramesses IV (KV 2), Ramesses V/VI (KV 9), Ramesses VII (KV 1), Ramesses IX (KV 6), and Ramesses XI

(KV 4). The largest number of Greek texts—almost half of all those recorded—occur in the tomb of Ramses V/VI (KV 9), once believed to be the tomb of the legendary Memnon (*I. Syringes* 1022–2017). KV 2, the last resting place of Ramesses IV, was the second most visited tomb according to the number of graffiti scratched into the plaster and rock and the dipinti written in black ink or painted in red (*I. Syringes* 133–789).

The graffiti and dipinti testify to almost 800 years of visitor presence in the royal wadi, with a climax in the first three centuries AD. Of the more than 2100 graffiti and dipinti, only 60 contain any chronological indication, with a mere 30 providing a precise date. The oldest documented inscription occurs in the tomb of Ramesses VII (KV 1) and dates to 278 BC or the reign of Ptolemaios II Philadelphos (*I. Syringes* 30). The youngest datable graffito comes from KV 2 (Ramesses IV) and the first half of the sixth century AD. It mentions Horion, the governor of the Thebaid from 537 AD onwards (*I. Syringes* 788; Baillet 1920–1926, xxiii, xxxviii, and lxxiii).

The ancient tourists visiting the valley appear to have come from all layers of society, from officials and dignitaries to soldiers and officers, philosophers and poets to common folk. They had journeyed from all corners of the Mediterranean region, including Asia Minor, Greece, Gaul, and Spain, but the vast majority of visitors were inhabitants of Thebes and immediately surrounding regions (both locals and immigrants: Bataille 1952, 170–171; Martin 1991, 356–357). A large number of the graffiti and dipinti containing an exact date fall in the early years of Roman Egypt, when one of the three Roman legions in Egypt was stationed in Thebes (until 23 AD; Speidel 1982) and soldiers from all over the ancient world serving in the Roman army paid a visit to the valley (e.g., *I. Syringes* 1733; Martin 1991, 359–360). The preferred season to visit the valley did not change dramatically through the millennia. More than half of the recorded visits had taken place between January and April, suggesting that ancient visitors, much like present day ones, preferred to journey to the royal wadi during the winter season. The tourists often did not limit their visit to a single tomb, but inscribed their names in several royal sepulchres (e.g., the Ptolemaic army commander Dryton in the tombs of Ramesses IV and V/VI: *I. Syringes* 306, 313, 413, 1780, and 1785). Most visitors did not journey on their own, but rather in groups with family members, friends, and/or colleagues, often leaving a mark of their joint visit by inscribing their names underneath one another (Baillet 1920–1926, xii–xix; Winnicki 1995a, 91).

The inscriptions often consist merely of the name of the visitor; at times the name of their father, their profession, city of origin, and a proskyneuma are added. Occasionally the author left behind a remark, often appreciating the workmanship that went into the scenes and inscriptions (the word *thauma*, "wonder," and its derivates regularly occur). There seems to be little evidence of a religious interest in the tombs (exceptions are *I. Syringes* 319 or 1054b) and hardly any understanding of the meaning of the decorative program depicted on their walls (e.g., *I. Syringes* 1405, but 1087 for a different point of view). One encounters poems (*I. Syringes* 1380), but also scathing comments (e.g., *I. Syringes* 1079, 1550, and 1613).

Except for references to the valley in the works of classical authors and the many graffiti and dipinti left behind on the tombs' walls, little else bears witness to the presence of visitors in the royal wadi in Greco–Roman times. A single coin dated to the reign of Emperor Maximian (287–305 AD), discovered in KV 9 (Ramesses V/VI), is one of the few objects left (accidentally) behind (Reeves and Wilkinson 1996, 165).

By the fourth century AD, there is an obvious decline in the number of visitors to the tombs and their original function seems to no longer be common knowledge. In Ammianus Marcellinus' *Res Gestae Libri* (22.15.30) the rock-cut tombs are considered to have been used as a safe haven at the time of natural calamities: "There are also subterranean syringes and winding passages which, it is said, those acquainted with the ancient rites, since they had foreknowledge that a deluge was coming and feared that the memory of the ceremonies might be destroyed, dug in the earth in many places with great labour; and on the walls of these caverns they carved many kinds of birds and beasts, and these countless forms of animals which they called hieroglyphic writing."

THE VALLEY OF THE KINGS IN BYZANTINE/ CHRISTIAN TIMES

The fourth century AD witnessed a dwindling number of tourists in the royal wadi and elsewhere on the Theban West Bank. With Christianity on the rise, the traditional religious landscape of Egypt was slowly being transformed beyond recognition. By the fifth to sixth centuries AD almost the entire population of the Theban West Bank had converted to Christianity. The town of Jeme, situated in and around the precinct of the temple of Ramesses III at Medinet Habu, became the main administrative and economic center. The town had already been in existence for almost 1500 years, but reached its peak in population and prosperity in the seventh and eight centuries AD. Other temples and monuments in this area were converted into monasteries and churches at that time. The monasteries of Phoibammon (Deir el–Bahri) and of Saint Mark (Gurnet Murai) belonged among the most important fully fledged monastic communities in the region, but smaller ones also existed, such as the Monastery of Epiphanius and the Monastery of Cyriacus. Many tombs on the Theban West bank served as refuges for hermits and monks or were reconstructed and turned into chapels or small churches, with a few simple dwellings constructed in the immediate vicinity to house small communities (Wilfong 1989; Wilfong 2002, 1–23; Lecuyot and Thirard 2008; Wipszycka 2009, 171–197).

Little activity took place in the Valley of the Kings during this period. It usually does not feature in overviews on Christianity in Egypt in general or on the Theban West Bank in particular, undoubtedly owing to the paucity of the material available and the general lack of interest in the Byzantine/Coptic period material culture during excavations in the royal wadi. Several of the tombs were at this time used as shelters by monks, with numerous graffiti and dipinti recording their names, prayers, and hymns in Coptic and depicting crosses and saints. A few of the tombs were also converted into chapels or small churches. The scantiness of the published archaeological material makes it difficult to establish whether the valley was inhabited continuously between the fourth/fifth and late sixth/early seventh century or whether individual monks and/or small communities settled repeatedly in the valley for limited periods of time. In general the Christian inhabitants of the tombs seem to have left most of the ancient Egyptian scenes and inscriptions undisturbed, in contrast to the destruction heaped upon many reliefs in numerous temples throughout the land. The ancient Egyptian imagery might have been seen as a portrayal of hell (and as such a vivid deterrent to sinners) by the anchorites dwelling in the tombs. The tomb of Ramesses VII (KV 1) is an exception as many of the figures of the ancient Egyptian deities in the burial chamber appear to have been damaged (especially the hands, feet, and faces) in Coptic times. The new residents also appear to have cleared out the debris that had collected in the entrance and the first sloping corridor(s) of several royal tombs. Whereas Greek and Latin graffiti and dipinti are located several meters above the original floor level in some tombs (e.g., KV 2), Coptic inscriptions and depictions can sometimes be found on a much lower level in the same location.

The main center of activities was located at and around the entrance to the eastern valley, especially in several smaller wadis branching off the main one, and concerns the royal tombs KV 1, KV 2, and KV 4 and the prince's tomb KV 3. The tomb of Ramesses IV (KV 2), located at the base of a hill on the northwest side of the main wadi, was reused as a chapel or small church. Herbert Winlock and Jules Baillet already considered it to be one of the most important Coptic sites in the royal wadi; the presence of more than 50 Coptic graffiti, including drawings of crosses and saints (e.g., TMP photos 10514 and 10515) on the walls of most corridors, two side chambers, and the burial chamber of the tomb confirms their assessment (Baillet 1920–1926, lxxii–lxxiii; Winlock and Crum 1926,18; Bickel 1990). KV 2 probably functioned in part as a cult place dedicated to Saint Ammônios and perhaps Saint Abraham (Delattre 2008, 188). Ammônios is depicted, together with an unidentified companion, in red ink on the right wall of corridor B (*I. Syringes* 780 = *SB Kopt.* I 474, TMP photo 10520). He is mentioned thrice more in the corridor: in an inscription in red ink by a certain Jacob, situated above the drawings of the two figures mentioned (Stern 1885: 100; Winlock and Crum 1926, 19 = *SB Kopt.* II 1058), in a sixth century inscription starting with an invocation that mentions, among other saints, Ammônios (*I. Syringes* 302 = *SEG* XLIV 1501; Derda and Łajtar 1994), and in the invocation of another inscription (*I. Syringes* 522). The name Ammônios also features several more times in Coptic inscriptions discovered in the vicinity of the Valley of the Kings, such as along the route leading from Deir el-Medina to the royal wadi (Delattre 2003, 371–373; Delattre 2008 for the complete dossier on saint Ammônios). The excavation of Edward R. Ayrton, employed by Theodore Davis, in the 1905–1906 season in the area in front of this tomb revealed the remains of a small limestone house and Coptic pottery and ostraca (e.g., Crum 1921, no. 388; O'Connell 2006, 130) located on top of a mud brick hut from Roman times. In front of the Roman house was an oven and two circular granaries (Davis and Ayrton 1908, 6–7; Winlock and Crum 1926, 18–19, 88 and plate 33b; Reeves 1984, 228 and plate 25a; Reeves 1990, 301, site 13).

KV 3, a small tomb most likely excavated for a son of Ramesses III in the first southeast branch of the main wadi, was transformed into a small yet elaborate chapel in the Byzantine period. The remains of the chapel found in the last but one chamber of the tomb (i.e., chamber H) consisted of a brick tiled floor and two Corinthian capitals, two bases and a part of a column, all carved from parts of an older sandstone temple located elsewhere. The tomb also yielded several Coptic lamps and jars (Winlock and Crum 1926, 19; Thomas 1966, 150–151; Romer 1981, 31; Reeves 1990, 133 and 319, site 37).

The tomb of the last Ramesside pharaoh Ramesses XI (KV 4) was used as a dwelling and stable in the Byzantine period. In the upper sections of the tomb, remains of a mud brick floor (corridors C–D) and a rough stone wall of a manger (between rooms E and F) testify to the adaptation of the tomb. Nine Coptic inscriptions and a depiction of a cross can be found in the entrance area of the tomb. A few decorated sherds, household debris, fragments of different cultivated plants, and a single, heavily corroded Byzantine copper coin were recovered during excavations in the tomb (Ciccarello and Romer 1979; Romer 1981, 31). Other royal tombs visited in Byzantine times were KV 1 (Ramesses VII), KV 8 (Merenptah) and KV 9 (Ramesses V/VI); all featured a few unpublished Coptic graffiti.

In the tombs of Ramesses II (KV 7), Merenptah (KV 8), Amenmesse (KV 10), Ramesses III (KV 11), Ramesses IV (KV 2), Ramesses V/VI (KV 9), and Ramesses VII (inside KV 1 and in a pile of debris to the south of the tomb's entrance), pottery sherds dating to the Late Roman/Coptic period have been found and partially studied. Amphorae (especially Late Roman B type) and cooking pots occur most frequently and can in general be dated to the fourth to sixth/seventh century AD. A number of sherds still had painted floral or cruciform decoration, while others had been written upon. It is not always possible to establish whether the ceramic material was actually used inside the tombs or entered the tomb at a later stage, brought in by flood water from elsewhere, but it clearly testifies that the royal wadi was inhabited during this period (Ertman 1993, 42; Brock 1995, 51, 53, 61–63; Guillaume and Emery-Barbier 1995; Leblanc 1996, 188, 191, 193, 198–199; Leblanc 1997, 155, 162, 164; Aston, Aston, and Brock 1998, 145, 149, 150, 159–161; Leblanc 1998, 78–79, 81, 86–87; Leblanc 2000, 99, 108, 112; Schaden and Ertman 1998, 128). The discovery of a Coptic rectangular sandstone stela, belonging to a woman named Souaei (EA 409; Hall 1905, 10, pl. 9) and of a rough wooden coffin containing the remains of a child in the wadi between KV 4 and KV 21 (Reeves 1990, 295, site 3) indicates that the tombs not only housed a small community, but that the valley was also once again used as a cemetery.

The western valley, which seems to have escaped the attention of visitors during the Greco–Roman period as no visitors' graffiti was left behind, became once again frequented in Late Antiquity. Late Roman/Coptic ware, especially amphorae and cooking pot sherds, were discovered in and around the tomb of Aye (WV 23), WV 24, and WV 25. The remains of the New Kingdom workmen's huts near these tombs were apparently reused as simple lodgings by hermits residing in the wadi (Schaden 1979, 164, 167 and plates IIIb and VIb; Schaden 1981, 56–58, 60; Schaden 1984, 46, 57, 63; Wilkinson 2004,

200). The eastern and western valleys appear to have been deserted in the course of the sixth or early seventh century AD.

CONCLUSION: THE VALLEY OF THE KINGS AFTER THE KINGS

The abandonment of the valley as a royal necropolis at the end of the New Kingdom quickly led to the wadi becoming a backwater on the Theban West bank. Following the dismantling and caching of the royal mummies in the Twenty-first Dynasty and early Twenty-second Dynasty, the valley was used for non-royal burials of individuals of lower rank throughout the Third Intermediate Period. Following years of neglect, with not a single burial securely dated to the Late Period, growing interest from visitors from all corners of the ancient world can be observed in Ptolemaic and especially Roman times, with a wealth of graffiti and dipinti attesting their presence. In Late Antiquity the valley hosted a small Christian community that reused a few tombs as lodgings and converted KV 2 and KV 3 into a church and a chapel.

BIBLIOGRAPHY

Aston, D. 2003. "The Theban West Bank from the Twenty-Fifth Dynasty to the Ptolemaic Period." In Strudwick and Taylor, 138–166.

Aston, D., B. Aston and E. C. Brock. 1998. "Pottery from the Valley of the Kings – Tombs of Merenptah, Ramesses III, Ramesses IV, Ramesses VI and Ramesses VII." *Ägypten und Levante* 8: 137–214.

Baillet, J. 1920. "Les graffiti grecs dans les tombeaux des rois à Thèbes d'Égypte." *Comptes rendus de l'Académie des Inscriptions et Belles-lettres* 64(2): 107–116.

Baillet, J. 1920–1926. *Inscriptions grecques et latines des Tombeaux des Rois ou syringes.* MIFAO 42. Cairo.

Bataille, A. 1951. "Thèbes gréco–romaine." *Chronique d'Égypte* 26: 325–353.

Bataille, A. 1952. *Les Memnonia: Recherches de payrologie et d'épigraphie grecque sur la nécropole de la Thèbes d'Egypte aux époques hellénistiques et romaine.* Cairo.

Bernand, A. and E. Bernand. 1960. *Les inscriptions grecques et latines du Colosse de Memnon.* Cairo.

Bickel, S. 1990. "Die Koptische Graffiti." In Hornung, 134–137.

Brock, E. C. 1995. "The Clearance of the Tomb of Ramesses VII." In Wilkinson, 47–67.

Capasso, M., ed. 1995. *Papiri documentari greci: Papyrologica Lupiensia* 2. Galatina.

Ciccarello, M. and J. Romer. 1979. *Theban Royal Tomb Project: A Preliminary Report of the Recent Work in the Tombs of Rameses X and XI in the Valley of the Kings.* Brooklyn.

Crum, W. E. 1921. *Short Texts from Coptic Ostraca and Papyri.* London.

Cruz–Uribe, E. and S. Vinson. 2005–2006. "Two Early Demotic Ostraca from the Valley of the Kings." *Journal of the American Research Center in Egypt* 42: 113–117.

Davis, T. M., ed. 1908. *The Tomb of Siptah: The Monkey Tomb and the Gold Tomb.* London.

Davis, T. M. and E. R. Ayrton. 1908. "The Excavations during the Winters of 1905–1906." In Davis, 6–8.

Delattre, A. 2003. "Graffitis de la montagne thébaine. II." *Chronique d'Égypte* 78: 371–380.

Delattre, A. 2008. "Inscriptions grecques et coptes de la montaigne thébaine relatives au culte de saint Ammônios." In Delattre and Heilporn, 183–188.

Delattre, A. and P. Heilporn, eds. 2008. *"Et maintenant ce ne sont plus que des villages...". Thèbes et sa région aux époques hellénistique, romaine et byzantine. Actes du colloque tenu à Bruxelles les 2 et 3 décembre 2005.* Papyrologica Bruxellensia 34. Brussels.

Derda, T. and A. Łajtar. 1994. "A Christian Prayer from Ramses IVth Tomb in the Theban Valley of the Kings." *Journal of Juristic Papyrology* 24: 19–22.

Ertman, E. 1993. "A First Report on the Preliminary Survey of Unexcavated KV10." *Kmt* 4(2): 38–46.

Gauthier, H. 1908. "Rapport sur une campagne de fouilles à Drah Abou'l Neggah en 1906." *Bulletin de l'Institut Français d'Archéologie Orientale* 6: 121–171.

Guillaume, A. and A. Emery-Barbier. 1995. "Le remplissage sédimentaire de la tombe de Ramsès II." *Memnonia VI*: 148–173.

Hall, H. R. 1905. *Coptic and Greek Texts of the Christian Period from Ostraka, Stelae, etc. in the British Museum.* London.

Hawass, Z. A. and K. Daoud, eds. 2005. *Studies in Honor of Ali Radwan.* Supplement *ASAE* 34. Cairo.

Hayes, W. C. 1935. *Royal Sarcophagi of the XVIII Dynasty.* Princeton.

Hornung, E., ed. 1990. *Zwei Ramessidische Königsgräber: Ramses IV. und Ramses VII.* Mainz.

Kondo, J. "A Preliminary Report on the Re-clearance of the Tomb of Amenophis III (WV 22)." In Reeves, 41–54.

Łajtar, A. 2006. *Deir el-Bahari in the Hellenistic and Roman Period: A Study of an Egyptian Temple Based on Greek Sources. The Journal of Juristic Papyrology,* Supplement 4. Warsaw.

Łajtar, A. 2012. "The Theban Region under the Roman Empire." In Riggs, 171–188.

Leblanc, C. 1996. "Trois campagnes de fouille dans la tombe de Ramsès II. KV 7 – Vallée des Rois – 1993/1994/1995." *Memnonia VII*: 185–211.

Leblanc, C. 1997. "Quatrième campagne de fouille dans la tombe de Ramsès II (KV 7) – 1996–1997." *Memnonia VIII*: 151–172.

Leblanc, C. 1998. "Cinquième campagne de fouille dans la tombe de Ramsès II (KV 7) – 1997–1998." *Memnonia IX*: 73–91.

Leblanc, C. 2000. "Sixième et septième campagnes de fouille dans la tombe de Ramsès II (KV 7) – Années 1998/1999 et 1999/2000." *Memnonia XI*: 91–116.

Lecuyot, G. and C. Thirard. 2008. "La montagne thébaine à l'époque copte à travers ses vestiges archéologiques." In Delattre and Heilporn: 125–136.

Letronne, J. A. 1848. *Recueil des inscriptions grecques et latines d'Egypte II.* Paris.

Łukaszewicz, A. 1999. "Valley of the Kings. Epigraphical Survey in the Tomb of Ramesses VI (KV 9)." *PAMR* 11: 191–194.

Martin, A. 1991. "De quelques inscriptions des Syringes." *Chronique d'Égypte* 66: 356–360.

Mynářová, J. and P. Onderka, eds. 2007. *Thebes: City of Gods and Pharaohs.* Prague.

Niwiński, A. 2005. "The Three Phases of Robberies in the Valley of the Kings and New Archaeological Evidence of the Tomb Robbers' Technique obtained during works of the Polish–Egyptian Cliff Mission at Deir el–Bahari." In Hawass and Daoud, 213–222.

Niwiński, A. 2007. "The Story of Thebes in the Third Intermediate Period." In Mynářová and Onderka, 161–171.

O'Connell, E. R. 2006. "Ostraca from Western Thebes: Provenance and History of the Collections at the Metropolitan Museum of Art and at Columbia University." *The Bulletin of the American Society of Papyrologists* 43: 113–137.

Petrie, W. M. F. 1909. *Qurneh*. London.

Reeves, C. N. 1984. "Excavations in the Valley of the Kings 1905/6." *Mitteilungen des Deutschen Archäologischen Instituts, Abteilung Kairo* 40: 227–235.

Reeves, C. N. 1990. *Valley of the Kings: The Decline of a Royal Necropolis*. London.

Reeves, C. N., ed. 1992. *After Tutankhamun: Research and Excavation in the Royal Necropolis at Thebes*. London and New York.

Reeves, C. N. and R. H. Wilkinson. 1996. *The Complete Valley of the Kings: Tombs and Treasures of Egypt's Greatest Pharaohs*. London.

Riggs, C. 2003. "The Egyptian Funerary Tradition at Thebes in the Roman Period." In Strudwick and Taylor, 189–201.

Riggs, C., ed. 2012. *The Oxford Handbook of Roman Egypt*. Oxford.

Romer, J. 1981. *Valley of the Kings*. New York.

Rutherford, I. C. 2012. "Travel and Pilgrimage." In Riggs: 701–716.

Schaden O. J. 1979. "Preliminary Report on the Re-clearance of Tomb 25 in the Western Valley of the Kings." *Annales du Service des Antiquités de l'Égypte* 63: 161–168.

Schaden, O. J. 1981. "Preliminary Report on the Clearing of WV-24 in an Effort to Determine its Relationship to Royal Tombs 23 and 25." *Kmt* 2(3): 53–61.

Schaden, O. J. 1984. "Clearance of the Tomb of King Ay (WV-23)." *Journal of the American Research Center in Egypt* 21: 39–64.

Schaden, O. J. and E. Ertman. 1998. "The Tomb of Amenmesse (KV 10): The First Season." *Annales du Service des Antiquités de l'Égypte* 73: 115–155.

Speidel, M.-P. 1974. "Two Greek Graffiti in the Tomb of Ramses V." *Chronique d'Égypte* 49: 384–386.

Speidel, M.-P. 1982. "Augustus' Deployment of the Legions in Egypt." *Chronique d'Égypte* 57: 120–124.

Stern, L. 1885. "Koptische Inschriften an alten Denkmälern." *Zeitschrift für Ägyptische Sprache und Altertumskunde* 22: 96–102.

Strudwick, N. 2003. "Some Aspects of the Archaeology of the Theban Necropolis in the Ptolemaic and Roman Periods." In Strudwick and Taylor, 167–188.

Strudwick, N. and J. Taylor, eds. 2003. *The Theban Necropolis: Past, Present and Future*. London.

Taylor, J. H. 1992. "Aspects of the History of the Valley of the Kings in the Third Intermediate Period." In Reeves, 186–206.

Thomas, E. 1966. *The Royal Necropoleis of Thebes*. Princeton.

Tod, M. N. 1925. "Notes on Some Greek Graffiti." *Journal of Egyptian Archaeology* 11: 256–258.

Vinson, S. 2006. "Djedor Was Here: Ancient Graffiti in the Valley of the Kings." *BARCE* 189: 19–21.

Vinson, S. 2010–2011. "A Bi-graphic (Greek and Demotic) Graffito from the Tomb of Ramses IV in the Valley of the Kings (KV 2)." *Enchoria* 32: 131–134.

Wilfong, T. C. 1989. "Western Thebes in the Seventh and Eighth Centuries: A Bibliographic Survey of Jême and Its Surroundings." *Bulletin of the American Society of Papyrologists* 26(1–2): 89–145.

Wilfong, T. C. 2002. *Women of Jeme: Lives in a Coptic Town in Late Antique Egypt*. Ann Arbor.

Wilkinson, R. H., ed. 1995. *Valley of the Sun Kings: New Explorations in the Tombs of the Pharaohs*. Tucson.

Wilkinson, R. H., ed. 2004. "University of Arizona Egyptian Expedition: Western Valley of the Kings Project (2000–2001). Final Report." *Annales du Service des Antiquités de l'Égypte* 78: 199–204.

Winlock, H. E. and W. E. Crum. 1926. *The Monastery of Epiphanius at Thebes. I The Archaeological Material; The Literary Material.* New York.

Winnicki, J. K. 1987. "Vier demotische Graffiti in den Königsgräbern von Theben." *Enchoria* 15: 163–167.

Winnicki, J. K. 1995a. "Der Besuch Drytons in de Königsgräbern von Theben." In Capasso: 89–94.

Winnicki, J. K. 1995b. "Zwei demotische Namen." *Journal of Juristic Papyrology* 25: 171–174.

Wipszycka, E. 2009. *Moines et communautés monastiques en Egypte (IVe–VIIIe siecles). The Journal of Juristic Papyrology*, Supplements 11. Warsaw.

CHAPTER 32

THE HISTORY OF KV EXPLORATION PRIOR TO THE LATE TWENTIETH CENTURY

JOYCE TYLDESLEY

THE Valley of the Kings was never a "lost" archaeological site; many of its emptied tombs remained open and obvious throughout the postdynastic age. But its original purpose—reflected in its local name, Wadi Biban el-Moluk (Valley of the Gates of the Kings)—quickly became a hazy memory. No one knew how many tombs there were, no one knew when they had been built, and as the hieroglyphic script had become unreadable, no one knew who had built them.

EARLY EXPLORERS

The Arab invasion of 641/642 C.E. had effectively isolated Egypt from the west. Southern Egypt, in particular, was regarded as lawless territory, and few visitors felt the need to travel beyond the relative safety of Cairo (Clayton 1982, 9). This situation continued until the European Renaissance saw a new western interest in the ancient world. With stability restored, Egypt started to attract increasing numbers of merchants and pilgrims, who concentrated their activities in the north of the country, and missionaries and explorers who were determined to discover what lay in the "interior." Having made their way to Luxor, they saw rubbish-covered ruins but failed to recognize Homer's "Hundred-gated Thebes," despite the fact that it had been mapped by the Flemish geographer Abraham Ortelius in 1595 (Reeves and Wilkinson 1996, 52).

In 1668 Father Charles François visited "the place of the mummies called Biban el Melouk" without understanding its true nature. Forty years later, Father Claude Sicard, the French supervisor of the Jesuit mission in Cairo, made the connection: he recognized the Karnak and Luxor temples as the remains of ancient Thebes and identified ten tombs in the valley (quoted in Romer 1981, 32):

> These sepulchres of Thebes are tunnelled into the rock and are of astonishing depth. Halls, rooms, all are painted from top to bottom. The variety of colours, which are almost as fresh as the day they were painted, gives an admirable effect. There are as many hieroglyphs as there are animals and objects represented, which makes us suppose that we have there the story of the lives, virtues, acts, combats and victories of the princes who are buried there, but it is impossible for us to decipher them for the present.

The Danish captain, author, and artist Frederic Norden explored Egypt in 1737–1738 at the request of King Christian VI; his visit was recorded in his illustrated *Voyage d'Egypte et de Nubie* (1755). Norden's English contemporary, Reverend Richard Pococke, also visited in the 1730s; his account of his adventures, *A Description of the East, and Some Other Countries* (1743), included a beautifully drawn but highly inaccurate map (Pococke 1743, 246):

> The vale where these grottos are, may be about one hundred yards wide. There are signs of about eighteen of them. However, it is to be remarked that Diodorus says seventeen of them only remained till the time of the Ptolemies; and I found the entrances to about that number, most of which he says were destroyed in his time, and now there are only nine that can be entered into.

The Scottish explorer James Bruce visited the valley in 1768. He was able to enter at least two open tombs and found himself fascinated by a wall scene showing three harpists. He started to draw the musicians, but was forced to abandon his work when his guides encouraged him to leave lest he be attacked by bandits. The inclusion of his fanciful sketch in his *Travels to Discover the Source of the Nile* (1790) caused great public interest, and the tomb became known as the "Tomb of the Harpists," or "Bruce's Tomb." Today it is identified as KV 11 (Ramesses III).

In 1792, William George Browne was able to enter three tombs, including KV 11. After noting that Bruce's now famous scene must have been drawn "from memory," he added to the decoration by inscribing his own name. It is from his *Travels in Africa, Egypt and Syria* that we learn of the first excavation in the valley, conducted by the son of Sheikh Hamam in the previous thirty years "in expectation of finding treasure."

Napoleon's Savants

On July 1, 1798, Napoleon Bonaparte invaded Egypt. Included on Napoleon's civilian staff was the Commission des Sciences et Arts d'Égypte, a group of eminent scholars tasked with investigating and recording the natural and ancient history of Egypt (Reeves 2000, 11–12). The army reached Thebes in January 1799. Two commission members—engineers Prosper Jollois and Édouard de Villiers du Terrage—were subsequently able to identify and map sixteen open or partially blocked tombs in the main valley (KV 1–11, 13–15, 18, 20) and to discover a tomb in the newly identified Western Valley (WV 22, Amenhotep III).

Working alongside the commission was Baron Dominique Vivant Denon, a renowned artist, writer, and diplomat. Traveling with the army as they pursued the remains of the Mameluk forces southward, Denon recorded many of Egypt's sites under the most difficult conditions (quoted in Clayton 1982, 23):

> Circumstances arising from the unsettled state of the country, and the necessary subserviance of my own particular designs to the military operations, had in many instances prevented me from taking a more than hasty glimpse of objects that would have amply recompensed a longer stay; but even if my researches shall have no other effects than abridging the future labours of those who may succeed me in a time of greater tranquility.

In 1802 Denon anticipated the findings of the commission by publishing his *Voyages dans la Basse et la Haute Égypte*. This included an account of his visit to the valley. In just three hours Denon had visited six open tombs, noting that although the heavy stone sarcophagi remained in place, "all the tombs are violated."

The work of the commission was published between 1809 and 1828 as nine volumes of text and eleven volumes of plates (two volumes of which were dedicated to the Theban monuments), entitled *Description de l'Égypte, ou, Recueil des Observations et des Recherches qui ont été faites en Égypte pendant l'expédition de l'armée française*. Ancient Egypt was already fashionable among the western elite, and the hugely popular *Description* sparked a new interest in "Nile style," which was intensified by Jean Francois Champollion's 1822 decoding of the hieroglyphic script. It was now possible to read the texts on the tomb walls. As Egypt's long history was revealed, Egyptian antiquities—until then admired for their beauty but considered to be artistic dead ends irrelevant to the development of western civilization—were suddenly in demand (Tyldesley 2005, 44–67).

THE GREAT BELZONI

Giovanni Battista Belzoni was an Italian-born hydraulic engineer who became an Egyptologist by accident (Mayes 1959). Having traveled to Egypt in 1815 to demonstrate a water-lifting device to Mohamed Ali (the demonstration was a failure), he started to work for the British consul-general, Henry Salt. Salt, and his French counterpart and rival, Bernadino Drovetti, were busy collecting—with a view to selling—Egypt's large-scale antiquities. Each was to amass a significant private collection, and these eventually formed the basis of the collections in the British Museum and the Louvre Museum (Salt) and Turin Museum and the Louvre (Drovetti).

Salt sent Belzoni to Luxor to acquire the "Young Memnon," a colossal head of Ramesses II. His mission accomplished and other adventures concluded Belzoni visited the valley to assess the red granite sarcophagus of Ramesses III in KV 11. Here he discovered and retrieved the lid, breaking it in the process, and shipped it to Alexandria. Ultimately, the lid would be displayed in the Fitzwilliam Museum, Cambridge, while the base would enter the collection of the Louvre Museum (Mojsov 2012, 277).

In 1816 Belzoni accidentally discovered WV 23 (Aye). He showed little interest in his find (Belzoni 1820, 150):

> I cannot boast of having made a great discovery in this tomb, though it contains several curious and singular painted figures on the walls; and from its extent, and part of a sarcophagus remaining in the centre of a large chamber, have reason to suppose, that it was the burial place of some person of distinction. . . . I declare, that I owe this discovery merely to fortune, not to any premeditated research, as I went into these mountains only to examine the various places where the water descends from the desert into the valleys after rain.

WV 23 was finally cleared by American Egyptologist Otto Schaden in 1972. In 1817 Belzoni found a second entrance near WV 23 and forced his way through its doorway with a battering ram. This unfinished tomb (WV 25) housed eight intrusive Twenty-second Dynasty mummies.

In search of an intact royal tomb, Belzoni returned to the main valley. He knew that Strabo had been told by the Egyptian priest that there might be as many as forty-seven tombs, a mixture of royal and nonroyal, yet the commission had only recorded sixteen (Belzoni 1820, 198). His engineer's eye allowed him to scan the cliffs and detect hidden tombs at an astonishing rate, discovering KV 16, 17, 19, 21, 30, and 31 plus WV 23 and 25. In addition, he pointed out two likely find-spots to Lord and Lady Belmore, who conducted their own excavation and discovered the private tombs KV 30 and 31 (Reeves and Wilkinson 1996, 56–60).

Belzoni's first discovery, made on October 9, 1817, was KV 19: the unfinished, beautifully painted tomb built for Mentuherkhepeshef, son of Ramesses IX, and home to two intrusive mummies. On the same day Belzoni found an uninscribed and undecorated tomb (KV 21) holding two more intrusive mummies. On October 10, 1817, Belzoni discovered KV 16 (Ramesses I) (Belzoni 1820, 200):

> Having proceeded through a passage thirty-two feet long and eight feet wide, I descended a staircase of twenty-eight feet, and reached a tolerably large and well-painted room. . . . We found a sarcophagus of granite, with two mummies in it, and in a corner a statue standing erect, six feet six inches high, and beautifully cut out of sycamore wood.

The Two Mummies Were Intrusive Burials

On October 16, 1817, Belzoni made his most spectacular discovery: a long, deep tomb, which he identified as the "tomb of Apis," but which we now know to be the tomb of Seti I (KV 17). Belzoni found hundreds of wooden shabtis, plus the remains of an embalmed bull, but the real treasure was Seti's alabaster sarcophagus, carved with scenes and verses from the Book of Gates. Belzoni took ten days to empty KV 17. He then recorded the wall scenes, making a series of hasty and inaccurate watercolors and taking wax impressions that, unknown to him, dulled the once-bright paintwork. Belzoni left the valley for the last time in January 1819. He had some words of advice for those who might be tempted to follow in his footsteps (Belzoni 1820): "It is my firm opinion, that in the Valley of Beban el Malook, there are no more [tombs] than are now known."

NUMBERING AND RECORDING THE TOMBS

As there was no official numbering system employed in the valley, individual excavators used their own alphabetical or numerical systems to order the tombs. English Egyptologist John Gardner Wilkinson ended this confusion when, in 1827, he surveyed, numbered, and mapped the twenty-one known tombs, personally painting a number beside each entrance (Reeves and Wilkinson 1996, 61–62). The tombs in the Western Valley were given their own numbering system (W1–W4). Today, Wilkinson's system is still in use, with some modifications. Tombs KV (Kings' Valley) 1–21 are the tombs identified by Wilkinson, their distribution reflecting the walk he took around the valley with his paint pot. The tombs in the Western Valley have been added into the number sequence and are known as either KV or as WV tombs. Subsequent "tombs," be they royal tombs, elite tombs, unfinished tombs, or simple pits, have been added to the list as and when discovered.

While Wilkinson numbered twenty-one tombs in the valley, his unpublished sketch map confirms that as many as twenty-eight were known (Reeves and Wilkinson 1996, 61–62). James Burton surveyed the valley in 1825 and was able to identify twenty-five tombs. His work in the valley included brief examinations of KV 20 and KV 5 (both of which proved impassable) and important work to reduce flood risk in the valley. This work was never published, but it is recorded in his diaries and notebooks, which are now part of the British Museum collection. Meanwhile, Burton's distant cousin, Robert Hay, was another enthusiastic visitor to the valley. Basing himself in KV 2 (Ramesses IV), he recorded up to twenty-three tombs. His work, too, is unpublished; his notebooks and drawings are now in the British Library.

In 1828–1829 Champollion made his first and only visit to Egypt. As part of a joint Franco-Tuscan expedition, working alongside Ippolito Rosselini, he spent two months living in KV 9 (Ramesses VI). From this base he recorded the tomb walls, concentrating on the hieroglyphic inscriptions, which would allow him to allocate owners to the tombs. A letter written to his brother confirms that his team had access to sixteen tombs (Reeves and Wilkinson 1996, 65):

> Arriving in Biban el-Molouk, I impatiently assured myself that the sixteen tombs (I am only talking here about the tombs whose sculpture has been preserved and the names of kings for whom they were hewn) were really, as I had previously argued for several reasons, those of kings belonging to Theban dynasties, that is princes whose family came from Thebes.

His team also carried out some clearance work in KV 16 (Ramesses I) and KV 7 (Ramesses II), and conducted what they considered to be an act of conservation. A flash flood had invaded Seti's now-open tomb, and some of the wall paintings had been damaged. Champollion's solution was to cut out two scenes, which were sent to the collections in Florence and the Louvre. Seti's tomb suffered further damage when the Prussian expedition, led by Karl Richard Lepsius, demolished a painted column in order to secure a scene. The Prussians spent four years in Egypt, with October 1844–February 1845 dedicated to recording the valley. A map was made showing twenty-one tombs in the main valley and four in the Western Valley, tomb scenes were copied, and there was some excavation in KV 7 (Ramesses II), KV 8 (Merenptah), and KV 20 (Thutmose I and Hatshepsut). This work was published as part of the *Denkmäler aus Aegypten und Aethiopien* (1849–1859).

During the 1850s Scotsman Alexander Rhind conducted trial excavations in the valley. He discovered nothing, and left the valley echoing Belzoni's words (Rhind 1862, 145):

> As for the Bab el-Molook, having dug at I believe every available spot it presented, not bearing evidence of previous search, I feel reasonably confident that no more sepulchres except those already known, exist within its proper limits

By the later nineteenth century it was recognized that Egypt's monuments were a valuable and finite resource in need of protection. In 1858 Said Pasha established the National Antiquities Service and appointed French Egyptologist Auguste Mariette as its director-general. The next year, Said Pasha established a national museum in the Bulaq area of Cairo. There was now official control over work in the valley, with Mariette alone able to license excavations. This was important: tourists were descending on Luxor in ever-increasing numbers, and antiquities, real or fake, legally excavated or not, were in great demand.

Mariette himself undertook an extensive program of excavation, which included the valley. He increased the number of known tombs from the twenty-one known in 1835 to twenty-five; unfortunately his workmen were untrained and badly supervised, and Mariette himself was rarely present on site, so it is not possible to determine which new tombs he added to the list.

VICTOR LORET

Many royal tombs had been discovered in the valley, but none was intact. Where were Egypt's ancient kings? In 1881 this question was in part answered when a cache of New Kingdom royal mummies, housed in a private tomb at Deir el-Bahri (DB 320), was discovered. Here were, among others, the labeled bodies of Ahmose I, Amenhotep I, Thutmose I–III, Ramesses I, Seti I, Ramesses II, Ramesses III, and Ramesses IX. It was now apparent that at least some of the royal tombs had been officially emptied, and their stripped mummies put into storage, long before the end of the dynastic age (Reeves 2000, 64–66).

The discovery of the Deir el-Bahri cache inspired Eugène Lefébure, director of the French Archaeological Mission in Cairo, to conduct a survey of the valley, incorporating tomb plans (including the previously unpublished KV 26–29, 37, 40, and 51, and WV 22 and 25) and all major texts and wall scenes. Lefébure worked at a frantic pace, producing copies which, despite being rough and ready, were extremely useful. His work, published in two volumes as *Les Hypogées royaux de Thèbes* (1886 and 1889), provided an invaluable reference manual for future archaeologists.

In 1888 George Daressey, of the Bulaq Museum, conducted clearance work in KV 9 (Ramesses VI) and KV 6 (Ramesses IX): his finds were, however, meager. Next came Victor Loret, the French director of the Antiquities Service from 1897 to 1899. Loret had all the luck that Daressey had lacked: in 1888 he discovered eight new tombs plus some pits, and in 1889 he discovered a further seven tombs (KV 26–32, 34–41, KV L–M). In addition, he systematically cleared and re-explored some of the previously known tombs.

On February 12, 1898, Loret's team discovered KV 34 (Thutmose III), high within the southern cliffs of the valley. The beautifully decorated tomb yielded an impressive assortment of damaged funerary goods plus a fine, cartouche-shaped quartzite sarcophagus. On March 9, 1898, the team found KV 35 (Amenhotep II). The new tomb was long and dangerous, with steep stairways, low ceilings, and an open well-shaft. In the corridor there was a small wooden boat, and on the boat there was a body (Loret 1899),

> all black and hideous, its grinning face turning towards me and looking at me, its long brown hair in sparse bunches around its head. I did not dream for an instant that this was just an unwrapped mummy. The legs and arms seemed to be bound. A hole exposed the sternum, there was an opening in the skull. Was this a victim of a human sacrifice? Was this a thief murdered by his accomplices in a bloody division of the loot, or perhaps he was killed by soldiers or by police interrupting the pillaging of the tomb?

The burial chamber housed an open quartzite sarcophagus holding a (noncontemporary) coffin. And in the coffin lay Amenhotep II himself, the first king to have been found lying in his own tomb in the valley. Like the Deir el-Bahri cache mummies, he had been stripped of his original bandages and jewelry and carefully rewrapped.

A side chamber in the same tomb held nine coffins bearing royal names. Here, among others, lay mummies identified as Thutmose IV, Amenhotep III, Seti II, Siptah, and Ramesses IV–VI. A sealed side chamber leading off the main pillared hall yielded a further three mummies (two male and one female), each unwrapped and uncoffined, with a damaged head and abdomen. The mummies were all left in the tomb, just as they had been found.

PROTECTING THE TOMBS

The highly efficient French Egyptologist Gaston Maspero had two spells as director of the national museum and head of the Antiquities Service, from 1881 to 1886 and 1899 to 1914. During his second period of office he transferred the museum to central Cairo. In order to improve administration within the Antiquities Department, he created posts for two chief inspectors, one based in the north and one based in the south, at Luxor. Each inspector would take responsibility for excavation and conservation in his own area; he would ensure that the sites were properly excavated, guarded, and conserved, and would investigate any theft or act of vandalism. The first southern inspector was the young English archaeologist Howard Carter. He assumed responsibility for a 500-mile stretch of sites, including the Theban monuments and the valley.

A robbery in KV 35—the mummy on the boat was stolen, and Amenhotep II was stripped of his bandages—demonstrated just how vulnerable the exposed tombs were. One of Carter's first acts was therefore to fit secure iron gates and grilles to the open tombs. At the same time he installed electric lights in the six most popular tombs (KV 6, 9, 11, 16, 17, 35). There was conservation work in several tombs (KV 16, 11, 9, 6), and Amenhotep II was restored and returned to KV 35 (he would be transferred to the safety of Cairo Museum in 1931). To cater for the ever-increasing numbers of tourists, the valley paths were widened and a donkey park and shelter was established.

In 1900–1901 Carter cleared KV 42 (originally identified as Thutmose II; now known to be Hatshepsut-Meryet-Ra) and KV 44 (a private tomb housing intrusive Twenty-second Dynasty burials). In 1901–1902 he excavated near the entrance to KV 18 (Ramesses X) and elsewhere in the main valley. In 1903–1904, Robert Mond financed Carter's restoration of KV 17 (Seti I), and a "Mrs. Goff" donated £10, which was used to restore KV 15 (Seti II).

THEODORE DAVIS

Theodore Davis was a retired American businessman who, having visited Egypt as a tourist, became obsessed with the idea of finding an intact royal tomb. Davis was extremely wealthy, but he lacked practical archaeological skills and so, in 1902, he agreed to fund Carter's excavations on behalf of the Antiquities Service. This was an arrangement that suited everyone. The Antiquities Service, always short of money, would be able to conduct excavations in the valley, while Davis—now the only person allowed to excavate in the valley—seemed assured of a good find. As Carter explains (unpublished sketch quoted in Reeves and Wilkinson 1996, 73):

> I put the following proposition to him. The Egyptian Government would be willing, when my duties permitted, for me to carry out researches in the Valley of the tombs of the Kings on his behalf, if he would be wiling on his part to cover the costs thereof, that the Egyptian Government in return for his generosity would be pleased, wherever it was possible, to give him any duplicate antiquities resulting [from] these researches.

Work began in the area between KV 2 (Ramesses IV) and KV 7 (Ramesses II), but the results were poor. Carter moved his workmen and, near KV 4 (Ramesses XI), uncovered KV 45, a small shaft tomb holding two Twenty-second Dynasty mummies, each in a double coffin. Moving closer to KV 36 (the courtier Maiherpre), he discovered an assortment of finds, including a painted wooden box housing a pair of Maiherpre's leather loincloths, and fragments of a wooden box or coffin bearing the name of Amenhotep III.

In 1903 Carter moved to the area near KV 21 (owner unknown) and discovered KV 60 (the royal nurse Sit-Ra, called In), a simple, single-chambered tomb. On January 18 he discovered KV 43 (Thutmose IV). This elaborately decorated tomb yielded some of the original grave goods: broken vessels, the remains of a war-chariot, and a quartzite sarcophagus. Less typically there was a male mummy—the king's son Webensenu, perhaps—propped against the wall of a side chamber. The next month saw a brief investigation in KV 60 followed by a more detailed investigation into the complex, uninscribed KV 20 (built for Thutmose I; subsequently extended to include Hatshepsut). This was a far from "lost" tomb; it had been known since the time of the Napoleonic expedition, but it had always been deemed impassable, its corridors blocked by a solid mass of rubble, mud, and small stones. It was to take two seasons to reach the burial chamber (Davis [1906] 2004, xiii):

> [T]he air had become so bad, and the heat so great, that the candles carried by the workmen melted, and would not give enough light to enable them to continue their work; consequently we were compelled to install electric lights, in the form of hand wires. . . . As soon as we got down about 50 metres, the air became so foul that the men could not work. In addition to this, the bats of centuries had built innumerable nests on the ceilings of the corridors and chambers, and their excrement had become so dry that the least stir of the air filled the corridors with a fluffy black stuff, which choked the noses and mouths of the men, rendering it most difficult for them to breathe.

When Carter was transferred to northern Egypt, Davis started to work with the replacement inspector, James Quibell. On February 5, 1905, Quibell discovered KV 46, the double burial of Yuya and Thuyu, parents of Queen Tiye. This was an astonishing discovery. Although the tomb had been robbed, it was to all intents complete, and the two mummies still lay in their golden coffins, surrounded by a remarkable collection of grave goods (Davis [1907] 2000).

In late 1905—when Arthur Weigall had replaced Quibell as southern inspector—Davis stopped financing excavations by the Antiquities Service and instead employed freelance Egyptologist Edward Ayrton. Weigall welcomed this as a positive development: he would continue to inspect Davis's work and would take charge of any major find, but in the meantime, he was free to attend to his many other responsibilities. But the change marked a downturn in the standard of Davis's already hurried archaeological work. Ayrton was well trained but young; he found it difficult to resist the demand for rapid results at the expense of scientific caution.

Ayrton's first task was to tidy up the excavations of previous years. He started work in the Western Valley, where he found nothing of importance. He then transferred to the main valley, where he worked first in the region of KV 12 (owner unknown), and then close by KV 43 (Thutmose IV). Here he found an unfinished tomb entrance (KV B). After working near KV 46 (Yuya and Thuya), he moved closer to KV 2 (Ramesses IV) and discovered an eclectic collection of Ramesside shabtis, ostraca, and postdynastic artifacts. Work then moved back to the area around KV 12, where further small antiquities were discovered.

In November 1905 Ayrton embarked on an archaeological sweep of the valley, working northward from KV 34 (Thutmose III). This led to more small finds and a new tomb. KV 47 (Siptah) was filled with hardened mud and proved extremely difficult to excavate. The work would eventually be finished by Harry Burton in 1912. This was followed by a series of finds: KV 49 (unfinished tomb), KV 50–52 (tombs housing mummified animals, possibly connected with Amenhotep II), KV 48 (vizier Amenemipet), and KV 53 (unknown owner).

The next season began on January 1, 1907. Just six days later Ayrton discovered KV 55, a uniquely complex Eighteenth Dynasty cache tomb housing material from the Amarna burials of Akhenaten, Tiye, Kiya, and (probably) Semenkhkare. By January 28 KV 55 had been (to a limited extent) photographed and emptied, the grave goods packed into boxes— "everything that is to be moved is out of the tomb"—and sent by steamer to the Cairo Museum. The male mummy, now reduced to a skeleton, had been identified as Tiye herself. Davis never wavered in his conviction that he had discovered the queen, and it was as *The Tomb of Queen Tiyei* that he published his findings (Davis [1910] 2001; see also Bell 1990).

Davis went on to make more finds, the most important of which was KV 57 (Horemheb). When Ayrton resigned in 1908—the strain of having worked for the demanding Davis having proved too much—he employed the Welsh archaeologist and draftsman Harold Jones as his successor. Jones made a series of minor discoveries until he became too ill to work. He was succeeded by Harry Burton, who did valuable conservation work, but who made no major finds.

Davis was bitterly disappointed. The sequence of Eighteenth Dynasty kings was now tolerably well understood, and it was clear that Tutankhamun had neither a tomb nor a mummy. Davis had always hoped that he would find his intact tomb. In fact he had found three important clues. In 1905–1906 Ayrton's team had discovered a faience cup bearing Tutankhamun's name. In 1907 they had found a small pit (KV 54) housing what were eventually identified as the remains of Tutankhamun's embalming materials (Winlock [1941] 2010). And in 1909 Jones's team had discovered a small chamber (KV 58) that yielded the gold foil from a chariot harness, inscribed with the cartouches of Tutankhamun and Aye. This "Chariot Tomb" was, Davis decided, the long lost tomb of Tutankhamun, and he published it as such. Included in his publication were the now-familiar words (Davis [1912] 2001, 3): "I fear that the Valley of the Tombs is now exhausted."

LORD CARNARVON AND HOWARD CARTER

When George Herbert, Fifth Earl of Carnarvon, was injured in a near-fatal car crash, he started to winter in Egypt (Carnarvon 2007, 37). He quickly developed a keen interest in archaeology, and like Davis before him, he needed a professional colleague who would persuade Weigall to grant him permission to excavate at major Theban sites. Carter, unemployed and strongly recommended by Maspero, was the obvious choice.

Carnarvon and Carter were convinced that there was an undiscovered royal tomb in the valley, but they could not act while Davis held the one and only concession to excavate. When, in 1914, Davis finally retired, Lord Carnarvon took over the concession (Carter and Mace [1923] 2003, 76):

> Sir Gaston Maspero, Director of the Antiquities department, who signed our concession, agree with Mr Davis that the site was exhausted, and told us frankly that he did not consider that it would repay further investigation. We remembered, however, that nearly a hundred years earlier Belzoni had made a similar claim, and refused to be convinced.

Official permission confirmed that "the work of excavation shall be carried out at the expense, risk and peril of the Earl of Carnarvon by Mr Howard Carter; the latter should be constantly present during excavation" (quoted in James 1992, 413–415). Article 8 made it clear that "mummies of the Kings, of Princes, and of High Priests, together with their coffins and sarcophagi, shall remain the property of the Antiquities Service." Western archaeologists could no longer expect to export a large share of any archaeological finds. This new approach caused intense resentment among old-school excavators, who relied on funding donated by museums and private individuals who expected to be rewarded with a share of any finds. There was a strong feeling that this might be the death of Egyptology.

The Great War caused a delay in excavation, and although 1915 did see some work in the Western Valley, work in the main valley did not start until 1917. The only way to be certain that there were no lost tombs was to clear the valley down to its bedrock. This was slow work; the valley was littered with old spoil heaps, which had to be inspected and then moved. In an article written for *The Times* on December 11, 1922, Carnarvon estimated that they had moved approximately 150,000–200,000 tons of rubbish.

The entrance to the virtually intact KV 62 (Tutankhamun) was discovered on November 4, 1922. The small tomb was packed with grave goods and included the mummy of the king himself. The clearance of the tomb was not completed until 1932, and the tomb remains substantially unpublished, although Carter did produce a three-volume popular account of his work (1923–1933), and various experts have since written on particular aspects of the tomb and its contents. Today Carter's records are freely available on the website of the Griffith Institute, Oxford.

ELIZABETH THOMAS

The clearance of Tutankhamun's tomb was followed by a lull in valley archaeology. The general assumption was that there was nothing more to find. There was, however, work still to be undertaken. The tombs were not well recorded, and few had been adequately published. The valley remained an archaeological muddle.

In February and early March 1938, American tourist Elizabeth Thomas paid her first visit to Luxor. This inspired her to study Egyptology at the Oriental Institute in Chicago. In the 1950s she returned to Luxor to study and record the tombs in the Valleys of the Kings and Queens; this mammoth undertaking evolved into *The Royal Necropoleis of Thebes*, privately published in 1966 with a print run of just ninety volumes. Thomas's research provided the first comprehensive history of the development and modern study of the royal cemeteries, and it remains an inspiration to Egyptologists today.

BIBLIOGRAPHY

Belzoni, G. B. 1820. *Narrative of the Operations and Recent Discoveries in Egypt and Nubia*. Edited by A. Siliotti (2001). London.

Bell, M. A. 1990. "An Armchair Excavation of KV 55." *Journal of the American Research Center in Egypt* 27: 97–137.

Carnarvon, F. 2007. *Carnarvon and Carter: The Story of the Two Englishmen who Discovered the Tomb of Tutankhamun*. Berkshire.

Carter, H. 1927. *The Tomb of Tut.ankh.Amen: The Burial Chamber*. London:. Reprinted with a foreword by N. Reeves. London, 2001.

Carter, H. 1933. *The Tomb of Tut.ankh.Amen: The Annex and Treasury*. London. Reprinted with a foreword by N. Reeves. London, 2000.

Carter, H., and A. C. Mace. 1923. *The Tomb of Tut.ankh.Amen: Search, Discovery and Clearance of the Antechamber*. London:. Reprinted with a foreword by N. Reeves. London, 2003.

Champollion, J. F. 1828–1830. *The Code-Breaker's Secret Diaries*. Translated by Martin Rynja. London.

Clayton, P. A. 1982. *The Rediscovery of Ancient Egypt*. London.

Cline, E. H., and D. O'Connor, eds. 2012. *Rameses III: The Life and Times of Egypt's Last Hero*. Ann Arbor, MI.

Davis, T. M., ed. 1906. *The Tomb of Hâtshopsîtû*. London:. Reprinted with a foreword by N. Reeves. London, 2004.

Davis, T. M. 1907. *The Tomb of Iouiya and Touiyou*. London. Reprinted with a foreword by N. Reeves. London, 2000.

Davis, T. M. 1910. *The Tomb of Queen Tiyei*. London. Reprinted with a foreword by N. Reeves. London, 2001.

Davis, T. M. 1912. *The Tombs of Harmhabi and Touatânkhamanou*. London. Reprinted with a foreword by N. Reeves. London, 2001.

Greener, L. 1967. *The Discovery of Egypt*. New York.

James, T. G. H. 1992. *Howard Carter: The Path to Tutankhamen*. London.

Loret, V. 1899. "Les Tombeaux de Thoutmés III et d'Amenophis II." In *Bulletin de l'Institut Égyptien*. Cairo. Translation after J. Romer, *Valley of the Kings* (London, 1981, repr. 1988), 161–162.

Mayes, S. 1959. *The Great Belzoni: The Circus Strongman Who Discovered Egypt's Ancient Treasures*. London.

Mojsov, B. 2012. "The Monuments of Rameses III." In *Rameses III: The Life and Times of Egypt's Last Hero*, edited by E. H. Cline and D. O'Connor, 271–304. Ann Arbor, MI.

Pococke, R. 1743. *A Description of the East and Some Other Countries*, Vol. 1. London. Full text reproduced in J. Pinkerton, ed., *A General Collection of the Best and Most Interesting Voyages and Travels in All Parts of the World* (London, 1814), 163–402.

Reeves, N. 2000. *Ancient Egypt: The Great Discoveries*. London.

Reeves, N., and R. H. Wilkinson. 1996. *The Complete Valley of the Kings: Tombs and Treasures of Egypt's Greatest Pharaohs*. London.

Rhind, A. H. 1862. *Thebes: Its Tombs and Their Tenants*. London.

Romer, J. 1981. *Valley of the Kings*. London.

Tyldesley, J. A. 2005. *Egypt: How a Lost Civilization Was Rediscovered*. London.

Winlock, H. E. 1941. *Materials Used at the Embalming of King Tutankhamun*. The Metropolitan Museum of Art Papers 10. New York. Reprinted with a foreword by D. Arnold, as *Tutankhamen's Funeral*. New York, 2010.

PART XIII

THE KV IN THE LATE TWENTIETH AND THE TWENTY-FIRST CENTURY AND BEYOND

CHAPTER 33

REMOTE SENSING IN THE VALLEY OF THE KINGS AND ITS HINTERLANDS

SARAH H. PARCAK AND GREGORY D. MUMFORD

INTRODUCTION

THE Valley of the Kings has attracted increasing attention since its initial recognition and explorations by Sicard (in 1707–1716); Pococke (in 1739); and many subsequent travelers, looters, scholars, and archaeologists (Romer 1981, 32–35). In the past century a few excavators, including Davis (in 1912), have declared that there was nothing left to find in this necropolis, but incomplete excavations and continuing discoveries negate this conclusion. Today most of the known royal tombs and pits cluster in the East Valley (KV), with less activity in the West Valley (WV), while this New Kingdom royal burial ground is actually far more complex and much wider spread: It contains many features other than tombs; it has been exploited variously in other time periods; many New Kingdom royal burials and mortuary complexes occur outside this necropolis; and it formed an integral part of a much broader ritual and secular landscape, interacting with diverse components in its hinterland (Weeks 2013, 6654–6661). A broad range of remote sensing techniques has only relatively recently begun to indicate how much more remains to be discovered here and in West Thebes. Before dealing with the current and potential applications of multiple remote sensing systems, however, it is necessary to review the types of past activities and features that occur and might yet materialize in this region (see map, Figure 33.1).

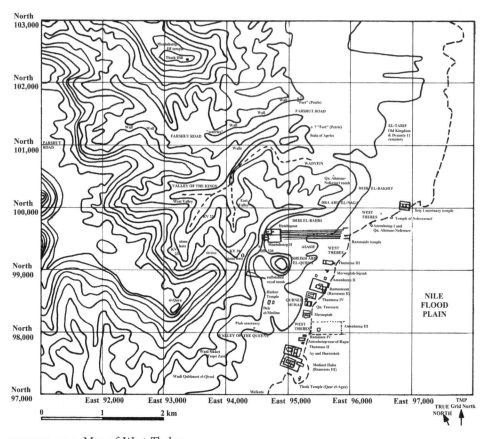

FIGURE 33.1 Map of West Thebes.

[Adapted by G. Mumford from Petrie (1909, pl. 4); Porter and Moss (1964, pls. 1, 4, 13), Porter and Moss (1972, pl. 33), and Weeks (2000a, 2, figs. 1–2, map 1/72).]

THE VALLEY OF THE KINGS

To date, the Valley of the Kings has yielded sixty-four New Kingdom tombs (KV 1–64), and twenty pits (A–T), which consist of twenty-five pharaohs' tombs from Thutmose I through Ramesses XI. At least one "missing" royal tomb belongs to Thutmose II (Baker 2008, 469). Such "lost" tombs may reflect undiscovered, unidentified, or unfinished tombs. For instance, Amenhotep I's tomb identification remains debated (Baker 2008, 38), and Prince Montuherkhepeshef usurped Ramesses VIII's initial tomb, KV 19 (Baker 2008, 329). Other unaccounted for tombs and burials include the transfer of royal family members from Amarna, namely the mummies of Nefertiti, Kiya, and Meketaten (Weeks 2000a, 10–13; Rose 2006). The remaining tombs and pits consist of unfinished tombs, burials for princes and other royal relatives (KV 5, 19), interments for nonroyal persons and pets (e.g., dogs, monkeys), embalming caches, and other features (Reeves 1992; Bickerstaffe 2007). Despite extensive plundering, many private and royal tombs retain significant portions of their mortuary furnishings (e.g., Thutmose IV; Davis 1904), while a few burials have survived virtually intact, such as Tuya/Yuya and Tutankhamun (Reeves 1990; Smith 1992).

The known location determinants and construction elements of New Kingdom royal tombs enable the formulation of predictive modeling (Renfrew and Bahn 2012, 89), suggesting what one might find in particular areas of the Valley of the Kings (and elsewhere). In general, the entrance to most Eighteenth Dynasty, type-1 royal tombs occurs along the foot of vertical cliff faces; type-2 royal tombs span the Eighteenth to Nineteenth Dynasties and are similar in design, but have rock-cut openings placed in varying locations, including above the valley floor; and type-3 royal tombs date from the Nineteenth to Twentieth Dynasties and display a different arrangement for rock-cut entryways, which lie at the base of sloping hillsides and spurs (Weeks 1999, 830). This royal cemetery has an underlying, fairly homogenous, deep band of shale (Esna shale formation), and an overlying and more complex series of marine bedding layers of limestone and shaly limestone (Theban limestone formation), which rise 300 meters at the peak of el-Qurn (Rutherford and Ryan 1995, 137–138). Over time landslides and erosion have created a thick layer of small to large pieces of limestone of varying types, conglomerates, sand, and other materials composing the New Kingdom floor of the necropolis, while subsequent flash floods, erosion, and human activity have covered this level. Although some tombs extend into the shale, the pharaonic workmen cut most tombs from different levels in the Theban limestone. Almost all of the tombs appear in the lowest bedding layer of marly limestone, including a very hard limestone capping layer with four gradually merging subdivisions that permitted the cutting and decoration of high-quality tombs; only a few tombs occur above this layer. The tomb cutters frequently used vertical faults to provide an already naturally prepared wall face and guide along which they could carve tombs into the bedrock (Rutherford and Ryan 1995, 138).

The Valley of the Kings has other components, particularly several clusters of rough stone workmen's structures near KV 24 and 25 in the West Valley, and more huts in the East Valley, including new discoveries near KV 18 and 62 (Weeks 2000a, map 1/72; Paulin-Grothe and Schneider 2001, 4). Of note, such huts, discarded tools, and construction debris are frequently found near tomb cuttings and may aid in finding new tombs. Černy and others have also found numerous graffiti from the New Kingdom through Coptic periods at the entry to Wadyein, in the East and West Valleys, along the pathway between these valleys, and near the workmen's "rest stop" to the west of KV 39 (Porter and Moss 1964, 590–591).

After the New Kingdom, various officials, priests, tomb robbers, tourists, hermits, and others continued to exploit or visit the Valley of the Kings during the Twenty-first to Thirtieth Dynasties (1069–332 B.C.E.) and the Ptolemaic-Roman through Coptic periods. Although the evidence for these interlopers comes mainly from graffiti, a number of Thebans reused private tombs for burials throughout the Twenty-first to Twenty-sixth Dynasties (Taylor 1992, 200–201), but avoided usurping royal tombs until the early Twenty-second Dynasty (e.g., KV 4, 19, 22, 34, 44, 45), after the final transfer of many royal mummies to DB 320 (Graefe and Belova 2010). The Theban population ceased interring people in the Valley of the Kings by the Twenty-sixth Dynasty, leaving graffiti here attesting to later visits (Strudwick 2003, 184). Some tombs became hermit dwellings in the Coptic period, while the royal necropolis has less tangible evidence for activity between the seventh century C.E. and 1707–1739 (Romer 1981, 32; Strudwick and Strudwick 1999, 206).

By the advent of the 1800s the Valley of the Kings witnessed a dramatic increase in visitors, plundering, and subsequently more scientific exploration (Weeks 1999, 828). The late 1800s to the present ushered in many discoveries, large-scale excavation, various disturbances, and major modifications to the topography of the Valley of the Kings (Reeves 1990). This includes the introduction of electricity (under Howard Carter), guard huts, offices, a tarmac roadway, parking lots, a tourist center, rest houses, and major landscaping and other facilities to provide tourists easier access to tombs (Weeks 1999, 829). Despite such intensive disturbances and investigations, the Valley of the Kings continues to yield startling discoveries, such as the KV 5 tomb of Ramesses II's sons (Weeks 2000b), and new tombs: KV 63–64 (Schaden 2011; Bickel and Paulin-Grothe 2012). In addition, many royal and private tombs remain incompletely excavated, often retaining old flood debris in side chambers and elsewhere. Of particular note, the 1998–2002 radar surveys by Reeves have also revealed that relatively large areas of New Kingdom strata remain undisturbed along the base of the Valley of the Kings, especially below tourist pathways (Rose 2006).

Hence, the presence of large areas of undisturbed debris, a few "missing" royal tombs, and continuing finds in this necropolis suggest that the Valley of the Kings still holds hidden tombs, pits, and other things. Any proposed remote sensing projects in this region must thereby take into account not only the localities and varying nature of past and recent activities here, but also the high potential for discovering many different features and artifacts in both the Valley of the Kings and the adjacent hills, valleys, and floodplain.

Northern Region

The northern side of the Valley of the Kings is accessed by a winding valley (Wadyein), beside which runs an east-west *wadi* (the Farshut Road) at the foot of Thoth Hill. The entrance to Wadyein contains the probable tomb of Queen Ahmose-Nefertari, New Kingdom graffiti, a quarry dating to Hatshepsut, a Twenty-sixth Dynasty rock stela (Apries), and other constructions (Porter and Moss 1964, 599–600). Petrie (1909, 2, pl. 4) noted southern and northern small, square rooms ("forts") flanking Wadyein and Farshut, which he described as thirteen feet and twenty-five feet square, respectively; he dated them to the late Roman period based on the brick sizes and a fourth-century C.E. potsherd from a brick.

Recent surveys along the eastern end of the Farshut Road, between el-Tarif and the Western Desert plateau, explored an overland route across the Qena Bend spanning the predynastic to early Islamic periods, with intense usage in the late Old Kingdom through Ramesside eras (Darnell and Darnell 2002, 4, fig. 1a). This route has small stretches of prepared trails, clusters of graffiti, lines of stone cairns, wind breaks, sentry posts, huts, camps, shrines (e.g., Gebel Antef), some walling systems, and potsherds and other artifacts. G. Mumford visited some sentry huts and the wall system in 1989, observing a fairly well-preserved, fieldstone construction with small, single-chambered guard huts along a ridge below Thoth Hill, overlooking the eastern end of Farshut Road (see Figure 33.2). This wall has an additional segment along the royal necropolis's eastern hilltop and probably helped secure this area (Strudwick and Strudwick 1999, 184; Weeks 2013, 6660). Another route, the 'Alamat Tal road, lies farther north and leads past a shrine at Gebel Tjauti, northwest to Hou, and west to Kharga Oasis.

Thoth Hill forms a major landmark yielding some prehistoric camps and flint tools in its vicinity and at el-Tarif (Kozlowski 1999). A Hungarian mission found an early dynastic stone structure below an Eleventh Dynasty temple on Thoth Hill, while a neighboring Oriental Institute survey recorded graffiti from this time and later periods (Vörös 1998, 61; Wilkinson 2000, 172–173; Darnell and Darnell 2002). Montuhotep (III) Sankhkare built a small Horus Temple and a sed-festival building here during the Eleventh Dynasty (Petrie 1909, 4–6; Porter and Moss 1972, 340, pl. 33; Vörös 1998, 64). A large cliff-tomb lay nearby in the side of Thoth Hill, with extensively plundered chambers and a broken-up sarcophagus; it may represent Montuhotep III's tomb, and thus be associated with the shrine (Vörös 1998, 65, 74; Dodson and Ikram 2008, 191). A graffito of King Senwosret attests to Twelfth Dynasty activity in the hilltop temple, while both the temple and cliff-tomb fell out of use at some point after the Middle Kingdom until their conversion into Coptic sanctuaries in the fourth to fifth centuries C.E.

FIGURE 33.2 Processed WorldView-2 imagery of part of a walling system to the north of the Valley of the Kings, running from the southeast (lower right) to northwest (upper left).

[Courtesy S. Parcak and Digital Globe.]

Eastern Region

Many structures lie to the east and southeast in West Thebes, including numerous private tombs along the West Theban hills, royal tombs in several areas, private and royal "mortuary" (i.e., memorial) temples and associated gardens along the cultivation's edge and elsewhere, and traces of some New Kingdom and later communities (Porter and Moss 1960; 1964, 600–605, 612–615). Aside from prehistoric through pharaonic period pit-graves, in West Thebes private rock-cut tombs span the Old Kingdom (Soliman 2009, 7–28), Middle Kingdom (Grajetzki 2009, 23, 94, 123, 140, 158), and New Kingdom (Kampp-Seyfried 1999a, 1999b), with much reuse in the Late Period to Coptic era (Strudwick 2003, 167–188; Riggs 2005, 175–244). This region also yields royal tombs and memorial temples dating to the Eleventh Dynasty at el-Tarif and Deir el-Bahri (Hölzl 1999), and to the Seventeenth and early Eighteenth Dynasties at Dra' Abu el-Naga' (Polz 2010, 343–353).

The royal tombs in the Valley of the Kings are physically separate from, but are linked to memorial temples, which contain mostly symbolic royal "residences" (Stadelmann 1996, 228) and lie along the floodplain's edge in West Thebes (Wilkinson 2000, 172–199). Many of these temples are undergoing reassessment (Haeny 1997; Wilkinson 2011), including their harbor and canal systems (Graham 2012) and display later usage. East Thebes also interacted with the West Bank, with an annual Festival of the Valley incorporating a ritual procession that departed from Karnak Temple to the western royal memorial temples. A procession of Amun of Opet also left Luxor Temple each year to visit a small Eighteenth Dynasty temple ("The Genuine Mound of the West"), which was later subsumed into Ramesses III's memorial temple at Medinet Habu (Kemp 2006, 266, fig. 97, 270, 274–276).

Regarding affiliated west bank communities, Amenhotep III built a massive palace complex at Malkata. It contained temples (Koltsida 2007), villas, servant housing, magazines, bakeries, and a harbor basin (Lacovara 1997, 113–115, figs. 20–22, 133, fig. 40, 141, fig. 48, 152, fig. 59; Kemp 2006, 277–280, fig. 101). A north-south road, outlying shrines, a royal rest-house(?), and other installations extend to the south (Kemp 1977).

Some information is known about the main West Theban settlement, which interacted with the adjacent temples and cemeteries. Papyrus BM 10068, probably from year 12 of Ramesses XI, furnishes a "town-roll" for West Thebes (James 1984, 194–196, 218–220). It lists 182 households and their owners from the memorial temple of Seti I southward along the floodplain's edge to the memorial temples of Amenhotep-son-of-Hapu and Medinet Habu, where excavations have revealed a small Eighteenth Dynasty temple, houses, and later town levels (Badawy 1968, 68–70, fig. 39; Kemp 2006: 351–355, fig. 122). The papyrus lists houses belonging to the West Theban mayor, district officers, high priests, priests, doctors, incense-roasters, scribes, inspectors, *medjay* (police), guards, gilders(?), goldsmiths, coppersmiths, sandal-makers, brewers, builders, wood-cutters, fishermen, washermen, stablemen, herdsmen, goat-herders, beekeepers, gardeners, porters, land-workers, and overseers of some of these personnel (Peet 1930, 93–98). A scribal school apparently lay behind the Ramesseum. One also finds winding streets, alleys, open areas, a great circular granary, garden plots, sinusoidal enclosures, ovens, reed housing, and mud brick residences and other buildings of varying sizes,

FIGURE 33.3 Processed WorldView-2 imagery of a large, subsurface structure at northern Qurnet Murai, southeast of the Hathor and Amun temples at Deir el-Medina.

[Courtesy of Sarah Parcak and Digital Globe.]

designs, functions, and quality (Hölscher 1939, 65–74, figs. 53–62; Lacovara 1997, 150–151, figs. 57–58). This settlement continued in various parts of West Thebes throughout the Twenty-first to Thirtieth Dynasties and into the Ptolemaic-Roman and Coptic periods, yielding diverse housing, temples (e.g., Ptolemaic "Thoth Temple" at Qasr el ʿAguz), monasteries, churches, and burials (Lacovara 1997, 156, fig. 63; Capuani 1999, 243–244; Horbury 2003; Kemp et al. 2004, 272–275, fig. 9; Bagnall and Rathbone 2004, 183–186, 192–203; Jenkins 2011; see Figure 33.3).

Southern Region

The region to the south contains many features associated directly and indirectly with the Valley of the Kings, including the sacred peak ("Quern"), which dominates West Thebes. About a hundred small shrines and a stone village lie near KV 39, along the northern and northeast slope of the Quern (Porter and Moss 1964, 589–590; Lacovara 1997, 140, fig. 47; Weeks 2000a, map 1/72). The parallels between this Theban stone village and one at Amarna are suggestive regarding their relationship to a nearby royal workmen's village. Their purpose is debated, however, and includes a police post, a workmen's rest stop, a female seclusion area, a servant's community, or a combination of these and other activities. Kemp (2012, 155–161) notes that ancient police paths skirt around the stone village at Amarna, which suggests that while it did not play as significant a role in facilitating patrols, it still formed a focal point along patrol routes. Helsinki University's (2009) current excavations at the Theban stone village may clarify its function.

The main New Kingdom royal workmen's village lay further south at Deir el-Medina, which included a walled settlement, adjacent shrines, a small Amun Temple, the Great Pit, and a cemetery (Meskell 2002, 201, fig. 7.8). Although the villagers transferred to Medinet Habu at the end of the Twentieth Dynasty, when royal burials ceased in the Valley of the Kings, some activity continued here in the Twenty-first through Twenty-sixth Dynasties (e.g., burials), the Ptolemaic period (a Hathor Temple), and the Roman period (e.g., an Isis shrine). In the Coptic period, Deir el-Medina and Qurnet Murai became a significant settlement ("Monastery of the City"; see Figure 33.4), with many tombs, burials, ostraca, a monastery of Saint Mark, and the conversion of the

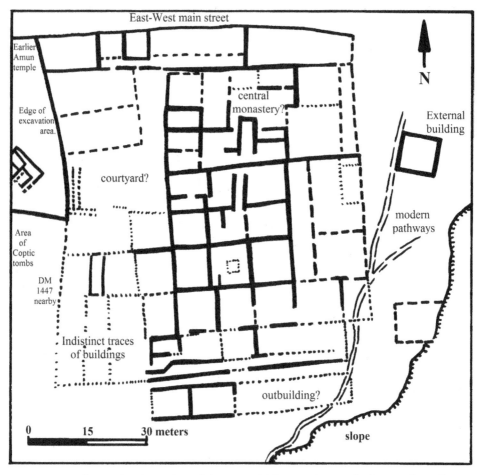

FIGURE 33.4 Extrapolated top plan of the potential "monastic complex" at northern Qurnet Murai, from processed WorldView-2 imagery.

[Image by Gregory Mumford.]

Hathor and Isis temples into a church and associated complex (Montserrat and Meskell 1997, 193–196; Kampp-Seyfried 1999a, 811–812; Wilkinson 2000, 189–190; Strudwick 2003, 176–178, fig. 6; Bagnall and Rathbone 2004, 200, 203).

During the Eighteenth Dynasty, some royal females were provided tombs in Wadis Sikket Taqet Zaid and Qubbanet el-Qirud, farther to the south. The former *wadi* contained an abandoned, earlier cliff-tomb and sarcophagus, begun for Hatshepsut during her tenure as a chief queen (Carter 1917, 114–118, pl. 22). Carter (1917, 108, pl. 19a) also noted some stone huts and three plundered tombs in this *wadi*, namely a corridor tomb and two pit-tombs, and asserted that this valley likely has other hidden tombs. The second valley lies farther south and yielded a cliff-tomb probably made for Hatshepsut's daughter, princess Neferure, whose cartouche lay on a nearby fallen limestone block, and a tomb for three princesses who lived during the reign of Thutmose III (Carter 1917, 109, pl. 19c; Porter and Moss 1964, 591–592).

During the Ramesside period, many queens, princes, and some important officials were interred in over ninety tombs in the "Valley of the Queens," which lay immediately south of Deir el-Medina (Leblanc 1999; Weeks 2013, 6660). This necropolis had an affiliated sanctuary of Ptah (Porter and Moss 1964, 706–709, 749–771). Some Late Period activity occurred in this region, including a tomb at the mouth of Wadi Qubbanet el-Qirud, which contained several monkey burials and funerary goods (Carter 1917, 109, pl. 19d; Porter and Moss 1964, 593).

REMOTE SENSING AND LANDSCAPES

Processing satellite-, aerial-, and ground-based remote sensing data is more than doing technical analysis (Lillesand et al. 2004; Parcak 2009a). It requires familiarity with the history and archaeology of a given place to assess fully all "findings" (Mumford and Parcak 2003; Parcak 2006). In the Valley of the Kings, locating features entails broader thinking: it is not only about tomb detection, but also about finding workmen's huts, guard posts, and trails. Until recently, Egyptology defined archaeological "sites" as specific locations rather than integrated landscapes of palimpsests (Parcak 2008), which form a "sitescape." Each royal tomb is a "site" unto itself, but is also simultaneously connected to the workmen's village at Deir el Medina, West Thebes, with its diverse supporting personnel, private tombs, memorial temples, and even the city and temples of East Thebes. Thus, much like Parker-Pearson and Ramilisonina's (2002) concept of zones of life and death around Stonehenge, the intended permanence of the New Kingdom royal tombs and their occupants is inextricably linked with multiple, interactive communities and temples throughout Thebes and external resources (Tilley 1994). Using remote sensing technologies allows us to locate previously unknown or unmapped features in the Valley of the Kings and its hinterland. One must also recognize the potential and limitations of each technology regarding the detection of surface and buried features (Parcak 2007).

Visual Applications of Aerial and Satellite Imagery

Aerial photography remains a useful archaeological mapping technique in Egypt, including high resolution Royal Air Force images of a largely rural, pristine Theban region in the 1920s and 1930s (e.g., Malkata). In 1979 the Theban Mapping Project (2002) commissioned the Remote Sensing Center of the Egyptian Academy of Scientific Research to take fourteen aerial photographs detailing the Theban West Bank, obtaining much clearer details (ca. 0.2–0.3 meter pixel resolution) of visible tomb facades, temples, stone huts, and other sites in the region.

Archaeologists have found satellite imagery less useful, albeit rapidly improving, in providing detailed images of surface architecture and features (Parcak 2009b). Corona imagery from the 1960s and 1970s recorded substantial standing monuments in Luxor and elsewhere, but has a 1 meter pixel resolution. Recent Quickbird imagery displays a 0.6 meter resolution and provides full coverage of West Thebes for under $1,000. Higher resolution imagery, like WorldView-2, is slightly more expensive, but has limited coverage. However, the resolution in such commercially available satellite imagery is improving rapidly, with 0.10 meter pixel resolutions projected in the next five to ten years.

Most archaeologists access Google Earth (GE) for visual assessments of surface sites (Handwerk 2006). GE is free, containing visual data from Geoeye and Quickbird, which have 0.5 and 0.6 meter resolutions, respectively. GE also allows one to view imagery draped over NASA digital elevation model data, thereby enabling archaeologists to study crude elevation differences between archaeological features. Regarding the Valley of the Kings, GE imagery displays significant reflectance and visual distortions at the entrance to most tombs. However, one can incorporate a three-dimensional fly-over tour for the necropolis. Researchers can also use a Geographic Information System (GIS: i.e., a layered data organization and synthesis tool) to overlay data and observe patterns that might otherwise remain obscured (Holcomb 2002), thus making GE an excellent research and teaching aid (Parcak 2009b). One project in Thebes adopted GE and other techniques to map changing field patterns and Nile River courses over time, revealing eastward and westward shifts and Karnak Temple's initial placement on an island (Hillier et al. 2007; Graham 2010, 133–138). Another study used X-SAR (RADAR) imagery to track Nile course meanderings at the Qena Bend to the north (Stern and Abdelsalam 1996).

Satellite Imagery Data Processing

Satellite imagery's main advantage is its ability to record diverse nonvisual data (i.e., outside the visible part of the light spectrum) that can detect unknown and obscured, subsurface archaeological features, such as a buried Thirtieth Dynasty temple wall at Tell Tebilla. Unlike visual applications of satellite imagery, the selection, acquisition, processing, and interpretation of nonvisual, high resolution satellite imagery data require extensive expertise, advance planning, and time (i.e., sometimes months), and may often be more costly. There is no single satellite imagery type for archaeological site and feature detection. Some types may be more useful than others depending on a given landscape. Satellite remote sensing specialists use multiple imagery types (e.g., ASTER; WorldView-1 and -2), algorithms, GIS, and statistical analysis to maximize finding potential new features. This study adopts a few of these techniques (e.g., WorldView-2) to assess the Valley of the Kings and its hinterland, which archaeologists have not yet examined using high resolution satellite imagery processing (more deeply buried structures, such as Amenhotep III's memorial temple, still require ground-based systems).

WorldView (WV) -1 and -2 represent the two main types of high resolution imagery available for assessing the archaeology of West Thebes. WV-1 provides an accurate, 0.5 meter resolution, panchromatic image (i.e., black and white). It is especially useful in detecting shallow buried features at multi-period sites. WV-2 has the highest commercially available resolution, consisting of 0.5 meter pixels in a panchromatic format and 1.85 meter pixels as multispectral data. Its eight multispectral bands are currently limited to the visual to near infrared, which enable the detection and differentiation of vegetation and soil types, and some geological identification (mainly through visual checks). By using known ground coordinates, its spatial accuracy can also be improved from 6.5 to 2 meters, while its initially high cost has dropped to $20 per square kilometer.

In selecting frequently updated satellite imagery, such as WV-1 or -2, one usually needs to consider local climatic conditions and other environmental factors (e.g., specific season, weather, vegetation, crop types). For instance, some archaeological features appear more clearly during times of greater moisture or materialize via changes in overlying vegetation health (e.g., structures below fields). Although the Valley of the Kings and adjacent hills have virtually no vegetation, other conditions may affect imagery data, including cloud cover, time of day, relative surface temperature, moisture levels, and the angle and reflectivity of sunlight (e.g., the cut limestone entries at tombs tend to be more reflective and obscured).

The next step involves determining the optimum processing techniques to detect and define new and little known archaeological sites and features. Such potential discoveries must be confirmed via published surveys and excavations and subsequent surface verification and investigation. In many cases earlier investigations are insufficiently published or mapped: Petrie's (1909, pl. 4) schematic map of New Kingdom sentry walls along Farshut Road is more accurately rendered here by processed WorldView-2 imagery (see Figure 33.2, above), while the small Roman "forts" (i.e., sentry huts) are insufficiently plotted and too small to relocate with confidence. Hence, some ambiguity may remain regarding such "new" discoveries.

WorldView-2 Findings

This study obtained a WV-2 image of West Thebes, dating to August 10, 2012, and combined its separate panchromatic and multispectral components to create a single, 0.5 meter multispectral image for the entire region. Implementing high pass imagery-filtering increased local details, while clipping individual areas containing potential new features enhanced contrast. In addition, further feature clarifications were obtained by experimenting with different band combinations and other enhancement techniques. Although this failed to reveal any obvious new features in the Valley of the Kings, multiple "new" findings appeared in the adjacent hills, which were confirmed by consulting published reports and maps.

For instance, the area of northern Qurnet Murai (Wilkinson 2000, 189), produced traces of a subsurface, rectilinear structure measuring 54 meters east-west by 80 meters north-south (see Figure 33.3). It had 1-meter-wide walls, enclosed twenty-six chambers ranging from 5–7 meters in area, and had an adjacent, 8-by-8-meter building. A perusal of visible building remains at Deir el-Medina from the 1798–1801 Napoleonic Expedition; Lane's 1827 topographical map of Thebes (Simpson 2003, pl. 127); and 2013 GE imagery, including multiple archaeological reports (Sauneron 1974; Horbury 2003), suggest that this structure was already long demolished, is practically invisible at the surface (i.e., one faint linear feature is apparent), and remains unexcavated (Dodson and Ikram 2008, 334 map 5E). It probably represents part of the Coptic settlement and monastery of Saint Mark (see above; Capuani 1999). Future excavations may confirm the exact date and nature of this complex. The authors subsequently visited this site in late December 2014, and observed a large, relatively flat-lying area to the north and east of the "Great Pit" and some traces of subsurface architecture, confirming some of the remote sensing results. The Theban hills have yielded other potential structures: a cluster of 10–12 huts lies to the southeast of the royal necropolis, but appears roughly built and more loosely spaced than the workmen's "rest stop." Several other probable huts, watch towers(?), and different constructions are visible along the hilltops, while additional possible structures might reflect natural outcrops. These suggestive findings need direct ground verification and assessment to determine their nature and date(s).

WorldView-3 Potential

The WV-3 satellite was launched in August 2014 and features 30–40 percent improvements in pixel resolution to 0.31 meter for panchromatic imagery, 1.24 meters for multispectral data, and 3.60 meters in the short-wave infrared. DigitalGlobe terms WV-3 as "superspectral" owing to its twenty-nine bands: a panchromatic band; eight visual and near infrared bands; eight short-wave infrared bands; and twelve other bands for tracking snow, ice, desert clouds, and aerosols. DigitalGlobe is preparing additional features that can aid archaeological applications, such as advanced algorithms for feature detection. Stereo pairs will enable data collection from large areas and the generation of very high resolution elevation models. In addition, unlike other satellite imagery, WV-3 will not require ground control points to correct each image.

LiDAR Applications

Light Detection and Ranging (LiDAR) is an airborne, three-dimensional, topographic mapping system with controlled availability in Egypt via NARSS (National Authority for Remote Sensing and Space Science). It works on airplanes and ultralights and has a differential GPS accuracy of 10–25 cm for elevation readings and 30 cm for horizontal coordinates. Depending on the survey area, it may take one or more flights for the LiDAR laser scanner to collect the data, at a rate of 100,000 points per second over fifteen acres, while specialists convert these point cloud data into digital terrain models, or contour maps, that are accurate to within a few centimeters. It can operate through all types of cloud and vegetation cover, detecting buried structures and archaeological features through faint surface traces and patterns. Although LiDAR has yet to be applied to archaeological surveys in much of the Middle East, it has been used very successfully elsewhere across the globe. LiDAR has mapped many new archaeological ground features below the dense rain forest at Caracol (Belize) (Chase et al. 2011) and detected a previously unknown Khmer-period site in Cambodia (Evans et al. 2013).

LiDAR would be quite useful in finding sites, tombs, and features in the Valley of the Kings and the Egyptian desert and floodplain. For instance, LiDAR could create a very detailed digital terrain model of the Valley of the Kings to aid in studying flash flooding zones and implementing water management and re-routing schemes. LiDAR data could also generate high resolution, three-dimensional maps of the Valley of the Kings, which could have satellite data or high resolution aerial photographs draped over them. LiDAR scans might reveal human-engineered surface features and patterns that have otherwise remained less visible or "invisible" to surface surveys. Although ground-based mapping is still essential (e.g., especially using a differential GPS; see Fenwick 2004), LiDAR could aid in the rapid, broad-scale mapping of walling systems, sentry huts, and other structures on the hilltops and ridges surrounding the royal necropolis. It would be time- and labor-prohibitive for ground surveys to replicate the millions of pulse plot points automatically generated by a LiDAR flight mission in a single day. Furthermore, the slopes and cliffs in this region would be much trickier and more dangerous to navigate in a differential GPS surface survey. Regarding potential tomb detection in the Valley of the Kings, LiDAR could help locate fracture traces, which extend up to twenty feet and allow water seepage into tombs. Thirty-three of the sixty-four tombs in the royal necropolis exploited such faults to aid in cutting entry passages (Parizek 2009), while some investigations have found vertical faults devoid of tomb cuttings. Of note, an aircraft-based radar survey, SLAR (sideways-looking airborne radar), might also provide similar success in mapping and finding surface features (Renfrew and Bahn 2012, 83).

Locating Buried Features

Finding hidden, rock-cut tombs, which frequently lie beneath talus slopes and construction debris, presents additional challenges. More traditional archaeological techniques range from cruder, broad-scale clearance to more careful, methodical excavation. Both excavation and chance played the main role in uncovering KV 63–64 in the Valley of the Kings: Bickel and Paulin-Grothe (2012, 28) found KV 64 while preparing the foundations for a shelter around KV 40. However, a few remote sensing systems can also detect more deeply buried features, including ASTER (Advanced Space-borne Thermal Emission and Reflection Radiometer).

ASTER currently has a 15–90 meter pixel resolution depending upon the selected data, but will soon attain almost a hundred times greater resolution using WV-3 data (Altaweel 2005; http://speclib.jpl.nasa.gov/). ASTER's hyperspectral data contain fifteen bands in the visible, near-mid, and thermal infrared (IR) portions of the electromagnetic spectrum. Each ASTER image covers 60 by 60 kilometers, which is available frequently as free data (via a cooperative agreement with NASA) or up to $50 per image, while ASTER elevation models are free. By draping processed ASTER satellite data (e.g., shortwave infrared bands) over ASTER elevation data, archaeologists can assess the local geology, topography (e.g., flash flood management and site protection), and potential archaeological site signatures (e.g., soil chemical signatures) in West Thebes. For instance, the thermal IR bands in ASTER data (i.e., 90-meter resolution) have already located previously unknown archaeological sites in the Nile Valley and delta floodplains (Parcak 2006).

This study applied ASTER short wave IR bands 5, 7, and 8 to create an RGB image focusing on the Valley of the Kings. An unsupervised classification organized the data pixels into their spectral classes using false color to compare the different geological layers in this region: limestone, Esna shale, and Dakhla chalk. Although this processing aided general comparisons of the imagery data across the region, its current 30-meter resolution prohibited the detection of smaller features. For the moment, the best archaeological application of these data includes overlaying them on a higher resolution, three-dimensional map of the Valley of the Kings to aid in flood management and site protection. However, the introduction of high resolution satellite thermal prospection (or higher resolution ground-based systems) in the near future offers great potential for locating hidden tombs in the Valley of the Kings by recording subtle ground temperature differences using a thermal IR camera.

For instance, within a twenty-four-hour period and throughout the year, the temperatures differ widely in different areas of the Valley of the Kings. Measuring local surface temperatures across the necropolis at various times of day may yield slight but significant differences between the debris covering the valley's floor and deeper rubble-filled and covered tomb shafts. Thermal prospection can measure temperature differences up to one-tenth of a degree (Renfrew and Bahn 2012, 99). The Valley of the Kings' natural suntrap generates very high temperatures from the late morning to late afternoon, while rock-cut tombs stay much cooler throughout the day. Hence, high resolution thermal surveys should theoretically detect increasing local differences in temperature as relatively cooler temperatures transfer slowly from hidden chambers and shafts to overlying debris across the necropolis's floor. Most royal and private rock-tombs contained substantial air pockets above flood debris, which should also affect the transference of cooler pockets to the overlying warmer surface debris. Presumably, the optimum point to record such differences occurs sometime between the late afternoon and dawn. One could easily run experiments on known pits that have been resealed (in the Valley of the Kings) to see what techniques work best before conducting a thermal survey.

A wide range of ground-based remote sensing technologies offers excellent options for the Valley of the Kings and its hinterland: SAR (Synthetic Aperture Radar), GPR (ground penetrating radar), magnetometry, electrical resistivity, acoustics and seismic methods, and thermography (Conyers 2007; Renfrew and Bahn 2012, 86, 97–103). In 1998–2002 Reeves and Watanabe applied a ground-based radar survey and detected two underground, shaft-like features (Rose 2006), which the 2005–2006 excavations by Schaden (2011) and Bickel and Paulin-Grothe (2012) also discovered independently, namely KV 63–64. The Theban Mapping Project's 1987 sonar survey failed to relocate KV 5 (Weeks 2000b, 4; contra Renfrew and Bahn 2012, 97), while a 10-meter trench uncovered it in a few days. In contrast, ground-based remote sensing techniques have worked better in the Theban floodplain and along the desert edge, such as magnetometers (Pavlish et al. 2002; Herbich 2012), GPR (Creasman and Sassen 2011), and electrical resistivity (Graham 2012).

CONCLUSIONS

Multiple space-, aerial-, and ground-based remote sensing tools are currently available for detecting potential archaeological and geological features in the Valley of the Kings and its hinterland. Some are accessible and relatively inexpensive, like WorldView-2 and ASTER, whereas other technologies, such as LiDAR, are currently harder and more expensive to obtain in Egypt. The release of WV-3 promises dramatic improvements in site detection, while the inclusion of a thermal IR camera in a LiDAR laser scanner should also aid greatly in locating buried tomb shafts and other features. Considering the pros and cons of individual remote sensing technologies, a multitiered approach using GIS represents the best option for finding new archaeological sites and features. This will allow scientists to compare the shapes, sizes, and characteristics of suggestive spectral signatures with known archaeological sites, structures, tombs, and other features. These variables can then be applied to a more effective predictive site modeling, while such multilayered data can also aid in isolating water entry points in tombs and thereby in formulating more effective flood management systems. Hence, the recent exponential improvements and trajectories in remote sensing technologies suggest that we will soon be able to map much of the subsurface and more deeply buried parts in the Valley of the Kings and elsewhere.

Authors' Note

Sarah Parcak furnished the remote sensing processing, analysis, and discussion in the second half of this study. Gregory Mumford provided the overall organization and editing; wrote the first half of this chapter (i.e., introduction through southern region); and contributed to the LiDAR, thermography, and ground-based remote sensing sections.

Bibliography

Altaweel, M. 2005. "The Use of ASTER Satellite Imagery in Archaeological Contexts." *Archaeological Prospection* 12: 151–166.

Badawy, A. 1968. *A History of Egyptian Architecture: The Empire (the New Kingdom) from the Eighteenth Dynasty to the End of the Twentieth Dynasty 1580–1085 BC.* Los Angeles.

Bagnall, R. S., K. Brodersen, C. B. Champion, A. Erskine, and S. R. Huebner, eds. 2013. *The Encyclopedia of Ancient History, Volumes I–XIII.* Oxford.

Bagnall, R. S., and D. W. Rathbone, eds. 2004. *Egypt from Alexander to the Copts: An Archaeological and Historical Guide.* London.

Baker, D. D. 2008. *The Encyclopedia of the Egyptian Pharaohs, Volume I: Predynastic through Twentieth Dynasty 3300–1069 BC.* Oakville.

Bard, K., ed. 1999. *Encyclopedia of the Archaeology of Ancient Egypt.* London.

Bickel, S., and E. Paulin-Grothe. 2012. "The Valley of the Kings: Two Burials in KV 64." *Egyptian Archaeology* 41 (Autumn): 36–40.

Bickerstaffe, D. 2007. "Embalming Caches in the Valley of the Kings." *KMT: A Modern Journal of Ancient Egypt* 18 (2, Summer): 46–53.

Bietak, M., ed. 1996. *House and Palace in Ancient Egypt: International Symposium in Cairo, April 8 to 11 1992, Volumes 1–2.* Österreiche Akademie der Wissenschaften Denkschriften der Gesamtakademie 14. Vienna.

Bietak, M., E. Czerny, and I. Forstner-Müller, eds. 2010. *Cities and Urbanism in Ancient Egypt: Papers from a Workshop in November 2006 at the Austrian Academy of Sciences.* Österreichische Akademie der Wissenschaften Denkschriften der Gesamtakademie 60. Vienna.

Capuani, M. 1999. *Christian Egypt: Coptic Art and Monuments through Two Millennia.* Cairo.

Carter, H. 1917. "A Tomb Prepared for Queen Hatshepsuit and Other Recent Discoveries at Thebes." *Journal of Egyptian Archaeology* 4 (2/3): 107–118.

Chase, A. F., D. Z. Chase, J. F. Weishampel, J. B. Drake, R. L. Shrestha, K. C. Slatton, J. J. Awe, and W. E. Carter. 2011. "Airborne LiDAR, Archaeology, and the Ancient Maya Landscape at Caracol, Belize." *Journal of Archaeological Science* 38: 387–398.

Conyers, L. B. 2007. "Ground-penetrating Radar for Archaeological Mapping." In *Remote Sensing in Archaeology.* Interdisciplinary Contributions to Archaeology, edited by J. R. Wiseman and F. El-Baz, 329–344. New York.

Creasman, P. P., and D. Sassen. 2011. "Remote Sensing." In *The Temple of Tausret: The University of Arizona Egyptian Expedition Tausret Temple Project, 2004–2011,* edited by R. H. Wilkinson, 150–159. Tuscon.

Darnell, J. C., and D. Darnell. 2002. *Theban Desert Road Survey in the Egyptian Western Desert.* Vol. 1, *Gebel Tjauti Rock Inscriptions 1–45 and Wadi el-Hol Rock Inscriptions 1–45.* Oriental Institute Publications 119. Chicago.

Davis, T. M. 1904. *The Tomb of Thoutmosis IV.* London:. Reprint 2002.

Dodson, A., and S. Ikram. 2008. *The Tomb in Ancient Egypt: Royal and Private Sepulchres from the Early Dynastic Period to the Romans.* Cairo.

Evans, D. H., R. J. Fletcher, C. Pottier, J.-B. Chevance, D. Soutif, B. S. Tan, S. Im, D. Ea, T. Tin, S. Kim, C. Cromarty, S. De Greef, K. Hanus, P. Bâty, R. Kuszinger, I. Shimoda, and G, Boornazian. 2013. "Uncovering Archaeological Landscapes at Angkor Using Lidar." *Proceedings of the National Academy of Sciences (USA), Early Edition* 110 (31): 1–6.

Fenwick, H. 2004. "Ancient Roads and GPS Survey: Modeling the Amarna Plain." *Antiquity* 78 (302): 880–885.

Graefe, E., and G. Belova, eds. 2010. *The Royal Cache TT 320: A Re-examination.* Cairo.

Graham, A. 2010. "Islands in the Nile: A Geoarchaeological Approach to Settlement Location in the Egyptian Nile Valley and the case of Karnak." In *Cities and Urbanism in Ancient Egypt: Papers from a Workshop in November 2006 at the Austrian Academy of Sciences,* edited by M. Bietak, E. Czerny, and I. Forstner-Müller, 125–143. Vienna.

Graham, A. 2012. "Investigating the Theban West Bank Floodplain." *Egyptian Archaeology* 41 (Autumn): 21–24.

Grajetzki, W. 2009. *Court Officials of the Egyptian Middle Kingdom.* Duckworth Egyptology. London.

Haeny, G. 1997. "New Kingdom 'Mortuary Temples' and 'Mansions of Millions of Years.'" In *Temples of Ancient Egypt,* edited by B. E. Shafer, 86–126. Ithaca, NY.

Handwerk, B. 2006. "Google Earth Satellite Maps Boost Armchair Archaeology." *National Geographic News,* November 7, 2006, 1–2. http://news.nationalgeographic.com/news/2006/11/061107-archaeology.html.

Helsinki University. 2009. "Researchers Dig through Millennia in the Valley of the Kings." *Science Daily,* February 15. http://www.sciencedaily.com/releases/2009/02/090203173651.htm.

Herbich, T. 2012. "Geophysical Methods and Landscape Archaeology." *Egyptian Archaeology* 41 (Autumn): 11–14.

Hillier, J. K., J. M. Bunbury, and A. Graham. 2007. "Monuments on a Migrating Nile." *Journal of Archaeological Science* 34 (7): 1011–1015.

Holcomb, D. 2002. "Remote Sensing and GIS Technology for Monitoring UNESCO World Heritage Sites: A Pilot Project." In *Proceedings of the Conference Space Applications for Heritage Conservation (ESA SP-515), 5–8 November 2002, Strasbourg, France,* edited by b. Warmbein, 8. Strasbourg.

Hölzl, C. 1999. "Thebes, el-Tarif, Saff-tombs." In *Encyclopedia of the Archaeology of Ancient Egypt,* edited by K. Bard, 826–828. London.

Hölscher, U. 1939. *The Excavation of Medinet Habu.* Vol. II, *The Temples of the Eighteenth Dynasty.* The University of Chicago Oriental Institute Publications 41. Chicago.

Horbury, M. E. 2003. "Egyptian Self-definition in the New Kingdom and Coptic Period." PhD diss., University College London. http://discovery.ucl.ac.uk/1382607/1/399530.pdf.

Ikram, S., and A. Dodson, eds. 2009. *Beyond the Horizon: Studies in Egyptian Art, Archaeology and History in Honour of Barry J. Kemp, Volumes 1–2.* Cairo.

James, T. G. H. 1984. *Pharaoh's People: Scenes from Life in Imperial Egypt.* London.

Jenkins, M. R. 2011. "Qasr el 'Aguz: The 'Temple of Thoth' on the West Bank at Luxor." *KMT: A Modern Journal of Ancient Egypt* 21 (4, Winter): 50–61.

Kampp-Seyfried, F. 1999a. "Thebes, el-Asasif, Dra' Abu el-Naga, el-Khokha, Qurnet Murai, and Sheikh Abd el-Qurna." In *Encyclopedia of the Archaeology of Ancient Egypt*, edited by K. Bard, 802–807, 811–812, and 822–824. London.

Kampp-Seyfried, F. 1999b. "Thebes, New Kingdom Private Tombs." In *Encyclopedia of the Archaeology of Ancient Egypt*, edited by K. Bard, 809–811. London.

Kemp, B. J., N. Moeller, K. Spence, and A. L. Gascoigne. 2004. "Egypt's Invisible Walls." *Cambridge Archaeological Journal* 14 (2): 261–288.

Kemp, B. J. 1977. "A Building of Amenophis III at Kôm el-'Abd." *Journal of Egyptian Archaeology* 63: 71–82.

Kemp, B. J. 2006. *Ancient Egypt: Anatomy of a Civilization*. 2nd ed. London.

Kemp, B. J. 2012. *The City of Akhenaten and Nefertiti: Amarna and Its People*. London.

Koltsida, A. 2007. "A Dark Spot in Ancient Egyptian Architecture: The Temple of Malkata." *Journal of the American Research Center in Egypt* 43: 43–57.

Kozlowski, J. K. 1999. "Thebes, el-Tarif, Prehistoric Sites." In *Encyclopedia of the Archaeology of Ancient Egypt*, edited by K. Bard, 824–826. London.

Lacovara, P. 1997. *The New Kingdom Royal City*. Studies in Egyptology. London.

Leblanc, C. 1999. "Thebes, Valley of the Queens." In *Encyclopedia of the Archaeology of Ancient Egypt*, edited by K. Bard, 833–836. London.

Lillesand, R., R. W. Kiefer, and J. Chipman. 2004. *Remote Sensing and Image Interpretation*. 5th ed. New York.

Maree, M., ed. 2010. *The Second Intermediate Period (Thirteenth-Seventeenth Dynasties): Current Research, Future Prospects*. Orientalia Lovaniensia Analecta 192. Leuven.

Meskell, L. 2002. *Private Life in New Kingdom Egypt*. Princeton, NJ.

Montserrat, D., and L. Meskell. 1997. "Mortuary Archaeology and Religious Landscape at Graeco-Roman Deir el-Medina." *Journal of Egyptian Archaeology* 83: 179–197.

Mumford, G., and S. Parcak. 2003. "Pharaonic Ventures into South Sinai: El-Markha Plain Site 346." *Journal of Egyptian Archaeology* 89: 83–116.

Murnane, W. J. 1999. "Thebes, Royal Funerary Temples." In *Encyclopedia of the Archaeology of Ancient Egypt*, edited by K. Bard, 814–818. London.

Parcak, S. H. 2006. "The Middle Egypt Survey Project, 2004–06." *Journal of Egyptian Archaeology* 92: 57–61.

Parcak, S. H. 2007. "Going, Going, Gone: Towards a Satellite Remote Sensing Methodology for Monitoring Archaeological Tell Sites under Threat in the Middle East." *Journal of Field Archaeology* 42: 61–83.

Parcak, S. H. 2008. "Site Survey in Egyptology." In *Egyptology Today*, edited by R. H. Wilkinson, 57–76. Cambridge.

Parcak, S. H. 2009a. *Satellite Remote Sensing for Archaeology*. London.

Parcak, S. H. 2009b. "The Skeptical Remote Senser." In *Beyond the Horizon: Studies in Egyptian Art, Archaeology and History in Honour of Barry J. Kemp, Volumes 1–2*, edited by S. Ikram and A. Dodson, 361–381. Cairo.

Parker-Pearson, M., and Ramilisonina. 2002. "Stonehenge for the Ancestors: The Stones Pass on the Message." *Antiquity* 72 (276): 308–326.

Paulin-Grothe, E., and T. Schneider. 2001. "New Workmen's Huts in the Valley of the Kings." *Egyptian Archaeology* 19 (Autumn): 3–5.

Parizek, K. 2009. "Fracture Trace-structures: Key to Discovery and Preservation of Tombs, Valley of the Kings and Queens, Egypt." Paper presented at GSA 2009 Annual Meeting, Portland, October 18–21, 2009.

Pavlish, L. A., A. C. D'Andrea, and K. R. Weeks, eds. 2002. "Results of a Magnetometer Survey over the Environs of the Mortuary Temple of Amenophis I, Luxor, Egypt." In *Proceedings of the 33rd International Symposium on Archaeometry, April 22–26, 2002, Amsterdam, Netherlands.*

Peet, T. E. 1930. *The Great Tomb Robberies of the Twentieth Egyptian Dynasty.* Vol. I, *Text.* Oxford.

Petrie, W. M. F. 1909. *Qurneh.* British School of Archaeology in Egypt 15. London.

Polz, D. 2010. "New Archaeological Data from Dra' Abu el-Naga and Their Historical Implications." In *The Second Intermediate Period (Thirteenth-Seventeenth Dynasties): Current Research, Future Prospects,* edited by M. Maree, 343–353. Leuven.

Porter, B., and R. B. L. Moss. 1960. *Topographical Bibliography of Ancient Egyptian Hieroglyphic Texts, Reliefs, and Paintings. Vol. I, The Theban Necropolis, Part I: Private Tombs.* 2nd ed. Oxford.

Porter, B., and R. B. L. Moss. 1964. *Topographical Bibliography of Ancient Egyptian Hieroglyphic Texts, Reliefs, and Paintings. Vol. I, The Theban Necropolis, Part II: Royal Tombs and Smaller Cemeteries.* 2nd ed. Oxford.

Porter, B., and R. B. L. Moss. 1972. *Topographical Bibliography of Ancient Egyptian Hieroglyphic Texts, Reliefs, and Paintings. Vol. II, Theban Temples.* 2nd ed. Oxford.

Reeves, C. N. 1990. *The Complete Tutankhamun: The King, the Tomb, the Royal Treasure.* London.

Reeves, C. N., ed. 1992. *After Tutankhamun: Research and Excavation in the Royal Necropolis at Thebes.* London.

Renfrew, C., and P. Bahn. 2012. *Archaeology: Theories, Methods and Practice.* 6th ed. London.

Riggs, C. 2005. *The Beautiful Burial in Roman Egypt: Art, Identity, and Funerary Religion.* Oxford Studies in Ancient Culture and Presentation. Oxford.

Romer, J. 1981. *Valley of the Kings.* London.

Rose, M. 2006. "Another Tomb in the Valley of the Kings?" *Archaeology* (August 3). http://archive.archaeology.org/online/interviews/reeves.html and http://www.nicholasreeves.com.

Rutherford, J., and D. P. Ryan. 1995. "Tentative Tomb Protection Priorities, Valley of the Kings, Egypt." In *Valley of the Sun Kings: New Explorations in the Tombs of the Pharaohs,* edited by R. H. Wilkinson, 134–156. Tuscon.

Sauneron, S. 1974. "Les travaux de l'Institut Français d'Archéologie Orientale en 1973–1974." *Bulletin de l'Institut Français d'Archeologie Orientale* 74: 183–233.

Schaden, O. J. 2011. "KV 63 Update: The 2011 Season." *KMT* 22 (2, Summer): 33–41.

Shafer, B. E., ed. 1997. *Temples of Ancient Egypt.* Ithaca, NY.

Simpson, C. 2003. "Modern Qurna—Pieces of an Historical Jigsaw." In *The Theban Necropolis: Past, Present and Future,* edited by N. Strudwick and J. H. Taylor, 244–249. London.

Smith, S. T. 1992. "Intact Tombs of the Seventeenth and Eighteenth Dynasties from Thebes and the New Kingdom Burial System." *Mitteilungen des Deutschen Archaologischen Instituts Abteilung Kairo* 48: 193–231.

Soliman, R. 2009. *Old and Middle Kingdom Theban Tombs.* Egyptian Site Series. London.

Stadelmann, R. 1996. "Temple Palace and Residential Palace." In *House and Palace in Ancient Egypt: International Symposium in Cairo, April 8 to 11 1992, Volumes 1–2*, edited by M. Bietak, 225–230. Vienna.

Stern, R. J., and M. G. Abdelsalam. 1996. "The Origin of the Great Bend of the Nile from Sir-C/X-SAR Imagery." *Science* 274 (5293): 1696–1698.

Strudwick, N. 2003. "Some Aspects of the Archaeology of the Theban Necropolis in the Ptolemaic and Roman Periods." In *The Theban Necropolis: Past, Present and Future*, edited by N. Strudwick and J. H. Taylor, 167–188. London.

Strudwick, N., and H. Strudwick. 1999. *Thebes in Egypt: A Guide to the Tombs and Temples of Ancient Luxor*. Ithaca, NY.

Strudwick, N., and J. H. Taylor, eds. 2003. *The Theban Necropolis: Past, Present and Future*. London.

Taylor, J. H. 1992. "Aspects of the History of the Valley of the Kings in the Third Intermediate Period." In *After Tutankhamun: Research and Excavation in the Royal Necropolis at Thebes*, edited by C. N. Reeves, 186–206. London.

Theban Mapping Project. 2002. *Theban Mapping Project: Atlas of the Theban Necropolis; Atlas of the Valley of the Kings*. http://www.thebanmappingproject.com/atlas/index.html.

Tilley, C. 1994. *A Phenomenology of Landscape: Places, Paths and Monuments*. Explorations in Anthropology. New York.

Vörös, G. 1998. *Temple on the Pyramid of Thebes: Hungarian Excavations on Thoth Hill at the Temple of Pharaoh Montuhotep Sankhkara 1995–1998*. Budapest.

Warmbein, B., ed. 2002. *Proceedings of the Conference Space Applications for Heritage Conservation (ESA SP-515), 5–8 November 2002, Strasbourg, France*. Strasbourg.

Weeks, K. R. 1999. "Thebes, Valley of the Kings." In *Encyclopedia of the Archaeology of Ancient Egypt*, edited by K. Bard, 828–831. London.

Weeks, K. R., ed. 2000a. *Atlas of the Valley of the Kings*. Publications of the Theban Mapping Project I. Cairo: American University in Cairo Press.

Weeks, K. R., ed. 2000b. *KV 5: A Preliminary Report on the Excavation of the Tomb of the Sons of Ramesses II in the Valley of the Kings*. Publications of the Theban Mapping Project II. Cairo: American University in Cairo Press.

Weeks, K. R. 2013. "Thebes, West." In *The Encyclopedia of Ancient History, Volumes I–XIII*, edited by R. S. Bagnall et al., 6654–6661. Oxford.

Wilkinson, R. H., ed. 1995. *Valley of the Sun Kings: New Explorations in the Tombs of the Pharaohs*. Tuscon.

Wilkinson, R. H. 2000. *The Complete Temples of Ancient Egypt*. London.

Wilkinson, R. H., ed. 2008. *Egyptology Today*. Cambridge.

Wilkinson, R. H., ed. 2011. *The Temple of Tausret: The University of Arizona Egyptian Expedition Tausret Temple Project, 2004–2011*. Tuscon.

Wiseman, J. R., and F. El-Baz, eds. 2007. *Remote Sensing in Archaeology*. Interdisciplinary Contributions to Archaeology. New York.

CHAPTER 34

THE SEARCH FOR OTHER TOMBS

STEPHEN W. CROSS

THREE famous explorers of the Valley of the Kings, at the conclusion of their excavations, all made similar statements. Giovanni Belzoni asserted, "It is my firm opinion, that in the Beban el Malook, there are no more (tombs) than are now known." Alexander Rhind said, "I feel reasonably confident that no more sepulchres except those already known, exist within its proper limits." Theodore Davis noted, "I fear that the Valley of the Tombs is now exhausted."

To date these gentlemen have been proved wrong three times, with the finding of KV 62, KV 63, and KV 64. Will they be proved wrong again in the future?

After the discovery of Tutankhamun's tomb, KV 62, by Carnarvon and Carter in 1922, the Valley of the Kings, the most famous cemetery in the world, had been virtually ignored by archaeologists. It is probable that most archaeologists agreed with the three explorers quoted above after the discovery of KV 62 and felt that Tutankhamun's tomb would be the last to be found in the valley. Toward the latter half of the twentieth century, interest in the valley was rekindled, and three large-scale expeditions have made clearances of sections of the valley with productive results, described below.

THE AMARNA ROYAL TOMBS PROJECT

The ARTP was a consortium of international Egyptologists whose mission was obvious from the title of their project: to find the missing Amarna royalty (discussed below). There was a very cogent reason for their search. At some indeterminate time before the end of the Twentieth Dynasty, a scribe, Wenenefer, visited almost every tomb in the valley (Peden, 2001, 184, 185). He left graffiti near each entrance, of his name and a stroke to signify his inspection of the tomb. Some graffiti had many strokes. His inspections were obviously to verify the intactness of the burials. But in the side *wadi* leading off from the central area, near to KV 58, were just such graffiti but with no associated tomb known. There was therefore a valid reason for this project and good reason to excavate.

The area of investigation chosen was from KV 11, Ramesses III, across the tourists' path to the northern side and down to the central area. KV 56 was carefully excavated of the flood debris that covered its floor, and it was discovered that the unusual shape of the burial chamber was because the tomb was unfinished. It was intended to provide a central column in the chamber, but this was never finished, leaving the curious stepped walls.

A spoil heap from an early twentieth-century excavator was found to the south of the entrance to KV 11. Here items of not only archaeological but also historical significance were discovered.

The first serious attempt at remote sensing was made across the central area of the valley using ground penetrating radar (GPR). The equipment used only penetrated to a depth of 2 meters, and bedrock is 5 meters deep in this area, so most of the anomalies in the scans proved to be of no archaeological significance, but two were closer to the surface and proved the usefulness of GPR. One feature, labeled no. 6 on later excavation, proved to be KV 63. A second feature, to the east of no. 6 and labeled no. 7, proved to be a natural cave.

As the excavation proceeded along the cliff face on the northern side, from KV 58 toward the central area, past the location of the graffiti, a series of three workmen's hut horizons was uncovered. These huts had previously been exposed by Ayrton's work for Davis in 1907. However, Carter tells us that Ayrton merely skimmed the surface of the huts and did not excavate thoroughly. The ARTP found that this was the case, and many antiquities were found, allowing them to date the three hut horizons: the upper top layer to the Twentieth Dynasty (Ramesses III to Ramesses VI), the middle layer to the Nineteenth Dynasty, and significantly, the lowest, bottom layer to the Eighteenth Dynasty. Although no tomb was found, underneath the lowest huts were found Amarna period artifacts.

The workmen's huts, as they can be dated from artifacts found within them, are very useful for working out the stratigraphy of the valley. Figure 34.1 shows a "guard hut" one of four in the western valley. There is also a complete section of workmen's huts. The significance of these has never been explored.

The success of this project was threefold. First is a "negative confession": the fact that no tomb was found during the excavation of the northern edge of the side *wadi* from KV 58 down to the huts means this area can be eliminated from further searches. Second, dating and mapping the three hut horizons, specifically mapping their elevations, meant that the stratigraphy of the central area could now finally be understood (Cross 2014). Third, remote sensing of the valley was conclusively proved to be valid with the finding of KV 63, although this could not be investigated at the time.

FIGURE 34.1 A "guard hut," one of four in the western valley. There is also a complete section of workmen's huts in this valley, the significance of which has never been explored.

THE AMENMESSE PROJECT: A SUPREME
COUNCIL OF ANTIQUITIES MISSION

The purpose of this mission was to completely clear KV 10, Amenmesses's tomb, in an attempt to work out the sequence of events that happened there. The tomb had also never been fully explored. Part of this clearance was the investigation of the area to the north surrounding the entrance in a search for any possible foundation deposits. An extensive group of previously unknown workmen's huts was uncovered and mapped, adding significantly to our knowledge of the valley.

At the very end of the 2005 season's work, Otto Schaden noticed that underneath the lowest group of huts was a layer of pure white limestone chippings (discussed below). Realizing its significance, but faced with its being too late in the season to investigate further, Schaden put off investigating this layer until the next season. Of course in 2006 he announced the discovery of KV 63.

Supreme Council of Antiquities

In 2007 the Supreme Council of Antiquities (SCA) began two extensive clearances of the valley, the eastern central area and the side *wadi* holding KV 8, Merenptah (Hawass et al. 2010). The object of both these clearances was to find a tomb, but for very different reasons.

The KV 8 clearance was based on a find of Carter's. During his excavation for Carnarvon at the entrance of this side *wadi*, an ostrakon was discovered. The ostrakon was a shard of limestone with hieratic writing on it. The writing mentioned a previously unknown Queen Isis and stated that her tomb was 200 cubits from the waterfall. The problem was that during a flash flood, there would have been two waterfalls in this side *wadi*: one from the top cliffs and another from a high step in the bedrock halfway down. Range arcs of 200 cubits were drawn on a map from both waterfalls, and excavation began. This in effect meant a complete clearance of the whole side *wadi*. Many unknown graffiti were uncovered on the side rock walls and recorded. An ancient dam built just above the entrance to KV 8 to protect the tomb from flooding was discovered. The dam was effective in stopping flow past the entrance, but it had the effect of blocking the flow and forming a small lake above the tomb. This leaked down through the joints in the bedrock, and the tomb was still damaged by water.

A large work area or perhaps workmen's hut was found on a leveled area above the tomb entrance. There were declivities in the bedrock to hold water pots (Hawass et al. 2010, figs. 13.1, 14, 15, 16, P. 76+77). This indicated that some work had been done *above* the tomb. As if to confirm this, as work progressed upward a staircase was found. The ancient workmen had cut away the rock between two parallel vertical joints in the bedrock to make a man-made stone staircase (Hawass et al. 2010, 80, figs. 22 and 23). Time and again we see the clever, if not elegant, alteration of the natural topography by the workmen to suit their own purposes. This work would not have progressed upward above KV 8 for no purpose, and it did appear that a tomb was about to be discovered. At the very top, under the cliff, the staircase turned left, south, and ended in a worked face; the cliff face had been smoothed by chisels to make it flat, and protruding flint nodules had been sheared off. But upon excavating beneath, nothing was found. It looked as though the intention was to build a tomb here, but it was abandoned. Why was it abandoned? Perhaps it rained? During a flash flood this site would have been vertically below the waterfall off the top of the surrounding cliff, not a good place to cut a tomb. The tomb of Queen Isis still awaits discovery, but it must be admitted that it might not lie within the valley.

The central area excavation was undertaken for a different historical reason. As Carter had excavated under workmen's huts on the western side and found a tomb, and as Schaden had also excavated under workmen's huts at the southern end and found a tomb, then perhaps under the huts known to be present on the eastern side would lie a tomb. Ayrton had previously uncovered these huts in 1907, but remembering Carter's comments on Ayrton's work and the experience of the ARTP with the huts near KV 11, if he had not dug down to bedrock, then there was the possibility of a discovery. A limited GPR survey was attempted, with inconclusive results. On excavating it was found that the tops of the huts were surprisingly near to the surface, and as excavation progressed lower a large amount of broken pottery, all dating to the Twentieth Dynasty, was found in Ayrton's backfill. The huts were found to be extremely well built and were more extensive than the 1907 map suggested. The huts continued south right up to the southern face of the cliff near KV 10. Once bedrock was reached, it was realized that Ayrton had indeed excavated down to bedrock, through the floors of the huts, and no tomb was going to be found. However, a square commencement or water storage pit was found at the southern end of the site. A complete surprise also was the finding of a natural cave under the cliff at the extreme southern end of the excavation. The cave was found to have been completely swept clean in antiquity (Cross 2014).

University of Basel Kings' Valley Project

The University of Basel Kings' Valley Project is probably the most important project in the valley since Carter and Carnarvon excavated in the 1920s. This mission has long been awaited and is seminal to our understanding of the history of the valley. The mission is to investigate, map, survey, and record the undecorated tombs in the valley. The early investigators, upon finding these tombs, thought they were uninteresting, and they were not recorded properly. For some of them, all we know is a number and a drawing in a field notebook, and even the exact locations of some are not known. In fact, the nature of the quest to which the title of this chapter refers has changed radically over the last hundred years. Davis stated openly that he was searching for kings' tombs and specifically for a queen's tomb. The blatant search for "treasure" is over. Finding a golden artifact tells us more about the skill of the metalworkers three and a half thousand years ago than about the intrinsic value of the metal itself.

The mission started at the southern end of the valley, in the *wadi* leading up to KV 34, Thutmose III's tomb, and has already paid handsome dividends. Previously there were ten known tombs in this side *wadi*, of which the occupants of only two were known. Early work allowed the previously anonymous tomb KV 32 to be identified as the tomb of Queen Tiaa, wife of Amenhotep II and mother of Thutmose IV.

One of the aims of the mission was to locate the lost tomb KV 59. This is one of those tombs about which almost nothing is known, even its location. The tomb was successfully found cut in the bedrock at the bottom of a trench 2 meters below the surface level. It is located between KV 26 and KV 37 on the east side of the *wadi* and opposite KV 31. The entrance shaft is filled with flood debris, and excavation is ongoing.

There are now eleven tombs in this *wadi*. While clearing the entrance of KV 40 for the fitting of an iron security door, a depression immediately to the northwest of the entrance was noted. Of course on clearing, KV 64 was discovered. It was an Eighteenth Dynasty noble's tomb that was robbed in antiquity; the tomb flooded and was then usurped and reused in the Twenty-second Dynasty for the burial of the chantress Nehmes Bastet.

In addition to recording the tombs, the mission is also measuring the topography, enabling new and accurate maps of the valley to be made. It is also finding during the clearances groups of previously unknown workmen's huts. The huts and the artifacts they contain are significantly adding to our understanding of the working practices of the men from the village of Deir el-Medina who built the tombs (Dorn 2012). The project is ongoing, and it is hoped that this mission will eventually study all of the anonymous tombs in the valley, increasing our knowledge significantly.

If one of the above clearances does discover another tomb, what would be its nature? To be specific, who could have been the owner of such a find? History dictates that, at a conservative estimate, omitting the above tomb of Queen Isis, there could be at least six more tombs in the valley, discussed below.

Thutmose II

It appears that from the start of the Eighteenth Dynasty, the preferential site for a king's burial was in or near the Eastern Valley. Although disputed, KV 39 may be the tomb of Amenhotep I. The entrance corridor and first chamber are certainly, by their cutting and architecture, evidence that it is a very early, if not the earliest, tomb in the valley, and it may have been for him, later added to twice. KV 20 was very probably the original tomb for Thutmose I, the large antechamber at the end of the winding corridor being the actual burial chamber. However, the tomb was altered. Hatshepsut, once she gained the crown, had KV 20 altered by the addition of a further staircase and large burial chamber leading off the antechamber. The change in cutting and architecture is marked, and as Romer has stated, the proportions conformed with and were the same as used in Hatshepsut's temple at Deir el-Bahri (Romer 1981, 102–195). Hatshepsut's intention was that she would be buried with her father. We should therefore expect that the tomb for Thutmose II would also lie within the confines of the Eastern Valley. To date no tomb has been located for this king.

Ramesses VIII

There is no known royal tomb for Ramesses VIII in the valley. That statement must be qualified, as KV 19, as Edwin Brock has observed, was originally commenced for him as prince Ramesses Sethherkhepeshef before he gained the throne. The cartouches at the base of the door jams were cut for him. But after he gained the throne, he never used this tomb; it was abandoned and later used for the burial of prince Mentuherkhepeshef, perhaps a son of Ramesses IX. As Brock also noted, two niches were cut in opposite walls at the end of the corridor. These were clearly for guardian statues as in Tutankhamun's tomb. These features are only found in a royal tomb, never in a prince's or noble's tomb. If this was not Ramesses VIII's intended tomb then as every Ramesside king from Ramesses I to Ramesses XI had a tomb cut into the valley, a tomb for this king must await discovery.

Ramesses V

KV 9 is variously known as the tomb of Ramesses VI or as the joint tomb of Ramesses V and Ramesses VI. Neither is strictly true. The tomb was indeed commenced for Ramesses V. The first four corridors were cut for him, and surprisingly, his cartouches were not erased or overwritten. A start was probably also made on the well-room E, and here his cartouches were usurped, but the rest of the tomb from here down to the eventual burial chamber was all cut for Ramesses VI. Ramesses VI was undoubtedly buried in this tomb, but was Ramesses V also buried here?

We know from the few intact burials that inclusion of items from previous kings found among the burial equipment, family heirlooms, was common. So finding a piece of a wooden box with Ramesses V's name in KV 9 certainly does not prove he was buried there. There is no known sarcophagus for Ramesses V, nor has any of his burial equipment come to light.

The condition of these two kings' mummies is also highly significant. According to Grafton Elliott Smith, who unwrapped both mummies, Ramesses V's mummy was "in an excellent state of preservation" (Smith 1912, 91), whereas "none of them (Royal Mummies) was so severely maltreated as that of Rameses VI." His body had been so hacked about that it had to be tied to a wooden piece from a coffin to hold it together (Smith 1912, 92). Such a different fate for these two mummies seems to preclude a robbery of the *same* tomb. Indeed, it looks as if Ramesses V's mummy was not robbed at all.

The final clue comes from Papyrus Turin 1923 (verso), which is basically an excuse about why so little work had been done for Ramesses VI in KV 9. The excuse given was that *after* the burial of Ramesses V, the workforce from Deir el-Medina was banned from the royal valley for six months, and that during this time they made six tombs in the Valley of the Queens. Ventura has speculated that it looks as if the king died of smallpox, due to the pustules on his skin, and obviously six royal ladies had also died, and that a plague had ravaged the royal household (Ventura 1988, 155). Therefore the valley, with its contaminated king, was put off limits until it was felt to be safe, a not unreasonable scenario.

The salient word above is *after* the burial of the king, Ramesses V. No work was done for Ramesses VI in KV 9 until six months after Ramesses V had been buried. There is also the problem that the only place within KV 9 that could have been used for Ramesses V's burial at this time was chamber E, which was unfinished and is far too small to hold a king's burial. There is also the fact that a burial here would have effectively blocked further work inside the tomb, especially the extraction of large amounts of stone. From all of the above it is clear that Ramesses V was not buried in KV 9, leaving it free to be usurped by his successor. Consequently, there may be, perhaps in the Western Valley, a hastily cut royal tomb that once held Ramesses V.

Amarna Royalty

Despite the ongoing controversy over the occupant of KV 55, the funerary equipment discovered inside it harks from Amarna. This shows that at least some of the royal dead were transferred from that city to the valley, presumably for safety after the demise of Atenism and the abandonment of Amarna. However, the Amarna royal family was extensive, with at least nine individuals, which leads to the possibility that more of the royal dead were also transferred to the valley. The ARTP finding of Amarna period artifacts underneath Eighteenth Dynasty workmen's huts is also an indication of activity in the valley at this specific time. It would not have been possible to install nine burials in the small chamber of KV 55, meaning that there may be another tomb containing at least some of these individuals awaiting discovery.

A Cache of Kings?

It is well known that at the end of the New Kingdom, all the royal tombs were emptied of their contents, and then the kings' mummies were restored and hidden away in two caches. With the finding of the DB 320 cache and the cache in KV 35, Amenhotep II's tomb, almost all of the kings' mummies were recovered. Almost, but not all. There are a few kings still to be discovered, notably Horemheb, Aye, and Thutmose I. It must be admitted that like Queen Isis above and with the precedent of DB 320, such a cache of kings might lie elsewhere in the Theban Mountain, but the possibility remains that there is just such a cache within the valley.

Another KV 64?

Of the sixty-four tombs so far found in the valley, only twenty-six are royal tombs. The other thirty-eight are the majority. It is therefore more likely that another of these private tombs will be found than another royal tomb. These minor tombs are usually called commoners' or nobles' tombs. Modern research is now leading us to the understanding that perhaps all of these tombs were for royalty, that is, members of the royal family of the time. Maiherpri, KV 36, and Yuya and Thuya, KV 46, were certainly members of the reigning royal family. This was the case from the middle to the end of the Eighteenth Dynasty. It was only in the Ramesside period that the Eastern Valley was reserved exclusively for royal men, kings and princes, hence the need for the Valley of the Queens. This is one reason that the University of Basel's work is so important. The discovery of KV 64 came as a complete surprise. It is entirely possible that yet another of these small nobles' tombs still awaits discovery.

Only further clearances of the valley will prove or disprove the validity of these conjectures. So how do we find tombs without digging haphazardly across the valley? There are methods and knowledge that can be gainfully applied to the search.

The first is that the ancient scribes actually told us where the tombs are. There are nearly 4,000 ancient graffiti scratched into the rocks of the Theban Mountain. A study of these reveals the enigmatic T graffito (Peden 2001, 236). It is enigmatic because until recently its significance had not been realized: it is a tomb marker. Sometime either at the end of the Twentieth Dynasty or the beginning of the Twenty-first Dynasty, a scribe (perhaps the famous father and son duo, Djheutymose and Butehamun?) (Peden 2001, 190–192, 208, 235, 237; Reeves and Wilkinson 1996, 205) went around all the known tombs and inscribed the T graffito, showing their location of the tombs. This was to show the teams tasked with clearing the tombs their location. The T graffito resembles a block drawing of a capital letter T (Litherland 2014, 24–25, figures 10, 11, 63). It is a crude representation of a basic tomb, a shaft and single chamber. Wherever it is found, either vertically below, or sometimes vertically above, will lie a tomb, although the graffito proves the tomb will not be intact. Note, only known tombs were so marked; some tombs, such as KV 55, KV 62, and KV 63, were already lost under the debris of a flash flood at the end of the Eighteenth Dynasty and were not marked with the T graffito (Cross 2008).

Second, scattered around the valley at various locations and elevations are sections of workmen's huts. Each group of huts was made for the construction of a specific royal tomb and was then abandoned. The foci of these huts therefore followed the location of the royal tombs. The workmen's huts, as most can be dated, are extremely useful in working out the stratigraphy of the valley. If a previously undiscovered section of huts can be found, then a tomb will lie near. Mapping of these huts and correlation with the known tombs is therefore a vital task for excavators.

Third, it is only recently that modern methods of remote sensing have been applied to the valley. As virtually all tombs in Egypt are rock-cut tombs, the most suitable equipment is GPR, which can see down through the sediments to bedrock and even through the bedrock to chambers below without the expense of excavating. Figure 34.2 shows the totally noninvasive use of GPR in the Valley of the Kings.

Although analysis of the GPR scans produced can be a difficult and expert task, the results can be spectacular. However, the equipment must be suitable to the task. During the two previous scans of the valley, in the 1970s and during the ARTP work described above, both sets of scans only penetrated down to a depth of 2 meters. Bedrock in the

FIGURE 34.2 The totally noninvasive use of Ground Penetrating Radar in the Valley of the Kings.

central area is 5 meters below the surface. A complete GPR survey scan of the valley might reveal the location of tombs, but would also finally provide a visual representation of the topography of the valley and the sequence of flash floods over the millennia. This is something the present writer plans for the future.

Finally, there can be no better (or perhaps more enjoyable!) method than the standard archaeological method of "walking the ground," pure observation of the site by simply walking the ground and looking for indications of tombs. This was how Belzoni discovered KV 17. He saw that a stream from a flash flood vanished into the ground instead of running off into the valley. The stream must have disappeared into a cavity in the bedrock, a tomb.

No matter what method is used to find a tomb, in every case, for the search to be successful, we must find previously untouched ground. Recognizing virgin ground is relatively simple. Freshly cut limestone is dazzlingly white, but over time the white surface weathers to the beautiful golden patina that we see in the valley now. If a horizon of pure white limestone chipping is found, then we will know that this layer has not been exposed since it was cut and the ground below has never been exposed. The search for a tomb literally becomes the search for white limestone. This was how Schaden located KV 63.

Where are the best locations to search for other tombs? Most books on the valley state that it has been fully excavated; it has not. Incredibly, there are still three areas, deep layers that date back to the Eighteenth Dynasty, two in the Eastern Valley and one in the Western Valley, that have never been excavated down to bedrock.

Is the Valley of the Kings exhausted? The answer must be a definite no!

BIBLIOGRAPHY

Amarna Royal Tomb Project. 2006. "Another New Tomb in the Valley of the Kings—
'KV64': II." July 31. http://www.nicholasreeves.com/item.aspx?category=Comment&id=81.

Bierbrier, M. L. 1992. *The Tomb Builders of the Pharaohs*. London.

Cerny, J. 1973, 2004. *A Community of Workmen at Thebes in the Ramesside Period*. Cairo.

Cerny, J. and A. A. Sadek, et al. 1969–1983. *Graffiti de la montagne thebaine*. 4 vols. Cairo.

Cross, S. W. 2008. "The Hydrology of the Valley of the Kings." *Journal of Egyptian Archaeology*
94: 303–310.

Cross, S. W. 2014. "The Workmen's Huts and Stratigraphy in the Valley of the Kings." *Journal of
Egyptian Archaelogy* 100: 135–152.

Dodson, A., and S. Ikram. 2008. *The Tomb in Ancient Egypt*. London.

Dorn, A. 2012. *Workmen's Huts in the Valley of the Kings: A Contribution to the Social History of
Ancient Egypt Because of New Source Material from the Mid-20th Dynasty (about 1150 BC)*.
Aegyptica Helvetica 23. Basel.

Hawass, Z., et al. 2010. "Preliminary Report of the Supreme Council of Antiquities (SCA)
Excavation in the Valley of the Kings (2007–2008)." In *Thebes and Beyond: Studies in Honour
of Kent Weeks*, edited by Z. Hawass and S. Ikram, 57–84. Cairo.

Hawass Z., and S. Ikram, eds. 2010. *Thebes and Beyond: Studies in Honour of Kent Weeks*. Cairo.

KV63. n.d. http://www.kv-63.com/.

Litherland, P. 2014. *The Western Wadis of the Thebam Necropolis*. New Kingdom Research
Foundation, London.

Peden, A. J. 2001. *The Graffiti of Pharaonic Egypt: Scope and Roles of Informal Writings (c.
3100–332 B.C.)*. Leiden.

Reeves, C. N., and R. H. Wilkinson. 1996. *The Complete Valley of the Kings: Tombs and Treasures
of Egypt's Greatest Pharaohs*. London.

Romer, J. 1981. *The Valley of the Kings*. London.

Romer, J. 1984. *Ancient Lives: The Story of the Pharaoh's Tombmakers*. London.

Smith, G. E. 1912. *Catalogue General Antiquites Egyptiennes du Musee du Caire: The Royal
Mummies*. Cairo.

Thomas, E. 1966. *The Royal Necropoleis at Thebes*. Princeton, NJ.

University of Basel, Deir el-Medina. n.d. http://aegyptologie.unibas.ch/forschung/editionen/
aegyptiaca-helvetica/.

University of Basel Kings' Valley Project. n.d. http://aegyptologie.unibas.ch/forschung/
projekte/university-of-basel-kings-valley-project/.

Ventura, R. 1988. "The Largest Project for a Royal Tomb in the Valley of the Kings." *Journal of
Egyptian Archaeology* 74: 1988. 137–156. Papyrus 1923.

....

CHAPTER 35

TOMB RECORDING

Epigraphy, Photography, Digital Imaging,
and 3D Surveys

....

ADAM LOWE

The authorities face agonizing decisions. Do they admit visitors to
royal graves and witness the near-certain deterioration and perhaps
disappearance of unique wall paintings from sheer people pressure?
Or do they close everything to save it for future generations?... The
dilemma pits the preservation of the priceless and finite archive that
is ancient Egypt against the pressing economic needs of a developing country—altruism for future generations against short-term
advantages.

(Fagan 2004, 252)

The Role of Recording and
Reconstruction and the Development
of Sustainable Tourism

....

In the eighteenth century Joachim Winckelmann proposed that sites and artifacts
should be conserved and preserved, not restored, renovated, or reconstructed. At the
time Winckelmann and others were excavating Rome and shaping our image of ruins
and antiquity—an image that embraced Greek, Etruscan, Roman, and Egyptian influences. The comment was aimed at the imaginative and active approach of many of his
contemporaries, especially Piranesi, who was restoring, renovating, and reconstructing, treating the remains he found as a sourcebook for ideas and information. Piranesi
was an artist. Winckelmann was an academic who represents the philological approach
that was in tune with the twentieth century, and his views reflect those of most heritage

professionals today. This approach was enshrined in the 1964 Venice Charter and other charters issued by ICOMOS, UNESCO and heritage professionals. However, as new technologies become available to record and study objects with forensic accuracy, it is clear that the decision-making processes of heritage managers and the practical tasks of conserving and preserving the past are neither simple nor an exact science.

However discreet the attempts to conserve might be, they alter the appearance of the original and often have unforeseen consequences that can be irreversible. They impose changes in color, tone, texture, and sheen, they condition the look and character of the sites and how we perceive them. They raise both moral and aesthetic issues. In the Valley of the Kings the glass panels installed in some tombs introduce a museum language that has nothing to do with the function or character of the tomb. The lighting, text panels, smell of human sweat, guards, tour groups, and a ban on photography all play their part in imposing an aesthetic dimension on the act of preservation.

When Winckelmann was writing in the middle of the eighteenth century, tourism was limited to a few wealthy and acquisitive individuals. The problem facing the heritage managers of today is how to ensure that our cultural heritage is preserved for the next generation in a meaningful way. Whatever practical and political arguments are put forward, an essential part of every approach is documentation: we have a duty to record what we have inherited. Twenty years ago it was not possible to digitize, store, and then rematerialize an object that, side by side with the original and at a normal viewing distance, looked identical. Now this is possible. It requires time, understanding, technology, and a different mindset. It demands new intellectual and professional frameworks. It also requires the development of hardware and software designed in conjunction with the people who are working to preserve and conserve. It involves collaborations among disciplines that struggle to share a common language.

Since the tomb of Tutankhamun was discovered, tourism has been the biggest threat to its survival. Yet Egypt's economy is dependent on tourism. Andrea Byrnes has described the problems clearly in her essay "Replication of the Tomb of Tutankhamun: Conservation and Sustainable Tourism in the Valley of the Kings" (Byrnes, 2013). She observes that Flinders Petrie and others were aware of the problem and that Howard Carter commented on the impact on the fabric of the tomb caused by the humidity and dust brought in by the visitors. She sites Michael Jones's chapter in Wilkinson's *Egyptology Today* and provides figures: "In 2005, for example, Egypt earned 6.4 billion US dollars in tourist revenue, providing work for around 12 percent of the nation's workforce." According to Kent Weeks and Nigel Hetherington's *The Valley of the Kings: A Site Management Handbook* (2013), during the height of the 2004 season the Valley of the Kings received 7,000 visitors per day and more than 1.8 million visitors in total for that year. The site management plan operates on the assumption that visitor numbers in the Valley of the Kings will have reached 15,000–20,000 per day by 2014. The tombs were built to last, but they were not built to receive visitors.

At the entrance to the tomb of Tutankhamun is a yellow sign that reads "EXTRA TICKET FOR TUTANKH AMON TOMB 100L.E." The celebrity of the tomb adds to its value and attracts visitors. While political unrest in recent years has led to a temporary downturn, the growth of tourism and the continued public interest in Egyptology will undoubtedly lead to the return of the visitors once public confidence in political stability returns. In the twenty-first century the Valley of the Kings has to play a dual role. On the one hand it is a repository of paintings and written texts that reveal essential insights into who we are. On the other it is essential for the economy of Egypt in general and Luxor in particular.

Tutankhamun's tomb is a tourist magnet. Schools around the world fill receptive and imaginative minds with the great stories of the boy king, pharaonic culture, adventure and archaeology, Howard Carter and curses, gold, and symbolism. Hollywood and computer games turn this interest into entertainment. The treasures from the tomb were moved to the Cairo Museum following the discovery, where they are seen by many more people than if they had remained in Luxor. Touring exhibitions of selected objects attract wider audiences and remain popular. In London, the 1972 exhibition *Treasures of Tutankhamun* attracted 1,650,000 visitors. Now, in addition to exhibitions of original objects, several identical commercial touring exhibitions based on tourist-quality copies and dramatized documentaries are successfully touring the world. All of these generate interest and result in increased tourism.

Some of the measures carried out by the Supreme Council of Antiquities to protect the tombs have had a positive effect, but all involve restricting access and keeping people moving through the tombs. Banning guided tours inside the tombs has made a significant difference and prevents large concentrations of people in one area. The restriction of each visitor to only three tombs per visit, the closure of the tomb of Seti I, and the imposition of severe limitations on visits to the tomb of Nefertari and the use of a rotation system (similar to that used to protect the Etruscan tombs in Tarquinia) all help. But ultimately, as with the caves at Lascaux and Altamira, the only solution for long-term preservation is to radically reduce visitor numbers. The question is: Can this be done in a way that keeps attracting the visitors and enhances our understanding of the importance of the site and the knowledge it contains? The use of new recording technologies is central to any answer. The role of facsimiles still needs to be defined and demonstrated. Since 1988 the Society of Friends of the Royal Tombs of Egypt, under the direction of Erik Hornung and Theodor Abt, has been championing this approach. The Supreme Council of Antiquities initiated a research project in the tomb of Seti I in 2001, and the recording work in the tomb of Tutankhamun started in 2009. In 2012 the facsimiles of the burial chamber, the sarcophagus, and the re-creation of the missing fragment from the tomb of Tutankhamun were given to the people of Egypt by the Society of Friends of the Royal Tombs of Egypt, the Factum Foundation, and Factum Arte (see Figure 35.1). The work has taken almost four years to complete and has involved a large group of individuals, each with different skills, working together as a team. Permission has been granted by the ministries of tourism and antiquities to install the facsimile on a site next to Howard Carter's house at the entrance to the Valley of the Kings. The aim is to encourage the conservation

FIGURE 35.1 The final installation of the facsimile of the burial chamber of Tutankhamun, during its temporary installation at the Conrad Hotel as part of the EU Task Force, November 2012.

[Photo by I. della Valle, courtesy of Factum Arte.]

community and the general public to visit both the original tomb (while it remains open) and the facsimile and contribute to the debate about the problems of preserving and safeguarding fragile sites.

The work that was carried out by Factum Arte over the past decade in the tombs of Tutankhamun and Seti I is a start—it reflects a coherent approach to the development and use of digital technology to record the surfaces and structure of the tombs in astonishing detail. These data are essential for objective study and to monitor the decay that is taking place. The fact that the data are of sufficient quality to reproduce physically in three dimensions is evidence of their correspondence to the original. This work has involved the development of new technologies to record, inspect, archive, and reveal the complex histories of these two tombs. It has involved the development of a complete working practice to rematerialize the data that can be communicated and taught. It is an approach that is rapidly gaining acceptance and has led to the creation of the Factum Foundation for Digital Technology in Conservation. The foundation funded most of the work in Egypt and has two main aims: to provide the technology and human skills to satisfactorily record the condition of the tombs and to convert public interest into a force that understands the difficulties of preserving the past and makes a positive contribution to its preservation.

Technical Considerations Based
on Non-Contact-Surface Observations

The craftsmen who made these tombs had a highly developed understanding of materials. It is probable that they attached symbolic significance to the materials they used, the order in which they were applied, the way they were mixed, and their final appearance. They certainly understood the physical properties of the materials they worked with. They prepared the plaster layers and the application of the paint so the walls could breathe. They understood how to draw long black lines with even edges, they understood how to make and prepare both natural pigments and those that required human artifice in their production. It is equally probable that they knew that when the tomb was sealed the natural environmental stability would ensure their work lasted, guaranteeing immortality for the pharaoh. The enemy of preservation is dynamic change: changes in temperature, humidity, and the levels of dust; chemical changes; and other diverse environmental fluctuations about which we are not yet aware.

The tomb was hacked out of the bedrock. Tool marks are visible underneath the plaster layers and brick holes. There is a visible raised line to the left of center of the north wall, as if the burial chamber was cut from both sides. The walls are coated with several layers of thinly applied plaster to smooth the irregularities in the bedrock before application of the priming coat and painted decoration. There is a skim of greyish coarse plaster and then a coat of a creamy brown plaster wash. On the north wall there are many air bubbles that appear to be in this "wash" layer. On the lower part of the west wall there appear to be two layers of plaster, while on the south wall there seem to be three, although it generally looks as if the plaster was applied quickly and reapplied where necessary. On the west and north walls there are tool marks in the plaster, as if it was applied by trowel, but there are also areas where it has been smoothed by hand, and traces of fingers can be observed. Over the plaster there is a coat of white priming paint in many places, but it is neither uniform nor consistent, and on the south and east walls the golden ochre paint was applied onto the plaster without the priming layer.

There are many dark brown spots that are the subject of ongoing research by the Getty Conservation Institute. These microorganisms cover most of the painted area of the tomb, appearing in places on the ceiling but not on the sarcophagus. Based on the evidence of Harry Burton's photographs[1], they haven't changed since Carter opened the tomb, suggesting that the walls were not fully dry when the tomb was sealed. Damp walls and the decaying offerings in the tomb provided the conditions that the micro-bacteria needed to grow. They "grew" in interesting ways on the painted areas and seem to prefer the light red under drawing and the areas in or around cracks. They also seem to be attracted to fibers within the paint or plaster. The photograph by Harry Burton of the "missing fragment" shows that there was no micro-bacterial growth on this area of the decoration. This section of the south wall could breathe and would have dried faster than the painted areas in contact with the bedrock.

On the north, west, and east walls some areas of missing plaster were repainted at the time of the original painting and as a result are now covered with brown spots. Others areas of loss have been filled since the opening of the tomb, and the restorer has covered his work with splashes of brown paint in imitation of the micro-bacteria. Based on observational information, it seems likely that the binder of the paint is primarily gelatin, while the binder in the black lines is more glossy and brittle, suggesting a natural resin; gum arabic was (and still is) readily available in and around Luxor.

A close study reveals that the baboons on the west wall were painted in the following order: 1. plaster, 2. white priming coat, 3. yellow paint, 4. red under drawing, 5. red face, 6. blue, 7. white hair, 8. black lines. The baboons are painted with a variety of tones of blue, which appears to suggest a mixed color varying in tone and hue. The leopard on the north wall was painted in a slightly different way: 1. plaster, 2. white priming coat, 3. yellow paint, 4. white paint, 5. red under drawing, 6. pale yellow skin, 7. red dots, 8. black outlines. There are many drips and splashes of yellow and red paint, suggesting haste or a lack of care.

Problems Inherent in Remedial and Aesthetic Restorations

Even from a distance it is clear that the surface of the painted walls is heavily cracked, and there is significant paint loss (see Figure 35.2). The surface reveals that the paint layer is in a friable and fragile state. The surface decay suggests that what is going on under the surface may be more serious. Observation of the dust deposits reveals that in places the plaster is detaching from the wall. From the high-resolution photographs it is possible to see shadows behind some of the holes in the paint and plaster—it is clear that large sections of plaster are only held in place by the skim layer of plaster and the consolidant that has been applied. The scale and location of some of the refills and repainting (the largest is an area of about 1 square meter) confirm this and reveal the fragile condition of the paint surface.

On the west wall near the handrail there is clear evidence that human touch has smoothed and eroded the surface and that all areas within reach are significantly more degraded than the rest of the tomb. On the area around the figure of Tutankhamun, lying on his funeral sledge, one can see the cracked and flaking nature of the paint, with the slightly glossier black lines lifting from the background golden ochre. Even from the position by the handrail one can make out an irregular surface sheen, as if the large areas of the wall have at some point been given a wash of consolidant. The high resolution photographs make it possible to study the surface in great detail and then test these observations against the actual wall. From close up the fragile state of the paint surface is instantly clear. Hundreds of injection marks reveal that significant work has been done in an attempt to bind the paint layer and plaster to the bedrock; white residues and drip

FIGURE 35.2 The surface of the East Wall in the burial chamber of Tutankhamun, showing flaking paint and a sheen from surface painted Paraloid.

[Photo by G. Dupond, courtesy of Factum Arte.]

marks from local surface applications of Paraloid can be found in many places. To fully understand what is happening, the conservators from the Getty Conservation Institute will need to see if the application of Paraloid is the problem or the solution. If it has limited the ability of the paint surface to breathe it will cause a buildup of moisture, and this will encourage the growth of salt crystals, which are capable of pushing the paint off the wall. This mix of a fragile surface and dynamic change caused by fluctuations in temperature and humidity will eventually result in collapse. There has been significant paint loss since the tomb was opened. If the means of consolidation are now a cause for concern, the treatment will need to be reversed.

REVERSIBILITY—A TERM IN NEED OF CLARIFICATION

Reversibility is a central principle of conservation practice. The term refers to the ability to remove any addition or change that is made. Since the 1970s Paraloid, a product originally designed to make printing ink more flexible, has been used extensively in the tombs. Now many conservators have serious reservations about its use and reversibility over time. When used to consolidate the painted surfaces in the tomb of Tutankhamun or Seti I, Paraloid cannot be removed without significant paint loss. The application of this acrylic resin also changes the color and tone of the paint; this is an irreversible change. Paraloid injected under the surface of the paint to stick the paint and plaster layer to the bedrock is also irreversible and changes the way the surface moves and breathes.

In the 1999 ARCE condition report on the tomb of Seti I, Dr. Bojana Mojsov comments: "[D]uring recent 'restoration' efforts plaster and several pigments have been added on top of uncleaned surfaces with varying results. This is particularly disturbing since it was done just recently and now only adds to the relatively numerous problems of the reliefs. All of this layer of *pentimento* ought to be removed and the surfaces cleaned before we can see what is left of the original decorations underneath or make any decisions about future restoration."

At the time that the ARCE report was being prepared a new "test" restoration was being carried out in Seti's tomb (room F). This test has resulted in a significant change in tone and color to a section of about 50 by 50 centimeters. Fifteen years after it was done, this test clearly demonstrates the problems inherent in using Paraloid, but it also reveals the way restorations change the appearance of the image. The white area on the left of the restoration has been over-painted with a white that both is a different "color" and has a different character than the original white. The unrestored area to the left of the restoration reveals a matte white (almost certainly huntite) painted over a greyish underpainting that could be either the plaster base or an intentional undercoat. The restored area appears to be a recently applied acrylic or gouache under a layer of Paraloid—the surface consolidation has slightly yellowed and the paint it covers is now flaking off the wall. All of this demonstrates the inherent difficulties of keeping things stable if the environment is dynamic and confirms the importance of high-resolution documentation.

REASONS FOR OPTIMISM

Despite all the reasons for concern, the twenty-first century is providing us with new high-resolution recording technologies that can digitize the tombs with sufficient accuracy to monitor the speed of decay. With the correct political support and infrastructure, the documentation could be carried out by Egyptian teams, providing employment in Luxor and the surrounding area—in theory it could also be self-financing. The fact that it is possible to record the tombs in color and three dimensions with forensic accuracy should become a central part any preservation policy. New technologies and software applications are resulting in innovative ways to study, analyze, and elaborate information. The developments in technology are moving fast, but a divide between technicians who understand the equipment and managers who understand the technical possibilities interferes with their application. The practical solution at present is to take advantage of the successful mechanisms that are in place and already applying technology—the Theban Mapping Project is one example.

In 2001 the Theban Mapping Project began work with Quantapoint to use their laser measuring system to produce accurate 3D plans and models. The Theban Mapping Project website was launched in August 2002, and its impact was immediate—by the end if its first month it had 150,000 unique visitors, clearly demonstrating a need and a receptive audience.

While the Quantapoint system can produce an accurate survey of the shape of a tomb, it cannot map the details of the surface texture or color. This requires different equipment and a different set of skills. The work that Factum Arte carried out in the tombs of Seti I and Tutankhamun recorded the surface of the walls with 100 million measured points per square meter. Color was recorded at a resolution of 800 dpi at a scale of 1:1. These data could be aligned and added to the Theban Mapping Project website. This would allow the virtual visitor to study the structure and layout of the tomb, zoom into any area and see the decoration in color, select any section and magnify it in order to inspect details, shift between color and 3D data, and connect to archives of historical photographs and other source material. The availability of this quantity of information in a virtual form does not reduce the desire to visit Egypt. On the contrary, it encourages it. It nurtures an intimacy with the site and facilitates new ways of study. But equally important, it allows us to know what damage we are doing—to monitor the speed of decay and to make informed decisions about how to safeguard the Theban necropolis and assist in the long-term preservation of the site.

The Practical Application of Digital Technology in Non-Contact Conservation

Outlined below are the stages involved in the non-contact recording (dematerialization) and the construction of a facsimile (rematerialization).

The digitalization of the surface of a work of art is a relatively new field: if carried out at sufficient resolution, it can be used to both study and monitor the surface of any object. It can also be used to rematerialize the object in diverse forms, ranging from multimedia presentations to the construction of exact facsimiles. The validity of this type of recording is dependent on the quality of the data gathered. Since their invention in the 1920s, photographically based 3D recording systems have focused on capturing the shape of an object. It is only recently that the technology has been able to record surface data. Recording the relief and texture of a surface is now possible and is leading to new insights into why the surface looks the way it does.

Dematerializing 1: The Lucida Laser Scanner—Designed to Record the Tombs

Lucida is a 3D laser scanner designed by artist and engineer Manuel Franquelo, custom built by Factum Arte, and funded by Factum Foundation. This system, the result of more than ten years of investigation into the high-resolution recording of the surface of paintings and relief objects, uses two cameras and one laser. A thin strip of red light is projected onto the surface of the object. As the line moves over the surface, it is recorded by the two cameras, positioned on either side of the laser. The distortions of the line produced by the relief of the surface are recorded as a tonal depth map, which is then converted into 3D information. The scanner moves parallel to the surface plane of the object, controlled by linear guides. Lucida uses a system of double exposure to extract the optimum data from both dark and glossy surfaces. The relationship between noise and information is critical; for any recording technology to be meaningful for cultural applications, it is essential that there be a close correspondence between the surface and the recording of the surface.

The Lucida scanner stores the data as raw black-and-white video. This is a radical innovation that significantly distances Lucida from other scanning systems, which use software algorithms to convert the photographic data into a three-dimensional mesh—this transformation is an irreversible abstraction of the data that results in a loss of information. Lucida condenses the raw (unprocessed) information, thus removing many of the obstacles that could limit future generations from accessing and reprocessing it.

Lucida uses the raw files to generate 3D and rendered simulations of the surface relief. These can be exported into triangulated meshes (.stl), point clouds, or a variety of different renderings. It is by virtue of the renderings that the recorded data can be accessed without specialized (and usually expensive) 3D software: it can easily be opened with standard image viewers. Moreover, it can be incorporated into accurately aligned, multilayered files that can also include additional types of recording, such as infra-red, X-ray, and color information. Multilayered files are proving very helpful for researchers and conservators alike and facilitate an accurate, objective, and meaningful method for analyzing the artwork.

The Lucida scanner is easy to use and transport. Due to its size, lightness, and physical configuration, it allows the user to work in conditions that are normally incompatible with computer-based technologies. It can be powered by electricity or battery. The battery can be recharged with solar energy by using a simple solar panel. In all the equipment that has been developed for use in Egypt, the aim has been to reduce cost, reduce complexity, and produce robust systems that can be used in the dusty, harsh conditions that exist in the tombs of the Theban necropolis.

Dematerializing 2: White Light Recording

There are several white light scanning systems that could be used in the tombs of the Theban necropolis. Each has advantages and disadvantages. The system chosen and

FIGURE 35.3 The SIDIO white light scanning system recording the surface of the sarcophagus of Tutankhamun.

[Photo by G. Dupond, courtesy of Factum Arte.]

used by Factum Arte in 2009 was the NUB3D SIDIO (see Figure 35.3). While it is heavier than many comparable systems and only has one camera, the data it records have a close correspondence to the surface being recorded. The SIDIO system employs a conjunction of optical technology, 3D topometry, and digital image processing to extract 3D coordinates from the surface of the object, a technique known as triangulation. Three-dimensional information is acquired by analyzing the deformation caused when parallel lines are projected onto the surface of an object and recorded by the camera. With these images, SIDIO integrated software calculates a coordinated XYZ point cloud relating to the surface and shape of the object. The SIDIO records the surface from many individually positioned shots that are then aligned. It requires a skilled and experienced operator to achieve good results.

Dematerializing 3: A Panoramic Photographic System

After working with a parallel photographic recording system for many years, Factum Arte switched to panoramic recording when the technology became available to produce high-resolution images quickly and accurately. At the end of 2010 we started working with German company CLAUSS. They have been developing panoramic photographic equipment since 1993 and launched their pan-and-tilt head in 2003.

The automated equipment consists of a motorized, panoramic head and a computer (to control the head), as well as the recording device (camera) and the archiving software to download and name the resulting photographs. The lighting, distance, speed of recording, and resolution all depend on factors specific to each recording task. When recording the image many photographs are automatically taken in sequence and then stitched together at subpixel accuracy. The aim is to record a high-resolution image that is in focus and has a resolution of at least 600 dpi at a scale of 1:1. The camera used to record the tomb of Tutankhamun was a Canon EOS7DII DSLR with various lenses depending on distance. The use of a UV-filtered, high-speed flash is recommended, but in conservation recording there is resistance to the use of flash. In the tomb a low-level cold light source was used. Depth of focus can be a problem, but this can be overcome by combining a mix of focus stacking and panoramic recording. The different planes of photographs are stitched together using focus-stacking software technology. The merging process consists of multiplying control points between photographs on the same plane and photographs on different planes, until a stitching result of subpixel accuracy is achieved. The result is a gigapixel image with uniform sharpness.

When carrying out photographic recording for conservation purposes, all the normal color and greyscale references are used. However, Factum Arte have found it essential to develop their own color reference system for use when printing the data. The main difficulty of recording the color is to understand the extreme complexity of the painted surface. The paintings were executed as broad areas of paint with a limited palette, but a combination of centuries of aging and modern interference has resulted in an inconsistent and intricate surface.

Rematerializing

At a time when many people are just starting to understand the role virtual models can play in studying and presenting cultural heritage, the technology is making it possible to go one stage further and return the data into a physical form. What has been carried out in the tomb of Tutankhamun is a two-way process—from the real world to the digital archive and then from the digital files back into the physical world without significant change or loss of detail.

This has been possible for some time, but the costs have been prohibitive. Now, due to a highly focused and motivated team at Factum Arte, the protocol has been put in place to vastly reduce the costs and break down all stages of the work into tasks that can be taught to a local workforce in Luxor. The details of this work are not the subject of this text, but it is important to outline the many stages that are involved.

The most time-consuming and expensive part of the rematerialization process is routing the 3D data at high resolution. To rout a 1-by-1-square-meter panel in 3D at a resolution of 250 microns takes approximately 400 hours. Once routed, the sections need to be cast and joined together. A skeleton has to be made to hold the panels in place and allow the entire surface of the tomb to be assembled with a floor and a ceiling.

Printing onto a relief surface presents its own difficulties, and after experimenting with various transfer systems Factum Arte developed its own elastic membrane that can be printed as a flat sheet. The membrane is a layered mixture of three materials: a thin, flexible inkjet ground, an acrylic gesso, and an elastic acrylic support. It is built in seven layers rolled onto a slightly textured silicon mold. The printing of the facsimile was done using a purpose-built flatbed inkjet printer. For many years this printer has been at the center of Factum Arte's approach to the production of facsimiles, as it allows the image to be built up in layers, each printed in perfect registration. This approach means that both the color and the tone can be controlled and locally altered to ensure a perfect match.

The printed flexible skins are positioned using a slow-cure contact adhesive. Sight and touch are both essential to ensure the exact relationship between the surface and the color. Working with a raking light, the skin is positioned and repositioned until all details in the printing correspond to the underlying surface. Once positioned correctly the skin and the relief are put into a vacuum chamber, and pressure is applied evenly until the adhesive has cured. Due to the gossamer-like character of the skin when it is fixed to the surface, it takes on the character of the wall of the tomb.

The burial chamber is assembled from interlocking panels that are bolted together from the outside. It has been designed for ease of transport and assembly. Once the tomb is assembled the final joins are filled and retouched.

The proposed lighting for the facsimile in its eventual location should match the lights used in the Valley of the Kings. The acoustics, smell, and temperature can also be controlled to increase the similarities between the original and the facsimile. Special effects can be used to control humidity and temperature, and projections onto the surface can inform the visitor of the problems in the tomb and the impact of these dynamic conditions.

THE BIOGRAPHY OF OBJECTS—THE OBJECT AS SUBJECT

The biography of any cultural artifact reveals various levels of human intervention at different times in its life. Many of these interventions have been made to preserve the object, but others reflect changing attitudes toward our relationship with the past. Some actions that have disastrous consequences are well intentioned, while others are not. The tombs in the Valley of the Kings contain examples of mindless vandalism as well as acts of love, care, and possession that have had equally ruinous and unpredictable consequences. The tomb of Seti I contains numerous examples of both; graffiti from the nineteenth and twentieth centuries cover the walls, and sections have been removed and are now in museums and collections around the world (the largest two sections are in the Musée du Louvre and the Museo Archeologico in Florence—interestingly, these two fragments now look very different from the original tomb and from each other). Belzoni cast large sections of the tomb in wax and vegetable fiber to make the "first" facsimile, which introduced the wonders of pharaonic culture to London in the 1820s. The travel agents used to sell plaster-casting kits to their tourists so they could take their own "handmade" souvenirs home; both had grave consequences for the tomb. Evidence of erosion of the surfaces and accidental damage can be found everywhere.

Values and opinions change from generation to generation. Winckelmann's statement that we must conserve and preserve is obviously correct, but we now have tools that he never had. Perhaps we can engage once again with the act of reconstructing and rethinking our relationship to the past in a way that makes it more accessible. Culture has wrongly been connected to leisure. This has led to many of today's problems. The tombs are not being preserved to give future generations something to do when they are on holiday; they are being protected to safeguard the important knowledge they contain. It is essential that this is done without impositions on the original. The aim is not to turn an original into a reproduction of itself by altering its appearance, but to allow the next generation to inherit the past in full knowledge of the complexity this involves.

If the facsimile, in its site next to Carter's house, can capture the public imagination in a similar way to the discovery of the tomb, then Tutankhamun can secure his immortality—at least for a while longer. With the right approach, new technologies are making it possible to have both an altruistic approach that preserves the site for future generations and the commercial benefits of tourism that the people of Egypt need right now.

POSTSCRIPT

This text was written in 2012 after the facsimile of the burial chamber had been presented to the Egyptian people by Baroness Ashton on behalf of the European Union. Between January and April 2014 and Egyptian team under the direction of the Egyptian architect Tarek Waly and a team from Factum Arte worked to install the facsimile in an underground space next to Howard Carter's house at the entrance to the Valley of the Kings. This initiative has met with extensive press coverage and almost universal praise. The same team is now awaiting the final permission to restore Stoppelaere house and create a training centre devoted to high-resolution recording in 3D and colour. As local operators are trained they will begin the epic task of recording all the decorated surfaces in the tomb of Seti I. A transfer of equipment and knowledge on this scale is redefining how we think about the long-term protection of heritage sites in an age of mass tourism.

ACKNOWLEDGMENTS

Many people have played a part in this work, but special thanks go to all of the team at Factum Arte, both those who worked to do the recording and those who spent thousands of hours processing and returning the digital data into a physical object that redefines the word "facsimile." The Factum Foundation for Digital Technology in Conservation and the Society of Friends of the Royal Tombs of Egypt provided logistical and financial support. The Universiy of Basel and AUC provided academic support. In Egypt our special thanks go to the SCA, specifically to Dr. Gaballah, Dr. Hawass, and our inspectors Mohamed Khalil and Mahmoud Mousa. Also very special thanks to Fayza Haikal, who has been supportive from the beginning. Since the facsimile was finished we have received essential support from James Moran, Charles-Edouard Held, Dominik Furgler, Dominic Asquith, Kent Weeks, Nigel Hetherington, Jaromir Malek, Nataliya Apostolova, Raquel Cabrera Álvarez, Bernadino León, Salima Ikram, the Ministry of Tourism, Egypt Air and everyone at the Griffith Institute in Oxford.

NOTE

1. Photographs by Harry Burton in *Tutankhamun: Anatomy of an Excavation*, Oxford: Griffith Institute, University of Oxford, 2006. <http://www.griffith.ox.ac.uk/gri/carter/gallery/>

BIBLIOGRAPHY

Abt, T., and E. Hornung. 2003. *Knowledge for the Afterlife: The Egyptian Amduat—a Quest for Immortality.* Zurich.

Andrew Byrnes. 2013. Egyptological, Magazine Edition 8, April 18th 2013; *Replicating the Tomb of Tutankhamun. Conservation and sustainable tourism in the Valley of the Kings.*

de la Torre, M., ed. 1997. *The Conservation of Archaeological Sites in the Mediterranean Region.* Los Angeles.

de la Torre, M., ed. 2002. *Assessing the Values of Cultural Heritage.* Los Angeles.

Demas, M. 2002. "Planning for Conservation and Management of Archaeological Sites: A Values-Based Approach." In *Management Planning for Archaeological Sites*, edited by J. Teutonico and G. Palumbo, 27–54. Los Angeles.

Eaton-Krauss, M. 1993. *The Sarcophagus in the Tomb of Tutankhamun.* Oxford.

Fagan, B. 2004. *The Rape of the Nile. Tomb Robbers, Tourists and Archaelogists in Egypt.* Boulder.

Gagliardi, P. 2011. *The Miracle of Cana: The Originality of the Re-Production.* Venice.

Hornung, E. and B. Bryan. 2002. *The Quest for Immortality: Treasures of Ancient Egypt.* Washington, DC and Copenhagen.

Hornung, E., A. Wiese, and C. Loeben. 2005. *Immortal Pharaoh: The Tomb of Thutmose III.* Madrid and Copenhagen.

ICOMOS. 1999. "International Cultural Tourism Charter: Managing Tourism at Places of Heritage Significance." WWW.ICOMOS.org/tourism/charter.html.

Lowe, A., and J. MacMillan-Scott. 2012. *The Authorised Facsimile of the Burial Chamber of Tutankhamun*. Madrid.

Mason, R. 2002. "Assessing Values in Conservation Planning: Methodological Issues and Choices." In *Assessing the Values of Cultural Heritage*, edited by M. de la Torre, 5–30. Los Angeles.

Mason, R., and E. Avrami. 2002. "Heritage Values and Challenges of Conservation Planning." In *Management Planning for Archaeological Sites*, edited by J. Teutonico and G. Palumbo, 13–26. Los Angeles.

McDonald, J. K. 1996. *House of Eternity: In the Tomb of Nefertari*. London.

Reeves, C. N., ed. 1992. *After Tut'ankhamun: Research and Excavation in the Royal Necropolis at Thebes*. London and New York.

Reeves, C. N., and R. H. Wilkinson. 1996. *The Complete Valley of the Kings: Tombs and Treasures of Egypt's Greatest Pharaohs*. London.

Sullivan, S. 1997. "A Planning Model for the Management of Archaeological Sites." In *Assessing the Values of Cultural Heritage*, edited by M. de la Torre, Los Angeles.

Teutonico, J., and G. Palumbo, eds. 2002. *Management Planning for Archaeological Sites: Proceedings from the International Workshop. . .* Los Angeles.

Vazio, C. 1999. *Study of the State of Preservation of the Decoration in the Tomb of Seti I, Valley of the Kings, Luxor, Egypt. 2 vols.: Survey of the Wall Paintings in KV17 and Polimethodological Research on Samples Taken from the Wall Paintings Found in the Tomb of Seti I (XIX Dynasty)*. Prepared for ARCE's Antiquities Development Project under USAID Grant no. 263-G-00-96-00016-00. Cairo.

Weeks, K. R. 1990. "Anatomy of a Concession." *K.M.T.: A Modern Journal of Ancient Egypt* 1(1, Spring): 42–47.

Weeks, K. R. 1992. "The Theban Mapping Project and Work in KV5." In *After Tut'ankhamun: Research and Excavation in the Royal Necropolis at Thebes*, edited by C. N. Reeves, 99–121. London and New York.

Weeks, K. R. 1994. "Protecting the Theban Necropolis." *Egyptian Archaeology* 4: 23–27.

Weeks, K. R. 1995. "The Work of the Theban Mapping Project and the Protection of the Valley of the Kings." In *Valley of the Sun Kings: New Explorations in the Tombs of the Pharaohs*, edited by R. H. Wilkinson, 122–128. Tucson, AZ.

Weeks, K. R., and N. J. Hetherington. 2013. *The Valley of the Kings: A Site Management Handbook*. Cairo: American University in Cairo Press.

Wiese, A., and A. Brodbeck. 2004. *Tutankhamun—The Golden Beyond: Tomb Treasures from the Valley of the Kings*. Cairo.

Wilkinson R. H., ed. 1995. *Valley of the Sun Kings: New Explorations in the Tombs of the Pharaohs*. Tucson, AZ.

....

CHAPTER 36

CONSERVATION AND FLOOD PROTECTION

....

MICHAEL JONES

THE Valley of the Kings is part of a natural drainage system in an arid environment that is activated by occasional heavy rainfall. The valley and all the tombs have been subject to periodic flooding numerous times during their history, in many cases with devastating consequences. Flooding and drainage are therefore major conservation issues. Any flood protection measures must acknowledge two important factors. The first is that the valley has always been a natural watercourse within a larger drainage system, and water will continue to enter it and must be channeled away as swiftly and efficiently as possible in ways that safeguard the tombs while respecting the archaeological character of the landscape. The second is that the valley is more than just the tombs; it is a historic landscape modified by natural and human activities in the past and today, a witness to all the events that have contributed to its present state. It is a major resource for research and documentation and holds an iconic value in the popular imagination relating to modern exploration and discovery, one reason that it is one of the most famous heritage sites in the world and the most important cultural tourist attraction in Egypt after the Giza pyramids. A conservation approach must therefore respond to the values and significance of this landscape in the perception of modern interest groups, including scholars, visitors, and locals. In its current condition, without comprehensive measures designed to address all the possible effects of the periodic downpours that threaten the valley and its heritage values, any other conservation measures may well be jeopardized or completely eliminated, and its principle modern purpose as a resource for scholarly activities and a major tourist attraction will be endangered.

On October 8 and November 4, 1994, heavy rains and subsequent runoff flooding caused extensive damage in the Valley of the Kings. In the aftermath of the first of these storms, sediments and loose stones entered at least thirteen tombs. The second downpour, which lasted only forty minutes, was heavier, and water and debris entered twenty or more tombs. The force of the runoff tore up pathways and steps made to facilitate access and destroyed several concrete emplacements around tomb entrances too weak to stand up against such events (see Figure 36.1). Further heavy rainfall occurred in May 1995, but with a lesser impact than the storms of the previous autumn. Storms of equal and even greater strength have occurred many times throughout the history of the valley. Evidence from the tombs themselves shows that since the New Kingdom at least twenty-four major flood events and many lesser storms have caused devastation comparable to that in 1994 in which waterborne debris has entered tombs.

The Valley of the Kings is part of a complex system of deep valleys and lesser stream beds that serve to drain a much larger area of sub-basins on the upper level of the desert. For most of the time these are dry, except when activated by periodic heavy rainfall. When it rains, water collects on the upper levels of the hillsides overlooking the valley and either runs off the slopes into the deeper ravines or ponds in depressions; when these depressions are full, water overflows and cascades down the cliffs into the valleys below, usually through well-worn gullies.

At least seven active stream beds run into the central area of the valley, which functions as a main drainage basin. The total basin area of the valley is 45.26 ha. Of this, 67 percent corresponds to the upper valley sub-basins and 33 percent to the lower valley system. Thus the amount of water that collects in the upper levels and potentially flows down into the valley itself is much greater than the volume of water that can collect in the valley.

FIGURE 36.1 The modern path in the natural flood channel between banks of redeposited excavation debris, destroyed by the flood of October 8, 1994.

Water entering the tombs carries silt, sand, natural stones, and limestone flakes made by the ancient tomb workers. In a major flood, standing water can remain in the deeper chambers of deeply cut tombs for many weeks after the storm that initiated it, and during this time the heavier materials will sink to the bottom, while finer graded sediments will be suspended and eventually fall much more slowly in the drying and thickening mixture. The grade and amount of material depend on the volume and velocity of the flood. KV 7 (Ramesses II) is among the worst affected and because of its size and accessibility is one of the clearest examples for study of what repeated infiltration of water and waterborne materials can do. The walls of the descending corridors have been scoured and the lower rooms filled with solidified sediments and stones.

Water also drains through the natural cavities in the strata of the Thebes formation limestone beds, into which many of the tombs with the finest carved decoration were cut. In deeper tombs, such as KV 17 (Seti I), the lowest chambers are actually cut into the top of the Esna shale. When water percolates into the Esna shale, this much more absorbent material expands and in so doing lifts the limestone beds overlying it, creating enormous pressure on pillars, walls, and ceilings. The result is increased fissuring and eventual structural failure of the tomb architecture, with accompanying losses to carved and painted reliefs and increasing instability and unsafety of the tomb interiors (see Figure 36.2). In the lower chambers of KV 7 (Ramesses II), 8 (Merenptah), and 11 (Ramesses III), and in KV 17 (Seti I) Room P especially, there is evidence that the pillars have literally exploded as they were squashed between the floor and ceiling by the force of the lift following serious flooding.

Storms of the kind witnessed in 1994 are well documented from the beginning of modern exploration in the valley some two centuries ago, when record-keeping began, although this documentation is mostly anecdotal. The tomb of Seti I is a case study for conditions, conservation issues, and their adverse effects throughout the whole valley, resulting in a steady decline through exposure to the weather and over-exploitation by scholars, collectors, and visitors in the nineteenth and twentieth centuries.

Belzoni's early account of the rains that entered and damaged parts of KV 17 in 1818 describes a situation that has become all too common after tombs are left uncovered and exposed. After removing chippings that blocked the entrance and filled the upper corridors, Belzoni dumped them in the gulley in front of the tomb, raising the ground level. He noticed that the tomb entrance lay at the foot of a hill with traces of runoff from rainwater, and he had begun, but left incomplete, a "small canal" to divert water in the event of rain. While he was in Nubia rain, "finding the entrance open, ran into the tomb, and though not much, was enough to occasion some damage to some of the figures. . . . The dryness of the calcareous stone. . . absorbed the dampness, and consequently cracked in many places, particularly in the angles of the pillars of the doorways, &c." Belzoni goes on to describe detached painted reliefs and continues:

> The damage done at that time was inconsiderable in a place of such an extent; but I fear, that in the course of a few years it will become much worse; and I am persuaded,

FIGURE 36.2 KV 7 (Ramesses II). Room J, the burial chamber, showing shattered ceiling and pillar, with fallen debris suspended in the sediments deposited during flooding.

[Reproduced by permission of the American Research Center in Egypt, Inc. (ARCE). 96-630-26. Photo: M. Jones.]

that the damp in the rainy days has caused as much damage in the tombs as has been occasioned in any other way.

(Belzoni 1820, 371)

Belzoni set the process in motion in KV 17 by filling the well-shaft to create an easy passage out for extracting the alabaster sarcophagus from the burial chamber to the surface, where it was packed for removal to London. The rainwater that followed soon afterward thus had an easy route in and penetrated as far as the lower parts of the tomb.

Robert Hay, writing in his diary on February 27, 1825, also describes the effect of rains on "Belzon's" tomb, that is, KV 17, noting that "every part is strewed with fragments. The painting is very perfect and worth copying, and the more of it the better, for in a few years I fear but little will remain" (Hay 1834). Edward Lane, who spent fifteen days in the valley with Hay in August 1826, also noted the water channel in the hillside over the tomb and showed it clearly in his drawing of the entrance, commenting:

[I]ts [the tomb's] situation is ill-chosen; for it is at the bottom of the bed of a small torrent; and though rain is a very rare phenomenon in Upper Egypt it has occasionally done great damage to this magnificent tomb. A rude wall has lately been built to divert this torrent as much as possible.

(Lane 2000, 382, and fig. 119)

An anonymous photograph, probably taken before 1880 in Room N of KV 17—the chamber with two pillars opening off the burial chamber—appears to show erosion, probably from water damage, along the lower parts of the walls below the cavetto cornice shelf that runs around the sides of this room, and a broken corner section at the base of one of the pillars (Vaczek and Buckland 1981, 5).

During the twentieth century both Harry Burton and Howard Carter were eyewitnesses to flooding. Burton, while working for the Metropolitan Museum of Art expedition in March 1914, recorded that "there was a terrible flood that ran down through the valley and entered several tombs. The tombs of Ramesses II and III were both again flooded, the latter blocked again by debris after having been long since partly excavated and made accessible by Salt and Lepsius." Burton took workmen into the tombs in an attempt to clear them, but the damage in the tomb of Ramesses III was so intense due to the expansion and shattering of the rock that he deemed it too dangerous to work there. The structural stability of the tomb of Ramesses II had held up, and Theodore Davis had workmen carry the wet mud out. Burton recorded conditions in the tomb during the first days after the flood, in which wet pools of mud were standing in a temperature of over 90 degrees Fahrenheit.

Carter, writing in 1918, recorded a thunderstorm that occurred a considerable distance from the Valley of the Kings, which itself remained completely unaffected by the rain. Nevertheless, the desert *wadi* system, of which the Valley of the Kings is a natural branch, was activated by the resulting runoff, which poured through the valley with tremendous force. Carter wrote:

> [I]n consecutive Octobers, we have had heavy downpours, and this time a particular phenomenon occurred. While we [were] dry as a bone, the larger valleys suddenly became seething rivers. Late in the afternoon, toward sunset, as the desert cooled, a terrific storm was evidently raging northwest. Far away at the back of the hills, incessant lightening was visible amongst great ominous clouds. . . but so far away that only faint rumblings of distant thunder were to be heard. Then, gradually the rush of water became audible—this grew to a roar—when suddenly. . . tidal waves came rushing down the valleys. Wadi Biban el Maluk, joined by the Great Northern Valley, in a few moments became little more than great mountain rivers—seething waters, reaching from side to side of the valley taking practically everything with them. The torrent cut wide furrows as much as four feet deep and stones as large as two feet in diameter rolled before the waters.
>
> (Carter 1918, October 25)

Carter described events that were only the most recent of many similar storms and resulting floods in a continuing pattern of intermittent heavy rainfall that have formed the topography of the valley and its surroundings before, during, and after its period of use as the location of an ancient elite cemetery some 3,000 years ago. The long-term conservation issues ensuing from such a sudden and prolonged increase in temperature and humidity in a closed environment are devastating, as can be seen from the conditions in tombs that have been repeatedly subjected to this. Belzoni's account also emphasizes how the damage need not be the result of repeated flooding but of a single event.

Interwoven with these storms and floods are the relatively short-lived periods of human activity that have also had a dramatic impact on the landscape and long periods of little or no activity in the valley when rainfall continued to occur. During these periods of inactivity, the natural and man-made environments forming the topography evolved into an equilibrium between a stable landscape and a suddenly volatile one, only to be interrupted by renewed human interest and work.

The first intense phase of use was that of digging out the tombs over the roughly 500 years of the New Kingdom. Occupation in the form of stone-built constructions and the dumping of large amounts of stone chippings and other material in the natural water-worn gullies and on the sloping hillsides within the confines of the valley not only altered the appearance of the landscape, but also interfered with or changed the configuration of watercourses that had evolved over millennia on the hillsides and in the gullies running down to the valley bottom. As tombs increased in size during the reigns of Seti I and Ramesses II (e.g., KV 17, 5, and 7), the volume of stone turned into chippings by the ancient workmen and dumped in the flood paths of the valley and surroundings increased exponentially.

Toward the end of the fourteenth century B.C.E., heavy rainfall in the region of the valley caused dramatic floods that moved natural boulders and pebbles, rock chippings, sand, shale, and fine silt through the central part of the valley. Several of the later Eighteenth Dynasty tombs, including KV 55, 62, and 63, were buried under this deposit. Water undoubtedly entered the tombs as a result of this event, causing damage, but ironically the depth of material on the surface sealed the entrances and preserved their ancient contexts until they were discovered by excavation in modern times (Cross 2008).

After a period of relative inactivity during the first millenium B.C.E., when storms and floods periodically activated the dry watercourses, renewed interest in the Hellenistic and Roman periods, also involving settlement in and around certain open tombs such as KV 2 (Ramesses IV), introduced another phase of use.

Most recently, following many centuries of relative abandonment the valley again became a focus of intense interest and activity. Excavations pursued so vigorously in the search for buried tombs over roughly the last 200 years have resulted in moving from place to place immense quantities of the chippings produced by the ancient workers, together with material deposited naturally by floods. Just as the ancient workings had created a new and contemporary landscape within the valley, modern excavations and the resulting formation of spoil dumps have dramatically altered it again. Both challenged the natural drainage of the valley (see Figure 36.3).

Tourist access as well as excavations have also contributed to significant topographical changes. During the twentieth century, facilities for visitors have been created focused more on visitors' comfort and experience than on the general preservation aspects of the area. A catalyst for improved visitor access was the discovery in 1922 of the tomb of

FIGURE 36.3 View of the central part of the valley in 1924 looking south, with KV 9, 10, 11, and 62 at center; bedrock exposed at lower left; banks of chippings from excavations on slopes and redeposited in the ravine to create pathways in the natural flood channels of the valley.

[Reproduced by permission of the Epigraphic Survey, Oriental Institute, University of Chicago; No. 130319.]

Tutankhamun (KV 62) and resulting publicity. In response, pathways were widened and graded, and walls were constructed around the entrances to tombs.

Explorers and archaeologists have been made acutely aware of the destructive effects of rain and floods in the valley by the conditions they discovered in most of the tombs they have excavated. Some, as noted above, have witnessed heavy storms and flooding for themselves. One of the most salient warnings provided by both the archaeological conditions recorded by excavators and the eyewitness accounts of modern floods is that sporadic unpredictable and uncontrolled flooding poses the greatest threat to any aspect of the valley's preservation.

In the aftermath of the 1994 floods, the hydraulic response of the Valley of the Kings was studied by the following projects: the Theban Mapping Project (Weeks 2000, 1997–2013; the California Academy of Science for the American Research Center in Egypt (ARCE) (Rutherford 2001), and C. C. Johnson and P. C. Malhotra (CCJM) for ARCE (Gokhale and Patel 2003). Supplementary work by ARCE was carried out in a separate project in KV 17 (Jones 2003, 2010a). Of these only the results of the Theban

Mapping Project and ARCE's investigation of KV 17 have been published. The studies by the California Academy of Science and CCJM are archived at ARCE in Cairo.

The California Academy of Science study carried out hydrological analyses, the objective of which was to assess conditions in the valley watershed to determine the maximum depth of surface water during a flood as it might pass the tomb entrances and to calculate the velocity of the water stream during such an event. It contains useful information about past floods, beginning with evidence from the Palaeolithic period, ca. 20,000 years B.P., through evidence for ancient floods in historical times, to the floods witnessed by modern excavators and archaeologists, including in 1994.

In the absence of any data collection in the region of the valley, the study used data from Las Vegas, Nevada, where similar climatic conditions pertain on a similar latitude, in a hilly desert environment. The rainfall data used in calculations in this study employ a level close to the maximum precipitation that has been recorded worldwide. Therefore they are probably a good guide to the maximum likely for the valley.

The study differentiates between the direct and long-term effects of floods. Direct effects on the tombs may comprise scouring the walls accompanied by the removal of plaster and painted decoration, spalling of walls and pillars, and erosion of reliefs carved directly on the limestone walls. Debris and sediments introduced into the tombs by flood water also falls under direct effects. Long-term effects are the most destructive. These are caused by the expansive properties of the geological structure of the valley, exerted by the clay and marl shales, and lead to rock joint movements that fracture the rock and ultimately lead to collapse. Migration of water within the rock sustains a moisture imbalance in the internal environments inside tombs, leading to increased humidity and temperatures over a long period, with additional spalling of surfaces and salt efflorescence that adds another component to the destruction of both decorated and undecorated surfaces. The expansions are followed by shrinkage as the clay and marl dry, adding further stress on the rock. The process may take many months after a particularly heavy flood, during which very large quantities of water may have entered tombs and seeped through the rock joints into the underlying shale.

A similar study was carried out by the Theban Mapping Project using rainfall data collected at Luxor Airport over a period of sixty-one years. It utilizes extreme analysis to estimate rainfall depth at various periods, and a model produced by the Massachusetts Institute of Technology was used to perform the hydraulic response of sub-catchment areas.

The main difference between these two studies lies in the methodology used. The California Academy of Sciences approach was based on the "probably maximum precipitation" method to calculate floods, while the Theban Mapping Project used the "soil concentration services" method, considering the maximum daily rainfall for storms of various return periods based on the information provided by the nearby weather station. Both methods and data sources are valuable, but both also have shortcomings. Las Vegas may not be an accurate comparison with Luxor, and Luxor Airport is located in flat desert where the collector systems and stream force effects are likely to be quite dissimilar from those of the steep cliffs and gullies of the region around the Valley of the

Kings. The California Academy of Sciences study presents a worst-case scenario that might occur, while the Theban Mapping Project calculations represent floods that are most likely to occur.

The study produced by CCJM in 2003 used a conceptual model of rainwater runoff of general applicability known as "watershed modeling simulation." This was preferred because the parametric and statistical models described above require long-term rainfall records, which are not available for the Valley of the Kings. The results showed that both of the previously mentioned studies provide important information.

Factors affecting risks of flooding are a combination of position and surrounding stratigraphic layering of debris, deposited either by floods or by excavators. Due to their position, some tombs that have been open since ancient times escaped serious flooding. Three such examples are KV 1, 2, and 9 (Ramesses VII, IV, and VI), whose entrances were cut well above the floodwater flow paths and remain so today, exposed only to minor runoff from the hillsides above.

Rutherford's recommendations for protecting tombs from flooding included a variety of measures based on the kind of tomb entrance (e.g., pit, steep stairs or sloping corridor, or gently sloping corridor) (Rutherford 2001, I: 7–31) and the location and proximity to cliffs, pathways, or narrow gullies acting as water conduits. The degree of exposure to flooding risk was estimated based on the aftermath of the October and November 1994 storms. No adjustments to the existing valley flood paths were included in these recommendations; rather, they favored an engineered response that imposed more layers of construction and intervention on the topography. However, as Romer pointed out more than thirty years ago, flood protection measures must include modifying the present shape of the valley floor (1988, 108). By designing and implementing a comprehensive archaeological project with research and documentation components, a plan could be devised that would restore, or partially restore, the natural drainage system. Such a project would be in keeping with the heritage values of the site and result in an achievable and acceptable conservation program.

For tombs mildly affected in 1994, for example KV 1 and 2 (Ramesses VII and IV), where the only infiltration came from small amounts of water draining off the hillside above the entrance, low-level intervention was proposed, involving the clearance of loose scree from the slopes around the entrance and construction of drains to channel water away. At KV 6 (Ramesses IX), however, where a gradually sloping passage starts at the modern ground level outside the tomb, recommended measures included removal of loose debris and cutting watertight drainage channels in the rock on either side of the slopes beside the entrance. In addition, a low deflection wall was suggested to project into the valley path on the upstream side of the entrance. Similar arrangements were proposed outside KV 7 (Ramesses II) and opposite KV 6 (Ramesses IX), with a low wall projecting diagonally outward and designed to deflect floodwater pouring downslope past these tombs.

KV 9 (Ramesses VI), another long sloping corridor tomb with a gradual incline and an entrance at the modern external ground level, is higher up the valley and adjacent to KV 62 (Tutankhamun). Although there was no significant flooding in this tomb after the

1994 rainfalls, there is a risk that water running off the hillside into which the tomb was cut would fall into the entrance corridor. Drainage slots and debris clearance around the entrance were recommended here, together with a deflection wall of the same kind designed for KV 6 and 7. An additional risk in KV 9 is posed by flooding in KV 12, which was broken into by the masons excavating KV 9, creating a cavity that connects the two tombs that should be sealed.

Tombs located close to the base of the cliffs, such as KV 13 (Bey) and KV 14 (Tausret/Sethnakhte), are severely threatened by the direct waterfall effect of water pouring over the cliffs from the catchment areas above. Substantial concrete roofing over the deeply cut entrances is the only way to stop the devastating floods that affected these tombs in earlier centuries and in modern times. KV 13 was particularly seriously affected in 1994 after having been excavated and studied by Hartwig Altenmüller from 1984 onwards, many of whose finds, stored in the tomb, were irretrievably lost in the flood. Such a roof was constructed over the entrance of KV 14 by the SCA after 1994. Another similarly located tomb is KV 35 (Amenhotep II). In 1994 the entrance chamber was filled with water-lain sediments despite the metal door recently installed by the SCA, although that effectively stopped larger rocks and other detritus from entering the tomb. At least 60 cubic meters of water was caught in the well-shaft, demonstrating the effectiveness of these elements of Eighteenth and Nineteenth Dynasty tomb design. Rutherford's recommendation here was to construct a second vaulted reinforced concrete roof over the existing entrance cover to protect the tomb from water, falling rock, and landslide material.

KV 34 (Thutmose III) is constructed in a rock cleft at the northern end of the valley and is approached by climbing a metal ladder. It is a deep, steeply descending tomb, and both its position and design give it "high-risk" status. An eroded gully that passes the west side of the tomb entrance carries water, sediments, and fine silt to an area around the entrance. Early photographs of the cliffs show the heaps of accumulated debris, and when Loret discovered the tomb in 1898 he found the entrance and chambers above the shaft filled with this material, so that the lower rooms had been protected from damage. At least 90 cubic meters of water flooded the tomb in 1994 and flowed into the burial chamber. Diversion walls around the entrance to divert water away and down the cliff face and a roof over the entrance would provide much-needed protection. In addition, some form of protective structure on the ground above the cliffs would be needed.

KV 62, the high-profile tomb of Tutankhamun, has received the best precautionary structures at the entrance. The walled courtyard in front of the steeply cut entrance steps has been covered by a reinforced concrete flat roof that provides shade for the crowds of visitors waiting to enter the tomb and shelters the entrance from direct rainfall. However, the opening into the courtyard is vulnerable to water draining from the direction of KV 8, Merenptah. Rutherford proposed deflection walls here.

Undecorated tombs, such as KV 12, 20, 22, 24, 36, 37, and 40, many of which have been left open and have partly filled with debris and rubbish through neglect, should be thoroughly documented, backfilled, and then sealed. To these might be added KV 55, which though famous for the objects discovered inside it, now removed, particularly the enigmatic late Eighteenth Dynasty coffin, is kept permanently closed and has little to offer a visitor beyond what could be seen in a thoroughly documented record. Numerous small shafts and openings exist, and those close to the cliff base are especially likely to fill with water, acting as underground reservoirs from which water can leach through the rock into more significant tombs. They are hard to access and cannot easily be pumped out when they are flooded. By eliminating these tombs as a risk factor, the amount of seepage would be considerably reduced, helping to control damage and monitor the effects of dampness and its sources in accessible tombs.

Following the 1994 floods, electrical supply was cut off and the roads leading to the valley were broken and blocked by debris. Emergency response was thus slow in coming and difficult to implement. Future storms will undoubtedly pose the same problems. Large quantities of standing water remained in deeper tombs, such as KV 57 (Horemheb), for days and in some cases weeks, as no power was available for electric pumps and no gas-driven pumps could be brought to the site. KV 57 was particularly hard hit in the 1994 floods, as was KV 11, on the opposite side of the narrow defile at a constricted point in the pathway through the valley. This feature is a bottleneck that increases the velocity of water flow and poses one of the most serious difficulties to managing floods, as it cannot be modified without altering the natural topography.

While many of the measures proposed in Rutherford's report are valuable suggestions, only one was implemented, as a prototype. It remained in place for less than a year and was never put to the test in a real flood. All are based on accepting the existing stratigraphy, modern ground levels, and visitor routes as they are today without modification. It is highly likely that tombs that were flooded in the past will be flooded again if conditions remain unchanged and no further protection measures are put in place. However, one of the difficulties posed by the proposed deflection walls is that by protruding into the pathways, they would potentially hinder visitor access and possibly impede exit in an emergency such as a flash flood. They emphasize how often approaches to work in the valley particularize the tombs and overlook their place as part of an overall archaeological context and natural environment.

The one measure that was installed, in 2001, involved a heavily engineered reinforced concrete armature around the entrances to KV 16 and 17, originally approved by the Supreme Council of Antiquities. However, the initiative failed on several counts, none associated with flooding. First, it was carried out with minimal archaeological supervision, although this area was known to have a stratigraphic sequence containing deposits relating to ancient activities overlain by material brought out of the tombs by Belzoni and possibly intermixed with other evidence for undocumented modern excavation and exploration of this part of the valley. Second, on aesthetic grounds it imposed an enormous, undisguised, and isolated modern edifice on a landscape in which strongly held views of authenticity lend important weight to how the valley should look. No integration was attempted between this modern emplacement and the ancient significance of the tombs and their surroundings, a factor that led to dismay among many of the archaeological community working in the valley at the time.

Within a year, additional studies were done to determine the feasibility of removing the "prototype," and it was eventually dismantled by hand and the rubble removed by lorry outside the valley. A new design was implemented in 2003 that included an archaeological monitoring program carried out by Edwin Brock. The flood path in the gulley in front of the tomb entrances was lowered, and baffle walls 2 meters high were constructed as separate units at the tomb entrances, with a stepped-up L shaped approach opening downstream. While this solution responded more sensitively to the valley's heritage significance and value as a historic landscape, it is not very successful aesthetically and in the end may not withstand a flash flood of the magnitude described by Carter in 1918. Indeed, as decades may pass between such events, regular inspections and follow-up maintenance and repairs are needed to keep these installations effective, and without such infrastructure in place constructions designed to safeguard the tombs will deteriorate before they are put to the test.

It is well established that floods endanger the tombs, but runoff will also endanger the approach road to the valley, the present vehicle parking arrangements, shops, and the visitors' center, which are located in the flood path, where a strong torrent of water might easily tear up the asphalt road and undermine building foundations. Carter's graphic account of how fast the water can arrive, and with what force, should be taken seriously in considering how the lives of visitors might also be put at risk.

The various studies carried out and the reports produced have contributed greatly to knowledge about the geological, topographic, and meteorological conditions in the Valley of the Kings. Nevertheless, as has been mentioned above, a comprehensive plan to investigate and document the valley archaeologically, aimed at providing a record of the natural and man-made stratigraphy, has yet to be fully carried out, systematically recorded, and made available. Recent deep digging in the valley by the Supreme Council of Antiquities, directed by Zahi Hawass, might have contributed to this investigative stage, but the results have not yet been published. Any interventions should be based on archaeological research and respect for heritage and aesthetic values. Solutions should be designed that require minimal maintenance, such as lowering pathways to enhance the landscape while protecting the tombs.

Yet while solutions in the valley itself are crucial, they represent only a fraction of the work required to reduce the amount of water entering the drainage basin from the hills above. Here engineering works would certainly be necessary to create a ring of protection measures capable of deflecting the most dangerous runoff away from its habitual routes into the valley. This would incorporate the Western Valley as well, where KV 22 (Amenhotep III) and KV 23 (Aye) are endangered, both being located close to the foot of cliffs. Implementation of such a large-scale conservation and preservation project would rely on agreement among all the interest groups involved in the valley. Foremost among these is the Ministry of Antiquities, which has stewardship of this heritage site. The international teams of archaeologists working in the valley, usually with individual research agendas, would need to contribute and perhaps adjust their programs, with more attention to the conservation ethic introduced into archaeological practice in the early 1990s and now standard elsewhere (Cleere 1993; Startin 1993).

Specialists in many disciplines who rarely collaborate simultaneously in archaeological projects—engineers, hydrologists, geologists, cultural heritage managers, and
conservators—as well as Egyptologists and archaeologists, would be involved in making
decisions throughout the work that would determine what future generations will be
able to experience and enjoy in the valley. A comparable project currently working in
the Valley of the Queens is addressing many of the same issues of rainfall, flooding, and
conservation and has already established helpful guidelines and a report with extensive references to previous work (Demas and Agnew 2012). There is no doubt that an
effective project can be carried out in the Valley of the Kings that would protect it from
further destruction by flooding. Ultimately the decision to implement it will depend on
the relative value and significance that its most influential interest groups attach to it and
their commitment to applying these principles to its conservation and preservation.

BIBLIOGRAPHY

Baer, N. S., and F. Snickars, eds. 2001. *Rational Decision-Making in the Preservation of Cultural
   Property*. Report on the 86th Dahlem Workshop, Berlin, 26–31 March 2000. Berlin.
Belzoni, G. 1820. *Narrative of the Operations and Recent Discoveries within the Pyramids,
   Temples, Tombs, and Excavations in Egypt and Nubia*. London.
Brock, E. C. 2010. "Conservation of the Sarcophagus of Ramesses VI: Piecing Together a
   Three-Dimensional Puzzle." In *Preserving Egypt's Cultural Heritage: The Conservation Work
   of the American Research Center in Egypt 1995–2005*, edited by R. Danforth, 63–67. Cairo and
   San Antonio, TX.
Carter, H. 1903. "Report of Work Done in Upper Egypt, 1902–1903." *Annales du Service des
   Antiquités de l'Égypte* 4: 171–180.
Carter, H. 1918. "*Western Thebes*." Unpublished Carter notebook G. Griffith Institute Archives,
   Oxford.
Cleere, H. 1993. "Managing the Archaeological Heritage." *Antiquity* 67 (255): 400–405.
Cross, S. W. 2008. "The Hydrology of the Valley of the Kings." *Journal of Egyptian Archaeology*
   94: 303–310.
Curtis, G. H. 1995. "Deterioration of the Royal Tombs." In *Valley of the Sun Kings: New
   Explorations in the Tombs of the Pharaohs*, edited by R. H. Wilkinson, 129–133. Tucson.
Danforth, R. 2010. *Preserving Egypt's Cultural Heritage: The Conservation Work of the American
   Research Center in Egypt 1995–2005*. Cairo and San Antonio, TX.
De la Torre, M. 1995. *The Conservation of Archaeological Sites in the Mediterranean
   Region: Proceedings of an International Conference Organized by the Getty Conservation
   Institute and the J. Paul Getty Museum, 6–12 May 1995*. Los Angeles.
Demas, M., and N. Agnew. 2012. *Valley of the Queens Assessment Report*, Vol. 1. Los Angeles.
Feilden, B. M., and J. Jokilehto. 1993. *Management Guidelines for Cultural Heritage Sites*. Rome.
Gokhale, S., and R. Patel, eds. 2003. "Flood Hydrology Study, Valley of the Kings, Luxor,
   Egypt." Unpublished report prepared by C. C. Johnson and P. C. Malhotra, (CCJM) in asso-
   ciation with Chemonics and Access Engineers, submitted to the American Research Center
   in Egypt, August 10, 2003.
Hassan, F. A., G. J. Tassie, A. de Trafford, L. Owens, and J. van Wetering, eds. 2009. *Managing
   Egypt's Cultural Heritage*. Discourses on Heritage Management Series No. 1. London.

Hawass, Z., ed. 2003. *Egyptology at the Dawn of the Twenty-first Century: Proceedings of the Eighth International Congress of Egyptologists, Cairo, 2000*, Vol. I. Cairo and New York.

Hay, R. 1834. "Diary of Robert Hay." Unpublished manuscript. British Library, London; Add. Ms. 31054.

Hetherington, N. J. 2009. "An Assessment of the Role of Archaeological Site Management in the Valley of the Kings, Luxor, Egypt." In *Managing Egypt's Cultural Heritage*, edited by F. A. Hassan et al., 149–163. London.

Hornung, E. 1991. *The Tomb of Pharaoh Seti I/Das Grab Sethos' I*. Zurich and Munich.

Jones, M. 2003. "The Work of the American Research Center in Egypt in the Tomb of Sety I in the Valley of the Kings, 1998–1999." In *Egyptology at the Dawn of the Twenty-first Century: Proceedings of the Eighth International Congress of Egyptologists, Cairo, 2000*, edited by Z. Hawass, 252–261. Cairo and New York.

Jones, M. 2010a. "The Tomb of Sety I in the Valley of the Kings: Creating a Plan for an Important Tomb at Risk." In *Preserving Egypt's Cultural Heritage: The Conservation Work of the American Research Center in Egypt 1995–2005*, edited by R. Danforth, 55–58. Cairo and San Antonio, TX.

Jones, M. 2010b. "Protective Walls in the Valley of the Kings: Floodwater Diversion Measures." In *Preserving Egypt's Cultural Heritage: The Conservation Work of the American Research Center in Egypt 1995–2005*, edited by R. Danforth, 59–62. Cairo and San Antonio, TX.

Kirshenblatt-Gimblett, B. 1998. *Destination Culture: Tourism, Museums and Heritage*. Berkeley, CA.

Lane, E. W. 2000. *Description of Egypt*. Edited by J. Thompson. Cairo and New York.

Leask, A., and A. Fyall. 2006. *Managing World Heritage Sites*. Amsterdam and Boston.

Mac Lean, M., M. de la Torre, and N. Agnew, eds. 1995. *The Tomb of Tutankhamun: The History of the Tomb and Its Conditions; A Summary of Research Prepared by the Getty Conservation Institute, October 1995*. Los Angeles.

Mallory, L. 2007. "Geophysics in the Valley of the Kings." *Geotimes: Earth, Energy and Environment News* (January) http://www.geotimes.org/jan07/feature_ValleyKings.html.

McLane, J., and R. Wüst. 2000. *Flood Hazards and Protection Measures in the Valley of the Kings. Cultural Resource Management*, 23, 6: 35–38.

Romer, J. 1988. *Valley of the Kings*. London.

Rutherford, J., et al. 2001. "Valley of the Kings Tomb Flood Protection Project." Unpublished report in three parts, submitted to the American Research Center in Egypt, February 11, 2003.

Rutherford, J., and D. P. Ryan. 1995. "Tentative Tomb Protection Priorities, Valley of the Kings, Egypt." In *Valley of the Sun Kings: New Explorations in the Tombs of the Pharaohs*, edited by R. H. Wilkinson, 134–156. Tucson.

Sharpley, R., and D. J. Telfer. 2004. *Tourism and Development: Concepts and Issues*. Clevedon.

Smith, G. S., P. M. Messenger, and H. A. Soderland. 2010. *Heritage Values in Contemporary Society*. Walnut Creek, CA.

Stanley-Price, N., and R. Burch, eds. 2004. "Site Reburial." Special issue, *Conservation and Management of Archeological Sites* 6 (3, 4).

Startin, B. 1993. "Preservation and the Academically Viable Sample." *Antiquity* 67 (255): 421–426.

Timothy, D. J., and G. P. Nyaupane. 2009. *Cultural Heritage and Tourism in the Developing World: A Regional Perspective*. London and New York.

Vaczek, L., and G. Buckland. 1981. *Travellers in Ancient Lands: A Portrait of the Middle East, 1839–1919*. Boston.

Weeks, K. R. 1995. "The Work of the Theban Mapping Project and the Protection of the Valley of the Kings." In *Valley of the Sun Kings: New Explorations in the Tombs of the Pharaohs*, edited by R. H. Wilkinson, 122–128. Tucson.

Weeks, K. R., ed. 2000. *KV 5: A Preliminary Report on the Excavation of the Tomb of the Sons of Ramesses II in the Valley of the Kings*. Cairo and New York.

Weeks, K. R., et al. 1997–2013. http://www.thebanmappingproject.com.

Weeks, K. R., and N. J. Hetherington. 2014. *The Valley of the Kings: A Site Management Handbook*. Cairo and New York.

Wilkinson, R. H., ed. 1995. *Valley of the Sun Kings: New Explorations in the Tombs of the Pharaohs; Papers from the University of Arizona International Conference on the Valley of the Kings*. Tucson.

CHAPTER 37

···

TOURISM IN THE VALLEY
OF THE KINGS

···

KENT R. WEEKS

THE royal necropolises at Thebes, including the East and West Valleys of the Kings (KV), were a restricted area in the New Kingdom, open only to a select group of priests, officials, and craftsmen. Others (including women) were banned, and guards were stationed around the sacred area's perimeter to enforce the no-entry rule (Černý 1973a, 1973; Ventura 1986, 170ff.). But there was at least one exception, recorded in a graffito scratched on a cliff face in the West Valley of the Kings during the reign of Ramesses IV (perhaps on June 26, 1150 B.C.E., according to Sadek 1990, 117; see also Dorn, ch 3, and Weeks, ch 2). It stated that the scribe Amennakht, son of Ipuy, had brought his three sons to the valley to marvel at a lake created by an unseasonal and apparently heavy rainstorm near KV 22. Amennakht's sons could perhaps be considered KV's first recorded tourists.

It was not until Graeco-Roman and Coptic Christian times, from 278 B.C.E. (the date of the first Greek graffito in KV) to 537 C.E. (the date of the last Latin text), that visitors came to the valley in any number. Jules Baillet (1926) recorded 2,105 graffiti written during those eight centuries, by tourists who left their names and comments on the walls of ten tombs (KV 1, 2, 4, 6, 7, 8, 9, 10, 11, and 15): 995 graffiti in KV 9, 656 in KV 2, 132 in KV 1, 121 in KV 8, and 60 or fewer in each of the others (Foertmeyer 1989). The tourists were a remarkably diverse lot: they came from Spain and Persia and every country in between, though most were Greek and Roman residents in Egypt (Rutherford 2012). They identified themselves as kings and emperors, governors and bureaucrats, priests, soldiers, poets, orators, philosophers, physicians and artisans, servants and slaves. The graffiti they left reflect their different backgrounds and interests. Some are praising of the valley, some dismissive, some confused: "Tatianus, governor of Upper Egypt [says]: O! admirable wonders of Egyptian sages, [you] cause us great astonishment" (Baillet 1926, entry 1380); "I visited, but I admired nothing" (entry 1613); "I, Dioskorammon, looked at this nonsense and found it bewildering" (entry 1550).

After the sixth century C.E., Thebes collapsed into a period of economic and political turmoil that lasted for over a millennium. Tourism in the valley stopped. There are no tourist graffiti in the Valley of the Kings during this time, and no texts have been found from the sixth to the eighteenth centuries that even mention the valley. Indeed, there is no evidence of travelers to the valley for the next 1,200 years, until the visits of Claude Sicard in 1708, Richard Pococke in 1739, and a few others (Greener 1966; Weeks 2001; Simpson 2003; el-Daly 2005). Even then, visitors were rare, and tourism would not reach the levels of Graeco-Roman times until the mid-nineteenth century.

The growth of nineteenth-century tourism has been tracked by Reid (2002, 300), who counted the number of books for travelers to Egypt published each decade. Between 1790 and 1799, 9 guidebooks were published in Europe, the United Kingdom, and the United States; in 1800–1809 there were 26; in 1850–1859, 86; in 1890–1899, 90; and in 1900–1914 there were 158, of which 97 were published in the United States, 27 in the United Kingdom, and 34 in continental Europe. Americans and British were Egypt's principal visitors in those years, followed by French and Germans (see also Kalfatovic 2001). The rapid late nineteenth- to twentieth-century rise in tourist numbers was due to several factors: the end of the American Civil War; industrialization and the rise of the middle class in the United States and Britain; the opening of the Suez Canal; the economic growth of Germany; the growing fascination in Europe and America with orientalism; and the development of mass tourism, pioneered by Thomas Cook (Sattin 2011; Searight 1979; Pudney, 1953).

Prior to the discovery in 1922 of the tomb of Tutankhamun, tourists came to the valley in small groups, by donkey or on foot. They spent a leisurely morning visiting half a dozen decorated royal tombs before taking lunch in one of them. Eliot Warburton ([1845] 1908, 160) was one such visitor. Inside the tomb he chose for a picnic, "a fire was lighted, carpets spread, and coffee was already diffusing its fragrance. . . many a pipe smoked incense to the spirits of the departed kings."

Tombs then were lit by guards holding candles or lanterns and mirrors, and decorated walls could only be seen in small, dimly lit sections. The guides visitors hired in Luxor often had limited knowledge, and some tourists depended on explanations given by valley guards, who, knowing little English and less Egyptology, happily spouted gibberish. Nevertheless, in spite of bad lighting and bad information, the tombs left a strong impression. "Nothing that has ever been said about them [the valley tombs] had prepared me for their extraordinary grandeur. . . white stucco brilliant with colours, fresh as they were thousands of years ago, but on a scale, and with such a splendor, that I can only compare to the frescoes of the Vatican Library" (Stanley 1911, 260–261).

After the railway was extended south from Cairo in 1898, the time it took to reach Luxor was cut from about ten days to only twelve hours. This change, and others, quickly brought about a new kind of tourism. Tourists now were likely to come in relatively large groups, strangers a travel agency had brought together solely for the purpose of making the trip, and they would spend a relatively short time in the country. What formerly had been leisurely one- or two- or even three-month-long sojourns on the Nile for small groups of wealthy friends now became two-week getaways for middle-class tourists who could spare little time away from work, and who therefore had to "do Egypt" quickly. The usual week-long tour of Luxor was compressed into two or three days (Sattin 2011, 220–225). Donkeys were replaced by motor coaches (the first automobiles came to Luxor in the early 1920s), and these required that roads be cut across east and west bank archaeological sites. But still, visitor numbers were relatively small and did little to threaten the monuments.

All this changed in the 1960s and 1970s. The great interest in ancient Egypt generated by the *Treasures of Tutankhamun* exhibitions in the United States and the United Kingdom and the construction of the Aswan High Dam and its well-publicized archaeological salvage program made Egypt a much sought-after destination. The mass tourism that resulted had a dramatic effect on Luxor and the Valley of the Kings (Searight 1969; Clayton 1982; Manley 1991; Greener 1996; Starkey and Starkey 1998; Kalfatovic 1992, 2001; Manley and Abdel-Hakim 2004; Sattin 2011). Over the next few years, as commercial jets made travel to Egypt easier and more affordable, new hotels were built in Luxor to accommodate ever-larger groups, more Nile cruise ships were launched, tour coaches and taxis grew in number, restaurants and souvenir shops multiplied, and more monuments were opened to visitors. Tourism quickly became Luxor's biggest industry and a major source of income for Egypt. By the late 1990s, over one million tourists came to Luxor annually, 40,000 a week in high season. The vast majority (93 percent) visited the Valley of the Kings (Abt Associates 2000a, annex 7; Weeks and Hetherington 2013). In 1997, the sale of tickets to the valley alone earned the government nearly 90 million Egyptian pounds, then about $3 million (Abt Associates 2000b, 87). By 2004, the numbers had risen to 1.8 million visitors and over 150 million Egyptian pounds, about $9.3 million (Weeks and Hetherington 2013).

FACILITATING TOURISM

Beginning in the 1970s, but especially between 1985 and 1989, the Egyptian Antiquities Organization (later the Supreme Council of Antiquities, still later the Ministry of State for Antiquities) undertook to make the Valley of the Kings more accessible and visitor-friendly. Electric lighting was first installed by Howard Carter in 1903 (in KV 6, 9, 11, 16, 17, and 35) and turned on for a few hours a day (Carter 1903). Now it was installed in eleven more tombs—KV 1, 2, 8, 15, 22, 23, 34, 43, 47, 57, and 62—and with generators that kept it running from 6:00 a.m. to 6:00 p.m. Carter's wall-mounted incandescent bulbs were replaced by fluorescent tubes laid on chamber floors. Iron gates were added to tomb entrances for security. Wooden stairs, walkways, and handrails were installed, mounted by drilling into floors and walls. Side chambers were cleared, fractured and fissured walls were patched, pillars were strengthened, and ceilings were reinforced (sometimes damaging ancient texts and paintings in the process). Huge glass panels were mounted in iron frames to prevent tourists from touching the fragile walls. Paths in the valley were widened to accommodate more tourists, and a rest house was built in the middle of the valley to offer snacks and drinks, shade, and toilets (which leached raw sewage into nearby tombs for decades). Signs were installed at the entrances of selected tombs, giving brief descriptions of their plans and history. The dirt track from the Nile floodplain to the valley was leveled and paved. Amennakht would not have recognized the valley to which he had brought his sons.

Today, organized visits to the Valley of the Kings are no longer leisurely affairs, but quick-marches meant to get "clients" into the valley and out in the shortest time possible. Tourists are herded from buses into long lines under the burning sun, waiting to be jostled through three crowded tombs (the number allowed on a single ticket), then back to their buses and on to the next site. Since 2008, tour guides have not been allowed to lecture in tombs—a good thing, since it reduces noise and congestion—but for tourists who did not read their guidebook in advance, the ninety-minute-long visit to the valley can be, as it was for Dioskorammon, "bewildering."

The Valley of the Kings is likely to become even more crowded. The development plan for the city of Luxor (its implementation well under way until the 2011 revolution brought a pause) predicts that the number of visitors to Luxor (and therefore to the valley) will increase to 4.2 million annually by 2017. Egypt's Tourism Development Authority hopes the number will reach 8 million (Abt 2000a). The revolution has slowed tourism's growth, but that is certainly only temporary. The total number of tourists to Egypt in 2010 was 14.7 million, dropping in 2011 to 9.8 million, then rising to 11.5 million in 2012 (Demas and Agnew 2012; various news reports).

NEEDED TOURIST FACILITIES

Mass tourism and poor site management are already creating problems for valley tombs. They are threatening their survival more than long-standing hydrological, geological, or structural concerns. Cleaning and conservation projects and badly needed upgrades to the valley's infrastructure have for decades been underfunded or ignored, and in many cases what is being done now will not alleviate the pressures of mass tourism (Weeks and Hetherington 2013).

Too many people in a tomb results in decorated walls being touched or hit by elbows and bags. Hot, sweaty tourists result in dramatic fluctuations in temperature and humidity. The Theban Mapping Project (TMP) has determined that the temperature in heavily visited tombs can climb from 21 degrees Celsius at 6:00 a.m. (when the tombs have been closed to visitors for over twelve hours) to 33 degrees Celsius at 2:00 p.m. (when they have been open for eight hours), and the humidity can rise from 18 to 71 percent. Such changes can seriously damage plaster and pigments. Before the 2011 revolution, the Valley of the Kings was visited by as many as 7,000 tourists a day, nearly all of them coming between 7:00 and 11:00 a.m.—1,500 per hour. Some tombs, which TMP estimates could safely accommodate no more than 100 tourists at a time, were often packed with 300 or more.

Such problems could be alleviated by installing environmental monitoring devices and silent air exchange or extraction systems and, most important, by controlling tourist numbers. For example, temperature and humidity levels could be monitored and tourist entry into a tomb temporarily halted when they reached unsafe levels. Until they returned to acceptable levels, tourists would be diverted to other tombs nearby. Timed tickets and entry controls also offer possible solutions. Other suggestions include keeping the valley open to visitors sixteen hours a day instead of the current eleven hours, or levying special admission fees for more popular tombs (such as KV 9 and 62), which reduces the number of group tourists who visit (Weeks and Hetherington 2013).

Inappropriate protective measures can exacerbate problems: the chemicals used to treat wooden walkways can damage pigments and often hinder tomb cleaning and dust control. Some are toxic, and they are used inside the tombs without any ventilation. Walkways made of composite materials rather than wood, treated with nontoxic varnishes and built using removable modules, would permit regular maintenance outside the tomb and would not harm the tomb's environment.

Conservation of decorated walls and structural repairs in valley tombs still often fall below international standards. In 1940, Davies (1940, 115) commented that "Egypt is a vast museum, the most extensive and most unique that exists, and it appears to be without effective curatorship." Effective curatorship is closer to becoming a reality today, but there are still many upgrades to be made. Better materials should be used for protective devices in tombs, and valley personnel at all levels should receive better training.

The large panels of reflective glass installed in many tombs to protect decorated walls actually cause damage and make for an unpleasant visitor experience. The glass is highly reflective, making it difficult to see the decorated walls. The panels quickly become dusty, and to clean them, a man with a rag slides along the 30-centimeter-wide space between glass and tomb wall, rubbing against the decorated plaster, spraying Windex onto the painted scenes as he moves. The panels were specially made for installation in the valley, and if cracked or broken, they cannot be replaced. They should be removed, and railings and small, unobtrusive, non-electrostatic Plexiglas panels should be installed instead.

Lighting in tombs currently consists of fluorescent lights placed on the floor. They provide poor-quality illumination that is unevenly distributed across the walls. Each tube generates substantial heat and is on from 6:00 a.m. to 5:00 p.m. each day. In KV 9 alone, there are 100 such tubes, and they alone raise the temperature in the tomb by several degrees. Replacing the tubes with LED lighting would be a highly effective way to provide better quality light, reduce ambient temperature, and cut operating costs.

Toilet facilities are inadequate and malodorous. New installations must be carefully located to avoid damaging tombs, and a system should be installed to carry waste away from the valley to a much-needed west bank waste treatment facility, which would also serve a vital role for local communities. (All these proposals are discussed in Weeks and Hetherington 2013.)

POSITIVE DEVELOPMENTS

At the same time that the tombs must be protected, visitors' experiences can be improved. Several recent tourist-related upgrades in the valley offer successful examples of what can be done.

The visitors' center, built in 2004 by the government of Japan, with displays designed by the TMP, has been well-received by guides, who use the displays to introduce their groups to the Valley of the Kings and its history. Displays include panels in Arabic, English, and Japanese, offering basic data on gods, rulers, excavators, hieroglyphs, and other subjects; a transparent, three-dimensional model of the valley shows how the tombs lie in relation to each other; and a video shows Howard Carter at work in the tomb of Tutankhamun.

Adjacent to the center, a new sales area where local vendors offer visitors curios and postcards is a clean, well-organized alternative to what formerly was a dirty and cluttered collection of kiosks that made many tourists uncomfortable. The sales area is one of the few ways in which local villagers benefit economically from the valley, and anecdotal evidence suggests that the new sales area has increased their profits.

New interpretive signs were installed in the valley by the TMP in 2002. They include valley maps, individual tomb plans and descriptions, and lists of tombs currently open to the public. The TMP's signs, laser-etched on aluminum panels, have now been adopted by the SCA as the standard for new signage at all Egyptian archaeological sites.

The TMP has completely photographed the walls of open valley tombs (except KV 17, 19, and 62, which are available elsewhere) and made available Zoomifiable images on its website. The images provide a baseline against which future condition surveys can be evaluated (http://www.thebanmappingproject.com; Weeks and Hetherington 2013; see also Dziobek and Abdel el-Raziq 1990).

By modifying pathways and installing entry ramps, the TMP has made six valley tombs wheelchair and handicapped accessible (Weeks and Hetherington 2013).

The TMP recently established a library of Egyptology and general knowledge on Luxor's west bank. It is open every day from 3:00 to 9:00 p.m., and inspectors, guides, conservators, students, and children are all welcome to use its collections free of charge. The library currently has nearly 2,000 volumes, over half of them in Arabic, and is extensively used by dozens of local people every week. Its goal is to better educate those directly involved with Egypt's ancient monuments and to make the Luxor public more aware of the importance of protecting their country's archaeological and environmental heritage (http://www.thebanmappingproject.com).

The future of Valley of the Kings tourism cannot be foretold in detail, but it is safe to assume that, in spite of recent setbacks, it will continue to grow, exerting even greater pressure on the tombs. The possible use of computer-generated, full-size replicas of selected tombs to accommodate tourists, while the original tombs remain closed, a plan successfully implemented in France at Lascaux, for example, is now receiving serious discussion (Lowe 2012). But replicas are expensive, and selecting a site at which to install them poses problems.

The primary goal of Egyptologists, conservators, and site managers must be to protect the valley for future generations. But they must be mindful of another, equally important, concern: Egypt depends economically on tourism, and Luxor relies especially heavily on tourist dollars. The goals of site protection and an ever-growing tourist industry may seem incompatible. But it is essential that both be given a fair hearing. Safeguarding the works of Egypt's ancient dead must be balanced with serving the needs of Egypt's living. With proper planning, these goals need not be in irreconcilable conflict. But to achieve them, that planning must begin *now*.

BIBLIOGRAPHY

Abt Associates. 2000a. *The Comprehensive Development of the City of Luxor Project, Egypt: Final Structure Plan*. [Vol] 2, *Supplementary Documents*. Cambridge, MA.

Abt Associates. 2000b. *The Comprehensive Development of the City of Luxor Project, Egypt: Phase I, Heritage Concept*. Cambridge, MA.

Baillet, J. 1926. *Inscriptions grecques et latines des tombeaux des rois ou syringes*. Mémoires publiés par les membres de l'Institut français d'archéologie orientale, 42. 2 vols. Cairo.

Carter, H. 1903. "Report on General Work Done in the Southern Inspectorate." *Annales du Service des antiquités de l'Egypte* 4: 43–50.

Černý, J. 1973. *The Valley of the Kings: Fragments d'un manuscrit inachevé*. Bibliotheque d'etudes, Institut francais d'archeologie orientale, 61. Cairo.

Clayton, P. 1982. *The Rediscovery of Ancient Egypt: Artists and Travellers in the Nineteenth Century*. London.

El-Daly, O. 2005. *Egyptology: The Missing Millennium; Ancient Egypt in Medieval Arabic Writing*. London.

Davies, N. de G. 1940. "The Defacement of the Tomb of Rekhmire." *Chronqiue d'Egypte* 15: 115.

Demas, M., and N. Agnew. 2012. *Valley of the Queens Assessment Report, 1: A Joint Project of the Getty Conservation Institute and the Supreme Council of Antiquities, Egypt for the Conservation and Management of the Valley of the Queens*. Los Angeles.

Dziobek, E., and M. Abdel Raziq. 1990. *Das Grab des Sobekhotep, TT Nr. 63*. Archäologische Veröffentlichungen des Deutschen Archäologischen Instituts, Abteilung Kairo, 71). Mainz.

Foertmeyer, V. A. 1989. "Tourism in Graeco-Roman Egypt." PhD thesis, Princeton University.

Greener, L. 1966. *The Discovery of Egypt*. London.

Kalfatovic, M. R. 1992. *Nile Notes of a Howadji: A Bibliography of Travelers' Tales from Egypt, from the Earliest Time to 1918*. Metuchen, NJ.

Kalfatovic, M. R. 2001. "Nile Notes of a Howadja: American Travellers in Egypt, 1837–1908." In *Unfolding the Orient: Travellers in Egypt and the Near East*, edited by P. Starkey and J. Starkey, 239–260. Reading and Ithaca, NY.

[Lowe, A.] 2012. *The Authorized Facsimile of the Burial Chamber of Tutankhamun, with Sarcophagus, Sarcophagus Lid and the Missing Fragment from the South Wall*. Madrid.

Manley, D., ed. 1991. *The Nile: A Traveller's Anthology*. London.

Manley, D., and S. Abdel-Hakim, eds. 2004. *Traveling Through Egypt: From 450 B.C. to the Twentieth Century*. Cairo.

Pudney, J. 1953. *The Thomas Cook Story*. London.

Reeves, C. N., and R. H. Wilkinson. 1996. *The Complete Valley of the Kings: Tombs and Treasures of Egypt's Greatest Pharaohs*. London and Cairo.

Reid, D. M. 2002. *Whose Pharaohs? Archaeology, Museums, and Egyptian National Identity from Napoleon to World War I*. Berkeley.

Riggs, C., ed. 2012. *The Oxford Handbook of Roman Egypt*. Oxford.

Roehrig, C. H. 2001. *Explorers and Artists in the Valley of the Kings*. Vercelli.

Romer, J. 1981. *Valley of the Kings*. London and New York.

Rutherford, I. C. 2012. "Travel and Pilgrimage." In *The Oxford Handbook of Roman Egypt*, edited by C. Riggs, 701–717, Oxford.

Sadek, A. A. 1990. "Varia graffitica." *Varia Aegyptiaca* 6: 109–120.

Sakr, M., N. Massoud, and H. Sakr. 2009. *Tourism in Egypt: An Unfinished Business* Egyptian Center for Economic Studies, Working Paper 147. Cairo.

Sattin, A. 2011. *Lifting the Veil: Two Centuries of Travellers, Traders and Tourists in Egypt*. London.

Searight, S. 1969. *The British in the Middle East*. London.

Simpson, C. 2003. "Qurna: Pieces of an Historical Jigsaw." In *The Theban Necropolis: Past, Present and Future*, edited by N. Strudwick and J. Taylor, 244–249. London.

Singleton, E., ed. 1911. *Egypt, As Described by Great Writers*. New York.

Stanley, D. 1911. "Tombs of the Kings." In *Egypt, As Described by Great Writers*, edited by E. Singleton, n.p. New York.

Starkey, P., and J. Starkey, eds. 1998. *Travellers in Egypt*. London.

Starkey, P., and J. Starkey, eds. 2001. *Unfolding the Orient: Travellers in Egypt and the Near East*. Reading and Ithaca, NY.

Strudwick, N., and J. Taylor, eds. 2003. *The Theban Necropolis: Past, Present and Future*. London.

Ventura, R. 1986. *Living in a City of the Dead: A Selection of Topographical and Administrative Terms in the Documents of the Theban Necropolis*. Orbis et Biblia Orientalia, 69. Göttingen.

Warburton, E. 1845. *The Crescent and the Cross, or Romance and Realities of Eastern Travel*. London. Reissued in 1908.

Weeks, K. R. 1995. "The Work of the Theban Mapping Project and the Protection of the Valley of the Kings." In *Valley of the Sun Kings: New Explorations in the Tombs of the Pharaohs*, edited by R. H. Wilkinson, 122–128. Tucson, AZ.

Weeks, K. R. 2001a. "The Exploration of Thebes." In *Valley of the Kings: The Tombs and the Funerary Temples of Thebes West*, edited by K. R. Weeks, 36–53. Vercelli and Cairo.

Weeks, K. R., ed. 2001b. *Valley of the Kings: The Tombs and the Funerary Temples of Thebes West*. Vercelli and Cairo.

Weeks, K. R., and N. J. Hetherington. 2013. *The Valley of the Kings: A Site Management Handbook*. Cairo. (In Arabic and English eds). Previously published as *The Valley of the Kings, Luxor, Egypt: Site Management Masterplan*. Cairo: Theban Mapping Project, 2006. (Funded in part by the World Monument Fund and Mr. Bernard Selz.)

Wilkinson, R. H., ed. 1995. *Valley of the Sun Kings: New Explorations in the Tombs of the Pharaohs; Papers of the University of Arizona International Conference on the Valley of the Kings*. Tucson, AZ.

CHAPTER 38

THE VALLEY OF THE KINGS IN THE LIVES OF MODERN EGYPTIANS

The People of Qurna[1]

KEES VAN DER SPEK

THE THEBAN NECROPOLIS AS SOCIAL LANDSCAPE

EVER since the early nineteenth-century operations of Giovanni Battista Belzoni, archeological fieldwork in the Valley of the Kings has relied on and been made possible by the manual labor provided by the villagers of nearby Qurna, the Qurnawi. In fact, the argument must be made that the relationship between Qurnawi and the surrounding archeological landscape is an integral part of the development of Egyptological presence and practice in the wider necropolis of the Theban west bank. It is in this alignment of diverse yet shared interests that the social anthropologist finds his place alongside the excavating field archeologist and the translating philologist. Qurnawi may indeed be seen to represent the most recent and final deposit in the stratigraphy of human landscape use in the Theban Necropolis, with both archeologist and anthropologist concerning themselves with their respective sequences and separated only by relative time and trench depth. What they share is a focus on the central place of human agency and action in the wādīs and surrounding foothills of the Theban west bank both during ancient and more recent times.

Much of Qurna village[2] originally consisted of scattered hamlets several of which dotted the foothills below the Valley of the Kings' eastern escarpment (Figure 38.1), although no longer so. Qurna's colorful mud-brick foothills architecture was demolished between 2006 and 2010 and its historic and social landscape destroyed. Amidst the roar and insidious vibrations of the bulldozers exacting their destruction in this fragile archeological landscape, Qurnawi were relocated to three new northern communities at several kilometers distance of the Theban Mountain.

FIGURE 38.1 The central area of the Theban foothills below the eastern escarpment of the Valley of the Kings, with the hill of Shaykh 'Abd al-Qurna on the right and the hamlet of al-Hurubāt at its foot, prior to demolition commencing December 2006.

(Photograph by Kees van der Spek.)

International visitors may view the Valley of the Kings along a spectrum ranging from the mysterious to the romantic, notions that will readily allow their association with an isolated archeological site in an out-of-the-way desert location and rich in both historical and material terms. What may be less evident to them is that the royal valley is also integrated in and defined by the historical and continuing social life of its nearby resident community. Members of that community experience the larger necropolis and the proximity of noble and royal tombs as a real-time and active force in their lives, for better or worse bestowing on Qurnawi a certain reputation and identity, and offering at once economic benefits and imposing hardship.[3] This chapter explores in turn some of the historical, political, and cultural facets of Qurnawi society: Western literary representations, the politics of heritage management and the role of UNESCO, and Qurnawi oral literary traditions.

QURNAWI AND EARLY TRAVELERS' FIRST IMPRESSIONS

A first distant glimpse linking Qurna with the Valley of the Kings dates to 1668, when two French Capuchin missionary brothers—Fathers Protais and Charles François d'Orléans—visited fellow Christians in Luxor. According to Father Protais, who authored the original account (Thévenot 1672; Sauneron 1983, 141–143), they learned from their Luxor informants about the west bank city of Habu with its many antiquities "incomparably more beautiful than those at Karnak." They were also told of a place called "Biout el Melouc" as a source for mummies which "the Arabs burn every day, as well as their wooden idols." Although there may be confusion here with the larger necropolis as to the origin of the mummies, the name "Biout el Melouc," the "Houses of the Kings," a variant attribution of today's "Biban al-Muluk," the "Doors of the Kings," that is, the Valley of the Kings, is beyond dispute.

Protais goes on to say that "nearby there is a place called Legourné, where the temples and statues are in such a well-preserved state, and the colors are so vivid, that it seems, so say the inhabitants in their own words, that the master-craftsman is yet to wash his hands since finishing his work" (Thévenot 1672, 3). We may assume here that these "inhabitants" are the people of "Legourné," al-Qurna, even if the observation comes from Protais' Christian informants in Luxor. They make no mention of tombs, but there can be little doubt that their reference to "vivid colors" included the decorated noble and royal tombs.

Although Protais regretted not to have visited the west bank, his account documents both the Valley of the Kings and a resident west bank community with names we can recognize, enshrining their presence in the Western literary record and providing early geographic and linguistic markers for a relationship that continues to this day.

QURNAWI SOCIAL BEHAVIOR OLD AND NEW

In part, Protais' account of the inhabitants of "Legourné" concerns their assessment of the state of preservation of the ancient monuments and their implied admiration for the master-craftsmen of old. Protais thereby establishes an unexpected connection with today's Qurnawi, a number of whom are employed by the Supreme Council of Antiquities as restorers of those same monuments (Figure 38.2), while others are indeed themselves master-craftsmen, creating works of art for sale to visitors (Van der Spek 2011, 219–287). As such, Protais offers a more positive image of seventeenth-century Qurnawi than do most other European accounts, the earliest of which dates back to the late sixteenth century.

Predating the visit of the two Capuchin missionaries by close to 80 years, that earliest narrative recounts a sojourn in Upper Egypt in 1589 by an anonymous Venetian traveler. Owing to the inundation, the "Anonymous Venetian" never visited the Luxor west bank and he could observe certain monuments there only from a distance, including the Memnon Colossi (Burri 1971, 81–83). Although the Venetian does not mention any villages there by name, his description of certain social characteristics in relation to the surrounding archeological landscape clearly points to a locally resident community we can now recognize as Qurnawi (Van der Spek 2011, 64–71).

FIGURE 38.2 Supreme Council of Antiquities restorer from Qurna at work in the Shaykh ʿAbd al-Qurna tomb of Amenemope, TT41.

(Photograph by Kees van der Spek.)

But the Venetian's account is rather different from the certain "connoisseurship" high-lighted by Father Protais, with the Venetian observing that the Luxor west bank "is an area where the boat captains refuse to lodge you, and all go and put you on the other bank, for this area of land is inhabited by certain cursed tribes of insubordinate Arabs" (Burri 1971, 81). He also comments how west bank inhabitants use the mountain for refuge during times of political unrest: "Each time the Turks have tried to attack, they have withdrawn themselves into the mountain, which is their fortress" (Burri 1971, 81). Similar observations by later travelers confirm that it is not just the natural geography of the mountain that provides shelter, but rather the tombs and underground passages of the Theban Necropolis (Bruce 1790, 125; Denon 1803(II), 86–87; (III), 30–32, 47–51, 177–178).

Thus, and commencing with the Venetian in 1589, European accounts come to increasingly relate the Theban Necropolis and its inhabitants not to "vivid colors" and "ancient craftsmen," but to antisocial behavior toward strangers and to open conflict with the country's ruling elite and system of governance. Beyond disputes over taxa-tion and strained village–state relations (Van der Spek 2011, 122–127), this behavior may possibly be linked with the procurement of an allegedly medicinal resin-like substance known as *mumiya* and extracted from ancient human remains excavated by Qurnawi from the tombs and mummy-pits in the necropolis. Owing to its perceived spiritu-ally defiling aspects, Qurnawi will have been considered as outcasts by other devout Muslims, likely resulting in their fierce disposition toward outsiders. Additional reasons for local discontent may have been any associated exploitative labor relations enforced by European merchants overseeing the *mumiya* operations, and European ignorance of local rules of hospitality when crossing tribal boundaries, among others (Van der Spek 2011, 72–78, 117–130). Mediated by boat captains' views infusing the attitudes of their sixteenth- and seventeenth-century passengers, generally negative impressions about Qurnawi have become perpetuated in the Western documentary record.

Whatever the cause for these negative relations, what may be said is that, first, the trade in *mumiya* was an early form of European consumption located in certain resources obtained from the Theban Necropolis. It predated that other form of European consumption: the extraction of antiquities by Western private and institutional collectors that has likewise resulted in negative perceptions about Qurnawi, this time resulting from Western concepts of heritage value and linked views about involvement in an illicit antiquities trade.

Second, the several early accounts that document the tombs' use for refuge and shelter during times of political unrest provide historical connections with the more recent habitation of the Theban foothills. Yet, emerging views about the adaptive reuse of the archeological landscape through the domestic occupation of subterranean tombs, and later during the twentieth century when above-ground mud-brick dwellings became the norm, were similarly informed by Western concepts of heritage value and therefore equally seen in negative terms, first by European and later by Egyptian officials.

DIVERGING VIEWS ON INDIGENOUS PRESENCE

Literary references to the Valley of the Kings and nearby population groups typically view the relationship between the ancient cemeteries and the villagers of the Theban west bank in one of two ways. For some, the modern Theban communities generally, and the villagers from Qurna specifically, are "the only living link with the people of ancient Egypt. They are directly descended from the embalmers, craftsmen, painters, sculptors and artists who lived here three thousand years ago" (Zakaria Goneim, in Cottrell, 1950, 144, 120–121), a view also informed by the evident artistic skills of modern Qurnawi craftsmen.

But a second perspective follows, for this broad range of claimed continuities with ancient Egypt also implies that Qurnawi are the descendants of the ancient tomb-robbers. The point is made repeatedly, including by such notable early twentieth-century Egyptologists as James Henry Breasted (1916, 525) and Howard Carter (Carter and Mace 1923, 70). Arguably, this view was carried into the modern era by Christiane Desroches-Noblecourt in her popular and influential 1963 study of Tutankhamun, which provided a first glimpse of Qurnawi for mid- and late-twentieth-century readers.

Her narrative situates the account of Howard Carter's search for the tomb of Tutankhamun against a backdrop of the activities of local tomb-robbers, both during ancient Egyptian and more recent times. Her account is accompanied by a photograph of a male Qurnawi, credited to have come from the collection of Gaston Maspero, the Director General of the *Service des antiquités* (Desroches-Noblecourt 1963, 57, 308; Van der Spek 2011, 24). Tellingly, this image (nr. 25) is preceded by one (nr. 24) that she identifies as the clearance in 1881 of the Dayr al-Bahari Royal Cache (DB320), the ancient royal burial site discovered and exploited by the 'Abd al-Rasul family from Qurna (Desroches-Noblecourt 1963, 55). She also attributes this photograph to Maspero, even though he was in Paris at the time. While showing the removal of royal mummies, that photograph was in fact taken in January 1900 during the clearance of the Tomb of Amenhotep II (KV 35) in the Valley of the Kings after its discovery by Victor Loret in 1898 (Orsenigo 2012, 28; Romer 1981, 180). Yet, its misidentification and the sequencing of the two illustrations linking Qurnawi with an alleged tomb-robbing episode served to strengthen further their reputation in the modern public imagination.

Despite episodes of activity by local tomb-robbers across the ages, any continuity between ancient and contemporary population groups cannot be conclusively argued and is therefore contentious at best. However, accounts such as that by Desroches-Noblecourt do turn the focus to the phenomenon of modern human presence in this archeological landscape—a fact that remains understated in most archeological field reports—and that highlights the contested nature of the "conflict-ridden spaces" (Tilley 1994, 11) that archeological sites often are. This contestation arises out of the conflict between what is essentially a Western academic practice with its own history, values and conventions being imposed on locally resident indigenous communities, whose behavior in sensitive archeological landscapes effectively came to be seen as a form of social deviance enacted against the greater cultural consciousness of the West. We may see these sentiments reflected in Sir Alan Gardiner's scathing assessment: "The inhabitants of Gurnah are inveterate and incorrigible tomb-robbers; (. . .) It must be remembered that the natives of Gurnah are for the most part born and bred to the habit of tomb-robbery; there is no hole so small that a native will not creep into it, undeterred by darkness, dirt, or lack of air" (Gardiner and Weigall 1913, 8, 9).

Thus, we may find that sentiments surrounding the "certain cursed tribes of insubordinate Arabs" of which the Anonymous Venetian wrote in 1589, when linked to contemporary heritage values associated with the "incomparably beautiful" antiquities of Medinat Habu and the Theban Necropolis mentioned by Protais in 1668, also carries over into modern writing. Archeological field reports and specialist Egyptological publications influence representations in the modern media and inspire a broader genre of popular and fictional archeological writing. In their totality, they continue the suspicion and tension between local people and those with vested interests in the west bank archeological landscape that is already evident in the accounts of early travelers.

The interrelationships and connections between past and present are a blessing and a curse for Egyptology and Qurnawi alike. Egyptologists benefit from the availability of local labor as much as they remain ambivalent about an indigenous community in a fragile archeological landscape. Qurnawi may find employment with Egyptian and for-eign archeological missions or earn a living from tourism, yet face restrictions imposed by their archeological surroundings. The varying sets of possible relationships can be mutually beneficial as much as they can strain relations (Fábián 2011, 13). This is not sim-ply some benign tension between Qurnawi and academic or tourism industry objectives infiltrating the social landscape of the necropolis. Qurnawi also feel the political power that the monuments exert over their lives. The practical outworking of the politicized nature of heritage selection and management of Egypt's archeological sites is evidenced in the government-initiated but economically and tourism industry-motivated eviction of Qurnawi from the Theban foothills and the demolition of their vernacular hamlets at the foot of the Kings Valley escarpment.

Mismanaging Heritage Management: The Role of UNESCO

Historically, observations of Qurnawi behavior dating back to 1589 have crystallized into three elements: (1) the unruly character of west bank villagers; (2) the use of the moun-tain for refuge; and (3) their relationship with the emerging art-historical and archeo-logical significance of the Theban Necropolis. The first of these would eventually feed into narratives of tomb-robbing and illicit antiquities dealings; the second ultimately evolved into subterranean tomb habitation and the development of the above-ground village of Qurna; and the third would translate into a heritage management discourse used to justify the removal of Qurnawi from the necropolis.

In combination they capture the issues and themes that have typified modern heritage management views: (1) alleged continued Qurnawi dealings in illegal antiquities; (2) claimed Qurnawi recalcitrance for refusing to leave the necropolis to protect illicit economic activi-ties; and (3) the need for protection of the deteriorating condition of the necropolis' World Heritage–listed artistic legacy. Taken together, they would strengthen the resolve to remove Qurnawi from the necropolis (Fakhry 1947), commencing in 1947 with the construction of "New Qurna" by renowned Egyptian architect Hassan Fathy—who indeed attributed the project's failure to Qurnawi resistance in order to protect their livelihood (Fathy 1973, 176)—and culminating in the evictions and demolitions executed between 2006 and 2010. Despite pronouncements of "Outstanding Universal Value" and World Heritage–listing, the result has been the final destruction of the socio-historical, contemporary, vernacular, and cul-tural landscape of the Theban Necropolis as well as, it must be said, the now severely com-promised state of much of the surrounding archeological stratigraphy.

Concentrating the heritage management of the Theban Necropolis under the aus-pices of UNESCO, "Ancient Thebes with its Necropolis" was inscribed in the World Heritage List in October 1979 (UNESCO 1979). Since its inscription, the World Heritage Committee has examined and adopted decisions on the state of conservation of the

Theban Necropolis where it concerns the presence of Qurna in 1998 (UNESCO 1999), 2001 (UNESCO 2001a), 2006 (UNESCO 2006), 2007 (UNESCO 2007), and 2008 (UNESCO 2008).

Yet, UNESCO through its Bureau of the World Heritage Committee (the World Heritage Centre, Paris) has proven itself to be a toothless tiger. Despite numerous "reactive monitoring missions" and commissioned expert reports (among these: Braun 2001; Michaelides and Dauge 2008); despite calls for comprehensive site impact assessment studies (UNESCO 1999, 2001a); and despite recommendations and requests made to the Egyptian government, the World Heritage Committee has been powerless to prevent the destruction of the Theban foothills communities. This has been despite their stated commitments to cultural landscapes (UNESCO 1992) and the conservation of earthen architecture (UNESCO 2001b, 2007, WHC-07/31.COM/21C; WHC-07/31.COM/24).

Studying the published deliberations of the World Heritage Committee's annual meetings, it is difficult to escape the impression that the scope of any UNESCO influence is governed by diplomatic convention and that any real "clout" either to prevent serious adverse impact on its World Heritage–listed properties or achieve any practical positive heritage management outcomes are ostensibly constrained by a perceived fear of being seen as meddling in internal affairs. In the face of much international lobbying on behalf of a more broadly conceived Theban west bank cultural landscape, UNESCO's efficacy rate in coordinating, managing, and enforcing holistic heritage management solutions for its World Heritage–listed Theban property has effectively been nil.

Practical UNESCO assistance includes commissioning expert assessments, of which the 2008 reactive monitoring mission to Luxor was significant. Its final report (Michaelides and Dauge 2008) incorporates earlier ICOMOS advice dated July 2006 (UNESCO 2007, WHC-07/31.COM/7B.Add.2, 9–10), with both documents articulating the heritage values of the necropolis' historic and social landscape:

> The information made available demonstrates that (. . .) little attention has been given as to how best to maintain the complex set of historic layers which underlie the Thebes inscription on the [World Heritage] List, and that indeed many significant parts of the site are being needlessly discarded. The demolition of (. . .) substantial parts of Gurnah are neither acceptable approaches within contemporary conservation theory (which demands that changes be limited to only those essential to meet critical functional needs, and here, only where this can be done without loss to heritage values), nor respectful of the property's Outstanding Universal Value. Even if some of these places are not what would be described as "antiquities", they should be protected as being indissociably connected to the development of the site, and therefore worthy of the strongest protection efforts. In particular, the loss of Gurnah, whose residents have provided the bulk of the excavation effort at Thebes from the 19th century forward, would involve loss of a place of great importance within the original nomination. Removal of the population of Gurnah, and reduction of the village to a few surviving designated (and empty) historic buildings is an act which goes against all the principles of conservation.
>
> (Michaelides and Dauge 2008, 7).

The report provides a poignant case study of the manner in which such commissioned expert opinion may be treated by the international delegations present at the annual sessions of the World Heritage Committee. The report was tabled at its Thirty-second Session in Quebec, Canada, in July 2008. A summary of issues was circulated in advance, stating that "the loss of Gurnah impairs the historical integrity and continuity of land-scape use and occupation highlighted a decade ago by the World Heritage Bureau" (UNESCO 2008, WHC-08/32.COM/7B.Add.2, 12).

The report and the state of conservation of "Ancient Thebes with its Necropolis" were discussed on July 5, 2008 (UNESCO 2008, WHC-08/32.COM, 128–129). Deliberations largely involved protestations from the Egyptian delegation that were vacuous, irrele-vant, emotive, and—in the case of claimed approvals by an international committee of experts—outright dishonest. There exists no independent confirmation[4] of this "com-mittee of experts" supporting Egyptian heritage management measures that would result in the destruction of the foothills' hamlets, and its invention is disingenuous and self-serving.

The transcript suggests that the Director of the World Heritage Centre simply surren-dered. The issue of the "committee of experts" was not further pursued, notwithstanding that "the World Heritage Centre has received no information about the composition of the committee of experts, its mandate or its discussions" (UNESCO 2008, WHC-08/32. COM/7B.Add.2, 11). Instead of supporting the report and at least requesting serious and substantive consideration of its findings, the Director simply acknowledged Egypt's part in the maintenance and restoration of its archeological sites and blamed UNESCO's ongoing concerns over the Theban property on a "misunderstanding" resulting from "the lack of response from the State Party over the past years" (UNESCO 2008, WHC-08/32.COM, 129). A detailed examination of the Michaelides and Dauge report's content there was not.

Instead, the Jordanian delegation requested the deletion of several items in the draft decision (UNESCO 2008, WHC-08/32.COM, 129). Specifically, item 13(d) (UNESCO 2008, WHC-08/32.COM/7B.Add.2, 12–13), where the World Heritage Committee requests to "Institute a moratorium on any further demolition at Gurnah and reloca-tion of the population until such time as the studies and impact assessments initially requested are carried out" was not retained in the final decision (UNESCO 2008, WHC-08/32.COM/24Rev, 92–93). This item essentially concerned the outstanding 1998 and 2001 issues noted by Michaelides and Dauge (2008, 7). However, included was a new paragraph (3) proposed by the delegation of Kenya to congratulate Egypt for its efforts in managing its World Heritage sites. That proposal was supported by the del-egations of Jordan, Tunisia and Peru (UNESCO 2008, WHC-08/32.COM, 129). Beyond these deliberations and resolutions, the documentation records no input from the other 16 member-state delegations that would have been present.

The impression one is left with is that the objective is to secure mutually beneficial political and diplomatic outcomes and that a degree of "horse-trading" must be going on behind the scenes by member-states' senior representatives who are in the main career diplomats or senior government bureaucrats well versed in diplomatic maneuvering. In this milieu, African and Middle Eastern delegations can align themselves on regional, cultural, or linguistic grounds and support the Egyptian delegation. Peru can offer its vote in exchange for treatment in kind (UNESCO 2008, WHC-08/32.COM, 134), including Egyptian assistance with the repatriation from Yale University of artifacts removed from Machu Picchu between 1912 and 1916 (el-Aref 2010). In the absence of strong international resolve to achieve substantive outcomes, Egypt can continue to ignore repeated UNESCO requests (UNESCO 2010, WHC-10/34.COM/7B, 128).

The concluding indictment must be that in such a process any tangible heritage management results are sacrificed. Despite World Heritage–listing, the Valley of the Kings and the larger Theban Necropolis with its indigenous community are pawns to be traded in the context of larger political objectives over which UNESCO has either little or no control, or in which it chooses not to interfere. The outcomes can be palpable: as late as April 2009, the demolitions in Qurna included buildings that were in excess of 100 years old and that were of great significance for the history of Egyptological practice in the necropolis. Most disconcerting, a community that constituted an important facet of Egypt's rural cultural diversity had its fate sealed by questionable decision making while a living earthen architectural landscape was willfully destroyed.

These issues must be of serious concern, not only because UNESCO first approved its program for the conservation of earthen architecture as early as 2001 (UNESCO 2001b), but also because UNESCO documents for 2008 and 2010 evidence a sharp contrast in the position of the World Heritage Centre in relation to the conservation of earthen architecture more broadly and the issue of Qurna specifically (UNESCO 2008, WHC-08/32.COM, 128–129; UNESCO 2010, WHC-10/34.COM/INF.20, 83).

Qurnawi Oral Literary Traditions: Folk Stories from the Theban Necropolis

As a consequence of this questionable heritage management process, the previously existing visual appeal of the necropolis' social landscape is now gone, and its current denuded state will likely resemble what the Anonymous Venetian and Father Protais might have seen had they been able to visit the Theban west bank when tomb habitation still obscured most occupants from view.

Qurnawi now live several kilometers to the north and have had their geographical and historical roots severed from the area that has always been intrinsic to their identity. Excavating Egyptologists may rejoice at this but for those who value the distinct element of rural cultural diversity that the necropolis community represented, their departure and the destruction of their vernacular earthen architecture is a loss. Their resettlement in what is effectively a new Luxor suburb will come with the homogenization that such wholesale relocation brings. For historians and archeologists there is to salvage what remains of the old ways (Fábián 2011), while anthropologists may monitor the consequent social changes taking place, mourning the loss of culturally-specific practices as modernity continues apace.

However, this is not to say that modernizing trends were not already manifest in the foothills hamlets before their demolition: modern appliances were already ubiquitous even then. Among these, the advent of televised entertainment has largely replaced traditional storytelling.

There is indeed evidence that there was once a rich oral literary corpus in existence in the villages of the Theban west bank, as is indicated by such actual stories occasionally referenced in the archeological literature. Examples include: "The Parable of the Sultan's Lion" recounted by Henry Rhind (1862, 305–307); "The Tale of the Rat and the Snake" as told to Howard Carter (Carter n.d.; Van der Spek 2011, 383–386); his reference to recitations containing "a deal of history and romance" (James 1992, 94); Gaston Maspero's reference to stories "partly satirical, partly sentimental" (Maspero 1911, 202–203); and the existence of "songs for every occasion" mentioned by Zakaria Goneim (in Cottrell, 1950, 145–146).

A part of the broader genre will have been intended for entertainment and amusement in the company of friends. Howard Carter was familiar with much of the narrative material in circulation at that time, observing that "reciters of romances, who, without book, commit their subjects to memory, afford attractive entertainment, and are often highly amusing," adding that "unfortunately many of their stories, such as fables of questionable moral teaching, are extremely indecent" (Carter n.d.; Van der Spek 2011, 383–384).

Nevertheless, during premodern times in the predominantly illiterate rural areas of Upper Egypt, storytelling will conceivably have been an important local instructional device intended to guide appropriate social behavior. One example of this may be found in the repertoire of stories that deals with the illicit excavation of antiquities. One story tells of a *shaykh* who was engaged to open a tomb for a family who wanted gold, but the tomb closed while the daughter was still inside, and the *shaykh*'s assistance could only work once. On the level of folklore, these literary narratives may not simply recount mythical or remembered accounts of illicit antiquities searches, but they will have served didactic purposes as well, if only to warn youngsters of the dangers of the caves and crevices of the Theban Mountain.

Collecting these folkloric oral literary narratives is a focus of ongoing anthropological fieldwork in Qurna (Figure 38.3), bridging the observations of those earlier archeologists and twenty-first-century Qurnawi. Further analysis will seek to locate possible sources and to integrate this material in the established broader thematic framework of the oral literary and folkloric traditions of rural Upper Egypt (el-Shamy 1980, 2004).

Such research is indeed one practical example of the relative proximity in which archeologists and anthropologists work when Qurna is their field site. That is to say, not only Egyptologists are digging up literary texts in the Theban Necropolis, but ethnographers can equally be engaged with textual sources, even if these are obtained in a different way. In a sense, we are all scratching at surfaces to uncover information and increase our understanding.

FIGURE 38.3 Only remnants of traditional storytelling remain as the voices of the last generation of Qurnawi to have experienced premodern times fall silent. Qurnawi elder Hasham Ibrahim Abdullah passed away in March 2013.

(Photograph by Kees van der Spek.)

What follows, in closing, is one of the stories collected during anthropological field-work in Qurna, to serve as an example of the Qurnawi folkloric corpus and to expand the repertoire commenced by some of those nineteenth- and twentieth-century archeologists who have been so closely connected to the Valley of the Kings and the men and boys from Qurna who worked alongside them.

PATIENCE IS THE HEAD OF WISDOM[5]

Once there was a couple called Salama and Fatima who were deeply in love and ready to do anything and everything for each other. When they were married Fatima wondered how she could keep Salama as her husband for ever. She thought of a way that might help him to be ever faithful to her and asked her husband this question: "Where can one find wisdom?" The husband could not answer but she gave him another chance by asking: "How can one be wise?" adding that she would not consider him her husband unless he replied to her question. In vain he tried, upon which Salama decided to leave home to go looking for the correct answer. He took some food and spare clothes and said goodbye to his wife. He went everywhere looking for an answer. He asked everyone he met. People accused him of being a madman. Days passed, weeks, months, the years—they all passed. He spent some 10 years without getting the right answer. One day, while he was walking along the bank of the river he saw a little girl playing beside a cottage. He was hungry and thought: "Why not ask this little girl to bring me some food from her house?" and he did. He then asked the girl about her father. "He went to irrigate water with water," she replied. He asked her where her mother was. She told him that her mother "went to fight." At last he asked her where her brother was. She said: "He was playing with the air." Salama was very surprised at these mysterious answers and decided to wait until her father returned to resolve the girl's riddles. He sat down and waited for several hours before the girl's father came home. He greeted the guest, made him welcome, and brought him food. But Salama refused to eat anything until his host explained his daughter's strange answers, to which the father agreed. Salama told him that the girl had said: "My father went to irrigate water with water." The father said: "Yes. I have a field of water melons. A water melon is irrigated with water." Then Salama said: "The girl told me that her mother went to fight. How was that"? His host explained: "A relative of ours has died, and as soon as she had heard so, she began to cry and shout. She put dust on her head and that was against Islam. That behaviour expressed objection against Allah, so she was fighting God's will." Salama then asked him how his son had played with the air. The father said: "My son is newly born and babies grasp at air." Then the father asked his guest where he came from. Salama said: "I come from far away looking for wisdom, and how to be a wise man." His host then told him that: "Patience is the head of Wisdom. The more patient you are the wiser you will be." Salama thanked him profusely and asked his permission to leave as he was most anxious to return home, having spent 10 years away from his beloved. When he finally arrived back home, it was midnight and he quietly opened the door of the bedroom. To his astonishment he saw two persons sleeping, covered with one blanket. Salama became very angry, thinking: "Did my wife deceive me and found herself another man during my absence?" He got his *janbiya* [dagger] out and decided to kill both of them. Then he remembered the advice of the little girl's father: "the more patient you are the wiser you will be." He waited and woke up his wife. She was very happy to see him but asked: "Do you know where we can find wisdom?" He answered: "Yes, in patience." She said: "That is right. If you had not been wise enough you would have killed our son." He said: "How?" She then told him that she had fallen pregnant before he left, and that their only son was now 10 years old.

NOTES

1. This chapter is dedicated to the memory of Sheelagh Schneemann (1926–2011) of Canberra, Australia, and Dirk Bakker (1927–2012) of Rotterdam, The Netherlands.
2. For a description of operative naming conventions and the various localities that make up larger al-Qurna, see Van der Spek, 2011, 39–51.

3. For a discussion of Qurnawi beyond what can be offered in these pages, see Van der Spek (2011). For a visual representation see Siron and Corradi (2008). For Upper Egyptian society more broadly, see Hopkins and Saad (2004).

4. Supporting evidence held by the author. Informants' identities withheld.

5. Recorded at al-Suālim, al-Qurna, 10 July, 1999. Translation of raw audio-file by Qurnawi English teacher Hassan Ibrahim, edited by Kees van der Spek.

BIBLIOGRAPHY

el-Aref, N. 2010. "Peru recovers artifacts from Yale University, thanks Egypt." *AhramOnline*, Saturday 18 December 2010. Retrieved from: http://english.ahram.org.eg/News/2159.aspx

Braun, J. P. 2001. *La question des villages de Qurna installés sur les tombes des Nobles de la Nécropole de Thèbes (Egypte)*. UNESCO-Commissioned Report. Paris.

Breasted, J. H. 1916. *A History of Egypt – From the Earliest Times to the Persian Conquest*. New York.

Bruce, J. 1790. *Travels to Discover the Source of the Nile*. Vol. I. London.

Burri, C. 1971. "Le Voyage en Égypte du Vénitien Anonyme: Août-Septembre 1589." In Burri and Sauneron, 5–153.

Burri, C., and S. Sauneron, eds. 1971 *Voyages en Egypte des années 1589, 1590 & 1591*. Cairo.

Carter, H. (n.d.). "Autobiographical sketches." *Notebook* 16, Sketch V, Pages 115–121, "Summer Life and a Tale from the Coffee-hearth." Oxford.

Carter, H., and A. C. Mace. 1923. *The Tomb of Tut.Ankh.Amen*. Vol. I. New York.

Cottrell, L. 1950. *The Lost Pharaohs*. London.

Denon, D.V. 1803. *Travels in Upper and Lower Egypt*. Volumes I, II, and III. London.

Desroches-Noblecourt, C. 1963. *Tutankhamen: Life and Death of a Pharaoh*. London.

Fábián, Z. I. 2011. "A thébai el-Hoha domb déli lejtőjének feltárása Nefermenu TT 184 számú sziklasírjának körzetében – 2010. 1. rész: Qurna egy sarka." *Orpheus Noster* III(1): 5–26.

Fakhry, A. 1947. "A Report on the Inspectorate of Upper Egypt: The Theban Necropolis—The Project of the Expropriation of the Village of Gurna." *Annales du Service des Antiquités de l'Égypte* 46: 34–35.

Fathy, H. 1973. *Architecture for the Poor: An Experiment in Rural Egypt*. Chicago.

Hopkins, N. S., and R. Saad, eds. 2004. *Upper Egypt: Identity and Change*. Cairo.

Gardiner, A. H., and A. E. P. Weigall. 1913. *A Topographical Catalogue of the Private Tombs of Thebes*. London.

James, T. G. H. 1992. *Howard Carter: The Path to Tutankhamun*. London and New York.

Maspero, G. 1911. *Egypt: Ancient Sites and Modern Scenes*. New York.

Michaelides, D., and V. Dauge. (2008). *Report of the Joint World Heritage Centre/ICOMOS Reactive Monitoring Mission to the World Heritage Site of Thebes and its Necropolis, April 18–24, 2008*. Paris: UNESCO. Retrieved from: http://whc.unesco.org/en/documents/100786.

Orsenigo, C. (2012). "Moving the KV35 Royal Mummies." *Kmt* 23(4) Winter 2012–13: 18–31.

Rhind, A.H. 1862. *Thebes: Its Tombs and Their Tenants*. London.

Romer, J. 1981. *Valley of the Kings: Exploring the Tombs of the Pharaohs*. New York.

Sauneron, S. 1983. *Villes et Légendes d' Égypte*. Cairo.

el-Shamy, H.M. 1980. *Folktales of Egypt*. Chicago.

el-Shamy, H.M. 2004. *Types of the Folktale in the Arab World: A Demographically Oriented Tale-Type Index*. Bloomington.

Siron, J., and P. Corradi. 2008. *Thèbes à l'ombre de la tombe*. DVD. Ennetbaden, Switzerland.

Thévenot, M. 1672. *Relations De Divers Voyages Curieux—Relation Du Voyage Du Sayd Ou De La Thebayde, Fait en 1668. par les PP. Protais & Charles-François d'Orleans, Capucins Missionaires*. Vol. 2. Paris.

Tilley, C. 1994. *A Phenomenology of Landscape–Places, Paths and Monuments*. Oxford and Providence.

UNESCO. 1979. *World Heritage Committee, Third Session, Cairo and Luxor, Egypt*. CC-79/ CONF.003/13, pp. 11–12. Retrieved from: http://whc.unesco.org/en/documents/730

UNESCO. 1992. *World Heritage Committee, Sixteenth Session, Santa Fe, USA*. WHC-92/ CONF.002/12. Retrieved from: http://whc.unesco.org/en/documents/940 http://whc. unesco.org/en/culturallandscape

UNESCO. (1999). *World Heritage Committee, Twenty-second Session, Kyoto, Japan*. WHC–98/ CONF.203/18, p. 105. Retrieved from: http://whc.unesco.org/en/documents/183

UNESCO. (2001a). *Bureau of the World Heritage Committee, Twenty-fifth Session, Paris, France*. WHC–2001/CONF.205/10, p. 37. Retrieved from: http://whc.unesco.org/en/ documents/1145/

UNESCO. (2001b). *World Heritage Committee, Twenty-fifth Session, Helsinki, Finland*. WHC-01/CONF.208/24, p. 63. Retrieved from: http://whc.unesco.org/document/1269

UNESCO. 2006. *World Heritage Committee, Thirtieth Session, Vilnius, Lithuania*. WHC-06/30. COM/INF.19; WHC-06/30.COM/7B.Add; WHC-06/30.COM/19. Retrieved from: http:// whc.unesco.org/en/documents/6587/ http://whc.unesco.org/document/6651 http://whc. unesco.org/en/documents/6728/

UNESCO. (2007). *World Heritage Committee, Thirty-first Session, Christchurch, New Zealand*. WHC-07/31.COM/21C; 07/31.COM/7B.Add.2; WHC-07/31.COM/24. Retrieved from: http://whc.unesco.org/archive/2007/whc07-31com-21Ce.pdf http://whc.unesco.org/ document/9022 http://whc.unesco.org/en/documents/9192

UNESCO. 2008. *World Heritage Committee, Thirty-second Session, Quebec City, Canada*. WHC-08/32.COM/7B.Add.2; WHC-08/32.COM/24Rev; WHC-08/32.COM. Retrieved from: http://whc.unesco.org/document/100768 http://whc.unesco.org/en/docu- ments/100946 http://whc.unesco.org/document/102287

UNESCO. 2010. *World Heritage Committee, Thirty-fourth Session, Brasilia, Brazil*. WHC-10/34. COM/7B; WHC-10/34.COM/INF.20. Retrieved from: http://whc.unesco.org/docu- ment/103459 http://whc.unesco.org/document/117078

Van der Spek, K. 2011. *The Modern Neighbors of Tutankhamun: History, Life, and Work in the Villages of the Theban West Bank*. Cairo.

APPENDIX

···

MEASUREMENTS OF KV
ROYAL
TOMB COMPONENTS

···

KENT R. WEEKS

APPENDIX table 1 gives a list of KV royal tombs discussed in Chapter 8 and described below in Appendix tables 2–16. (KV 62 is not included.) Tombs are listed in the probable order of their cutting which, except for KV 20 and 38, is also the regnal order of their owners (see, most recently, Preys 2011, Eaton-Krauss 2012, cited in Chapter 8.)

In tables 2–16, tombs are listed by their KV number left to right in chronological order (see Appendix table 1). Tombs are grouped into Stages 1–4 as defined by Hornung (see Chapter 8). The data in this appendix was checked for accuracy by Lori Lawson.

The following symbols and abbreviations are common to all tables. (Symbols unique to a single table are defined in the notes to that table):

H = height of chamber in meters.
Hc = height of chamber in cubits and palms: 1 cubit = 52.3 cm.; 1 palm = 1/7 cubit = 0.07 m. (Weeks 1979, 1998; Ventura 1988; Rossi 2004). For example, the figure 5–2 is to be read as 5 cubits and 2 palms.
W = chamber width in meters.
Wc = chamber width in cubits and palms.
L = chamber length in meters.
H/W = proportion of height to width.
Area and Volume take into account vaulted ceilings, recesses, ramps, pillars, irregularities, and other features, and are not simply an averaged HxWxL.
/ = chamber is absent.

Appendix Table 1 KV Royal Tombs Included in Tables 2–16 and Chapter 8

Dynasty 18

KV 20	Thutmosis II (?)/Hatshepsut
KV 38	Thutmosis I
KV 34	Thutmosis III
KV 35	Amenhotep II
KV 43	Thutmosis IV
KV 22	Amenhotep III
KV 23	Aye
KV 57	Horemhab

Dynasty 19

KV 16	Ramesses I
KV 17	Seti I
KV 7	Ramesses II
KV 8	Merenptah
KV 10	Amenmesse
KV 15	Seti II
KV 14	Tausert/Setnakht
KV 47	Siptah

Dynasty 20

KV 11	Ramesses III
KV 2	Ramesses IV
KV 9	Ramesses V/VI
KV 1	Ramesses VII
KV 6	Ramesses IX
KV 18	Ramesses X
KV 4	Ramesses XI

Appendix Table 2 Occurrence of Chambers in KV Royal Tombs

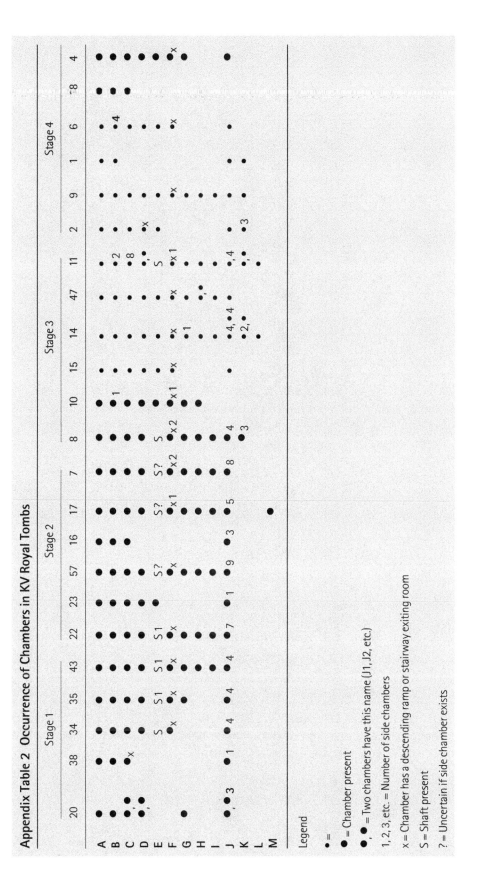

Legend

• =

● = Chamber present

•,● = Two chambers have this name (J1, J2, etc.)

1, 2, 3, etc. = Number of side chambers

x = Chamber has a descending ramp or stairway exiting room

S = Shaft present

? = Uncertain if side chamber exists

Appendix Table 3 Dimensions of Chamber B

	Stage 1					Stage 2						Stage 3						Stage 4					
	20	38	34	35	43	22	23	57	16	17	7	8	10	15	14	47	11	2	9	1	6	18	4
H	2.15		1.91	2.44	1.94	2.76	2.66	2.56	2.63	2.58	2.82	3.23	3.25	3.30	2.75	3.11	3.44	4.23	3.84	4.04	4.47	3.90	4.15
Hc	4-1		3-5	4-5	3-5	5-2	5-1	4-6	5-0	4-7	5-3	6-1	6-1	6-2	5-2	5-7	6-4	8-1	7-2	7-5	8-4	7-3	7-7
W	1.65	2.29	2.16	1.70	1.98	2.45	2.64	2.65	2.61	2.62	2.61	2.64	2.59	2.74	2.13	2.60	2.70	3.16	3.17	3.17	3.22	3.15	3.29
Wc	3-1	4-3	4-1	3-2	3-5	4-5	5-0	5-0	4-7	5-0	4-7	5-0	4-7	5-2	4-1	4-7	5-1	6-0	6-0	6-0	6-1	6-0	6-2
L	23.58	5.71	8.35	9.83	11.04	11.20	11.37	13.24	9.33	10.61	12.33	15.66	14.20	15.32	7.56	14.34	14.43	15.17	14.94	15.28	15.33	15.19	15.21
H/W	1.30		0.88	1.44	0.98	1.13	1.01	0.97	1.01	0.98	1.08	1.22	1.25	1.20	1.29	1.20	1.27	1.34	1.21	1.27	1.39	1.24	1.26
Area	38.54	12.58	17.71	16.51	21.88	27.44	29.91	34.98	24.34	27.79	32.07	41.38	36.78	42.93	16.03	37.32	38.68	47.95	48.24	48.13	49.42	47.81	50.10
Vol	82.86		33.83	39.72	43.68	75.73	79.21	91.49	63.89	70.93	90.44	140.86	129.30	138.66	44.22	115.21	133.05	202.87	180.45	197.04	222.75	192.32	206.66

Appendix Table 4 Dimensions of Chamber C

	Stage 1					Stage 2						Stage 3						Stage 4					
	20	38	34	35	43	22	23	57	16	17	7	8	10	15	14	47	11	2	9	1	6	18	4
H	*	2.16	3.77	3.44	5.33	4.85	5.44	5.37	4.96	3.81	3.86	3.15	3.16	3.31	2.61	3.11	3.31	4.23	3.65	/	4.11	4.W4–	3.96
Hc		4-1	7-1	6-4	10-1	9-2	10-3	10-2	9-3	7-2	7-3	6-0	6-0	6-2	4-7	5-7	6-2	8-1	6-7		7-6	8-3	7-4
W		5.78	1.62	1.50	1.98	3.36	2.63	2.59	2.60	2.60	2.62	2.65	2.63	2.81	2.11	2.61	2.71	3.15	3.18		3.22	3.16	3.24
Wc		11-0	3-1	2-6	3-5	6-3	5-0	4-7	4-7	4-7	5-0	5-0	5-0	5-3	4-0	4-7	5-1	6-0	6-1		6-1	6-0	6-1
L		4.89	3.61	4.05	4.19	4.70	7.95	7.92	7.66	7.72	7.37	8.03	8.87	14.27	6.70	8.79	11.63	12.66	12.37		9.95	10.44	12.56
H/W		0.37	2.33	2.29	2.69	1.44	2.07	2.07	1.91	1.47	1.47	1.19	1.20	1.18	1.24	1.19	1.22	1.34	1.15		1.28	1.41	1.22
Area		26.99	5.73	5.23	8.28	15.79	20.73	20.38	19.77	19.97	19.31	21.22	23.55	40.05	14.17	23.02	30.97	39.89	39.04		32.01	32.19	40.60
Vol		58.30	23.24	22.14	36.81	76.58	89.43	81.33	78.28	63.15	74.53	67.88	73.54	133.08	36.66	115.57	102.51	168.73	143.32		131.56	113.59	161.41

Legend

* = Multiple, irregular chambers have been labeled C

Appendix Table 5 Dimensions of Corridor D

	Stage 1						Stage 2									Stage 3				Stage 4					
	20(D1)	20(D2)	38	34	35	43	22	23	57	16	17	7	8	10	15	14	47	11(D1)	11(D2)	2	9	1	6	18	4
H	2.08	1.76	/	1.99	2.03	2.24	2.74	2.64	2.62	/	2.78	2.54	3.49	3.15	3.34	2.61	3.36	3.12	3.19	5.00	3.65	/	3.69	/	3.97
Hc	3-7	3-3		3-6	3-6	4-2	5-2	5-0	5-0		5-2	4-6	6-5	6-0	6-3	4-7	6-3	5-7	6-1	9-4	6-7	6-7	7-0		7-4
W	2.05	2.27		2.04	1.67	1.97	2.64	2.63	2.63		2.61	2.60	2.64	2.66	2.80	2.13	2.59	6.48	2.63	3.12	3.18		3.20		3.20
Wc	3-6	4-2		3-6	3-1	3-5	5-0	5-0	5-0		4-7	4-7	5-0	5-1	5-2	4-1	4-7	12-3	5-0	5-7	6-1		6-1		6-1
L	23.41	46.52		4.38	5.17	8.19	8.42	13.94	10.51		9.09	8.54	9.80	7.88	14.36	6.83	10.52	4.47	11.93	12.17	10.37		11.52		12.48
H/W	1.01	0.78		0.98	1.22	1.14	1.04	1.00	1.00		1.07	0.97	1.32	1.18	1.19	1.23	1.30	0.48	1.21	1.60	1.15		1.15		1.24
Area	47.68	98.58		8.57	8.55	16.00	22.20	36.63	27.50		23.65	22.15	25.80	20.92	40.27	14.36	27.55	28.40	31.21	38.05	32.86		36.84		39.69
Vol	99.17	136.49		17.78	17.36	35.86	60.88	96.68	73.02		62.56	58.08	89.60	65.90	134.70	37.77	92.57	88.61	100.26	191.29	120.14		135.94		157.57

Appendix Table 6 Dimensions of Hall E

	Stage 1					Stage 2							Stage 3				Stage 4						
	20	38	34	35	43	22	23	57	16	17	7	8	10	15	14	47	11	2	9	1	6	18	4
H*	/	/	1.70	2.25	2.33	2.50	2.98	2.39	/	2.46	2.62	3.74	3.07	3.39	2.59	2.97	3.19	4.09	3.63	/	3.51	/	3.67
Hc*			3-2	4-2	4-3	4-5	5-5	4-4		4-5	5-0	7-1	5-6	6-3	4-7	5-5	6-1	7-6	6-7		6-5		7-0
W			5.06	4.96	4.16	4.38	4.14	4.16		4.17	4.15	4.25	4.16	4.38	3.16	4.14	4.21	4.20	4.15		5.25		4.43
Wc			9-5	9-3	7-7	8-3	7-6	7-7		7-7	7-7	8-1	7-7	8-3	6-0	7-6	8-0	8-0	7-7		10-0		8-3
L			4.16	4.12	4.17	3.64	4.01	3.37		3.65	3.65	3.58	2.71	3.19	2.26	3.27	3.16	3.66	4.51		4.91		4.46
H/W*			0.34	0.45	0.56	0.57	0.72	0.57		0.59	0.63	0.88	0.74	0.77	0.82	0.72	0.76	0.97	0.87		0.67		0.83
Area			21.03	20.26	17.24	15.94	16.52	15.55		15.17	15.14	15.20	11.22	13.92	7.14	13.41	13.30	15.36	18.81		25.78		19.74
Vol*			38.80	45.14	40.18	39.85	49.35	37.17		37.32	39.66	57.89	34.43	47.94	18.50	40.21	42.18	62.82	68.28		90.49		72.45

Legend

* = Measurement does not include shaft

Appendix Table 7 Dimensions of Hall F

	Stage 1						Stage 2							Stage 3						Stage 4			
	20	38	34	35	43	22	23	57	16	17	7	8	10	15	14	47	11	2	9	1	6	18	4
H	/	/	2.72	2.19	2.53	2.46	/	2.72	/	3.16	3.23	3.26	3.10	3.51	2.58	2.76	2.74	/	3.96	/	3.41	/	3.57
Hc			5–1	4–1	4–6	4–5		5–1		6–0	6–1	6–2	5–6	6–5	4–7	5–2	5–2		7–4		6–4		6–6
W			6.69	10.16	10.26	6.21		6.88		7.95	8.40	9.42	9.48	8.07	5.27	7.94	7.90		8.44		8.55		8.33
Wc			12–5	19–3	19–4	11–6		13–1		15–1	16–0	18–0	18–1	15–3	10–1	15–1	15–1		16–1		16–2		15–6
L			11.35	6.39	6.15	10.26		7.53		8.43	8.40	8.95	8.84	8.56	4.75	8.40	9.10		7.22		8.51		10.99
H/W			0.41	0.22	0.25	0.40		0.40		0.40	0.38	0.35	0.33	0.43	0.49	0.35	0.35		0.47		0.40		0.43
Area			75.38	64.77	63.11	63.71		51.61		66.75	70.60	84.11	82.91	69.36	24.91	66.17	72.24		60.83		72.10		91.87
Vol			205.03	141.85	159.43	156.72		157.75		207.84	225.84	274.20	257.02	242.49	64.58	183.96	208.55		223.54		245.86		327.99

Appendix Table 8 Dimensions of Corridor G

	Stage 1						Stage 2							Stage 3				Stage 4					
	20	38	34	35	43	22	23	57	16	17	7	8	10	15	14	47	11	2	9	1	6	18	4
H	1.36	/	/	2.45	2.23	2.57	/	2.60	/	2.64	2.52	3.97	3.85	/	2.65	3.41	3.07	/	3.70	/	/	/	3.97
Hc	2-4			4-5	4-2	4-6		4-7		5-0	4-6	7-4	7-3		5-0	6-4	5-6		7-1				7-4
W	1.93			1.58	1.97	2.46		2.62		2.62	2.58	2.70	2.59		2.09	2.58	2.64		3.17				3.14
Wc	3-5			3-0	3-5	4-5		5-0		5-0	4-7	5-1	4-7		3-7	4-7	5-0		6-0				6-0
L	6.11			4.94	8.21	5.47		7.60		8.94	8.54	8.99	9.77		4.25	7.55	6.98		7.31				4.78
H/W	0.70			1.55	1.13	1.04		0.99		1.01	0.98	1.47	1.49		1.27	1.32	1.16		1.17				1.26
Area	9.81			6.13	16.15	13.46		19.85		23.40	22.11	24.26	25.34		8.84	19.47	18.39		23.09				15.01
Vol	13.34			14.42	36.45	34.59		51.65		61.78	55.72	86.95	92.66		23.51	66.39	56.46		85.43				59.59

Appendix Table 9 Dimensions of Corridor H

	Stage 1						Stage 2						Stage 3						Stage 4					
	20	38	34	35	43	22	23	57	16	17	7	8	10	15	14	47(H1)	47(H2)#	11	2	9	1	6	18	4
H	/	/	/	/	3.95	4.98*	/	2.99	/	2.70	2.38	3.12	2.87	/	2.60	3.26	4.01	3.05	/	5.04	/	/	/	/
Hc					7-4	9-4		5-5		5-1	4-4	5-7	5-3		4-7	6-2	7-5	5-6		9-4				
W					1.90	2.50		3.12		2.63	2.60	7.40	2.52		2.09	2.56	3.68	5.25		3.16				
Wc					3-4	4-5		5-7		5-0	4-7	14-1	4-6		3-7	4-6	7-0	10-0		6-0				
L					3.14	3.88		4.93		5.28	6.38	7.37	6.30		4.52	8.41	8.76	4.37		9.73				
H/W					2.08	1.99		0.96		1.03	0.92	0.42	1.14		1.24	1.27	1.09	0.58		1.59				
Area					5.96	9.70		15.40		13.81	16.50	54.40	15.80		9.30	21.70	31.73	22.94		30.50				
Vol					23.57	48.31		41.68		35.91	39.27	169.73	45.35		24.18	70.74	127.24	69.97		139.09				

Legend

* = Ceiling height is irregular.

= What was labeled J1 of KV 47 in the TMP Atlas is more accurately to be labeled H2. See text, Chamber J.

Appendix Table 10 Dimensions of Hall I

	Stage 1						Stage 2						Stage 3					Stage 4					
	20	38	34	35	43	22	23	57	16	17	7	8	10	15	14	47	11	2	9	1	6	18	4
H	/	/	/	/	2.23	2.64	/	2.66	/	2.53	2.05	3.28	/	/	2.61	3.12	3.17	/	3.75	/	/	/	/
Hc					4-2	5-0		5-1		4-6	3-6	6-2			4-7	5-7	6-0		7-1				
W					3.62	3.83		4.12		4.16	7.28	2.71			4.17	6.28	5.25		4.16				
Wc					6-6	7-2		7-6		7-7	13-6	5-1			7-7	12-0	10-0		7-7				
L					5.19	5.14		5.21		5.17	5.74	9.89			3.23	5.29	5.28		4.53				
H/W					0.62	0.69		0.65		0.61	0.28	1.21			0.63	0.50	0.60		0.90				
Area					18.73	20.02		21.32		21.84	41.87	26.81			13.39	33.20	27.80		18.83				
Vol					41.89	52.85		57.34		54.46	105.09	72.66			34.95	103.58	88.13		70.61				

Appendix Table 11 Dimensions of Burial Chamber J

	Stage 1						Stage 2							Stage 3						Stage 4					
	20 (J1)	20 (J2)	38	34	35	43	22	23	57	16	17	7	8	10	15	14 (J1)	14 (J2)	47*	11	2	9	1	6	18	4
H	4.53	2.70	2.64	3.31	3.16	4.45	3.12	3.92	4.27	3.23	6.05	5.83	6.47	/	3.25	5.41	6.02	5.30	6.55	5.22	6.93	4.25	3.60	/	5.01
Hc	8-5	5-1	5-0	6-2	6-0	8-4	5-7	7-3	8-1	6-1	11-4	11-1	12-3		6-1	10-2	11-4	10-1	12-4	9-7	13-2	8-1	6-6		9-4
W	7.18	5.45	5.43	8.53	8.69	8.36	8.14	8.89	8.95	6.26	8.38	13.07	14.87		2.77	10.77	13.31	13.73	13.86	8.33	13.04	5.18	5.34		11.30
Wc	13-5	10-3	10-3	16-2	16-4	15-7	15-4	16-7	17-1	11-7	16-0	24-7	28-3		5-2	20-4	25-3	26-2	26-3	15-6	24-7	9-6	10-1		21-4
L	10.11	11.10	10.47	14.64	14.93	14.42	15.40	6.46	14.12	5.16	14.26	13.81	13.75		8.04	10.57	12.63	9.07	12.69	7.30	8.90	8.53	6.83		12.50
H/W	0.63	0.50	0.49	0.39	0.36	0.53	0.38	0.44	0.48	0.52	0.72	0.45	0.44		1.17	0.50	0.45	0.39	0.47	0.63	0.53	0.82	0.67		0.44
Area	59.07	61.66	53.03	116.87	128.42	120.18	125.36	57.29	117.19	32.20	126.55	180.49	204.37		21.51	114.28	170.48	125.26	174.40	60.53	118.53	44.26	36.32		139.94
Vol*	268.49	166.48	140.00	386.84	405.81	451.18	391.12	225.53	466.31	104.07	503.00	870.45	1111.77		63.54	473.90	790.35	554.67	882.22	317.23	506.49	188.10	130.04		638.88

Legend

* = What was labeled J1 of KV 47 in the TMP *Atlas* is more accurately to be labeled H2. What is labeled J2 in the *Atlas* is here labeled J. See text, Chamber J.

Appendix Table 12 Dimensions of Corridor K

	Stage 1					Stage 2										Stage 3					Stage 4					
	20	38	34	35	43	22	23	57	16	17	7	8	10	15	14 (K1)	14 (K2)	47	11 (K1)	11 (K2)	2	9	1	6	18	4
H	—	—	—	—	—	—	—	—	—	—	—	3.05	—	—	3.50	2.56	—	2.56	2.50	3.46	4.28	3.72	—	—	—
Hc												5–6			6–5	4–6		4–6	4–5	6–4	8–1	7–1			
W												4.22			2.48	2.35		2.61	2.58	2.58	2.48	3.13			
Wc												8–1			4–5	4–3		4–7	4–7	4–7	4–5	5–7			
L												8.00			14.96	9.96		2.61	2.71	6.96	4.06	3.58			
H/W												0.72			1.41	1.09		0.98	0.97	1.34	1.73	1.19			
Area												33.73			36.18	22.67		6.79	6.95	17.87	10.06	11.21			
Vol												102.88			120.62	54.68		17.38	17.38	62.23	38.02	41.70			

Appendix Table 13 Occurrences of Single– and Double–Leaf Wooden Doors

	Stage 1			Stage 2							Stage 3							Stage 4					
	20	38	34	35	43	22	23	57	16	17	7	8	10	15	14	47	11	2	9	1	6	18	4
B											D	D	D	D	D	D		D	D	D	D		D
Ba–Bd																	S(Ba, Bb)						
C												D	D		D	D		D	D		D		D
Ca–h																	S(Ca–Ch)						
D											D			D			S(D1), D(D2)	D	D		D		D
E											D			D				D					
Ea																							
F											S	S					D		S		D		D
Fa											S	S					S						
Faa																							
G												D											D
Ga																							
H											S	D											
I								S		S	S												
J			S	S	S	S		S		S	S	D		D	D(J2)			D	D	D	D		
Ja–Jf			S(Ja–Jd)	S(Ja–Jd)	S(Ja–Jd)	S(Ja–Je)					S(Ja–Jf)												
Jaa–Jdd											S(Jdd)												
Jccc–Jddd											S(Jddd)												
K																	D(K1)	D		D			
Ka–Kc																							
L																							

Legend

Shading indicates chamber and its entrance are present. If no S or D in shaded box, entrance has no door.

S = single-leaf door

D = double-leaf door

Appendix Table 14 Occurrences of Single and Compound Jambs in Gates

	Stage 1					Stage 2						Stage 3						Stage 4					
	20	38	34	35	43	22	23	57	16	17	7	8	10	15	14	47	11	2	9	1	6	18	4
B	G	G	G	G	/	X	X	G	X	G	G	X	X	X	X	X	X	G	G	G	G	G	G
Ba–Bd													G(Ba)			X	G(Ba, Bb)				X(Ba–Bd)	G	G
C	G(C1, C2)	G	G	G	G	G	G	G	G	G	G	G	X	X	X	X	X	G	G	G	G	G	G
Ca–h																X	G(Ca–Ch)						
D	G(D1)		G	G	G	G	G	G	G	G	G	G	X	X	X	X	X(D1, D2)	G	G	G	G	G	G
Da			G	G	G	G	G	G		G	G	G	X	X	X	X	X	G	G	G	G	G	G
E			G	G	G	G	G	G		G	G	G	X	X	X	G	X	G	X	G	X		G
Ea				G	G	G						X	X	X	X	G	X		X				
F			G	G	G	G		G		X	G	X	X	X	X	G	X		X	G	X		G
Fa				G	G	G					X	G				G	X		X				
Faa				G	G	G						G											
G	G		G	G	G	G	G	G	G	G	G	G	G		X	G	G	G	G			G	G
Ga														G	G	G	G		G				
H					G	/		G		G	G	X	G	G	G	G(H1, H2*)	X	G	G	X		G	
I	G(J1)	G	G	G	G	G	G	X	G	X	X	G	G	G	X	G	X	X	X	X	X		/
Ja–Jf	G(J2a–Jc)	G(Ja)	G(Ja–Jd)	G(Ja–Jd)	G(Ja–Jd)	G(Ja–Je)	G(Ja)	G(Ja–Jb, Jd–Je, XJc)	G(Ja, Jc, /Jb)	G(Ja, Je, X(Jb–Jd))	X(Ja–Jf)	G(Ja–Jd)		G	G(J1), X(J2) / G(J1a–J1d, J2a–J2d)	X* / G(Ja–Jd)	G(Ja–Jd)	X	G / X	X	X		/
Jaa–Jdd						G(Jbb, Jcc)		G(Jaa–Jcc)			X(Jdd)												
Jccc–Jddd								G(Jccc)			X(Jddd)												
K												X / G(Kb), X(Ka, Kc)		X(K1), G(K2)	X(K1), G(K2)		X(K1), G(K2)						
Ka–Kc										/								G / G(Ka–Kc)		G			
L														G	G		G	G		G			

Legend

G = simple jamb

X = compound jamb

blank = Tomb lacks this chamber and entrance

/ = entrance only, no gate

* = What was labeled J1 of KV 47 in the TMP *Atlas* is more accurately to be labeled H2. What is labeled J2 in the *Atlas* is here labeled J. See text, Chamber J.

Appendix Table 15 Occurrences, Dimensions and Number of Pillars

	Stage 1					Stage 2									Stage 3					Stage 4			
	20	38	34	35	43	22	23	57	16	17	7	8	10	15	14#	47	11	2	9	1	6	18	4
No. of pillars																							
F			2	2	2	2		2		4	4	4	4	4		4	4		4		4	4	4
J	3(J2)	1@	2	6	6	6		6		6	8	8	4	4	8(J1) 8(J2)	4(J2)	8		4*			4	4
Fa										2	4	2	2										
Ja–Jddd						1(Jb) 1(Jc)				2(Jb) 4(Jc)	2(Jc) 2(Jd) 2(Jddd)												
Size of pillars																							
F			1.27	1.08	0.97	0.99		1.07		0.99	0.93	1.08	1.07	1.08		1.11	1.06		1.06		1.09	1.45	
J	1.47	0.88	1.24	1.11	1.05	0.97		1.07		1.04	1.10	1.07			0.64(J1) 1.11(J2)	1.07	1.04		1.12			2.19	
Fa										1.18	0.95	0.8	%										
Ja–Jddd						0.72(Jb) 0.87(Jc)				0.99–1.02	0.90–0.95												

Legend

* = Chamber also contains 4 pilasters.

= Pillar in K1a is 1.04m; there is also an unfinished pillar in K1b.

@ = Most likely a construction pillar. See text, section V.

% = Unfinished pillar

Appendix Table 16 Occurrences and Number of Niches and Recesses

	Stage 1					Stage 2							Stage 3					Stage 4					
	20	38	34	35	43	22	23	57	16	17	7	8	10	15	14	47	11	2	9	1	6	18	4
B	N3																						
C	N1 (C1) N1 (C2)		R2	R2	R2	R2	R2	R2	R2	R2	R2	R2	R2	R2			R2	R2	R2		R2	R2	R2
D	N1 (D1) N2 (D2)											N2	N2	N2	N2	N2	N2	N2	N2		N2		
E																							
F																		R2					
G				N1																			
H										R2													
I																							
J				B4	B4, N3	B4	B4	B4	B4	B4, N4	B4	N8, R3											
K																	N2	R2					
L															N2		R5						

Legend

N = Niche present

B = Magical brick niche present

R = Recess present

1, 2, 3,etc. = Number of N, B, or R present

Index